T0325918

Progress in Brain Research
Volume 228

Brain-Computer Interfaces: Lab Experiments to Real-World Applications

Serial Editor

Vincent Walsh
Institute of Cognitive Neuroscience
University College London
17 Queen Square
London WC1N 3AR UK

Editorial Board

Mark Bear, *Cambridge, USA.*
Medicine & Translational Neuroscience

Hamed Ekhtiari, *Tehran, Iran.*
Addiction

Hajime Hirase, *Wako, Japan.*
Neuronal Microcircuitry

Freda Miller, *Toronto, Canada.*
Developmental Neurobiology

Shane O'Mara, *Dublin, Ireland.*
Systems Neuroscience

Susan Rossell, *Swinburne, Australia.*
Clinical Psychology & Neuropsychiatry

Nathalie Rouach, *Paris, France.*
Neuroglia

Barbara Sahakian, *Cambridge, UK.*
Cognition & Neuroethics

Bettina Studer, *Dusseldorf, Germany.*
Neurorehabilitation

Xiao-Jing Wang, *New York, USA.*
Computational Neuroscience

Progress in Brain Research
Volume 228

Brain-Computer Interfaces: Lab Experiments to Real-World Applications

Edited by

Damien Coyle
Intelligent Systems Research Centre,
Ulster University, Derry, Northern Ireland, United Kingdom

ELSEVIER AMSTERDAM · BOSTON · HEIDELBERG · LONDON · NEW YORK · OXFORD
PARIS · SAN DIEGO · SAN FRANCISCO · SINGAPORE · SYDNEY · TOKYO

Elsevier
Radarweg 29, PO Box 211, 1000 AE Amsterdam, Netherlands
The Boulevard, Langford Lane, Kidlington, Oxford OX5 1GB, United Kingdom
50 Hampshire Street, 5th Floor, Cambridge, MA 02139, United States

First edition 2016

Copyright © 2016 Elsevier B.V. All rights reserved

No part of this publication may be reproduced or transmitted in any form or by any means,
electronic or mechanical, including photocopying, recording, or any information storage and
retrieval system, without permission in writing from the publisher. Details on how to seek
permission, further information about the Publisher's permissions policies and our
arrangements with organizations such as the Copyright Clearance Center and the Copyright
Licensing Agency, can be found at our website: www.elsevier.com/permissions.

This book and the individual contributions contained in it are protected under copyright by the
Publisher (other than as may be noted herein).

Notices

Knowledge and best practice in this field are constantly changing. As new research and
experience broaden our understanding, changes in research methods, professional practices, or
medical treatment may become necessary.

Practitioners and researchers must always rely on their own experience and knowledge in
evaluating and using any information, methods, compounds, or experiments described herein.
In using such information or methods they should be mindful of their own safety and the safety
of others, including parties for whom they have a professional responsibility.

To the fullest extent of the law, neither the Publisher nor the authors, contributors, or editors,
assume any liability for any injury and/or damage to persons or property as a matter of products
liability, negligence or otherwise, or from any use or operation of any methods, products,
instructions, or ideas contained in the material herein.

ISBN: 978-0-12-804216-8
ISSN: 0079-6123

For information on all Elsevier publications
visit our website at https://www.elsevier.com/

www.elsevier.com • www.bookaid.org

Publisher: Zoe Kruze
Acquisition Editor: Kirsten Shankland
Editorial Project Manager: Hannah Colford
Production Project Manager: Magesh Kumar Mahalingam
Cover Designer: Greg Harris

Typeset by SPi Global, India

Contributors

H.A. Agashe
Noninvasive Brain-Machine Interface Systems Lab, University of Houston, Houston, TX, United States

K.K. Ang
Neural and Biomedical Technology Department, Institute for Infocomm Research, A*STAR; School of Computer Science and Engineering, College of Engineering, Nanyang Technological University, Singapore

P. Aricò
University of Rome "Sapienza"; BrainSigns srl; Neuroelectrical Imaging and BCI Lab, IRCCS Fondazione Santa Lucia, Rome, Italy

L. Astolfi
Neuroelectrical Imaging and Brain-Computer Interface Laboratory, Fondazione Santa Lucia IRCCS; Sapienza University of Rome, Rome, Italy

F. Babiloni
University of Rome "Sapienza"; BrainSigns srl, Rome, Italy

R. Beveridge
Intelligent Systems Research Centre, Ulster University, Derry, Northern Ireland, United Kingdom

N. Birbaumer
Institute of Medical Psychology and Behavioral Neurobiology, University of Tübingen, Tübingen, Germany; Wyss-Center for Bio- and Neuro-Engineering, Geneva, Switzerland

G. Borghini
University of Rome "Sapienza"; BrainSigns srl; Neuroelectrical Imaging and BCI Lab, IRCCS Fondazione Santa Lucia, Rome, Italy

U. Chaudhary
Institute of Medical Psychology and Behavioral Neurobiology, University of Tübingen, Tübingen, Germany

F. Cincotti
Neuroelectrical Imaging and Brain-Computer Interface Laboratory, Fondazione Santa Lucia IRCCS; Sapienza University of Rome, Rome, Italy

A. Colosimo
University of Rome "Sapienza", Rome, Italy

J.L. Contreras-Vidal
Noninvasive Brain-Machine Interface Systems Lab, University of Houston, Houston, TX, United States

D. Coyle
Intelligent Systems Research Centre, Ulster University, Derry, Northern Ireland, United Kingdom

D. Cruse
School of Psychology, University of Birmingham, Birmingham, United Kingdom

G. Di Flumeri
University of Rome "Sapienza"; BrainSigns srl; Neuroelectrical Imaging and BCI Lab, IRCCS Fondazione Santa Lucia, Rome, Italy

T. Fomina
International Max Planck Research School for Cognitive and Systems Neuroscience; Max Planck Institute for Intelligent Systems, Tübingen, Germany

R. Formisano
Post-Coma Unit, Fondazione Santa Lucia IRCCS, Rome, Italy

C. Förster
Max Planck Institute for Intelligent Systems, Tübingen, Germany

R.M. Gibson
The Brain and Mind Institute, University of Western Ontario; University of Western Ontario, London, ON, Canada

M. Grosse-Wentrup
Max Planck Institute for Intelligent Systems, Tübingen, Germany

C. Guan
Neural and Biomedical Technology Department, Institute for Infocomm Research, A*STAR; School of Computer Science and Engineering, College of Engineering, Nanyang Technological University, Singapore

M.R. Hohmann
International Max Planck Research School for Cognitive and Systems Neuroscience; Max Planck Institute for Intelligent Systems, Tübingen, Germany

V. Jayaram
International Max Planck Research School for Cognitive and Systems Neuroscience; Max Planck Institute for Intelligent Systems, Tübingen, Germany

C. Jeunet
Laboratoire Handicap Activité Cognition Santé, University of Bordeaux; Project-Team Potioc/LaBRI, Inria Bordeaux Sud-Ouest, Bordeaux, France

J. Just
Hertie Institute for Clinical Brain Research; German Center for Neurodegenerative Diseases (DZNE), Tübingen, Germany

A. Korik
Intelligent Systems Research Centre, Ulster University, Derry, Northern Ireland, United Kingdom

F. Lotte
Project-Team Potioc/LaBRI, Inria Bordeaux Sud-Ouest, Bordeaux, France

D. Mattia
Neuroelectrical Imaging and Brain-Computer Interface Laboratory, Fondazione Santa Lucia IRCCS, Rome, Italy

D.J. McFarland
National Center for Adaptive Neurotechnologies, Wadsworth Center, Albany, NY, United States

M. Molinari
Spinal Cord Unit, IRCCS Santa Lucia Foundation, Rome, Italy

G.R. Müller-Putz
Graz University of Technology, Institute of Neural Engineering, Graz, Austria

B. N'Kaoua
Laboratoire Handicap Activité Cognition Santé, University of Bordeaux, Bordeaux, France

P. Ofner
Graz University of Technology, Institute of Neural Engineering, Graz, Austria

A.M. Owen
The Brain and Mind Institute, University of Western Ontario; University of Western Ontario, London, ON, Canada

A.Y. Paek
Noninvasive Brain-Machine Interface Systems Lab, University of Houston, Houston, TX, United States

J. Pereira
Graz University of Technology, Institute of Neural Engineering, Graz, Austria

K.S. Phua
Neural and Biomedical Technology Department, Institute for Infocomm Research, A*STAR, Singapore

F. Pichiorri
Neuroelectrical Imaging and Brain-Computer Interface Laboratory, Fondazione Santa Lucia IRCCS; Sapienza University of Rome, Rome, Italy

S. Pozzi
DeepBlue srl, Rome, Italy

A. Ramos-Murguialday
Institute of Medical Psychology and Behavioral Neurobiology, University of Tübingen, Tübingen, Germany; TECNALIA, San Sebastian, Spain

A. Riccio
Neuroelectrical Imaging and Brain-Computer Interface Laboratory, Fondazione Santa Lucia IRCCS, Rome, Italy

M. Risetti
Neuroelectrical Imaging and Brain-Computer Interface Laboratory, Fondazione Santa Lucia IRCCS, Rome, Italy

F. Schettini
Neuroelectrical Imaging and Brain-Computer Interface Laboratory, Fondazione Santa Lucia IRCCS, Rome, Italy

B. Schölkopf
Max Planck Institute for Intelligent Systems, Tübingen, Germany

L. Schöls
Hertie Institute for Clinical Brain Research; German Center for
Neurodegenerative Diseases (DZNE), Tübingen, Germany

A. Schwarz
Graz University of Technology, Institute of Neural Engineering, Graz, Austria

N. Siddique
Intelligent Systems Research Centre, Ulster University, Derry, Northern Ireland,
United Kingdom

S.R. Soekadar
Applied Neurotechnology Laboratory, University Hospital of Tübingen, Tübingen,
Germany

R. Sosnik
Hybrid BCI Lab, Holon Institute of Technology, Holon, Israel

M. Synofzik
Hertie Institute for Clinical Brain Research, Tübingen, Germany

J. Toppi
Neuroelectrical Imaging and Brain-Computer Interface Laboratory, Fondazione
Santa Lucia IRCCS; Sapienza University of Rome, Rome, Italy

J. Ushiba
Faculty of Science and Technology, Keio University, Kohoku-ku, Yokohama,
Kanagawa, Japan

T.M. Vaughan
National Center for Adaptive Neurotechnologies, Wadsworth Center, Albany, NY,
United States

C. Wang
Neural and Biomedical Technology Department, Institute for Infocomm
Research, A*STAR, Singapore

N. Widmann
Max Planck Institute for Intelligent Systems, Tübingen, Germany

S. Wilson
Intelligent Systems Research Centre, Ulster University, Derry, Northern Ireland,
United Kingdom

H. Yang
Neural and Biomedical Technology Department, Institute for Infocomm
Research, A*STAR, Singapore

Contents

PART II   NON-INVASIVE DECODING OF 3D HAND AND ARM MOVEMENTS

Preface

Progress in noninvasive electroencephalography (EEG)-based brain–computer interface (BCI) research, development and innovation has accelerated in recent years. New brain signal signatures for inferring user intent and more complex control strategies have been the focus of many recent investigations. Major advances in recording technology, signal processing techniques, and clinical applications, tested with patient cohorts, as well as nonclinical applications, have been reported. This volume presents a timely snapshot of some of the current trends and state of the art in these areas, with an emphasis placed on the underlying neurology and neurophysiologic signaling underpinning the BCIs presented, with all contributions centered around EEG but relevant to all other neuroimaging/brain recording modalities.

Contributions cover some of the current hottest topics in BCI research, including a thorough review of psychological factors affecting user training in BCI and their associated neural correlates, elucidating how knowledge of such factors can be very informative when designing training protocols for BCI participants and end-users. Three contributions are centered around decoding three-dimensional hand/arm movements and discriminating arm movement in different planes from EEG, including a thorough review delineating classical motor imagery detection against more complex movement intentions decoding. A second study highlights the importance of information encoded in EEG mu and beta band power, whereas many 3D hand movement decoding studies involving EEG to date have focused on lower delta bands for 3D movement decoding. A reaching and grasping study with end-users of this specific research—upper limb amputees—highlights the potential for exploiting motion trajectory prediction BCIs for neuroprosthetic control. This clinical application study is followed by a further five chapters, which review and highlight methodological considerations and results for a range of other clinical applications of noninvasive BCIs. These include an informative and cogent historical perspective of BCI development and an overview of BCIs intended to provide a means of communication for patients with locked-in syndrome due to amyotrophic lateral sclerosis (ALS) and for the restoration of motor function to patients who have suffered severe stroke. This is followed by a chapter, which highlights the powerful prospects for BCI in promoting neural plasticity for rehabilitation in poststroke hemiplegia, with an emphasis on BCI paradigms where motor cortical output and input are simultaneously activated by translating motor cortical activity associated with the attempt to move paralyzed fingers into actual exoskeleton-driven finger movements. Beyond upper limb and hand rehabilitation in stroke, another chapter addresses a potentially new application for BCIs, namely, dysphagia rehabilitation, providing a thorough review of neural and cortical correlates of swallowing and detection of the motor imagery of swallow. This is followed by an ALS patient study of a newly proposed paradigm that targets higher-level cognitive processes, namely, activation of self-referential memory and cognitive tasks devoid of mnemonic content, to transmit information and infer user intent. The hypothesis is that higher cognitive tasks to modulate brain activity may be better than tasks that involve sensorimotor processes for ALS sufferers, as sensorimotor processes are impaired in ALS. This hypothesis may have implications for the topic of the chapter that follows, which focuses on a thorough review of the literature on applying BCI for assessment of awareness and communication in patients with disorders of consciousness following brain injury. This application of BCI has received increased attention in recent years following a number of studies showing that patients diagnosed in vegetative state or minimally consciousness state, who cannot respond or communicate with overt behavioural responses, are capable of modulating brain activity through imagery or by attending stimuli presented visually or auditorily. These clinical studies are complemented with coverage of two distinct nonclinical applications. The first focuses on assessment of cognitive load or mental workload of professional air traffic controllers during realistic air traffic control tasks using a passive BCI, demonstrating the feasibility of passive BCIs in operative environments. The second focuses on exploring the impact of graphical complexity and display modality on visual evoked potentials, ie, a standard display monitor vs a virtual reality wearable display headset, when used in a neurogaming context. This study focuses on a motion-onset visual evoked potentials (mVEP) paradigm, which has received less attention compared to its VEP counterpart paradigms such as the P300 paradigm and the steady-state visual evoked potentials (SSVEP) paradigm. The last two chapters in the volume focus around usability of BCI, with a focus on clinical applications highlighting issues that impact on fostering BCI outside the laboratory and the practical issues for use in real life. These include BCI technology meeting requirements such as being simple to operate, requiring minimal expert oversight, being usable by the people who need them, in essence, following a user-centered design for developing practical BCI products with an emphasis on translational BCI research.

In summary, this book volume deals with both the advanced, fundamental research and practical considerations involved in taking *EEG-based BCIs from laboratory experiments to real-world applications*. All contributors have done an excellent job in highlighting the advances and challenges in their respective research topics. The fact that the majority of studies presented in this volume involve end-users, and cover a range of human conditions caused by disease and injury, is a strong endorsement of how the field is progressing toward the translation of BCI research into viable neurotechnology that can improve the quality of life for many and that can change lives for many. There are, no doubt, still significant challenges and, therefore, a need for continued fundamental and translational research. It is hoped that this book volume serves as a valuable source of information and a key reference point for the next wave of research and development in the evolution of BCIs.

Damien Coyle

User Training

PART

I

User Training

Advances in user-training for mental-imagery-based BCI control: Psychological and cognitive factors and their neural correlates

1

C. Jeunet*,†,1, B. N'Kaoua*, F. Lotte†

*Laboratoire Handicap Activité Cognition Santé, University of Bordeaux, Bordeaux, France
†Project-Team Potioc/LaBRI, Inria Bordeaux Sud-Ouest, Bordeaux, France
1Corresponding author: Tel.: +33-5-24574067, e-mail address: camille.jeunet@inria.fr

Abstract

While being very promising for a wide range of applications, mental-imagery-based brain–computer interfaces (MI-BCIs) remain barely used outside laboratories, notably due to the difficulties users encounter when attempting to control them. Indeed, 10–30% of users are unable to control MI-BCIs (so-called BCI illiteracy) while only a small proportion reach acceptable control abilities. This huge interuser variability has led the community to investigate potential predictors of performance related to users' personality and cognitive profile. Based on a literature review, we propose a classification of these MI-BCI performance predictors into three categories representing high-level cognitive concepts: (1) users' relationship with the technology (including the notions of computer anxiety and sense of agency), (2) attention, and (3) spatial abilities. We detail these concepts and their neural correlates in order to better understand their relationship with MI-BCI user-training. Consequently, we propose, by way of future prospects, some guidelines to improve MI-BCI user-training.

Keywords

Brain–computer interfaces, Interuser variability, User-training, Predictors of performance, Neural correlates, Sense of agency, Computer anxiety, Attention, Spatial abilities, Improving training protocols

Progress in Brain Research, Volume 228, ISSN 0079-6123, http://dx.doi.org/10.1016/bs.pbr.2016.04.002
© 2016 Elsevier B.V. All rights reserved.

1 INTRODUCTION

Brain–computer interfaces (BCIs) are communication systems that enable their users to send commands to computers by means of brain signals alone (Wolpaw and Wolpaw, 2012). These brain signals are usually measured using electroencephalography (EEG), and then processed by the BCI. For instance, a BCI can enable a user to move a cursor to the left or to the right of a computer screen by imagining left- or right-hand movements, respectively. Since they make computer control possible without any physical activity, EEG-based BCIs have promised to revolutionize many application areas, notably to control assistive technologies (eg, control of text input systems or wheelchairs) for motor-impaired users (Millán et al., 2010; Pfurtscheller et al., 2008) and rehabilitation devices for stroke patients (Ang and Guan, 2015) or as input devices for entertainment and human–computer interaction (Graimann et al., 2010), to name but a few (Van Erp et al., 2012). Despite this promising potential, such revolutions have not yet been delivered, and BCIs are still barely used outside research laboratories (Van Erp et al., 2012; Wolpaw and Wolpaw, 2012). The main reason why current BCI fail to deliver is their substantial lack of reliability and robustness (Van Erp et al., 2012; Wolpaw and Wolpaw, 2012). In particular, BCI too often fail to correctly recognize the user's mental commands. For example, in a study with 80 users, the average classification accuracy was only 74.4%, for a BCI using two imagined movements as commands (Blankertz et al., 2010). Moreover, it is estimated that between 10% and 30% of BCI users, depending on the BCI type, cannot control the system at all (so-called BCI illiteracy/deficiency) (Allison and Neuper, 2010).

BCIs, as the name suggests, require the interaction of two components: the user's brain and the computer. In particular, to operate a BCI, the user has to produce EEG patterns, eg, using mental imagery tasks, which the machine has to recognize using signal processing and machine learning. So far, to address the reliability issue of BCI, most research efforts have been focused on EEG signal processing and machine learning (Allison and Neuper, 2010; Bashashati et al., 2007; Makeig et al., 2012). While this has contributed to increased performances, improvements have been relatively modest, with classification accuracy being still relatively low and BCI illiteracy/deficiency still high (Allison and Neuper, 2010; Wolpaw and Wolpaw, 2012). To make BCI truly reliable and thus useful, it is also necessary to ensure the user can produce clear, stable, and distinct EEG patterns. Indeed, BCI control is known to be a skill that must be learned and mastered by the user (Wolpaw and Wolpaw, 2012). This means that (1) the BCI performances of a user become better with practice and thus that (2) the user needs to learn how to produce these stable, clear, and distinct EEG patterns to successfully control a BCI (Lotte et al., 2013a; Neuper and Pfurtscheller, 2010). This need for training is particularly salient for BCI based on mental-imagery (MI) tasks. With the so-called mental-imagery-based brain–computer interfaces (MI-BCIs), users send mental commands by performing MI tasks, eg, movement imagination or mental mathematics, which are then recognized by the BCI and translated into commands for the application.

In this chapter, we focus on this type of BCI which is prominent in many BCI applications such as stroke rehabilitation (Ang and Guan, 2015), the control of wheelchairs or prosthetics (Millán et al., 2010), and entertainment applications (Lotte et al., 2013b), among many others.

Designing a reliable MI-BCI thus requires that the MI-BCI user has been properly and specifically trained to control that BCI. Current training approaches have been rather similar across the different MI-BCI designs so far, and can be divided into two main families: the operant conditioning approach (Wolpaw et al., 1991) and the machine learning approach (Millán et al., 2002). While these two training approaches differ in the way the classifier is defined (manually defined vs optimized on EEG data), both approaches require to provide feedback to user. Such feedback is generally visual, indicating both the mental task recognized by the classifier together with the system's confidence in the recognized task. A typical and very popular example is the Graz BCI protocol (Pfurtscheller and Neuper, 2001). In this protocol, users are instructed to perform kinesthetic imagination of left- or right-hand movements following the on-screen display of an arrow pointing either left or right, respectively. They then receive visual feedback in the form of a bar extending toward the left or the right, depending on whether a left- or right-hand movement was recognized by the BCI. The length of the bar is proportional to the classifier output. Users are typically trained with such an MI-BCI protocol over several sessions (ie, on several days), each session being composed of 4–6 runs, and a run comprising about 15–20 trials per mental task.

However, even with state-of-the-art signal processing and classification algorithms, a tremendous inter-, and intra-subject variability has been observed in terms of performance (command classification accuracy) in virtually every MI-BCI paper, both with the machine learning and the operant conditioning approaches (Allison and Neuper, 2010; Kübler et al., 2013; Wolpaw and Wolpaw, 2012). Thus, it is now clear that one of the major aspects contributing to MI-BCI control performances is the individual characteristics of the BCI user (Kübler et al., 2013). However, it is neither entirely clear which characteristics do impact BCI performances, why they have such an impact nor what the extent of this impact is. This has led the BCI community to look for predictors of MI-BCI performance, ie, individual characteristics that correlate with the command classification accuracy. Indeed, identifying such predictors would allow BCI designers to find the most suitable BCI for a given user. Alternatively, or additionally, identifying such predictors would enable BCI researchers to identify what makes some users fail to control MI-BCI and thus to work on designing specific solutions. In particular, a promising research direction would be to propose MI-BCI training approaches that are adapted to users, according to their characteristics (Lotte and Jeunet, 2015; Lotte et al., 2013a). Interestingly enough, a number of neurophysiological predictors have been identified, as reviewed in Ahn and Jun (2015). Some psychological predictors have also been identified for P300-based BCI and BCI based on sensorimotor rhythms (SMR) (Kleih and Kübler, 2015). However, to the best of our knowledge, there is no comprehensive and up-to-date review that surveys the psychological and cognitive factors that impact MI-BCI performances, presents some cognitive mechanisms that could explain why they have such an impact, sheds light on the underlying neural correlates of these factors and proposes theoretical solutions that could take these factors into account to improve MI-BCI training. This is therefore what this chapter sets out to offer.

First, this chapter surveys the BCI literature in order to identify the psychological and cognitive factors that correlate with MI-BCI performance (Section 2). This survey allowed the identification of different predictors that can be organized into three main categories, each representing a higher-level cognitive concept. In particular, it was found that existing predictors of MI-BCI performance were mostly related to the relationship between users and technology, their attention and their spatial abilities. Thus, the following sections define each of these concepts in more detail, and describe their neural correlates: the user–technology relationship is dealt with in Section 3, attention is discussed in Section 4 and spatial abilities are attended to Section 5. Finally, Section 6 proposes some future prospects and theoretically promising levers to improve MI-BCI training by taking into account each of these three high-level factors.

2 PSYCHOLOGICAL AND COGNITIVE FACTORS RELATED TO MI-BCI PERFORMANCE

This first section offers a review of the latest developments in our understanding of the psychological and cognitive factors reported to influence MI-BCI performance (ie, control accuracy). These factors can be divided into three groups. The first group includes the factors associated with the *States* of the user. Users' states are described by Chaplin et al. (1988) as "temporary, brief, and caused by external circumstances." The second group gathers the factors related to the users' *Traits*, characterized as "stable, long-lasting, and internally caused" with respect to one's environment and experience (Chaplin et al., 1988). Finally, the third group comprises the factors that can be qualified neither as *Traits* nor as *States*, ie, demographic characteristics, habits, and environment-related factors.

2.1 EMOTIONAL AND COGNITIVE STATES THAT IMPACT MI-BCI PERFORMANCE

Some aspects of users' states, and more specifically of their cognitive and emotional states, have been reported to influence their MI-BCI performance in terms of control accuracy. First, Nijboer et al. (2008) have shown that mood (measured using a subscale of the German Inventory to assess Quality of Life—Averbeck et al., 1997) correlates with BCI performance. On the other hand, both attention (Daum et al., 1993; Grosse-Wentrup et al., 2011; Grosse-Wentrup and Schölkopf, 2012), assessed for instance by means of digit spans or block taping spans (Daum et al., 1993), and motivation (Hammer et al., 2012; Neumann and Birbaumer, 2003; Nijboer et al., 2008) levels have repeatedly been shown to positively correlate with performance, both in the context of slow cortical potential (SCP) and SMR-based BCI. Furthermore, in their study, Nijboer et al. (2008) suggested that higher scores in mastery confidence, ie, how confident the participant was that the training would be successful, were correlated to better SMR regulation abilities, whereas higher rates of fear of incompetence were correlated to lower SMR regulation abilities. This last point has also been suggested in Kleih et al. (2013) for stroke patients taking part in BCI-based rehabilitation. More generally speaking, fear of the BCI system has been shown to affect performance (Burde and Blankertz, 2006; Nijboer et al., 2010; Witte et al., 2013). In the same vein, control beliefs (Witte et al., 2013), ie, participants' beliefs that their efforts to learn would result in a positive outcome, and self-efficacy (Neumann and Birbaumer, 2003), which can be defined as participants' beliefs in their own abilities to manage future events, have been suggested to play a role in BCI performance, in an SMR and an SCP paradigm, respectively. Mastery of confidence, control beliefs, and self-efficacy can be classed as context-specific states, ie, states triggered each time a person faces a specific situation.

2.2 PERSONALITY AND COGNITIVE TRAITS THAT INFLUENCE MI-BCI PERFORMANCE

On the one hand, several aspects of the cognitive profile have been related to BCI control ability. Memory span and attentional abilities have been shown to correlate with the capacity to regulate SCP in patients with epilepsy (Daum et al., 1993). Hammer et al., (2012) also showed that attention span played a role in one-session SMR-BCI control performance. In addition, active learners seem to perform better than reflective learners (Jeunet et al., 2015a) in a context of MI-BCI control. This dimension, active vs reflective, is one of the four dimensions of the Learning Style that can be assessed using the Index of Learning Style test (Felder and Spurlin, 2005). Abstractness, ie, imagination abilities, has also been shown to correlate with classification accuracy in an MI-BCI experiment (Jeunet et al., 2015a). Furthermore, Hammer et al. (2012) have proposed a model for predicting SMR-BCI performance—which includes visuomotor coordination (assessed with the Two-Hand Coordination Test) and the degree of concentration (assessed with the Attitudes Towards Work)—that reaches significance. More recently, Hammer et al. (2014) tested this model in a four session experiment (one calibration and three training sessions) within a neurofeedback-based SMR-BCI context (ie, involving no machine learning). Their results showed that these parameters explained almost 20% of SMR-BCI performance in a linear regression. However, the first predictor, ie, visual–motor coordination, failed significance. With this model, the average prediction error was less than 10%. Moreover, kinesthetic imagination and visual–motor imagination scores have both been shown to be related to BCI performance by Vuckovic and Osuagwu (2013). Finally, a strong correlation [$r = 0.696$] between mental rotation scores and MI-based BCI performance has been reported (Jeunet et al., 2015a) in a six session experiment, during which participants had to learn to perform three MI tasks (motor imagery of the left hand, mental subtraction, and mental rotation of a 3D shape). This finding has recently been replicated in an experiment based purely on motor imagery (imagination of left- and right-hand movements) in which mental rotation scores correlated with participants' peak performance [$r = 0.464$] (Jeunet et al., 2016).

On the other hand, concerning personality traits, Burde and Blankertz (2006) have obtained a positive correlation between a Locus of control score related to dealing with technology and the accuracy of BCI control. More recently, tension and self-reliance (ie, autonomy toward the group) were related to MI-BCI performance (measured in terms of classification accuracy) in a model also including abstractness abilities and the active/reflective dimension of the learning style (Jeunet et al., 2015a). This model enabled prediction of more than 80% of the between-participant variance in terms of performance with an average prediction error of less than 3%.

2.3 OTHER FACTORS IMPACTING MI-BCI PERFORMANCE: DEMOGRAPHIC CHARACTERISTICS, EXPERIENCE, AND ENVIRONMENT

Some other factors that have also been related to the ability to control a BCI, cannot be classified as either traits or states. These factors can be divided into three categories: (1) demographic characteristics, (2) experience/habits, and (3) environment. Concerning the first point, demographic characteristics, age, and gender have been related to SMR-BCI performance (Randolph, 2012): women being more capable than men and over 25 year-olds being more competent than their younger counterparts. On the other hand, some habits or experiences have been shown to increase SMR-BCI control abilities (Randolph, 2012; Randolph et al., 2010). More specifically, playing a musical instrument, practicing a large number of sports, playing video games (Randolph, 2012), as well as spending time typing and the ability to perform hand and arm or full-body movements (Randolph et al., 2010) positively impact SMR-BCI performance. However, the consumption of affective drugs seems to have the opposite effect (Randolph et al., 2010). Finally, the user's environment, and more particularly the quality of caregiving for patients, has been suggested in an anonymous report to play a role in SMR-BCI performance (Kleih and Kübler, 2015).

2.4 TO SUMMARIZE: MI-BCI PERFORMANCE IS AFFECTED BY THE USERS' (1) RELATIONSHIP WITH TECHNOLOGY, (2) ATTENTION, AND (3) SPATIAL ABILITIES

To summarize, the predictors of MI-BCI performance can be gathered into the three following categories, as depicted in Table 1:

- Category 1—*The user–technology relationship and the notion of control* (spades, see Table 1): indeed, based on the literature, it appears that people who apprehend the use of technologies (and more specifically the use of BCIs) and who do not feel in control, experience more trouble controlling BCIs.

Table 1 This Table Summarizes the Different Predictors (State, Trait, and Others) That Have Been Related to MI-BCI Performance in the Literature

States	Emotional state	♣	Mood (Nijboer et al., 2008)
	Cognitive state	♣	Attention level (Grosse-Wentrup and Schölkopf, 2012; Grosse-Wentrup et al., 2011)
		♣	Motivation (Hammer et al., 2012; Neumann and Birbaumer, 2003; Nijboer et al., 2008)
		♠	Mastery confidence (Nijboer et al., 2008)
		♠	Fear of the BCI (Burde and Blankertz, 2006; Nijboer et al., 2010; Witte et al., 2013)
		♠	Control beliefs (Witte et al., 2013)
		♠	Fear of incompetence (Kleih et al., 2013; Nijboer et al., 2008)
		♠	Self-efficacy (Neumann and Birbaumer, 2003)
Traits	Personality	♠	Locus of control for dealing with technology (Burde and Blankertz, 2006)
		♠	Tension (Jeunet et al., 2015a)
		♠	Self-reliance (Jeunet et al., 2015a)
	Cognitive profile	♣	Attention span (Hammer et al., 2012)
		♣	Attentional abilities (Daum et al., 1993)
		♣	Attitude toward work (Hammer et al., 2012)
		♣	Memory span (Daum et al., 1993)
		♦	Visual–motor coordination (Hammer et al., 2012, 2014)
		♦	Learning style: active vs reflective learners (Jeunet et al., 2015a)
		♦	Kinesthetic imagination score (Vuckovic and Osuagwu, 2013)
		♦	Visual–motor imagination score (Vuckovic and Osuagwu, 2013)
		♦	Mental rotation scores (Jeunet et al., 2015a)
		♦	Abstractness (Jeunet et al., 2015a)
Other factors	Demographic data	•	Age (Randolph, 2012)
		•	Gender (Randolph, 2012)
	Experience	♦	Playing a music instrument (Randolph, 2012)
		♦	Practicing sports (Randolph, 2012)
		♦	Playing video games (Randolph, 2012)
		♦	Hand and arm movements (Randolph et al., 2010)
		♦	Time spent typing (Randolph et al., 2010)
		♦	Full body movements (Randolph et al., 2010)
		♣	Consumption of affective drugs (Randolph et al., 2010)
	Environment	•	Quality of caregiving (Kleih and Kübler, 2015)

The predictors related to the user–technology relationship are associated to spades, while those related to attention are associated to clubs and those related to spatial abilities are associated to diamonds.

- Category 2—*Attention* (clubs, see Table 1): this category includes both attentional abilities (trait) and attention level (state). The latter can fluctuate with respect to different parameters such as environmental factors, mood, or motivation. Both these aspects of attention have been repeatedly evoked as being predictors of BCI performance.
- Category 3—*Spatial Abilities* (diamonds, see Table 1): many predictors depicted in the previous brief review are related to motor abilities (eg, two-hand coordination, sports, or music practice) or to the ability to produce mental images (eg, kinesthetic imagination scores or abstractness abilities). These predictors can be gathered under the label of "spatial abilities."

It is noteworthy that in the vast majority of the experiments during which the predictors were computed, users were BCI-naïve and thus novices. Indeed, as stated earlier, predictors were generally computed during the first training session, whereas learning to control an MI-BCI requires several training sessions (McFarland et al., 2010; Neuper and Pfurtscheller, 2010; Pfurtscheller and Neuper, 2001). In the next paragraph, we will argue that the involvement of the predictors in Category 1, ie, *the User–Technology Relationship and the Notion of Control*, can be explained by the fact that users were BCI-naïve while the involvement of the predictors in Categories 2 and 3, ie, *Attention and Spatial Abilities*, can be explained by the fact they were novices.

First, when confronted with a new technology, and even more so when this technology is associated with a new interaction paradigm (as is the case here with MI), users are likely to experience anxiety and a related low feeling of control during their first interaction attempts. Yet, the level of control perceived by a user (ie, to what extent they consider being responsible for the perceived outcome of their actions) has been shown to positively correlate with motivation, performance, and general skill acquisition (Achim and Al Kassim, 2015; Saadé and Kira, 2009; Simsek, 2011). These elements, which will be described in further detail in Section 3, both explain why the notions of anxiety and control are involved in BCI performance and how they are related to other predictors.

Second, the definition of attention and spatial abilities as two major categories of MI-BCI performance predictors is consistent with *Phase # 1* of the Ackerman model of interindividual differences during skill acquisition (Ackerman, 1988). In his model, Ackerman argues that skill acquisition is divided into three phases and that interindividual differences are explained by different factors according to the phase in which the user is (Neumann and Birbaumer, 2003):

- Phase #1: Slow and error prone performance—During this phase, interindividual differences are mainly explained (1) by task-appropriate abilities and (2) by "cognitive-intellectual general ability, involving a strong demand on the cognitive attentional system" (Neumann and Birbaumer, 2003).
- Phase #2: Redefinition and strengthening of the stimulus-response connections of the skill—During this second phase, speed of perception plays a major role in interindividual differences.

- Phase #3: Automatic phase—During this third phase, noncognitive psychomotor abilities are mostly responsible for interindividual differences (Wander et al., 2013).

As stated earlier, BCI users were in an early stage of learning, ie, in Phase #1 of the Ackerman model, when the predictors were computed. This is coherent with the fact that BCI literature reports a strong involvement of (1) spatial abilities and (2) attention. Spatial abilities correspond to the ability to produce, transform, and interpret mental images (Poltrock and Brown, 1984). Thus, they can be defined as "task-appropriate" abilities for an MI-BCI control task. On the other hand, the involvement of attentional state and trait is consistent with the second factor responsible for inter-individual differences in Phase #1, namely, "cognitive-intellectual general ability" and the "cognitive attentional system."

The concepts associated with each of the three categories of predictors, ie, relationship with technology, attention, and spatial abilities are introduced, and their neural correlates are described in the following sections.

3 THE USER–TECHNOLOGY RELATIONSHIP: INTRODUCING THE CONCEPTS OF COMPUTER ANXIETY AND SENSE OF AGENCY—*DEFINITION AND NEURAL CORRELATES*

In the previous section, we stated that some predictors of MI-BCI performance could be gathered under the label "user–technology relationship." These factors can be divided into two categories: (1) the apprehension of the use of technology and (2) the notion of control.

On the one hand, the fear of the BCI system (Burde and Blankertz, 2006; Nijboer et al., 2010; Witte et al., 2013), the fear of incompetence (Kleih et al., 2013; Nijboer et al., 2008), and tension (Jeunet et al., 2015a), all having been shown to negatively impact MI-BCI performance, reflect a certain apprehension of the user toward BCI use. This apprehension can be defined as *computer anxiety* (CA).

On the other hand, the locus of control related with dealing with the technology (Burde and Blankertz, 2006) will influence the extent to which users feel in control while using the BCI. In the same vein, levels of mastery confidence (Nijboer et al., 2008), control beliefs (Witte et al., 2013), and self-efficacy (Neumann and Birbaumer, 2003) will impact the experience of control of the technology. An experimental study (Brosnan, 1998) suggested that self-efficacy would determine the way the person attempts to solve the task and that it would explain around 50% of the variance in the task performance. Besides, self-efficacy has been suggested to be related to motivation, work engagement, and performance (Achim and Al Kassim, 2015). This would be consistent with the MI-BCI literature as both self-efficacy and motivation were involved in MI-BCI users' control abilities. It appears that people with high a self-efficacy level perceive failure as a challenge, and not as a threat (Achim and Al Kassim, 2015) which could explain why they are prone to persevere, and thus more likely to reach good performances. Furthermore, Vlek et al. (2014) indicate that when users feel in control, their attitude toward the BCI system is more positive which enables them to replenish mental resources and increase motivation which in turn induces a better task engagement. Both these studies and the predictors stress the importance of the notion of control to reach better MI-BCI control abilities. This notion of control can be conceptualized as the *sense of agency*.

These two aspects of the user–technology relationship, namely the apprehension of the technology and the notion of control, are much related. In the following sections, we will further detail these two phenomena and the neural correlates associated to the sense of agency (indeed, to our knowledge, no studies have investigated the neural correlates of the specific concept of CA). We will notably see that the *sense of agency* (ie, the feeling of being in control) actually mediates CA (ie, the apprehension of the technology).

3.1 APPREHENSION OF TECHNOLOGY: THE CONCEPT OF CA—*DEFINITION*

Computer Anxiety (CA), also called "Tech-Stress" (Achim and Al Kassim, 2015), can be classed as a *context-specific anxiety*, ie, a transitory neurotic anxiety ranging between anxiety trait and anxiety state (Saadé and Kira, 2009). Indeed, it is a kind of anxiety specifically associated to one context: the use of a computer or of a computer-based technology.

Brosnan (1998) has shown that CA has a direct influence over performance when an unforeseen or unknown event occurs during the interaction process. Moreover, CA has been shown to impact the perceived ease-of-use of the technology, ie, high CA will result when perceived difficulty is high. Both these elements explain why CA plays a major part when people are first exposed to new technologies, especially when the paradigm of interaction is new for them, as is the case for MI-BCI control. Brosnan (1998) insists on the fact that even those who do not usually experience it, may undergo CA when confronted with a piece of technology that is new to them. Besides, around one-third of the population is thought to experience CA to some degree: from preferring not to use the technology to palpitations while using it (Brosnan, 1998). The relationship between anxiety and performance could be explained, according to Brosnan (1998), by the fact that anxious people devote more cognitive resources to "off-task" efforts (such as worrying about their performance), which induces shifts in attention between task and "off-task" considerations. As a consequence, the focused attention level dedicated to the task is decreased and fewer resources are available to perform the task. Thus, the task takes longer to complete, and performances drop in the case of tasks in which a limited amount of time is allocated. Furthermore, Simsek (2011) identifies CA as being an affective response due to one's beliefs about one's lack of ability to control the technology. This perception of the level of control that one can exert on the task corresponds to the concept of self-efficacy. Simsek (2011) argues that decreasing CA, and thus increasing self-efficacy, would lead to a better skill acquisition.

To summarize, based on empirical and theoretical studies, it seems that CA levels could enable to predict one's level of self-efficacy, which in turn could enable prediction of one's performance. More specifically, self-efficacy mediates the impact of CA on performance (Saadé and Kira, 2009).

3.2 "I DID THAT!": THE CONCEPT OF SENSE OF AGENCY—*DEFINITION*

The sense of agency can be defined as "the sense that I am the one who is causing or generating an action" (Gallagher, 2000). The sense of agency is of utmost importance when a person is controlling an external device, since it will influence their affect toward the technology, and thus their commitment to the task and their performance (Vlek et al., 2014). However, in the context of MI-BCI, experiencing this sense of agency is not straightforward. Indeed, as a component of the "who" system (De Vignemont and Fourneret, 2004; Farrer and Frith, 2002), ie, a mechanism which allows one to attribute one's own actions to oneself, the sense of agency depends on the sensory feedback resulting from the action. In other words, it depends upon a bodily experience (Damasio, 1999). Yet, the absence of proprioceptive feedback when performing MI tasks prevents this bodily experience from occurring (Haselager, 2013), and should theoretically inhibit the sense of agency. However, evidence exists that the sense of agency does not only depend on the outcome of an action, but also that it is triggered before the action takes place (Gallagher, 2012; Synofzik et al., 2008) which explains why MI, under certain conditions, can be associated with a sense of agency (Peres-Marcos et al., 2009).

The sense of agency can be divided into two components (Farrer and Frith, 2002; Gallagher, 2012; Synofzik et al., 2008): (1) the feeling of agency and (2) the judgement of agency (also called feeling of ownership). The feeling of agency is pre-reflective, implicit, low-level, and nonconceptual while the judgement of agency is reflective, explicit, high-order, belief-like, and conceptual. In other words, the feeling of agency precedes the action, and triggered during the preparation of the action, while the judgement of agency results from the computation of the comparison between the predicted and actual outcomes of the action. Synofzik et al. (2008) explains that a feeling of agency must be conceptually processed for a judgement or an attribution of agency to occur. The judgement of agency has been investigated in more depth than the feeling of agency in the literature (Chambon et al., 2013).

In order to experience a judgement of agency, three principles must be respected (Vlek et al., 2014): (1) the priority principle: the conscious intention to perform an act must immediately precede the action, (2) the consistency principle: the sensory outcome must fit the predicted outcome, and (3) the exclusivity principle: one's thoughts must be the only apparent cause of the outcome (ie, one must not believe there to be an outside influence). Moreover, several indicators influencing the judgement of agency have been proposed (Wegner, 2003; Wegner et al., 2004): bodily and environmental cues (Where am I?), bodily feedback (proprioceptive and kinesthetic information), bodily feedforward (ie, the predicted sensory feedback), sensory feedback, social cues, action consequences, and action-relevant thoughts (thinking about doing beforehand, in other words: the feeling of agency). On the one hand, the absence of some of these markers can lead to "a case of automatism" (Wegner, 2003), that is to say to the absence of judgement of agency: the agent is "doing without feeling." On the other hand, the manipulation of the same markers can lead to "an illusion of agency/ownership" (Wegner, 2003): agents who are "feeling without doing," and thus think they are in control although they are not.

3.3 "I DID THAT!": THE CONCEPT OF SENSE OF AGENCY—*NEURAL CORRELATES*

As stated by Ehrsson et al. (2004), the neural correlates underlying the sense of agency remain poorly understood. However, some brain regions have been repeatedly associated with this phenomenon. More specifically, here we will focus on the premotor cortex (PMC), and more precisely on its ventral part, ie, the supplementary motor area (SMA), as well as on the angular gyrus (AG) which is part of the posterior parietal cortex (PPC), on the anterior insula and on the cerebellum. All of the aforementioned brain areas have been reported to be involved in sensorimotor transformation and motor control as well as in the sense of agency (David et al., 2008).

Self-agency has been shown to be underlain by an increased activity in the PMC (Ehrsson et al., 2004; Farrer and Frith, 2002) and more specifically in its ventral part, the SMA (Farrer and Frith, 2002; Kühn et al., 2013). The neural populations in the ventral PMC (SMA) and parietal PMC have been stated to represent both the seen and felt position of the limbs (Ehrsson et al., 2004). Thus, it is thought that the PMC enables a multisensory integration and thus provides a mechanism for bodily attribution (Ehrsson et al., 2004). Farrer and Frith (2002) have also suggested that the insula may play a role in the experience or agency. More specifically, they measured an increase in activity in the anterior insula when a person was aware of causing an action. The authors justify this implication by the fact that the insula's role is to integrate all the concordant multimodal sensory signals associated with voluntary movements. This result seems very consistent with the literature, since the activation of both these regions has been linked to awareness and execution of self-generated actions, to action preparation and to subjects' own intention to act (David et al., 2008).

Contrariwise, the activation of the PPC has been shown to negatively correlate with the sense of agency: the more a person tends to attribute the action to another person, the more the PPC is activated (Farrer and Frith, 2002). In other words, the activity in the PPC—and more specifically in the AG—increases when discrepancies are noticed between the predicted and the actual sensory outcomes of the action (Chambon et al., 2013). Indeed, PPC activation is linked to the processing of visual–motor incongruence during self-generated actions (David et al., 2008). In this process, the cerebellum acts as a relay to inform about the sensorimotor discrepancies between the predicted and actual outcomes of the action (David et al., 2008). But it seems that the AG also monitors the signals linked to action selection in the dorsolateral prefrontal cortex to prospectively provide information about the subjective feeling of control over action outcomes (Chambon et al., 2013). Thus, the online monitoring of these signals by the AG may provide the subject with "a subjective marker of volition, prior to the action itself" (Chambon et al., 2013). While consistent, these correlates are still discussed. For instance, Kühn et al. (2013) report no correlation between AG activation and their subjective measure of agency.

The fact that these brain areas belong to different functional brain networks could explain their role in self-agency. For instance, the insula and the PPC have been shown to be involved in complex representations of the self (Farrer and Frith, 2002). Farrer and Frith (2002) suggested that the relocation from the insula (when experiencing self-agency) to the PPC (when attributing the outcome to another person) could correspond to a shift in the attentional process from the egocentric to the allocentric point of view. In a similar vein, the PPC and the SMA are the key nodes in the human mirror neuron system: they encode motor aspects of actions performed by oneself or by another person (David et al., 2008).

To summarize, the sense of agency seems to be related to complex interconnections between several brain areas enabling one to experience (1) a feeling of agency before the action outcome (through the involvement of the PMC/SMA and cerebellum among others) but also (2) a judgement of agency by comparing the predicted and perceived outcomes (notably through the activation of the insula and the AG/PPC). However, the neural processes involved in each of these phenomena, namely the feeling and judgement of agency, as well as the differences between both, require further investigation (David et al., 2008).

4 ATTENTION—*DEFINITION AND NEURAL CORRELATES*

The second category of factors that have been found to correlate with BCI performances contains attention-related predictors. Indeed, both attentional traits, ie, the BCI user's intrinsic attentional capacities, and attentional states, ie, the amount of the user's attentional resources dedicated to the BCI task, were found to be correlated to BCI performances. To summarize (see Table 1), the attentional traits predicting BCI performances include attention span (Hammer et al., 2012), attentional abilities (Daum et al., 1993), attitude toward work (Hammer et al., 2012) which also measures the capacity to concentrate on a task, and memory span (Daum et al., 1993) which measures the ability to maintain attention (Engle et al., 1999). The higher the attentional abilities of BCI users, the better the BCI classification accuracy they will reach. There is also some evidence that the attentional state of BCI users seems to be correlated to their BCI performances. Indeed, two different neurophysiological markers based on neural correlates of the attentional state were defined and measured in single-trial EEG signals. They were both found to be significantly correlated to the classification accuracy obtained for these trials (Bamdadian et al., 2014; Grosse-Wentrup and Schölkopf, 2012; Grosse-Wentrup et al., 2011) (see Section 4.2 for more details on these two EEG predictors based on attentional states).

Another factor, which is not a result of attention alone but is, however, related to it, is the user's motivation for a given BCI session, which has also been found to be predictive of their BCI performances (Hammer et al., 2012; Neumann and Birbaumer, 2003; Nijboer et al., 2008). Indeed, attention appears to be a critical factor in many models of motivation (Keller, 2008, 2010).

Finally, there are a number of other factors that have been found to be correlated to BCI performances that are not related to attention per se, but that are likely to impact the attentional resources that users devote to the BCI task. These include mood (Nijboer et al., 2008), the consumption of affective drugs (Randolph et al., 2010), as well as environmental factors for patients such as room temperature, sleep quality, or headaches (Neumann and Birbaumer, 2003).

The following sections define and describe in more detail some of the cognitive mechanisms of attention, their associated neural correlates, and their relevance to BCI control.

4.1 ATTENTION—*DEFINITION*

Attention could be defined as the "the ability to focus cognitive resources on a particular stimulus" (Frey et al., 2014b). According to Posner and Petersen (1990), the attention system can be divided into three main subsystems, each of which corresponds to a major attentional function. These three subsystems are the alerting system, the orienting system, and the executive control system. The alerting function is responsible for maintaining a state of vigilance over long periods of time, ie, it is responsible for sustained attention. Sustained attention (or vigilance) is necessary to perform long and usually tedious tasks. The orienting function is involved in selecting information among different information streams, such as different modalities (sounds, images) or different spatial or temporal locations. It is implicated in ignoring distracting events, and is thus involved in what is known as selective attention. The third function, executive control, is involved in the awareness of events and in the management of attentional resources, which are limited. Indeed, two tasks competing for attention will interfere with each other, thus possibly reducing performances for these tasks. Executive control is therefore involved in what is known as focal attention. For further details concerning the different components of attention, the interested reader can refer to Petersen and Posner (2012), Posner and Boies (1971), and Posner and Petersen (1990). It is also important to note that attentional abilities and resources vary between individuals (Petersen and Posner, 2012).

Attention has been known for many years to be necessary in ensuring successful learning (Nissen and Bullemer, 1987). Indeed, if learners do not assign enough attentional resources to a given learning task, eg, because they have to perform dual-attentional tasks (ie, split their attentional resources between two tasks), their learning performance will be greatly reduced, or they may even fail to be aware of relevant learning material and fail the learning task altogether (Nissen and Bullemer, 1987). Keller even stated that "attention is a prerequisite for learning" (Keller, 1987). This gave birth to the ARCS model of instructional design, a well-known model used to design learning material and training tasks (Keller, 1987, 2008). ARCS stands for attention, relevance, confidence and satisfaction, which are the four main components of human motivation that are necessary to ensure successful learning. In order to ensure an efficient instruction and training, the ARCS model states that it is necessary to get the attention of students on the relevant learning stimulus (thus ignoring distractors), and to sustain this attention over the duration of the instruction, in order to focus the attentional resources on training-relevant problems (Keller, 1987). We can see here that the three subsystems of attention (sustained attention, selective attention, and focal attention) are therefore involved in the learning process. Since BCI control requires training, it therefore makes sense that it also requires the user's attentional resources, and thus that attention and motivation are predictors of BCI performance.

4.2 ATTENTION—*NEURAL CORRELATES*

Interestingly enough, the attention system corresponds to specific anatomical structures in the brain that are different than those dedicated to information processing (Posner and Petersen, 1990). Each of the three attention subsystems (alerting, orienting, and executive control) corresponds to a specific brain network (Petersen and Posner, 2012; Posner and Petersen, 1990). The alerting network, although still not fully understood, seems to primarily involve the right hemisphere (frontal and parietal lobes), including the right inferior parietal lobule with the AG and thalamic areas (Petersen and Posner, 2012; Seghier, 2013). The orienting network notably involves the frontal eye fields, the intraparietal sulcus and the superior parietal lobe, the temporoparietal junction, the AG, and the ventral frontal cortex (Petersen and Posner, 2012; Seghier, 2013). Finally, the Executive Network involves multiple brain areas, including the medial frontal cortex, the anterior cingulate cortex, the dorsolateral prefrontal cortex, the anterior prefrontal cortex, the precuneus, the thalamus, the anterior insula, the intraparietal sulcus, and the intraparietal lobule. There is large interindividual variability in the efficiency of these networks which explains, at least in part, the interindividual variations in attentional abilities, ie, attentional traits (Petersen and Posner, 2012).

There are also a number of electrophysiological neural correlates, in particular spectral variations in EEG signals that are related to change in attention levels. Regarding the alerting system, decreased vigilance levels are associated with a slowing of EEG frequencies, ie, in an increased power for low frequency EEG rhythms (delta ~1–4 Hz, theta ~4–7 Hz, low alpha ~7–10 Hz), and a decreased power for higher frequency EEG rhythms (Frey et al., 2014a,b; Roy, 2015). The amplitude of event-related potentials such as the P300 or the parietal N100 also decreases with lower vigilance. Concerning the orienting system, alpha activity (~8–12 Hz) has also been shown to be related to selective attention, with higher alpha power indicating lower attention, and occipital alpha providing information on the location of spatial visual attention (Frey et al., 2014a,b). A delta (3–8 Hz) over beta (16–24 Hz) power ratio has also been used as a marker of sustained attention (Bamdadian et al., 2014).

Finally, it seems that the Gamma (55–85 Hz) power in attentional networks related to the executive control system also correlates with the attentional level (Grosse-Wentrup et al., 2011).

Consistent with the cognitive literature stressing the impact of attention on success in task-learning, the BCI community has also identified a number of neural correlates of attention that are related to BCI performance. For instance, variation in Gamma power, notably in executive control attentional brain networks, has been found to be correlated to SMR-BCI performance and can be used to predict successful or unsuccessful classification both for SMR-BCI (Grosse-Wentrup and Schölkopf, 2012; Grosse-Wentrup et al., 2011) and for general MI-BCI (Schumacher et al., 2015). Moreover, the extent of activation of the dorsolateral prefrontal cortex (involved in executive control as seen earlier), was also found to differ between SMR-BCI users with high performances and SMR-BCI users with low performances (Halder et al., 2011). Finally, an EEG predictor based on frontal Theta, occipital Alpha, and midline Beta power, which are all neural correlates of sustained attention (thus involving the alerting system) as described previously, has been shown to correlate with SMR-BCI performances (Bamdadian et al., 2014).

5 SPATIAL ABILITIES—*DEFINITION AND NEURAL CORRELATES*

As already seen, many studies have highlighted the role of spatial abilities on BCI performance variation across subjects. The general hypothesis is that low BCI performers have less-developed abilities to generate or maintain mental images.

For example, Vuckovic and Osuagwu (2013) relate the results of kinesthetic and visual–motor imagery questionnaires to performances obtained with a BCI based on object-oriented motor imagery. They show that the kinesthetic score could be a relevant predictor of performance for an SMR-BCI. Moreover, the physical presence of the object of an action facilitates motor imagination in poor imagers. It is important to note that the impact of imagery abilities on BCI performances might be mediated by differences in brain activation. Guillot et al. (2008) attempted to identify the functional neuroanatomical networks that dissociate able vs poor imagers. They used functional magnetic resonance imaging (fMRI) to compare the pattern of cerebral activations in able and poor imagers during both the physical execution and MI of a sequence of finger movements. Results show that good imagers activated the parietal and ventrolateral premotor regions to a greater degree, both having been shown to play a critical role in the generation of mental images.

Another spatial skill that has been shown to be related to MI-BCI performance is mental rotation ability. Mental rotation scores (measured using a mental rotation test) are a robust measure of spatial abilities, particularly for mental representation and manipulation of objects (Borst et al., 2011; Poltrock and Brown, 1984). Mental rotation scores have been shown to be correlated with scores obtained with other tests of spatial abilities such as space relation tests or spatial working memory (Just and

Carpenter, 1985; Kaufman, 2007), suggesting that they may be related to more general spatial skills (Thompson et al., 2013). Jeunet et al. (2015a) have explored the relationships between MI-BCI performance and the personality and cognitive profile of the user. The main result is a strong correlation between MI-BCI performances and mental rotation scores.

In the same vein, Randolph (2012) has shown that video game experience is likely to enhance BCI performance. Many studies have noted a link between video game experience and spatial abilities. For example, spatial abilities can be improved through playing action video game (Dorval and Pepin, 1986; Subrahmanyam and Greenfield, 1994). Feng et al. (2007) observe that performances in a mental rotation test are enhanced after only 10 h of training with an action video game. More remarkably, these authors found that playing an action video game can decrease the well-known gender disparity in mental rotation tasks (see also Ventura et al., 2013). All these elements strongly suggest that the link between video game experience and BCI performance could be mediated by spatial ability levels.

Moreover, Randolph (2012) showed that using hand and arm movements, or full-body movements (such as playing sports or musical instruments) also favors BCI performances. Many authors have also observed a link between spatial abilities and motor processes (Hoyek et al., 2014). For example, Moreau et al. (2011) compared elite and novice athletes and found a significant relationship between sports performance, activity, sport-specific training, and mental rotation abilities. In the Hoyek et al. (2014) study, the motor performance of 7- to 8-year-old and 11- to 12-year-old children was measured in a steeple chase and an equivalent straight distance sprint. Data revealed that the time taken to complete the chase was influenced by speed and sex, but also by the individual mental rotation ability. These links between motor performances and spatial abilities are also attested by neuroimaging studies, which provide evidence that motor areas are involved in mental rotation (eg, Lamm et al., 2007). Thus, it can be assumed that the relationship between BCI performance and motor processes are mediated by spatial ability levels.

Finally, Hammer et al. (2012) found that visual–motor coordination abilities constitute a predictor of BCI efficiency, and Scordella et al. (2015) showed a relationship between motor coordination and visual-spatial skills (measured by a visual-constructive task). We can again assume that the link between visual–motor coordination and BCI efficiency is mediated by visual-spatial abilities.

5.1 SPATIAL ABILITIES—*DEFINITION*

As mentioned earlier, spatial abilities embody the ability to produce, transform, and interpret mental images (Poltrock and Brown, 1984). Lohman (1993) greatly highlighted the pivotal role of spatial abilities and particularly MI in all models of human abilities. This author reports that high levels of spatial abilities have frequently been linked to creativity in many domains (arts, but also science and mathematics) (see also Shepard, 1978). He also indicates that Albert Einstein, as well as other well-known physicists (such as James Clerk Maxwell, Michael Faraday, and

Herman von Helmholtz) and inventors, have been reported to have had high spatial abilities, and that these abilities played an important role in their creativity. Furthermore, studies on developmental cognitive skills have consistently shown that spatial aptitude and mathematical aptitude are closely related (Geary et al., 2000). Moreover, the importance of spatial ability in educational pursuits and in the professional world was examined by Wai et al. (2009), with particular attention devoted to STEM (science, technology, engineering, and mathematics) domains. Participants (Grades 9–12, $N = 400{,}000$) were tracked for 11 years. Results showed that spatial abilities were a significant predictor of achievement in STEM, even after taking into account possible third variables such as mathematical and verbal skills (see also Humphreys et al., 1993; Shea et al., 2001).

The key role of MI in human cognition has also been highlighted by the fact that it is involved in certain pathological situations such as Posttraumatic Stress Disorders (Brewin et al., 1996), schizophrenia (Oertel-Knöchel et al., 2013), depression (Rogers et al., 2002), social phobia (Clark and Wells, 1995), and bipolar disorder (Holmes et al., 2008) (for a review, see Pearson et al., 2013). For example, impairment in image generation or in mental rotation of letters has been shown in unipolar major depression (Rogers et al., 2002).

Furthermore, the potential role of imagery for motor skill learning has been demonstrated in many situations, such as learning new skills in sports (Murphy, 1994), improving performance both in novice and expert surgeons (Cocks et al., 2014), and in Paralympics athletes (Martin, 2012).

Today, it is common to distinguish between large scale and small-scale spatial abilities (Hegarty et al., 2006). Large scale abilities refer to the notion of wayfinding (or spatial navigation) defined as "the process of determining and following a path or route between origin and destination" (Golledge, 1999). Wayfinding is assessed by tasks such as search, exploration, route following, or route planning in contexts including outdoor and urban environments, indoor spaces and virtual reality (VR) simulations (Wiener et al., 2009).

By contrast, small-scale spatial abilities are usually assessed by paper and pencil tests, which involve perceptually examining, imagining, or mentally transforming representations of small shapes or easy-to-handle objects (Hegarty et al., 2006). These abilities also refer to the notion of MI consisting of several component processes. For example, the classical model of Kosslyn (1980, 1994) proposes a distinction between four components, namely image generation (the ability to form mental images), image maintenance (the ability to retain images over time), image scanning (the ability to shift one's attention over an imaged object), and image manipulation (the ability to rotate or otherwise transform images) (see also Marusan et al., 2006).

5.2 SPATIAL ABILITIES—*NEURAL CORRELATES*

The neural correlates of visual MI are subject to much debate. Some authors claim a functional equivalence between visual perception and visual MI, with the retinotopic areas in the occipital lobe acting as common substrate (for a review, see Bartolomeo,

2008). However, some brain lesion studies indicate that visual imagery is possible without the involvement of primary visual areas (Chatterjee and Southwood, 1995). Nevertheless, the frontal eye fields and the superior parietal lobule seem to play a crucial role in generating visual mental images (Mechelli et al., 2004). These results have been confirmed by Zvyagintsev et al. (2013) showing that the visual network comprises the fusiform gyrus bilaterally and a frontoparietal network involving the superior parietal lobule and frontal eye field bilaterally.

Motor imagery is a particular case of MI defined as the mental simulation of a specific action without any corresponding motor output (Jeannerod, 1994). The neural substrate that underlies motor imagery has also been subject to many debates. Miller et al. (2010) measured cortical surface potentials in subjects during overt action and imagery of the same movement. They demonstrated the role of primary motor areas in movement imagery and showed that imagery activated the same brain areas as actual motor movement. In their study, the magnitude of imagery-induced cortical activity was reduced compared to real movement, but this magnitude was largely enhanced when subjects learned to use imagery to control a cursor in a feedback task. It is important to note that a distinction has been made between two types of motor imagery depending on the point of view adopted to imagine an action: the third person perspective point-of-view consists in self-visualizing an action, whereas the first person point of view perspective implies somesthetic sensations elicited by the action. Some evidence suggested that visual (third person) and somesthetic/kinesthetic (first person) motor imagery recruit distinct neural networks. Guillot et al. (2004) showed that visual imagery predominantly activated the occipital regions and the superior parietal lobules, whereas kinesthetic imagery preferentially activated the motor-associated structures and the inferior parietal lobule. Finally, Ridderinkhof and Brass (2015) specify that activation during kinesthetic MI is not just a subliminal activation of the same brain areas involved in the real action. For these authors the activation during kinesthetic imagery is similar to the activation associated with the preparatory planning stages that eventually lead to the action (Jeannerod, 2006).

Interestingly enough, it has been shown that kinesthetic motor imagery leads to better MI-BCI performances than visual–motor imagery (Neuper et al., 2005). Nevertheless, the distinction between these different forms of MI, their neural correlates, and their relationships with the neural circuits involved in motor processes remain to be elucidated.

To conclude this section, spatial skills play a crucial role in human cognition as they are involved in many activities including art, music, mathematics, engineering, literature, etc. Jeunet et al. (2015a) demonstrated that spatial skills and particularly mental rotation scores are a relevant predictor of BCI efficiency. Moreover, many skills related to spatial abilities (such as playing sports, musical instruments, and action video games) have been shown to be likely to improve BCI performance. It is an attractive hypothesis to consider that imagery abilities could contribute to explaining the "BCI illiteracy" phenomenon, but further investigations are needed to make a more systematic study of the relationship between certain cognitive and personality predictors, spatial abilities, and BCI efficiency.

6 PERSPECTIVES: THE USER–TECHNOLOGY RELATIONSHIP, ATTENTION, AND SPATIAL ABILITIES AS THREE LEVERS TO IMPROVE MI-BCI USER-TRAINING

6.1 DEMONSTRATING THE IMPACT OF THE PROTOCOL ON CA AND SENSE OF AGENCY

In Section 3, we stressed the impact of the notion of control on performance, notably through its mediating role on CA. The notion of control can be conceptualized as a *Sense of Agency*, ie, "the sense that I am the one who is causing or generating an action" (Gallagher, 2000). Given the strong impact that the sense of agency has on performance, it seems important to increase it as far as possible. Yet, in the context of MI-BCI control, it is not straightforward. Indeed, the sense of agency is mainly based on a bodily experience, whereas performing MI tasks does not provide the participant with any sensory feedback. Thus, here we would like to insist on the importance of the feedback, especially during the primary training phases of the user (Coyle et al., 2015; McFarland et al., 1998). Indeed, in the first stages, the fact that the technology and the interaction paradigm (through MI tasks) are both new for the users is likely to induce a pronounced CA associated with a low sense of agency. Providing the users with a sensory feedback informing them about the outcome of their "action" (MI task) seems necessary in order to trigger a certain sense of agency at the beginning of their training. This sense of agency will in turn unconsciously encourage users to persevere, increase their motivation, and thus promote the acquisition of MI-BCI related skills, which is likely to lead to better performances (Achim and Al Kassim, 2015; Saadé and Kira, 2009; Simsek, 2011). This process could underlie the (experimentally proven) efficiency of biased feedback for MI-BCI user-training. Indeed, literature (Barbero and Grosse-Wentrup, 2010) reports that providing MI-BCI users with a biased (only positive) feedback is associated with improved performances while they are novices. However that is no longer the case once they have progressed to the level of expert users. This result could be due to the fact that positive feedback provides users with an illusion of control which increases their motivation and will to succeed. As explained by Achim and Al Kassim (2015), once users reach a higher level of performance, they also experience a high level of self-efficacy which leads them to consider failure no longer as a threat (Kleih et al., 2013) but as a challenge. And facing these challenges leads to improvement.

However, to be efficient, this feedback must follow certain principles (Vlek et al., 2014). First, the priority principle, ie, the conscious intention to perform an act must immediately precede the act: here, the feedback must appear after the users become conscious they have to perform the act and have started to do it. Second, the consistency principle, ie, the sensory outcome must fit the predicted outcome. And third, the exclusivity principle, ie, one's thoughts must be the only apparent cause of the outcome. This last point suggests that the user should not think that another person is controlling the feedback. Thus, if the feedback is biased, it has to be subtle enough so that the user is not aware of it. Otherwise, the user will not feel in control anymore. The two latter principles could explain why biased feedback is efficient for novices but not for experts. Indeed, experts develop the ability to generate a precise predicted outcome that usually matches the actual outcome (when the feedback is not biased). This explains why when the feedback is biased, and therefore the predicted and actual outcomes do not match, expert users attribute the discrepancy to external causes more easily. In other words, it can be hypothesized that experts might be disturbed by a biased feedback because they can perceive that it does not truly reflect their actions, thus decreasing their sense of being in control.

Furthermore, Beursken (2012) tested the impact of the concept of transparent mapping in a pseudo-BCI experiment. A protocol is said to be transparent when the task and the feedback are consistent. In the experiment, the sense of agency of the participants was tested in two conditions: one transparent and one nontransparent. The participants had to imagine movements of their left and right hands. In the transparent condition, a virtual left or right hand moved on the screen when left- or right-hand imagination was recognized, respectively. In the nontransparent condition however, the same tasks were associated with both hands making "thumbs-up" or "okay" movements. Participants felt more in control in the transparent condition and reported that less effort was required to understand the instructions and remember the meaning of the feedback. Consequently, more resources were available to perform the task. This result means that when designing the feedback, researchers must be careful to propose a feedback that fits the mental task. Yet, in standard training protocols such as Pfurtscheller and Neuper's (2001), MI tasks are associated with a bar extending in a specific direction. Although the direction of the bar is consistent with the task when participants are asked to perform left- and right-hand motor imagery, it is not particularly natural. In a recent study (Jeunet et al., 2015b), we showed that an equivalent tactile feedback provided on users' hands was more efficient. With reference to the Ackerman model (1988), when the outcome (the feedback) is consistent with the task, during the Phase #1 the "task-appropriate" abilities, here spatial abilities, decrease in influence and thus the between-subject variability in terms of performance also decreases. However, when the outcome is inconsistent with the task, the requirements for information processing are important and the impact of the user-profile, here in terms of attentional abilities and spatial abilities, remains constant (Neumann and Birbaumer, 2003) which makes the between-subject variability due to these factors stable even in advanced phases of the training.

To summarize, we can derive three guidelines for MI-BCI protocol design that could enable users to experience a better sense of agency. First, providing the users, especially novices, with a sensory feedback is essential as it will increase their potential sense of agency. While positively biasing the feedback can improve novice users' sense of agency, motivation, and will to succeed, this is not the case for expert users who can be disturbed by biased feedback. Second, in order to be efficient the feedback must follow the principles of priority, consistency, and exclusivity. And finally, transparent protocols, ie, protocols in which the feedback fits with the MI task, should be associated with better MI-BCI performance as (1) they induce a greater sense of agency and (2) they require less workload to be processed and thus grant more cognitive resources to be devoted to the task.

6.2 RAISING AND IMPROVING ATTENTION

As mentioned previously, attention is a major predictor of BCI performances, and it has been shown that the better the users' attentional abilities and the more attentional resources they devote to BCI training, the better their BCI performances. Therefore, BCI performances could be improved by designing BCI training protocols that (1) train users to increase their attentional abilities and (2) ensure the attentional resources of users are directed toward and maintained on the BCI training tasks.

A first suggestion to improve BCI training is to include attention-training tasks, to improve users' attentional abilities and thus their BCI performance. A number of approaches may be used, but recently researchers have identified meditation and neurofeedback as promising approaches for attention training (Brandmeyer and Delorme, 2013). Indeed, it has been shown that meditation is actually a successful form of attention training that improves the ability of practitioners to focus their attentional resources on a given task, possibly for long periods of time, as well as their ability to ignore distractors. Expert meditators have been found to show different activation levels than nonmeditators in the frontoparietal and the default mode networks, in fMRI studies (Braboszcz et al., 2010). The Gamma EEG power in these areas also differs between expert meditators and nonmeditators (Lutz et al., 2008). Such brain networks are notably involved in sustained attention. Interestingly enough, these areas, and gamma activity originating from there, have both been identified as being related to BCI performance (Grosse-Wentrup and Schölkopf, 2012; Halder et al., 2011). The promising usefulness of meditation practice for BCI training is further supported by research from a number of groups who have found that meditation increases SMR-BCI performances (eg, Eskandari and Erfanian, 2008; He et al., 2015). In other words, meditation improves attentional abilities, which in turn improves BCI performances.

Attentional capabilities can also be improved using neurofeedback training, eg, by providing users with games in which they have to increase an EEG measure of their attentional level to win (Lim et al., 2010, 2012). For instance, in Lim et al. (2012), children with attention deficit hyperactivity disorder (ADHD) were asked to play a game in which the speed of the character they were controlling was directly proportional to their attentional level, as measured by EEG. Thus, they had to focus as much attention as possible on the game in order to move fast enough to complete it in the allotted time. This was shown to be a successful form of attention training, which reduced the children's ADHD symptoms (Lim et al., 2010, 2012). Gamma neurofeedback was also shown to be useful in improving visual attention abilities

(Zander et al., 2013). To the best of our knowledge, such neurofeedback training of attentional capabilities has not been explored with the aim of MI-BCI control abilities, and thus could be a promising direction to investigate.

A second suggestion to improve BCI training is to design BCI training tasks, feedbacks, and environments that capture and maintain the attention of the user on the BCI training. In the ARCS model for instructional design, Keller suggests a number of approaches to get and maintain users' attention (Keller, 1987). In particular, this includes ensuring the active participation of the learners, adding game-like training, having a variety of supports, training materials and tasks, ensuring concrete training tasks, and feedbacks as well as encouraging inquiry and curiosity from the learners (Keller, 1987). In practice, for MI-BCI, this could be achieved by having BCI users control video games or VR applications with their BCI, hence ensuring game-like training, active user participation, and concrete training tasks. The fact that VR and game-based BCI training were actually shown to improve BCI performances (Lotte et al., 2013b) further supports this suggestion. Moreover, rather than using the same standard training protocol continuously and repeatedly, variety in training can be obtained by adding other training tasks, with different objectives. For instance, users can be asked to practice each MI task separately, or to perform a given MI task as fast as possible as in Ramsey et al. (2009) for instance. Finally, to encourage enquiry and add concreteness to the training, BCI users could be provided with richer and more motivating visualization and feedbacks that enable them to see the impact of a given MI task on their EEG signals in real time, thus motivating them to explore different strategies. This could be achieved using recently proposed EEG visualization techniques such as Teegi (Frey et al., 2014a,b). With this approach, users can see their own brain activity and EEG features in real time, displayed in a user-friendly way on the head of a physical puppet they can manipulate.

Other considerations could be taken into account to ensure users assign an appropriate amount of attentional resources to the BCI training. For instance, the training protocol should avoid requiring split attention, ie, requiring users to divide their attentional resources between two different subtasks, especially if these tasks involve the same modality, eg, two visual processing tasks. This would indeed deplete the user's cognitive resources and lead to poorer performances and lower learning efficiency for any training task (Sweller et al., 1998). This is a relevant point to consider as BCI feedback is often provided on the visual modality, while the controlled BCI application generally also requires visual processing, eg, to control a game or a visual speller. Interestingly enough, it has been shown that providing tactile instead of visual feedback in such a split-attentional task leads to improved BCI performance (Jeunet et al., 2015b). Thus, it would be worth studying as well auditory feedback, see, eg, (McCreadie et al., 2014), in similar contexts. Finally, since it is possible to measure users' attentional level from EEG signals, this could be used in real time to detect whether they are paying enough attention, and warn them to refocus their attention, if necessary, as suggested in Schumacher et al. (2015).

6.3 INCREASING SPATIAL ABILITIES

If it appears that the training of spatial abilities could improve BCI performance, it is necessary to review the studies that have tried to better understand the effects of training on spatial skills.

For instance, it is well known that men perform better than women in spatial perception and mental rotation tests (see for example, Linn and Petersen's, 1985). In a meta-analysis, Baenninger and Newcombe (1989) found that improvements in men and women remain parallel in response to practice and training, so that gender differences remain constant. However, other studies have shown greater performance improvement in women than in men (Okagaki and Frensch, 1994), or a waning of gender differences (Kass et al., 1998).

In a meta-analysis of training studies, Uttal et al. (2013) indicated that spatial skills are highly malleable and that training in spatial thinking is effective, durable, and transferable (to skills that have not been subject to specific training). The authors outline that many studies in which transfer effects were present administered large numbers of trials during training, which allowed to conclude that such a transfer is possible if sufficient training or experience is provided. The meta-analysis did not show a significant effect of age or a significant effect of the type of training on the degree of improvement. Finally, the initial level of spatial skills affected the degree of malleability. Participants who started at lower levels of performance improved more in response to training than those who started at higher levels (Uttal et al., 2013).

Terlecki et al. (2008) confirmed the impact of long-term practice or repeated testing, and training capacity to improve mental rotation performances. However, neither mental rotation practice nor video game training reduced gender differences. It is also important to note that these effects can last over several months and the effects of video game experience are transferable to tasks that have not been trained for.

All these results are extremely interesting as they show that training and practice can improve spatial skills. Mental training has been used to improve performances in many domains such as sports, surgical performances, and music. However, very few studies have focused on BCI practice.

Erfanian and Mahmoudi (2013) have investigated the role of mental practice and concentration on a natural EEG-based BCI for hand grasp control. The imagery task used was the imagination of hand grasping and opening. For imagery training, the authors used a video-based method where subjects watched themselves performing hand-closing and -opening while undertaking imagery. The results showed that mental and concentration practice increased the classification accuracy of the EEG patterns. Moreover, mental practice more specifically affected the motor areas. This study shows very promising results on the way spatial training could improve BCI performances.

In the study of Jeunet et al. (2015a), participants followed a standard training protocol composed of six identical sessions during which they had to learn to perform three MI tasks: mental rotation, mental subtraction, and left-hand motor imagery. On the one hand, no improvement in performance was noticed between the 1st and 6th session on average, suggesting that participants did not learn despite the large number of sessions. On the other hand, the BCI performance appeared to be strongly correlated to participants' mental rotation scores. In the near future, the authors propose to test the impact of spatial training and particularly mental rotation training on BCI efficiency. The authors also considered applications in the context of patients suffering from motor impairments, since MI abilities can be preserved after brain injury. In any case, it is a challenging project to study the impact of spatial training on reducing the "BCI illiteracy" phenomenon, and thus enabling BCI to be more systematically used outside laboratories.

7 CONCLUSION

In this chapter, we performed a literature survey in order to identify the psychological and cognitive factors related to MI-BCI performance. This survey enabled us to classify most of the predictors into three categories representing higher-level cognitive concepts: (1) the user–technology relationship (comprising the notions of anxiety and control during the interaction), (2) attention, and (3) spatial abilities. These three categories appear to be extremely relevant in the context of MI-BCI training. Indeed, the predictors were computed during the early stages of training, ie, during the first or first few sessions. Moreover, most studies were performed on BCI-naïve users who were confronted with a BCI for the first time. Yet, the literature suggests that this situation (early training phase and first exposition to the technology) can induce an important level of anxiety associated to a low sense of agency, both having potential negative repercussions on performance (Achim and Al Kassim, 2015; Saadé and Kira, 2009; Simsek, 2011). This first point justifies the involvement of the *category 1* predictors, ie, those related to the users' relationship with the technology. Besides, the Ackerman model (Ackerman, 1988) suggests that during the early stages of learning (phase #1), the interuser variability in terms of performance in mainly due to (1) differences in "task-appropriate" abilities and (2) high-level cognitive abilities such as attention. These two aspects correspond to the two other predictor categories that we identified. Indeed, spatial abilities (*category 3*), ie, the ability to produce, transform, and interpret mental images (Poltrock and Brown, 1984) can be considered as "task-appropriate" abilities in the context of MI-BCI training, while attention (*category 2*) clearly corresponds to the second parameter influencing interuser variability in Ackerman's model. Hence the elaboration of these three categories: the inclusion of the predictors in different categories was justified, the associated cognitive models were introduced, and the neural correlates related to each concept were described. This work was intended to provide a better understanding of the different factors impacting MI-BCI training and thus to provide, in the prospects section, a discussion about how these factors could be taken into account when designing future protocols in order to optimize user-training. More specifically, the impact of the training protocol on users' CA and sense of agency was demonstrated. It has been suggested that a biased positive feedback could increase novice users' sense of agency and thus increase their performance. Also, the significance of respecting the principles of priority, consistency, exclusivity, and a transparent mapping between the task and the feedback was emphasized. Furthermore, it should also be possible to increase BCI training efficiency by considering the user's attention. In particular, attention capabilities can be improved using meditation or neurofeedback. Moreover, attentional resources can be optimally directed toward BCI training by using gamified BCI training tasks, varied tasks, rich and friendly feedback, as well as multimodal feedbacks. BCI efficiency could also be improved by using training procedures of spatial skills, since spatial training has proved to enhance performances in many domains (sport, music, surgical practice, etc.). Moreover, this improvement has been shown to be effective, durable, and transferable (to skills that have not been subject to specific training) when the training duration is long enough. Finally, the user's mental rotation ability seems to be a very good candidate to be trained, since this ability has been identified as a relevant predictor of BCI performance and since the consequences of mental rotation training on spatial and more general skills have been clearly identified.

To conclude, we hope that this work will be useful to guide the design of new protocols and improve MI-BCI user-training so that these technologies become more accessible to their end-users. Nevertheless, it is important to note that improving training protocols is not enough. The roles of the researcher and experimenter are also of utmost importance, notably concerning: (1) the demystification of the BCI technology to reduce a priori CA, through scientific mediation and communication with the media; (2) the writing of informed-consent forms and explanations, which should be clear and informative, and provide an objective estimation of the benefit on risk balance and enable to regulate any form of hope that may be generated (Nijboer et al., 2013); and (3) the social presence and trust relationship with the user, which are essential in facilitating the learning process (Kleih et al., 2013).

REFERENCES

Achim, N., Al Kassim, A., 2015. Computer usage: the impact of computer anxiety and computer self-efficacy. Proc. Soc. Behav. Sci. 172, 701–708.

Ackerman, P.L., 1988. Determinants of individual differences during skill acquisition: cognitive abilities and information processing. J. Exp. Psychol. Gen. 117 (3), 288.

Ahn, M., Jun, S.-C., 2015. Performance variation in motor imagery brain–computer interface: a brief review. J. Neurosci. Methods 243, 103–110.

Allison, B., Neuper, C., 2010. Could Anyone Use a BCI? Brain Computer Interfaces. Springer, London.

Ang, K.K., Guan, C., 2015. Brain–computer interface for neurorehabilitation of upper limb after stroke. Proc. IEEE 103 (6), 944–953.

Averbeck, M., Leiberich, P., Grote-Kusch, M.T., Olbrich, E., Schroder, A., Brieger, M., et al., 1997. Skalen zur Erfassung der Lebensqualitat (SEL)—Manual. Swets & Zeitlinger B.V, Frankfurt.

Baenninger, M., Newcombe, N., 1989. The role of experience in spatial test performance: a meta-analysis. Sex Roles 20, 327–344.

Bamdadian, A., Guan, C., Ang, K.K., Xu, J., 2014. The predictive role of pre-cue EEG rhythms on MI-based BCI classification performance. J. Neurosci. Methods 235, 138–144.

Barbero, A., Grosse-Wentrup, M., 2010. Biased feedback in brain-computer interfaces. J. Neuroeng. Rehabil. 7, 34.

Bartolomeo, P., 2008. The neural correlates of visual mental imagery: an ongoing debate. Cortex 44 (2), 107–108.

Bashashati, A., Fatourechi, M., Ward, R.K., Birch, G.E., 2007. A survey of signal processing algorithms in brain-computer interfaces based on electrical brain signals. J. Neural Eng. 4 (2), R32–R57.

Beursken, E., 2012. Transparency in BCI: the effect of the mapping between an imagined movement and the resulting action on a user's sense of agency (bachelor thesis). Radboud University, The Netherlands.

Blankertz, B., Sannelli, C., Halder, S., Hammer, E., Kübler, A., Müller, K.-R., Curio, G., Dickhaus, T., 2010. Neurophysiological predictor of SMR-based BCI performance. NeuroImage 51 (4), 1303–1309.

Borst, G., Kievit, R.A., Thompson, W.L., Kosslyn, S.M., 2011. Mental rotation is not easily cognitively penetrable. J. Cogn. Psychol. 23 (1), 60–75.

Braboszcz, C., Hahusseau, S., Delorme, A., 2010. Meditation and neuroscience: from basic research to clinical practice. In: Carlstedt, R. (Ed.), Integrative Clinical Psychology, Psychiatry and Behavioral Medicine: Perspectives, Practices and Research. Springer Publishing, New York, pp. 1910–1929.

Brandmeyer, T., Delorme, A., 2013. Meditation and neurofeedback. Front. Psychol. 4, 688.

Brewin, C.R., Dalgleish, T., Joseph, S., 1996. A dual representation theory of posttraumatic stress disorder. Psychol. Rev. 103 (4), 670–686.

Brosnan, M.J., 1998. The impact of computer anxiety and self-efficacy upon performance. J. Comput. Assist. Learn. 14 (3), 223–234.

Burde, W., Blankertz, B., 2006. Is the locus of control of reinforcement a predictor of brain-computer interface performance? In: Paper Presented at the PASCAL Pattern Analysis, Statistical Modelling and Computational Learning.

Chambon, V., Wenke, D., Fleming, S.M., Prinz, W., Haggard, P., 2013. An online neural substrate for sense of agency. Cereb. Cort. 23 (5), 1031–1037.

Chaplin, W.F., John, O.P., Goldberg, L.R., 1988. Conceptions of states and traits: dimensional attributes with ideals as prototypes. J. Personal. Soc. Psychol. 54 (4), 541–557.

Chatterjee, A., Southwood, M.H., 1995. Cortical blindness and visual imagery. Neurology 45 (12), 2189–2195.

Clark, D.M., Wells, A., 1995. A cognitive model of social phobia. In: Heimberg, R.G., Liebowitz, M.R., Hope, D. et al., (Eds.), Social Phobia: Diagnosis, Assessment, and Treatment, vol. 41(68). John Wiley & Sons, Chichester, pp. 22–23.

Cocks, M., Moulton, C.A., Luu, S., Cil, T., 2014. What surgeons can learn from athletes: mental practice in sports and surgery. J. Surg. Educ. 71 (2), 262–269.

Coyle, D., Stow, J., McCreadie, K., McElligott, J., Carroll, Á., 2015. Sensorimotor modulation assessment and brain-computer interface training in disorders of consciousness. Arch. Phys. Med. Rehabil. 96 (3), 62–70.

Damasio, A.R., 1999. The Feeling of What Happens: Body and Emotion in the Making of Consciousness. Hartcourt Brace, New York.

Daum, I., Rockstroh, B., Birbaumer, N., Elbert, T., Canavan, A., Lutzenberger, W., 1993. Behavioural treatment of slow cortical potentials in intractable epilepsy: neuropsychological predictors of outcome. J. Neurol. Neurosurg. Psychiatr. 56, 94–97.

David, N., Newen, A., Vogeley, K., 2008. The "sense of agency" and its underlying cognitive and neural mechanisms. Conscious. Cogn. 17 (2), 523–534.

DeVignemont, F., Fourneret, P., 2004. The sense of agency: a philosophical and empirical review of the "who" system. Conscious. Cogn. 13 (1), 1–19.

Dorval, M., Pepin, M., 1986. Effect of playing a video game on a measure of spatial visualization. Percept. Mot. Skills 62 (1), 159–162.

Ehrsson, H.H., Spence, C., Passingham, R.E., 2004. That's my hand! Activity in premotor cortex reflects feeling of ownership of a limb. Science 305 (5685), 875–877.

Engle, R.W., Kane, M.J., Tuholski, S.W., 1999. Individual differences in working memory capacity and what they tell us about controlled attention, general fluid intelligence, and functions of the prefrontal cortex. In: Miyake, A., Shah, P. (Eds.), Models of Working Memory: Mechanisms of Active Maintenance and Executive Control. Cambridge University Press, Cambridge, pp. 102–134.

Erfanian, A., Mahmoudi, B., 2013. A Natural EEG-Based Brain-Computer Interface for Hand Grasp Control: The Role of Mental Practice and Concentration. Department of Biomedical Engineering, Faculty of Electrical Engineering, Iran University of Science & Technology, Tehran, Iran.

Eskandari, P., Erfanian, A., 2008. Improving the performance of brain-computer interface through meditation practicing. In: Engineering in Medicine and Biology Society, 2008. EMBS 2008. 30th Annual International Conference of the IEEE, pp. 662–665.

Farrer, C., Frith, C.D., 2002. Experiencing oneself vs another person as being the cause of an action: the neural correlates of the experience of agency. Neuroimage 15 (3), 596–603.

Felder, R.M., Spurlin, J., 2005. Applications, reliability and validity of the index of learning styles. Int. J. Eng. Educ. 21 (1), 103–112.

Feng, J., Spence, I., Pratt, J., 2007. Playing an action video game reduces gender differences in spatial cognition. Psychol. Sci. 18 (10), 850–855.

Frey, J., Gervais, R., Fleck, S., Lotte, F., Hachet, M., 2014a. Teegi: tangible EEG interface. In: Proceedings of the 27th Annual ACM Symposium on User Interface Software and Technology, pp. 301–308.

Frey, J., Mühl, C., Lotte, F., Hachet, M., 2014b. Review of the use of electroencephalography as an evaluation method for human-computer interaction. In: Proc. of PhyCS, pp. 214–223.

Gallagher, S., 2000. Philosophical conceptions of the self: implications for cognitive science. Trends Cogn. Sci. 4 (1), 14–21.

Gallagher, S., 2012. Multiple aspects in the sense of agency. New Ideas Psychol. 30 (1), 15–31.

Geary, D.C., Saults, S.J., Liu, F., Hoard, M.K., 2000. Sex differences in spatial cognition, computational fluency, and arithmetical reasoning. J. Exp. Child Psychol. 77, 337–353.

Golledge, R.G., 1999. Human way finding and cognitive maps. In: Golledge, R.G. (Ed.), Wayfinding Behavior: Cognitive Mapping and Other Spatial Processes. Johns Hopkins Press, Baltimore, pp. 5–45.

Graimann, B., Allison, B., Pfurtscheller, G., 2010. Brain-Computer Interfaces: Revolutionizing Human-Computer Interaction. Springer Science & Business Media.

Grosse-Wentrup, M., Schölkopf, B., 2012. High gamma-power predicts performance in sensorimotor-rhythm brain-computer interfaces. J. Neur. Eng. 9 (4), 046001.

Grosse-Wentrup, M., Schölkopf, B., Hill, J., 2011. Causal influence of gamma oscillations on the sensorimotor rhythm. NeuroImage 56, 837–842.

Guillot, A., Collet, C., Dittmar, A., 2004. Relationship between visual and kinesthetic imagery, field dependence-independence, and complex motor skills. J. Psychophysiol. 18 (4), 190–198.

Guillot, A., Collet, C., Nguyen, V.A., Malouin, F., Richards, C., Doyon, J., 2008. Functional neuroanatomical networks associated with expertise in motor imagery. Neuroimage 41 (4), 1471–1483.

Halder, S., Agorastos, D., Veit, R., Hammer, E.M., Lee, S., Varkuti, B., Bogdan, M., Rosenstiel, W., Birbaumer, N., Kübler, A., 2011. Neural mechanisms of brain–computer interface control. Neuroimage 55 (4), 1779–1790.

Hammer, E.M., Halder, S., Blankertz, B., Sannelli, C., Dickhaus, T., Kleih, S., et al., 2012. Psychological predictors of SMR-BCI performance. Biol. Psychol. 89 (1), 80–86.

Hammer, E.M., Kaufmann, T., Kleih, S.C., Blankertz, B., Kübler, A., 2014. Visuo-motor co-ordination ability predicts performance with brain-computer interfaces controlled by modulation of sensorimotor rhythms (SMR). Front. Hum. Neurosci. 8, 574.

Haselager, P., 2013. Did I do that? Brain–computer interfacing and the sense of agency. Minds Mach. 23 (3), 405–418.

He, B., Baxter, B., Edelman, B.J., Cline, C.C., Ye, W.W., 2015. Noninvasive brain-computer interfaces based on sensorimotor rhythms. Proc. IEEE 103 (6), 907–925.

Hegarty, M., Montello, D.R., Richardson, A.E., Ishikawa, T., Lovelace, K., 2006. Spatial abilities at different scales: individual differences in aptitude-test performance and spatial-layout learning. Intelligence 34 (2), 151–176.

Holmes, E.A., Geddes, J.R., Colom, F., Goodwin, G.M., 2008. Mental imagery as an emotional amplifier: application to bipolar disorder. Behav. Res. Ther. 46 (12), 1251–1258.

Hoyek, N., Collet, C., Rienzo, F., Almeida, M., Guillot, A., 2014. Effectiveness of three-dimensional digital animation in teaching human anatomy in an authentic classroom context. Anatom. Sci. Educ. 7 (6), 430–437.

Humphreys, L.G., Lubinski, D., Yao, G., 1993. Utility of predicting group membership and the role of spatial visualization in becoming an engineer, physical scientist, or artist. J. Appl. Psychol. 78 (2), 250.

Jeannerod, M., 1994. Motor representations and reality. Behav. Brain Sci. 17 (2), 229–245.

Jeannerod, M., 2006. Motor Cognition: What Actions Tell the Self, vol. 42. Oxford University Press.

Jeunet, C., N'Kaoua, B., Subramanian, S., Hachet, M., Lotte, F., 2015a. Predicting mental imagery based BCI performance from personality, cognitive profile and neurophysiological patterns. PLoS One10 (12), e0143962.

Jeunet, C., Vi, C., Spelmezan, D., N'Kaoua, B., Lotte, F., Subramanian, S., 2015b. Continuous tactile feedback for motor-imagery based brain-computer interaction in a multitasking context. In: Human-Computer Interaction–INTERACT 2015. Springer International Publishing, pp. 488–505.

Jeunet, C., Jahanpour, E., Lotte, F., 2016. Why standard training protocols should be changed: an experimental study. J. Neural Eng. Accepted.

Just, M.A., Carpenter, P.A., 1985. Cognitive coordinate systems: accounts of mental rotation and individual differences in spatial ability. Psychol. Rev. 92 (2), 137.

Kass, S.J., Ahlers, R.H., Dugger, M., 1998. Eliminating gender differences through practice in an applied visual spatial task. Hum. Perform. 11 (4), 337–349.

Kaufman, S.B., 2007. Sex differences in mental rotation and spatial visualization ability: can they be accounted for by differences in working memory capacity? Intelligence 35 (3), 211–223.

Keller, J.M., 1987. Development and use of the ARCS model of instructional design. J. Instruct. Dev. 10 (3), 2–10.

Keller, J., 2008. An integrative theory of motivation, volition, and performance. Technol. Instruct. Cogn. Learn. 6, 79–104.

Keller, J., 2010. Motivational Design for Learning and Performance: The ARCS Model Approach. Springer Science & Business Media.

Kleih, S., Kübler, A., 2015. Psychological factors influencing brain-computer interface (BCI) performance. In: Proceedings of the BCI Workshop of the SMC2015 Conference, pp. 3192–3196.

Kleih, S.C., Kaufmann, T., Hammer, E., Pisotta, I., Picchiori, F., Riccio, A., Mattia, D., Kübler, A., 2013. Motivation and SMR-BCI: fear of failure affects BCI performance. In: del R. Millan, J., Gao, S., Müller-Putz, G., Wolpaw, J.R., Huggins, J.E. (Eds.), Proceedings of the 5th International Brain-Computer Interface Meeting: Defining the Future, Asilomar Conference Center, Pacific Grove, California, USA, June 3–7, pp. 160–161.

Kosslyn, S.M., 1980. Image and Mind. Harvard University Press, Cambridge.

Kübler, A., Holz, E., Kaufmann, T., Zickler, C., 2013. A user centred approach for bringing BCI controlled applications to end-users. In: Dr. Reza Fazel-Rezai (Ed.), Brain-Computer Interface Systems—Recent Progress and Future Prospects. InTech open. http://dx.doi.org/10.5772/55802. Available from: http://www.intechopen.com/books/brain-computer-interface-systems-recent-progress-and-future-prospects/a-user-centred-approach-for-bringing-bci-controlled-applications-to-end-users.

Kühn, S., Brass, M., Haggard, P., 2013. Feeling in control: neural correlates of experience of agency. Cortex 49 (7), 1935–1942.

Lamm, C., Windischberger, C., Moser, E., Bauer, H., 2007. The functional role of dorsolateral premotor cortex during mental rotation: an event-related fMRI study separating cognitive processing steps using a novel task paradigm. NeuroImage 36 (4), 1374–1386.

Lim, C., Lee, T., Guan, C., Fung, D.S., Cheung, Y., Teng, S., Zhang, H., Krishnan, K., 2010. Effectiveness of a brain-computer interface based programme for the treatment of ADHD: a pilot study. Psychopharmacol. Bull. 43, 73–82.

Lim, C.G., Lee, T.S., Guan, C., Fung, D.S.S., Zhao, Y., Teng, S.S.W., Zhang, H., Krishnan, K.R.R., 2012. A brain-computer interface based attention training program for treating attention deficit hyperactivity disorder. PLoS One 7 (10), e46692.

Linn, M.C., Petersen, A.C., 1985. Emergence and characterization of sex differences in spatial ability: a meta-analysis. Child Dev. 56 (6), 1479–1498.

Lohman, D.F., 1993. Spatial ability and G. In: Dennis, I., Tapsfield, P. (Eds.), Human Abilities: Their Nature and Measurement. Erlbaum, Mahwah, pp. 97–116.

Lotte, F., Jeunet, C., 2015. Towards improved BCI based on human learning principles. In: 3rd International Brain-Computer Interfaces Winter Conference.

Lotte, F., Larrue, F., Mühl, C., 2013a. Flaws in current human training protocols for spontaneous brain-computer interfaces: lessons learned from instructional design. Front. Hum. Neurosci. 7, 568.

Lotte, F., Faller, J., Guger, C., Renard, Y., Pfurtscheller, G., Lécuyer, A., Leeb, R., 2013b. Combining BCI with virtual reality: towards new applications and improved BCI. In: Towards Practical Brain-Computer Interfaces. Springer, Berlin, pp. 197–220.

Lutz, A., Slagter, H.A., Dunne, J.D., Davidson, R.J., 2008. Attention regulation and monitoring in meditation. Trends Cogn. Sci. 12 (4), 163–169.

Makeig, S., Kothe, C., Mullen, T., Bigdely-Shamlo, N., Zhang, Z., Kreutz-Delgado, K., 2012. Evolving signal processing for brain–computer interfaces. Proc. IEEE 100, 1567–1584.

Martin, J., 2012. Mental preparation for the 2014 winter paralympic games. Clin. J. Sport Med. 22 (1), 70–73.

Marusan, M., Kulistak, J., Zara, J., 2006. Virtual reality in neurorehabilitation: mental rotation. In: Proceedings of the Third Central European Multimedia and Virtual Reality Conference, pp. 77–83.

McCreadie, K.A., Coyle, D.H., Prasad, G., 2014. Is sensorimotor BCI performance influenced differently by mono, stereo, or 3-D auditory feedback? IEEE Trans. Neural Syst. Rehabil. Eng. 22 (3), 431–440.

McFarland, D.J., McCane, L.M., Wolpaw, J.R., 1998. EEG-based communication and control: short-term role of feedback. Rehabil. Eng. IEEE Trans. 6 (1), 7–11.

McFarland, D., Sarnacki, W., Wolpaw, J., 2010. Electroencephalographic (EEG) control of three-dimensional movement. J. Neural Eng. 7, 036007.

Mechelli, A., Price, C.J., Friston, K.J., Ishai, A., 2004. Where bottom-up meets top-down: neuronal interactions during perception and imagery. Cereb. Cortex 14, 1256–1265.

Millán, J.d.R., Franzé, M., Cincotti, F., Varsta, M., Heikkonen, J., Babiloni, F., 2002. A local neural classifier for the recognition of EEG patterns associated to mental tasks. IEEE Trans. Neural Netw. 13 (3), 678–686.

Millán, J.d.R., Rupp, R., Müller-Putz, G.R., et al., 2010. Combining brain–computer interfaces and assistive technologies: state-of-the-art and challenges. Front. Neurosci. 4, 161. http://dx.doi.org/10.3389/fnins.2010.00161.

Miller, K.J., Schalk, G., Fetz, E.E., Nijs, M.d., Ojemann, J.G., Rao, R.P.N., 2010. Cortical activity during motor execution, motor imagery, and imagery-based online feedback. PNAS 107 (9), 4430–4435.

Moreau, D., Mansy-Dannay, A., Clerc, J., Guerrien, A., 2011. Spatial ability and motor performance: assessing mental rotation processes in elite and novice athletes. Int. J. Sport Psychol. 42 (6), 525–547.

Murphy, S.M., 1994. Imagery interventions in sport. Med. Sci. Sports Exerc. 26, 486–494.

Neumann, N., Birbaumer, N., 2003. Predictors of successful self-control during brain-computer communication. J. Neurol. Neurosurg. Psychiatry 74, 1117–1121.

Neuper, C., Pfurtscheller, G., 2010. Neurofeedback training for BCI control. In: Graimann, B., Pfurtscheller, G., Allison, B. (Eds.), Brain-Computer Interfaces. Springer, Berlin, pp. 65–78.

Neuper, C., Scherer, R., Reiner, M., Pfurtscheller, G., 2005. Imagery of motor actions: differential effects of kinesthetic and visual-motor mode of imagery in single-trial EEG. Brain Res. Cogn. Brain Res. 25, 668–677.

Nijboer, F., Furdea, A., Gunst, I., Mellinger, J., McFarland, D.-J., Birbaumer, N., Kübler, A., 2008. An auditory brain-computer interface (BCI). J. Neurosci. Methods 167, 43–50.

Nijboer, F., Birbaumer, N., Kübler, A., 2010. The influence of psychological state and motivation on brain-computer interface performance in patients with amyotrophic lateral sclerosis—a longitudinal study. Front. Neurosci. 4.

Nijboer, F., Clausen, J., Allison, B.Z., Haselager, P., 2013. The asilomar survey: stakeholders' opinions on ethical issues related to brain-computer interfacing. Neuroethics 6 (3), 541–578.

Nissen, M.J., Bullemer, P., 1987. Attentional requirements of learning: evidence from performance measures. Cogn. Psychol. 19 (1), 1–32.

Oertel-Knöchel, V., Knöchel, C., Rotarska-Jagiela, A., Reinke, B., Prvulovic, D., Haenschel, C., et al., 2013. Association between psychotic symptoms and cortical thickness reduction across the schizophrenia spectrum. Cereb. Cortex 23 (1), 61–70.

Okagaki, L., Frensch, P., 1994. Effects of video game playing on measures of spatial performance: gender effects in late adolescence. J. Appl. Dev. Psychol. 15, 33–58.

Pearson, D.G., Deeprose, C., Wallace-Hadrill, S.M., Heyes, S.B., Holmes, E.A., 2013. Assessing mental imagery in clinical psychology: a review of imagery measures and a guiding framework. Clin. Psychol. Rev. 33 (1), 1–23.

Peres-Marcos, D., Slater, M., Sanchez-Vives, M.V., 2009. Inducing a virtual hand ownership illusion through a brain-computer interface. Neuroreport 20 (6), 589–594.

Petersen, S.E., Posner, M.I., 2012. The attention system of the human brain: 20 years after. Annu. Rev. Neurosci. 35, 73–89.

Pfurtscheller, G., Neuper, C., 2001. Motor imagery and direct brain-computer communication. Proc. IEEE 89, 1123–1134.

Pfurtscheller, G., Müller-Putz, G., Scherer, R., Neuper, C., 2008. Rehabilitation with brain-computer interface systems. IEEE Comput. 41, 58–65.

Poltrock, S.E., Brown, P., 1984. Individual differences in visual imagery and spatial ability. Intelligence. 8, 93–138.

Posner, M.I., Boies, S.J., 1971. Components of attention. Psychol. Rev. 78 (5), 391–408.

Posner, M.I., Petersen, S.E., 1990. The attention system of the human brain. Ann. Rev. Neurosci. 13, 25–42.

Ramsey, L., Tangermann, M., Haufe, S., Blankertz, B., 2009. Practicing fast-decision BCI using a "goalkeeper" paradigm. BMC Neurosci. 10 (1), P69.

Randolph, A.-B., 2012. Not all created equal: individual-technology fit of brain–computer interfaces. In: 45th Hawaii International Conference on System Science HICSS, pp. 572–578.

Randolph, A.-B., Jackson, M.-M., Karmakar, S., 2010. Individual characteristics and their effect on predicting Mu rhythm modulation. Int. J. Hum. Comput. Interact. 27 (1), 24–37.

Ridderinkhof, K.R., Brass, M., 2015. How kinesthetic motor imagery works: a predictive-processing theory of visualization in sports and motor expertise. J. Physiol. Paris 109 (1), 53–63.

Rogers, M.A., Bradshaw, J.L., Phillips, J.G., Chiu, E., Mileshkin, C., Vaddadi, K., 2002. Mental rotation in unipolar major depression. J. Clin. Exp. Neuropsychol. 24 (1), 101–106.

Roy, R., 2015. Étude de corrélats électrophysiologiques pour la discrimination d'états de fatigue et de charge mentale: apports pour les interfaces cerveau-machine passives (doctoral dissertation). Grenoble Alpes.

Saadé, R., Kira, D., 2009. Computer anxiety in e-learning: the effect of computer self-efficacy. J. Inf. Technol. Educ. Res. 8 (1), 177–191.

Schumacher, J., Jeunet, C., Lotte, F., 2015. Towards explanatory feedback for user training in brain–computer interfaces. In: IEEE International Conference on Systems Man & Cybernetics (IEEE SMC).

Scordella, A., Di Sano, S., Aureli, T., et al., 2015. The role of general dynamic coordination in the handwriting skills of children. Front. Psychol. 6, 580. http://dx.doi.org/10.3389/fpsyg.2015.00580.

Seghier, M.L., 2013. The angular gyrus multiple functions and multiple subdivisions. Neuroscientist 19 (1), 43–61.

Shea, D.L., Lubinski, D., Benbow, C.P., 2001. Importance of assessing spatial ability in intellectually talented young adolescents: a 20-year longitudinal study. J. Educ. Psychol. 93 (3), 604.

Shepard, R.N., 1978. The mental image. Am. Psychol. 33 (2), 125.

Simsek, A., 2011. The relationship between computer anxiety and computer self-efficacy. Contemp. Educ. Technol. 2 (3), 177–187.

Subrahmanyam, K., Greenfield, P.M., 1994. Effect of video game practice on spatial skills in girls and boys. J. Appl. Dev. Psychol. 15 (1), 13–32.

Sweller, J., van Merrienboer, J., Pass, F., 1998. Cognitive architecture and instructional design. Educ. Psychol. Rev. 10, 251–296.

Synofzik, M., Vosgerau, G., Newen, A., 2008. Beyond the comparator model: a multifactorial two-step account of agency. Conscious. Cogn. 17 (1), 219–239.

Terlecki, M.S., Newcombe, N.S., Little, M., 2008. Durable and generalized effects of spatial experience on mental rotation: gender differences in growth patterns. Appl. Cogn. Psychol. 22 (7), 996–1013.

Thompson, J.M., Nuerk, H.C., Moeller, K., Kadosh, R.C., 2013. The link between mental rotation ability and basic numerical representations. Acta Psychol. 144 (2), 324–331.

Uttal, D.H., Meadow, N.G., Tipton, E., Hand, L.L., Alden, A.R., Warren, C., Newcombe, N.S., 2013. The malleability of spatial skills: a meta-analysis of training studies. Psychol. Bull. 139 (2), 352.

Van Erp, J., Lotte, F., Tangermann, M., 2012. Brain-computer interfaces: beyond medical applications. IEEE Comput. 45, 26–34.

Ventura, M., Shute, V., Zhao, W., 2013. The relationship between video game use and a performance-based measure of persistence. Comput. Educ. 60 (1), 52–58.

Vlek, R., van Acken, J.P., Beursken, E., Roijendijk, L., Haselager, P., 2014. BCI and a user's judgment of agency. In: Grübler, G., Hildt, E. (Eds.), Brain-Computer-Interfaces in Their Ethical, Social and Cultural Contexts. Springer, The Netherlands, pp. 193–202.

Vuckovic, A., Osuagwu, B.-A., 2013. Using a motor imagery questionnaire to estimate the performance of a brain–computer interface based on object oriented motor-imagery. Clin. Neurophysiol. 124 (8), 1586–1595.

Wai, J., Lubinski, D., Benbow, C.P., 2009. Spatial ability for STEM domains: aligning over 50 years of cumulative psychological knowledge solidifies its importance. J. Educ. Psychol. 101 (4), 817.

Wander, J.D., Blakely, T., Miller, K.J., Weaver, K.E., Johnson, L.A., Olson, J.D., Fetz, E.E., Rao, R.P.N., Ojemann, J.G., 2013. Distributed cortical adaptation during learning of a brain–computer interface task. Proc. Natl. Acad. Sci. U. S. A. 110 (26), 10818–10823.

Wegner, D.M., 2003. The Illusion of Conscious Will. MIT Press, Cambridge.

Wegner, D.M., Sparrow, B., Winerman, L., 2004. Vicarious agency: experiencing control over the movements of others. J. Pers. Soc. Psychol. 86, 838–848.

Wiener, J.M., Büchner, S.J., Hölscher, C., 2009. Taxonomy of human way finding tasks: a knowledge-based approach. Spat. Cogn. Comput. 9 (2), 152–165.

Witte, M., Kober, S.-E., Ninaus, M., Neuper, C., Wood, G., 2013. Control beliefs can predict the ability to up-regulate sensorimotor rhythm during neurofeedback training. Front. Hum. Neurosci. 7.

Wolpaw, J.R., Wolpaw, E.W., 2012. Brain-Computer Interfaces: Principles and Practice. Oxford University Press, New York.

Wolpaw, J.R., McFarland, D.J., Neat, G.W., Forneris, C.A., 1991. An EEG-based brain-computer interface for cursor control. Electroencephalogr. Clin. Neurophysiol. 78, 252–259.

Zander, T.O., Battes, B., Schölkopf, B., Grosse-Wentrup, M., 2013. Towards neurofeedback for improving visual attention. In: 5th International Brain-Computer Interface Meeting.

Zvyagintsev, M., Clemens, B., Chechko, N., Mathiak, K.A., Sack, A.T., Mathiak, K., 2013. Brain networks underlying mental imagery of auditory and visual information. Eur. J. Neurosci. 37 (9), 1421–1434.

Non-Invasive Decoding of 3D Hand and Arm Movements

PART

II

Non-Invasive
Decoding of 3D
Hand and Arm
Movements

From classic motor imagery to complex movement intention decoding: The noninvasive Graz-BCI approach

2

G.R. Müller-Putz[1], A. Schwarz, J. Pereira, P. Ofner

Graz University of Technology, Institute of Neural Engineering, Graz, Austria
[1]Corresponding author: Tel.: +43-316-873-30700; Fax: +43-316-873-30702,
e-mail address: gernot.mueller@tugraz.at

Abstract

In this chapter, we give an overview of the Graz-BCI research, from the classic motor imagery detection to complex movement intentions decoding. We start by describing the classic motor imagery approach, its application in tetraplegic end users, and the significant improvements achieved using coadaptive brain–computer interfaces (BCIs). These strategies have the drawback of not mirroring the way one plans a movement. To achieve a more natural control—and to reduce the training time—the movements decoded by the BCI need to be closely related to the user's intention. Within this natural control, we focus on the kinematic level, where movement direction and hand position or velocity can be decoded from noninvasive recordings. First, we review movement execution decoding studies, where we describe the decoding algorithms, their performance, and associated features. Second, we describe the major findings in movement imagination decoding, where we emphasize the importance of estimating the sources of the discriminative features. Third, we introduce movement target decoding, which could allow the determination of the target without knowing the exact movement-by-movement details. Aside from the kinematic level, we also address the goal level, which contains relevant information on the upcoming action. Focusing on hand–object interaction and action context dependency, we discuss the possible impact of some recent neurophysiological findings in the future of BCI control. Ideally, the goal and the kinematic decoding would allow an appropriate matching of the BCI to the end users' needs, overcoming the limitations of the classic motor imagery approach.

Keywords

Motor imagery, Movement intention, Decoding, Natural control, Neuroprosthesis, Brain–computer interface, EEG

© 2016 Elsevier B.V. All rights reserved.

1 OVERVIEW

Generally, brain–computer interfaces (BCIs) enable users to interact with the environment only by thought. Experimental strategies for BCIs are either based on focused attention on external stimuli or based on specific mental tasks (Wolpaw et al., 2002). Developments of the last years have shown that BCI based on focused attention is used for fast selections and therefore communication purposes (Halder et al., 2015; Kübler and Birbaumer, 2008; Nijboer et al., 2008a,b; Pinegger et al., 2013), whereas BCIs with specific mental strategies are used for control, eg, of wheelchairs (Galán et al., 2008) or for restoration of grasping movements (Kreilinger et al., 2013; Rohm et al., 2013; Rupp et al., 2015). In the first the end user is located in front of a computer screen or table, whereas in the latter the end user needs free view, maybe is moving around and wants to endogenously control the application.

In this chapter, we are going to discuss the mental activity "motor imagery" (MI), and how this task was shaped from classic detection of a general motor imagination to more complex motor intention tasks. We start by describing classical mental strategies used by sensorimotor rhythm-based BCI, eg, left/right hand MI, and how they can be exploited for control and communication. The following sections focus specially on providing a more natural neuroprosthesis control for people with high spinal cord injury (SCI) to control grasping and reaching of their paralyzed upper limbs by applying functional electrical stimulation (FES). We review the literature about movement decoding and show how to decode trajectories from executed movements and discuss how these findings can be applied to motor imaginations. In the last sections, we address the decoding of movement targets and goals.

2 METHODS
2.1 CLASSIC MOTOR IMAGINATION

The Graz-BCI approach is based on the detection of changes in electroencephalographic (EEG) rhythms which are modulated by MI (Pfurtscheller et al., 2006). MI describes the mental rehearsal of a motor task without its execution. Typical kinesthetic MI tasks are (1) sustained imagination of squeezing a training ball, (2) repetitive opening and closing of the hand, or (3) sustained/repeated movement imagination of both feet, eg, dorsi or plantar flexion of both feet. These tasks induce a power increase or decrease of EEG amplitudes in certain frequency bands (mainly rolandic-mu and beta band) relative to a reference period and are referred to as event-related (de)synchronization (Pfurtscheller and Aranibar, 1979). These changes in brain oscillations are time locked but not phase locked to a given cue or event, which means that these changes occur after a certain time, but with random phase. These relative power changes can be shown in time–frequency plots as depicted in Fig. 1 (Graimann et al., 2002).

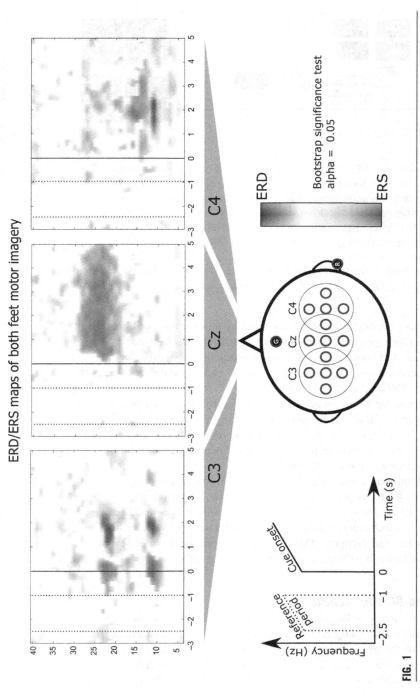

FIG. 1

Examples of ERD/ERS time–frequency maps for kinesthetic motor imagery of both feet (planar flexion/extension). Laplacian derivations were taken over C3, Cz, and C4 (signals referenced to the right ear lobe (R), ground (G) located at position AFz). *Hot (dark gray in the print version) colors* indicate significant ($p<0.05$) power decrease (ERD), and *cold (gray in the print version) colors* indicate significant ($p<0.05$) power increase. Seventy-five trials recorded using the Graz-BCI paradigm were used for calculation (see Fig. 2 for further explanation of the paradigm). The time axis (x-axis) is referenced to the cue onset (second 0, *solid black vertical line*). The frequency axis (y-axis) displays a bandwidth between 4 and 40 Hz. The *dashed perpendicular lines* indicate the reference period which was taken for calculation (−2.5 to −1 s before the cue). Notice the strong ERD (beta range) during the MI period over Cz, while simultaneously ERS occurs over C3 (alpha and beta) and C4 (beta).

Data taken from Schwarz, A., et al., 2015. A co-adaptive sensory motor rhythms brain–computer interface based on common spatial patterns and random forest. Conf. Proc. IEEE Eng. Med. Biol. Soc. 2015, 1049–1052.

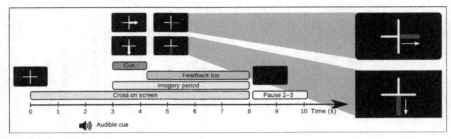

FIG. 2

A two-class version of the Graz-BCI paradigm. At second 0, a cross appears on the screen followed by an auditory tone to get the user's attention at second 2. At second 3, the imagery period starts with the appearance of a randomly chosen *arrow* pointing either right, indicating MI of the right hand or down, indicating MI of both feet. At second 4.25, the *arrow* disappears. If the system has already been calibrated for online feedback a *red* (*dark gray* in the print version) *bar graph* provides positive feedback. The *bar* grows in the direction of the *arrow*. Its length is proportional to the classifier output of the last second or any other heuristic deem necessary (eg, sham feedback). At second 8, the *bar* and cross disappear and an intertrial random pause of 2–3 s is introduced.

Furthermore, this phenomenon can be triggered by an external event, and users may induce it by actively performing the designated task (Pfurtscheller and Neuper, 1997). This fact is used in noncue-guided, asynchronous BCI scenarios, where users decide for themselves when to establish control (Müller-Putz et al., 2005; Pfurtscheller et al., 2006; Scherer et al., 2004).

Motor imagery can be an efficient strategy for controlling a BCI based on the modulation of rhythms of the sensorimotor cortex also known as SMR-based BCI (Faller et al., 2012; Kreilinger et al., 2013; Neuper et al., 2005, 2009; Scherer et al., 2008). The SMR-BCI uses the power decreases/increases as a feature for discriminating between two or more different MIs.

In the standard approach, users have to do several training runs to gather sufficient repetitions (40–80 trials per class) of the MI task to train classification algorithms. These repetitions are systematically collected using a cue-based paradigm. Especially well known and widely used is the Graz-BCI paradigm, which can be seen in Fig. 2 (Pfurtscheller and Neuper, 2001). The cue-based paradigm is designed to maximize the SMR-based information without disturbing influences.

2.1.1 SMR-based BCIs for control

Several control scenarios have been established, where users were able to control a FES-based neuroprosthesis using SMR-based BCIs. In 2003, Pfurtscheller et al. (2003) could restore the grasp function of the left hand of a tetraplegic end user (29 years, male, complete SCI at C5) using an FES motor neuroprosthesis and an SMR-based BCI: after a 4-month BCI training period the patient was able to control the neuroprosthesis by foot imagery and was able to grasp a drinking glass (Müller-Putz, 2004).

In a later case study, Müller-Putz et al. (2005) demonstrated the coupling of an implanted Freehand system (Peckham et al., 2001) with an SMR-based BCI: the BCI emulated the input of the shoulder joystick which is usually used to control the device. Within 3 days the tetraplegic end user was able to control the Freehand system only by movement imagination. He used the imagination of a left hand movement to trigger the Freehand-generated movements to his right hand.

In 2013, Rohm et al. (2013) showed in another single case study the possibility of combining the acquired control signal from an SMR-BCI with a shoulder position sensor (see Fig. 3). By protraction and retraction, or elevation and depression of the shoulder, the user could control elbow flexion and extension, or hand opening and closing, respectively. The routing of the analog signal from the shoulder position sensor to the control of the elbow or the hand and the access to a pause state was done by a digital brain-switch provided by the SMR-BCI (see Fig. 3). With this setup, a tetraplegic end user (41 years, male, SCI at C4, no preserved elbow, hand, or finger

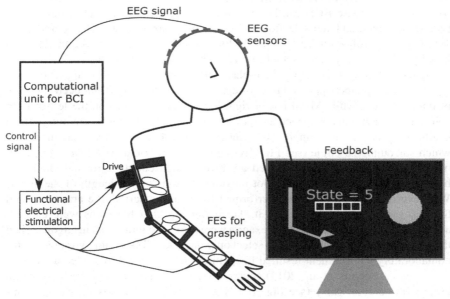

FIG. 3

Schematic of a hybrid BCI for controlling an upper extremity neuroprosthesis (Rohm et al., 2013). EEG is recorded, and the BCI determines a control signal from the EEG. The feedback monitor displays the current arm position and a feedback circle which grows or shrinks in diameter according to the classifier distance.

Modified from Kreilinger, A., et al., 2013. Neuroprosthesis control via noninvasive hybrid brain–computer interface. IEEE Intell. Syst. 28(5), 40–43.

movements) was able to perform several activities of daily living including eating a pretzel stick and signing a document (Rohm et al., 2013; Rupp et al., 2015). In Mueller-Putz et al. (2010), a pulse-width coded brain-switch was implemented which allowed subjects to use only one MI pattern for control of hand (grasp) as well as elbow (extension, flexion) movements. The latest development was a continuous elbow control (Kreilinger et al., 2013). Here, the users were able to control hand opening and closing as well as the flexion and extension of the elbow, only by different durations of one imagined motor task. It is obvious that such a control scheme is a help for end users with high level of SCI. Nevertheless, it is only used for simple control of predefined grasp patterns (open/close) and elbow angle (flexion/extension) and does not allow a tetraplegic end user to control his/her arm more naturally.

2.1.2 SMR-based BCIs for communication

Apart from controlling neuroprosthesis, several other attempts were made to use SMR-based BCIs for communication which resulted primary in different variations of virtual spelling devices. The main constraint for using virtual keyboards is that for letter selection only two to utmost four control signals can be used (eg, MI left hand, MI right hand, MI both feet, and MI of tongue movement; Schlögl et al., 2005). The performance of these BCIs can be measured by the spelling rate. Obermaier et al. (2003) implemented letter selection using a binary control signal and a dichotomous search routine followed by two levels for confirmation and correction. In three healthy subjects, they achieved a 0.67–1.02 letters/min spelling rate.

Scherer et al. (2004) used a three-class self-paced BCI for selecting letters (see Fig. 4B): the alphabet appeared in two separate columns. Foot MI induced scrolling of both columns, while MI of left or right hand selected a letter in the left or right column. This approach achieved an average spelling rate of 1.99 letters/min in three healthy subjects. In a later approach, Blankertz et al. (2006) used six hexagonal fields which surrounded a circle (see Fig. 4A). In each of the fields there were letters or other symbols. The circle contained an arrow which could be rotated clockwise by right hand MI. An imagined foot movement extended the length of the arrow. Whenever this imagination was performed for a longer period, the arrow touched the hexagon and thereby selected it. Thereafter all other hexagons were cleared, and the five letters of the selected hexagon were moved to individual hexagons. Then the same procedure was repeated to select only one letter. Tests with two subjects in a nonlaboratory environment resulted in spelling rates from 2.3 to 7.6 letters/min.

Recently, Scherer et al. (2015) centered their communication approach on end users with cerebral palsy (see Fig. 4C). They introduced MI-based, row–column-based scanning technique which enabled end users to select icons in a matrix solely based on right hand MI (sustained squeezing of a training ball). Icons in a matrix were highlighted one row after each other—when the row of the designated icon highlighted, users performed right hand MI for selection. Afterward, the columns of the row highlighted one at a time and users performed a second MI for final selection. To reduce the effect of false positive selections, evidence accumulation was implemented in a way that the user had to do the correct selection three out of five

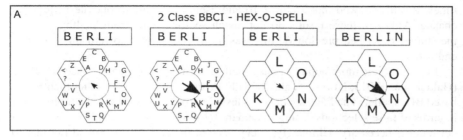

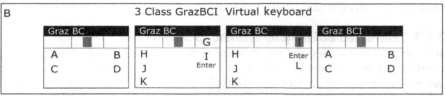

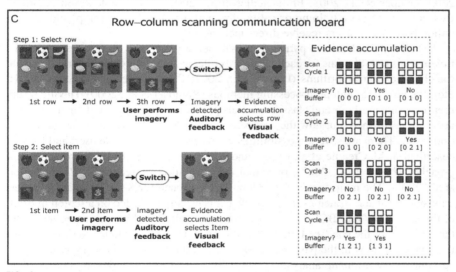

FIG. 4

BCI-communication boards (selection): (A) Hex-O-Spell typewriter: the two states classified by the B(erlin)BCI system control the turning and growing of the *gray arrow*, respectively. *Letters* can thus be chosen in a two step procedure. (B) Three-class Graz-BCI virtual keyboard: user scrolls through the alphabet (*symbols* move from the *bottom* to the *top* of the screen) and picks, by moving the feedback cursor, the desired symbol shown on the left or on the right half of the screen. This example shows the insertion of the letter "I" in order to spell the word "BCI." (C) BCI-based one-switch row–column communication board: the example illustrates the selection of the "Flower" item (3rd row, 2nd column). An example of the evidence accumulation for the selection of the 2nd row is shown on the right (*dotted box*): each time imagery is detected for the currently highlighted row, the buffer for the

(Continued)

times. Results showed that 7 out of 10 end users were able to operate better than chance. Although these results do not match spelling rates from healthy users in the studies described previously, this was the first approach toward this group of end users.

In general it is more popular to use spelling techniques which are based on P300 (Halder et al., 2015; Nijboer et al., 2008a,b; Pinegger et al., 2013) rather than SMR-based BCI speller. The P300 speller uses less electrodes and deems to be more robust in terms of false selections. Using a standard P300 speller matrix, only one selection per letter is necessary. Ultimately, acceptance of the end user is crucial in order to select an adequate communication method.

2.1.3 SMR-based BCI training (classic vs adaptive)

BCI use is a skill that users must learn. Overall, user training may take weeks or even months and binary (discrimination of one MI vs another, eg, right hand MI vs both feet MI) accuracies of 75% or less are typically achieved (Kübler and Neumann, 2005; Neuper et al., 2003; Pfurtscheller et al., 2000). The classical and common BCI consists of (1) a training or calibration part, (2) a classifier setup, and (3) the online part, where users receive direct feedback.

Usually, the calibration part is done without any feedback to the user until sufficient trials (40–80 trials for each class) are collected to provide enough training data for classification algorithms (Lotte et al., 2007; Pfurtscheller and Neuper, 2001; Steyrl et al., 2015) and preprocessing methods (Ramoser et al., 2000). Having setup preprocessing methods and classifiers, users proceed to the online part: again, the MI tasks are performed, but now the user receives feedback according to the classification result. There are several possibilities to present feedback to the user: auditory as described in McCreadie et al. (2014) and Nijboer et al. (2008a,b), vibrotactile approaches (Febo et al., 2007), or visual representation of feedback (Pfurtscheller et al., 2006). The main focus of the Graz-BCI approach for SMR-based BCIs relies on visual feedback strategies. Here, feedback is usually provided on a screen in front of the user. The Graz-BCI displays a horizontal feedback which increased length to the direction of the cue (see Fig. 2). The length is proportional to the number of correct classifications in the past second or to the certainty of the classification result, eg, linear discriminant analysis (LDA) distance. Over a series of consecutive

---

FIG. 4—CONT'D specific row is incremented by one. Assuming a three out five rule, ie, three out of the past five selections for a row have to be classified as imagery, then the 2nd row is selected during the 4th scan cycle. Note that no imagery was detected during the 3rd scan cycle.

Panel (A) Figure taken and modified from Blankertz, B., et al., 2006. The Berlin brain–computer interface presents the novel mental typewriter Hex-O-Spell. Verlag der Technischen Universität Graz, pp. 108–109. Panel (B) Modified from Scherer, R., et al., 2004. An asynchronously controlled EEG-based virtual keyboard: improvement of the spelling rate. IEE Trans Biomed Eng. 6(51), 979–84; Panel (C) Modified from Schwarz, A., et al., 2015. A co-adaptive sensory motor rhythms brain–computer interface based on common spatial patterns and random forest. Conf. Proc. IEEE Eng. Med. Biol. Soc. 2015, 1049–1052.

sessions mutual adaptation between brain and machine may occur which lead to an improved performance (Pfurtscheller and Neuper, 2001).

Whenever a person performs an action—like grasping a glass of water—an immediate reaction (feedback) to the action is perceived: haptic information of the touch of the glass and its weight, and visual information regarding reaching and grasping coordination. This feedback becomes even more essential when it comes to learning new processes, eg, learning to control a BCI-driven neuroprosthesis. Therefore, it is imperative to incorporate feedback as soon as possible—especially within the training and calibration part. This would induce a mutual training experience within the session: the system adapts online to the MIs of the user, while the user adapts to the feedback provided by the BCI.

An early step toward this so-called coadaptive BCIs was done by Vidaurre et al. who provided feedback to the user starting from the first trial using a standard classifier trained on data from a large pool of subjects. Thereafter, the system continuously adapted the underlying statistical model. In a supporting study with nine healthy subjects, they could show performance increase over three consecutive sessions. Consecutive studies by Vidaurre fine-grained the approach and proved to be highly effective in training both novice users and users who initially were not able to achieve stable BCI control (Vidaurre et al., 2011a,b).

In 2012, Faller and Vidaurre approached the coadaptive concept from a different angle. Instead of creating a basis classifier out of a pool of subjects, they gathered a small amount of training trials (10 trials per class) and trained their initial classifier on this set. Whenever five new trials per class were available, the classifier was retrained on the complete set of available data. The system was conceptualized in an autocalibrating manner: each gathered trial was investigated for artifacts—tainted trials were excluded from the retraining process. Furthermore, the system selected out of several predefined bandpower features, the feature with the highest class discriminability. In a supporting multisession study, 10 out 12 participants exceeded peak performances of 70% in their last session with a median accuracy of $80.2 \pm 11.3\%$. Postinterviews showed that all users preferred the online feedback training over the brief offline phase in the beginning (Faller et al., 2012).

This autocalibrating, coadaptive BCI was the basis for a study in individuals with SCI ($n = 6$); the system started collecting EEG data in a cue-guided task consisting of three classes: right hand MI, left hand MI, and a noncontrol state. After the initial short calibration, the system automatically selected the MI task that produced better discriminable activity patterns against the noncontrol state. All six tetraplegic participants scored significantly better than chance at an overall mean accuracy (peak) of $69.5 \pm 6.4\%$ (Faller et al., 2013). In a follow-up study with a larger group of end users ($n = 22$), similar results could be reached. In the same study, an attempt of controlling a paradigm in a self-paced manner was done, and 11 from 20 end users achieved performances significantly better than chance (Faller et al., 2014). One drawback in terms of pattern recognition in the studies mentioned earlier is that only a limited number of MI-specific frequency bands were examined and selected. Since the most discriminative features are user-dependent, the approach was suboptimal in terms of classification performance. In a later study, Schwarz et al. (2015) used filterbank common spatial patterns to overcome this issue: Here, a battery of narrow-banded passband filters was individually combined with a single common spatial patterns filter (Ramoser et al., 2000). To deal with the high number of emerging features, they used a random forest, a nonlinear ensemble classifier which is based on decision trees (Breiman, 2001; Steyrl et al., 2015). Though the coadaptive BCI implementation grew in complexity, their efforts were rewarded: 12 healthy subjects showed mean accuracies (peak) of $88.6 \pm SD$ 6.1%. Compared to Faller et al. (2012), this implementation turned out to be a significant ($p < 0.05$) improvement.

The concept of adaptation during runtime offers several crucial advantages for successful BCI control or communication. It is well known that EEG signal and brain pattern quality may change over time—even within session. Possible reasons for these changes are deteriorating levels of attentiveness, motivation of the user, or environmental conditions. Up to a certain point, a coadaptive system may reduce the effect of these influences, eg, by reducing the number of controllable classes if the user gets fatigued, or by excluding certain EEG sensors from processing if the signal becomes noisy. In Fallers follow-up study from 2014 (Faller et al., 2014), a simple EMG-artifact detector based on an autoregressive filter model was implemented and retrained in a coadaptive manner: a yellow dot was shown on the paradigm-screen every time users became anxious and started to move, indicating to them to relax.

The classic BCI approach typically requires a lengthy training period. This can be exhausting and fatiguing for the user as the data collection is usually done without any kind of feedback. With the coadaptive approaches shown, the training part without feedback can be reduced to a minimum. In the beginning, the feedback may not be as accurate as the classic BCI approach since the system is only trained with a couple of trials. However, with increasing runtime, accuracy increases as well. Last but not least, postinterviews done by Faller et al. (2012) and Schwarz et al. (2015) indicate a high user acceptance rate.

Current technology already provides vast computational resources, which easily cover the additional performance demand of a coadaptive system. Although more complex in development and implementation, these studies already present a convenient plug and play solution to possible end users and their caregivers; operating these systems only requires connecting the system to the user and starting it.

Despite improvements due to the coadaptive approach, SMR-based BCIs still lack a natural control. They rely on movement imaginations which do not necessarily correspond to the neuroprosthesis movements. Usually, movement imaginations which can be decoded by an SMR-based BCI are artificially assigned to neuroprosthesis movements, eg, a foot movement imagery is assigned to a hand open command. Furthermore, SMR-based BCI detects the brain state of imagining a movement but not the actual imaged movement. For instance they detect the limb which is subjected to MI but not the trajectories of the limb. In the following sections, we discuss approaches to overcome the limitations of the SMR-based BCI and to archive a natural control.

2.2 DECODING MOTOR EXECUTION

As seen in the previous section, one application of a BCI is the control of a motor neuroprosthesis for the restoration of hand and elbow function in tetraplegic end users by thoughts. The general idea is that an end user's intention of a movement of the arm is recognized by the BCI, and the neuroprosthesis executes this movement. An important objective is that the control of the neuroprosthesis should be natural to the user. It is important because the term "natural" has desirable implications. On the one hand, the control would be familiar and direct and therefore comfortable. On the other hand, the user would not have to learn complicated mental control strategies; thus, the training time could be shortened. To facilitate a natural control, two tough problems have to be solved first: (1) a highly sophisticated neuroprosthesis, which supports as many degrees of freedom as the human upper limb, has to be developed, and (2) the movements decoded by the BCI have to be as close as possible to the imagined ones. An overview of state-of-the-art neuroprosthesis can be found elsewhere (Jackson and Zimmermann, 2012), here we give an overview on how movement trajectories can be decoded from EEG, magnetoencephalography (MEG), and electrocorticography (ECoG) during executed movements, and then we present our Graz-BCI approach on movement decoding. Decoding imagined movements will be discussed in the next section.

To decode movements one first needs to know the neuronal features containing movement information about trajectories or movement directions. Sensorimotor rhythms in the mu or beta are rather associated with general movement activity but contain only little information about movement trajectories (Ball et al., 2009; Nakanishi et al., 2013; Waldert et al., 2008). However, low-frequency EEG signals (delta band) and to a lesser extent gamma band activity can provide information about movement trajectories.

The following studies decoded movement information from ECoG signals. Pistohl et al. (2008) decoded 2D hand positions during arm movements from low-frequency time-domain signals and broad band gamma (40–80 Hz) power modulations. Interestingly, a combination of time domain and power features did not improve the movement decoding. Schalk et al. (2007) decoded movement trajectories during 2D joystick control, and Milekovic et al. (2012) demonstrated an online classification of 1D joystick movement directions based on low-frequency ECoG signals. Movement directions during a center-out task to four and eight targets were decoded by Ball et al. (2009) with the movement-related potential (a low-frequency time-domain signal) and power modulations in the low-frequency band (<2 Hz) and broad gamma band (34–128 Hz) carrying most information. Nakanishi et al. (2013) reported 3D arm trajectory decoding from the delta (<4 Hz) and high-gamma band (50–90 Hz).

Movement decoding has also been analyzed in human MEG signals. Georgopoulos et al. (2005) reconstructed movement trajectories in a pentagon-copying task with a 2D joystick using time-domain features, and Bradberry et al. (2009) decoded hand velocities from time-domain features in a center-out drawing task. Three-dimensional velocity decoding of movements in a center-out task was reported by Yeom et al. (2013). Also hand movement direction was decoded from low-frequency time-domain signals (<3 Hz) and low-frequency power modulations

(0.5–7.5 Hz) in Waldert et al. (2008), and Wang et al. (2010) decoded movement directions in a 2D center-out task using wrist movements (radial/ulnar deviation, flexion/extension). Jerbi et al. (2007) found phase locking between oscillatory brain rhythms in low-frequencies (2–5 Hz) and time-varying hand speed. Fingertip positions were reconstructed in Toda et al. (2011) during pointing movements in various directions from time-domain features.

Finally, movements have been decoded from EEG too. Bradberry et al. (2010) decoded hand movement velocities in a center-out-reaching task. Kim et al. (2015) decoded trajectories, while subjects moved their hand around a predefined trajectory, and Lv et al. (2010) decoded hand movement velocities during a drawing task in four directions. Úbeda et al. (2015) analyzed the decoder performance in relation to the movement variability and found that continuous and slower movements improve the accuracy of the decoder. Also finger movements have been decoded from delta band EEG signals (Agashe et al., 2015; Paek et al., 2014). These papers propose that movement parameters (eg, position, velocity, movement directions) can be decoded noninvasively best from low-frequency time-domain signals.

Exploiting low-frequency time-domain signals, Bradberry et al. (2010) showed the decoding of hand velocities from EEG. We extended this work to decode also arm positions by an actual simplification of the original decoder. Fig. 5A shows

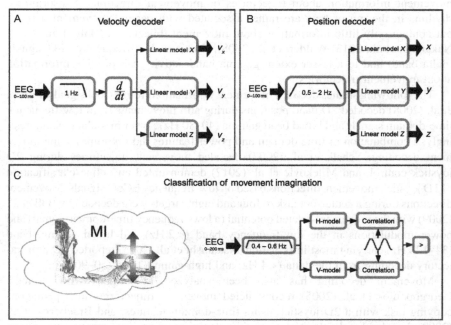

FIG. 5

Schemas of the different movement decoder. (A) Velocity decoder, (B) position decoder, and (C) classification of imagined movements in two movement planes (horizontal vs vertical).

the decoder elements as used in Bradberry et al. (2010). There, the EEG signals are low-pass filtered with a cutoff frequency of 1 Hz and subsequently differentiated. Subsequently, the signals including time lags up to 100 ms in the past are feed into three linear models. Each linear model calculates the velocity in the x, y, and z directions, respectively.

We replaced the differentiator and the low-pass filter with a band-pass filter and thereby were able to extract position data of the arm (Ofner and Müller-Putz, 2012). Position data are more general than velocity, because velocity and acceleration can be calculated from position data by simply differentiating position data. Furthermore, the decoder is simpler and easier to comprehend without a differentiator block (see Fig. 5B for a scheme of our position decoder). We band-pass filtered the EEG data between 0.5 and 2 Hz and used three linear models (for $x/y/z$ coordinates) to calculate the position of the right hand. The input to these linear models was all 49 band-pass filtered EEG channels at 11 time lags from 0 to 117 ms in the past. We trained these three models separately by using a multiple linear regression where we recorded the dependent variable, ie, x, y, or z positions of the hand, with a Kinect sensor device (Microsoft, Redmond, USA) and the OpenNI framework (formerly PrimeSense, Tel-Aviv, Israel).

Later on, a correlation between the EEG and hand position in a center-out-reaching task was also shown by exploiting power modulations in the delta and gamma band (Korik et al., 2014).

An often used similarity measure between decoded an actual movements is the Pearson's correlation coefficient. However, one has to be aware that a correlation measure is based on the number of common sign changes of the two signals to compare (eg, velocity signals); thus, it is crucial that the signals contain many zero-crossings (after mean subtraction), ie, signals should be like oscillations. When analyzing hand trajectories in center-out-reaching tasks this is often not taken into account and can lead to over-optimistic results suggesting better correlations. Antelis et al. (2013) discuss problems when using the correlation measure in movement decoding.

We tackled that problem by designing an experiment where subjects performed continuous movements instead of center-out-reaching movements. Subjects were not restricted to certain movement patterns and were asked to execute natural, round (not jaggy) and in speed varying arm movements in front of them. For the sake of suppressing eye movements we did not use external targets, eg, on a computer screen, resulting in self-chosen movements. Using the aforementioned position decoder and this paradigm, we reached average cross-validated correlation coefficients in the three dimensions x, y, and z of 0.70/0.78/0.62 with standard deviations of 0.12/0.07/0.14. We also applied the original velocity decoder to our data and reached correlations of $0.70/0.77/0.62 \pm 0.13/0.11/0.15$ (see Fig. 6A for an example of decoded and measured positions). In the literature, correlations of 0.19/0.38/0.32 (velocities, $x/y/z$) (Bradberry et al., 2010), 0.37/0.24 (velocities, x/y) (Lv et al., 2010), and around 0.6 (velocities, $x/y/z$) (Kim et al., 2015) were reported. However, although the correlation values reached in our experiment appear to be high, they are

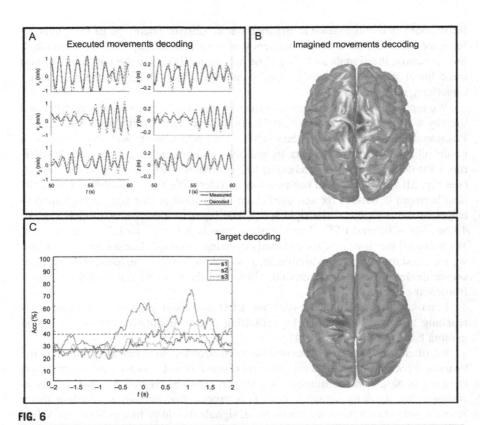

FIG. 6

(A) Example of decoded executed movements (Ofner and Müller-Putz, 2012).
(B) contributions of brain sources to the decoding averaged over nine subjects (Ofner
and Müller-Putz, 2015a,b). (C) *Left*: classification accuracies of three subjects when
decoding the movement target (time point 0 s corresponds to the movement onset,
the *dashed line* depicts the significance level), *right*: sources with discriminative information
about movement targets/directions for subject s2 at time point −47 ms relative to
movement onset (Ofner and Müller-Putz, 2015a,b).

probably still too low for an accurate neuroprosthesis control. For an accurate arm
neuroprosthesis 3D control we expect correlation values above 0.90.

One point to improve the decoder is to use more electrodes (above 100) in a
denser arrangement to better deal with the signal-to-noise ratio of the EEG. The next
point is to develop user training protocols. A conventional SMR-based BCI relies on
the fact that not only the classifier is trained but also the user itself is trained. The user
learns to express the patterns which can then be recognized by the classifier leading
to an improved classification accuracy (Friedrich et al., 2013). However, it is still
not researched if such a user training effect also exists when we decode from

low-frequency time-domain signals, and such training may provide a significant improvement in movement decoding. Another possibility to improve the decoder could be the implementation of alternative decoding algorithms, for example, particle filter (Zhang et al., 2014), kernel ridge regression (Kim et al., 2015), or artificial neural networks (ANN; Korik et al., 2015). Interestingly, Korik et al. (2015) found that not the delta and gamma bands, but the mu and beta bands contain the most information about movement trajectories when using an ANN. However, none of the mentioned methods provided yet substantial improvements to be suitable for a neuroprosthesis noninvasive online control. Thus, research should still focus on optimal decoding algorithms.

In addition to refining the algorithms, one could also try to decode other movement parameters which may be better decodable from EEG, eg, acceleration, joint angles, or different coordinate systems. However, as tempting as this may seem, one has to be aware that a decoder based on multiple linear models and multiple time lags is quite powerful. Thus, if, for example, the brain encodes arm positions but we try to decode arm velocities, the trained linear model can transform positions to velocities by simply subtracting the EEG signals between time lags. The linear model could also do a coordinate transformation so that the brain coordinate system matches the world coordinate system. Thus, the movement parameters and the choice of the coordinate system are not critical factors.

We are also interested in which features can be used for decoding, and what are the sources of these features. To answer which features the decoder uses we have to look at the signal processing chain of the decoder. The position decoder mainly comprises a band-pass filter and linear models. All of them apply linear operations to the EEG signal with the important consequence that no frequency component can be inserted or deleted in the signal processing chain. Existing frequency components in the EEG can only be amplified or attenuated. Thus, the passband of the band-pass filter has to be set so that it covers most of the movement frequencies. It is pointless to set the band-pass filter to an upper cutoff frequency of, eg, 50 Hz if the human limb cannot execute such fast movements. It will only decrease the signal-to-noise ratio and performance, because the subsequent model will then get additional frequency components unrelated to the movement. On the other side, we found frequency components below 0.5 Hz—although representing movement frequencies—not applicable for movement decoding. Either, frequencies below 0.5 Hz just do not contain much movement information or are covered by other movement unrelated EEG signals in that frequency range. Thus, we are not able to decode the absolute position, which is a 0 Hz frequency component, but only changes in position. To summarize, the frequencies of the decoded movements have to be represented one to one in the EEG and the information must be encoded in the amplitude/phase of the EEG signals.

To answer which neuronal sources contain movement information we have to analyze the weights of the decoder. However, a strong common weight pattern was not observable across subjects. Weights include a spatial filter—in addition to the actual decoder part—to reduce the signal-to-noise ratio of the measured velocity/position coding sources. If this spatial filter is highly tuned to the head properties of a person (eg, geometry, conductivity) and electrode impedances, each person would have an individual weight pattern. As presented in the following sections, there are better ways to analyze the neuronal sources. Furthermore, the position decoder is here a stationary model which assumes that the underlying sources do not change their spatial distribution over time. However, there is the possibility that the spatial distribution of the sources on the cortex changes slightly because of the recruitment of different muscles, depending on the position of the arm. In that case, a stationary model would be suboptimal and a nonstationary model could improve the decoder performance, yielding better interpretable patterns.

2.3 DECODING MOTOR IMAGINATION

Within the scope of BCI-based FES control for SCI persons it is necessary to decode imagined movements from the EEG. SMR-based BCIs rely on the fact that similar areas show power modulations whether one executes or imagines movements (Pfurtscheller and Neuper, 1997), and those areas are still modulated during MI in SCI persons, especially, when they train to imagine movements (Enzinger et al., 2008). However, the situation with movement decoding from low-frequency EEG during motor imagination, and the applicability to a SCI person is mostly unclear despite some first attempts that have been reported in the literature. Vuckovic and Sepulveda (2008, 2012) classified imagined wrist movements using delta band features. Gu et al. (2009a,b) found in healthy subjects and in amyotrophic lateral sclerosis patients that the speed of imagined wrist movements is encoded in movement-related cortical potentials. These papers show that in low-frequency components of the EEG information is encoded about imagined discrete hand movements. The next step is to generalize the decoder to imagined continuous hand/arm movements. In Bradberry et al. (2011) a computer cursor was controlled in 2D with decoded imagined finger/arm movements. However, only a single target was presented on a computer screen in each trial, and Poli and Salvaris (2011) showed that a random cursor also hits this target after a while, reaching similar decoding results. Recently, Kim et al. (2015) decoded imagined arm movements when subjects moved their arm along an infinity symbol (∞), and reasonable correlation values around 0.5 have been obtained. However, in the scalp maps in Kim et al. (2015) (1) no consistent correlation patterns are observable across subjects, (2) the average correlation of the channels correlating best with the movement is 0.15 ± 0.07, and (3) prefrontal electrodes were excluded from the maps. This makes the scalp maps hard to interpret with respect to the origin of the neural signals; however, this would have been important to rule out that eye movements contributed at least partly to the decoding results.

Eye movements are a problem in decoding experiments, because the eye movements often correlate with arm/hand movements, and the electrical field of the eye dipole can be measured easily in the EEG. Thus, a decoder could exploit the electrical field of the eye dipole instead of brain sources for decoding arm movements.

There exist EEG cleaning methods to remove eye movement-related influences from the EEG, like linear regression (Schlögl et al., 2007) or by inspecting ICA components and removing those contaminated with eye movements (Delorme et al., 2007). However, there is no proof that these methods remove these eye movement influences from the EEG completely—they rather attenuate them in the EEG. Thus, a decoder could still exploit eye movements. In addition to the influence caused by the electrical field of the eye dipoles, eye movements could also potentially modulate brain sources. In that case the decoder could pick up signals which actually originate from the brain but are due to eye movements and not due to MI. Indeed, Pesaran et al. (2006) discovered that eye movements modulate the neural activity in the dorsal premotor area in monkeys. However, a transfer of these findings to EEG is not proven. As a solution, we suggest a combination of eye movement avoidance by the experiment design (if possible) and the use of an EEG cleaning method. Furthermore, source analysis is mandatory to assure that the decoder's sources—either in the source or channel space—originate from the brain.

Considering the problem with eye movements, we designed a motor imagination decoding experiment where we avoided eye movements by the experiment design (Ofner and Müller-Putz, 2015a,b). Subjects imagined rhythmic arm movements in the horizontal or vertical plane, and we asked them to fixate their gaze to a cross on a computer screen. These movements were synchronized to the beats of a metronome. This allowed us to obtain the trajectories of the imagined arm movements without provoking eye movements. Fig. 6C shows schematically a subject performing right arm MI. Afterward, we decoded the trajectories of the imagined arm movements from low-frequency time-domain signals using a position decoder similar to the one described in the previous section. Based on the decoded trajectories, we classified the imagined movements as horizontal or vertical. In the end, it was a two-class classification based on a position decoder. We instructed subjects to synchronize the MIs to the metronome beep tones with a rhythm of 1 Hz presented by a computer. A beep tone corresponded to an end position of the imagined trajectories (left/right, bottom/top), and therefore MIs were done with 0.5 Hz. Furthermore, we assumed that subjects imagined arm trajectories similar to a sinus oscillation, ie, highest velocity in the middle of the trajectory and the lowest at the trajectory endpoints. For this reason, the frequency profile of the imagined movements presumably had most power around 0.5 Hz. Regarding the linear nature of the decoder (see the previous section), we expected the most informative EEG signals around 0.5 Hz and set the cutoff frequencies of the band-pass filter in the position decoder to 0.4 and 0.6 Hz (see Fig. 5C for an overview of the classifier and the decoder models). First, we decoded the positions in the horizontal and vertical planes, ie, x/y coordinates. Then, we correlated the decoded positions with a 0.5 Hz sine oscillation and assigned the imagined movement to the plane with the highest correlation. The reasoning behind it was: if subjects imagined a movement in the horizontal plane, the horizontal model should output a sine oscillation, ie, the imagined trajectory, while the vertical model should output noise because no-movement happened in the vertical direction, and vice versa in the case of a vertical movement. The band-pass filter and the two horizontal/vertical models constitute a position decoder, but the final "larger than" comparison makes it a classifier. This way, the successful classification is an indirect proof that imagined movement trajectories can be decoded from the EEG. This decoder validation approach was necessary to avoid eye movements. Seven out of nine subjects reached a significant classification accuracy (>59%). The average classification accuracy over all nine subjects was $64 \pm 10\%$. In case of horizontal movements, the horizontal model reached an average correlation of 0.30 with the sinus oscillation. For vertical movements, a correlation of 0.34 was reached. Despite the classification accuracies and correlations being rather low, they still show that imagined movements can be decoded from the EEG.

As mentioned earlier, also the sources of the decoder are of interest, to rule out the usage of invalid sources like eye movements or muscle artifacts, and to enrich the knowledge in the neuroscience field. Due to large channel correlations, the weights of a multiple linear regression (as used in the previous section) are not interpretable, a problem known in statistics as multicollinearity (Farrar and Glauber, 1967). Intuitively, when two variables are correlated, weights have to be shared between them. A variable which highly correlates with other variables tends to get a lower weight than when not correlated with others. A multiple linear regression still predicts the response variable, but the weights are not interpretable when channels are highly correlated. Instead, our method relies on partial least squares (PLS), see Ofner and Müller-Putz (2015a,b) and Wold et al. (2001) for more details. PLS can be used to find the weights of a linear model similar to a multiple linear regression but allows us to find the sources exploited by the linear model. Basically, PLS finds latent (hidden) variables in the data which can be used for movement decoding. These latent variables are weighted and summed up, yielding the position in the horizontal and vertical plane. The back projection of all latent variables—weighted with their importance for decoding—to the source space (=voxel space) is from now on called "contribution." The contributions are proportional to the amplitudes of the latent variables projected to the voxels and the importance of the latent variables for the decoding. Fig. 6B shows the contribution values averaged over all nine subjects.

It can be observed that the most contributing region is the supplementary motor area (SMA) when decoding imagined movement trajectories. The SMA is involved in higher-level motor tasks, and furthermore this observation is consistent with the MEG studies (Waldert et al., 2008; Yeom et al., 2013), showing that central regions carry movement trajectory/direction information. Notably, Yuan et al. (2010) showed that also SMR power modulations accompanying MI can occur on the SMA, but in general they occur on the sensorimotor cortex (Pfurtscheller and Silva, 1999; Yuan et al., 2008). Power modulations in a certain frequency band and low-frequency time-domain signals are different features, and as they also appear on different areas on the brain, they are probably related to different underlying processes.

In general, the literature about macroscale brain sources carrying movement trajectory/direction information during motor-related tasks is not entirely consistent. Jerbi et al. (2007) observed phase locking between slow oscillatory MEG activity and hand speed on the contralateral primary motor cortex. The contralateral motor area and the left inferior frontal gyrus (IFG) were found by Wang et al. (2010) to encode the intended wrist movement direction. An involvement of primary sensorimotor, higher motor, and parietal regions during 2D finger trajectory decoding from MEG is shown in Toda et al. (2011). Motor, posterior parietal, and occipital areas were found to be associated with hand movement velocities in Lv et al. (2010). When decoding arm movement trajectories from EEG, Bradberry et al. (2010) found an involvement of the contralateral primary sensorimotor region and the inferior parietal lobule (IPL). All of these studies found motor-related areas containing movement information on a macroscale level. However, a single and consistent pattern is not observable in these studies. Probably, this has to be attributed to the different movement conditions, eg, self-chosen/targets, (non)repetitive, movement execution/ imagination, trajectory/direction decoding. However, this has not been systematically studied yet.

Interestingly, in functional magnetic resonance imaging (fMRI) studies, Grahn and Brett (2007) found a higher activation in the SMA and basal ganglia during rhythm perception. Bengtsson et al. (2009) showed a higher activation of the dorsal premotor cortex, SMA, pre-SMA, and lateral cerebellum when listening to rhythmic sequences. These studies indicate an involvement of the SMA during beat perception. As in our experiment subjects perceived metronome beats and showed an involvement of the SMA, the role of the metronome beats in movement decoding has to be questioned. The metronome beats may have caused class-unspecific brain oscillations which were subsequently class specifically (horizontal vs vertical) modulated by the MI. However, the metronome beats could not have influenced the classification results as the beats were the same in both classes. The metronome beats could at most be a necessary condition but not a sufficient condition for decoding MI. The relation between beat perception and decoding from low-frequency signal is yet unclear but has to be kept in mind when designing movement studies with rhythmic beats.

We made a first attempt to decode movement imaginations from the brain and ruled out other invalid sources like muscle, eye, or cable movement artifacts. It was possible to decode imagined movements of the arm in two different planes with low—but significant—accuracies. Furthermore, we showed that the brain region containing most movement information when decoding from low-frequency time-domain EEG signals is the SMA. How can these findings be translated to FES control? We think that although movement trajectory decoding is possible in principle, the decoder performance is still too low to be a used in an online control scenario. However, such an online control study will be one of our next steps. A remedy can be the reduction of information needed for neuroprosthesis control which will be explored in the next section.

2.4 DECODING MOVEMENT TARGETS

The previous sections covered continuous decoding of movements which would allow a maximum user control over the neuroprosthesis. However, continuous decoding requires a BCI to extract a lot of information from the brain which is problematic since the decoded signals can be noisy or even they can lack movement information. As a solution, we propose an intelligent neuroprosthesis control which is informed about the target to reach and then plans and executes the movement on its own. Thus, the BCI decodes only the intended target, and the trajectory to that target is calculated by the neuroprosthesis itself leading to a mutual control between the user and the neuroprosthesis. Decoding the target corresponds to a one-time classification of all possible targets in reach distance. This is still a difficult problem, but requires less information extraction from the brain than continuously decoding 3D trajectories. Furthermore, it actually does not restrict the user as we normally do not consciously plan the actual movement trajectory. We rather identify the target to reach and execute the reaching movement, leaving the details of the movement, ie, the trajectory, to lower level motor systems. Hence, the combination of movement target decoding and intelligent neuroprosthesis control complies with the hierarchical motor system of the brain.

Some success regarding the decoding of the target or the movement direction corresponding to a target from EEG has already been reported in the literature. Hammon et al. (2008) showed the classification of the target location during a reach movement; self-chosen center-out joystick movements were classified by Waldert et al. (2008); Li et al. (2012) classified movements in a delayed saccade-or-reach task; and Robinson et al. (2013) and Lew et al. (2014) decoded movement directions in a center-out-reaching task. These papers show that low-frequency EEG signals (delta band) encode information about movement directions or targets in the planning phase of the movement. Decoding the movement within the planning phase, ie, before movement onset, is of crucial importance. There, the decoding is based on the actual motor intention and cannot be based on somatosensory feedback because no-movement happens at this time. Thus the decoding can at least be based on a planned, upcoming movement which is of high importance for persons with SCI where we want to restore movements.

In a preliminary study, we analyzed the suitability of EEG signals for movement target decoding (Ofner and Müller-Putz, 2015a,b) and combined it with source imaging to show the origin of the neural signals containing movement target information. A ball serving as the target was presented in one of the four corners of a computer screen and subjects had to reach that target with the right hand in a self-paced manner. Afterward we analyzed if the movement targets can be decoded from the brain and calculated the classification accuracies relative to the movement onset. As in most movement studies based on low-frequency EEG signals one has to take care of eye movements. A target presented on a computer usually attracts the gaze of a subject. It induces eye movements which can affect the decoder, ie, the decoder is then based on eye movements instead on brain signals. We took care of eye movements by a careful design of our paradigm. We instructed subjects to look immediately at the target when it appeared, but the self-paced movement to the target started more than 5 s later. That way, no eye movements were provoked during the movement. Fig. 6C shows the obtained classification accuracies based on three subjects.

One subject stands out showing two classification accuracy peaks around movement onset (63%), and when the target was hit (73%). To reveal the brain sources essential for classification, we calculated discriminative spatial patterns (Liao et al., 2007) in the source space obtained by sLORETA. Similar to the previous section one should not interpret the weights of an LDA classifier. Those weights have to be treated as filters and not as patterns. However, if one wants to interpret the sources used by an LDA classifier, one has to calculate the patterns with, for example, the discriminative spatial patterns method. Fig. 6C shows the LDA pattern of the best performing subject. This pattern was calculated at the time of highest classification accuracy before the movement onset. It shows that the LDA classifier uses sources on the primary motor cortex and partly on the SMA, which corresponds to a similar pattern as in Waldert et al. (2008) where subjects moved a joystick in four directions (MEG), or as in our previous work where subjects imagined movements in a horizontal or vertical plane (EEG; Ofner and Müller-Putz, 2015a,b), see previous section.

Planned movements to targets can be decoded from the EEG, and the decoding is indeed based on neural sources. In combination with an intelligent neuroprosthesis which can plan a trajectory to a target, a proper restoration of movement functions could be possible in the future. However, it is unclear if the target itself or the movement direction to that target is coded in the brain because a target corresponded always to the same movement direction in our study. This was often ignored in movement studies and needs to be clarified in future studies.

2.5 DECODING MOVEMENT GOALS

The approaches mentioned earlier (Sections 2.2–2.4) focus on the kinematic level. As seen, a valid option to improve the current decoders would be to identify the target of an action before even knowing the movement-by-movement details of the movement—as proposed in Section 2.4. Nevertheless, prior to this kinematic level, there is the goal level, which also contains relevant information on the upcoming action. In this section, we will overview some of the most important neurophysiological findings at the goal level and discuss their potential impact in BCI research.

Ideally, the goal level—describing the short-term goals necessary to achieve some action—and the kinematic level—describing the arm movement in space and time—would be merged to achieve an optimal and intuitive neuroprosthesis control. This distributed hierarchy of action representation, where the goal and kinematic level take part, has been proposed by Grafton and Hamilton (2007).

Since what matters the most when we initiate a goal-directed action is the goal we have in mind, there is also the hypothesis that certain actions show stronger patterns of activations when there is a clear goal defined.

In this context, it is of utmost importance to define the so-called goal-directed movements. As proposed by Byron et al. (2007) goal-directed movements (also known as object-directed or transitive movements) are movements directed to a target available at the subject's vicinity. These movements do not need to involve a direct contact or manipulation of the object (eg, grasping an apple or pointing to an apple are both examples of goal-directed movements). The goals may be physical objects located near the subject or visual targets displayed on a screen. The planning of a goal-directed movement starts by identifying the goal, and only then the trajectories for the intended motor behavior are planned (Desmurget and Sirigu, 2009). This also implies that repeated movements directed toward the same goal are not necessarily identical, due to the existence of variability in movement kinematics. A goal-directed action therefore covers all movements that occur in an intentional relationship with particular goals rather than by chance (Csibra and Gergely, 2007). In the past decade, several progresses have been made in understanding the neural correlates behind such behaviors.

Considering that goal-directed movements imply the interaction with a target, they are of utmost importance for BCIs, when comparing to movements that are nonobject directed (aimless or intransitive movements). For instance, in a grasp neuroprosthesis, the device only needs to be active when in the presence of a goal. In fact, one of the recurrent problems in achieving a reliable neuroprosthesis asynchronous control is to know when to activate the device, maximizing the number of true positives, while making sure that the number of false positives is still minimal. If one could determine the differences between goal-directed and aimless movements, then this information could be used to establish thresholds for an earlier and correct activation during asynchronous control.

In Table 1, we summarize the meaning of some terms that are used in this section to describe voluntary motor actions and behavior. Furthermore, we condensed some of the neurophysiological studies that are reviewed in this section, within the context of goal-directed movements during movement observation, execution, and imagination tasks.

Observing or imagining actions triggers the motor programs necessary for action execution implying that actions are naturally related to perception. This strict link has been investigated in the past years, through fMRI, EEG, and other neuroimaging techniques. The focus has been in the posterior superior temporal sulcus (pSTS) and the frontoparietal cortical networks. Both regions are thought to describe the goal of actions. It was shown that the pSTS is implicated in movement planning, containing semantic information concerning objects and their corresponding actions, being also an input to the IPL (Saxe et al., 2004).

In respect to the frontoparietal cortical networks, most of the experiments—trying to support the existence of the homologous mirror network in humans—focus on the inferior frontal cortex (IFC), encompassing both IFG and ventral premotor cortex (PMCv), and the IPL (Rizzolatti et al., 2014). Both the IFC and IPL are cortical regions whose function is predominantly motor, being active during both observation and execution of movements (Agnew et al., 2007). These and other brain areas important for the understanding of motor actions are represented in Fig. 7. Though debating the exact functional role of the frontoparietal motor resonance system in action understanding is beyond the scope of this chapter, some of the findings in this field can be of interest for BCI research. The greatest implication is that the motor system is not just a movement controller and programmer but also a preponderant player in high-level cognitive functions (Rizzolatti et al., 2014).

Table 1 Terms Used to Describe Movements and Object–Context Interaction

Terms and Meanings		
Movement	*Movement*: a displacement of at least a body part (eg, elbow extension). *Motor act*: a sequence of movements (eg, reaching). *Motor action*: sequence of motor acts temporally structured (eg, reaching followed by a palmar grasp) that allows the user to fulfill his/her intention (eg, eating).	
	Goal-directed movement (=object-directed/related or transitive)	**Aimless movement** (=nonobject-directed or intransitive)
Object interaction	A movement that, alone or integrated in a motor act, allows the person to reach a desired goal (typically an object). Example: *pointing to/reaching/grasping an apple.*	A movement without an intention to manipulate a particular object. Example: *pointing to/reaching/ grasping as "empty" postures.*
Studies	Buccino et al. (2001): observation, fMRI Muthukumaraswamy et al. (2004): execution, EEG Caplan et al. (2003) and Ekstrom et al. (2005): execution, ECoG Cornwell et al. (2008): execution, MEG Wamain et al. (2014): observation, EEG Pereira et al. (2015): execution, EEG Aflalo et al. (2015): tetraplegic patient, imagination, spike activity	
	Meaningful goal-directed movement	**Meaningless goal-directed movement**
Object and context interaction	A movement, part of a motor action, where there is a close effector–object–context relationship, strongly dependent on the reason (or final intention) of the motor action. Example: *grasping an apple and bringing it to the mouth.*	There is no close relationship between the object and the context of the action. Example: *grasping an apple and bringing it to the ear.*
Studies	Fogassi et al. (2005): monkey brain, execution and observation, neural population activity Iacoboni et al. (2005): observation, fMRI Newman-Norlund et al. (2010): observation, fMRI	

So what are then the differences between the neural correlates of goal-directed and nonobject-directed (or aimless) movements? An fMRI study showed that, during the observation of object-related actions, subjects had a greater activation in the posterior parietal lobe when comparing with observations of the same actions without target interaction. In both action observation conditions, the premotor cortex was equally activated (Buccino et al., 2001). These results support the view that the goals of actions are mapped onto the parietal lobe. Later, Muthukumaraswamy et al. (2004) found differences in EEG oscillations between goal-directed and nonobject-directed grasps, concretely demonstrating that the mu rhythm suppression was stronger when subject observed a precision grip related to an external object than when that same movement was simply an empty posture.

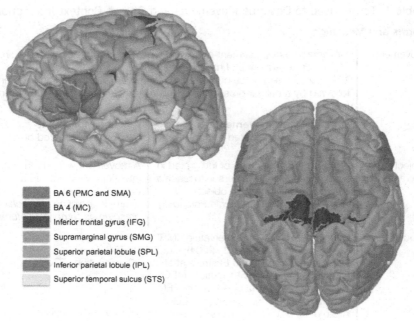

BA 6 (PMC and SMA)

BA 4 (MC)

Inferior frontal gyrus (IFG)

Supramarginal gyrus (SMG)

Superior parietal lobule (SPL)

Inferior parietal lobule (IPL)

Superior temporal sulcus (STS)

FIG. 7

Lateral and superior views of the human brain, showing the areas involved in movement observation, execution, and encoding of action goals. The inferior frontal cortex—encompassing both ventral premotor cortex (PMCv) and inferior frontal gyrus (IFG)—and the inferior parietal lobule (IPL) are active during movement observation and execution. This frontoparietal circuit is thought to be closely related to other areas, like the dorsal premotor cortex and the superior parietal lobule. Differences between transitive and intransitive actions have been localized in the parietal cortex: specifically, studies show an important role of the IPL in encoding the goal of actions and additionally the influence of the supramarginal gyrus (SMG) in discriminating actions depending on their context (semantic meaningfulness of motor actions).

Despite being based on movement observation, these studies showed that object-directed movements lead to different and more salient neural responses than equivalent—but intransitive—movements. In consistency with previous ECoG studies (Caplan et al., 2003; Ekstrom et al., 2005), an MEG study in a movement execution task showed increased power in the 4–8 Hz theta band in the hippocampus and surrounding parahippocampal structures during a goal-directed navigation on a screen, when compared to nonobject-directed navigation (Cornwell et al., 2008).

We investigated whether there were EEG-detectable differences between the execution of goal-directed actions and aimless movements (Pereira et al., 2015). In a reach-and-touch paradigm, subjects were presented with a small red ball on the touchscreen monitor (*Goal condition*) or with a red screen (*No-Goal condition*).

After 2 s and in 50% of the trials, a change of color (from red to purple) indicated that the subjects should move. By doing this, we separated the *Movement* conditions from the *No-Movement* conditions (where there was no change of the stimuli color) In the *Goal Movement* condition, the subjects should reach and touch the target as accurately as possible. In the *No-Goal Movement* condition the subjects decided where to touch. The existence of a 2-s period between *Goal/No-Goal* and *Movement/No-Movement* cues assured that the patterns of cortical activation during this period were due to the differences between *Goal* and *No-Goal* conditions and not due to movement preparation oscillations. Significant differences between both conditions were found in both event-related potentials and event-related desynchronization/synchronization phenomena. ERP components differed depending on the goal directedness of the task. Specifically, it was shown that the N200 amplitude was increased after the *No-Goal* stimulus, while an earlier and stronger P300 was present in the *Goal* condition.

The results are consistent with the work from Wamain et al. (2014), where they used EEG to assess the temporal dynamics of object-related action processing during an observation task. Similarly, Wamain et al. observed an increased P300 amplitude when subjects perceived object-related actions compared to nonobject-related actions, further proving that the neural differences observed were not simply due to differences in visual complexity of the stimuli but due to additional activation of object motor features.

In addition to the time-domain differences, we also showed that the upper alpha band in the central–parietal electrodes was suppressed longer in the goal-directed condition and that this ERD magnitude was also stronger for the majority of subjects (Pereira et al., 2015). These results indicate an increased processing load on the *Goal* condition, similarly to the studies from Muthukumaraswamy et al. (2004) and Cornwell et al. (2008). Thus, it seems that the neural circuits of both goal-directed movement observation and execution largely overlap.

What about movement imagination? Very recently, Aflalo et al. (2015) successfully showed that movement imaginations of goals, trajectories, and types of movements could be decoded from spike activity in the posterior parietal cortex of a tetraplegic patient. This study again supports the view that the human PPC encodes and represents high-level, cognitive aspects of action, being a rich source of control signals for neuroprosthesis control. Using a masked-memory reach paradigm, where the subject imagined a continuous reaching movement to a target after a delay period during which the goal disappeared from the screen, they proved the existence of specialized goal-tuned units and trajectory-tuned units, further supporting the hierarchy of action representation proposed by Grafton and Hamilton (2007).

Through the past decade, many other progresses have been made in understanding the neurophysiological mechanisms behind action representation and organization. Simply recognizing an action as goal directed is only one of the many aspects that can be useful for natural MI decoding.

Fogassi et al. (2005) first tried to understand which brain mechanisms link action understanding to a particular context. Studying the IPL of the monkey brain, they found out that discharges in neurons were context dependent: the neurons code the same act in a different way according to the final goal of the action. Specifically, they studied two different goal-directed action contexts: monkeys reached, grasped, and ate food or they reached, grasped an object, and placed it inside a container. In both tasks, the same grasping action was involved but the final goal was different. Some neurons showed higher discharge rates during the grasp-to-eat task, others showed increased responses in the grasp-to-place task. Though it could be argued that the differences could be due to the existence of different targets or even differences in movement kinematics—control experiments successfully discarded this possibility. The same results were obtained when the monkeys simply observed the exact same task executed by the experimenter. The authors proved the coexistence of mirror properties and context-dependent action encoding in the IPL, suggesting this area as the basis for action intention understanding.

So, aside from the hand–object interaction existent in goal-directed actions, also the context of the action seems to have an important role in action organization and planning. For example, grasping-to-eat is considered semantically meaningful, since there is a close relationship between the effector and the reason why the object (in this case food) is used. The ability to discriminate between meaningful and meaningless (or less meaningful) actions has been further explored in humans using fMRI (Iacoboni et al., 2005; Newman-Norlund et al., 2010). Newman-Norlund et al. (2010) showed short video clips of hand and foot transitive actions in which the relationship between those and the object was either meaningful (eg, hand pressing on a stapler or foot stepping a pedal) or meaningless (eg, foot pressing on a stapler or hand pressing a pedal). Interestingly, they showed that meaningful interactions between object and hand/foot evoked extra activations in the right supramarginal gyrus (SMG) and that the left SMG responded more to meaningless actions (Fig. 7). Despite the fact that most of the results derive from execution and observation tasks, they may match to action imagination, as Aflalo et al. (2015) work shows. To what extent imagined actions will have identical patterns as the ones already detected in movement execution and observation still needs to be investigated with EEG.

3 CONCLUSION

A promising way to achieve an intuitive control of a neuroprosthesis based on FES is by using a noninvasive BCI. However, in its current state, MI-based BCIs lack natural control and have a limited number of classes (often, only a brain-switch BCI can be implemented). This means that current BCIs are only capable of detecting the SMRs associated to the imagination of a certain movement and then to transfer this into a digital control signal. To address this gap, it would be necessary to decode the person's real intention of a hand/arm movement. For instance, the user thinks about grasping a bottle, and the BCI translates this signal into continuous movement commands to the motor neuroprosthesis, which executes the exact imagined action.

Despite several attempts of achieving a reliable decoder—during movement execution and specially during movement imagination tasks—to continuously decode movement parameters is a challenge, and it is not yet mature enough. Significant but rather low decoder performances can be obtained, which till now are not suitable for a reliable online control. An alternative to the continuous decoding is the target decoding, before movement onset. This consists in a more plausible alternative, since we no longer decode the movement-by-movement details but we focus exclusively on the final target (or final position) of the movement. In addition to the kinematic level, new findings in the neurophysiological processes behind movement planning associated to the goal level should be considered in future BCI research. While the kinematic level describes the arm movements in space and time, the goal level describes the high-level cognitive aspects in motor action. Examples are hand–object interaction and context dependency of actions, which have been shown to increase the brain patterns in specific regions during both movement observation and execution in EEG recordings. If movement imaginations lead to similar results, then—along with the natural movement imaginations decoding at the kinematic level—the subjects should be instructed to imagine the kinesthetic interaction with the object and the context of the action itself.

We believe that these intuitive movement imaginations are the future for BCI control, having several advantages for rehabilitation applications: online classification accuracies would be improved, training time would be reduced, and easier training strategies could be developed for helping users to reach and maintain control. However, two points are still missing. First, transferring these results to persons with SCI or other damage of the central nervous system. The decoder performance has to be reliable enough to be a valuable support to the end user. Second, moving out of the lab and applying the decoder in a real environment during daily living. Finally, we will be able to see, whether intact pathways to and from the periphery are necessary to produce all these effects we are able to observe in healthy people.

ACKNOWLEDGMENT

This work was partly funded by the Horizon 2020 project MoreGrasp Nr. H2020-ICT-2014-1 643955 and ERC Consolidator Grant "Feel Your Reach."

REFERENCES

Aflalo, T., et al., 2015. Neurophysiology. Decoding motor imagery from the posterior parietal cortex of a tetraplegic human. Science 348 (6237), 906–910.

Agashe, H.A., Paek, A.Y., Zhang, Y., Contreras-Vidal, J.L., 2015. Global cortical activity predicts shape of hand during grasping. Front. Neurosci. 9 (121), 1–11.

Agnew, Z.K., Bhakoo, K.K., Puri, B.K., 2007. The human mirror system: a motor resonance theory of mind-reading. Brain Res. Rev. 54 (2), 286–293.

Antelis, J.M., et al., 2013. On the usage of linear regression models to reconstruct limb kinematics from low frequency EEG signals. PLoS One 8 (4), 1–14.

Ball, T., Schulze-Bonhage, A., Aertsen, A., Mehring, C., 2009. Differential representation of arm movement direction in relation to cortical anatomy and function. J. Neural Eng. 6 (1), 1–16.

Bengtsson, S.L., et al., 2009. Listening to rhythms activates motor and premotor cortices. Cortex 45 (1), 62–71.

Blankertz, B., et al., 2006. The Berlin Brain–Computer Interface Presents the Novel Mental Typewriter Hex-O-Spell. In: Proceedings of the 3rd International Brain-Computer Interface Workshop and Training Course. Technischen Universität Graz, Graz, pp. 108–109.

Bradberry, T.J., Rong, F., Contreras-Vidal, J.L., 2009. Decoding center-out hand velocity from MEG signals during visuomotor adaptation. Neuroimage 47 (4), 1691–1700.

Bradberry, T.J., Gentili, R.J., Contreras-Vidal, J.L., 2010. Reconstructing three-dimensional hand movements from noninvasive electroencephalographic signals. J. Neurosci. 30, 3432–3437.

Bradberry, T.J., Gentili, R.J., Contreras-Vidal, J.L., 2011. Fast attainment of computer cursor control with noninvasively acquired brain signals. J. Neural Eng. 8 (3), 1–9.

Breiman, L., 2001. Random forests. Mach. Learn. 45 (1), 5–32.

Buccino, G., et al., 2001. Action observation activates premotor and parietal areas in a somatotopic manner: an fMRI study. Eur. J. Neurosci. 13 (2), 400–404.

Byron, M.Y., et al., 2007. Mixture of trajectory models for neural decoding of goal-directed movements. J. Neurophysiol. 97 (5), 3763–3780.

Caplan, J.B., et al., 2003. Human theta oscillations related to sensorimotor integration and spatial learning. J. Neurosci. 23 (11), 4726–4736.

Cornwell, B.R., et al., 2008. Human hippocampal and parahippocampal theta during goal-directed spatial navigation predicts performance on a virtual Morris water maze. J. Neurosci. 28 (23), 5983–5990.

Csibra, G., Gergely, G., 2007. 'Obsessed with goals': functions and mechanisms of teleological interpretation of actions in humans. Acta Psychol. 124 (1), 60–78.

Delorme, A., Sejnowski, T., Makeig, S., 2007. Enhanced detection of artifacts in EEG data using higher-order statistics and independent component analysis. Neuroimage 34 (4), 1443–1449.

Desmurget, M., Sirigu, A., 2009. A parietal-premotor network for movement intention and motor awareness. Trends Cogn. Sci. 13 (10), 411–419.

Ekstrom, A.D., et al., 2005. Human hippocampal theta activity during virtual navigation. Hippocampus 15 (7), 881–889.

Enzinger, C., et al., 2008. Brain motor system function in a patient with complete spinal cord injury following extensive brain–computer interface training. Exp. Brain Res. 190 (2), 215–223.

Faller, J., Vidaurre, C., Solis-Escalante, T., et al., 2012. Autocalibration and recurrent adaptation: towards a plug and play online ERD-BCI. IEEE Trans. Neur. Syst. Rehabil. Eng. 20 (3), 313–319.

Faller, J., et al., 2013. Online Co-adaptive Brain–Computer Interfacing: Preliminary Results in Individuals with Spinal Cord Injury. IEEE, San Diego, CA, pp. 977–980.

Faller, J., et al., 2014. A co-adaptive brain–computer interface for end users with severe motor impairment. PLoS One 9 (7), 1–10.

Farrar, D.E., Glauber, R.R., 1967. Multicollinearity in regression analysis: the problem revisited. Rev. Econ. Stat. 49 (1), 92–107.

Febo, C., et al., 2007. Vibrotactile feedback for brain–computer interface operation. Comput. Intell. Neurosci. 2007, 1–12.

Fogassi, L., et al., 2005. Parietal lobe: from action organization to intention understanding. Science 308 (5722), 662–667.

Friedrich, E.V.C., Neuper, C., Scherer, R., 2013. Whatever works: a systematic user-centered training protocol to optimize brain–computer interfacing individually. PLoS One 8 (9), e76214.

Galán, F., et al., 2008. A brain-actuated wheelchair: asynchronous and non-invasive brain–computer interfaces for continuous control of robots. Clin. Neurophysiol. 119 (9), 2159–2169.

Georgopoulos, A.P., Langheim, F.J.P., Leuthold, A.C., Merkle, A.N., 2005. Magnetoencephalographic signals predict movement trajectory in space. Exp. Brain Res. 167 (1), 132–135.

Grafton, S.T., Hamilton, A.F.D.C., 2007. Evidence for a distributed hierarchy of action representation in the brain. Hum. Mov. Sci. 26 (4), 590–616.

Grahn, J.A., Brett, M., 2007. Rhythm and beat perception in motor areas of the brain. J. Cogn. Neurosci. 19 (5), 893–906.

Graimann, B., Huggins, J.E., Levine, S.P., Pfurtscheller, G., 2002. Visualization of significant ERD/ERS patterns in multichannel EEG and ECoG data. Clin. Neurophysiol. 113 (1), 43–47.

Gu, Y., Dremstrup, K., Farina, D., 2009a. Single-trial discrimination of type and speed of wrist movements from EEG recordings. Clin. Neurophysiol. 120 (8), 1596–1600.

Gu, Y., et al., 2009b. Offline identification of imagined speed of wrist movements in paralyzed ALS patients from single-trial EEG. Front. Neurosci. 3 (62), 1–7.

Halder, S., et al., 2015. Brain-controlled applications using dynamic P300 speller matrices. Artif. Intell. Med. 63 (1), 7–17.

Hammon, P.S., et al., 2008. Predicting reaching targets from human EEG. IEEE Signal Process. Mag. 25 (1), 69–77.

Iacoboni, M., et al., 2005. Grasping the intentions of others with one's own mirror neuron system. PLoS Biol. 3 (3), e79.

Jackson, A., Zimmermann, J.B., 2012. Neural interfaces for the brain and spinal cord—restoring motor function. Nat. Rev. Neurol. 8 (12), 690–699.

Jerbi, K., et al., 2007. Coherent neural representation of hand speed in humans revealed by MEG imaging. Proc. Natl. Acad. Sci. U.S.A. 104 (18), 7676–7681.

Kim, J.-H., Biessmann, F., Lee, S.-W., 2015. Decoding three-dimensional trajectory of executed and imagined arm movements from electroencephalogram signals. IEEE Trans. Neural Syst. Rehabil. Eng. 23 (5), 867–876.

Korik, A., Siddique, N., Sosnik, R., Coyle, D., 2014. Correlation of EEG Band Power and Hand Motion Trajectory. Graz University of Technology Publishing House, Graz, pp. 1–4.

Korik, A., Siddique, N., Sosnik, R., Coyle, D., 2015. 3D Hand Movement Velocity Reconstruction Using Power Spectral Density of EEG Signals and Neural Network. IEEE, Milano, pp. 8103–8106.

Kreilinger, A., et al., 2013. Neuroprosthesis control via noninvasive hybrid brain–computer interface. IEEE Intell. Syst. 28 (5), 40–43.

Kübler, A., Birbaumer, N., 2008. Brain–computer interfaces and communication in paralysis: extinction of goal directed thinking in completely paralysed patients? Clin. Neurophysiol. 119 (11), 2658–2666.

Kübler, A., Neumann, N., 2005. Brain–computer interfaces—the key for the conscious brain locked into a paralyzed body. Prog. Brain Res. 150, 513–525.

Lew, E.Y., Chavarriaga, R., Silvoni, S., Millan, J.D.R., 2014. Single trial prediction of self-paced reaching directions from EEG signals. Front. Neurosci. 8, 222.

Li, J., Wang, Y., Zhang, L., Jung, T.P., 2012. Combining ERPs and EEG spectral features for decoding intended movement direction. Conf. Proc. IEEE Eng. Med. Biol. Soc. 769–772.

Liao, X., Yao, D., Wu, D., Li, C., 2007. Combining spatial filters for the classification of single-trial EEG in a finger movement task. IEEE Trans. Biomed. Eng. 54 (5), 821–831.

Lotte, F., et al., 2007. A review of classification algorithms for EEG-based brain–computer interfaces. J. Neural Eng. 2 (4), R1–R13.

Lv, J., Li, Y., Gu, Z., 2010. Decoding hand movement velocity from electroencephalogram signals during a drawing task. Biomed. Eng. Online 9 (64), 1–21.

McCreadie, K.A., Coyle, D.H., Prasad, G., 2014. Is sensorimotor BCI performance influenced differently by mono, stereo, or 3-D auditory feedback? IEEE Trans. Neural Syst. Rehabil. Eng. 22 (3), 43–50.

Milekovic, T., et al., 2012. An online brain–machine interface using decoding of movement direction from the human electrocorticogram. J. Neural Eng. 9 (4), 1–14.

Mueller-Putz, G., Scherer, R., Pfurtscheller, G., Neuper, C., 2010. Temporal coding of brain patterns for direct limb control in humans. Front. Neurosci. 4, 34.

Müller-Putz, G., 2004. New Concepts in Brain–Computer Communication: Use of Steady-State Somatosensory Evoked Potentials, User Training by Telesupport and Control of Functional Electrical Stimulation. Graz University of Technology, Graz.

Müller-Putz, G.R., Scherer, R., Pfurtscheller, G., Rupp, R., 2005. EEG-based neuroprosthesis control: a step towards clinical practice. Neurosci. Lett. 382, 169–174.

Muthukumaraswamy, S.D., Johnson, B.W., McNair, N.A., 2004. Mu rhythm modulation during observation of an object-directed grasp. Cogn. Brain Res. 19 (2), 195–201.

Nakanishi, Y., et al., 2013. Prediction of three-dimensional arm trajectories based on ECoG signals recorded from human sensorimotor cortex. PLoS One 8 (8), 1–9.

Neuper, C., et al., 2003. Clinical application of an EEG-based brain–computer interface: a case study in a patient with severe motor impairment. Clin. Neurophysiol. 114, 399–409.

Neuper, C., Scherer, R., Reiner, M., Pfurtscheller, G., 2005. Imagery of motor actions: differential effects of kinesthetic versus visual-motor mode of imagery on single-trial EEG. Brain Res. Cogn. Brain Res. 25, 668–677.

Neuper, C., Scherer, R., Wriessnegger, S., Pfurtscheller, G., 2009. Motor imagery and action observation: modulation of sensorimotor brain rhythms during mental control of a brain–computer interface. Clin. Neurophysiol. 120, 239–247.

Newman-Norlund, R., et al., 2010. The role of inferior frontal and parietal areas in differentiating meaningful and meaningless object-directed actions. Brain Res. 1315, 63–74.

Nijboer, F., et al., 2008a. An auditory brain–computer interface (BCI). J. Neurosci. Methods 167 (1), 43–50.

Nijboer, F., et al., 2008b. A P300-based brain–computer interface for people with amyotrophic lateral sclerosis. Clin. Neurophysiol. 119, 1909–1916.

Obermaier, B., Müller, G.R., Pfurtscheller, G., 2003. "Virtual keyboard" controlled by spontaneous EEG activity. IEEE Trans. Neural Syst. Rehabil. Eng. 11, 422–426.

Ofner, P., Müller-Putz, G.R., 2012. Decoding of Velocities and Positions of 3D Arm Movement from EEG. IEEE, San Diego, pp. 6406–6409.

Ofner, P., Müller-Putz, G.R., 2015a. Movement Target Decoding from EEG and the Corresponding Discriminative Sources: A Preliminary Study. IEEE, Milano, pp. 1468–1471.

Ofner, P., Müller-Putz, G.R., 2015b. Using a noninvasive decoding method to classify rhythmic movement imaginations of the arm in two planes. IEEE Trans. Biomed. Eng. 62 (3), 972–981.

Paek, A.Y., Agashe, H.A., Contreras-Vidal, J.L., 2014. Decoding repetitive finger movements with brain activity acquired via non-invasive electroencephalography. Front. Neuroeng. 7 (3), 1–18.

Peckham, P., et al., 2001. Efficacy of an implanted neuroprosthesis for restoring hand grasp in tetraplegia: a multicenter study. Arch. Phys. Med. Rehabil. 82 (10), 1380–1388.

Pereira, J., Ofner, P., Muller-Putz, G.R., 2015. Goal-Directed or Aimless? EEG Differences During the Preparation of a Reach-and-Touch Task. IEEE, Milano, pp. 1488–1491.

Pesaran, B., Nelson, M.J., Andersen, R.A., 2006. Dorsal premotor neurons encode the relative position of the hand, eye, and goal during reach planning. Neuron 51 (1), 125–134.

Pfurtscheller, G., Aranibar, A., 1979. Evaluation of event-related desynchronization (ERD) preceding and following voluntary self-paced movements. Electroencephalogr. Clin. Neurophysiol. 46, 138–146.

Pfurtscheller, G., Neuper, C., 1997. Motor imagery activates primary sensorimotor area in humans. Neurosci. Lett. 239 (2–3), 65–68.

Pfurtscheller, G., Neuper, C., 2001. Motor imagery and direct brain–computer communication. Proc. IEEE 89, 1123–1134.

Pfurtscheller, G., Silva, F.H.L.D., 1999. Event-related EEG/MEG synchronization and desynchronization: basic principles. Clin. Neurophysiol. 110 (11), 1842–1857.

Pfurtscheller, G., et al., 2000. Brain oscillations control hand orthosis in a tetraplegic. Neurosci. Lett. 292, 211–214.

Pfurtscheller, G., et al., 2003. "Thought"-control of functional electrical stimulation to restore handgrasp in a patient with tetraplegia. Neurosci. Lett. 351, 33–36.

Pfurtscheller, G., et al., 2006. 15 years of BCI research at Graz University of Technology: current projects. IEEE Trans. Neural Syst. Rehabil. Eng. 14 (2), 205–210.

Pinegger, A., Wriesnegger, S., Müller-Putz, G., 2013. Introduction of a universal P300 brain–computer interface communication system. Biomed. Tech. 58, 1–2.

Pistohl, T., et al., 2008. Prediction of arm movement trajectories from ECoG-recordings in humans. J. Neurosci. Methods 167 (1), 105–114.

Poli, R., Salvaris, M., 2011. Comment on 'fast attainment of computer cursor control with noninvasively acquired brain signals'. J. Neural Eng. 8 (5), 1–3.

Ramoser, H., Müller-Gerking, J., Pfurtscheller, G., 2000. Optimal spatial filtering of single trial EEG during imagined hand movement. IEEE Trans. Rehabil. Eng. 8, 441–446.

Rizzolatti, G., Cattaneo, L., Fabbri-Destro, M., Rozzi, S., 2014. Cortical mechanisms underlying the organization of goal-directed actions and mirror neuron-based action understanding. Physiol. Rev. 94 (2), 655–706.

Robinson, N., et al., 2013. Multi-class EEG classification of voluntary hand movement directions. J. Neural Eng. 10 (5), 1–11.

Rohm, M., et al., 2013. Hybrid brain–computer interfaces and hybrid neuroprostheses for restoration of upper limb functions in individuals with high-level spinal cord injury. Artif. Intell. Med. 59 (2), 133–142.

Rupp, R., et al., 2015. Functional rehabilitation of the paralyzed upper extremity after spinal cord injury by noninvasive hybrid neuroprostheses. Proc. IEEE 103 (6), 954–968.

Saxe, R., et al., 2004. A region of right posterior superior temporal sulcus responds to observed intentional actions. Neuropsychologia 42 (11), 1435–1446.

Schalk, G., et al., 2007. Decoding two-dimensional movement trajectories using electrocorticographic signals in humans. J. Neural Eng. 4 (3), 264–275.

Scherer, R., et al., 2004. An asynchronously controlled EEG-based virtual keyboard: improvement of the spelling rate. IEEE Trans. Biomed. Eng. 6 (51), 979–984.

Scherer, R., et al., 2008. Toward self-paced brain–computer communication: navigation through virtual worlds. IEEE Trans. Biomed. Eng. 55, 675–682.

Scherer, R., et al., 2015. Thought-based row-column scanning communication board for individuals with cerebral palsy. Ann. Phys. Rehabil. Med. 58 (1), 14–22.

Schlögl, A., Lee, F., Bischof, H., Pfurtscheller, G., 2005. Characterization of four-class motor imagery EEG data for the BCI-competition. J. Neural Eng. 4, L14–L22.

Schlögl, A., et al., 2007. A fully automated correction method of EOG artifacts in EEG recordings. Clin. Neurophysiol. 118 (1), 98–104.

Schwarz, A., et al., 2015. A co-adaptive sensory motor rhythms brain–computer interface based on common spatial patterns and random forest. Conf. Proc. IEEE Eng. Med. Biol. Soc. 2015, 1049–1052.

Steyrl, D., Scherer, R., Faller, J., Müller-Putz, G., 2015. Random forests in non-invasive sensorimotor rhythm brain–computer interfaces: a practical and convenient non-linear classifier. Biomed. Tech. (Berl.) 60, 77–86.

Toda, A., Imamizu, H., Kawato, M., Sato, M.A., 2011. Reconstruction of two-dimensional movement trajectories from selected magnetoencephalography cortical currents by combined sparse Bayesian methods. Neuroimage 54 (2), 892–905.

Úbeda, A., et al., 2015. Movement factors in upper limb kinematics decoding from EEG signals. PLoS One 10 (5), 1–12.

Vidaurre, C., Sannelli, C., Müller, K.-R., Blankertz, B., 2011a. Co-adaptive calibration to improve BCI efficiency. J. Neural Eng. 8, 025009.

Vidaurre, C., Sannelli, C., Müller, K.R., Blankertz, B., 2011b. Machine-learning based co-adaptive calibration for brain–computer interfaces. Neural Comput. 23, 791–816.

Vuckovic, A., Sepulveda, F., 2008. Delta band contribution in cue based single trial classification of real and imaginary wrist movements. Med. Biol. Eng. Comput. 46 (6), 529–539.

Vuckovic, A., Sepulveda, F., 2012. A two-stage four-class BCI based on imaginary movements of the left and the right wrist. Med. Eng. Phys. 34 (7), 964–971.

Waldert, S., et al., 2008. Hand movement direction decoded from MEG and EEG. J. Neurosci. 28 (4), 1000–1008.

Wamain, Y., Pluciennicka, E., Kalenine, S., 2014. Temporal dynamics of action perception: differences on ERP evoked by object-related and non-object-related actions. Neuropsychologia 63, 249–258.

Wang, W., et al., 2010. Decoding and cortical source localization for intended movement direction with MEG. J. Neurophysiol. 104 (5), 2451–2461.

Wold, S., Sjöström, M., Eriksson, L., 2001. PLS-regression: a basic tool of chemometrics. Chemometr. Intell. Lab. Syst. 58 (2), 109–130.

Wolpaw, J.R., et al., 2002. Brain–computer interfaces for communication and control. Clin. Neurophysiol. 113 (6), 767–791.

Yeom, H.G., Kim, J.S., Chung, C.K., 2013. Estimation of the velocity and trajectory of three-dimensional reaching movements from non-invasive magnetoencephalography signals. J. Neural Eng. 10 (2), 1–9.

Yuan, H., Doud, A., Gururajan, A., He, B., 2008. Cortical imaging of event-related (de)synchronization during online control of brain–computer interface using minimum-norm estimates in frequency domain. IEEE Trans. Neural Syst. Rehabil. Eng. 16 (5), 425–431.

Yuan, H., et al., 2010. Negative covariation between task-related responses in alpha/beta-band activity and BOLD in human sensorimotor cortex: an EEG and fMRI study of motor imagery and movement. Neuroimage 49 (3), 2596–2606.

Zhang, J., et al., 2014. Nonlinear EEG decoding based on a particle filter model. BioMed Res. Int. 2014, 1–13.

3D hand motion trajectory prediction from EEG mu and beta bandpower

A. Korik*,[1], R. Sosnik[†], N. Siddique*, D. Coyle*

*Intelligent Systems Research Centre, Ulster University, Derry, Northern Ireland, United Kingdom
[†]Hybrid BCI Lab, Holon Institute of Technology, Holon, Israel
[1]Corresponding author: Tel.: +44-28-716-75170, e-mail address: korik-a@email.ulster.ac.uk

Abstract

A motion trajectory prediction (MTP) - based brain–computer interface (BCI) aims to reconstruct the three-dimensional (3D) trajectory of upper limb movement using electroencephalography (EEG). The most common MTP BCI employs a time series of bandpass-filtered EEG potentials (referred to here as the potential time-series, PTS, model) for reconstructing the trajectory of a 3D limb movement using multiple linear regression. These studies report the best accuracy when a 0.5–2 Hz bandpass filter is applied to the EEG. In the present study, we show that spatiotemporal power distribution of theta (4–8 Hz), mu (8–12 Hz), and beta (12–28 Hz) bands are more robust for movement trajectory decoding when the standard PTS approach is replaced with time-varying bandpower values of a specified EEG band, ie, with a bandpower time-series (BTS) model. A comprehensive analysis comprising of three subjects performing pointing movements with the dominant right arm toward six targets is presented. Our results show that the BTS model produces significantly higher MTP accuracy ($R \sim 0.45$) compared to the standard PTS model ($R \sim 0.2$). In the case of the BTS model, the highest accuracy was achieved across the three subjects typically in the mu (8–12 Hz) and low-beta (12–18 Hz) bands. Additionally, we highlight a limitation of the commonly used PTS model and illustrate how this model may be suboptimal for decoding motion trajectory relevant information. Although our results, showing that the mu and beta bands are prominent for MTP, are not in line with other MTP studies, they are consistent with the extensive literature on classical multiclass sensorimotor rhythm-based BCI studies (classification of limbs as opposed to motion trajectory prediction), which report the best accuracy of imagined limb movement classification using power values of mu and beta frequency bands. The methods proposed here provide a positive step toward noninvasive decoding of imagined 3D hand movements for movement-free BCIs.

Keywords

3D motion trajectory prediction, Brain–computer interface, Decoding hand velocity, Electroencephalography, Sensorimotor rhythms, Multiclass classification, Inner–outer (nested) cross-validation

Progress in Brain Research, Volume 228, ISSN 0079-6123, http://dx.doi.org/10.1016/bs.pbr.2016.05.001
© 2016 Elsevier B.V. All rights reserved.

1 INTRODUCTION

A brain–computer interface (BCI) aims to decode brain signals directly without using natural neuromuscular pathways to provide alternative communication or movement control options for the physically impaired (Wolpaw et al., 2002). BCI research has investigated a wide range of application areas from orthosis control in the spinal injured (Pfurtscheller et al., 2000), virtual and real wheelchair control (Leeb et al., 2007; Rebsamen et al., 2010), stroke rehabilitation (Prasad et al., 2010; Silvoni et al., 2011), and entertainment and gaming applications (Lecuyer et al., 2008; Marshall et al., 2013) to applications involving reading of visual imagery by online detection of visuospatial working memory (Hamamé et al., 2012) or collecting information about ongoing cognitive neural activity for monitoring, for instance, situational interpretations and emotional states (Zander and Kothe, 2011) among many others. A large proportion of BCI applications are aimed at enabling people to gain control of objects in real or virtual three-dimensional (3D) spaces with motor imagery (MI), where imagined movement enables voluntary modulation of the neural activity in the sensorimotor cortex (Huang et al., 2012; LaFleur et al., 2013; McFarland et al., 2010; Royer et al., 2010), which can be decoded for control.

Two different approaches have been used in noninvasive MI BCIs, namely multiclass (MC) sensorimotor rhythm (SMR) BCIs and time-series-based motion trajectory prediction (MTP) BCIs (Coyle and Sosnik, 2015). MC SMR BCIs enable multidimensional control in the real or virtual spaces using a classifier trained to distinguish between the imagined movement of different limbs, with normally two limbs being classified involving discrimination of the imagined movement of four limbs have (Coyle et al., 2005; McFarland et al., 2000; Pfurtscheller et al., 1993; Qin and He, 2005; Royer et al., 2010; Wolpaw et al., 1991) but up to four class BCIs also been investigated (Morash et al., 2008; Pfurtscheller et al., 2006). MC SMR BCIs use a multidimensional feature space and classifier for control. As the spatiotemporal SMR amplitude is modulated differently for the executed/imagined movement of different limbs, the executed or imagined movement of different limbs can normally be classified with varying degrees of success from electroencephalography (EEG) originating in sensorimotor areas (Pfurtscheller, 2001; Wolpaw et al., 2002). Signal amplitude modulation occurs as a result of event-related desynchronization (ERD) or synchronization (ERS) in large neural networks in sensorimotor areas. ERD and ERS originate from the decreased or increased phase-locked synchronous activity of specific neural populations and are manifested by decreased or increased power in mu (8–12 Hz) and central beta (18–26 Hz) frequency bands over the central and parietal cortex (Pfurtscheller and Lopes da Silva, 1999; Pfurtscheller et al., 1993, 2000, 2006; Qin and He, 2005; Wolpaw et al., 1991). Common SMR BCIs typically control different directions by classifying imaginary motion or rest status of the specified limbs, which are regularly left hand, right hand, foot (single for both feet), and tongue (Ge et al.,

2014; Morash et al., 2008; Pfurtscheller et al., 2006). More advanced applications use a self-regulatory scheme in which the user learns to modulate the SMR to gain control over different dimensions independently (McFarland et al., 2010; Royer et al., 2010; Wolpaw and McFarland, 2004). Classical MC SMR BCIs (Yuan and He, 2014) involving imagery of limb movements have been shown to be very effective for many tasks including communication (Wolpaw et al., 2002), word processing (Kübler et al., 2005), games control (Coyle et al., 2015), hand orthosis control (Baxter et al., 2013; King et al., 2011), and robotic arm control in a shared control strategy where the user specifies the target with the BCI and the robot's intelligent controller performs the movement (Fatima et al., 2015). While classical MC SMR BCIs can decode a certain number of end target positions, this technique does not aim to decode the trajectory of a real or imagined limb movement from EEG.

In contrast to MC SMR BCIs, common MTP BCIs aim to reconstruct the limb movement trajectory itself, ie, estimating the track of the limb coordinates or velocity vectors during an executed or imagined movement (Korik et al., 2014). A commonly investigated MTP BCI involves decoding a single upper limb movement toward multiple targets in 3D space (Bradberry et al., 2010; Choi, 2013; Yeom et al., 2013), but finger movement (Paek et al., 2014), drawing tasks (Georgopoulos et al., 2005), or such complex movements as walking (Presacco et al., 2011) or drinking a glass of water (Heger et al., 2012) have also been investigated based on noninvasively recorded brain activity using EEG or magnetoencephalography techniques. In contrast to classical MC SMR BCIs which normally involve discrete classification of movements into different classes (eg, left arm movement vs right arm movement imagination) (Coyle et al., 2005; McFarland et al., 2000; Pfurtscheller et al., 1993; Qin and He, 2005), MTP BCIs reconstruct the 3D trajectory from a time series of bandpass-filtered EEG potentials using multiple linear regression (mLR) (Bradberry et al., 2010; Georgopoulos et al., 2005) as presented in Section 2.4. SMR BCIs report the best accuracy when power values of mu (8–12 Hz) and beta (12–30 Hz) bands are used for classifying the movement (Coyle et al., 2010; McFarland et al., 2000, 2010; Wolpaw and McFarland, 2004). In contrast, MTP BCIs usually report the best results when a low delta (0.5–2 Hz) bandpass filter is applied to the EEG before the input time-series is fed to an mLR-based kinematic data estimation module (Bradberry et al., 2010; Paek et al., 2014; Robinson et al., 2015; Yeom et al., 2013).

Other studies using invasive recording techniques also report the relationship between the trajectory of a limb movement and low-frequency component of neural signals. For example, Nakanishi et al. (2013) reconstructed arm movement from time-varying electrocorticography (ECoG) potentials registered in the sensorimotor cortex using an mLR model. They reported the highest accuracy when a 0–4 Hz bandpass filter was applied to the ECoG. In one another study, Hall et al. (2014) confirmed a strong correlation of hand velocity trajectories of monkeys and amplitude modulation of the local field potentials (LFPs) in the ($\sim$3 Hz) low-frequency band in the primary motor cortex (M1). As ECoG and EEG signals are composed of LFPs, this relationship provides an explanation of successfully decoded limb movement trajectories based on time series of low delta (0.5–2 Hz) bandpass-filtered ECoG or EEG potentials.

Although MTP BCI approaches employing the bandpass-filtered EEG potentials as input to the mLR model have been shown to provide the highest accuracy in the 0.5–2 Hz frequency band, Antelis et al. (2013) pointed out the possible misinterpretation of these results. Antelis et al. (2013) investigated the mLR-based MTP BCI using center-out task when the executed movement follows a periodic rhythm, demonstrating how this setup can lead to an overestimated accuracy in the low-frequency band if the accuracy is measured by correlation of the executed and reconstructed trajectories.

Here, we present evidence that time-varying power pattern of mu and beta bands provide more information for 3D MTP BCIs than the lower frequency bands. Moreover, we show that spatiotemporal power patterns of subject-specific EEG bands, ie, the time series of bandpower values from the selected EEG channels in specific frequency bands (bandpower time-series, BTS, model) as opposed to the time series of bandpass-filtered EEG potentials (potential time-series, PTS, model) provides more robust information for decoding the 3D trajectory of a limb movement. We compare the commonly used PTS model with the proposed BTS model where bandpower is calculated in 500 ms width time-varying window of the EEG in selected channels.

Our pilot analysis (Korik et al., 2015) provided evidence that significantly higher accuracy rates are achievable for the BTS-based MTP compared to the PTS-based MTP. Furthermore, in line with MC SMR BCI results, we showed that the BTS-based MTP provided the highest accuracy when power values were taken from the mu (8–12 Hz) and low-beta (12–18 Hz) bands. Here, we present further evidence of the approach with additional data, refined preprocessing and feature selection methods, and advanced analysis on an EEG–kinematic dataset, comprising three subjects and two runs, and 3D movements to six targets.

In summary, the aims of the chapter are

1. To compare the commonly used PTS-based MTP approach (Bradberry et al., 2010) with the BTS-based MTP model presented here.
2. To show that mu and beta rhythms provide information for decoding 3D hand motion trajectory from spatiotemporal power pattern of these specific EEG bands and that this information is more reliable that the commonly used low delta band.
3. To illustrate why MTP BCIs have focused on lower frequency components exclusively and occlude information in mu and beta bands for MTP.
4. To show that the BTS-based MTP approach might provide a synthesis of methods that are commonly used for classifying limb movement with an MC-based SMR BCI and reconstructing the track of the movement by a PTS-based MTP BCI.

We must note that all the work presented in this study, similar to most of the published MTP studies to date, is focused on motor execution (ie, reconstructing track of a realized hand movement) as opposed to MI which is the subject of our ongoing experiments (Korik et al., 2016).

2 METHODS

EEG-based 3D hand MTP poses many challenges regardless of the movement type, being actual or imagined. It is, therefore, valid to assume that multiple stages of high performing signal processing is necessary to extract the relevant information. This section presents the details of the various signal preprocessing and prediction procedures that have been used in this work. Fig. 1 illustrates the various steps and processing blocks used for the analysis. These blocks are discussed in detail in the following subsections, whereas the experimental paradigm is discussed in Section 2.1, data recording in Section 2.2, preprocessing in Section 2.3, details of the kinematic data reconstruction in Section 2.4, and architecture optimization and calculation of the final results are described in Section 2.5.

2.1 EXPERIMENTAL PARADIGM

Three healthy subjects (males, aged 25–46 years) gave informed consent and participated in the study, which was conducted in the Hybrid BCI lab at Holon Institute of Technology (HIT), Israel. The study was performed with the informed consent of the subjects and had full ethical approval from Wolfson Medical Center Research Ethics Committee. All subjects were right-handed, without any medical or psychological illness and/or medication and had normal or corrected to normal vision. The subjects were informed about the experimental task to be undertaken prior to the experiment.

Subjects sat on a chair, 1.5 m in front of a Kinect sensor (Kinect, 2010), looking forward and were requested to maintain a constant head position, refrain from teeth grinding and to minimize unrequired movement during the experiment. They were also asked to minimize eye blinks during the movement cycles (described later) and to rest during the intertask resting periods. The experimental tasks were executed by their right, dominant hand.

The experiment comprised two runs of executed hand movement tasks, where runs were separated by an interrun resting (IRR) lasting one minute. During the IRR, subjects were asked to relax and not to move or talk. The runs comprised repeated movements between the home position and one of the six targets. Targets 3, 2, and 1 lay in the shoulder plane forming 0, 30, and 60 degrees, respectively, between the torso and the shoulder (Fig. 2). Target 5 lays 30 degree below the shoulder plane, forming 0 degree between the torso and the shoulder. Targets 4 and 6 lay 30 degree above the shoulder plane, forming 0 and 60 degree, respectively, between the torso and the shoulder. The format of the runs, which match the experimental paradigm of our pilot analysis (Korik et al., 2015), is presented in Fig. 3.

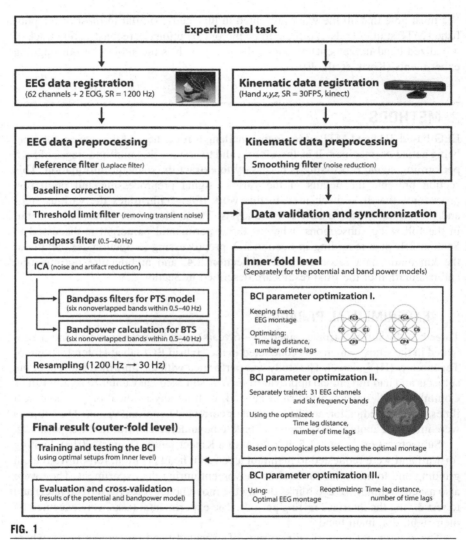

FIG. 1

Signal processing pipeline—from data acquisition to evaluation of the decoding accuracy.

Each run comprised six blocks, each comprising 15 hand movements between the home position and one of the six targets. Eight seconds before run initiation, the subject was asked to get ready for the task. The movement between the home position and a target was synchronized with an 800 ms auditory cue (6 kHz tone), which was followed by an 800 ms pause epoch. The backward movement from the target to the home position was synchronized with an 800 ms auditory cue (4 kHz tone), which was followed by an 800 ms resting epoch at the home position. Thus, a movement cycle lasted for 3200 ms (Fig. 3A), a movement block lasted for 48 s (Fig. 3B), and a

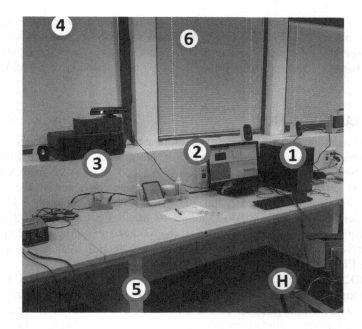

FIG. 2

Illustration of the experimental setup. The circle with label H and circles with numbers indicate the home position and six target positions, respectively.

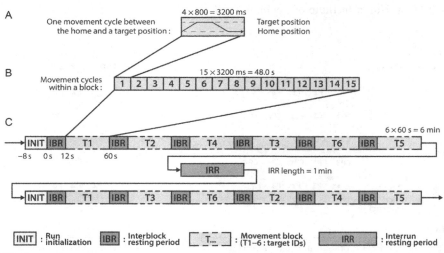

INIT : Run initialization IBR : Interblock resting period T... : Movement block (T1–6 : target IDs) IRR : Interrun resting period

FIG. 3

The timing of the experimental paradigm. (A) A movement cycle between the home position (*H*) and one of the six targets (T1–6). (B) Structure of one block comprising 15 movement cycles between the H and one of the targets. (C) Structure of the runs, where each run comprises six movement blocks to one of the six targets (T1–6).

run lasted 6 min, comprising six blocks each followed by an interblock resting (IBR) period, lasting for 12 s (Fig. 3C). For each IBR, a recorded voice message was played for 4 s before the subsequent block initiation, informing the subject about the identity of the next target. The runs were separated by an IRR period lasting 1 min.

2.2 DATA ACQUISITION

EEG and kinematic data were acquired simultaneously. EEG signals were recorded in 61 channels. Two electrooculography (EOG) electrodes were attached inferiorly to the orbital fossa of the left eye. Both EEG and EOG were recorded using g.HIamp80 (2013). The EEG reference electrode was positioned on the right ear lobe. The EEG was amplified (gain: 20,000), filtered (Butterworth 0.5–100 Hz, eighth order), and sampled (A/D resolution: 24 bits, sampling rate: 1200 samples/s). The ground electrode was positioned on the forehead above the nose. Impedance for all active electrodes was below 50 KΩ. In the following section, Fig. 4A illustrates the EEG montage.

The 3D Microsoft Kinect camera system (Kinect, 2010) was developed for Xbox 360 to record 3D limb movements. We decided to use this device for registering kinematic data as it provides 3D coordinates of limbs' joints to sufficient accuracy. Kinematic data were recorded from the right dominant hand, elbow, and shoulder at 30 frames per second (FPS). The kinematic data acquisition does not require the placement of markers on the joints of the arm because the Kinect camera system can identify the limb joints without markers. All datasets were acquired at the Hybrid BCI lab at Holon Institute of Technology (HIT), Israel.

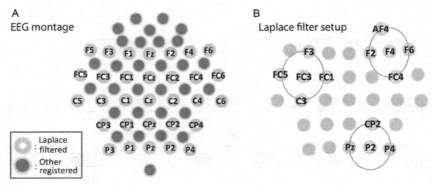

FIG. 4

Illustration of EEG montage and Laplace filter setup. (A) EEG montage and those channel locations that were used as center points for the Laplace filtering. (B) Three representative examples of Laplace filter electrode sets. For each of the three sets, the Laplace center electrode and those electrodes, which were selected as surrounding electrodes for Laplace filtering are labeled.

2.3 DATA PREPROCESSING

2.3.1 EEG data preprocessing

EEG preprocessing involved a reference filter for reducing common mode artifacts, baseline filter for DC shift correction, a threshold limit filter for filtering out data intervals with high-level transient noise, a wide range (0.5–40 Hz) bandpass filter for filtering out nonrelevant frequency bands, and independent component analysis (ICA) for removal of EOG, muscle artifacts, and noise reduction. Following ICA, the data were parallel filtered by six nonoverlapped bandpass filters within the 0.5–40 Hz frequency range, serving as an input for the PTS model. In addition, the fast Fourier transform (FFT) was applied to the ICA outputs in six frequency bands, serving as an input for the BTS model. Details of the two models are presented in Section 2.4. Additional details of the applied preprocessing methods are described later.

2.3.1.1 Re-referencing and bandpass filtering

EEG channels are usually charged with a common mode artifact, which distorts the registered EEG signals. There are numerous referencing methods commonly used in EEG preprocessing for reducing common mode artifacts, including bipolar referencing, common average referencing (CAR), Laplace filter, and common spatial patterns (Fehmi and Collura, 2007; Lu et al., 2013; McFarland et al., 1997; Ramoser et al., 2000). As part of a limited pilot analysis on data not included in this study (unpublished), we compared the filters' noise and artifact reduction performance of referencing methods. CAR and Laplace filters in four different distances of the Laplace center and surrounding electrodes were applied separately to the raw EEG data.

As the ICA technique provided slightly better separation of the noise components when the small Laplace filter was applied, we selected the small Laplace filter for the current analysis. Out of the 61 registered EEG channels, 31 channels (Fig. 4A) were re-referenced using a small Laplace filter as described in Eq. (1) according to McFarland et al. (1997) and Lu et al. (2013):

$$x_i^{LAP} = x_i^{ER} - \sum_{j \in S_i} g_{ij} x_j^{ER} \tag{1}$$

where x_i^{ER} is the potential between electrode i and the reference Eq. (2),

$$g_{ij} = \frac{1/d_{ij}}{\sum_{j \in S_i} 1/d_{ij}}. \tag{2}$$

S_i is the set of electrodes surrounding the electrode i and d_{ij} is the distance between electrodes i and j ($j \in S_i$).

The surrounding electrodes for the small Laplace filter have been selected as shown in Fig. 4B (eg, for the FC3 central electrode, the surrounding electrodes were F3, C3, FC5, and FC1). For EEG channels that resided at the edge of the montage, the Laplace filtering was applied to a reduced number of surrounding electrodes. For example, for P2 central electrode, only three surrounding electrodes (CP2, Pz, and P4) were used for the Laplace filter because the EEG montage did not involve the PO_2 electrode location above P2. Our analysis showed the optimal electrode subset, which results in the highest accuracy for MTP (Section 2.5) may involve such EEG electrode locations, where the Laplace filter was applied to a reduced number of surrounding electrodes. Therefore, in cases where all four surrounding electrodes are not available, it is appropriate to use the earlier described modified Laplacian in order to keep these electrode locations in the analysis.

As the baseline of the re-referenced signals was not zero, DC shift was calculated separately for each re-referenced channel and subtracted from the re-referenced signals. To avoid processing data intervals with low signal-to-noise ratio (SNR), preprocessed EEG data intervals with a high-level transient noise ($>|\pm300\,\mu V|$) were removed from further analysis. In order to keep the EEG and kinematic datasets synchronized, indices of removed intervals were registered and fed into the data synchronization algorithm. As valuable information for MTP could be gained from 0.5–40 Hz EEG frequency band (Korik et al., 2015), the data were filtered in this frequency band by an eighth order Butterworth filter.

2.3.1.2 Independent component analysis

EEG is a multidimensional interrelated signal that is generated by numerous independent neural sources and noise components as defined in Eq. (3):

$$EEG[t] = f(s(t)) + n(t) \qquad (3)$$

where $EEG[t]$ is the EEG signals, $f(s(t))$ is a mixture function of the unknown sources, and $n(t)$ is the noise. Therefore, using a coordinate transformation it is possible to convert the raw signals into a vector space wherein the basis coordinates are related to the most prominent sources as shown in Eq. (4):

$$EEG[t] = \mathbf{A}s(t) + n(t) \qquad (4)$$

where $\mathbf{A}$ is a mixing matrix that is used on $s(t)$ sources for reconstructing the EEG signals. ICA gives a solution for converting the original N-dimensional vector space, where N is the number of registered EEG channels, into a new vector space where the number of signals sources is given by $s(t)$ and noise sources is given by $n(t)$ (Kachenoura et al., 2008; Makeig et al., 1995). Those ICA components, which may be related to artifacts such as EOG, electromyography (EMG), or noise components, can be identified by their tempo-spectral features and scalp distribution (Mognon et al., 2010). The noise-reduced EEG signals can be constructed using the inverse ICA transformation on the components that were considered not to be artifactual or noise sources.

Thus, ICA was performed on the 31 preprocessed Laplacian channels shown in Fig. 4A. The components that were identified as related to EOG, EMG, or noise, were removed and the remaining components were transferred back to the original 31-dimensional data space using the inverse ICA transformation.

2.3.1.3 The potential time-series model

In order to detect the frequency band that provides the highest accuracy for the kinematic data reconstruction (Sections 2.4 and 2.5), an eighth order Butterworth filter was applied to the ICA-filtered EEG, separately in the following six frequency bands: lower delta (0.5–2 Hz), theta (4–8 Hz), mu (8–12 Hz), lower beta (12–18 Hz), upper beta (18–28 Hz), and gamma (28–40 Hz). The PTS model was trained and tested separately based on preprocessed EEG, respectively, to the above defined six bands. The preprocessing method for the PTS model, described in present chapter, provides such kind of EEG dataset, which is commonly used in the standard PTS-based MTP BCI studies (Antelis et al., 2013; Bradberry et al., 2010; Choi, 2013; Georgopoulos et al., 2005; Ofner and Müller-Putz, 2012; Paek et al., 2014; Sicard et al., 2014).

2.3.1.4 The bandpower time-series model

The BTS model is a standard model applied in traditional MC SMR BCIs but here we apply it to MTP BCIs for the first time. In the BTS model, each of the six nonoverlapped bandpass filters was extended with a time-varying bandpower calculation, which provided the power of the ICA-filtered EEG signals in a 500 ms width sliding time window for the six specified frequency bands with 33.3 ms time lag between two adjacent windows. This time, lag was chosen to match the kinematic sampling rate (30 FPS). The bandpower within a time window was calculated by averaging the absolute values of the bandpass-filtered EEG potentials within the window as described in Eq. (5):

$$B_{fn}[t] = \frac{\sum_{m=1}^{M} \left| S(m)_{fn}[t] \right|}{M} \tag{5}$$

where $B_{fn}[t]$ is the bandpower value calculated from EEG channel n, using bandpass filter f, within a 500 ms width time window t. M is the number of samples within the time window and $S(m)$ is the mth bandpass-filtered sample within the time window. Thus, the BTS model was trained separately with the time series of bandpower values that were calculated from the ICA-filtered EEG in each of the following six frequency bands: 0.5–4, 4–8, 8–12, 12–18, 18–28, and 28–40 Hz, and compared. These bands are similar to the bands that were used for the PTS model. The only difference is the lowest band, was selected to narrower (0.5–2 Hz) for the PTS model. This modification was applied because a number of published studies (Bradberry et al., 2010; Ofner et al., 2015; Paek et al., 2014; Robinson et al., 2015; Sicard et al., 2014) reported the highest accuracy of MTP for the PTS model in a narrow band around 1 Hz center frequency. Nevertheless, as in the case of the BTS model, our prior analysis (unpublished) did not show any significant difference in accuracy using 0.5–2 or 0.5–4 Hz bands; therefore, we tested the BTS model in the 0.5–4 Hz band.

2.3.2 Kinematic data preprocessing

A high-frequency noise (>10 Hz) was detected in the registered kinematic data, which did not originate from real movement. This noise was reduced before further processing. As we observed a low-pass filter would cause a significant distortion in the kinematic data during the movement periods, a moving average smoothing filter with a five sample window was applied separately for each kinematic coordinate. The quality of the smoothed kinematic data was validated manually as described in Section 2.3.1.2.

2.3.3 Data synchronization, data validation, and task interval separation

As MTP BCIs aim to reconstruct movement kinematics from the corresponding EEG signals (Section 2.4), accurate data synchronization between EEG and kinematic signals is crucial. This subsection highlights critical issues related to EEG–kinematic data synchronization, data validation, and task interval separation, which is the basis for proper selection of training data and test data (Section 2.5).

As it was found that the Kinect sampling rate was not stable throughout the recording sessions, the two datasets were synchronized by a time stamp array that was stored for both data types based on the onset and offset time points of the movement tasks. The preprocessed EEG dataset was downsampled from 1200 to 30 Hz to reduce the size of the EEG dataset and to match the sampling rate of the kinematic data.

The preprocessed EEG and kinematic data were validated manually. Preprocessed EEG data intervals containing high-level transient noise were marked as invalid intervals and removed from further analysis along with their corresponding kinematic data. The preprocessed kinematic data were investigated separately for hand coordinates in x, y, and z directions. Data intervals that were charged with a high-level transient noise (detected with manual validation) were marked and removed from further processing along with their corresponding EEG data.

Based on the registered kinematic data, the onset and the offset trigger points of each block were registered manually in each run. These trigger points were used for preparing an inner- and outer-fold level-based EEG–kinematic dataset, which was used in the framework of the inner–outer cross-validation (CV) system for optimizing, training, and testing the investigated MTP models (Section 2.5).

2.4 KINEMATIC DATA RECONSTRUCTION

The core module in an MTP BCI is the kinematic data estimator block, which reconstructs the kinematic trajectory based on the input EEG time-series. In the training stage, the key parameters of the estimation block are optimized.

Fig. 5 illustrates the configuration for training the estimation block. The parameters of the kinematic data estimation block are regulated by the comparison module

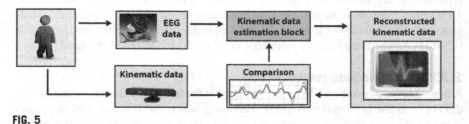

FIG. 5

Block diagram for training an MTP BCI.

which calculates the difference between the registered and reconstructed kinematic trials, in order to attain maximal correlation between them. The mLR models are tested on several configurations of the EEG features in order to find the feature setup that provides the highest MTP accuracy. The model coefficients (parameters) for each investigated configuration are optimized separately to minimize the prediction (or reconstruction) error. The following subsection describes mLR for MTP.

2.4.1 Multiple linear regression

Here, we describe the mLR-based MTP method used for kinematic trajectory reconstruction separately in each of the three orthogonal spatial dimensions, separately. mLR combined with the PTS model was presented by Bradberry et al. (2010) as shown in Eq. (6):

$$x_i[t] = a_{if} + \sum_{n=1}^{N} \sum_{k=0}^{L} b_{ifnk} S_{fn}[t-k] + \varepsilon[t] \tag{6}$$

where a_{if} and b_{ifnk} are regression parameters that learn the relationship between $S_{fn}[t-k]$ input and $x_i[t]$ output data. $x_i[t]$ contains the three orthogonal velocity components, $S_{fn}[t-k]$ is standardized temporal difference of EEG potentials on which bandpass filter f is applied at EEG sensor n, at time lag k according to Eq. (6). The i index denotes spatial dimensions in the 3D orthogonal coordinate system, N is the number of EEG sensors, L is the number of time lags, and $\varepsilon[t]$ is the residual error. The embedding dimension is the number of time lags plus one ($L+1$), ie, the number of those time lagged samples that are selected from each channel for estimating kinematic data at time point t. The standardized difference for the PTS model is described in Eq. (7):

$$S_{fn}[t] = \frac{P_{fn}[t] - \mu_{P_{fn}}}{\sigma_{P_{fn}}} \tag{7}$$

where $P_{fn}[t]$ is the value of the input time-series at time t (ie, a potential value for the PTS model), $\mu_{P_{fn}}$ is the mean value, and $\sigma_{P_{fn}}$ is standard deviation of P_{fn}.

The BTS model presented here uses the same equation for mLR as described above in Eq. (6) but the $S_{fn}[t-k]$ standardized temporal difference is calculated from bandpower values of the specified EEG band rather than bandpass-filtered EEG potentials. As bandpower values are limited to positive value, therefore, the standardized difference was calculated differently for the BTS model that of for the PTS model is described in Eq. (7) in which case the input was roughly symmetric. The standardized difference for the BTS model is described in Eq. (8):

$$S_{fn}[t] = \frac{B_{fn}[t]}{\sigma_{B_{fn}}} \tag{8}$$

where $B_{fn}[t]$ is the value of the input time-series at time t (ie, a bandpower value for the BTS model) and $\sigma_{B_{fn}}$ is the standard deviation of B_{fn}.

The input–output structure of the kinematic data estimation module is similar for the PTS and BTS models. The only difference is the optimal number of time lags

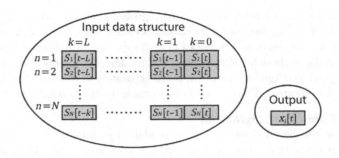

FIG. 6

Illustration of the input data structure and the output data for the kinematic data estimation block at time point t. The input dataset is prepared using a time series of the preprocessed EEG data that was registered at 0 to L time lag distance from t according to channel IDs 1 to N. The corresponding output data is the kinematic data at time point t.

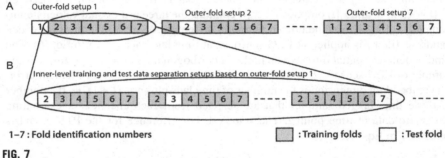

FIG. 7

Illustration of the inner–outer (nested) cross-validation technique. This figure provides an example of training and test data separation options in the inner-fold level (B) from the outer-fold setup (A), which uses fold 2–7 for training and fold 1 for testing purposes.

(ie, embedding dimension minus one) that is selected during parameter optimization as described in the following section (Section 2.5). The structure of the input and output data at time point t, according to Eq. (6), is illustrated in Fig. 6.

2.5 ARCHITECTURE OPTIMIZATION, TRAINING, TEST, AND CROSS-VALIDATION

The inner–outer cross-validation technique was employed (Fig. 7) to optimize the MTP architecture. This involved testing and selecting a range of parameters using an inner-fold CV (Fig. 7B) and calculating the final results in the outer-fold CV (Fig. 7A) using the optimal architecture that is selected by the inner-fold CV. The MTP accuracy is assessed by estimating the correlation value of the measured and the reconstructed kinematic trials. The final results were calculated by averaging MTP accuracy across the outer folds for each subject, separately. We applied a six-fold CV on the inner folds and sevenfold CV in the outer folds.

2.5.1 Data separation for inner–outer cross-validation

Preparing a proper training dataset is very important for the homogeneity of training. The kinematic data estimation block will be trained properly for each kind of movement only if the training dataset contains a similar amount of data for each target. As inner–outer CV uses all combinations of the outer folds, the homogenous distribution of movement dependent data intervals is an additional criterion for the outer folds.

The analyzed dataset involves two runs, each run contains six separated blocks, respectively, with the six different targets and each block involves 15 full movement cycles between the home and the actual target as illustrated in Fig. 3. A 40-s length interval, comprising approximately 12 movement cycles, centered at the middle of each block was selected for further processing as shown in Fig. 8A. Each 40 s length interval slice was divided into seven nonoverlapped subintervals and then the order of the subintervals within each block was randomized separately as presented in Fig. 8B. From this data structure, the randomized subintervals were redistributed into seven outer folds as illustrated in Fig. 8C (ie, the data content of each outer fold were drawn from six unique movement intervals with similar length for each of the six targets). This kind of data separation guaranteed the homogenous distribution of

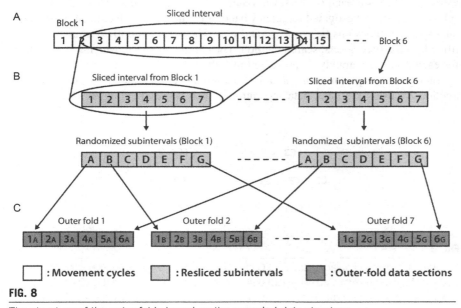

FIG. 8

The structure of the outer folds based on the recorded data structure.

movement dependent data intervals for each outer fold. The inner-fold data were drawn from the outer folds (Fig. 8C) as shown in Fig. 7.

As the global parameter space is too large for practical one-step optimization, ie, there are multiple parameters that can affect performance, it is a challenge to optimize globally. A three steps approach was taken for optimization with the first optimization phase having a fixed EEG montage, while time lag and embedding dimension were optimized. The second optimization phase used the parameters optimized in the first optimization phase, while the importance of channels was identified by evaluating all single channels independently and subsequently ranking channels by their importance and selecting a subset. The third phase involved reoptimization of time lag and embedding dimension with the chosen subset of channels from the second phase of optimization. The following subsections describe the optimization phases.

2.5.2 Optimization 1: Time lag and embedding dimension

For the first phase of optimization, the EEG montage was kept fixed and only the time lag and the embedding dimension were varied. Our recent analysis (Korik et al., 2015) in accordance with other studies (Bradberry et al., 2010; Choi, 2013; Ofner and Müller-Putz, 2012) showed that the best MTP accuracy is obtained when EEG signals are selected over the sensorimotor cortex. Thus, 10 re-referenced (ie, Laplace-filtered) and preprocessed EEG channels over the sensorimotor cortex were selected for the initial EEG montage as illustrated in Fig. 9.

For both of the PTS and BTS models, the time lag and embedding dimension were optimized for each of the seven outer folds using the inner-level CV for each subject, run, and investigated frequency band, separately for each of the three orthogonal spatial dimensions (ie, $v_{(x)}$, $v_{(y)}$, and $v_{(z)}$). The optimal configuration was identified by a heuristic global search method. The parameter space, which was searched for each option separately, is presented in Table 1.

Input and output training and test datasets were prepared as discussed in Section 2.4 using the inner data separation, which is presented in Fig. 7B.

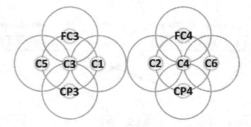

FIG. 9

Illustration of the 10 Laplace-filtered EEG channel locations, which were selected as input EEG montage for the first step of the BCI parameter optimization. Each of the 10 labeled input signals is the result of the EEG preprocessing method described in Section 2.3.1, which includes small Laplacian derivation area illustrated with the *circles*.

Table 1 The Investigated Parameter Space

Parameter	Investigated Parameter Space	
	PTS Model	**BTS Model**
Time lag	33–200 ms	33–600 ms
Embedding dimension	1–17 samples	1–15 samples
Input frequency band	0.5–2, 4–8, 8–12, 12–18, 18–28, 28–40 Hz	0.5–4, 4–8, 8–12, 12–18, 18–28, 28–40 Hz

Table 2 The Typical Range of the Optimal Time Lag-Related Parameter Values Based on the First Step of the MTP Parameter Optimization

	PTS Model		BTS Model	
Subject	**Time Lag (ms)**	**Embedding Dimensions ($L+1$)**	**Time Lag (ms)**	**Embedding Dimensions ($L+1$)**
1	33–100	9–11 samples	100–300	9–11 samples
2	66–100	9–13 samples	100–300	7–11 samples
3	66–100	7–11 samples	100–300	9–11 samples

2.5.3 Optimization 2: Channel selection and topological analysis

Our prior analysis showed the optimal time lag and embedding dimension are not identical but similar for different EEG channel setups. Therefore, in the second optimization step, the time lag and embedding dimension were kept fixed using the values obtained in the first step and the kinematic data reconstruction was calculated with each of the 31 preprocessed EEG channels, separately. Thus, in this step, the model was trained and tested based on a single input channel setup. The importance of the EEG channels was identified by evaluating the results of each channel independently and subsequently ranking channels by their importance based on the achieved accuracy. According to Eq. (6), the number of inputs for kinematic data reconstruction is equal to N multiplied by the embedding dimension L, where N is the number of the input EEG channels. In order to maintain a tractable number of the input parameters for the kinematic data reconstruction the number of the selected input EEG channels, N, should be limited. As the average optimal embedding dimension resulted in $(L+1) \sim 11$ (Table 2), we decided to limit the maximal number of the selected input EEG channels to eight. Therefore, the eight highest ranked channels were selected as the optimal channel subset. The optimal channel subset selection was performed for each of those options separately, which was discussed in the previous subsection describing the first step of parameter optimization.

In order to illustrate the most prominent cortical areas, the calculated single channel accuracy values for each subject and frequency band separately were averaged across all inner folds, runs, and spatial directions. The averaged accuracy values were plotted in the form of a topological map for the two models and each subject separately in each of the six frequency bands. The averaged accuracy values were used only for this illustration which is presented in Section 3.

2.5.4 Optimization 3: Reoptimization of time lag and embedding dimension
In this step, the time lag and embedding dimension were optimized once again separately for all of those options that were discussed in optimization 1 using the relevant EEG subsets from parameter optimization 2.

2.5.5 Calculating the final results and cross-validation
After the three optimization phases, which were completed using inner-fold data, the final results were calculated based on the outer fold data using best subject-specific parameter setups, selected based on inner-fold CV performance. Accuracy metrics (ie, the correlation value) of the hand velocity trial reconstruction was calculated separately for the PTS and BTS models in the selected frequency bands for the seven outer test folds and three orthogonal vector components in x, y, and z directions. The mean value of the accuracies calculated across the seven outer test folds was averaged and compared for the PTS and BTS models at each of the three directions, respectively. The accuracy rates of the PTS model and the proposed BTS model were compared and differences were analyzed using the Student's t-test.

3 RESULTS
3.1 THE OPTIMAL TIME LAG AND EMBEDDING DIMENSION
The optimal time lag and embedding dimension were selected in the first optimization phase on each of the inner-fold cross-validations using a fixed preselected input channel setup for the PTS and BTS models for each, subject, run, frequency band, and spatial dimension combinations, separately. The resulted optimal time lag and embedding dimension values varied for different options. Table 2 presents the typical range of the optimal values for the two compared models.

3.2 THE OPTIMAL CHANNEL SETS
Fig. 10A–C, presents the topological maps that were plotted to illustrate the cortical areas, which provided the highest accuracy in the second optimization phase based on single EEG channel inputs.

The highest accuracy of the PTS model was achieved for each subject when a low delta (0.5–2 Hz) bandpass filter was applied to the preprocessed EEG. In contrast, the most prominent frequency bands for the BTS model were the mu (8–12 Hz) and low-beta (12–18 Hz) bands. For the BTS model, the theta (4–8 Hz) and high-beta

(18–28 Hz) bands also provided a reasonable high level of accuracy. Table 3 presents the frequency bands, which provided the highest accuracies during the inner-fold CV tests.

A comparison between topological results of PTS and BTS models in the delta band is presented in Fig. 10A and B. Fig. 10A and C illustrates the important cortical areas for MTP in the case of the most prominent frequency bands for the PTS and BTS model, respectively.

Using the optimal EEG montages which have been selected separately for different options (as described for optimization 1), the time lag and embedding dependent parameters were reoptimized in the inner-fold cross-validations. However, the reoptimization using the optimal montages yielded similar time lag and embedding dimension values to those that are reported for the preselected montages in Table 2.

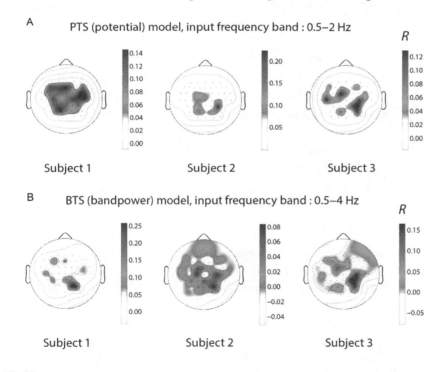

FIG. 10

(A) Topological maps of correlation values (R) obtained using the PTS model in the most prominent frequency band (ie, low delta (0.5–2 Hz)). The plots show the R-value for each Laplacian channel by averaging across all inner folds, two runs, and three orthogonal spatial dimensions. (B) Topological maps of correlation values (R) obtained using the BTS model in the low delta (0.5–2 Hz). The plots show the R-value for each Laplacian channel by averaging across all inner folds, two runs, and three orthogonal spatial dimensions.

(Continued)

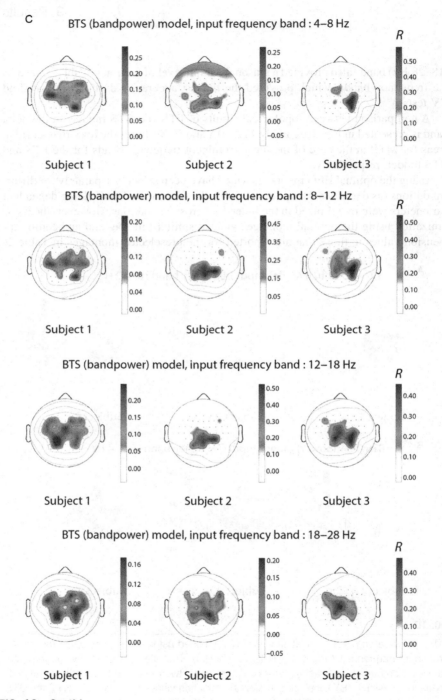

FIG. 10—Cont'd

(C) Topological maps of correlation values (*R*) obtained using the BTS model in prominent frequency bands (ie, theta (4–8 Hz), mu (8–12 Hz), low beta (12–18 Hz), and high beta (18–28 Hz)). The plots show the *R*-value for each Laplacian channel by averaging across all inner folds, two runs, and three orthogonal spatial dimensions.

Table 3 Summary of the Frequency Bands That Provided the Highest Accuracy in the Inner Cross-Validations

Subject	PTS Model	BTS Model
1	Low delta (0.5–2 Hz)	Theta (4–8 Hz), low beta (12–18 Hz)
2	Low delta (0.5–2 Hz)	Mu (8–12 Hz), low beta (12–18 Hz)
3	Low delta (0.5–2 Hz)	Theta (4–8 Hz), mu (8–12 Hz), low beta (12–18 Hz), high beta (18–28 Hz)

3.3 ACCURACY OF TRAJECTORY RECONSTRUCTION

The final results were calculated on the outer-fold level using the optimal setups based on the three steps of optimization performed in each of the inner-level cross-validations. Correlation values were calculated separately for the seven outer test folds according to the three spatial dimensions and were averaged across all folds and the three spatial dimensions. Fig. 11 presents a comparison of the achieved

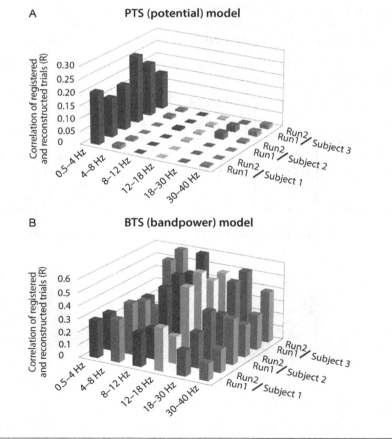

FIG. 11

Comparison of the kinematic trial reconstruction accuracy of the PTS model (A) and the BTS model (B) in the six analyzed input frequency bands for two runs for each of the three subjects.

accuracy for hand velocity trial reconstruction based on the six investigated frequency bands across each of the three subjects and two runs.

The final results were calculated on the outer-fold level using the optimal setups that were calculated based on the inner-level tests. Correlation values were calculated separately for the seven outer test folds according to the three spatial dimensions and were averaged across all folds and the three spatial dimensions.

In accordance with the inner-fold results, the low-delta (0.5–2 Hz) band was found to be the most prominent frequency band for the PTS model (Fig. 11A). The most prominent frequency band for the BTS model across all subjects was found typically to be the mu (8–12 Hz) and low-beta (12–18 Hz) bands. However, for subjects 1 and 3 the theta (4–8 Hz) band and for subject 3 the high-beta (18–28 Hz) band also provided a high level of accuracy (Fig. 11B).

The best accuracy of the PTS model resulted in $R \sim 0.2$ ($p < 0.02$) in the low-delta (0.5–2 Hz) band, while the BTS model achieved significantly higher $R \sim 0.45$ ($p < 0.02$) accuracy rates typically in the mu (8–12 Hz) and low-beta (12–18 Hz) bands. Table 4 summarizes the typical parameter ranges, which typically resulted the best outer-level accuracy across the investigated options in the inner-level tests, and Fig. 12 provides a comparison of the achieved outer-level test accuracy by the two investigated models using the earlier mentioned parameter setup.

Table 4 Summary of the Optimal Parameter Range for the PTS and BTS Models Based on the Inner-Level CV

		PTS Model	BTS Model
Time lag		66–100 ms	100–300 ms
Embedding dimension		9–11 samples	9–11 samples
Prominent band(s)	Subject 1	Low delta (0.5–2 Hz)	Theta (4–8 Hz), low beta (12–18 Hz)
	Subject 2		Mu (8–12 Hz), low beta (12–18 Hz)
	Subject 3		Theta (4–8 Hz), mu (8–12 Hz), low beta (12–18 Hz), high beta (18–28 Hz)

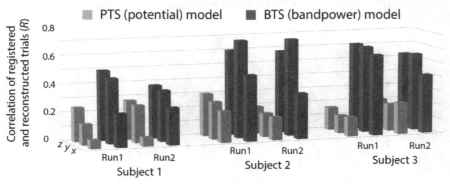

FIG. 12

Comparison of the kinematic trial reconstruction accuracy for PTS model and BTS model in x, y, and z directions using the optimal MTP architectures.

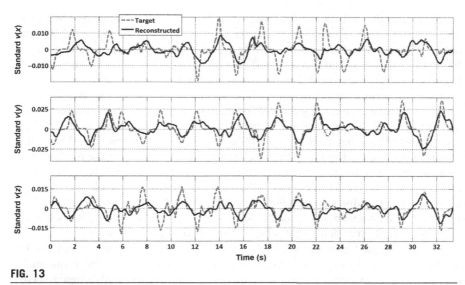

FIG. 13

Illustration of the actual and the reconstructed hand velocity trials.

Finally, Fig. 13 presents an example of the target and reconstructed kinematic velocity trials based on subject 2, run1, and outer test fold 1 for the BTS model using the best BCI architecture selected based on the three step optimization on the corresponding inner folds.

4 DISCUSSION

MTP BCIs commonly use the time series of bandpass-filtered EEG potentials for trajectory reconstruction. In this study, we compared the EEG PTS-based MTP approach (Bradberry et al., 2010) with the proposed BTS-based MTP approach (Korik et al., 2015). A number of papers, for example (Bradberry et al., 2010; Liu et al., 2011; Paek et al., 2014; Robinson et al., 2015), report the best accuracy for MTP in the low-delta (0.5–2 Hz) band using the PTS approach. These studies, showing prominence in the low-delta band, are in conflict with the extensive literature on classical SMR BCIs, which report the highest accuracies using power values of mu (8–12 Hz) and beta (12–30 Hz) bands (McFarland et al., 2000, 2010; Pfurtscheller et al., 1993, 2006; Qin and He, 2005; Wolpaw et al., 1991). Classical SMR BCI performance is explained with reference to ERD and ERS (Pfurtscheller and Lopes da Silva, 1999; Wolpaw et al., 1991), which are detectable over the sensorimotor cortex in mu and beta bands. In contrast, Hall et al. (2014) demonstrated how the hand velocity trajectories of monkeys and amplitude modulation of the LFPs in low-frequency band (~3 Hz) in the M1 correlate. This modulation is scaled in a similar frequency range that is regularly applied to the bandpass filter for preparing the input time series of a common MTP BCI. It is, therefore, logical to assume that the success of decoding of the limb movement trajectory is due to this modulation. As SMR BCIs classify limb movements by power spectral density (PSD) of the mu (8–12 Hz) and beta (12–30 Hz) bands, we assumed that the time-varying power pattern of these frequency bands might hold more significant information for limb movement decoding compared to that available in the low-delta band.

Here, we present mathematical evidence to indicate why low-frequency band information is being selected by the PTS-based motion trajectory prediction approach and the other higher frequency components are being neglected. As the highest accuracy of MTP achieved using the PTS model is achieved when a 0.5–2 Hz bandpass is applied to the EEG, it is hypothesized that the trajectory of the movement is coded in the low-delta band (Bradberry et al., 2010; Paek et al., 2014; Robinson et al., 2015; Yeom et al., 2013). In essence, the common conclusion is as follows: although the moving and resting state of a limb is coded in the PSD of mu and beta bands, the trajectory of the movement is coded in the low-delta band. We show this conclusion is not necessarily true and might reveal a limitation of the PTS model.

We investigated how the time-delayed samples of EEG potentials in the PTS model match the rhythm of an executed movement. The PTS model in our study resulted in similar values for the optimal time lag ($\sim$66–100 ms) and the optimal embedding dimension ($\sim$11 samples) (Table 4) which are reported in other MTP studies (Bradberry et al., 2010; Korik et al., 2015). For the PTS model these parameters result in taking samples across a window of approximately 1 s (11 time-delayed sample points) which correspond with cycles of the executed movement, as the length of a movement between the home and a target position was 800 ms.

To further analyze this, we investigated through simulation how the time-delayed samples points of the input PTS fit the bandpass-filtered EEG signals when the EEG is bandpass filtered in different frequency bands (Fig. 14A1 and A2). In this simulation, the first synthetic potential dataset is derived from a 1 Hz attenuated sine wave (Fig. 14A1) and the second synthetic dataset is derived from a 23 Hz attenuated sine wave (Fig. 14A2). These are used to simulate bandpass-filtered EEG signals when the filter is applied to the 0.5–2 Hz and 18–28 Hz bands, respectively, and assumes that the movement trajectory is encoded in the attenuation. As Fig. 14A1 shows, if the 1 Hz synthetic data is sampled every 100 ms over 1000 ms as is done with the PTS model (indicated by markers), the signal can be reconstructed from the samples points. Nevertheless, higher bands (>4 Hz) illustrated by the 23 Hz attenuated sine in Fig. 14A2, with inputs selected every 100 ms are composed of quasi-random potential values because the width of the time lag is longer than the period of the input signals and the movement encoded in the attenuation could not be reconstructed from these samples. Therefore, the input signal is represented properly by the time-delayed sample points of the PTS model if, and only if, the input signal belongs to the 0.5–2 Hz frequency range.

On the other hand, the comparison between Fig. 14A1, A2, B1, and B2 highlights that, in the case of the BTS model the time variance of the EEG bandpower is represented properly by the input BTS in both (lower and higher) investigated frequency bands (Fig. 14B1 and B2) as well as in any other EEG bands.

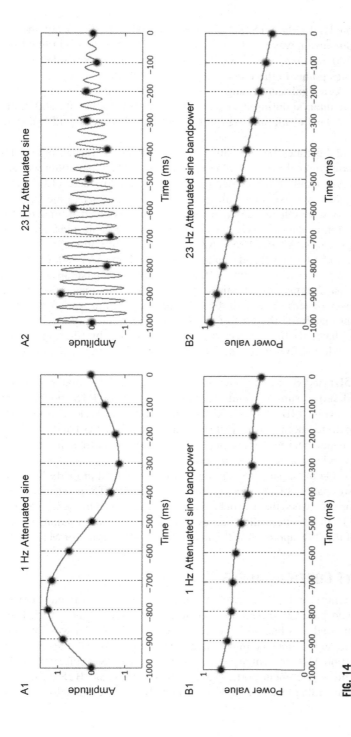

FIG. 14

(A1 and A2) illustration of time-delayed samples points are selected from a 1- and a 23-Hz attenuated sine wave for preparing input time series using 100 ms time lag (*vertical marker lines*). (B1 and B2) illustration of the selected time-delayed samples points based on bandpower values of those signals, which are presented in A1 and A2, respectively. In the case of 1 Hz signal, the fast Fourier transform (FFT) was applied to the 0.5–2 Hz band. In the case of 23 Hz signal, the FFT was applied to the 18–28 Hz band.

The optimal time lag for the BTS model is between 100 and 300 ms, and the optimal embedding dimension was $L + 1 = 11$ (Table 4). Therefore, the optimal time lag was higher (~200 ms) compared to the PTS model (~100 ms). Nevertheless, the time-delayed samples points in the input BTS still matched the rhythms of the executed movement. As a significant change in the SMR PSD occurs typically within a 100...300 ms time interval during the executed movement (Ball et al., 2008), the input BTS using a 200 ms width time lag can follow the variance of the PSD during the movement.

Fig. 15A1 and A2 illustrates the same situation as that described earlier for the PTS model, this time, based on real EEG data. In this example, the bandpass filter was applied to two different bands (ie, low-delta (0.5–2 Hz) and low-beta (12–18 Hz) bands). In order to make the example realistic, the EEG channel sets, time lag, and embedding dimension were selected based on the values that provided optimal results in the present study for the datasets have been investigated (see Table 4 in Section 3).

Comparing Figs. 14A1, A2 and 15A1, A2 similar results are observable for the simulation data (Fig. 14A1 and A2) and for the real signals (Fig. 15A1 and A2) where valuable content is represented by the input PTS if, and only if, the bandpass filter is applied to the delta band. If movement trajectory relevant information is coded in the spatiotemporal power pattern of specific EEG bands and the time variance of this information content match the rhythms of the executed movement, the commonly applied PTS model has only limited access to this information by filtering out the delta band from the whole EEG spectrum, otherwise, for higher frequencies, aliasing occurs.

Finally, Fig. 15B1 and B2 provides an illustration for the BTS model based on real EEG data and shows similar results to those obtained for BTS model using the synthetic dataset (Fig. 14B1 and B2). If movement trajectory relevant information is coded in spatiotemporal power pattern of any specific EEG band, the BTS model can detect band-specific information by selecting the correct inputs from the relevant time-varying bandpower time-series.

In conclusion, while the input BTS can reconstruct movement properly from the spatiotemporal power pattern of any specific EEG subband, the PTS model can select relevant information only when the low-delta band is filtered out from the whole EEG spectrum. As the BTS input pattern allows access to more specific information, we recommend the use of the BTS approach with mu and beta band activity for MTP BCIs.

4.1 PROMINENT CORTICAL AREAS

MTP BCI studies report the highest accuracy when the input EEG montage covers the sensorimotor and parietal cortical areas (Choi, 2013; Ofner et al., 2015; Paek et al., 2014). In our study, in line with the literature, the PTS model was found to cover premotor and supplementary motor area (Fig. 10A), whereas the spectrum model was focused on M1 and primary somatosensory areas (S1) (Fig. 10C). The difference of the most prominent cortical areas for the PTS and BTS models in the delta band is comparable by checking Fig. 10A and B. The presented topological

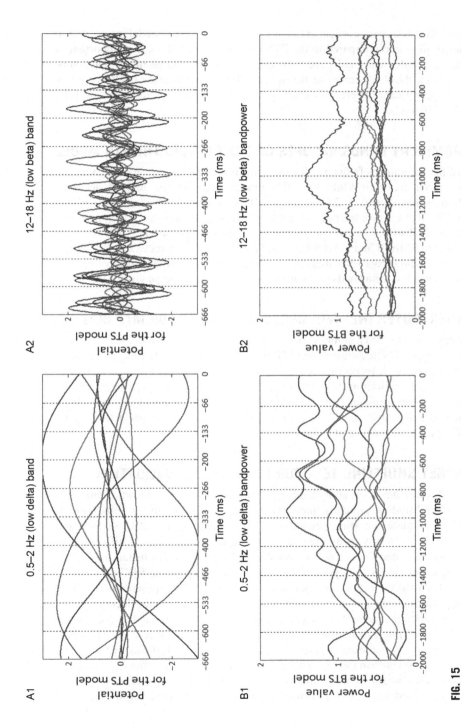

FIG. 15

An example of input data set preparation for the PTS model (A1 and A2) and for the BTS model (B1 and B2) in the case of two different frequency bands (0.5–2 and 12–18 Hz). EEG channel sets, time lag, and embedding dimension were selected based on Table 4. The *colored (gray shades in the print version) lines* show the input signals (ie, bandpass-filtered EEG for the PTS model (A1 and A2) and bandpower values for the BTS model (B1 and B2)), while the *vertical marker lines* indicate the selected samples based on the optimal time lag.

maps show the prominent cortical areas in the case of the BTS model are shifted in the posterior direction compared to the PTS results. Nevertheless, it is important to highlight the topological results are very variant across the three investigated subjects; therefore, the low number of the subjects limits the analysis in showing any statistically significant difference between topological results of the PTS and BTS model (Fig. 10A–C).

4.2 PROMINENT BANDS/RESULTS OF THE PTS AND THE BTS MODEL

The identified prominent frequency bands confirmed our expectations (Korik et al., 2015) for both models. While the PTS model achieved the highest accuracy ($R \sim 0.2$) in the low-delta (0.5–2 Hz) band, the BTS model yielded significantly higher accuracy ($R \sim 0.45$) across the three subjects typically in the mu (8–12 Hz), and low-beta (12–18 Hz) bands. The current findings show not only consistency between classical MC-based SMR BCIs and BTS-based MTP BCI results, wherein the best accuracy is achieved in similar bands but suggest that replacing the potential values with power values of mu and low-beta bands might improve the achievable accuracy in MTP BCIs.

4.3 INNER–OUTER (NESTED) CROSS-VALIDATION FOR MTP BCIs

In this study, we provided a guideline for preparing a proper dataset in the framework of the inner–outer CV technique for MTP purposes. We presented the inner–outer CV technique, which is recommended for MTP studies because it provides an opportunity to separate the optimization, training, and test steps using a global dataset. We also provided an example of how to ensure homogeneity in the training and testing data when applying inner–outer CV (Fig. 8), which is essential in order to train the MTP BCI with the same weights for each type of movement.

4.4 TARGET SHUFFLING TEST FOR FINAL RESULT VALIDATION

As outlined, there has been considerable discussion around the decoding methods applied in MTP studies, typically linear regression models, and the correlation metrics used to evaluate decoding performance (see Antelis et al., 2013 or Poli and Salvaris, 2011). One way to assure that decoding performance is significant is to compute again the decoding process with shuffled input data (for instance by shuffling the different movement cycles within a block but keeping the EEG data order). This provides a value of randomness that can be statistically compared with actual decoding performance (similar to the way we have compared both the decoding techniques). To verify if indeed that the correlations attained by the models applied we have applied shuffling to a number of similar datasets. In (Korik et al., 2016) a preliminary study using a similar experimental setup, the target shuffling test was performed in order to confirm the reconstructed trajectories are valid: the reconstructed trajectories were calculated in the same way as outlined in this chapter for both shuffled and unshuffled test data on each of the outer folds. Comparing data for one subject, the correlation in the case of the shuffled kinematic data for all folds was close to zero ($R \sim 0$) as expected for shuffled targets, compared to $R \sim 0.6$ for unshuffled data. The differences are significant and provide clear evidence that the methods applied and results attained here are not due random fluctuations in the data nor are the evaluation methods applied suboptimal. Therefore, the results provide clear evidence that EEG can be used to decode real 3D hand movement trajectories and that mu, beta, and, in some cases, theta bands provide more information than the low delta band.

4.5 LIMITATIONS AND FUTURE WORK

1. We should highlight the present study is limited to reconstructing an executed movement; however, decoding the trajectory of an imagined movement is possible (Ofner and Müller-Putz, 2015). In the earlier cited study Ofner and Müller-Putz used low-frequency information to decode imagined movement. As PSD of the mu and beta EEG bands are changing in a similar way for an executed and imagery movement (Höller et al., 2013), we expect that the outcomes gained from the BTS MTP model will be adaptable to an imagery movement-based BTS MTP model. Thus, we are currently testing the BTS MTP model for decoding imagery 3D movement of limbs (Korik et al., 2016). Real-time feedback of imagined limb movement is likely to enhance performance also.

2. The present study was carried out on a limited dataset, including only three subjects and two runs. We are planning to collect data from additional subjects to further test our hypothesis that the BTS model provides higher accuracy compared to the PTS model. Although we significantly improved the accuracy of the MTP by replacing the PTS model ($R \sim 0.2$) with the BTS approach ($R \sim 0.45$), the obtained accuracy rates are relatively low compared to several studies reporting accuracy rates of $R \sim 0.5...0.7$ for motion trajectory prediction (Choi, 2013; Ofner and Müller-Putz, 2012; Paek et al., 2014); however, the target setup of these studies differs from the setup presented in this analysis. In Choi (2013), five subjects performed a continuous arm-reaching task with their right arm in the following sequences: Home–C–A–B, Home–C–D–B, Home–D–B–A, Home–D–C–A, where A, B, C, and D are target positions located around the center Home position in a two-dimensional plane. In Ofner and Müller-Putz (2012), five subjects performed continuous self-chosen right arm movements in the three-dimensional spaces without specified targets. In Paek et al. (2014), five subjects tapped their right index finger three times on the target and angular velocity trajectory of the finger metacarpal–phalangeal (MCP) joint in one dimension was reconstructed. The difference in the accuracy of our study compared to Choi (2013), Ofner and Müller-Putz (2012), and Paek et al. (2014) may be as a result of the different experimental paradigm. In addition, our study had six specific targets increasing the complexity of the task for the user and signal processing framework. There have been no other MTP with EEG studies to date involving limb movements toward six targets has been reported.

3. Differences in accuracy between our results and those of Choi (2013), Ofner and Müller-Putz (2012), and Paek et al. (2014) may also originate from a relatively high noise level that was identified in our EEG records. We are working to improve the quality of our EEG records in order to increase the SNR. ICA is applied to remove nonneural artifacts, keeping only EEG relevant components. It is important to note that an over sensitive ICA component removal could also have an impact where in some cases executed movement could have some influence on the signals in low-frequency bands, ie, actual physical movement distortion on the EEG electrodes, which could be picked up in studies that report low-frequency band prominence. ICA is not applied in Choi (2013) and Ofner and Müller-Putz (2012); however in Paek et al. (2014), ICA was applied where the decoded task (ie, tapping only one target with the index finger and decoding one-dimensional angular velocity profile of the MCP joint) was not as complex as the paradigm presented in our study involving 3D hand movement between the home and six target positions.

4. As the present study focused only on an mLR model, it will be important to compare the efficiency of different estimation methods. As brain activity is nonlinear, it is plausible to assume that replacement of the linear regression module with a nonlinear estimation method could further improve the accuracy of the MTP. There is preliminary evidence that feed forward neural network (NN) can improve performance for MTP BCIs (Korik et al., 2015; Sicard et al., 2014). Future work will involve investigating improvement in MTP accuracy when mLR methods are replaced with a nonlinear estimation methods such as kernel ridge regression (Kim et al., 2014), NNs (Coyle, 2009, 2013; Coyle et al., 2005), or self-organization fuzzy neural network (Coyle and Sosnik, 2015; Coyle et al., 2009; Siddique and Adeli, 2013).

The feature selection method applied involves identification of the most prominent cortical areas and frequency bands but the number of the input parameters (ie, selected input EEG channels multiplied by the embedding dimension) is relatively high. The number of inputs has less impact for mLR-based kinematic data reconstruction as the training provided reasonable high accuracy within a short time period, but in the case of the more computational demanding multiple nonlinear regression methods, such as NNs, the number of inputs should be reduced because these methods are impacted more by the "course of dimensionality" (Priddy and Keller, 2005) compared to mLR-based training (Jang, 1993). A more advanced feature selection method is recommended for future with mLR methods, which can reduce the number of the input parameters by eliminating the redundancy through mutual information assessment (Coyle, 2013) and keeping the most important information in the input data vector. There are several possible approaches for improving our feature selection method, for example, applying a PCA-based dimension reduction algorithms (Xiao and Ding, 2013), or the distinction sensitive learning vector quantization application (Pregenzer and Pfurtscheller, 1995) among others.

5 CONCLUSION

In this study, we investigated why low-delta band information is commonly found to be predictive for motion trajectory prediction and mu and beta bands are neglected in 3D limb motion trajectory prediction BCIs even though mu and beta band activity have been exploited extensively for distinguishing or classifying of the executed and imagined movement of two or more limbs. We highlighted a possible shortcoming in the commonly used PTS-based MTP BCI model, which results in reasonable accuracy using the time series of bandpass-filtered EEG potentials, only when the filter is applied in the low-delta (0.5–2 Hz) band. In contrast, we showed that spatiotemporal power pattern of various frequency bands (theta, mu, and beta bands) hold significant information about movement trajectory and this information can be decoded using time-varying bandpower with optimal time embedded parameters and mLR. We found a significant increase in the MTP accuracy when the time series of bandpass-filtered EEG potentials (PTS model) was replaced with the time series of bandpower values (BTS model). While the PTS-based model provided acceptable results only in the low-delta band (0.5–2 Hz), the BTS model provided the highest accuracy across three subjects typically in the mu (8–12 Hz), and low-beta (12–18 Hz) bands. Our results show consistency between the extensive literature on MC-based SMR BCIs and BTS-based MTP BCIs as the highest decoding accuracy for both types of BCI are obtained when similar frequency bands are used.

Although the present study focused on executed 3D movement reconstruction, the ultimate goal is to decode assumed trajectory of an imagined movement, which is likely to be more challenging (Korik et al., 2016). It is expected that the findings presented here will have an impact on developing BCIs, which offer movement-free communication and control.

REFERENCES

Antelis, J.M., et al., 2013. On the usage of linear regression models to reconstruct limb kinematics from low frequency EEG signals. PLoS One 8 (4), 1–14.

Ball, T., et al., 2008. Movement related activity in the high gamma range of the human EEG. NeuroImage 41 (2), 302–310.

Baxter, B.S., Decker, A., He, B., 2013. Noninvasive control of a robotic arm in multiple dimensions using scalp electroencephalogram. In: 6th Annual International IEEE EMBS Conference on Neural Engineering San Diego, California, 6–8 November, pp. 6–8.

Bradberry, T.J., Gentili, R.J., Contreras-Vidal, J.L., 2010. Reconstructing three-dimensional hand movements from noninvasive electroencephalographic signals. J. Neurosci. 30 (9), 3432–3437.

Choi, K., 2013. Reconstructing for joint angles on the shoulder and elbow from non-invasive electroencephalographic signals through electromyography. Front. Neurosci. 7, 190.

Coyle, D., 2009. Neural network based auto association and time-series prediction for biosignal processing in brain-computer interfaces. IEEE Comput. Intell. Mag. 4 (4), 47–59.

Coyle, D., 2013. Channel and class dependent time-series embedding using partial mutual information improves sensorimotor rhythm based brain-computer interfaces. In: Pedrycz, W., Chen, S.-M. (Eds.), Time Series Analysis, Modeling and Applications: A Computational Intelligence Perspective. Springer, Berlin Heidelberg, pp. 249–278.

Coyle, D., Sosnik, R., 2015. Neuroengineering (sensorimotor-computer interfaces). In: Kacprzyk, J., Pedrycz, W. (Eds.), Springer Handbook of Computational Intelligence. Springer, Berlin Heidelberg, Berlin, Heidelberg. Available at: http://link.springer.com/10.1007/978-3-662-43505-2.

Coyle, D., Prasad, G., McGinnity, T.M., 2005. A time-frequency approach to feature extraction for a brain-computer interface with a comparative analysis of performance measures. EURASIP J. Adv. Signal Process. 2005 (19), 3141–3151.

Coyle, D., et al., 2009. Faster self-organizing fuzzy neural network training and a hyperparameter analysis for a brain–computer interface. IEEE Trans. Syst. Man Cybern. B Cybern. 39 (6), 1458–1471.

Coyle, D., et al., 2010. Predictive-Spectral-Spatial Preprocessing for a Multiclass Brain-Computer Interface. In: The International Joint Conference on Neural Networks. IEEE, Barcelona, Spain, pp. 18–23.

Coyle, D., et al., 2015. Action games, motor imagery, and control strategies: toward a multi-button controller. In: Handbook of Digital Games and Entertainment Technologies. Springer Singapore, Singapore, pp. 1–34.

Fatima, M., Shafique, M., Khan, Z.H., 2015. Towards a Low cost brain-computer interface for real time control of a 2 DOF robotic arm. In: Emerging Technologies (ICET), Peshawar, pp. 1–6.

Fehmi, L.G., Collura, T., 2007. Effects of electrode placement upon EEG biofeedback training; the monopolar-bipolar controversy.pdf. J. Neurother. 11 (2), 45–63.

g.HIamp80, 2013. g.tec medical engineering GmbH, Schiedlberg, Austria. Available at: http://www.gtec.at/Products/Hardware-and-Accessories/g.HIamp-Specs-Features.

Ge, S., Wang, R., Yu, D., 2014. Classification of four-class motor imagery employing single-channel electroencephalography. PLoS One 9 (6), e98019.

Georgopoulos, A.P., et al., 2005. Magnetoencephalographic signals predict movement trajectory in space. Exp. Brain Res. 167 (1), 132–135. Experimentelle Hirnforschung. Expérimentation cérébrale.

Hall, T.M., de Carvalho, F., Jackson, A., 2014. A common structure underlies Low-frequency cortical dynamics in movement, sleep, and sedation. Neuron 83 (5), 1185–1199.

Hamamé, C.M., et al., 2012. Reading the mind's eye: online detection of visuo-spatial working memory and visual imagery in the inferior temporal lobe. NeuroImage 59 (1), 872–879.

Heger, D., et al., 2012. Filling a glass of water: continuously decoding the speed of 3D hand movements from EEG signals. Conf. Proc. IEEE. Eng. Med. Biol. Soc. 2012, 4095–4098.

Höller, Y., et al., 2013. Real movement vs. motor imagery in healthy subjects. Int. J. Psychophysiol. 87 (1), 35–41.

Huang, D., et al., 2012. Brain–computer interface (BCI): a 2-D virtual wheelchair control based on event-related desynchronization/synchronization and state control. IEEE Trans. Neural. Syst. Rehabil. Eng. 20 (3), 379–388.

Jang, J.-S.R., 1993. ANFIS: adaptive-network-based fuzzy inference system. IEEE Trans. Syst. Man Cybern. 23 (3), 665–685.

Kachenoura, A., et al., 2008. ICA: a potential tool for BCI systems. IEEE Signal Process. Mag. 25 (1), 57–68.

Kim, J., Biessmann, F., Lee, S., 2014. Reconstruction of hand movements from EEG signals based on non-linear regression. In: Brain-Computer Interface (BCI), International Winter Workshop. IEEE, Jeongsun-kun, pp. 1–3.

Kinect, 2010. Kinect for Xbox 360. Available at: https://support.xbox.com/en-GB/browse/xbox-360/accessories/Kinect.

King, C.E., et al., 2011. Noninvasive brain-computer interface driven hand orthosis. In: 33rd Annual International Conference of the IEEE Eng. Medicine and Biology Society, Boston, MA, USA, pp. 5786–5789.

Korik, A., et al., 2014. Brief review of non-invasive motion trajectory prediction based brain-computer interfaces. In: The 8th IEEE EMBS UK & RI Postgraduate Conference in Biomedical Engineering & Medical Physics. University of Warwick, Warwick, p. 2. pp. 23–24.

Korik, A., et al., 2015. 3D hand movement velocity reconstruction using power spectral density of EEG signals and neural network. In: 35th Annual International Conference of the IEEE Engineering in Medicine and Biology Society, Milan, pp. 8103–8106.

Korik, A., et al., 2016. Imagined 3D hand movement trajectory decoding from sensorimotor EEG rhythms. In: IEEE International Conference on Systems, Man, and Cybernetics, Budapest, Hungary, in press.

Kübler, A., et al., 2005. Patients with ALS can use sensorimotor rhythms to operate a brain-computer interface. Neurology 64 (10), 1775–1777.

LaFleur, K., et al., 2013. Quadcopter control in three-dimensional space using a noninvasive motor imagery-based brain-computer interface. J. Neural Eng. 10 (4), 046003.

Lecuyer, A., et al., 2008. Brain-computer interfaces, virtual reality, and videogames. Computer 41 (10), 66–72.

Leeb, R., et al., 2007. Self-paced (asynchronous) BCI control of a wheelchair in virtual environments: a case study with a tetraplegic. Comput. Intell. Neurosci. 2007, 79642.

Liu, J., Perdoni, C., He, B., 2011. Hand movement decoding by phase-locking low frequency EEG signals. In: 33rd Annual International Conference of the IEEE Eng. Medicine and Biology Society, Boston, MA, USA, pp. 6335–6338.

Lu, J., McFarland, D.J., Wolpaw, J.R., 2013. Adaptive Laplacian filtering for sensorimotor rhythm-based brain–computer interfaces. J. Neural Eng. 10 (1), 1–14.

Makeig, S., Bell, A.J., Jung, T.P., Sejnowski, T.J., 1995. Independent component analysis of electroencephalographic data. In: Advances in Neural Information Processing Systems, Neural Information Processing Systems (NIPS) Conference, vol. 8.

Marshall, D., et al., 2013. Games, gameplay, and BCI: the state of the art. IEEE Trans. Comp. Intell. AI Games 5 (2), 82–99.

McFarland, D.J., et al., 1997. Spatial filter selection for EEG-based communication. Electro-encephalogr. Clin. Neurophysiol. 103 (3), 386–394.

McFarland, D.J., et al., 2000. Mu and beta rhythm topographies during motor imagery and actual movements. Brain Topogr. 12 (3), 177–186.

McFarland, D.J., Sarnacki,, W.A., Wolpaw, J.R., 2010. Electroencephalographic (EEG) control of three-dimensional movement. J. Neural Eng. 7 (3), 036007.

Mognon, A., et al., 2010. ADJUST: an automatic EEG artifact detector based on the joint use of spatial and temporal features. Psychophysiology 48, 229–240.

Morash, V., et al., 2008. Classifying EEG signals preceding right hand, left hand, tongue, and right foot movements and motor imageries. Clin. Neurophysiol. 119 (11), 2570–2578.

Nakanishi, Y., et al., 2013. Prediction of three-dimensional arm trajectories based on ECoG signals recorded from human sensorimotor cortex. PLoS One 8 (8), e72085.

Ofner, P., Müller-Putz, G.R., 2012. Decoding of velocities and positions of 3D arm movement from EEG. Conf. Proc. IEEE Eng. Med. Biol. Soc. 2012, 6406–6409.

Ofner, P., Müller-Putz, G.R., 2015. Using a noninvasive decoding method to classify rhythmic movement imaginations of the arm in two planes. IEEE Trans. Biomed. Eng. 62 (3), 972–981.

Ofner, P., Member, S., Gernot, R.M., 2015. Using a noninvasive decoding method to classify rhythmic movement imaginations of the arm in two planes. IEEE Trans. Biomed. Eng. 62 (3), 972–981.

Paek, A.Y., Agashe, H., Contreras-vidal, J.L., 2014. Decoding repetitive finger movements with brain activity acquired via non-invasive electroencephalography. Front. Neuroeng. 7 (3), 1–18.

Pfurtscheller, G., 2001. Functional brain imaging based on ERD/ERS. Vis. Res. 41 (10-11), 1257–1260.

Pfurtscheller, G., Lopes da Silva, F.H., 1999. Event-related EEG/MEG synchronization and desynchronization: basic principles. Clin. Neurophysiol. 110 (11), 1842–1857.

Pfurtscheller, G., Flotzinger, D., Kalcher, J., 1993. Brain-computer interface—a new communication device for handicapped persons. J. Microcomput. Appl. 16 (3), 293–299.

Pfurtscheller, G., et al., 2000. Brain oscillations control hand orthosis in a tetraplegic. Neurosci. Lett. 292 (3), 211–214.

Pfurtscheller, G., et al., 2006. Mu rhythm (de)synchronization and EEG single-trial classification of different motor imagery tasks. NeuroImage 31 (1), 153–159.

Poli, R., Salvaris, M., 2011. Comment on 'Fast attainment of computer cursor control with noninvasively acquired brain signals'. J. Neural Eng. 8, 058001, 3 pp.

Prasad, G., et al., 2010. Applying a brain-computer interface to support motor imagery practice in people with stroke for upper limb recovery: a feasibility study. J. Neuroeng. Rehabil. 7 (1), 60.

Pregenzer, M., Pfurtscheller, G., 1995. Distinction sensitive learning vector quantization (DSLVQ) application as a classifier based feature selection method for a brain computer interface. In: Fourth International Conference on Artificial Neural Networks. IET, Cambridge, pp. 433–436.

Presacco, A., et al., 2011. Neural decoding of treadmill walking from noninvasive electroencephalographic signals. J. Neurophysiol. 106 (4), 1875–1887.

Priddy, K.L., Keller, P.E., 2005. Artificial Neural Networks: An Introduction. SPIE Press, Bellingham, Washington, USA.

Qin, L., He, B., 2005. A wavelet-based time-frequency analysis approach for classification of motor imagery for brain-computer interface applications. J. Neural Eng. 2 (4), 65–72.

Ramoser, H., Muller-Gerking, J., Pfurtscheller, G., 2000. Optimal spatial filtering of single trial EEG during imagined hand movement. IEEE Trans. Rehabil. Eng. 8 (4), 441–446.

Rebsamen, B., et al., 2010. A brain controlled wheelchair to navigate in familiar environments. IEEE Trans. Neural Syst. Rehabil. Eng. 18 (6), 590–598.

Robinson, N., Guan, C., Vinod,, A.P., 2015. Adaptive estimation of hand movement trajectory in an EEG based brain-computer interface system. J. Neural Eng. 12 (6), 066019.

Royer, A.S., et al., 2010. EEG control of a virtual helicopter in 3-dimensional space using intelligent control strategies. IEEE Trans. Neural Syst. Rehabil. Eng. 18 (6), 581–589.

Sicard, G., Katz, R., Zacksenhouse, M., 2014. Decoding of hand kinematics from a noninvasive brain-computer interface. In: Computational Motor Control Workshop (CMCW), Israel (Be'er Sheva).

Siddique, N., Adeli, H., 2013. Computational Intelligence: Synergies of Fuzzy Logic, Neural Networks and Evolutionary Computing, first ed. Wiley J., Chichester, UK.

Silvoni, S., et al., 2011. Brain-computer interface in stroke: a review of progress. Clin. EEG Neurosci. 42 (4), 245–252.

Wolpaw, J.R., McFarland, D.J., 2004. Control of a two-dimensional movement signal by a noninvasive brain-computer interface in humans. Proc. Natl. Acad. Sci. U.S.A. 101 (51), 17849–17854.

Wolpaw, J.R., et al., 1991. An EEG-based brain-computer interface for cursor control. Electroencephalogr. Clin. Neurophysiol. 78 (3), 252–259.

Wolpaw, J.R., et al., 2002. Brain computer interfaces for communication and control. Front. Neurosci. 4 (113), 767–791.

Xiao, R., Ding, L., 2013. Evaluation of EEG features in decoding individual finger movements from one hand. Comput. Math. Methods Med. 2013, 243257.

Yeom, H.G., Kim, J.S., Chung, C.K., 2013. Estimation of the velocity and trajectory of three-dimensional reaching movements from non-invasive magnetoencephalography signals. J. Neural Eng. 10 (2), 026006.

Yuan, H., He, B., 2014. Brain-computer interfaces using sensorimotor rhythms: current state and future perspectives. IEEE Trans. Biomed. Eng. 61 (5), 1425–1435.

Zander, T.O., Kothe, C., 2011. Towards passive brain-computer interfaces: applying brain-computer interface technology to human-machine systems in general. J. Neural Eng. 8 (2), 025005.

Multisession, noninvasive closed-loop neuroprosthetic control of grasping by upper limb amputees

4

H.A. Agashe[1], A.Y. Paek, J.L. Contreras-Vidal

Noninvasive Brain-Machine Interface Systems Lab, University of Houston, Houston, TX, United States

[1]Corresponding author: Tel.: +1-512-924-6296; Fax: +1-713-743-4444, e-mail address: hagashe@uh.edu

Abstract

Upper limb amputation results in a severe reduction in the quality of life of affected individuals due to their inability to easily perform activities of daily living. Brain–machine interfaces (BMIs) that translate grasping intent from the brain's neural activity into prosthetic control may increase the level of natural control currently available in myoelectric prostheses. Current BMI techniques demonstrate accurate arm position and single degree-of-freedom grasp control but are invasive and require daily recalibration. In this study we tested if transradial amputees (A1 and A2) could control grasp preshaping in a prosthetic device using a noninvasive electroencephalography (EEG)-based closed-loop BMI system. Participants attempted to grasp presented objects by controlling two grasping synergies, in 12 sessions performed over 5 weeks. Prior to closed-loop control, the first six sessions included a decoder calibration phase using action observation by the participants; thereafter, the decoder was fixed to examine neuroprosthetic performance in the absence of decoder recalibration. Ability of participants to control the prosthetic was measured by the success rate of grasping; ie, the percentage of trials within a session in which presented objects were successfully grasped. Participant A1 maintained a steady success rate ($63 \pm 3\%$) across sessions (significantly above chance [$41 \pm 5\%$] for 11 sessions). Participant A2, who was under the influence of pharmacological treatment for depression, hormone imbalance, pain management (for phantom pain as well as shoulder joint inflammation), and drug dependence, achieved a success rate of $32 \pm 2\%$ across sessions (significantly above chance [$27 \pm 5\%$] in only two sessions). EEG signal quality was stable across sessions, but the decoders created during the first six sessions showed variation, indicating EEG features relevant to decoding at a smaller timescale (100 ms) may not be stable. Overall, our results show that (a) an EEG-based BMI for grasping is a feasible strategy for further investigation of prosthetic control by amputees, and (b) factors that may affect brain activity such as medication need further examination to improve accuracy and stability of BMI performance.

Progress in Brain Research, Volume 228, ISSN 0079-6123, http://dx.doi.org/10.1016/bs.pbr.2016.04.016
© 2016 Elsevier B.V. All rights reserved.

Keywords

Brain–machine interfaces, Grasping, Electroencephalography, Amputee

1 INTRODUCTION

Upper limb amputation, stroke, or severe spinal cord injury result in loss or significant reduction in bimanual motor function and dexterous hand movements in the affected limb(s). Recent advances in robotic prosthetics for the upper limb potentially allow amputees to control a multitude of dexterous tasks (Cipriani et al., 2011a; Resnik et al., 2012, 2014). In addition to positioning the arm in space, an important challenge is to be able to control the preshaping of fingers during grasping. Targeted muscle reinnervation (TMR; Kuiken et al., 2009) and myoelectric control using residual limb muscle activity offer exciting possibilities (Cipriani et al., 2011a, 2014; Resnik et al., 2014). Brain–machine interfaces (BMIs), which directly translate neural activity in the cortex to control external devices, may increase the level of natural control currently available in myoelectric prostheses (Contreras-Vidal et al., 2012; Lebedev and Nicolelis, 2006).

There are currently multiple myoelectric controlled hand prostheses available commercially, such as the i-limb (Touch Bionics, UK), the (FDA approved) DEKA arm (Deka Integrated Solutions Corporation, USA), and the (FDA approved) Axon-Bus Peripheral System/Michelangelo hand (Otto Bock Healthcare Product GmbH, Austria). In this study, we used the IH2 Azzurra, a hand prosthesis developed as research platform at Prensilia s.r.l., Italy. Amputee-relevant behavioral testing methods have so far focused on peripheral neural interfaces (Zhou et al., 2007). Notably, electromyography (EMG)-based systems have shown reasonably reliable 7-dof (degree of freedom) control of a prosthetic limb using EMG after TMR—a surgical technique pioneered by Dr. Kuiken involving the transfer of residual nerves in the amputated arm to the remaining muscle, which then provide EMG signals that correlate to the original nerve functions allowing a virtual or physical prosthetic arm to respond directly and more naturally to the brain signals (Kuiken et al., 2009; Li et al., 2010). However, some critical challenges of this approach concern the stability of EMG recordings, interference from muscles controlling remaining joints, effects of tissue loading, control of fine dexterous movements, and the cognitive burden of operating the device (Kuiken et al., 2009). Other studies have shown that dexterous control of robotic hands is possible using surface/intramuscular EMG from the muscles in the residual limb (Cipriani et al., 2014).

Recent milestones in BMI research include real-time cortical control of robotic limbs in monkeys (Kim et al., 2006; Musallam et al., 2004; Serruya et al., 2002; Taylor et al., 2002), nonhuman primates (Carmena et al., 2003; Clanton et al., 2010; Velliste et al., 2008), and the control of 2D/3D computer cursors by able-bodied and/or paralyzed individuals (Bradberry et al., 2011; Ganguly and Carmena, 2009; Hochberg et al., 2006; McFarland et al., 2010; Schalk et al., 2008).

Hochberg et al (2006) reported results for a tetraplegic human (MN) implanted with a 96-microelectrode array in the primary motor cortex (MI). Subject MN was able to achieve, in the course of 57 consecutive sessions over 9 months, BMI control of 2D cursor movement that MN used to open and close e-mail, operate devices such as a television, and open/close a prosthetic hand to grasp and transport an object from one location to another. More recently, results from two tetraplegics demonstrating their ability to control 3D reach and grasp movements with the DEKA robotic arm (Resnik et al., 2014) were published (Hochberg et al., 2012). Collinger et al. (2012) showed that over a period of 13 weeks, a tetraplegic could learn to control a robotic arm with seven dof (including one for grasping) in 3D space. Overall, intracranial BMIs have showed control of arm positioning with a high degree of accuracy in tetraplegic users but have a single dof to control grasping (Collinger et al., 2012; Hochberg et al., 2012; Velliste et al., 2008). In a recent study, Wodlinger et al. (2015) show tuning of individual neurons to hand shape in a 4D space; however, the number of tuned units decreases over time. In amputees who are able to produce muscular activity in residual limbs, intracortical BMIs present an unfavorable risk to benefit ratio compared to myoelectric prosthetics. In such cases, noninvasive BMIs to control prosthetic limbs could potentially augment myoelectric control, but have not been demonstrated yet.

Proximal and distal upper extremity movement information has been shown to be encoded as the power in specific frequency bands in cortical field potentials at different spatial scales: local field potentials (LFPs), electrocorticography (ECoG), electroencephalography (EEG), and magnetoencephalography (Ball et al., 2008; Kubánek et al., 2009; Pistohl et al., 2012; Waldert et al., 2009; Zhuang et al., 2010). More recently, researchers have shown that information is also encoded in the time-domain amplitudes of these field potentials in the lowest frequency band (0–5 Hz) (Acharya et al., 2010; Bansal et al., 2011; Bradberry et al., 2009, 2010; Hall et al., 2014; Kubánek et al., 2009; Mollazadeh et al., 2011). In our previous work we showed that grasping movements in able-bodied individuals can be decoded from time-domain low delta band (0.1–1 Hz) electroencephalographic (EEG) activity, a noninvasive modality to record cortical potentials at the scalp (Agashe and Contreras-Vidal, 2011, 2013; Agashe et al., 2015; Paek et al., 2014). Further, we showed that principal components (PCs) of finger kinematics are decoded with the same level of accuracy as finger joint angles during grasp preshaping. In a closed-loop BMI scenario, it is advantageous to control the kinematic PCs as they allow grasp preshaping with fewer dof. In our most recent study (Agashe et al., 2015) we demonstrated an amputee's (single session) control over the grasp preshaping by controlling two kinematic PCs in a closed-loop BMI scenario.

In recent years, concerns over the long-term stability of intracortical neural recordings have been raised, and studies show a decrease in BMI performance over time (Chestek et al., 2011; Dickey et al., 2009; Perge et al., 2014), although there are indications of stability over a week (Blakely et al., 2009). In intracortical implanted electrode studies, changes in recorded signals and the resulting changes in BMI performance are attributed to formation of scar tissue and migration of neurons, as well as unstable electrode material characteristics (Chestek et al., 2011; Dickey et al., 2009). Simeral et al. (2011) investigated the stability and reliability of intracortical microelectrode arrays in a human with tetraplegia 1000 days postimplantation and showed viable recordings for decoding and satisfactory performance of a cursor control task during five consecutive days of testing. The same subject S3 also demonstrated continuous neuronal ensemble control of simulated arm reaching using a Kalman decoder in days 1049, 1057, and 1080 postimplant (Chadwick et al., 2011). Chao et al. (2010) evaluated ECoG-based decoding of hand position and arm joint angles during reaching movements in nonhuman primates over a period of several months. This study showed that decoding performance did not significantly degrade with time and that decoding performance and the time between decoder model generation and decoder testing were not negatively correlated. Perge et al. (2014) studied two tetraplegics implanted with multielectrode arrays over the period of 1 year. Decoding accuracy during a motor imagery task declined at the rate of 3.6 [5.65]%/month (for subjects T2 and [S3], respectively), using a multiunit spiking activity-based decoder. For the LFP-based decoder, a similar decline (2.4[2.85]%/month) was reported.

In the case of EEG, the reasons for session-to-session variability include variability in electrode placement, gradual changes in impedance between scalp and electrodes due to changes in environmental conditions, such as humidity, temperature, channel motion, and sweat, and changes in emotional, hormonal, and pharmacological states of subjects. However, similar questions regarding the long-term signal quality and BMI performance hold in the case of EEG and have not yet been investigated. In this study, we look at stability of EEG signals as well as changes in BMI performance over multiple sessions performed on different days in two chronic transradial amputees.

2 MATERIALS AND METHODS
2.1 STUDY PARTICIPANTS

This study was approved by the institutional review board at the University of Houston. Three amputee volunteers participated in this study after giving written informed consent. The inclusion criteria for this study were: (a) traumatic transradial amputation in right arm, (b) right hand dominant before amputation, (c) no untreated pain/neuromas in residual limb and no untreated phantom pain, and (d) should be able to carry weight of prosthetic (640 g) fitted to their stump socket. Participant A3 was a 67-year-old right transradial amputee who opted out of the study after three sessions due to phantom pain. Data from participant A3 are therefore not included in further analyses. Participant A1 was a 56-year-old healthy male who underwent bilateral transradial upper limb amputation following an electrocution injury 32 years before this study. At the time of testing, he used a body-powered hook prosthetic which he had been using for the past 25 years. Participant A2 was a 59-year-old woman who underwent right transradial upper limb amputation following an automotive accident 14 years before this study. At the time of testing, she used a myoelectric controlled electric hook prosthetic which she had been using for the past 14 years. Both participants did not show any indications of cognitive deficits and were right hand dominant before amputation. Participant A1 was under supervised pharmacological treatment to manage hypertension and urinary bladder function. Participant A2 was under supervised pharmacological treatment for depression, hormone imbalance, pain management (for phantom pain as well as shoulder joint inflammation), and drug dependence.

2.2 DATA ACQUISITION AND INSTRUMENTATION/HARDWARE

Participants were fitted with an anthropomorphic prosthetic hand (IH2 Azzurra, Prensilia s.r.l., Italy) to their residual limb sockets (Fig. 1) fitted by a Certified Prosthetist Orthotist specialist (Cipriani et al., 2011b). Whole head 64 channel active EEG (BrainAmpDC with actiCAP, Brain Vision LLC, USA) was recorded at 100 Hz during the experiment. Simultaneous recording of EEG, real-time data processing, and control of the robotic hand was achieved using the BCI2000 software framework (Schalk et al., 2004). Although EEG was recorded at 100 Hz, data packets were sent from EEG amplifiers at a rate 50 Hz, constraining the real-time loop to 20 ms. Consequently, robotic hand control was also sampled at 50 Hz.

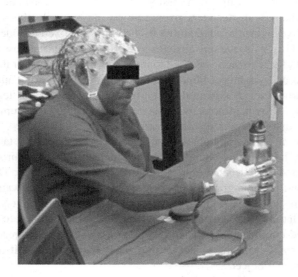

FIG. 1

Experimental setup. Amputee participants were fitted with the IH2 Azzurra robotic hand to their residual limb sockets. Sixty-four channel active EEG was recorded simultaneously, while participants performed the grasping task (Agashe and Contreras-Vidal, 2014).

The IH2 Azzurra robotic hand has five dof: one each for the flexion–extension of the thumb, index finger, and middle finger; one for the combined flexion–extension of the ring and little finger; and one for the thumb rotation (Cipriani et al., 2011b). The IH2 Azzurra hand uses a differential mechanism via which a single dof is used to control both the MCP (metacarpal–phalangeal) and PIP (proximal interphalangeal) finger joints in such a way that when the MCP joint encounters an obstruction (due to grasping an object), the PIP continues to flex until the object is fully grasped (Cipriani et al., 2011a). Finger kinematics for a single dof were specified at an 8-bit resolution, with 0 and 255 corresponding to open and fully flexed positions, respectively. Nominally, two synergies of grasping based on PC analysis of the joint angles were identified based on previous work (Agashe and Contreras-Vidal, 2011; Agashe et al., 2015; Santello et al., 1998) corresponding to the correlated movement of the flexion–extension across all fingers and the thumb (PC1), and the thumb rotation (PC2).

2.3 EXPERIMENT DESIGN

Participants performed 13 sessions over a period of 5 weeks, with each session being performed on a different day. In the first six sessions, participants performed a "training" phase (used to create a BMI decoder) followed by a "testing" phase (closed-loop control using the decoder created in the training phase). In the next six sessions (sessions 7–12), only the testing phase was performed, using the decoder from the training phase of the sixth session. The first six sessions allowed us to investigate the changes in decoders over multiple days, while the sessions 7–12 allowed us to investigate the adaptability of the brain to a fixed decoder, the consistency of the EEG signals, and any changes in BMI performance across multiple sessions. The final (13th) session was used to measure chance levels for the continuous time predictions using a subject-blind paradigm: unknown to participants, computer-generated Brownian noise was used to control the robotic hand instead of participants' EEG. The Brownian noise was generated as a cumulative sum of Gaussian white noise, so that its power spectrum varied as $1/f^2$.

In both training and testing phases, participants were seated at a table with their attached robotic hand resting on a flat switch, which served to synchronize onset of hand transport and EEG decoder output controlling grasp preshaping. During the behavioral task, participants grasped an object (either an aluminum water bottle or a credit card, corresponding to cylindrical and lateral grasps, respectively) with the robotic hand. Each trial consisted of the researcher presenting an object to be grasped at a predetermined comfortable distance (20–30 cm) away from the resting position. Following presentation of the object to be grasped, participants self-initiated hand transport toward the object.

During the training phase, initiation of hand transport triggered a predetermined grasping sequence in the robotic hand, suitable to the object being presented. The predetermined finger joint trajectories were created so as to have typical human grasp aperture time profiles seen during grasping (Castiello, 2005). A Gaussian

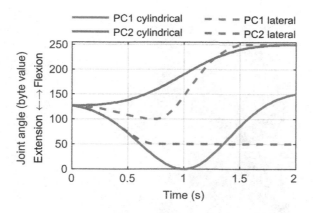

FIG. 2

PC1 and PC2 training phase trajectories. During the training phase, participants observed as the robotic hand performed predetermined grasp trajectories. The predetermined trajectories were based on two synergies of movement, PC1 and PC2, shown above for the two objects. PC1 controlled the flexion–extension of the fingers and the thumb, while PC2 controlled the thumb rotation. The initial resting grasp position was set midway between complete flexion and extension.

profile was used for PC1 activation, while a Gaussian profile was used for PC2 velocity, with a total time lengths 2 and 1.5 s, respectively (Fig. 2). The thumb rotation (PC2) was held constant during the second half of the trajectory in the case of the lateral grasp. Participants timed their hand transport in conjunction with hand preshaping, so that the object was grasped by the end of the hand transport. Participants were instructed to imagine themselves controlling the hand preshaping and grasping. In addition to the visual feedback, participants were asked to imagine kinesthetic feedback as well. The grasp was held steady for 2 s, followed by an opening of the grasp and a return to the resting position (reverse of the grasping trajectory). During the grasp release trajectory, participants transported the hand back to its resting position (Fig. 3). Participants performed 100 trials during the training phase. The order in which objects (bottle or card) were presented varied in a pseudorandom fashion.

A mapping (BMI decoder) between the 64-channel EEG data and the two synergies (PC1 and PC2) was created using data recorded in the training phase. In the testing phase, this mapping was applied to EEG to make real-time predictions of PC1 and PC2, allowing closed-loop control of the robotic hand preshaping. Initiation of hand transport by the participant, following presentation of an object to be grasped, triggered the start of closed-loop control (Fig. 4). Thereafter, participants had 5 s to grasp the presented object. The outcome of each trial was marked as a "success" or "failure" depending on whether the participant was able to grasp the object or not within the allotted preset time (5 s). Monitoring current drawn by the actuator motor for each dof allowed us to detect when an object was grasped,

FIG. 3

Grasp trajectories in the training phase. Snapshots of the grasp trajectory are shown above for the cylindrical grasp (*top row*) and the lateral grasp (*bottom row*) (Agashe and Contreras-Vidal, 2014).

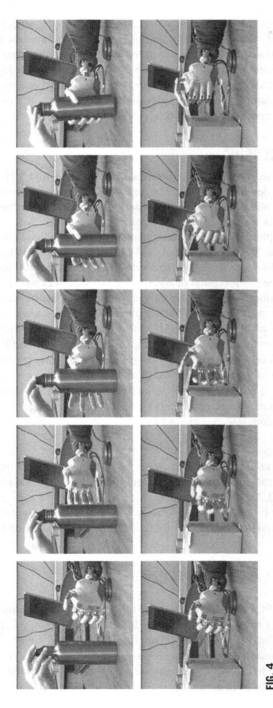

FIG. 4

Grasp preshaping with closed-loop control. Examples of successful grasps during the closed-loop control are shown for the cylindrical (*top row*) and the lateral (*bottom row*) grasps (Agashe and Contreras-Vidal, 2014; Agashe et al., 2015).

since the current drawn increases rapidly if resistance due to the object is encountered. Once an object was successfully grasped, closed-loop control ceased and the grasp was held steady for 2 s. Following either outcome, the hand shape was returned to resting position according to the predetermined grasp release trajectory suitable for the presented object, as used in the training phase. Participants performed 100 trials during the testing phase. The order in which objects (bottle or card) were presented varied in a pseudorandom fashion.

2.4 SIGNAL PROCESSING

A causal filter was used to band-pass filter data between 0.1 and 1 Hz. This was implemented as cascaded high-pass and low-pass second-order Butterworth filters. The maximum group phase delay in the passband was 300 ms. Both training phase and testing phase EEG were filtered in this manner.

After the training phase, EEG and kinematics were extracted and processed offline in MATLAB (The Mathworks, Inc., USA). A lag of 100 ms was introduced in the EEG so that kinematics at time t aligned with EEG at time $t - 100$ ms. This was done to account for the corticospinal delay; the lag estimate was based on previous decoding studies (Bradberry et al., 2010). EEG data were standardized by their mean and standard deviation over the entire training phase. Kinematics were upsampled to 100 Hz (from 50 Hz) using the MATLAB *pchip* (piecewise cubic hermite interpolating polynomial) method, followed by a transformation to PC1 and PC2 by multiplying with the PC coefficient matrix for the predetermined grasp trajectories. PC1 was set to the average of the four finger and thumb flexion values, corresponding to PC loadings of 0.25 for each of the four joints. PC2 was set to the thumb rotation value. Data were segmented into movement periods, from movement onset to completion of grasp, and concatenated along trials.

2.4.1 Decoding

These data were then used to construct a linear mapping using robust linear regression, which mitigates the effect of outliers by weighting them less. This method was implemented in MATLAB (The Mathworks, Inc., USA) using the *robustfit* function which uses iteratively reweighted least squares with a bisquare weighting function. PC1 and PC2 were modeled independently as a linear combination of EEG sensor data:

$$PC_i[t] = \beta_{i0} + \sum_j \beta_{ij} S_j[t - 100\text{ms}],$$

where $PC_i[t]$ is the ith PC being decoded at time t, β_{ij} are the model parameters, and S_j are the processed EEG from the jth electrode. In the testing phase, this linear mapping was used to predict PC1 and PC2 values from filtered and standardized EEG. Standard deviation from the training phase was used to scale EEG. These PC predictions were then scaled using a gain parameter so that when transformed back to the kinematic space of joint actuators, they represent movements which spanned the kinematic range. A few (typically 5–10) trials were conducted before the testing phase to manually tune the gain parameters according to the subjects' preference of the range of motion. Final predicted kinematic actuator values were constrained to the range 0–255 by applying a saturating linear transfer function (MATLAB function *satlin*).

3 RESULTS

3.1 CLOSED-LOOP GRASPING PERFORMANCE WAS STABLE OVER SESSIONS

During closed-loop BMI operation, participants were allowed 5 s from movement onset to grasp the presented object in each trial. If the object was grasped successfully, we marked it as a "success," and as a "failure" otherwise. Fig. 4 shows examples of successful closed-loop grasps for the two objects. We used the percentage of successful trials (success rate) within a session as a performance metric to measure BMI performance. In addition to correctly decoded kinematics, this metric also depended on the ability of participants to position and time the hand transport to successfully grasp the presented object. Correct decoding of hand grasp kinematics (finger extension followed by flexion with suitable amplitude and timing) but incorrect hand orientation resulted in a failure to grasp the object functionally and was counted as such. Thus, while functionally relevant, success rate as a metric was a compounded measure of participants' ability to position and time the hand transport in synchrony with the decoded kinematics. The first six sessions included observation-based decoder training immediately preceding the closed-loop operation (see Section 2). In sessions 7–12, participants performed only the closed-loop control (testing) phase. In the 13th session, blind to subjects, we controlled the two synergies using Brownian noise. In this case, the success rate is an isolated measure of their ability to time their hand transport and position to successfully grasp an object, when the prosthetic hand randomly opens and closes. Brown noise was used as it is spectrally similar to EEG, with the power spectra of both signals following a characteristic $\frac{1}{f^{|\alpha|}}$ curve (Nunez and Srinivasan, 2006). For the generated Brown noise, $\alpha = 2$. It should be noted that chance levels are not 50%, since the two outcomes (success vs failure) do not necessarily have equal probabilities and because the decoding task was not discrete and depended on appropriate EEG-based scaling and timing of prosthetic grasp suitable for the test object.

Success rates were significantly above chance levels ($p < 0.05$) for participant A1, except for one session (Fig. 5). For participant A2, success rates were significantly above chance levels in only two sessions. Participant A2 had greater difficulty with hand transport, in part due to shoulder pain, resulting in lower chance levels than participant A1. Bootstrapped 95% confidence intervals were calculated for each session and used to determine the significance levels when comparing to chance levels. Across the first six sessions, when the decoder was calibrated before each

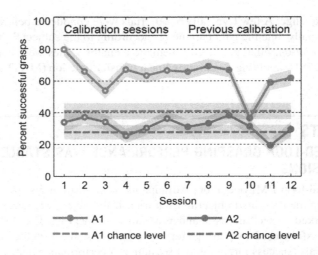

FIG. 5

Closed-loop BMI performance. The percentage of successful grasps during closed-loop operation was used as a metric of BMI performance and is shown across sessions for both participants. *Shaded* regions indicate the bootstrapped 95% confidence intervals. The first six sessions (*open circles*) represent sessions in which a training phase preceded the testing phase. The last six sessions (*solid circles*) used the decoder calibration from the sixth session. Chance levels (*dashed line*) indicate the performance when the robotic hand was controlled by brown noise (blind to the participants).

closed-loop phase, mean performance for participant A1 remained stable at $66 \pm 3\%$, indicating that BMI performance is consistent across multiple decoders created on different days. With the exception of one session, performance across sessions 7–12 was also stable at $65 \pm 2\%$, indicating that the brain is able to recall decoders from previous sessions.

3.2 LONG-TERM STABILITY OF EEG SIGNAL FEATURES AND DECODERS

Three factors determine BMI performance: the quality and stability of the input signals (EEG features), the decoder, and the user's changing internal states. Stability of EEG features used as inputs to the BMI across sessions has not been investigated previously. In this regard, we tracked delta-band EEG standard deviation and amplitude changes at the timescale of 10 s, across multiple sessions (Fig. 6A and B) for participant A1 who had BMI performance above chance levels. We did not observe any discernible differences between the observation-based calibration phases and the closed-loop phase. Across all sessions, EEG amplitude is higher in the prefrontal and temporal scalp regions, likely due to these areas being farther away from the reference, as well as high amplitude ocular and myographic artifacts. One of the sessions (session 9) had high EEG amplitudes and standard deviation across all scalp regions,

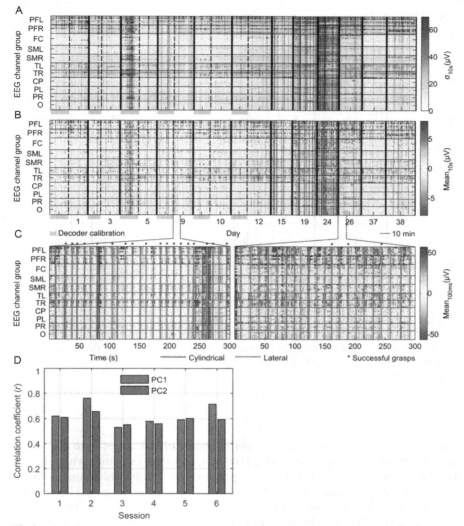

FIG. 6

Longitudinal stability of EEG for subject A1. Decoders were calibrated and tested for the first six sessions, while sessions 7–12 were performed with the decoder calibrated in session 6. Longitudinal stability of all EEG channels during BMI use across sessions is shown above for participant A. EEG channels were grouped by scalp location: *CP*, central-parietal; *FC*, frontal-central; *O*, occipital; *PFL*, prefrontal left; *PFR*, prefrontal right; *PL*, parietal left; *PR*, parietal right; *SML*, sensorimotor left; *SMR*, sensorimotor right; *TL*, temporal left; *TR*, temporal right. (A) The standard deviation in the delta band, at a timescale of 10 s. (B) The mean at the same timescale. EEG amplitude is markedly higher in the prefrontal and temporal regions, which may be due to high amplitude ocular and myographic artifacts. (C) The changes in EEG at the timescale of 100 ms (timescale relevant for decoding) for sessions 4 (high performance) and 10 (low performance), respectively. Movement onset is indicated by the *vertical red* (*gray* in the print version) (cylindrical grasp) or *green* (*gray* in the print version) (lateral grasp) *lines*. Successful grasps are indicated by an *asterisk* (*) above the movement onset. (D) Performance of the decoder on the calibration data was assessed by computing the correlation coefficient (*r*) between predicted and actual PC trajectories. The *r* value was stable across sessions for both PC1 (mean $r=0.63\pm0.09$) and PC2 (mean $r=0.59\pm0.04$), indicating consistent decoder performance.

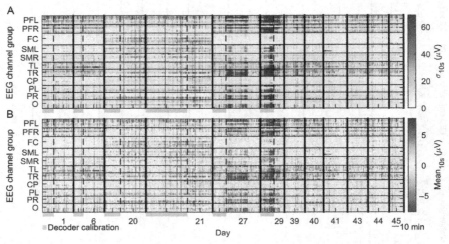

FIG. 7

Longitudinal stability of EEG for subject A2. (A) The standard deviation in the delta band, at a timescale of 10 s. (B) The mean at the same timescale. High EEG amplitudes were observed in prefrontal and temporal areas. High amplitudes in sessions 5 and 6 did not correlate with a low success rate.

but did not correspond to lower BMI performance. EEG features were also stable over timescales relevant for decoding (100 ms), and across sessions with differing BMI performance (Fig. 6C). Decoder performance on the calibration data, as assessed by the correlation coefficient (r) between predicted and actual kinematics, was also stable across sessions for both PC1 (mean $r = 0.63 \pm 0.09$) and PC2 (mean $r = 0.59 \pm 0.04$). EEG stability patterns were similar for participant A2 (high prefrontal and temporal amplitudes; Fig. 7).

To visualize the changes in the decoders across the first six sessions for participant A1, we plotted the model parameters on a scalp map for PC1 and PC2 (Fig. 8). In each BMI calibration (training) phase, models were created so as to minimize the least square error between the model predicted and actual kinematic trajectories. Since the BMI performance was stable, changes in the model over sessions indicate underlying EEG signal changes. Interestingly, although models for PC1 and PC2 were created independently, they showed very similar sets of EEG channels over which the magnitude of model parameters was high, within each session (Fig. 8). This indicates that signals over similar scalp areas control both PC1 and PC2 amplitudes, and is expected from the smoothly coordinated and temporally coupled synergies during natural grasping (Santello et al., 1998, 2002). The spatial distribution of model parameters on the scalp for A2 (Fig. 9) showed variation as well.

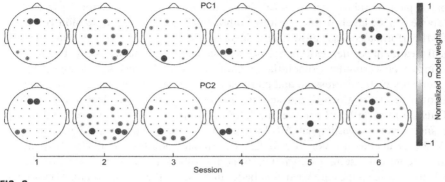

FIG. 8

Stability of decoder across sessions for A1. During the first six sessions, decoders were calibrated after the training phase to evaluate stability of the decoder parameters across sessions. Decoder parameters for PC1 (*top row*) and PC2 (*bottom row*) were plotted on a scalp map, for participant A1.

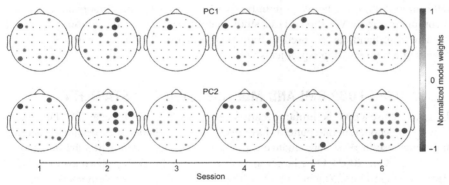

FIG. 9

Stability of decoder across sessions for A2. During the first six sessions, decoders were calibrated after the training phase to evaluate stability of the decoder parameters across sessions. Decoder parameters for PC1 (*top row*) and PC2 (*bottom row*) were plotted on a scalp map, for participant A2.

4 DISCUSSION

4.1 MULTISESSION, CLOSED-LOOP BMI PERFORMANCE

Over all sessions, BMI success rate was $63 \pm 3\%$ for participant A1 (above chance levels in 11 sessions) and $32 \pm 2\%$ for participant A2 (above chance levels in two sessions). With a fixed decoder (sessions 7–12), the success rate was $60 \pm 5\%$ for participant A1 (above chance levels in five sessions) and $30 \pm 3\%$ for participant A2 (above chance levels in one session). Although EEG was stable in session 10 for A1, BMI performance was below chance levels. Participant A2 was under pharmacological treatment for depression, hormone imbalance, pain management (for phantom pain as well as shoulder joint inflammation), and drug dependence. Pharmacological interventions for depression and pain management, and hormonal interventions are known to affect global brain activity as measured in EEG (Becker et al., 1980; Guisado et al., 1975; Hunter et al., 2006) and may explain the lower BMI performance levels in participant A2. In addition, shoulder pain resulted in participant A2 being unable at times to smoothly coordinate hand transport. These conditions may represent useful exclusion criteria for future EEG-based neuroprosthetics. Clearly, more studies are needed to better understand the effects of pharmacological agents on brain activity.

In the absence of overt kinematics in amputees, being able to train decoders presents a challenge for researchers. In the past, movement observation has been used to train BMI models in primates for 3D reaching movements (Wahnoun et al., 2004, 2006). A similar approach has been used to calibrate intracortical BMI systems to control positioning of an arm in space in humans (Hochberg et al., 2012). Bradberry et al. (2011) have shown that it is possible to use action observation to determine a mapping between noninvasive EEG activity and cursor movement on a computer screen. We show in this study that observing grasping actions performed by a robotic hand can be used to train time-domain EEG-based neural interfaces, allowing amputees to grasp objects.

4.2 CLOSED-LOOP BMI AND MULTISESSION EEG STABILITY

Learning to use a BMI is similar to learning a new tool (Bradberry et al., 2011). Given a new fixed decoder, neural patterns have been shown to change over sessions, resulting in an increase in BMI performance (up to a limit) as the brain learns the new "tool" (Carmena et al., 2003). Over larger timescales of months, BMI performance may also decay, owing to loss in signal quality (Perge et al., 2014). A complementary approach to keeping the decoder fixed and letting the brain adapt is to adapt the decoder itself to changing neural activity, such that BMI performance is maximized (Orsborn et al., 2012). There are typically a characteristic timescale associated with changes in BMI performance over sessions due to changes in neural patterns, and a timescale at which the BMI model is adaptive (DiGiovanna et al., 2009). In our study, we used two extremes on the closed-loop BMI system adaptation timescale spectrum: the first six sessions, when the decoder was changed every session, represent the fastest timescale (single session), while sessions 7–12, when a fixed decoder was used, represent the other extreme in which adaptation was limited to the user's brain.

Changing the decoder every session is generally accepted to be detrimental to BMI performance (Orsborn et al., 2012), and strategies have been proposed to make optimal use of the interaction between the adaptive BMI algorithm and the learning process of the brain itself (DiGiovanna et al., 2009; Orsborn et al., 2012).

Nevertheless, we created a new decoder every session for the first six sessions as we wanted to study the stability of such decoder over sessions, with respect to the input EEG features. Our results show that as a result of changing EEG features, decoders are not stable. The performance drop in session 3 for participant A1 could possibly be associated with unstable EEG signal quality during the training phase for this session (Fig. 6A and B). During sessions 7–12, the decoder was fixed, allowing us to examine the potential for cortical plasticity, given that performance was stable, except for one session. Surprisingly, the performance was stable for this duration, and possibly because the timescale of BMI user learning may be longer than six sessions (Collinger et al., 2012; Hochberg et al., 2012; Perge et al., 2014).

4.3 IMPLICATIONS FOR NONINVASIVE BMIS

In this study, an amputee participant (A1) was able to control a robotic hand to grasp two objects (bottle and credit card) with a success rate of 63% over 5 weeks. We previously showed that low-frequency time-domain EEG contains information about a variety of upper limb movement intentions, such as hand transport (Bradberry et al., 2010), grasping (Agashe and Contreras-Vidal, 2011, 2013), and finger movements (Paek et al., 2014). Studies from other groups show similar results from field potentials at smaller spatial scales, like LFPs (Bansal et al., 2011; Hall et al., 2014; Mollazadeh et al., 2011; Zhuang et al., 2010) and ECoG (Acharya et al., 2010; Kubánek et al., 2009; Pistohl et al., 2012). Closed-loop studies with implanted intracortical electrodes also show significant information in low-frequency time-domain LFP (Perge et al., 2014). Traditionally, BMIs for motor control have used power modulation in specific frequency bands such as the mu (8–13 Hz) and beta (20–30 Hz) bands (McFarland et al., 2010). Advances in pattern recognition techniques have improved upon these approaches (Korik et al., 2015), and continued research is essential to explore the limits of this traditional approach. Our approach differs from traditional motor imagery BCIs based on mu and beta modulations in several ways: (1) we decode over the whole scalp representation therefore capturing amplitude signal modulations over large distributed neural networks in contrast to the usually restricted localized scalp areas over sensorimotor scalp areas in mu/beta approaches. (2) mu/beta are usually involved in initiation (eg, mu suppression) or termination (eg, beta rebound) of movements that scales with movement speed (Yuan et al., 2010). (3) mu/beta usually require operant conditioning or neurofeedback and (4) not all subjects show detectable mu rhythms which make it difficult to decode movement (Ahn and Jun, 2015). Here, we show for the first time that the low-frequency time-domain feature space is viable for extracting grasping-related movement intent from amputees, and can be used to control closed-loop neuroprosthetics over a period of several weeks.

Our current BMI relies on subject-initiated hand transport to trigger BMI control of the hand via a switch, constraining the system to laboratory use. BMI systems which are able to detect initiation of hand transport for grasping without a switch, would be more suited for use outside the lab and is a target for future innovation.

Further studies with a larger time window that will be able to detect changes in BMI learning over the scale of months are also needed. Tactile feedback from fingertip sensors may also help neuroprosthetic embodiment and closed-loop performance. Further studies are also needed to investigate the generalizability of decoders to different grasp types. Results from this study show that EEG-based BMIs are feasible when the right input feature space is used.

ACKNOWLEDGMENTS

This work was supported by the National Science Foundation award IIS-1219321. The authors thank Ted Muilenburg for help with participant recruitment and socket fabrication.

REFERENCES

Acharya, S., Fifer, M.S., Benz, H.L., Crone, N.E., Thakor, N.V., 2010. Electrocorticographic amplitude predicts finger positions during slow grasping motions of the hand. J. Neural Eng. 7, 046002. http://dx.doi.org/10.1088/1741-2560/7/4/046002.

Agashe, H.A., Contreras-Vidal, J.L., 2011. Reconstructing hand kinematics during reach to grasp movements from electroencephalographic signals. In: 3th Annual International Conference of the IEEE Engineering in Medicine and Biology Society (EMBC) (Boston, USA), pp. 5444–5447. http://dx.doi.org/10.1109/IEMBS.2011.6091389.

Agashe, H.A., Contreras-Vidal, J.L., 2013. Decoding the evolving grasping gesture from electroencephalographic (EEG) activity. Conf. Proc. IEEE Eng. Med. Biol. Soc. 2013, 5590–5593. http://dx.doi.org/10.1109/EMBC.2013.6610817.

Agashe, H.A., Contreras-Vidal, J.L., 2014. Observation-based training for neuroprosthetic control of grasping by amputees. Conf. Proc. IEEE Eng. Med. Biol. Soc. 2014, 3989–3992. http://dx.doi.org/10.1109/EMBC.2014.6944498.

Agashe, H.A., Paek, A.Y., Zhang, Y., Contreras-Vidal, J.L., 2015. Global cortical activity predicts shape of hand during grasping. Front. Neurosci. 9, 121. http://dx.doi.org/10.3389/fnins.2015.00121.

Ahn, M., Jun, S.C., 2015. Performance variation in motor imagery brain–computer interface: a brief review. J. Neurosci. Methods 243, 103–110.

Ball, T., Demandt, E., Mutschler, I., Neitzel, E., Mehring, C., Vogt, K., et al., 2008. Movement related activity in the high gamma range of the human EEG. Neuroimage 41, 302–310. http://dx.doi.org/10.1016/j.neuroimage.2008.02.032.

Bansal, A.K., Vargas-Irwin, C.E., Truccolo, W., Donoghue, J.P., 2011. Relationships among low-frequency local field potentials, spiking activity, and three-dimensional reach and grasp kinematics in primary motor and ventral premotor cortices. J. Neurophysiol. 105, 1603–1619. http://dx.doi.org/10.1152/jn.00532.2010.

Becker, D., Creutzfeldt, O.D., Schwibbe, M., Wuttke, W., 1980. Electrophysiological and psychological changes induced by steroid hormones in men and women. Acta Psychiatr. Belg. 80 (5), 674–697.

Blakely, T., Miller, K.J., Zanos, S.P., Rao, R.P.N., Ojemann, J.G., 2009. Robust, long-term control of an electrocorticographic brain-computer interface with fixed parameters. Neurosurg. Focus 27, E13. http://dx.doi.org/10.3171/2009.4.FOCUS0977.

Bradberry, T.J., Rong, F., Contreras-Vidal, J.L., 2009. Decoding center-out hand velocity from MEG signals during visuomotor adaptation. Neuroimage 47, 1691–1700. http://dx.doi.org/10.1016/j.neuroimage.2009.06.023.

Bradberry, T.J., Gentili, R.J., Contreras-Vidal, J.L., 2010. Reconstructing three-dimensional hand movements from noninvasive electroencephalographic signals. J. Neurosci. 30, 3432–3437. http://dx.doi.org/10.1523/JNEUROSCI.6107-09.2010.

Bradberry, T.J., Gentili, R.J., Contreras-Vidal, J.L., 2011. Fast attainment of computer cursor control with noninvasively acquired brain signals. J. Neural Eng. 8, 036010. http://dx.doi.org/10.1088/1741-2560/8/3/036010.

Carmena, J.M., Lebedev, M.A., Crist, R.E., O'Doherty, J.E., Santucci, D.M., Dimitrov, D.F., et al., 2003. Learning to control a brain-machine interface for reaching and grasping by primates. PLoS Biol. 1, E42. http://dx.doi.org/10.1371/journal.pbio.0000042.

Castiello, U., 2005. The neuroscience of grasping. Nat. Rev. Neurosci. 6, 726–736. http://dx.doi.org/10.1038/nrn1744.

Chadwick, E.K., Blana, D., Simeral, J.D., Lambrecht, J., Kim, S.P., Cornwell, A.S., et al., 2011. Continuous neuronal ensemble control of simulated arm reaching by a human with tetraplegia. J. Neural Eng. 8, 034003. http://dx.doi.org/10.1088/1741-2560/8/3/034003.

Chao, Z.C., Nagasaka, Y., Fujii, N., 2010. Long-term asynchronous decoding of arm motion using electrocorticographic signals in monkeys. Front. Neuroeng. 3, 3. http://dx.doi.org/10.3389/fneng.2010.00003.

Chestek, C.A., Gilja, V., Nuyujukian, P., Foster, J.D., Fan, J.M., Kaufman, M.T., et al., 2011. Long-term stability of neural prosthetic control signals from silicon cortical arrays in rhesus macaque motor cortex. J. Neural Eng. 8, 045005. http://dx.doi.org/10.1088/1741-2560/8/4/045005.

Cipriani, C., Antfolk, C., Controzzi, M., Lundborg, G., Rosén, B., Carrozza, M.C., et al., 2011a. Online myoelectric control of a dexterous hand prosthesis by transradial amputees. IEEE Trans. Neural Syst. Rehabil. Eng. 19, 260–270.

Cipriani, C., Controzzi, M., Carrozza, M.C., 2011b. The SmartHand transradial prosthesis. J. Neuroeng. Rehabil. 8, 29. http://dx.doi.org/10.1186/1743-0003-8-29.

Cipriani, C., Segil, J., Birdwell, J., Weir, R., 2014. Dexterous control of a prosthetic hand using fine-wire intramuscular electrodes in targeted extrinsic muscles. IEEE Trans. Neural Syst. Rehabil. Eng. 22, 828–836.

Clanton, S.T., Zohny, Z., Velliste, M., Schwartz, A.B., 2010. Simultaneous 7-dimensional cortical control of an arm and hand robot via direct brain interface. In: Neuroscience Meeting Planner. Society for Neuroscience, San Diego, CA. Program No. 494.6.

Collinger, J.L., Wodlinger, B., Downey, J.E., Wang, W., Tyler-Kabara, E.C., Weber, D.J., et al., 2012. High-performance neuroprosthetic control by an individual with tetraplegia. Lancet 6736, 1–8. http://dx.doi.org/10.1016/S0140-6736(12)61816-9.

Contreras-Vidal, J.L., Presacco, A., Agashe, H.A., Paek, A., 2012. Restoration of whole body movement: toward a noninvasive brain-machine interface system. IEEE Pulse 3, 34.

Dickey, A.S., Suminski, A., Amit, Y., Hatsopoulos, N.G., 2009. Single-unit stability using chronically implanted multielectrode arrays. J. Neurophysiol. 102, 1331–1339. http://dx.doi.org/10.1152/jn.90920.2008.

DiGiovanna, J., Mahmoudi, B., Fortes, J., Principe, J.C., Sanchez, J.C., 2009. Coadaptive brain–machine interface via reinforcement learning. IEEE Trans. Biomed. Eng. 56, 54–64.

Ganguly, K., Carmena, J.M., 2009. Emergence of a stable cortical map for neuroprosthetic control. PLoS Biol. 7, e1000153. http://dx.doi.org/10.1371/journal.pbio.1000153.

Guisado, R., Arieff, A.I., Massry, S.G., Lazarowitz, V., Kerian, A., 1975. Changes in the electroencephalogram in acute uremia. Effects of parathyroid hormone and brain electrolytes. J. Clin. Invest. 55, 738.

Hall, T.M., de Carvalho, F., Jackson, A., 2014. A common structure underlies low-frequency cortical dynamics in movement, sleep, and sedation. Neuron 1–15. http://dx.doi.org/10.1016/j.neuron.2014.07.022.

Hochberg, L.R., Serruya, M.D., Friehs, G.M., Mukand, J.A., Saleh, M., Caplan, A.H., et al., 2006. Neuronal ensemble control of prosthetic devices by a human with tetraplegia. Nature 442, 164–171. http://dx.doi.org/10.1038/nature04970.

Hochberg, L.R., Bacher, D., Jarosiewicz, B., Masse, N.Y., Simeral, J.D., Vogel, J., et al., 2012. Reach and grasp by people with tetraplegia using a neurally controlled robotic arm. Nature 485, 372–375.

Hunter, A., Leuchter, A., Morgan, M., Cook, I., 2006. Changes in brain function (quantitative EEG cordance) during placebo lead-in and treatment outcomes in clinical trials for major depression. Am. J. Psychiatry 163, 1426–1432.

Kim, S.P., Sanchez, J.C., Rao, Y.N., Erdogmus, D., Carmena, J.M., Lebedev, M.A., et al., 2006. A comparison of optimal MIMO linear and nonlinear models for brain–machine interfaces. J. Neural Eng. 3, 145–161.

Korik, A., Siddique, N., Sosnik, R., Coyle, D., 2015. E3D hand movement velocity reconstruction using power spectral density of EEG signals and neural network. In: Engineering in Medicine and Biology Society (EMBC), 2015 37th Annual International Conference of the IEEE (IEEE), pp. 8103–8106.

Kubánek, J., Miller, K.J., Ojemann, J.G., Wolpaw, J.R., Schalk, G., 2009. Decoding flexion of individual fingers using electrocorticographic signals in humans. J. Neural Eng. 6, 066001. http://dx.doi.org/10.1088/1741-2560/6/6/066001.

Kuiken, T.A., Li, G., Lock, B.A., Lipschutz, R.D., Miller, L.A., Stubblefield, K.A., et al., 2009. Targeted muscle reinnervation for real-time myoelectric control of multifunction artificial arms. JAMA 301, 619–628.

Lebedev, M.A., Nicolelis, M.A.L., 2006. Brain-machine interfaces: past, present and future. Trends Neurosci. 29, 536–546. http://dx.doi.org/10.1016/j.tins.2006.07.004.

Li, G., Schultz, A.E., Kuiken, T.A., 2010. Quantifying pattern recognition-based myoelectric control of multifunctional transradial prostheses. IEEE Trans Neural Syst. Rehabil. Eng. 18, 185–192.

McFarland, D.J., Sarnacki, W.A., Wolpaw, J.R., 2010. Electroencephalographic (EEG) control of three-dimensional movement. J. Neural Eng. 7, 36007.

Mollazadeh, M., Aggarwal, V., Davidson, A.G., Law, A.J., Thakor, N.V., Schieber, M.H., 2011. Spatiotemporal variation of multiple neurophysiological signals in the primary motor cortex during dexterous reach-to-grasp movements. J. Neurosci. 31, 15531–15543. http://dx.doi.org/10.1523/JNEUROSCI.2999-11.2011.

Musallam, S., Corneil, B.D., Greger, B., Scherberger, H., Andersen, R.A., 2004. Cognitive control signals for neural prosthetics. Science 305 (80), 258–262.

Nunez, P.L., Srinivasan, R., 2006. Electric Fields of the Brain: The Neurophysics of EEG. Oxford University Press, USA.

Orsborn, A.L., Dangi, S., Moorman, H.G., Carmena, J.M., 2012. Closed-loop decoder adaptation on intermediate time-scales facilitates rapid BMI performance improvements independent of decoder initialization conditions. IEEE Trans. Neural Syst. Rehabil. Eng. 20, 468–477.

Paek, A.Y., Agashe, H.A., Contreras-Vidal, J.L., 2014. Decoding repetitive finger movements with brain activity acquired via non-invasive electroencephalography. Front. Neuroeng. 7, 3.

Perge, J. a, Zhang, S., Malik, W.Q., Homer, M.L., Cash, S., Friehs, G., et al., 2014. Reliability of directional information in unsorted spikes and local field potentials recorded in human motor cortex. J. Neural Eng. 11, 046007. http://dx.doi.org/10.1088/1741-2560/11/4/046007.

Pistohl, T., Schulze-Bonhage, A., Aertsen, A., Mehring, C., Ball, T., 2012. Decoding natural grasp types from human ECoG. Neuroimage 59, 248–260. http://dx.doi.org/10.1016/j.neuroimage.2011.06.084.

Resnik, L., Meucci, M.R., Lieberman-Klinger, S., Fantini, C., Kelty, D.L., Disla, R., et al., 2012. Advanced upper limb prosthetic devices: implications for upper limb prosthetic rehabilitation. Arch. Phys. Med. Rehabil. 93, 710–717.

Resnik, L., Borgia, M., Latlief, G., Sasson, N., Smurr-Walters, L., 2014. Self-reported and performance-based outcomes using DEKA arm. J. Rehabil. Res. Dev. 51, 351–362.

Santello, M., Flanders, M., Soechting, J.F., 1998. Postural hand synergies for tool use. J. Neurosci. 18, 10105.

Santello, M., Flanders, M., Soechting, J.F., 2002. Patterns of hand motion during grasping and the influence of sensory guidance. J. Neurosci. 22, 1426–1435.

Schalk, G., McFarland, D.J., Hinterberger, T., Birbaumer, N., Wolpaw, J.R., 2004. BCI2000: a general-purpose brain-computer interface (BCI) system. IEEE Trans. Biomed. Eng. 51, 1034–1043. http://dx.doi.org/10.1109/TBME.2004.827072.

Schalk, G., Miller, K.J., Anderson, N.R., Wilson, J.A., Smyth, M.D., Ojemann, J.G., et al., 2008. Two-dimensional movement control using electrocorticographic signals in humans. J. Neural Eng. 5, 75–84. http://dx.doi.org/10.1088/1741-2560/5/1/008.

Serruya, M.D., Hatsopoulos, N.G., Paninski, L., Fellows, M.R., Donoghue, J.P., 2002. Brain-machine interface: instant neural control of a movement signal. Nature 416, 141–142.

Simeral, J.D., Kim, S.-P., Black, M.J., Donoghue, J.P., Hochberg, L.R., 2011. Neural control of cursor trajectory and click by a human with tetraplegia 1000 days after implant of an intracortical microelectrode array. J. Neural Eng. 8, 025027. http://dx.doi.org/10.1088/1741-2560/8/2/025027.

Taylor, D.M., Tillery, S.I.H., Schwartz, A.B., 2002. Direct cortical control of 3D neuroprosthetic devices. Science 296 (80), 1829.

Velliste, M., Perel, S., Spalding, M.C., Whitford, A.S., Schwartz, A.B., 2008. Cortical control of a prosthetic arm for self-feeding. Nature 453, 1098–1101. http://dx.doi.org/10.1038/nature06996.

Wahnoun, R., Tillery, S.I.H., He, J., 2004. Neuron selection and visual training for population vector based cortical control. Conf. Proc. IEEE Eng. Med. Biol. Soc. 2, 4607–4610. http://dx.doi.org/10.1109/IEMBS.2004.1404277.

Wahnoun, R., He, J., Helms Tillery, S.I., 2006. Selection and parameterization of cortical neurons for neuroprosthetic control. J. Neural Eng. 3, 162–171. http://dx.doi.org/10.1088/1741-2560/3/2/010.

Waldert, S., Pistohl, T., Braun, C., Ball, T., Aertsen, A., Mehring, C., 2009. A review on directional information in neural signals for brain-machine interfaces. J. Physiol. Paris 103, 244–254. http://dx.doi.org/10.1016/j.jphysparis.2009.08.007.

Wodlinger, B., Downey, J.E., Tyler-Kabara, E.C., Schwartz, A.B., Boninger, M.L., Collinger, J.L., 2015. Ten-dimensional anthropomorphic arm control in a human brain-machine interface: difficulties, solutions, and limitations. J. Neural Eng. 12, 016011. http://dx.doi.org/10.1088/1741-2560/12/1/016011.

Yuan, H., Perdoni, C., He, B., 2010. Relationship between speed and EEG activity during imagined and executed hand movements. J. Neural Eng. 7, 26001. http://dx.doi.org/10.1088/1741-2560/7/2/026001.

Zhou, P., Lowery, M.M., Englehart, K.B., Huang, H., Li, G., Hargrove, L., et al., 2007. Decoding a new neural machine interface for control of artificial limbs. J. Neurophysiol. 98, 2974–2982. http://dx.doi.org/10.1152/jn.00178.2007.

Zhuang, J., Truccolo, W., Vargas-Irwin, C.E., Donoghue, J.P., 2010. Decoding 3-D reach and grasp kinematics from high-frequency local field potentials in primate primary motor cortex. IEEE Trans. Biomed. Eng. 57, 1774–1784. http://dx.doi.org/10.1109/TBME.2010.2047015.

Patients Studies and Clinical Applications

PART

III

Patients Studies
and Clinical
Applications

Brain–computer interfaces in the completely locked-in state and chronic stroke

U. Chaudhary*,1, N. Birbaumer*,†, A. Ramos-Murguialday*,‡,1

*Institute of Medical Psychology and Behavioral Neurobiology, University of Tübingen,
Tübingen, Germany
†Wyss-Center for Bio- and Neuro-Engineering, Geneva, Switzerland
‡TECNALIA, San Sebastian, Spain
1Corresponding authors: Tel.: +49-174-1368031 (U.C.), +49-178-8753929 (A.R.);
Fax: +49-7071-295956,
e-mail address: uchau001@fiu.edu; ander.ramos@med.uni-tuebingen.de

Abstract

Brain–computer interfaces (BCIs) use brain activity to control external devices, facilitating paralyzed patients to interact with the environment. In this chapter, we discuss the historical perspective of development of BCIs and the current advances of noninvasive BCIs for communication in patients with amyotrophic lateral sclerosis and for restoration of motor impairment after severe stroke.

Distinct techniques have been explored to control a BCI in patient population especially electroencephalography (EEG) and more recently near-infrared spectroscopy (NIRS) because of their noninvasive nature and low cost. Previous studies demonstrated successful communication of patients with locked-in state (LIS) using EEG- and invasive electrocorticography-BCI and intracortical recordings when patients still showed residual eye control, but not with patients with complete LIS (ie, complete paralysis). Recently, a NIRS-BCI and classical conditioning procedure was introduced, allowing communication in patients in the complete locked-in state (CLIS). In severe chronic stroke without residual hand function first results indicate a possible superior motor rehabilitation to available treatment using BCI training. Here we present an overview of the available studies and recent results, which open new doors for communication, in the completely paralyzed and rehabilitation in severely affected stroke patients. We also reflect on and describe possible neuronal and learning mechanisms responsible for BCI control and perspective for future BMI research for communication in CLIS and stroke motor recovery.

Keywords

Brain–computer interface, Amyotrophic lateral sclerosis, Locked-in state, Complete locked-in state, Stroke, Electroencephalography, Functional near-infrared spectroscopy, Classical conditioning, Communication, Rehabilitation

Progress in Brain Research, Volume 228, ISSN 0079-6123, http://dx.doi.org/10.1016/bs.pbr.2016.04.019
© 2016 Elsevier B.V. All rights reserved.

Brain–computer interface (BCI) is an emerging technology that uses brain activity directly without any motor involvement, for activation of a computer or other external devices. This chapter presents an overview of BCI in locked-in state (LIS) and completely locked-in state (CLIS) due to amyotrophic lateral sclerosis (ALS). LIS can also be caused due to brainstem stroke (León-Carrión et al., 2002; Smith and Delargy, 2005) (not discussed in this chapter) and chronic stroke. The topics discussed in this chapter are outlined below:

(1) Historical perspective—This section traces the initiation of BCI research, its early setback, and successes.
(2) Types of BCI—The beginning of 21st century witnessed a rapid rise in BCI studies, where different types of brain signals were used, which forms the topic of this section.
(3) BCIs for communication in paralysis due to ALS—This section describes various studies performed till date to provide communication to patient in locked-in state (LIS) and completely locked-in state (CLIS) due to ALS. This section also describes the learning mechanism entailing BCI control in paralysis.
(4) BCIs for chronic stroke—This section focuses on several BCI studies performed on chronic stroke patient.
(5) Future perspective—Finally the chapter ends with the future perspective.

1 HISTORICAL PERSPECTIVE

Hans Berger, who discovered the human EEG, speculated in his first comprehensive review of his experiments with the "Elektrenkephalogramm" (1929) about the possibility of reading thoughts from the EEG traces by using sophisticated mathematical analyses. Grey Walter, the brilliant EEG pioneer who described the contingent negative variation, often called the "expectancy wave," built the first automatic frequency analyzer and the computer of "average transients" with the intention of discriminating covert thoughts and language in the human EEG (Walter, 1964). In 1973, Jacques Vidal presented a system that was capable of translating EEG signals into computer control signals, and coined the term "brain–computer interface" (BCI). He predicted in 1973 the prospective applications of direct brain–computer control. Vidal concluded in this visionary paper:

> As the reader undoubtedly realizes, direct brain-computer communication still lies somewhat in the future. Even the relatively modest experimental program outlined in this paper may take several years to reach maturity, at which time new directions probably will have emerged. In summary, it can be said that the feasibility of the communication concept rests on three basic assumptions. The first assumption is that mental decisions and reactions can be probed, in a dimension that both transcends and complements overt behavior, from the array of observable bioelectric signals and, in particular, from the electroencephalographic

potential fluctuations as measured on the human scalp. A second assumption is that all meaningful EEG phenomena should be viewed as a complex structure of elementary wavelets, similar in nature to components of evoked responses that sequentially reflect individual cortical events and create a continuous flow of neuroelectric messages. The third assumption is that operant conditioning procedures can increase the reliability and stability of these time signatures and patterns. Admittedly the validity and implications of these assumptions are far from universally accepted.

1.1 INITIAL SETBACK

During the late 1960s and early 1970s, Neal E. Miller and collaborators opposed the traditional wisdom of the autonomous nervous system (ANS) as autonomous and independent of voluntary control of the somatic central nervous system (CNS). Miller (1969), in a landmark paper in *Science*, challenged the view that voluntary control is acquired through operant (instrumental) conditioning, whereas modification of involuntary ANS functions is learned through classical (Pavlovian) conditioning, a distinction first emphasized by Skinner (Holland and Skinner, 1961; Skinner, 1953). Miller presented experimental evidence in curarized and artificially ventilated rats showing that even after long-term curarization of several weeks, the animals learned to increase and decrease heart rate, renal blood flow, and dilation and constriction of peripheral arteries in an operant conditioning paradigm rewarding the animals for increases and decreases of these specific physiological functions. These studies stirred an enormous interest in the scientific and clinical community, particularly in psychosomatic medicine and behavior modification. The results suggested that instrumental (voluntary) control of autonomic functions is possible without any mediation of the somatic-muscular system. Operant training of any internal body function seemed possible, opening the door for psychological and learning treatment of many medical diseases such as high blood pressure, cardiac arrhythmias, vascular pathologies, renal failure, gastrointestinal disorders, and many others. In the clinic, biofeedback of these functions replaced the operant conditioning in rats; the feedback from the specific physiological variable constituted the reward (Kamiya, 1971). During the next two decades, Miller and his students at Rockefeller University tried to replicate their own findings but the size of the conditioning effect declined with each replication. Finally, by the mid-1980s, it was impossible to replicate the previous effects. Barry Dworkin, Neal Miller's last and most prolific student, continued to try and build the most sophisticated "intensive care unit" for curarized rats, but again, operant training of autonomic function or nerves in the curarized rat was impossible. In contrast, classical conditioning succeeded even in single facial nerve fibers (Dworkin, 1993; Dworkin and Miller, 1986). Dworkin attributed the failure of operant techniques to the missing homeostatic effect of the reward. The reward acquires its positive effect through homeostasis-restoring effects (ie, ingestion of food restores glucostatic and fluid balance). In the curarized rat (and the completely paralyzed respirated and fed patient?), where all body functions are kept artificially constant, the homeostatic function of the reward is no longer present because imbalances of the equilibrium do not occur. The chronically curarized rat and the completely paralyzed artificially ventilated and fed locked-in patient share many similarities; difficulties in communicating with these patients may be understood based on these similarities.

The difficulties in replicating the operant learning of autonomic variables were accompanied by an "awakening" in the clinical arena of biofeedback applications. The most impressive clinical results were achieved with electromyographic feedback in chronic neuromuscular pain (Flor and Birbaumer, 1993), neuromuscular rehabilitation of various neurological conditions, particularly external sphincter control in enuresis end encopresis, and posture control in kyphosis and scoliosis (Birbaumer et al., 1994), but there were clinically unimpressive or negligible results in essential hypertension, heart rate (Cuthbert et al., 1981), and gastric hyperfunction. It became painfully clear that only very limited positive effects of biofeedback on visceral pathology with clinically and statistically relevant changes occur. There was one notable exception, however, neurofeedback of brain activity (Berger et al., 1979).

1.2 EARLY SUCCESSES

The most spectacular and popularized results in the emerging field of biofeedback were the self-regulation of brain waves (Kamiya, 1971). Increase and decrease of alpha frequency of the EEG were supposed to create "meditative" states with many beneficial effects in the periphery and on behavior. Theta wave augmentation and reduction had profound effects on vigilance and attention (Birbaumer, 1977). Slow cortical potentials (SCPs) control allowed anatomically specific voluntary regulation of different brain areas with area-specific effects on behavior and cognition (Birbaumer et al., 1990). Warning voices such as experiments by Mulholland and his group demonstrating perfect control of alpha waves through manipulation of the oculomotor system and decoupling of eye fixation went largely unheard. Sterman (Sterman, 1981; Sterman and Friar, 1972) was the first to propose self-control of epileptic seizures by an augmentation of sensorimotor rhythm (SMR). SMR in human subjects is recorded exclusively over sensorimotor areas with frequencies of 10–20 Hz and variable amplitudes. Pfurtscheller and colleagues (2005) localized the source of human SMR in the sensorimotor regions following the homuncular organization of the motor and somatosensory cortical strip. Imagery of hand movement abolishes SMR over the hand region; imagery or actual movement of the legs blocks SMR in the interhemispheric sulcus. Pfurtscheller called this phenomenon event-related desynchronization and synchronization. On the basis of careful animal experiments (Sterman and Clemente, 1962a,b), Sterman demonstrated incompatibility of seizures in motor and premotor areas in the presence of SMR. Cats exhibited maximum SMR during motor inhibition and various sleep stages. Presence of spindles during different sleep stages, particularly during rapid eye movement sleep indicated recruitment of inhibitory thalamocortical circuits and blocked experimentally induced seizures. Sleep spindles and SMR share identical physiological mechanisms. Epileptic cats and humans were trained to increase SMR, and, after extensive training ranging from 20 to more than 100 sessions, Sterman (Sterman and MacDonald, 1979) was able to demonstrate seizure reduction and complete remission in some patients with drug-resistant epilepsy. The results of SMR control in animals and patients seem to demonstrate that manipulation (mediation) of the peripheral motor efferent is not a necessary requirement of SMR control, at least on the basis of EMG recordings of the arm muscles showing no measurable variation during motor imagery with CNS event-related desynchronization.

Beginning in 1979, Birbaumer's group published an extensive series of experiments that demonstrated operant control of SCPs in the EEG. These demonstrations differed from previous brain biofeedback work as they documented the following in well-controlled experimental paradigms.

1. Strong and anatomically specific effects of self-induced cortical changes on behavior and cognition;
2. Solid neurophysiological evidence about anatomical sources and physiological function of SCPs (Birbaumer, 1999; Birbaumer and Roberts, 1992; Birbaumer et al., 1990).

Of particular interest in the context of CNS motor mediation of voluntary control of brain activity was the fact that SCPs originating from posterior parietal sources were resistant to operant learning, whereas central and frontal SCPs could be brought under voluntary, operant control after one to five training sessions (Lutzenberger et al., 1993). Several clinical studies confirmed the critical importance of the anterior brain systems for physiological regulation of CNS functions. Lutzenberger et al. (1993) showed that patients with extended prefrontal lobe lesions were unable to learn SCP control despite intact intellectual functioning. Disorders with prefrontal dysfunctions such as attention deficit disorder (Birbaumer et al., 1986) and schizophrenia (Schneider et al., 1992) exhibited extreme difficulties in acquiring SCP control, and attentional improvement after SCP or SMR neurofeedback training required long training periods. Again, peripheral motor function played no role in SCP conditioning, but intact prefrontal systems seemed to be a prerequisite for successful brain control.

Subjects received visual feedback of positive and negative SCPs of 6-s duration and were rewarded for the production of target amplitudes (Hinterberger et al., 2005a,b). The successful voluntary brain control depends on activity in premotor areas and the anterior parts of the basal ganglia. Birbaumer et al. (1990) had proposed earlier that physiological regulation of SCP and attention depends critically on anterior basal ganglia activity regulating local cortical activation thresholds and SCP in selective attention and motor preparation. Braitenberg created the term "thought pump" ("Gedankenpumpe" in German) for this basal ganglia–thalamus–cortical loop. Taken together, the extensive literature on the SCP also suggests that operant-voluntary control of local cortical excitation thresholds underlying goal-directed thinking and preparation depends on an intact motor or/and premotor cortical and subcortical system. Encouraged by the reliable and lasting effects of brain self-regulation on various behavioral variables and by Sterman's case demonstrations, Birbaumer and colleagues conducted several controlled clinical studies on the effect of SCP regulation on intractable epilepsy (Kotchoubey et al., 2001b; Rockstroh et al., 1993). Based on their neurophysiological model of SCP regulation, patients with focal epileptic seizures were trained to downregulate cortical excitation by rewarding them for cortical positive potentials and perception of SCP changes. After extremely long training periods, some of these patients gained close to 100% control of their SCPs and seizure suppression, tempting Birbaumer and colleagues to apply cortical regulation as a BCI for paralyzed patients. Given that epileptic patients suffering from a dysregulation of cortical excitation and inhibition and consequent brain lesions learn to control their brain responses both within the laboratory and in daily life, it is not unreasonable to ask whether a paralyzed patient could learn to activate an external device or computer in order to move a prosthetic armor to convey messages to a voice system. However, only a few years later, the entire field of NFB-related behavioral effects fell into disrepute, as many premature claims based on successes in single patients diagnosed with various disorders could not be validated in larger, controlled trials.

2 TYPES OF BCI

The beginning of 21st century witnessed a rapid progress in BCI research with the number of published research papers rising exponentially. This rapid rise has been led by an increase in the number of techniques, both invasive and noninvasive, used to acquire different kinds of brain signals.

The invasive BCI approach is divided into four main types: (1) local field potentials (LFPs) (Lebedev and Nicolelis, 2006), (2) single-unit activity (Velliste et al., 2008), (3) multiunit activity, and (4) electrocorticography (ECoG) (Felton et al., 2007). The invasive BCI approach involves implantation of electrode grids or multielectrode grids, via surgical procedure in rodents (Chapin et al., 1999; Talwar et al., 2002) and nonhuman primates (Donoghue, 2002; Nicolelis, 2003; Serruya et al., 2002; Wessberg et al., 2000). During these experiments animals learned to utilize their brain activity to control the displacements of computer cursors (Serruya et al., 2002) or one-dimensional (1D) to three-dimensional (3D) movements of simple and elaborate robot arms (Chapin et al., 1999; Wessberg et al., 2000). The single neuron recording was later tested in tetraplegic human patient by research group of Hochberg (Hochberg et al., 2006) and Donoghue (Donoghue et al., 2007). Despite the initial setback and incomplete understanding of the mechanism underlying NFB-related behavioral effects, a number of well-controlled studies have now provided evidence about the influence of operant conditioning of brain activity on neuronal functions and some selected brain pathologies (Fuchs et al., 2003; Kotchoubey et al., 2001a; Monastra et al., 2006).

The noninvasive BCI approach is divided into six types: (1) SCPs (Birbaumer et al., 1990; Kubler et al., 2001), (2) SMR and motor-related beta rhythms

(13–30 Hz) (Kübler et al., 2005; Wolpaw et al., 2002), (3) event-related potentials (ERPs), the most widely used is P300 (Farwell and Donchin, 1988), (4) steady-state visual- or auditory-evoked potentials (SSVEP/SSAEP) (Zhu et al., 2010), (5) blood oxygenation level-dependent (BOLD) imaging using fMRI (DeCharms et al., 2004; Weiskopf et al., 2003; Yoo et al., 2013), and (6) concentration changes of oxy/deoxy hemoglobin using near-infrared spectroscopy (NIRS) (Gallegos-Ayala et al., 2014; Naito et al., 2007). The user's brain signals obtained via invasive or noninvasive means are acquired via amplifiers, filtered, and decoded using an online classification algorithm. In turn, this output is fed back to users, which allows them to modulate their brain activity. The feedback may consist of sensory stimuli such as visual (Caria et al., 2007), auditory (Nijboer et al., 2008b), or vibrotactile stimuli varying proportionally to the classified brain activity; a discrete reward for a particular brain response, namely, a verbal response (such as "yes" or "no"); the movements of a prosthesis or wheelchair, or direct electrical stimulation of muscles or brain. Thus the BCI used in clinical environments can be divided into types, namely assistive BCI and rehabilitative BCI system. The assistive BCI system aims to substitute lost functions, for example, communication (Birbaumer et al., 1999), or to achieve continuous, high-dimensional control of robotic devices, or relies on functional electric stimulation (FES) (Pfurtscheller et al., 2003) to assist in daily-life environments, as shown in Fig. 1A. In contrast, the rehabilitative BCI systems (also termed restorative or biofeedback BCI) aim to facilitate the restoration of brain function by normalizing the neurophysiologic activity (Birbaumer and Cohen, 2007; Ramos-Murguialday et al., 2012; Soekadar et al., 2014), as shown in Fig. 1B.

A   BCI for communication in locked-in
                        patient

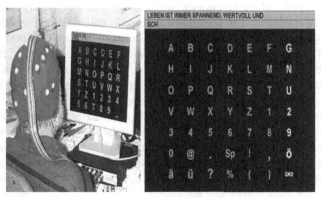

FIG. 1

(A) An assistive BCI based on P300 speller used for communication in locked-in patient.

(Continued)

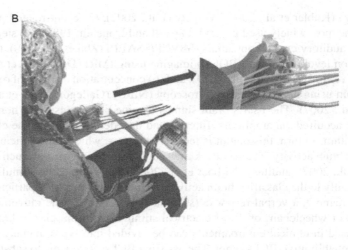

FIG. 1—CONT'D

(B) A rehabilitative BCI for hand movement restoration in stroke patient.

3 BCI FOR COMMUNICATION IN PARALYSIS DUE TO ALS

ALS is a progressive motor neuron disease that results in eventual complete destruction of the peripheral and central motor system affecting sensory or cognitive functions to a minor degree (Chou and Norris, 1993). The course is unyieldingly progressive. There is no treatment available; patients have to decide whether to accept artificial respiration and feeding for the rest of their lives after the disease destroys respiratory and bulbar functions or to die of respiratory or related problems. If they opt for life and accept artificial respiration, the disease progresses until the patient loses control of the last muscular response, which is usually the eye muscle or the external sphincter. The resulting condition is called complete locked-in state (CLIS) (Bauer et al., 1979). CLIS condition consists of virtually total immobility, including all eye movements, combined with preserved consciousness. If there is total immobility except for vertical eye movement and blinking, combined with preserved consciousness, then the patient is said to be in locked-in state (LIS) (Bauer et al., 1979). Almost all people with ALS experience a speech disorder as the disease progresses and ultimately most become unable to speak at all (Ball, 2007). For patients with several motor channels left, communication support involves a range of augmentative and alternative communication (AAC) strategies involving low- and high-technology (speech-generating devices) options (Beukelman and Mirenda, 2005). When patients are in LIS and later in CLIS due to the loss of all motor channels, none of the AACs work and the patients are rendered communication less. To address this critical issue of communication in LIS and CLIS, both invasive and noninvasive BCI approaches have been used but noninvasive methods have been utilized more extensively than invasive methods (Birbaumer and Cohen, 2007; Birbaumer et al., 2008). BCI-based communication involves generation of brain signal by the patient to control alphanumeric grids, binary cursers, and/or web browsing tools to formulate sentence or express the feelings and/or desire to the caregiver and/or family members.

3.1 INVASIVE BCI FOR COMMUNICATION

Invasive BCI records the neural cells firing pattern, which constitutes the substrate for behaviorally relevant information, via an implanted electrode array. Kennedy and Bakay (1998) implanted the first type of invasive BCI in humans, which was cortically implanted glass microelectrode filled with a neurotrophic growth factor. Kennedy et al. (2000, 2004) published several single cases with ALS in different stages, but none of the patients were either in LIS or CLIS. The patients learned to control the vertical or horizontal movement of a cursor on computer screen, by modulating the firing pattern of the axons grown into the electrode. A series of BCI studies on human patients with subdurally or epidurally implanted macroelectrodes recording ECoG in presurgically implanted patients with epilepsy (Hinterberger et al., 2008; Leuthardt et al., 2004) showed high classification rates of 70–90% accuracy in selecting letters from different speller systems using brain oscillations derived from motor-related areas with frequencies up to the high gamma range without extensive training times. Patients used different types of imagery to select or ignore a particular letter or object from a computer menu. The first implantation of 100 microelectrodes in the motor cortex of a tetraplegic patient by Hochberg et al. (2006) seems to allow improved BCI performance, where the patient learned to use the neural interface system to move and click a computer cursor. Gilja et al. (2015) demonstrated the use of an invasive neural prosthesis for cursor control to free typing of words in two patients with ALS, and reported a typing speed of 115 words in <19 min by one patient, but none of the patients were in LIS or CLIS. In Birbaumer's group, two patients in CLIS suffering from ALS were implanted with ECoG electrodes after failure to communicate with EEG and pH recordings (Murguialday et al., 2011; Wilhelm et al., 2006). Despite an already well-trained P300-based BCI, a paradigm based on detection of ERPs requiring directed attention in a specific sensory modality (eg, vision, hearing, touch) that was established during the LIS in one patient, neither of these two patients achieved reliable brain communication rates with ECoG-BCIs. Furthermore, improving the quality and degrees of freedom in the brain signals (eg, using single cell firing or LFP) was not superior to noninvasive recordings in these CLIS patients (Birbaumer, 2006; Birbaumer et al., 2008). This essentially negative result of invasive brain recording suggests a more fundamental theoretical problem of learning and attention in brain communication with BCI in CLIS. However, the database of invasive BCIs for communication purposes in paralyzed patients at present is too small to judge their efficacy, and the willingness of patients and their families to agree to implantation is weak as long as the noninvasive BCIs are available and functioning.

3.2 NONINVASIVE BCIs FOR COMMUNICATION

Several kind of EEG-based BCI has been developed and investigated for communication in LIS due to ALS, namely SCP-BCI, SMR-BCI, and P300-BCI.

3.2.1 The SCP-BCI

Birbaumer et al. (1999) were the first to demonstrate the feasibility of SCP-BCI for communication with two LIS patients diagnosed with ALS. In this study, a speller program presented a string of letters on the training screen. Both users were successful in learning volitional control of SCP activation and deactivation shifts to indicate a desired letter. SCP records the cortical activation potential from the central Cz location on scalp over 0.5–10.0 s. The shift can be either positive or negative; negative shifts are typically associated with movement and other functions involving cortical activation, while positive shifts are usually associated with reduced cortical activation (Birbaumer, 1999; Rockstroh et al., 1993). The users learn to select options appearing on the screen by decreasing or increasing the SCP voltage level. The voltage is displayed as vertical movement of a cursor and final selection is indicated in a variety of ways, as shown in Fig. 2A. The BCI can also operate in a mode that gives auditory or tactile feedback. In several studies Birbaumer and his colleagues have shown that people can learn to control SCPs and thereby control movement of an object on a computer screen (Birbaumer et al., 1999; Kübler and Birbaumer, 2008; Kubler et al., 2001). It has been tested extensively in people with late-stage ALS and has proved able to supply basic communication capability (Kübler and Birbaumer, 2008).

3.2.2 The SMR-BCI

Wolpaw and colleagues at the Wadsworth Laboratories in Albany, New York, did an extensive series of experiments, mainly with healthy persons, using SMR rather than SCP as the target brain response (Wolpaw et al., 2002). SMR refers to localized sinusoidal frequencies in the alpha and lower beta range of EEG activity, which can be recorded over somatosensory and motor cortical areas. SMR decreases or desynchronizes with movement, preparation for movement, or movement imagery, and it increases or synchronizes in the postmovement period or during motor quiescence (Pfurtscheller et al., 1998). In a group of patients, two with high spinal cord lesions, Wolpaw and McFarland (2004) demonstrated that multidimensional control of a cursor movement on a computer screen can be learned in just a few sessions of training. The subjects were able to move a cursor within 10 s into one of eight goals appearing randomly at one of the four corners of the screen. The patient's task is to move the cursor on the target, as shown in Fig. 2B. For example, low SMR amplitude during motor imagery moves the cursor to the bottom bar, high SMR amplitude moves the cursor toward the top bar (Bai et al., 2010; Kübler et al., 2005). The flexibility, speed, and learning performance are generally equal to that seen when invasive multielectrode BCI systems are tested in animals.

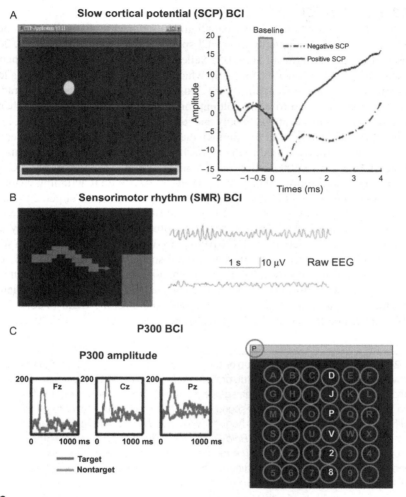

FIG. 2

Three types of BCI (*left*) and EEG analyses averaged over several trials (*right*). (A) SCP-BCI: targets are presented at the top or bottom of the screen. Patients' task is to move the cursor (*yellow dot* (*white*) in the print version) toward the target with the highlighted frame. The cursor moves steadily from left to right and its vertical deflection corresponds to the SCP amplitude. *Bottom right*: time course of the SCP amplitude averaged across 350 trials separated by task requirement. Negative SCP amplitude (*dashed line*) moves the cursor toward the top, positive SCP amplitude (*bold line*) toward the bottom target. Before each trial, a baseline is recorded indicated by the *green bar* (*light gray* in the print version). At time point 2 s the task is presented, at 500 ms the baseline is recorded, and at zero cursor movement starts. Positive and negative SCP amplitude shifts are clearly distinguishable, indicating that the patient learned to manipulate the SCP amplitude. (B) SMR-BCI: targets are

(Continued)

3.2.3 The P300-BCI

The P300-BCI is based on "oddball paradigm" introduced by Farwell and Donchin (1988). It is the most commonly used BCI speller application (Mugler et al., 2010; Nijboer et al., 2008a; Pires et al., 2011; Sellers et al., 2010). In P300-BCI, participants are presented with a 6×6 matrix in which each of the 36 cells contains a letter or a symbol (Farwell and Donchin, 1988). This design becomes an oddball paradigm by first intensifying each row and column for 100 ms in random order and then by instructing participants to attend to only one (the desired) of the 36 cells. Thus, in one trial of 12 flashes (6 rows and 6 columns), the target cell will flash only twice, constituting a rare event compared to the 10 flashes of all other rows and columns, and will therefore elicit a P300 (Sellers and Donchin, 2006), as shown in Fig. 2C.

In all cases, the majority of patient in LIS due to ALS with functioning vision and eye control demonstrated the ability to learn self-regulation of the targeted brain signals. The LIS patient who underwent EEG-based BCI studies never transitioned into CLIS state, prompting several researchers to hypothesize that BCI training may serve as a protective factor. Sellers et al. (2010) reported long-term follow-up data for an ALS patient that has been actively using a P300-speller BCI program for 2.5 years. The findings indicate that the BCI accuracy remained high and the device benefited the user by allowing him to interact, communicate, and work. However, when the technology was introduced after the participants had become CLIS (Thorns et al., 2010), Kübler and Birbaumer (2008) have shown that patients in CLIS do not reach

---

FIG. 2—CONT'D presented at the top or bottom right margin of the screen. Patients' task is to move the cursor into the target. Cursor movement is indicated by the *squares*; during feedback of SMR amplitude, only one square is visible. The cursor moves steadily from left to right, vertical deflections correspond to the SMR amplitude. *Top right panel* shows amplitude of the EEG as a function of frequency averaged across 230 trials separated by task requirement (top vs bottom target). *Bold line* indicates frequency power spectrum when the cursor had to be moved toward the top target; *dashed line* when the cursor had to be moved toward the bottom target. A difference in amplitude can be clearly seen around the 10 Hz SMR peak. (C) P300-BCI: a 6×6 letter matrix is presented. Rows and columns flash in random order, indicated by the *bright row*. In the copy spelling mode (Kübler et al., 2001), the patients' task is to copy the word presented in the top line (GEHIRN, German for "brain"). In each trial, patients have to count how often the target letter flashes. The target letter is presented in parentheses at the end of the word. Selected letters are presented in the second line below the word to copy. *Middle right panel* depicts EEG to target letters (*bold line*) averaged across 43 trials comprising 430 flashes of the target letter and 2150 flashes of all rows and columns not containing the target letter. *Dashed line* indicates the course of the EEG to all the nontarget rows and columns (for an exact description of letter selection, see, eg, Sellers and Donchin, 2006). EEG to target letters is clearly distinguishable from nontarget letters.

Panel (A): Figure from Kübler and Birbaumer, N., 2008. Brain-computer interfaces and communication in paralysis: extinction of goal directed thinking in completely paralysed patients? Clin. Neurophysiol. 119(11), 2658–2666.

sufficient BCI control for communication with EEG parameters. It has been postulated that some cognitive impairment and changes in EEG signatures in late-stage ALS may contribute to the lack of success using EEG-BCI technology as Kübler and Birbaumer (2008) speculated that extinction of goal-directed thinking may prohibit operant learning of brain communication. According to Birbaumer et al. (2009), it is still unclear whether BCI allow for voluntary control of brain responses and communications with CLIS patients. However, Murguialday et al. (2011) reported that passive limb movements and auditory stimuli continue to evoke ERP activity in CLIS patients, potentially permitting BCI communication. Hence, there is a need to find an alternative learning paradigm and probably another neuroimaging technique to design a more effective BCI to help ALS patient in CLIS with communication.

3.3 LEARNING BCI CONTROL IN PARALYSIS

Birbaumer et al. (2012) hypothesized that "loss of the contingency between a voluntary response and/or intention and its feedback" with loss of subsequent reward in individuals who are completely paralyzed, with vision problems, would prevent instrumental (voluntary) learning, even if auditory afferent input and cognitive processing (attention, memory, imagery) remained intact. If the voluntary response is cognitive, such as in covert goal-orientated imagery in CLIS, the feedback or reward does not follow a reliable behavioral or internal change and the response consequently extinguishes. In several investigations (Hinterberger et al., 2005a,b, 2008) with simultaneous registration of slow cortical brain potentials of the electroencephalogram and functional magnetic resonance imaging (fMRI) with epileptic and healthy people it was shown that in people who learned the neuroelectric control of slow brain activities well, regions in the basal ganglia, above all in the anterior striatum, are activated during the learning process. People who do not learn neuroelectric self-regulation of the brain do not show simultaneous activation of the basal ganglia.

Skill learning involves a discriminative stimulus (SD) that activates response planning, the actual response, and an effect (reward or punishment) that is time contingent upon the response. The response plan is modified based on the difference between the anticipated effect and the actual effect (Ziessler et al., 2004). Skill learning curves, like other forms of procedural learning and repetition priming, usually follow a positive exponential function (Gupta and Cohen, 2002). During the neurofeedback-based learning of metabolic or neuroelectric responses, no response plan exists at the start of training, because the response and its physiological and behavioral correlates are not in the repertoire of the organism's memory. Further, such responses usually do not fulfill a motivational drive-modulating function—except if brain regions with homeostatic properties are modified. Therefore, they need external reinforcement in order to become stable habits. Sensory feedback of the target physiological response acquires its anticipated effect by motivating learning from instruction (in humans) or through association with primary or secondary rewarding or punishing stimuli. As training progresses, however, an idiosyncratic response plan develops, usually hidden from the experimenter. The participants use imagery and other abstract cognitive activities, which become more and more "pruned" from irrelevant response elements until a final response concept reliably evokes the desired effect (Neumann et al., 2004). The hidden nature and idiosyncrasy of the initial response plan leads to large differences in variability of the learning curves in neurofeedback experiments, particularly during the initial training phases. Visual or auditory feedback stimuli that represent the response strength of the desired brain response are used most frequently in neurofeedback. Instructions to the participant may play a critical role in self-control of brain activity, if ambiguous instructions are given (eg, "try to produce an increase of the red colored bar on the screen"), the initially unstructured response plan may appear even less specific for the participant. Ambiguities in instruction and initial responses could lead to high variability, often extended training periods, and a substantial rate of nonlearners in neurofeedback (Birbaumer et al., 1999; Neumann et al., 2004). Neurofeedback of the BOLD signal and other metabolic brain signals, for example, as measured with NIRS, may produce smoother and more exponential learning curves than neuroelectric responses, comparable to motor skill acquisition, because feedback from the brain's vascular system to the critical brain areas responsible for skill learning (eg, the striatum and basal ganglia structures) constrains the abstract nature of the skill to be acquired (Koralek et al., 2012). The brain processes information from its vascular system, but it has no sensors for its neuroelectric responses. Changes in blood oxygenation, flow, and pressure are readily processed in the brain and thus may compensate for the lack of motor response components in brain self-regulation and allow faster "sharpening" of the response properties and pruning of irrelevant response components through feedback and reward.

Caria et al. (2007) demonstrated that participants who learned to regulate their own BOLD response in the anterior insula via rtfMRI (real time functional magnetic resonance imaging) feedback showed decrease in the number of clusters and an increase in the distance between the clusters, with increasing rtfMRI neurofeedback training.

3.3.1 The role of the basal ganglia in the learned acquisition of brain control

Brain responses are learned, stored, and retained in a manner that is comparable to a motor skill, following the rules of implicit learning (Squire, 1987). In contrast to explicit learning, implicit learning and memory do not require conscious and effortful search. In the neurofeedback situation, implicit learning is usually negatively defined by providing no explicit instruction to participants as to how they may control the brain activity represented by the feedback stimulus, such as imagery and other mental strategies. In animals, learned control of neuroelectric responses that range from single cell firing (Fetz, 1969) to cortical EEG (Elbert, 1993) has clearly indicated that neither instructions nor explicit mental strategies—as far as they can be assessed in animals—are necessary to learn brain control. A discriminative stimulus (SD) that indicates to the animal the occurrence of a reward after the particular physiological change is sufficient to guarantee learning. Whereas self-regulation and operant learning of peripheral vascular responses, such as blood pressure, blood flow, vascular diameter, and blood oxygenation, are well documented, instrumental learning of brain vascular responses in animals has not been investigated, but there is no evident reason to expect a difference in outcome for brain vascular responses and peripheral vascularity. The most compelling evidence for the procedural nature of neurofeedback-based learning and the critical role of cortical–basal ganglia loops responsible for procedural learning in learned brain control comes from a neurofeedback study with rodents (Koralek et al., 2012). For motor skills, the role of the cortical–basal ganglia loop is well established, but brain self-regulation does not involve any movement subjects have to learn the abstract skill of changing brain activity while motionless, to move a neuroprosthetic device or a computer cursor without activating the motor periphery. Koralek et al. (2012), using intracellular recordings, trained rats to modulate the firing rate of two adjacent neural ensembles in the primary motor cortex (M1) in order to obtain a reward. Modulation of activity in the two ensembles resulted in changes in the pitch of an auditory cursor, which provided constant auditory feedback of the task to the rodents. Reward was delivered when rodents precisely increased activity in one ensemble and decreased it in another ensemble, or vice versa, in order to move the auditory cursor to one of two target tones. When a successful effort was made to any of the targets, the rodent was rewarded with a sucrose solution for one target and with a food pellet for the other. Within 11 days of training, rats became proficient in both tasks and exhibited typical skill-learning acquisition rates. Omitting the feedback but retaining the reward did not result in learning. Degradation of the food–reward contingency or degradation of reward by satiety also rapidly impaired learning, even if correct auditory feedback was provided. Both feedback and reward are necessary for acquisition of the brain response. Striatal neuroplasticity in natural motor skills proved to be critical for learning of the neurofeedback task; cross correlations between the motor cortical cells and striatal neurons revealed increased oscillatory coupling in the 4–8 Hz range with learning. Finally, knockout rats that lacked N-methyl-D-aspartate receptors (NMDARs)—necessary for long-term potentiation in striatal neurons—did not learn the self-regulation task, despite intact movement. Pharmacological blockade of NMDARs in the dorsal striatum also impaired the task in the same way. These compelling data are complemented by earlier fMRI-brain imaging evidence in humans during learning of self-regulation of SCPs. Comparing good learners with poor learners in this neurofeedback task revealed activity of the basal ganglia and cortical motor structures in proficient learners (Hinterberger et al., 2005a,b). The participants received visual feedback of the amplitude of their SCP, increased cortical negativity (indicating stronger activation of the brain at central sites) moved a cursor up on the screen and decreased negativity moved the curser down, both movements being proportional to the change in amplitude of the SCP. Using neurofeedback and brain–machine interface (BMI) training of sensorimotor (8–15 Hz) rhythms, Halder et al. (2011) demonstrated that learned control of sensorimotor areas, which are an essential part of the cortico–basal–ganglia–loop, can be predicted from BOLD-response increase in those areas during pretraining motor imagery, particularly while observing movement in others. Overall, this converging evidence from animal and human neurofeedback paradigms strengthens the theoretical position that brain self-regulation and BMI control can be viewed as skill learning. Whereas an intact subcortical extrapyramidal motor system and dorsal striatum seem to be a *conditio sine qua non* for brain-regulation skill acquisition, the impact of the peripheral and central "pyramidal" voluntary motor system remains an open question (Birbaumer et al., 2013).

The interdependence of self-regulation of the brain and skill learning becomes particularly dramatic in CLIS, in whom contingencies between goal-directed thinking and intentions are lost because there is no environmental response to the particular intention. The learning process behind acquiring brain control—irrespective of whether it concerns neuroelectric activities of single cells or the electroencephalogram or metabolic changes of the cerebral circulation—is analogous to those learning procedures examined for the acquisition of skills (eg, sport, music) (Stocco et al., 2010). The automation and training in BCI as in any other skill runs exponentially, whereby in the course of the automated acquisition, increasingly less cortical areas are activated and the attention focus is restricted to the brain regions dealing with the particular behavior (Birbaumer and Chaudhary, 2015). Classical semantic conditioning of autonomic responses or brain responses does not depend on goal-directed motor systems and involves only minimal attentional resources and effort. Experiments with curarized rats resulted in excellent classical learning of autonomic functions but failed for instrumental operant control of physiological responses (Dworkin and Miller, 1986). Thus, classical semantic conditioning may circumvent extinction of volition, goal-directed thinking, effortful selective attention, and cognitive control, imagery, and working memory functions during learning and, thus, may allow to maintain communication in complete paralysis. These predictions were evaluated in a series of experiments involving healthy participants and ALS patients at various stages of their disease, all of them in LIS or CLIS (De Massari et al., 2013; Furdea et al., 2012; Ruf et al., 2013). These experiments showed that although classical conditioning paradigm seemed to work, the EEG alone as the clinical BCI signal could not be used reliably for successful communication.

3.4 FUNCTIONAL NEAR-INFRARED SPECTROSCOPY-BASED BCI FOR COMMUNICATION IN CLIS

Functional near-infrared spectroscopy (*f*NIRS) is an emerging neuroimaging modality that employs near-infrared light to noninvasively or invasively investigate cerebral oxygenation changes in healthy and neurologically impaired adults and children (Chaudhary et al., 2011, 2014; Obrig, 2014). Recently, *f*NIRS-BCI was developed in our lab, based on classical semantic conditioning, for communication in CLIS. A single case report by Gallegos-Ayala et al. (2014) for the first time described a CLIS patient with ALS achieving BCI control and "yes"–"no" communication to simple questions with known positive or negative answers and some open questions over an extensive time period of more than a year. *f*NIRS was used to measure and classify cortical oxygenation and deoxygenation following the questions. The BCI methodology used in this report departed radically from the previous BCI procedures (De Massari et al., 2013), a more "reflexive" mode based on learning principles of classical conditioning to simple questions was used. This "reflexive" mode served to train the classifier separating "yes" and "no" brain answers silently imagined by the patient. While EEG-BCI application resulted in significant (above 70%) classification of "yes" and "no" responses in only 7 of 37 sessions and no discriminatory response in brain oscillations to the images at frequencies between 3 and 30 Hz, *f*NIRS-BCI communication resulted in an overall stability of 72–100% correct answers across 14 consecutive sessions.

Hence, to further validate these preliminary findings of Gallegos-Ayala et al., 2014 and refine the technology of NIRS-based BCI for communication in CLIS patients extensive studies were performed on four ALS patients in CLIS using combined NIRS-EEG-based BCIs (submitted for publication). NIRS-EEG-based BCI was employed successfully to train four patients to regulate their frontocentral brain regions in response to auditorily presented questions. In Chaudhary et al. (submitted) patients learned to answer personal questions with known answers and open questions all requiring a "yes" or "no" thought (image) using frontocentral oxygenation changes measured with *f*NIRS. If replicated with ALS patients in CLIS, these positive results could indicate the abolition of complete locked-in states at least for ALS.

4 BCIs FOR CHRONIC STROKE

Current estimations place the percentage of people worldwide living with aftereffects of cerebrovascular accidents such as stroke at more than 1% of the world population. Very often, these conditions are accompanied with the deterioration or loss of functions, which can manifest itself, for example, as paralysis, speech apraxia, or cognitive deficits. 85% of all stroke survivors are affected by deficits for movement control (Cirstea et al., 2003; Langhorne et al., 2015; Saka et al., 2008; Young and Forster, 2007). This has a devastating effect on the quality of life of these patients, their ability to carry out activities of daily living, and in general their abilities to contribute to society. Although there exist many therapeutic strategies that attempt to help the patients to regain some functions, many patients do not benefit from the application of these approaches. It is estimated that around 80% of all stroke survivors with upper limb motor deficits do not fully regain their function (Hendricks et al., 2002), making tremendous efforts of caregivers and health-care systems necessary for long-term care.

There is an urgent need to recover the impaired functions in these patients, enabling them to lead a normal, healthy life as before the incident and to contribute again fully to the society. Solutions to this are profoundly required, because the aging of today's society will increase the already enormous pool of patients suffering from an impaired neural system year after year with millions of new patients worldwide. The foundation for functional recovery lies in the nervous system itself and in the remarkable plasticity of the brain which enables the brain to use the alternative pathways for the control of functions, if the original ones are lost or impaired (Pascual-Leone et al., 2005). Unfortunately, neurorehabilitation is an intricate process with successful recovery depending on a large number of factors, many of these related to environmental and psychological parameters of the patient (motivation, depression, and caregivers support). It is therefore necessary to employ methods that can compensate for these factors and actively guide the brain toward a state most beneficial for recovery. Current state-of-the-art rehabilitation strategies aim to support task-dependent reorganization (Pomeroy and Aglioti, 2011) without being able to directly influence this process. Several studies already explored the beneficial effects of robot therapy in chronic stroke when compared to conventional therapy, leaving the clinical relevance in question (Klamroth-Marganska et al., 2014). However, in these studies the robots only made passive movements and the contingency between intention and action was lost, which considerably diminished the robot's potential to induce neuroplastic changes (Turner et al., 2013).

4.1 STROKE REHABILITATION STRATEGIES

Traditional rehabilitation strategies following stroke are classed as bottom-up approaches. Such methods aim to generate motor recovery by manipulating at the distal level to elicit a subsequent change in neural circuits (Belda-Lois et al., 2011). Examples of traditional rehabilitation strategies include bilateral arm training and constrained induced therapies; for a comparison, see Lin et al. (2008). However, many bottom-up approaches may not be suitable for stroke patients, displaying limited residual hand movement, as active movement is often a necessary prerequisite for such rehabilitations (Birbaumer et al., 2008). Consequently, more modern approaches to stroke rehabilitation have begun to focus on top-down rehabilitation methods for stroke recovery; these therapies aim to assist reorganization of neural circuits still intact following stroke or to induce them if chronic stage is reached, in order to convalesce motor function (Belda-Lois et al., 2011). Examples of such methods included FES, cellular, and pharmacological interventions (Chollet et al., 2011; Krakauer et al., 2012; Savitz et al., 2014). A variety of robots for the upper and lower limb have been used as an addition to physical therapy for the training of different components of the CNS (spinal circuits and the brain). The addition of movement augmentation to the voluntary drive is greatly benefiting from the increased ability to perform the function, which greatly contributed to the motivation and arousal (Turner et al., 2013).

The hypothesis that was behind the augmented movement therapy by robots assumes that the greater recovery is partly due to the peripheral mechanisms, but mostly due to the cortical plasticity (Popovic and Popovic, 2006). This hypothesis has been confirmed in motor training tasks with physiological tests involving transcranial magnetic stimulation (TMS) (Tyč and Boyadjian, 2011) and imaging based on fMRI and EMG (Ramos-Murguialday et al., 2014). Another body actuator to move patients' paretic limbs is FES, which has been proven to induce motor plasticity and recovery (Quandt and Hummel, 2014). FES therapeutical effect might be mediated by the afferent fibers that are activated either during active movement or by passive movements produced by direct electrical stimulation (Jackson and Zimmermann, 2012). Furthermore, FES efficacy may be maximized when coupled with voluntary control neural mechanisms. Direct spinal cord stimulation (SCS) has been suggested as an alternative to FES and is a widespread and standard in clinical use as treatment for pain and spasticity (Minassian et al., 2012). Its use in primates suggests functional grasping movements are feasible using spinal microstimulation techniques (Moritz et al., 2007; Zimmermann et al., 2011). However, the invasiveness effects need to be further investigated in primates.

4.2 STROKE BCIs STUDIES

Although stroke patients exhibit a range of responses to various rehabilitation strategies, patients with severe hemiparesis generally display limited to no recovery in response to conventional treatment strategies (Belda-Lois et al., 2011). However, recent technological developments in modern rehabilitation methods, specifically BCIs, may represent an alternative rehabilitation strategy in severely impaired patients (Ang et al., 2011; Prasad et al., 2010). In a recent double-blinded controlled study Birbaumer's group has shown that even chronic stroke patients suffering from upper limb severe impairment can achieve significant improvement through proprioceptive BCIs training (Ramos-Murguialday et al., 2012), as shown in Fig. 3. The coupling of perception and action through contingent feedback using a robot controlled by the brain activity of the patient was the key element that leads to reorganization of neural networks and to improved motor abilities in the limbs with extremely severe movement deficits.

Patients learned over 20 sessions to control a neuroprosthetic device fixed to arm and hand of the paretic limb by decreasing the power of the sensorimotor rhythm of the ipsilesional motor cortex. Patients were instructed to change their brain rhythm with an actual movement of the paralyzed arm even if no movement was possible. While in a first proof of concept study (Buch et al., 2008) no generalization of improvement outside the laboratory occurred, an additional behavioral physiotherapy targeted at generalization of the BCI effects and online proprioceptive feedback of brain oscillations resulted in marked rehabilitation effects in a contingent reward-feedback group only (Ramos-Murguialday et al., 2012). A control group receiving random feedback of brain activity showed no improvement and no change in cortical and subcortical reorganization. A remarkable consistent pattern of brain

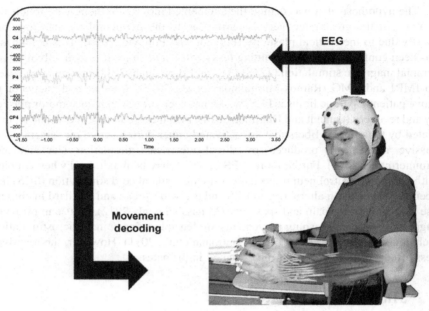

FIG. 3

Brain–machine interface in severe chronic stroke. In order to rewire motor intention and movement, EEG activity over the motor perilesional area (*left upper insert*) is used to drive an exoskeleton attached to patient's arm/hand (*bottom right insert*). The patients are instructed to try to move and if they "produce" a desynchronization of sensorimotor rhythm their hand/arm moves. This contingent and concurrent connection allows instrumental learning and rewiring of cortical areas responsible for motor execution/intention with the intended movement's afferent activity.

reorganization and connectivity changes occurred in the successfully treated patients. This randomized controlled double-blind study proved BCI efficacy in chronic stroke motor rehabilitation and assessed cortical and subcortical reorganization including functional and structural connectivity measures in stroke patients without residual movements (Ramos-Murguialday et al., 2012). Recent controlled clinical studies have confirmed these results (Ang et al., 2014; Ono et al., 2014; Pichiorri et al., 2015) and optimized using brain stimulation techniques (Kasashima-Shindo et al., 2015).

The choice of brain activity from the lesioned hemisphere originates in reports that stroke patients that recover motor function rely on activity in a motor network that highly resembles that in normal individuals (predominantly contralateral) (Calautti and Baron, 2003) and those indicating that upregulation of activity in ipsilesional regions and downregulation in contralesional areas (Hummel and Cohen, 2006; Pascual-Leone et al., 2005), at least in some patients result in clinical improvements.

Proficient neuroprosthetic control achieved through transform learning reversibly reshapes cortical networks through local effects (Ganguly et al., 2011) and can trigger a large-scale modification of the cortical network centered on the direct neurons, ie, those causally related to motor output, even in perilesional areas (Gulati et al., 2015).

Recent experiments (Nishimura et al., 2013) demonstrated corticospinal synaptic plasticity in vivo at the level of single neurons induced by normal firing patterns during free behavior. This was achieved using an autonomous recurrent neural interface that delivers electrical stimuli in the spinal cord triggered by action potentials of corticospinal cells in nonhuman primates during free behavior. Furthermore, Lucas and Fetz (2013) demonstrated that artificial afferent feedback could reorganize motor cortex outputs and suggested that under normal conditions corticomuscular relations are maintained through physiological feedback loops.

Most of the existing neural interfaces are used almost exclusively to control the "kinematics" and not the "kinetics" of paretic limb movement (Bensmaia and Miller, 2014). If only brain control is used, there is no involvement of the muscles. This might impede functional reorganization of the neural network involved in functional visuomotor tasks, becoming a simple brain control of assistive technology that once switched off or taken away condemns the patient to return to previous motor impairment level. Therefore, a hybrid approach should be explored, where residual muscle activity is included in the contingent connection between perilesional cortical areas and movement related afferent feedback.

Furthermore, residual EMG activity in paralyzed limbs in approximately 45% of severe chronic stroke patients can be used to decode movement intention and therefore, it can be used for rehabilitation robotics control (Ramos-Murguialday et al., 2014).

In BCI-based neurorehabilitation, plasticity has been shown to be induced if the response latency relative to the user's current intention is in the order of a few hundred milliseconds or smaller (Xu et al., 2014). While upper-limb recovery has been extensively investigated, lower limb and gait function have only recently been explored in combination with BCIs for the detection of movement intention (Jiang and Rehbaum, 2014).

4.3 TAKING ADVANTAGE OF BRAIN STIMULATION

Developing new motor rehabilitation neural interfaces for functional motor rehabilitation requires greater understanding of the neurophysiology of the neural network involved in functional recovery. Despite of all the molecular, cellular, and physiological changes that have been identified during recovery (Ganguly et al., 2013), their contribution to functional neuroplastic mechanisms remains unclear.

A key mechanism by which neuronal activity drives plasticity is credited to Hebb (1945) who proposed that "some growth process or metabolic change" occurs to strengthen the connectivity between two neurons when their activities exhibit a persistent causal relationship with one another (ie, "cells that fire together wire together"). This process involves synaptic potentiation as well as structural changes such as axon sprouting and the formation and stabilization of new dendritic spines and can be imposed artificially using three stimulation paradigms, namely, repetitive stimulation, paired stimulation, and closed-loop stimulation (Jackson and Zimmermann, 2012). Furthermore, recent empirical studies demonstrated how noninvasive brain stimulation (NIBS) might influence excitability of neural circuits at subcortical and spinal levels (Edwardson et al., 2013).

TMS-based brain stimulation techniques like intermittent theta burst stimulation (TBS) on the primary motor cortex (M1) have demonstrated M1 corticospinal excitability and M1 receptiveness to sensory input (Ackerley et al., 2014). Therefore, intermittent TBS at the ipsilesional M1 could be used to enhance ipsilesional sensorimotor integration and facilitate sensorimotor training after stroke. Cerebellar TDCS (cTDCS) could be used to strengthen the connection between the cerebellum and M1, which is known to change in association with motor learning. Recent findings are clinically promising, as cTDCS might provide a useful approach to enhance stroke rehabilitation strategies that focus on adaptive learning such as robot-assisted therapy (Grimaldi et al., 2016). However, the exact mechanisms and area of influence of cTDCS need to be further investigated.

Recent work has suggested transcranial lasers as a tool to enhance neural activity (Gonzalez-Lima and Barrett, 2014), despite failing to prove the efficacy of this technology to promote recovery in the acute phase when applied passively (Hacke et al., 2014).

Photoneuromodulation involves the absorption of photons by specific molecules in neurons that activate bioenergetic signaling pathways after exposure to red-to-near-infrared light. An effective transcranial near-infrared laser treatment (NILT) energy dose stimulates brain adenosine-5′-triphosphate (ATP) production (Lapchak and Taboada, 2010) and blood flow (Uozumi et al., 2010). ATP-dependent membrane ion pumps will be activated leading to greater membrane stability and resistance to depolarization, which has been shown to transiently reduce neuronal excitability (ie, neural inhibition) (Konstantinović et al., 2013). M1 TMS and TDCS are neural stimulation techniques generating electromagnetic fields, which corrupt many of the neurophysiological means to interface neural networks at brain level. NILT and maybe cTDCS could be applied before and during the neural interface intervention without generating electromagnetic stimulation artifacts. However, the neurophysiological changes due to NILT stimulation need to be further investigated. Furthermore, NILT noninvasively targets cytochrome oxidase, a key enzyme for energy production, with induced expression linked to energy demand. Hence NILT is mechanistically specific and noninvasive, while TMS and TDCS stimulation are nonspecific.

It is noteworthy to mention that for stroke recovery, protocols that aim at suppressing excitability of the contralesional hemisphere may be contraindicated for some patients, emphasizing that NIBS is not "one-size-fits-all." Therefore, more trials on stroke patients for a better understanding related to the neurophysiological effects of NIBS are needed.

5 FUTURE PERSPECTIVE

At present the database for the application of BCIs for communication in the completely paralyzed is thin and only available for LIS in ALS. EEG-based BCIs are currently being used to provide basic communication to patient in LIS but not in CLIS. Recently, fNIRS-based BCI was developed and tested successfully to provide basic communication to patient in CLIS. The effectiveness of current BCIs can be improved by using multiple neuronal signals, which is currently being investigated in several labs. Invasive and noninvasive BCIs using more than one type of brain signals have a bright future because no alternative exists for communication and no alternative to BCI will exist in the near future. Currently the use of BCI technologies is carried out in presence and supervision of technical expert. The BCI technologies can be taken out of the research laboratory only if the intricacy of the system is simplified and the need of technical support can be reduced. Thus the use of BCI technologies will depend on further improvements in the ease and convenience of their daily use. Extensive replication of the initial promising results in ALS and subcortical stroke to vast patient population (including patient with disorders of consciousness; Coyle et al., 2015; Cruse et al., 2011; Owen and Coleman, 2008) is of utmost clinical importance, with a good chance of at least minimal social interaction and communication in these uncommunicative patient groups. For severe chronic stroke without residual hand movement, noninvasive neuroelectric-based BCI training in continuation with physiotherapy targeted at the generalization to the social environment is a promising and economically feasible option. However, an increase of degree of freedom for motor restoration and probably also neuronal plasticity and recovery at a cellular level ask for an invasive approach with implanted and if possible wireless electrode arrays. Invasive BCI arrays will be permanently connected to peripheral neuroprosthetic devices, exoskeletons, and FES at the cortical, spinal, and neuromuscular level. These invasive approaches will largely profit from progress in the field of high spinal cord injury and vice versa, ie, invasive and noninvasive. Epidural electrical stimulation already resulted in an astonishing degree of spinal reorganization and neuromuscular recovery. The combination of BCI and facilitating brain reorganization using NIBS before or during BCI may benefit the induction of functional neuroplasticity. Motivation and engagement should be considered as a fundamental part of the rehabilitation and new gaming and inclusive approaches should be further developed and tested.

ACKNOWLEDGMENTS

We acknowledge the participation of all our patients, funding sources: Ministero della Salute, Rome, Italy Progetto No 2614726: Approchi reabilitativi, Baden-Wurttemberg Stiftung (GRUENS-Rob1), the Indian–European collaborative research and technological development projects (INDIGO-DTB2-051), the Natural Science Foundation of China (NSFC 31450110072), National Natural Science Foundation of China (Grant number: 61550110252), EU COST action

TD1006, Deutsche Forschungsgemeinschaft (DFG, Koselleck), Volkswagen Stiftung and Bundes Ministerium fur Bildung und Forschung BMBF MOTOR-BIC (FKZ 13GW0053), Ministry of Science, Research and the Arts of Baden Wüttemberg (Az: 32-729.63-0/5-5), and EMOIO from the Federal ministry of Education and Research (524-4013-16SV7196).

Declaration of interests: The authors declare no conflicts of interests.

REFERENCES

Ackerley, S.J., Stinear, C.M., Barber, P.A., Byblow, W.D., 2014. Priming sensorimotor cortex to enhance task-specific training after subcortical stroke. Clin. Neurophysiol. 125 (7), 1451–1458.

Ang, K.K., et al., 2011. A large clinical study on the ability of stroke patients to use an EEG-based motor imagery brain-computer interface. Clin. EEG Neurosci. 42 (4), 253–258.

Ang, K.K., Guan, C., Phua, K.S., Wang, C., Zhou, L., Tang, K.Y., Joseph, G.J.E., Kuah, C.W.K., Chua, K.S.G., 2014. Brain-computer interface-based robotic end effector system for wrist and hand rehabilitation: results of a three-armed randomized controlled trial for chronic stroke. Front. Neuroeng. 7.

Bai, O., et al., 2010. Towards a user-friendly brain-computer interface: initial tests in ALS and PLS patients. Clin. Neurophysiol. 121 (8), 1293–1303.

Ball, L.J.B., 2007. Duration of AAC technology use by persons with ALS. J. Speech Lang. Path. 15 (4), 371.

Bauer, G., Gerstenbrand, F., Rumpl, E., 1979. Varieties of the locked-in syndrome. J. Neurol. 221 (2), 77–91.

Belda-Lois, J.-M., et al., 2011. Rehabilitation of gait after stroke: a review towards a top-down approach. J. Neuroeng. Rehabil. 8 (1), 66.

Bensmaia, S.J., Miller, L.E., 2014. Restoring sensorimotor function through intracortical interfaces: progress and looming challenges. Nat. Rev. Neurosci. 15 (5), 313–325.

Berger, W.L., et al., 1979. Self-regulation of slow cortical potentials in normal subjects and patients with frontal lobe lesions. Prog. Brain Res. 54, 427–430.

Beukelman, D.R., Mirenda, P., 2005. Augmentative & Alternative Communication: Supporting Children & Adults with Complex Communication Needs, third ed. Paul H. Brookes Publishing, Baltimore, MD.

Birbaumer, N., 1977. Operant enhancement of EEG-theta activity: aspiration and reality. In: Beatty, In J., Legewie, H. (Eds.), Biofeedback and Behavior. Plenum Press, New York, pp. 135–146.

Birbaumer, N., 1999. Slow cortical potentials: plasticity, operant control, and behavioral effects. Neuroscientist 5 (2), 74–78.

Birbaumer, N., 2006. Breaking the silence: brain-computer interfaces (BCI) for communication and motor control. Psychophysiology 43 (6), 517–532.

Birbaumer, N., Chaudhary, U., 2015. Learning from brain control: clinical application of brain–computer interfaces. e-Neuroforum 6 (4), 87–95.

Birbaumer, N., Cohen, L.G., 2007. Brain-computer interfaces: communication and restoration of movement in paralysis. J. Physiol. 579 (Pt. 3), 621–636.

Birbaumer, N., Roberts, L., 1992. Area-specific self-regulation of slow cortical potentials on the sagittal midline and its effects on behavior. Electroencephalogr. Clin. Neurophysiol. 84 (4), 353–361.

Birbaumer, N., Elbert, T., Rockstroh, B., Lutzenberger, W., 1986. Biofeedback of slow cortical potentials in attentional disorders. Cerebral Psychophysiology: Studies in Event-Related Potentials. pp. 440–442.

Birbaumer, N., Elbert, T., Canavan, A.G., Rockstroh, B., 1990. Slow potentials of the cerebral cortex and behavior. Physiol. Rev. 70 (1), 1–41.

Birbaumer, N., et al., 1994. Behavioral treatment of scoliosis and kyphosis. J. Psychosom. Res. 38 (6), 623–628.

Birbaumer, N., et al., 1999. A spelling device for the paralysed. Nature 398 (6725), 297–298.

Birbaumer, N., Murguialday, A.R., Cohen, L., 2008. Brain-computer interface in paralysis. Curr. Opin. Neurol. 21 (6), 634–638.

Birbaumer, N., et al., 2009. Chapter 8 neurofeedback and brain-computer interface. Clinical applications. Int. Rev. Neurobiol. 86 (09), 107–117.

Birbaumer, N., et al., 2012. Ideomotor silence: the case of complete paralysis and brain-computer interfaces (BCI). Psychol. Res. 76 (2), 183–191.

Birbaumer, N., Ruiz, S., Sitaram, R., 2013. Learned regulation of brain metabolism. Trends Cogn. Sci. 17 (6), 295–302.

Buch, E., et al., 2008. Think to move: a neuromagnetic brain-computer interface (BCI) system for chronic stroke. Stroke 39 (3), 910–917.

Calautti, C., Baron, J., 2003. Functional neuroimaging studies of motor recovery after stroke in adults a review. Stroke 34 (6), 1553–1566.

Caria, A., et al., 2007. Regulation of anterior insular cortex activity using real-time fMRI. Neuroimage 35 (3), 1238–1246.

Chapin, J.K., et al., 1999. Real-time control of a robot arm using simultaneously recorded neurons in the motor cortex. Nat. Neurosci. 2 (7), 664–670.

Chaudhary, U., et al., 2011. Frontal activation and connectivity using near-infrared spectroscopy: verbal fluency language study. Brain Res. Bull. 84 (3), 197–205.

Chaudhary, U., et al., 2014. Motor response investigation in individuals with cerebral palsy using near infrared spectroscopy: pilot study. Appl. Opt. 53 (3), 503–510.

Chollet, F., et al., 2011. Fluoxetine for motor recovery after acute ischaemic stroke (FLAME): a randomised placebo-controlled trial. Lancet Neurol. 10 (2), 123–130.

Chou, S.M., Norris, F.H., 1993. Issues & opinions: amyotrophic lateral sclerosis: lower motor neuron disease spreading to upper motor neurons. Muscle Nerve 16 (8), 864–869.

Cirstea, M.C., Ptito, A., Levin, M.F., 2003. Arm reaching improvements with short-term practice depend on the severity of the motor deficit in stroke. Exp. Brain Res. 152 (4), 476–488.

Coyle, D., et al., 2015. Sensorimotor modulation assessment and brain-computer interface training in disorders of consciousness. Arch. Phys. Med. Rehabil. 96 (3), S62–S70.

Cruse, D., et al., 2011. Bedside detection of awareness in the vegetative state: a cohort study. Lancet 378 (9809), 2088–2094.

Cuthbert, B., et al., 1981. Strategies of arousal control: biofeedback, meditation, and motivation. J. Exp. Psychol. Gen. 110 (4), 518.

DeCharms, R.C., et al., 2004. Learned regulation of spatially localized brain activation using real-time fMRI. NeuroImage 21 (1), 436–443.

De Massari, D., et al., 2013. Brain communication in the locked-in state. Brain 136 (6), 1989–2000.

Donoghue, J.P., 2002. Connecting cortex to machines: recent advances in brain interfaces. Nat. Neurosci. 5, 1085–1088.

Donoghue, J.P., et al., 2007. Assistive technology and robotic control using motor cortex ensemble-based neural interface systems in humans with tetraplegia. J. Physiol. 579 (3), 603–611.

Dworkin, B., 1993. Learning and Physiological Regulation. University of Chicago Press, Chicago.

Dworkin, B.R., Miller, N.E., 1986. Failure to replicate visceral learning in the acute curarized rat preparation. Behav. Neurosci 100 (3), 299.

Edwardson, M.A., Lucas, T.H., Carey, J.R., Fetz, E.E., 2013. New modalities of brain stimulation for stroke rehabilitation. Exp. Brain Res. 224 (3), 335–358.

Elbert, T., 1993. Slow Cortical Potentials Reflect the Regulation of Cortical Excitability.

Farwell, L.A., Donchin, E., 1988. Talking off the top of your head: toward a mental prosthesis utilizing event-related brain potentials. Electroencephalogr. Clin. Neurophysiol. 70 (6), 510–523.

Felton, E., et al., 2007. Electrocorticographically controlled brain-computer interfaces using motor and sensory imagery in patients with temporary subdural electrode implants: report of four cases. J. Neurosurg. 106 (3), 495–500.

Fetz, E., 1969. Operant conditioning of cortical activity unit. Science 163, 955–958.

Flor, H., Birbaumer, N., 1993. Comparison of the efficacy of electromyographic biofeedback, cognitive-behavioral therapy, and conservative medical interventions in the treatment of chronic musculoskeletal pain. J. Consult. Clin. Psychol. 61 (4), 653.

Fuchs, T., et al., 2003. Neurofeedback treatment for attention-deficit/hyperactivity disorder in children: a comparison with methylphenidate. Appl. Psychophysiol. Biofeedback. 28 (1), 1–12.

Furdea, A., Ruf, C.A., Halder, S., De Massari, D., Bogdan, M., Rosenstiel, W., Matuz, T., Birbaumer, N., 2012. A new (semantic) reflexive brain–computer interface: in search for a suitable classifier. J. Neurosci. Methods 203 (1), 233–240.

Gallegos-Ayala, G., et al., 2014. Brain communication in a completely locked-in patient using bedside near-infrared spectroscopy. Neurology 82 (21), 1930–1932.

Ganguly, K., et al., 2011. Reversible large-scale modification of cortical networks during neuroprosthetic control. Nat. Neurosci. 14 (5), 662–667.

Ganguly, K., Byl, N.N., Abrams, G.M., 2013. Neurorehabilitation: motor recovery after stroke as an example. Ann. Neurol. 74 (3), 373–381.

Gilja, V., et al., 2015. Clinical translation of a high-performance neural prosthesis. Nat. Med. 21 (10), 1142–1145.

Gonzalez-Lima, F., Barrett, D.W., 2014. Augmentation of cognitive brain functions with transcranial lasers, Front. Syst. Neurosci. 8, 36.

Grimaldi, G., Argyropoulos, G.P., Bastian, A., Cortes, M., Davis, N.J., Edwards, D.J., Ferrucci, R., Fregni, F., Galea, J.M., Hamada, M., Manto, M., 2016. Cerebellar transcranial direct current stimulation (ctDCS): a novel approach to understanding cerebellar function inhealth and disease. Neuroscientist 22 (1), 83–97.

Gulati, T., et al., 2015. Robust neuroprosthetic control from the stroke perilesional cortex. J. Neurosci. 35 (22), 8653–8661.

Gupta, P., Cohen, N.J., 2002. Theoretical and computational analysis of skill learning, repetition priming, and procedural memory. Psychol. Rev. 109 (2), 401–448.

Hacke, W., Schellinger, P.D., Albers, G.W., Bornstein, N.M., Dahlof, B.L., Fulton, R., Kasner, S.E., Shuaib, A., Richieri, S.P., Dilly, S.G., Zivin, J., 2014. Transcranial laser therapy in acute stroke treatment results of neurothera effectiveness and safety trial 3, a phase III clinical end point device trial. Stroke 45 (11), 3187–3193.

Halder, S., et al., 2011. Neural mechanisms of brain-computer interface control. NeuroImage 55 (4), 1779–1790.

Hebb, D.O., 1945. Man's frontal lobe: a critical review. Arch. Neurol. Psychiatry 54, 421–438.

Hendricks, H.T., et al., 2002. Motor recovery after stroke: a systematic review of the literature. archives of physical medicine and rehabilitation. Arch. Phys. Med. Rehabil. 83 (11), 1629–1637.

Hinterberger, T., et al., 2005a. Neuronal mechanisms underlying control of a brain–computer interface. Eur. J. Neurosci. 21 (11), 3169–3181.

Hinterberger, T., Birbaumer, N., Flor, H., 2005b. Assessment of cognitive function and communication ability in a completely locked-in patient. Neurology 64 (7), 1307–1308.

Hinterberger, T., et al., 2008. Voluntary brain regulation and communication with electrocorticogram signals. Epilepsy Behav. 13 (2), 300–306.

Hochberg, L.R., et al., 2006. Neuronal ensemble control of prosthetic devices by a human with tetraplegia. Nature 442 (7099), 164–171.

Holland, J., Skinner, B., 1961. The Analysis of Behavior: A program for Self-Instruction. Mc Graw-Hill, New York.

Hummel, F., Cohen, L., 2006. Non-invasive brain stimulation: a new strategy to improve neurorehabilitation after stroke? Lancet Neurol. 5 (8), 708–712.

Jackson, A., Zimmermann, J., 2012. Neural interfaces for the brain and spinal cord-restoring motor function—restoring motor function. Nat. Rev. Neurol. 8 (12), 690–699.

Jiang, N., Rehbaum, H., 2014. Intuitive, online, simultaneous, and proportional myoelectric control over two degrees-of-freedom in upper limb amputees. IEEE Trans. Neural Syst. Rehab. 22 (3), 501–510.

Kamiya, J., 1971. Biofeedback and Self-control: An Aldine Reader on the Regulation of Bodily Processes and Consciousness.

Kasashima-Shindo, Y., et al., 2015. Brain–computer interface training combined with transcranial direct current stimulation in patients with chronic severe hemiparesis: proof of concept study. J. Rehabil. Med. 47 (4), 318–324.

Kennedy, P.R., Bakay, R.a., 1998. Restoration of neural output from a paralyzed patient by a direct brain connection. Neuroreport 9 (8), 1707–1711.

Kennedy, P.R., et al., 2000. Direct control of a computer from the human central nervous system. IEEE Trans. Rehabil. Eng. 8 (2), 198–202.

Kennedy, P., et al., 2004. Using human extra-cortical local field potentials to control a switch. J. Neural Eng. 1 (2), 72–77.

Klamroth-Marganska, V., et al., 2014. Three-dimensional, task-specific robot therapy of the arm after stroke: a multicentre, parallel-group randomised trial. Lancet Neurol. 13 (2), 159–166.

Konstantinović, L., et al., 2013. Transcranial application of near-infrared low level laser can modulate cortical excitability. Lasers Surg. Med. 45 (10), 648–653.

Koralek, A.C., et al., 2012. Corticostriatal plasticity is necessary for learning intentional neuroprosthetic skills. Nature 483 (7389), 331–335.

Kotchoubey, B., Strehl, U., Uhlmann, C., Holzapfel, S., Ko, M., et al., 2001. Modification of slow cortical potentials in patients with refractory epilepsy: a controlled outcome study. Epilepsia 42 (3), 406–416.

Krakauer, J.W., et al., 2012. Getting neurorehabilitation right: what can be learned from animal models? Neurorehabil. Neural Repair 26 (8), 923–931.

Kübler, A., Birbaumer, N., 2008. Brain-computer interfaces and communication in paralysis: extinction of goal directed thinking in completely paralysed patients? Clin. Neurophysiol. 119 (11), 2658–2666.

Kubler, A., et al., 2001. Brain-computer communication: self-regulation of slow cortical potentials for verbal communication. Arch. Phys. Med. Rehabil. 82 (11), 1533–1539.

Kübler, A., Nijboer, F., Mellinger, J., Vaughan, T.M., Pawelzik, H., Schalk, G., McFarland, D.J., Birbaumer, N., Wolpaw, J.R., 2005. Patients with ALS can use sensorimotor rhythms to operate a brain-computer interface. Neurology 64 (10), 1775–1777.

Langhorne, P., Bernhardt, J., Kwakkel, G., 2015. Stroke rehabilitation. Lancet 377 (9778), 1693–1702.

Lapchak, P., Taboada, L.D., 2010. Transcranial near infrared laser treatment (NILT) increases cortical adenosine-5′-triphosphate (ATP) content following embolic strokes in rabbits. Brain Res. 1306, 100–105.

Lebedev, M.a., Nicolelis, M.a.L., 2006. Brain-machine interfaces: past, present and future. Trends Neurosci. 29 (9), 536–546.

León-Carrión, J., et al., 2002. The locked-in syndrome: a syndrome looking for a therapy. Brain Inj. 16 (7), 571–582.

Leuthardt, E.C., et al., 2004. A brain–computer interface using electrocorticographic signals in humans. J. Neural Eng. 1 (2), 63–71.

Lin, K., et al., 2008. Effects of constraint-induced therapy versus bilateral arm training on motor performance, daily functions, and quality of life in stroke survivors. Neurorehabil. Neural Repair 23, 441–448.

Lucas, T.H., Fetz, E.E., 2013. Myo-cortical crossed feedback reorganizes primate motor cortex output. J. Neurosci. 33 (12), 5261–5274.

Lutzenberger, W., Roberts, L., Birbaumer, N., 1993. Memory performance and area-specific self-regulation of slow cortical potentials: dual-task interference. Int. J. Psychophysiol. 15 (3), 217–226.

Miller, N.E., 1969. Learning of visceral and glandular responses. Science 163 (866), 434–445.

Minassian, K., et al., 2012. neuromodulation of lower limb motor control in restorative neurology. Clin. Neurol. Neurosurg. 114 (5), 489–497.

Monastra, V.J., et al., 2006. Electroencephalographic biofeedback in the treatment of attention-deficit/hyperactivity disorder. J. Neurother. 9 (4), 5–34.

Moritz, C.T., et al., 2007. Forelimb movements and muscle responses evoked by stimulation of cervical micro spinal cord in sedated monkeys. J. Neurophysiol. 97 (1), 110–120.

Mugler, E.M., et al., 2010. Design and implementation of a P300-based brain-computer interface for controlling an internet browser. IEEE Trans. Neural Syst. Rehabil. Eng. 18 (6), 599–609.

Murguialday, A.R., 2011. Transition from the locked in to the completely locked-in state: a physiological analysis. Clin. Neurophysiol. 122 (5), 925–933.

Naito, M., et al., 2007. A communication means for totally blood volume measured with. IEICE Trans. Inf. Syst. E90-D (7), 1028–1037.

Neumann, N., et al., 2004. Automatic processing of self-regulation of slow cortical potentials: evidence from brain-computer communication in paralyzed patients. Clin. Neurophysiol. 115 (3), 628–635.

Nicolelis, M.A.L., 2003. Neural Circuits. Neuroscience 4 (May), e27488.

Nijboer, F., Sellers, E.W., et al., 2008a. A P300-based brain-computer interface for people with amyotrophic lateral sclerosis. Clin. Neurophysiol. 119 (8), 1909–1916.

Nijboer, F., Furdea, A., et al., 2008b. An auditory brain–computer interface (BCI). J. Neurosci. Methods 167 (1), 43–50.

Nishimura, Y., et al., 2013. Spike-timing-dependent plasticity in primate corticospinal connections induced during free behavior. Neuron 80 (5), 1301–1309.

Obrig, H., 2014. NIRS in clinical neurology - a "promising" tool? NeuroImage 85, 535–546.

Ono, T., et al., 2014. Brain-computer interface with somatosensory feedback improves functional recovery from severe hemiplegia due to chronic stroke. Front. Neuroeng. 7, 19.

Owen, A.M., Coleman, M.R., 2008. Functional neuroimaging of the vegetative state. Nat. Rev. Neuroscience 9 (3), 235–243.

Pascual-Leone, A., et al., 2005. The plastic human brain cortex. Ann. Rev. Neurosci. 28, 377–401.

Pfurtscheller, G., et al., 1998. Separability of EEG signals recorded during right and left motor imagery using adaptive autoregressive parameters. IEEE Trans. Rehabil. Eng. 6 (3), 316–325.

Pfurtscheller, G., et al., 2003. Thought" – control of functional electrical stimulation to restore hand grasp in a patient with tetraplegia. Neurosci. Lett. 351 (1), 33–36.

Pfurtscheller, G., Neuper, C., Birbaumer, N., 2005. Human brain–computer interface (BCI). In: Riehle, A., Vaadia, E. (Eds.), Motor Cortex in Voluntary Movements. A Distributed System for Distributed Functions. CRC Press, Boca Raton, FL, pp. 367–401.

Pichiorri, F., et al., 2015. Brain–computer interface boosts motor imagery practice during stroke recovery. Ann. Neurol. 77 (5), 851–865.

Pires, G., Nunes, U., Castelo-Branco, M., 2011. Statistical spatial filtering for a P300-based BCI: tests in able-bodied, and patients with cerebral palsy and amyotrophic lateral sclerosis. J. Neurosci. Methods 195 (2), 270–281.

Pomeroy, V., Aglioti, S., 2011. Neurological principles and rehabilitation of action disorders rehabilitation interventions. Neurorehabil. Neural Repair 25 (5 suppl.), 33S–43S.

Popovic, D., Popovic, M., 2006. Hybrid assistive system for rehabilitation: lessons learned from functional electrical therapy in hemiplegics. In: Engineering in Medicine and Biology Society, 2006. EMBS'06. 28th Annual International Conference of the IEEE (pp. 2146-2149). IEEE.

Prasad, G., et al., 2010. Applying a brain-computer interface to support motor imagery practice in people with stroke for upper limb recovery: a feasibility study. J. Neuroeng. Rehabil. 7 (1), 60.

Quandt, F., Hummel, F., 2014. The influence of functional electrical stimulation on motor recovery in stroke patients hand. Exp. Transl. Stroke Med. 6, 9.

Ramos-Murguialday, A., et al., 2012. Proprioceptive feedback and brain computer interface (BCI) based neuroprostheses. PLoS One 7 (10), e47048.

Ramos-Murguialday, A., et al., 2014. Brain-machine-interface in chronic stroke rehabilitation: a controlled study. Ann. Neurol. 74 (1), 100–108.

Rockstroh, B., et al., 1993. Cortical self-regulation in patients with epilepsies. Epilepsy Res. 14 (1), 63–72.

Ruf, C.a., 2013. Semantic conditioning of salivary pH for communication. Artif. Intell. Med. 59 (2), 1–8.

Saka, O., McGuire, A., Wolfe, C., 2008. Cost of stroke in the United Kingdom. Age Ageing 38 (1), 27–32.

Savitz, S.I., et al., 2014. Stem cells as an emerging paradigm in stroke 3: enhancing the development of clinical trials. Stroke 45 (2), 634–639.

Schneider, F., Koch, J.D., Mattes, R., 1992. Heimann Das erkennen von emotionen ans dem gesichtsausdruck bie viseullen halbfelddarbietungen durch schizophrene und depressive patienten. Nervenarzt 63, 545–550.

Sellers, E.W., Donchin, E., 2006. A P300-based brain-computer interface: initial tests by ALS patients. Clin. Neurophysiol. 117 (3), 538–548.

Sellers, E.W., Vaughan, T.M., Wolpaw, J.R., 2010. A brain-computer interface for long-term independent home use. Amyotroph. Lateral Scler. 11 (5), 449–455.

Serruya, M., Hatsopoulos, N., Paninski, L., 2002. Brain-machine interface: instant neural control of a movement signal. Nature 416 (6877), 141–142.

Skinner, B.F., 1953. Science and Human Behavior. Macmillan. Private events, New York.

Smith, E., Delargy, M., 2005. Locked-in syndrome. BMJ 330 (February), 3–6.

Soekadar, S.R., et al., 2014. Brain–machine interfaces in neurorehabilitation of stroke. Neurobiol. Dis. 83, 172–179.

Squire, L., 1987. Memory and Brain. Oxford University Press, New York.

Sterman, M., 1981. EEG biofeedback: physiological behavior modification. Neurosci. Biobehav. Rev. 5 (3), 405–412.

Sterman, M., Clemente, C., 1962a. Forebrain inhibitory mechanisms: cortical synchronization induced by basal forebrain stimulation. Exp. Neurol. 6 (2), 91–102.

Sterman, M., Clemente, C., 1962b. Forebrain inhibitory mechanisms: sleep patterns induced by basal forebrain stimulation in the cat behaving. Exp. Neurol. 6 (2), 103–117.

Sterman, M., Friar, L., 1972. Suppression of seizures in epileptic Following on sensorimotor EEG feedback training. Electroencephalogr. Clin. Neurophysiol. 33 (1), 89–95.

Sterman, M.B., MacDonald, L.R., 1979. Effects of central cortical EEG feedback training on incidence of poorly controlled seizures. In: Mind/Body Integration. Springer, pp. 347–362.

Stocco, A., Lebiere, C., Anderson, J.R., 2010. Conditional routing of information to the cortex: a model of the basal Ganglia's role in cognitive coordination. Psychol. Rev. 117 (2), 541–574.

Talwar, S., et al., 2002. Behavioural neuroscience: rat navigation guided by remote control. Nature 417 (6884), 37–38.

Thorns, J., et al., 2010. Movement initiation and inhibition are impaired in amyotrophic lateral sclerosis. Exp. Neurol. 224 (2), 389–394.

Turner, D.L., et al., 2013. Neurophysiology of robot-mediated training and therapy: a perspective for future use in clinical populations. Front. Neurol. 4 (November), 1–11.

Tyč, F., Boyadjian, A., 2011. Plasticity of motor cortex induced by coordination and training. Clin. Neurophysiol. 122 (1), 153–162.

Uozumi, Y., Nawashiro, H., Sato, S., Kawauchi, S., Shima, K., Kikuchi, M., 2010. Targeted increase in cerebral blood flow by transcranial near-infrared laser irradiation. Lasers Surg. Med. 42 (6), 566–576.

Velliste, M., et al., 2008. Cortical control of a prosthetic arm for self-feeding. Nature 453 (7198), 1098–1101.

Walter, W., 1964. Contingent negative variation-electrocortical sign of significant association in human brain. In: 364 Science146, American Association Advancement Science, Washington, DC, p. 434.

Weiskopf, N., et al., 2003. Physiological self-regulation of regional brain activity using real-time functional magnetic resonance imaging (fMRI): methodology and exemplary data. Neuroimage 19 (3), 577–586.

Wessberg, J., et al., 2000. Real-time prediction of hand trajectory by ensembles of cortical neurons in primates. Nature 408, 361–365.

Wilhelm, B., Jordan, M., Birbaumer, N., 2006. Communication in locked-in syndrome: effects of imagery on salivary pH. Neurology 67 (3), 534–535.

Wolpaw, J.R., McFarland, D.J., 2004. Control of a two-dimensional movement signal by a noninvasive brain-computer interface in humans. Proc. Natl. Acad. Sci. U. S. A. 101 (51), 17849–17854.

Wolpaw, J.R., et al., 2002. Brain-computer interfaces for communication and control. Clin. Neurophysiol. 113 (6), 767–791.

Xu, R., Jiang, N., Lin, C., Mrachacz-Kersting, N., Dremstrup, K., Farina, D., 2014. Enhanced low-latency detection of motor intention from EEG for closed-loop brain-computer interface applications. IEEE Trans. Biomed. Eng. 61 (2), 288–296.

Yoo, S.-S., et al., 2013. Non-invasive brain-to-brain interface (BBI): establishing functional links between two brains. PLoS One 8 (4), e60410.

Young, J., Forster, A., 2007. Review of stroke rehabilitation. BMJ 334 (7584), 86–90. Clinical research ed.

Zhu, D., Bieger, J., Molina, G.G., Aarts, R.M., 2010. A survey of stimulation methods used in SSVEP-based BCIs. Comput. Intell. Neurosci. 2010, 1.

Ziessler, M., Nattkemper, D., Frensch, P.A., 2004. The role of anticipation and intention in the learning of effects of self-performed actions. Psychol. Res 68 (2-3), 163–175.

Zimmermann, J., Seki, K., Jackson, A., 2011. Reanimating the arm and hand with intraspinal microstimulation. J. Neural Eng. 8 (5), 054001.

Brain–machine interfaces for rehabilitation of poststroke hemiplegia

J. Ushiba[*,1], S.R. Soekadar[†]

Faculty of Science and Technology, Keio University, Kohoku-ku, Yokohama, Kanagawa, Japan
†Applied Neurotechnology Laboratory, University Hospital of Tübingen, Tübingen, Germany
1Corresponding author: Tel.: +81-45-566-1678; Fax: +81-45-566-1678,
e-mail address: ushiba@brain.bio.keio.ac.jp

Abstract

Noninvasive brain–machine interfaces (BMIs) are typically associated with neuroprosthetic applications or communication aids developed to assist in daily life after loss of motor function, eg, in severe paralysis. However, BMI technology has recently been found to be a powerful tool to promote neural plasticity facilitating motor recovery after brain damage, eg, due to stroke or trauma. In such BMI paradigms, motor cortical output and input are simultaneously activated, for instance by translating motor cortical activity associated with the attempt to move the paralyzed fingers into actual exoskeleton-driven finger movements, resulting in contingent visual and somatosensory feedback. Here, we describe the rationale and basic principles underlying such BMI motor rehabilitation paradigms and review recent studies that provide new insights into BMI-related neural plasticity and reorganization. Current challenges in clinical implementation and the broader use of BMI technology in stroke neurorehabilitation are discussed.

Keywords

Brain–computer interface, Brain–machine interface, Sensorimotor cortex, Corticospinal tract, Neural plasticity, Motor learning, Rehabilitation, Hemiplegia

1 INTRODUCTION

Brain–computer interface (BCI), or alternatively, brain–machine interface (BMI) technology allows for the direct translation of brain activity into the control signals for a machine, robot, or computer (Wolpaw et al., 2002). After versatile robotic arm control via a real-time readout of motor intentions from cortical neural activity in rodents (Chapin et al., 1999) and nonhuman primates (Carmena et al., 2003) was recently demonstrated, an increasing number of human BMI studies exemplify the vast potential of this technology for the restoration of movement (Bouton et al., 2016; Hochberg et al.,

Progress in Brain Research, Volume 228, ISSN 0079-6123, http://dx.doi.org/10.1016/bs.pbr.2016.04.020
© 2016 Elsevier B.V. All rights reserved.

2012; for review: Birbaumer and Cohen, 2007; Soekadar et al., 2015a). For example, the control of a robotic arm (Hochberg et al., 2012; Yanagisawa et al., 2011), motor-driven orthosis (Pfurtscheller et al., 2000; Soekadar et al., 2011), neuromuscular functional electrical stimulation (FES) (Bouton et al., 2016; Heasman et al., 2002; Pfurtscheller et al., 2003), and virtual reality (Leeb et al., 2007) have been demonstrated in patients who are experiencing severe paralysis because of stroke, spinal cord injury, or muscular dystrophy. Besides being an innovative technological solution to replace or substitute for a lost function, BMI technology may serve as an effective tool to strengthen damaged neural pathways or induce cortical plasticity, eg, in the context of neurorehabilitation (Daly and Wolpaw, 2008; Soekadar et al., 2015a; Ushiba and Kasuga, 2015). As all established treatment strategies, eg, constraint-induced movement therapy (CIMT) (Taub et al., 1999), require some remaining voluntary movement ability (Kwakkel et al., 2015) or muscle contractions, 30–50% of all stroke survivors do not qualify for these strategies and might thus substantially benefit from recent advances in BMI technology and research.

Recently, it has been shown that repeated use of a BMI can promote the neural plasticity of motor maps and increase functional connectivity influencing motor behavior, eg, reaction time (Boulay et al., 2011). Based on this finding, BMIs are currently being tested as therapeutic tools for various brain disorders, such as attention-deficit disorder (Lim et al., 2012), epilepsy (Strehl et al., 2014), and depression (Zotev et al., 2016). Here, we provide an overview of the current state and future clinical applications of BMI technology in neurorehabilitation, while stressing the main challenges for the effective implementation of this novel technology into broader clinical practice. While focusing on noninvasive BMI strategies, particularly based on electroencephalography (EEG), successful translation of such approach from bench to bedside will be described as a pilot example for the auspicious perspectives, but also complex challenges that translational clinical neuroscience is currently facing. Besides introducing the rationale of current BMI designs and approaches targeting functional recovery, the advantages and disadvantages of either approach, eg, implantable and noninvasive BMIs, will be discussed. The basic concept of BMI-based neurorehabilitation relates to the idea that a functional deficit is reflected by a physiological "biomarker," which can be used (directly or indirectly) as target for a therapeutic (BMI) intervention (Fig. 1A). Besides depicting such rationale and basic principles of BMI-based neurorehabilitation, the broader context and integration of BMI technology into a comprehensive rehabilitation concept as basis for future evidence-based stroke neurorehabilitation guidelines will be introduced (Fig. 2B). Finally, unsolved technical and nontechnical issues and challenges, as well as a one-decade perspective for BMI neurorehabilitation will be addressed.

2 SIGNAL MODALITY OF BMI

There are various types of brain activity recordings used for human BMI applications. Whereas microelectrode arrays and electrocorticography offer high temporal

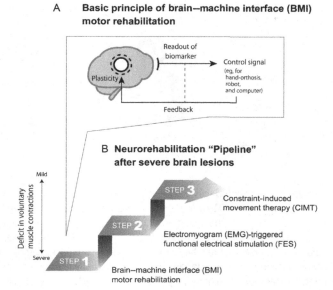

A   **Basic principle of brain—machine interface (BMI) motor rehabilitation**

B **Neurorehabilitation "Pipeline" after severe brain lesions**

FIG. 1

Basic principles and role of brain—machine interface (BMI) motor rehabilitation training in restoration of movements in poststroke hemiplegia. (A) Basic principle of BMI motor rehabilitation training. Brain physiological measures, such as electric, magnetic of metabolic activity, that were identified as "biomarkers" of a specific brain function or behavior are recorded and translated into control signals of external devices, such as hand-orthoses, robots, or computers. Control of these objects results in immediate sensory feedback contingently related to the physiological measure. Recently, paradigms were developed in which physiological measures are directly linked to electric or magnetic brain stimulation (indicated by the *black dotted line*), termed closed-loop stimulation paradigms.
(B) Neurorehabilitation "pipeline" after severe brain lesions. Depending on the severity of deficits in voluntary muscle contractions, a different rehabilitation approach is selected. In absence of any voluntary electromyographic (EMG) activity, brain physiological measures are used to restore movements as exemplified in (A). Once EMG activity is detectable, but insufficient to perform a movement related to daily life activities, such EMG-activity is used as trigger for functional electrical stimulation (FES) of the affected muscles. Once movements are sufficient to perform actions of daily life, constraint-induced movement therapy (CIMT) (Taub et al., 1999) becomes applied.

and spatial resolution in signal recordings resulting in high information transfer rates (Murphy et al., 2016), the invasiveness of such recordings represents a mental and physical burden for BMI users. Besides issues related to the implantation of the electrodes, there are several other challenges that relate to the long-term application of such devices, particularly related to biocompatibility, risk of infections, maintenance

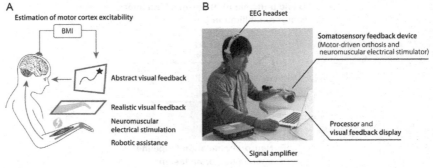

FIG. 2

Illustration of a brain–machine interface (BMI) system for motor rehabilitation used at Keio University, Japan (Ushiba et al., 2014). (A) System setup for BMI motor rehabilitation. Brain electric signals are recorded using electroencephalography (EEG) translated into various forms of feedback, eg, visual or proprioceptive, using an orthotic device, functional electric stimulation (FES), or virtual reality. (B) Photograph of a user engaging in BMI motor rehabilitation at Keio University, Japan. Brain electric activity, as measured by sensorimotor rhythm (SMR) event-related desynchronization (ERD) is recorded and analyzed by a laptop. Once SMR-ERD exceeds a predetermined level, control signals are sent to a hand orthosis opening or closing the user's hand.

of electrode positions, and the preservation of electric properties between the brain and the electrodes (eg, Fernández et al., 2014).

EEG, near-infrared spectroscopy (NIRS), and magnetoencephalography (MEG) are noninvasive measures of brain signals (Shibasaki, 2008). These techniques have inherent limitations regarding spatial resolution and signal quality because the electrodes or sensors are rather distant from the cortical source. Taking EEG, for instance, the distance between neural sources in the cortex and EEG electrodes causes summation of electrical activity that derives from a wide range of cortex (Cooper et al., 1965). This makes separation of the sources challenging. As the voltage from a dipole falls off by the inverse of the square of the distance from the dipole, the amplitude of EEG signals is very small, ranging in the tens of microvolts. Moreover, the skull and tissue between the cortex and EEG electrode have a large capacitance, leading to inherent electric dampening affecting several tens of Hertz. While physiological studies have suggested that modulation in gamma or higher frequency bands in the parietotemporal regions is related to sensorimotor processing, these signals are significantly diminished in EEG for the above-mentioned reasons. EEG is also susceptible to artifact contamination from facial muscle activity or eye movements (Cooper et al., 1965; Wolpaw and McFarland, 2004). Because of these factors, readouts of cortical signals using EEG are generally not as accurate as those from intracranial brain recordings.

Despite these limitations, EEG remains the gold standard for obtaining neural information from patients in a clinical setting without the need for surgery, posing a lower mental and physical burden to BMI users. Recent advancements in electrode technology promise reliable long-term use, as well as safe and easy mounting and unmounting in daily life situations. EEG is also suitable for use in acute settings, making EEG-based BMIs applicable for clinical rehabilitation. For these reasons, EEG-based BMI technology has recently made major advances in clinical applications, eg, in restoration of communication and paralysis (Birbaumer et al., 2014; Hashimoto et al., 2010; Soekadar et al., 2015a).

3 IDENTIFICATION OF BIOMARKERS FOR BMI MOTOR REHABILITATION

EEG or MEG recorded over the sensorimotor cortex is characterized by the arc-shaped mu-rhythm (also called the sensorimotor rhythm, SMR), typically oscillating at a frequency of 8–13 Hz. Participants can learn to control the amplitude of the SMR when provided with real-time feedback (Ono et al., 2013). Therefore, SMR-based BMIs were first used to allow paralyzed patients to communicate, to control virtual reality, or to control robotic arms. SMR-BMI proficiency has been successfully shown in severely paralyzed individuals with cerebral palsy (Daly et al., 2013), muscular dystrophy (Hashimoto et al., 2010), spinal cord injury (Müller-Putz et al., 2014), or stroke (Soekadar et al., 2011).

Most SMR-BMI paradigms quantify SMR modulations by calculating event-related desynchronization (ERD) recorded over the sensorimotor cortex. It has been shown that SMR-ERD covaries with blood–oxygen-level-dependent (BOLD) signals as measured by magnetic resonance imaging (MRI) deriving from the same cortical areas (Formaggio et al., 2008, 2010; Yuan et al., 2010). Studies using transcranial magnetic stimulation (TMS) delivered to the primary motor cortex (M1) have shown that an increase of corticospinal tract excitability is associated with a SMR-ERD decrease (Hummel et al., 2002) and is accompanied with decrease of GABAergic intracortical inhibition (Takemi et al., 2013). Despite the absence of any overt muscle contractions during motor imagery-related SMR-ERD, the potentiation of spinal motoneurons was recently demonstrated (Takemi et al., 2015).

Besides the modulation of sensorimotor cortex excitability associated with motor imagery or movement preparation, planning, or execution, it has been shown that the application of electric current targeting the sensorimotor cortex, eg, by using transcranial direct current stimulation (tDCS), can modulate SMR. This underlines the importance of the sensorimotor cortex as part of the SMR's neural substrate (Matsumoto et al., 2010). Recently, it was shown that even individuals in minimally conscious state may have the capacity to regulate SMR-ERD (Coyle et al., 2015) and use this ability for communication. Another tDCS study evidenced a causal link between M1 function and the successful acquisition of abstract skills such as control over SMR-ERD (Soekadar et al., 2015b).

4 BMI MOTOR REHABILITATION AND ITS OUTCOME

Based on these fundamental findings on SMR, real-time SMR feedback paradigms using visual and/or somatosensory modalities, termed *BMI motor rehabilitation* in this chapter, have been proposed as a possible tool to mediate the functional reorganization of the motor nervous system, even in the absence of any overt physical movements or voluntary electromyographic (EMG) activity. BMI systems generally consist of electrodes or sensors recording electric, magnetic, or metabolic brain signals (such as EEG, MEG, or NIRS), an algorithm for real-time analysis and translation of the recorded signals embedded in a central processing unit, and last but not least an output device (eg, robots, exoskeletons, virtual reality goggles, or brain stimulators) (Fig. 1A). Various types of feedback stimuli have been tested, eg, abstract visual feedback such as bar-type level meters (Ortner et al., 2012) or time series trend graphs (Broetz et al., 2010; Buch et al., 2008; Mukaino et al., 2014; Prasad et al., 2010; Shindo et al., 2011), realistic visual feedback that mimics physical movement (Ortner et al., 2012; Pichiorri et al., 2015), FES (Mukaino et al., 2014), and movement assistance via electromechanical exoskeletons (Shindo et al., 2011) (Fig. 2A). Fig. 2B illustrates an example of a BMI system recently used for stroke motor rehabilitation at Keio University, Japan (Liu et al., 2012; Ushiba et al., 2014). Here, EEG is used to record SMR-ERD related to the attempt to extend the paralyzed fingers. Signal processing is performed on a portable laptop, sending control signals to a BMI-driven hand orthosis and FES systems in case SMR-ERD exceeds a predetermined level.

Clinical studies investigating the feasibility and efficacy of BMI motor rehabilitation in poststroke hemiplegia assessed various neurophysiological and behavioral outcome measures, such as motor-evoked potentials (MEPs; eg, Mukaino et al., 2014; Shindo et al., 2011), cortical reorganization, as well as electrophysiological assays (eg, Fig. 3; Mukaino et al., 2014; Shindo et al., 2011), and clinical functional scores such as the Fugl–Meyer Assessment (Ang et al., 2015a,b; Ramos-Murguialday et al., 2013) or National Institute of Health Stroke Scale (Pichiorri et al., 2015), modified Ashworth Score for spasticity rating (Mukaino et al., 2014; Pichiorri et al., 2015) or goal-attainment score (Broetz et al., 2010). The first study that demonstrated that even stroke survivors with severe chronic motor deficits can learn to regulate SMR was reported by Buch et al. (2008). Several single-case studies have reported improved motor function in the context of SMR-BMI applications (Broetz et al., 2010; Caria et al., 2011; Daly et al., 2009). Larger case-series documented recovery along various modalities, eg, reappearance of EMG signals in the paralyzed hand, decrease in resting threshold of MEPs elicited from the ipsilesional motor cortex, as well as improved clinical motor function scores (Ang et al., 2011; Prasad et al., 2010; Shindo et al., 2011). Further studies have suggested that ERD feedback coupled with somatosensory stimuli might be more effective for functional recovery than simple visual stimuli (Ono et al., 2014). A controlled single case A-B-A-B design evidenced that SMR-triggered FES feedback promotes lateralized cortical activity (assessed by EEG and functional MRI), increased corticospinal excitability and EMG activity, and improved clinical scores compared with a simple

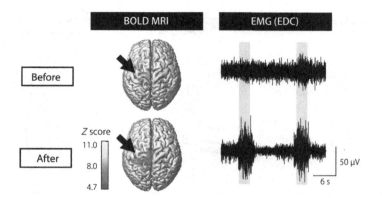

FIG. 3

Example of brain metabolic and electromyographic (EMG) differences before (*upper row*) and after (*lower row*) brain–machine interface (BMI) motor rehabilitation training in a representative stroke survivor. Data were recorded from a participant with severe hemiplegia after left-hemispheric stroke who underwent daily BMI motor rehabilitation training (Mukaino et al., 2014). (Left column) Blood–oxygen-level-dependent (BOLD) contrast as measured by magnetic resonance imaging (MRI), reflecting the metabolic activity of the cerebral cortex during the attempt to move the paralyzed finger, was assessed before (*top trace*) and after (*bottom trace*) the BMI motor rehabilitation training. After BMI motor rehabilitation training, there was a marked increase in BOLD contrast on the ipsilesional hemisphere, documenting lateralization of BOLD contrast similarly found in healthy controls. (*Right column*) Likewise, electromyographic (EMG) activity recorded over the paretic extensor digitorum communis (EDC) muscle increased after the BMI motor rehabilitation training (shaded time period: attempted finger opening) after the BMI motor rehabilitation training.
Figures adapted with permission from Mukaino, M., Ono, T., Shindo, K., Fujiwara, T., Ota, T., Kimura, A., Liu, M., Ushiba, J., 2014. Efficacy of brain-computer interface-driven neuromuscular electrical stimulation for chronic paresis after stroke. J. Rehabil. Med. 46 (4), 378–382.

combination of repeated motor attempts and FES unrelated to SMR-ERD (Mukaino et al., 2014). Functional MRI data have evidenced a focalized BOLD response in ipsilesional sensorimotor cortex following such SMR-BMI training (Caria et al., 2011; Mukaino et al., 2014; Ono et al., 2015). More recently, randomized controlled trials have demonstrated the feasibility and efficacy of BMI motor rehabilitation training in larger patient populations (Ang et al., 2014, 2015a; Pichiorri et al., 2015; Ramos-Murguialday et al., 2013).

5 POSSIBLE MECHANISMS UNDERLYING BMI MOTOR REHABILITATION TRAINING-RELATED FUNCTIONAL RECOVERY

In the healthy brain, activity of the sensory and motor system is highly integrated across different neural feedback loops (Fig. 4A). A brain lesion, eg, due to stroke

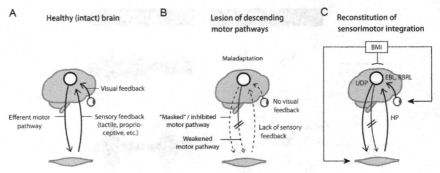

FIG. 4

(Re)integrating afferent and efferent activity in poststroke hemiplegia using brain–machine interface (BMI) motor rehabilitation. (A) Healthy (intact) brain. Efferent and afferent activity is integrated across different neural feedback loops involving vision, proprioception, and other senses. Volitional movements accompanied by sensorimotor rhythm event-related desynchronization (SMR-ERD) that are mediated by corticospinal (descending) pathways result in contingent sensory feedback mediated by afferent (ascending) pathways. (B) Poststroke hemiplegia results in disintegration of afferent and efferent activity weakening descending, but also ascending neural pathways. Learned nonuse may further weaken or mask intact descending and ascending pathways. Additionally, normal function of higher-order integrative cortical areas may be impacted by various maladaptive neural processes. (C) Direct translation of SMR-ERD into contingent sensory feedback results in reintegration of afferent and efferent activity and, thus, strengthening or unmasking of ipsilesional corticospinal pathways. Mechanisms underlying such paradigm may involve use-dependent plasticity (UDP), error-based learning (EBL), Hebbian plasticity (HP), or reward-based reinforcement learning (RBRL).

or a traumatic brain injury, can structurally damage these loops, resulting in disintegration of afferent and efferent neural activity. In severe hemiplegia, most daily life actions are performed with the unaffected hand which may result in neuroplasticity favoring the contralesional hemisphere and (further) weakening synaptic efficacy in the ipsilesional sensorimotor loop (Fig. 4B). Importantly, though weakened, the majority of stroke survivors with hemiplegia seem to have remaining intact afferent and efferent neural pathways as indicated by presence of MEPs in the affected upper extremity (Brasil et al., 2012). BMI motor rehabilitation training strategies strive, thus, to strengthen these weakened or masked pathways in order to promote (re)integration of ipsilesional neural feedback loops (Fig. 4C) (Soekadar et al., 2015a). Besides strengthening the ipsilesional corticospinal tract, acquiring the ability to control SMR may contribute to extensive functional reorganization of cortical and subcortical networks. Depending on the research background, BMI-related motor recovery has been mainly attributed to the following underlying concepts and mechanisms:

5.1 USE-DEPENDENT PLASTICITY

The functional organization of the motor nervous system, including the primary motor cortex, is modified by use (Bütefisch et al., 2000). It has been demonstrated in rats that synaptic efficacy is modifiable in an activity-dependent manner, resulting in long-term potentiation (Hess and Donoghue, 1994). Use-dependent plasticity, involving cortical reorganization within the thumb representation, has been demonstrated in the human motor cortex (Classen et al., 1998). A short period of training, consisting of simple, voluntary, repetitive thumb movements in a specific direction, elicits reorganization of the cortical representation of the thumb encoding kinematic details of the practiced movement. Similarly, relatively brief training periods involving synchronous movements of the thumb and foot elicit a medial expansion of the thumb representation (Liepert et al., 1999). In the context of BMI control, ie, through repeated self-regulation of SMR-ERD, learning to regulate such brain activity might involve such use-dependent plasticity in and between areas involved in motor initiation, planning, and execution.

5.2 HEBBIAN (TIMING DEPENDENT) PLASTICITY

Joint activity of distinct neuronal groups strengthens the synaptic links between active neurons. For instance, paired associative stimulation involving the repeated pairing of peripheral nerve stimulation and TMS over M1 operates with spike-timing-dependent plasticity (Müller-Dahlhaus et al., 2015), such that increases in corticospinal excitability occur when the neural spikes transmitted through the peripheral nerves and the neural activity elicited by TMS coincide temporally in the cortex (Carson and Kennedy, 2013). In the context of BMI motor rehabilitation training in which regulation of SMR-ERD is linked with sensory feedback, Hebbian (timing dependent) plasticity might strengthen the synaptic links between the compromised afferent and efferent pathways.

5.3 REWARD-BASED REINFORCEMENT LEARNING

Models of decision making have focused on yet another learning process, termed reinforcement learning, to account for how organisms learn to select the optimal response for a given context (Daw et al., 2006; Sutton and Barto, 1998; Taylor and Ivry, 2014). Based on Ivan Pavlov's and Burrhus F. Skinner's work in the 19th and 20th century, reinforcement learning has recently evolved as an area of machine learning. Reinforcement learning operates by comparing an expected and realized outcome (Sutton and Barto, 1998). If a behavior produces a greater than expected reward, the likelihood of repeating that behavior is increased; if the outcome is less than the expected reward, the likelihood of repeating that behavior is decreased. Dopamine activity in the basal ganglia, and in particular, the ventral striatum, was shown to correlate with the size of these prediction errors (Schultz, 1998), and categorical processing of such activity (ie, either obtaining or failing to obtain the reward) may play a dominant role in reinforcement learning. It is plausible to expect a similar process during BMI motor rehabilitation. Because severe paralysis after stroke results in lack of reward after the attempt to, eg, grasp a bottle and drink, the expected behavior (ie, using the paralyzed hand) will decrease or will even vanish (learned nonuse). In contrast, successful grasping mediated by a BMI system may reinforce such behavior, ie, attempting to grasp a bottle using the paralyzed hand.

5.4 ERROR-BASED LEARNING

As introduced by Diedrichsen et al. (2010), motor behavior such as reaching (Donchin et al., 2003; Shadmehr and Mussa-Ivaldi, 1994), eye movements (Srimal et al., 2008), walking (Morton and Bastian, 2006), and object manipulation (Witney et al., 2000) quickly adapt to the changing dynamics of the body and environment. Error-based learning in this context is generally conceptualized as an estimation problem. For example, for reaching movements, the motor system may estimate the forces that will act on the arm. If a perturbing force is experienced, the estimate will be updated using the prediction error, the difference between the predicted and observed forces. Crucially, during the next movement, the motor system is tuned to counteract the perturbation by translating the previous prediction error into a vectorial quantity (as in contrast to reinforcement learning). Error-based learning is a robust and well-studied phenomenon keeping motor behavior finely calibrated in a changing environment. Learning to regulate SMR-ERD through online feedback (eg, of its amplitude) might also involve error-based learning.

6 CLINICAL POSITIONING

In the Copenhagen study, Nakayama and colleagues assessed 421 stroke survivors after onset of their stroke using the Scandinavian Stroke Scale and the feeding and grooming items of the Barthel Index (Nakayama et al., 1994) on a weekly basis. They found that recovery mainly occurred within the first 2 months, and that full function was achieved by 79% of stroke survivors with mild paresis, compared with only 18% of stroke survivors with severe paresis. In the group with mild paresis, a valid prognosis could be made within the first 3 weeks, and further recovery was not expected later than 6 weeks after stroke. In the group with severe paresis, a valid prognosis was possible within the first 6 weeks, and further recovery was limited beyond 11 weeks after stroke.

However, the above study is limited in that the outcomes were assessed using the upper extremity-related items of the Barthel Index, which does not necessarily reflect the functions of the affected hand and arm per se because these activities could also be performed using the unaffected side. Furthermore, the study does not account for recent advances in basic and clinical findings (Liu et al., 2012) showing plasticity and learning even in stroke survivors with severe chronic paralysis (Kitago and Krakauer, 2013; Sharma and Cohen, 2012). For instance, use-dependent plasticity may play a major role in the recovery of function after stroke (Bütefisch et al., 1995, 2000). Facilitating plasticity and the learning process are thus important for functional recovery from motor impairment.

As all established rehabilitative measures target mild-to-moderate impairment, there is currently no rehabilitation strategy for stroke survivors with severe impairments and total loss of voluntary movements. This group accounts for 30–50% of all stroke survivors. For instance, CIMT requires overt physical movement (Taub et al., 1999), and EMG-triggered neuromuscular stimulation requires self-regulated (voluntary) EMG activity. In contrast, BMI motor rehabilitation training only requires SMR-ERD and no actual physical movements. Therefore, BMI motor rehabilitation is currently the only tool that promises to reanimate impaired limbs, even in stroke survivors without any residual overt movements. One possible endpoint of BMI motor rehabilitation training is the reappearance of voluntary EMG (Liu et al., 2012). Once restored, voluntary EMG activity can be used as trigger for FES (Fujiwara et al., 2009). While these studies strongly suggest that BMI technology is a powerful tool in stroke neurorehabilitation, larger clinical studies and studies that investigate the exact underlying mechanisms of action are urgently needed. Clearly, the required effort to train stroke survivors on a daily basis with expensive research equipment and under the supervision of specialized scientists, physicians, and physiotherapists as carried out in the described studies makes it presently hard to establish BMI training as a standard therapy in stroke. Thus, new ways to make BMI motor rehabilitation training more effective or substantially lower the costs for such BMI motor rehabilitation training are required. In this context, recent efforts to translate current BMI technology into the daily life environment of stroke survivors seem particularly promising. Such approach would additionally facilitate generalization of learned skills into the user's everyday life behavior.

7 FUTURE OF BMI MOTOR REHABILITATION

As previously conceptualized for the whole field of neurorehabilitation (Dimyan and Cohen, 2011), clinical outcomes of BMI motor rehabilitation training may be facilitated by combining it with other therapies, such as physiotherapy (Broetz et al., 2010), robotics (Ang et al., 2015a), and neuromodulation techniques such as tDCS (Ang et al., 2015b; Kasashima-Shindo et al., 2015). Studies on neural repair using pharmacological interventions and stem cell implantations also suggest that combination with other rehabilitation therapies can maximize the clinical outcome. In this context, BMI motor rehabilitation training might be conceptualized as a tool to promote neural plasticity preconditioning the damaged brain to undergo substantial reorganization further fostered and stabilized by goal-directed physiotherapy and other means leading to a generalization of learned skills.

Recently, BMI motor rehabilitation was extended from stroke to other motor disorders, such as spinal cord injuries (Takahashi et al., 2012) or writer's cramp (Hashimoto et al., 2014). While these examples demonstrate improvements in the motor domain, other domains, eg, those responsible for cognition and emotion regulation, might also be targeted by BMI neurorehabilitation paradigms.

Recent studies suggest that the anatomical and physiological characteristics of the brain itself might be used as a predictor of BMI performance or outcome of functional recovery. It was shown that BMI control performance in healthy individuals correlates with gray matter volume of the supplementary motor area, supplementary somatosensory area, and dorsal premotor cortex. MEG alpha oscillation in the peri-infarct region and alpha connectivity in stroke survivors predicted rehabilitation outcomes (Westlake et al., 2012). Poststroke loss and the recovery of sensorimotor function were also found to be associated with acute deterioration and the subsequent retrieval of functional MRI-based interhemispheric connectivity within the sensorimotor system (van Meer et al., 2010). These examples suggest that structural and functional characterization of the individual brain may be useful to determine whether and to what extend a person is eligible for BMI motor rehabilitation.

BMI motor rehabilitation in poststroke hemiplegia or spinal cord injury was also developed for restoration of lower limb movements and locomotive patterns. It was shown that peripheral nerve trunk stimulation accompanied by motor-related cortical potentials in EEG can increase M1 excitability, suggesting that the BMI neurorehabilitation concept can be also adapted to the rehabilitation of the lower limb. Locomotion, however, requires postural adjustment against gravity. Differences in the neural architecture between the upper and lower limb are also crucial for planning a specific BMI intervention. For example, central pattern generators for fundamental locomotion rhythm are located in the spinal cord, while brainstem nuclei corresponding to the mesenphalic locomotor region may also contribute to walking. Reticulospinal or other descending tracts also play a role in locomotion-related postural adjustment. Compared to voluntary movements of the hands, cortical activity related to locomotion is relatively low and due to its main activity peak in the interhemispheric fissure more difficult to record. Additionally, significant movement artifacts in the EEG during walking may impair cortical signal decoding.

Currently, two main approaches promise to improve BMI efficacy in neurorehabilitation: either the full implantation of a wireless BMI system capable of bridging weakened or nonexistent corticospinal pathways (for review, Murphy et al., 2016), or refining existent noninvasive systems by improving BMI paradigms toward increased efficacy in strengthening the thalamocortical sensorimotor circuit, including combination with tools improving BMI learning such as, eg, brain stimulation (Ang et al., 2015b; Kasashima-Shindo et al., 2015; Soekadar et al., 2015b). Yet, many questions related to BMI training in stroke neurorehabilitation remain unanswered; for instance, dose–response relationships, or the influence of BMI training on other brain functions, eg, the cognitive domain (Soekadar et al., 2015c).

BMI systems that can be used in daily life environments to perform daily life activities, helping stroke survivors to generalize learned grasping motions into their daily routines, might pave the way for broader clinical use of BMI technology in the near future. Such portable, robust, and reliable systems used in rehabilitation facilities and then in the patient's home environment would also allow the collection of large amounts of (neuro)-physiological data, which might help in addressing some of the above-mentioned questions. Additionally, recording and analysis of other physiological measures, such as heart rate, respiration rate, or body temperature, may result in optimized training schedules that are optimized for the individual user. The recent development of hybrid BMIs that integrate different bio-signals has demonstrated sufficiently robust and reliable control of simple exoskeletons (Soekadar et al., 2015d; Witkowski et al., 2014), eg, to perform activities of daily life outside the laboratory environment.

8 UNSOLVED ISSUES AND QUESTIONS

BMI motor rehabilitation consists of many elements: the repetition of motor attempts, movement support by motor-driven braces or orthotic devices, sensory feedback related to actuator movements, and contingent coupling of motor and sensory system activation. An exact understanding of each component's contribution toward the induction of neural plasticity and motor relearning facilitating functional recovery is, however, still lacking. Only a few preliminary studies have tested the efficacy of BMI components on the learning/rehabilitation process and are thus noted here. Daily BMI training over 5 days with healthy participants suggested that presentation of abstract visual feedback limits learning of SMR self-regulation, while visual feedback related to movements of a realistic limb facilitates learning (Ono et al., 2013). Presumably, a tangible visual image of animated limbs helps in body imaging, motor planning, and regulation of motor output (de Vignemont and Haggard, 2008). In a clinical BMI study involving hemiplegic stroke survivors, the gain in functional recovery was higher in a group that received somatosensory feedback compared to a group receiving visual feedback (Ono et al., 2013). Recent randomized and controlled clinical studies suggest that somatosensory feedback contingent to self-regulated motor-related EEG/NIRS signals, but not sham feedback unrelated to brain activity, promotes motor recovery (Mihara et al., 2012; Ramos-Murguialday et al., 2013). Another clinical study with a single-case A-B-A-B design reported that clinical outcome was unchanged or even worsened when a stroke survivor attempted to open his paralyzed fingers during the application neuromuscular electrical stimulation irrespective of his actual brain activity (Mukaino et al., 2014). This result is clinically interesting, because functional recovery was not promoted by a simple combination of motor imagery and continuous passive motion/neuromuscular electrical stimulation, both of which are standard rehabilitative measures.

While this chapter introduced a number of potential mechanisms involved in BMI-based rehabilitation of poststroke hemiplegia, also other mechanisms might be involved. Recent studies on neuron–glia interactions, epigenetic mechanisms, and large-scale network dynamics have revealed a number of plasticity mechanisms across multiple, overlapping spatial, and temporal scales (Buch et al., 2016) that have neither been investigated nor understood in the context of BMI stroke rehabilitation. Further

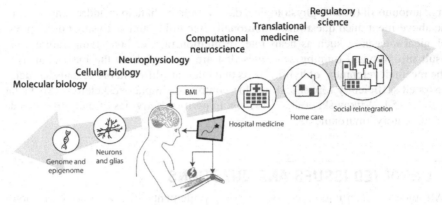

FIG. 5

Overview of the different disciplines involved in development, testing, and implementation of brain–machine interface (BMI) technology in broad clinical routine. The genetic/epigenetic and cellular mechanisms underlying BMI use are widely unknown, but should be further investigated, eg, to improve efficacy of BMI motor rehabilitation training in poststroke hemiplegia. Tight involvement of translational medicine and the regulatory sciences is required to facilitate the path from acute care in the hospitals toward the end user's home environment and their full social reintegration.

basic research studies on the underlying mechanisms are, thus, needed and should be embedded into the perspective of a multiscale, multidisciplinary context (Fig. 5).

To make BMI-based rehabilitation more mainstream in the clinical care of stroke survivors over the next 5–10 years, clinical trials involving BMI technology should adhere to highest scientific standards and use endpoint measures that are comparable across studies so that, eg, coverage by health insurances will come in reach. Additionally, tight involvement of the regulatory sciences is required to facilitate and promote interactions between research institutions, hospitals, private companies, and the end users. Recently, the Clinical Brain-Machine Interface (CBMI) Society (www.cbmi-society.org) was launched as a chapter of the International BCI Society (www.bcisociety.org). By building up a dynamic and integrative global community, the CBMI Society aims at fostering cross-institutional, international collaborations to facilitate implementation of BMI-based neurotechnology in health care.

9 CONCLUDING REMARKS

BMIs are powerful clinical tools enabling the paralyzed to move again. However, broader clinical use lags behind current technological possibilities. Now, one decade after the "coming of age" of BCI research (Birbaumer, 2006) and successful translation of BMI technology from bench to bedside, concerted multidisciplinary efforts are needed to add this powerful tool to the current mainstream repertoire in stroke neurorehabilitation. Besides lack of other treatment options for stroke survivors without any voluntary muscle contractions, three main factors have formed the basis for the current success of BMI technology in motor neurorehabilitation: First, the functional role of the sensorimotor cortex for limb movements was well documented. Second, the mechanisms underlying neural plasticity facilitating motor learning and recovery were increasingly understood through basic research studies that involved rodents, nonhuman primates, and humans. Third, a first reliable real-time biomarker that reflects cortical activity and corticospinal excitability has been identified and appeared to be a promising target for BMI neurorehabilitation.

The successful implementation of BMI motor rehabilitation in the clinical routine may in many ways serve as a role model for other BMI-related therapeutic applications. Additionally, transferring the insights gained in the context of BMI motor rehabilitation may help in the development of treatment strategies for other neuropsychiatric disorders.

ACKNOWLEDGMENTS

This work was supported by the Japan Agency for Medical Research and Development (AMED) under the projects of Strategic Research Program for Brain Sciences and Development of Medical Devices and Systems for Advanced Medical Services, and Japan Society for the Promotion of Science (JSPS) Graint-in-Aid for Scientific Research C (16K01469). This was also supported by the European Commission under the project AIDE (645322), the German Federal Ministry of Education and Research (BMBF, 01GQ0831, 16SV5838K), and the Deutsche Forschungsgemeinschaft (DFG, SO932-2).

REFERENCES

Ang, K.K., Guan, C., Chua, K.S., Ang, B.T., Kuah, C.W., Wang, C., Phua, K.S., Chin, Z.Y., Zhang, H., 2011. A large clinical study on the ability of stroke patients to use an EEG-based motor imagery brain-computer interface. Clin. EEG Neurosci. 42, 253–258.

Ang, K.K., Guan, C., Phua, K.S., Wang, C., Zhou, L., Tang, K.Y., Ephraim Joseph, G.J., Kuah, C.W., Chua, K.S., 2014. Brain-computer interface-based robotic end effector system for wrist and hand rehabilitation: results of a three-armed randomized controlled trial for chronic stroke. Front. Neuroeng. 7, 30.

Ang, K.K., Chua, K.S., Phua, K.S., Wang, C., Chin, Z.Y., Kuah, C.W., Low, W., Guan, C., 2015a. A randomized controlled trial of EEG-based motor imagery brain-computer interface robotic rehabilitation for stroke. Clin. EEG Neurosci. 46 (4), 310–320.

Ang, K.K., Guan, C., Phua, K.S., Wang, C., Zhao, L., Teo, W.P., Chen, C., Ng, Y.S., Chew, E., 2015b. Facilitating effects of transcranial direct current stimulation on motor imagery brain-computer interface with robotic feedback for stroke rehabilitation. Arch. Phys. Med. Rehabil. 96 (3 Suppl.), S79–S87.

Birbaumer, N., 2006. Brain-computer-interface research: coming of age. Clin. Neurophysiol. 117, 479–483.

Birbaumer, N., Cohen, L.G., 2007. Brain-computer interfaces: communication and restoration of movement in paralysis. J. Physiol. 579 (3), 621–636.

Birbaumer, N., Gallegos-Ayala, G., Wildgruber, M., Silvoni, S., Soekadar, S.R., 2014. Direct brain control and communication in paralysis. Brain Topogr. 27, 4–11.

Boulay, C.B., Sarnacki, W.A., Wolpaw, J.R., McFarland, D.J., 2011. Trained modulation of sensorimotor rhythms can affect reaction time. Clin. Neurophysiol. 122 (9), 1820–1826.

Bouton, C.E., Shaikhouni, A., Annetta, N.V., Bockbrader, M.A., Friedenberg, D.A., Nielson, D.M., Sharma, G., Sederberg, P.B., Glenn, B.C., Mysiw, W.J., Morgan, A.G., Deogaonkar, M., Rezai, A.R., 2016. Restoring cortical control of functional movement in a human with quadriplegia. Nature 533, 247–250. http://dx.doi.org/10.1038/nature17435.

Brasil, F., Curado, M.R., Witkowski, M., Garcia, E., Broetz, D., Birbaumer, N., Soekadar, S.R., 2012. MEP predicts motor recovery in chronic stroke patients undergoing 4-weeks of daily physical therapy. In: Human Brain Mapping Annual Meeting, Beijing. June 10–14, 2012.

Broetz, D., Braun, C., Weber, C., Soekadar, S.R., Caria, A., Birbaumer, N., 2010. Combination of brain-computer interface training and goal-directed physical therapy in chronic stroke: a case report. Neurorehabil. Neural Repair 24, 674–679.

Buch, E.R., Liew, S.L., Cohen, L.G., 2016. Plasticity of sensorimotor networks: multiple overlapping mechanisms. Neuroscientist (in press). pii:1073858416638641.

Buch, E., Weber, C., Cohen, L.G., Braun, C., Dimyan, M.A., Ard, T., Mellinger, J., Caria, A., Soekadar, S., Fourkas, A., Birbaumer, N., 2008. Think to move: a neuromagnetic brain-computer interface (BCI) system for chronic stroke. Stroke 39, 910–917.

Bütefisch, C., Hummelsheim, H., Denzler, P., Mauritz, K.H., 1995. Repetitive training of isolated movements improves the outcome of motor rehabilitation of the centrally paretic hand. J. Neurol. Sci. 130 (1), 59–68.

Bütefisch, C.M., Davis, D.C., Wise, S.P., Sawaki, L., Kopylev, L., Classen, J., Cohen, L.G., 2000. Mechanisms of use-dependent plasticity in the human motor cortex. Proc. Natl. Acad. Sci. U. S. A. 97, 3661–3665.

Caria, A., Weber, C., Brötz, D., Ramos, A., Ticini, L.F., Gharabaghi, A., Braun, C., Birbaumer, N., 2011. Chronic stroke recovery after combined BCI training and physiotherapy: a case report. Psychophysiology 48, 578–582.

Carmena, J.M., Lebedev, M.A., Crist, R.E., O'Doherty, J.E., Santucci, D.M., Dimitrov, D.F., Patil, P.G., Henriquez, C.S., Nicolelis, M.S., 2003. Learning to control a brain-machine interface for reaching and grasping by primates. PLoS Biol. 1 (2), E42.

Carson, R.G., Kennedy, N.C., 2013. Modulation of human corticospinal excitability by paired associative stimulation. Front. Hum. Neurosci. 7, 823.

Chapin, J.K., Moxon, K.A., Markowitz, R.S., Nicolelis, M.A., 1999. Realtime control of a robot arm using simultaneously recorded neurons in the motor cortex. Nat. Neurosci. 2 (7), 664–670.

Classen, J., Liepert, J., Wise, S.P., Hallett, M., Cohen, L.G., 1998. Rapid plasticity of human cortical movement representation induced by practice. J. Neurophysiol. 79, 1117–1123.

Cooper, R., Winter, A.L., Crow, H.J., et al., 1965. Comparison of subcortical, cortical and scalp activity using chronically indwelling electrodes in man. Electroencephalogr. Clin. Neurophysiol. 18, 217–228.

Coyle, D., Stow, J., McCreadie, K., McElligott, J., Carroll, Á., 2015. Sensorimotor modulation assessment and brain-computer interface training in disorders of consciousness. Arch. Phys. Med. Rehabil. 96, S62–S70.

Daly, J.J., Wolpaw, J.R., 2008. Brain-computer interfaces in neurological rehabilitation. Lancet Neurol. 7, 1032–1043.

Daly, J.J., Cheng, R., Rogers, J., Litinas, K., Hrovat, K., Dohring, M., 2009. Feasibility of a new application of noninvasive brain computer interface (BCI): a case study of training for recovery of volitional motor control after stroke. J. Neurol. Phys. Ther. 33 (4), 203–211.

Daly, I., Billinger, M., Laparra-Hernández, J., Aloise, F., Garcìa, M.L., Faller, J., et al., 2013. On the control of brain-computer interfaces by users with cerebral palsy. Clin. Neurophysiol. 124, 1787–1797. http://dx.doi.org/10.1016/j.clinph.2013.02.118.

Daw, N.D., O'doherty, J.P., Dayan, P., Seymour, B., Dolan, R.J., 2006. Cortical substrates for exploratory decisions in humans. Nature 441, 876–879.

de Vignemont, F., Haggard, P., 2008. Action observation and execution: what is shared? Soc. Neurosci. 3 (3–4), 421–433.

Diedrichsen, J., White, O., Newman, D., Lally, N., 2010. Use-dependent and error-based learning of motor behaviors. J. Neurosci. 30 (15), 5159–5166.

Dimyan, M.A., Cohen, L.G., 2011. Neuroplasticity in the context of motor rehabilitation after stroke. Nat. Rev. Neurol. 7 (2), 76–85.

Donchin, O., Francis, J.T., Shadmehr, R., 2003. Quantifying generalization from trial-by-trial behavior of adaptive systems that learn with basis functions: theory and experiments in human motor control. J. Neurosci. 23, 9032–9045.

Fernández, E., Greger, B., House PA, Aranda, I., Botella, C., Albisua, J., Soto-Sánchez, C., Alfaro, A., Normann, R.A., 2014. Acute human brain responses to intracortical microelectrode arrays: challenges and future prospects. Front. Neuroeng. 7, 24.

Formaggio, E., Storti, S.F., Avesani, M., Cerini, R., Milanese, F., Gasparini, A., Acler, M., Pozzi Mucelli, R., Fiaschi, A., Manganotti, P., 2008. EEG and fMRI coregistration to investigate the cortical oscillatory activities during finger movement. Brain Topogr. 21 (2), 100–111. http://dx.doi.org/10.1007/s10548-008-0058-1.

Formaggio, E., Storti, S.F., Cerini, R., Fiaschi, A., Manganotti, P., 2010. Brain oscillatory activity during motor imagery in EEG-fMRI coregistration. Magn. Reson. Imaging 28 (10), 1403–1412. http://dx.doi.org/10.1016/j.mri.2010.06.030.

Fujiwara, T., Kasashima, Y., Honaga, K., Muraoka, Y., Tsuji, T., Osu, R., Hase, K., Masakado, Y., Liu, M., 2009. Motor improvement and corticospinal modulation induced by hybrid assistive neuromuscular dynamic stimulation (HANDS) therapy in patients with chronic stroke. Neurorehabil. Neural Repair 23 (2), 125–132.

Hashimoto, Y., Ushiba, J., Kimura, A., Liu, M., Tomita, Y., 2010. Change in brain activity through virtual reality-based brain-machine communication in a chronic tetraplegic subject with muscular dystrophy. BMC Neurosci. 11, 117.

Hashimoto, Y., Ota, T., Mukaino, M., Liu, M., Ushiba, J., 2014. Functional recovery from chronic writer's cramp by brain-computer interface rehabilitation: a case report. BMC Neurosci. 15, 103.

Heasman, J.M., Scott, T.R., Kirkup, L., Flynn, R.Y., Vare, V.A., Gschwind, C.R., 2002. Control of a hand grasp neuroprosthesis using an electroencephalogram-triggered switch: demonstration of improvements in performance using wavepacket analysis. Med. Biol. Eng. Comput. 40 (5), 588–593.

Hess, G., Donoghue, J.P., 1994. Long-term potentiation of horizontal connections provides a mechanism to reorganize cortical motor maps. J. Neurophysiol. 71, 2543–2547.

Hochberg, L.R., Bacher, D., Jarosiewicz, B., Masse, N.Y., Simeral, J.D., Vogel, J., Haddadin, S., Liu, J., Cash, S.S., van der Smagt, P., Donoghue, J.P., 2012. Reach and grasp by people with tetraplegia using a neurally controlled robotic arm. Nature 485 (7398), 372–375. http://dx.doi.org/10.1038/nature11076.

Hummel, F., Andres, F., Altenmüller, E., Dichgans, J., Gerloff, C., 2002. Inhibitory control of acquired motor programmes in the human brain. Brain 125, 404–420.

Kasashima-Shindo, Y., Fujiwara, T., Ushiba, J., Matsushika, Y., Kamatani, D., Oto, M., Ono, T., Nishimoto, A., Shindo, K., Kawakami, M., Tsuji, T., Liu, M., 2015. Brain-computer interface training combined with transcranial direct current stimulation in patients with chronic severe hemiparesis: proof of concept study. J. Rehabil. Med. 47 (4), 318–324.

Kitago, T., Krakauer, J.W., 2013. Motor learning principles for neurorehabilitation. Handb. Clin. Neurol. 110, 93–103.

Kwakkel, G., Veerbeek, J.M., van Wegen, E.E.H., Wolf, S.L., 2015. Constraint-induced movement therapy after stroke. Lancet Neurol. 14, 224–334.

Leeb, R., Friedman, D., Muller-Putz, G.R., Scherer, R., Slater, M., Pfurtscheller, G., 2007. Self-paced (asynchronous) BCI control of a wheelchair in virtual environments: a case study with a tetraplegic. Comput. Intell. Neurosci. 2007, 79642.

Liepert, J., Terborg, C., Weiller, C., 1999. Motor plasticity induced by synchronized thumb and foot movements. Exp. Brain Res. 125 (4), 435–439.

Lim, C.G., Lee, T.S., Guan, C., Fung, D.S., Zhao, Y., Teng, S.S., Zhang, H., Krishnan, K.R., 2012. A brain-computer interface based attention training program for treating attention deficit hyperactivity disorder. PLoS One 7. e46692.

Liu, M., Fujiwara, T., Shindo, K., Kasashima, Y., Otaka, Y., Tsuji, T., Ushiba, J., 2012. Newer challenges to restore hemiparetic upper extremity after stroke: HANDS therapy and BMI neurorehabilitation. Hong Kong Physiother. J. 30 (2), 83–92.

Matsumoto, J., Fujiwara, T., Takahashi, O., Liu, M., Kimura, A., Ushiba, J., 2010. Modulation of mu rhythm desynchronization during motor imagery by transcranial direct current stimulation. J. Neuroeng. Rehabil. 7, 27. http://dx.doi.org/10.1186/ 1743-0003-7-27.

Mihara, M., Miyai, I., Hattori, N., Hatakenaka, M., Yagura, H., Kawano, T., Okibayashi, M., Danjo, N., Ishikawa, A., Inoue, Y., Kubota, K., 2012. Neurofeedback using real-time near-infrared spectroscopy enhances motor imagery related cortical activation. PLoS One 7 (3). e32234.

Morton, S.M., Bastian, A.J., 2006. Cerebellar contributions to locomotor adaptations during splitbelt treadmill walking. J. Neurosci. 26, 9107–9116.

Mukaino, M., Ono, T., Shindo, K., Fujiwara, T., Ota, T., Kimura, A., Liu, M., Ushiba, J., 2014. Efficacy of brain-computer interface-driven neuromuscular electrical stimulation for chronic paresis after stroke. J. Rehabil. Med. 46 (4), 378–382.

Müller-Dahlhaus, F., Lücke, C., Lu, M.K., Arai, N., Fuhl, A., Herrmann, E., Ziemann, U., 2015. Augmenting LTP-like plasticity in human motor cortex by spaced paired associative stimulation. PLoS One 10. e0131020.

Müller-Putz, G.R., Daly, I., Kaiser, V., 2014. Motor imagery-induced EEG patterns in individuals with spinal cord injury and their impact on brain–computer interface accuracy. J. Neural Eng. 11 (3), 035011. http://dx.doi.org/10.1088/1741-2560/11/3/035011. ISSN 1741-2560.

Murphy, M.D., Guggenmos, D.J., Bundy, D.T., Nudo, R.J., 2016. Current challenges facing the translation of brain computer interfaces from preclinical trials to use in human patients. Front. Cell. Neurosci. 9, 497.

Nakayama, H., Jørgensen, H.S., Raaschou, H.O., Olsen, T.S., 1994. Recovery of upper extremity function in stroke patients: the Copenhagen Stroke Study. Arch. Phys. Med. Rehabil. 75 (4), 394–398.

Ono, T., Kimura, A., Ushiba, J., 2013. Daily training with realistic visual feedback improves reproducibility of event-related desynchronisation following hand motor imagery. Clin. Neurophysiol. 124 (9), 1779–1786.

Ono, T., Shindo, K., Kawashima, K., Ota, N., Ito, M., Ota, T., Mukaino, M., Fujiwara, T., Kimura, A., Liu, M., Ushiba, J., 2014. Brain-computer interface with somatosensory feedback improves functional recovery from severe hemiplegia due to chronic stroke. Front. Neuroeng. 7, 19.

Ono, T., Tomita, Y., Inose, M., Ota, T., Kimura, A., Liu, M., Ushiba, J., 2015. Multimodal sensory feedback associated with motor attempts alters BOLD responses to paralyzed hand movement in chronic stroke patients. Brain Topogr. 28 (2), 340–351.

Ortner, R., Irimia, D.C., Scharinger, J., Guger, C., 2012. A motor imagery based brain-computer interface for stroke rehabilitation. Stud. Health Technol. Inform. 181, 319–323.

Pfurtscheller, G., Guger, C., Müller, G., Krausz, G., Neuper, C., 2000. Brain oscillations control hand orthosis in a tetraplegic. Neurosci. Lett. 292 (3), 211–214.

Pfurtscheller, G., Müller, G.R., Pfurtscheller, J., Gerner, H.J., Rupp, R., 2003. 'Thought'—control of functional electrical stimulation to restore hand grasp in a patient with tetraplegia. Neurosci. Lett. 351 (1), 33–36.

Pichiorri, F., Morone, G., Petti, M., Toppi, J., Pisotta, I., Molinari, M., Paolucci, S., Inghilleri, M., Astolfi, L., Cincotti, F., Mattia, D., 2015. Brain-computer interface boosts motor imagery practice during stroke recovery. Ann. Neurol. 77 (5), 851–865.

Prasad, G., Herman, P., Coyle, D., McDonough, S., Crosbie, J., 2010. Applying a brain-computer interface to support motor imagery practice in people with stroke for upper limb recovery: a feasibility study. J. Neuroeng. Rehabil. 7, 60.

Ramos-Murguialday, A., Broetz, D., Rea, M., Läer, L., Yilmaz, O., Brasil, F.L., Liberati, G., Curado, M.R., Garcia-Cossio, E., Vyziotis, A., Cho, W., Agostini, M., Soares, E., Soekadar, S., Caria, A., Cohen, L.G., Birbaumer, N., 2013. Brain–machine interface in chronic stroke rehabilitation: a controlled study. Ann. Neurol. 74, 100–108.

Schultz, W., 1998. Predictive reward signal of dopamine neurons. J. Neurophysiol. 80, 1–27.

Shadmehr, R., Mussa-Ivaldi, F.A., 1994. Adaptive representation of dynamics during learning of a motor task. J. Neurosci. 14 (5 Pt. 2), 3208–3224.

Sharma, N., Cohen, L.G., 2012. Recovery of motor function after stroke. Dev. Psychobiol. 54 (3), 254–262.

Shibasaki, H., 2008. Human brain mapping: hemodynamic response and electrophysiology. Clin. Neurophysiol. 119 (4), 731–743.

Shindo, K., Kawashima, K., Ushiba, J., Ota, N., Ito, M., Ota, T., Kimura, A., Liu, M., 2011. Effects of neurofeedback training with an electroencephalogram-based brain–computer interface for hand paralysis in patients with chronic stroke: a preliminary case series study. J. Rehabil. Med. 43, 951–957.

Soekadar, S.R., Witkowski, M., Mellinger, J., Ramos Murguialday, A., Birbaumer, N., Cohen, L.G., 2011. ERD-based online brain-machine interfaces (BMI) in the context of neurorehabilitation: optimizing BMI learning and performance. IEEE Trans. Neural Syst. Rehabil. Eng. 19, 542–549.

Soekadar, S.R., Birbaumer, N., Slutzky, M.W., Cohen, L.G., 2015a. Brain-machine interfaces in neurorehabilitation of stroke. Neurobiol. Dis. 83, 172–179.

Soekadar, S.R., Witkowski, M., Birbaumer, N., Cohen, L.G., 2015b. Enhancing Hebbian learning to control brain oscillatory activity. Cereb. Cortex 25 (9), 2409–2415. http://dx.doi.org/10.1093/cercor/bhu043.

Soekadar, S.R., Cohen, L.G., Birbaumer, N., 2015c. Clinical brain-machine interfaces. In: Tracy, J., Hampstead, B., Sathian, K. (Eds.), Plasticity of Cognition in Neurologic Disorders. Oxford University Press, New York, NY, pp. 347–362.

Soekadar, S.R., Witkowski, M., Vitiello, N., Birbaumer, N., 2015d. An EEG/EOG-based hybrid brain-neural computer interaction (BNCI) system to control an exoskeleton for the paralyzed hand. Biomed. Tech. 60 (3), 199–205.

Srimal, R., Diedrichsen, J., Ryklin, E.B., Curtis, C.E., 2008. Obligatory adaptation of saccade gains. J. Neurophysiol. 99, 1554–1558.

Strehl, U., Birkle, S.M., Wörz, S., Kotchoubey, B., 2014. Sustained reduction of seizures in patients with intractable epilepsy after self-regulation training of slow cortical potentials—10 years after. Front. Hum. Neurosci. 8, 604.

Sutton, R.S., Barto, A.G., 1998. Reinforcement Learning: An Introduction. MIT Press, Cambridge, MA.

Takahashi, M., Takeda, K., Otaka, Y., Osu, R., Hanakawa, T., Gouko, M., Ito, K., 2012. Event related desynchronization-modulated functional electrical stimulation system for stroke rehabilitation: a feasibility study. J. Neuroeng. Rehabil. 9, 56.

Takemi, M., Masakado, Y., Liu, M., Ushiba, J., 2013. Event-related desynchronization reflects downregulation of intracortical inhibition in human primary motor cortex. J. Neurophysiol. 110 (5), 1158–1166. http://dx.doi.org/10.1152/jn.01092.2012.

Takemi, M., Masakado, Y., Liu, M., Ushiba, J., 2015. Sensorimotor event-related desynchronization represents the excitability of human spinal motoneurons. Neuroscience 297, 58–67. http://dx.doi.org/10.1016/j.neuroscience.2015.03.045.

Taub, E., Uswatte, G., Pidikiti, R., 1999. Constraint-induced movement therapy: a new family of techniques with broad application to physical rehabilitation—a clinical review. J. Rehabil. Res. Dev. 36, 237–251.

Taylor, J.A., Ivry, R.B., 2014. Cerebellar and prefrontal cortex contributions to adaptation, strategies, and reinforcement learning. Prog. Brain Res. 210, 217–253.

Ushiba, J., Kasuga, S., 2015. ICT for neurorehabilitation. In: Ligthart, L.P., Prasad, R., Pupolin, S. (Eds.), Neuro-Rehabilitation with Brain Interface. River Publishers, Aalborg, Denmark, pp. 9–20.

Ushiba, J., Morishita, A., Maeda, T., 2014. A task-oriented brain-computer interface rehabilitation system for patients with stroke hemiplegia. In: 2014 4th International Conference on Wireless Communications, Vehicular Technology, Information Theory and Aerospace and Electronic Systems, VITAE 2014—Co-located with Global Wireless Summit. Article Number 6934416.

van Meer, M.P., van der Marel, K., Wang, K., Otte, W.M., El Bouazati, S., Roeling, T.A., Viergever, M.A., Berkelbach van der Sprenkel, J.W., Dijkhuizen, R.M., 2010. Recovery of sensorimotor function after experimental stroke correlates with restoration of resting-state interhemispheric functional connectivity. J. Neurosci. 30 (11), 3964–3972.

Westlake, K.P., Hinkley, L.B., Bucci, M., Guggisberg, A.G., Byl, N., Findlay, A.M., Henry, R.G., Nagarajan, S.S., 2012. Resting state α-band functional connectivity and recovery after stroke. Exp. Neurol. 237 (1), 160–169.

Witkowski, M., Cortese, M., Cempini, M., Mellinger, J., Vitiello, N., Soekadar, S.R., 2014. Enhancing brain-machine interface (BMI) control of a hand exoskeleton using electrooculography (EOG). J. Neuroeng. Rehabil. 11, 165.

Witney, A.G., Goodbody, S.J., Wolpert, D.M., 2000. Learning and decay of prediction in object manipulation. J. Neurophysiol. 84, 334–343.

Wolpaw, J.R., McFarland, D.J., 2004. Control of a two-dimensional movement signal by a noninvasive brain-computer interface in humans. Proc. Natl. Acad. Sci. U.S.A. 101 (51), 17849–17854.

Wolpaw, J.R., Birbaumer, N., McFarland, D.J., Pfurtscheller, G., Vaughan, T.M., 2002. Brain-computer interfaces for communication and control. Clin. Neurophysiol. 113 (6), 767–791.

Yanagisawa, T., Hirata, M., Saitoh, Y., Goto, T., Kishima, H., Fukuma, R., Yokoi, H., Kamitani, Y., Yoshimine, T., 2011. Real-time control of a prosthetic hand using human electrocorticography signals. J. Neurosurg. 114 (6), 1715–1722.

Yuan, H., Liu, T., Szarkowski, R., Rios, C., Ashe, J., He, B., 2010. Negative covariation between task-related responses in alpha/beta-band activity and BOLD in human sensorimotor cortex: an EEG and fMRI study of motor imagery and movements. Neuroimage 49, 2596–2606.

Zotev, V., Yuan, H., Misaki, M., Phillips, R., Young, K.D., Feldner, M.T., Bodurka, J., 2016. Correlation between amygdala BOLD activity and frontal EEG asymmetry during real-time fMRI neurofeedback training in patients with depression. Neuroimage Clin. 11, 224–238.

Neural and cortical analysis of swallowing and detection of motor imagery of swallow for dysphagia rehabilitation—A review

7

H. Yang*,1, K.K. Ang*,†, C. Wang*, K.S. Phua*, C. Guan*,†

**Neural and Biomedical Technology Department, Institute for Infocomm Research, A*STAR, Singapore*
†*School of Computer Science and Engineering, College of Engineering, Nanyang Technological University, Singapore*
1*Corresponding author: Tel.: +65-6408-2000; Fax: +65-6776-1378, e-mail address: hjyang@i2r.a-star.edu.sg*

Abstract

Swallowing is an essential function in our daily life; nevertheless, stroke or other neurodegenerative diseases can cause the malfunction of swallowing function, ie, dysphagia. The objectives of this review are to understand the neural and cortical basis of swallowing and tongue, and review the latest techniques on the detection of motor imagery of swallow (MI-SW) and motor imagery of tongue movements (MI-TM), so that a practical system can be developed for the rehabilitation of poststroke dysphagia patients. Specifically, we firstly describe the swallowing process and how the swallowing function is assessed clinically. Secondly, we review the techniques that performed the neural and cortical analysis of swallowing and tongue based on different modalities such as functional magnetic resonance imaging, positron emission tomography, near-infrared spectroscopy (NIRS), and magnetoencephalography. Thirdly, we review the techniques that performed detection and analysis of MI-SW and MI-TM for dysphagia stroke rehabilitation based on electroencephalography (EEG) and NIRS. Finally, discussions on the advantages and limitations of the studies are presented; an example system and future research directions for the rehabilitation of stroke dysphagia patients are suggested.

Keywords

Motor imagery of swallow, Motor execution of swallow, Motor imagery of tongue movements, Swallowing, Tongue protrusion, Tongue movements, Dysphagia, Stroke rehabilitation, Detection, Classification

Progress in Brain Research, Volume 228, ISSN 0079-6123, http://dx.doi.org/10.1016/bs.pbr.2016.03.014
© 2016 Elsevier B.V. All rights reserved.

1 BACKGROUND

1.1 INTRODUCTION

Human swallowing is a fundamental function that is essential to our daily life. Dysphagia is the difficulty in swallowing or the inability to swallow resulting from the injury to swallowing motor areas and their connection to the brain stem (Hamdy et al., 1999a,b, 2000, 2001). Dysphagia is usually caused by stroke or other neurodegenerative diseases and central nervous system disorders (Furlong et al., 2004; Jestrovic et al., 2015; Martin et al., 2004; Satow et al., 2004; Teismann et al., 2011; Yang et al., 2012, 2014). The initiation of swallowing is a voluntary action, which requires the integrity of sensorimotor areas of the cerebral cortex (Hamdy et al., 1999a,b), and a series of oral and pharyngesophageal peristaltic events (Furlong et al., 2004). Swallowing consists of a series of processes, namely, voluntary and reflex motor control, intraoral sensory processing, salivation, and visceral regulation (Satow et al., 2004). If any of these processes or connections to the brain stem were damaged, initiation of swallow would become difficult. The majority of dysphagia is caused by stroke, where most stroke patients experience dysphagia (Hamdy et al., 2000, 2001). Dysphagia can lead to series of consequences such as malnutrition, pulmonary aspiration, mortality, and poor quality of life.

Motor imagery is a mental process by which an individual rehearses or simulates a given action in his/her mind without actually performing the movement (Dickstein and Deutsch, 2007; Ge et al., 2014; Sharma et al., 2006). Brain–computer interfaces (BCIs) enable those patients who have lost control of their motor faculties to communicate with the external world through the imagination of actions such as movements of limbs and tongue (Morash et al., 2008; Wolpaw et al., 2002). Motor imagery is assumed to involve similar cortical brain areas as that activated during motor execution (Dickstein and Deutsch, 2007; Ge et al., 2014; Sharma et al., 2006), which has been employed to improve the sparsity and recovery of motor function for the rehabilitation of stroke patients (Ang et al., 2014a,b; Dickstein and Deutsch, 2007; Prasad et al., 2010; Sharma et al., 2006; Silvoni et al., 2011). Motivated by these works, several methods on the detection of motor imagery of swallow (MI-SW) have been proposed recently, with the aim of facilitating the motor imagery-based training of dysphagia stroke patients for rehabilitation (Yang et al., 2012, 2013a,b, 2014).

1.2 SWALLOWING PROCESS AND ASSESSMENT

Swallowing is a complex process that requires the sensory processing of ingested material; execution of oral, pharyngeal, and laryngeal movements; coordination with mastication and respiration (Martin et al., 2004). Swallowing consists of three interacting phases, ie, oral (oral preparatory and oral transfer), pharyngeal, and esophageal phases, which are of varying degrees of dependence on the central control mechanism (Ertekin and Aydogdu, 2003; Matsuo and Palmer, 2008; McKeown et al., 2002; Satow et al., 2004). Varying amount of functional and structural

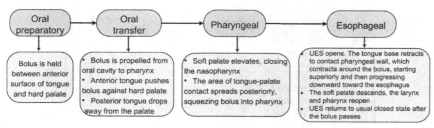

FIG. 1

Block diagram of swallowing a liquid bolus.

Adapted from Matsuo, K., Palmer, J.B., 2008. Anatomy and physiology of feeding and swallowing: normal and abnormal. Phys. Med. Rehabil. Clin. N. Am. 19 (4), 691–707.

abnormality exist in dysphagia patients in each of these phases (Matsuo and Palmer, 2008; Mckeown et al., 2002), eg, oral cavity, pharynx, larynx, or esophagus. To initiate and regulate swallowing, combination of feedback and motor planning is required (Furlong et al., 2004). A block diagram of swallowing a liquid bolus is shown in Fig. 1.

Swallowing assessment is used to evaluate how safe a patient can swallow, which is usually done by a skilled speech–language pathologist (Mckeown et al., 2002). The assessment includes bedside assessment and video fluoroscopy. The bedside assessment assesses the feeding status, posture, breathing and cooperation levels, oral reflexes, pharyngeal swallow, and a trial feed with water bolus. Videofluoroscopy is an X-ray technique that provides a detailed anatomical assessment by illuminating the path taken by the bolus (mixed with barium) as it completes the four phases of swallowing (Hamdy et al., 2000; McKeown et al., 2002). The newer fiberoptic endoscopic evaluation of swallowing (FEES) technique enables more direct assessment (McKeown et al., 2002). FEES examines motor and sensory functions of swallowing so that proper treatment can be given to patients with swallowing difficulties. Conventional therapeutic interventions include the changes in diet, posture, and adjustments of food; the physical exercises such as tongue strengthening exercises and pharyngeal maneuvers; and methods for sensitizing/desensitizing the oropharynx to alter swallow reflex (Hamdy et al., 2000; Kiger et al., 2006). Recently, stimulation techniques such as thermal stimulation and neuromuscular stimulation (eg, VitalStim) were employed (Kiger et al., 2006; Langdon and Blacker, 2010).

1.3 OBJECTIVES AND MOTIVATION

The objectives of this review are on the following aspects. Firstly, we review and summarize the typical methodologies that performed the neural cortical analysis of swallowing and tongue protrusion and movements on the modalities such as fMRI, PET, MEG, and NIRS. Secondly, we review the techniques that performed the detection of MI-SW, motor imagery of tongue protrusion/movements (MI-TM), and the analysis of the correlations between MI-SW and MI-TM, and between

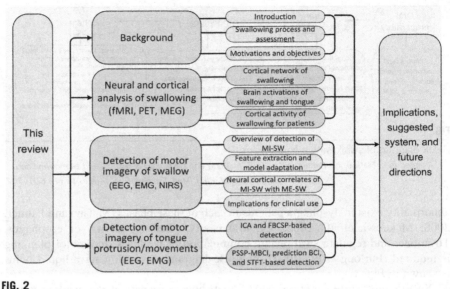

FIG. 2

Schematic illustration of the coverage in this review.

MI-SW and motor execution of swallow (ME-SW). Thirdly, we review existing work on the detection of MI-TM under multiclass settings. Finally, discussions on the advantages and limitations of the studies for swallowing are presented, and an example rehabilitation system and future research directions are suggested. The focus of this review is on BCI-based techniques, with the aim of proposing a motor imagery-based technique for the rehabilitation of stroke patients suffering from dysphagia. A schematic illustration of the coverage in this review is shown in Fig. 2. It is noted that the neurological origins of swallowing, cortical activations during swallowing, different modalities used for swallowing studies, and swallowing-related olfactory-based electroencephalography (EEG) studies have also been discussed in other reviews (Ertekin and Aydogdu, 2003; Jestrovic et al., 2015).

2 NEURAL AND CORTICAL ANALYSIS OF SWALLOWING

In this section, we review typical techniques used for neural and cortical analysis of the components of swallowing and summarize the details of the major articles in Table 1.

2.1 CORTICAL NETWORK OF SWALLOWING

The neuroanatomical representation of the cortical network involved in swallowing has been identified using transcranial magnetic stimulation (TMS) (Hamdy et al., 1996), functional magnetic imaging (Hamdy et al., 1999a,b), and positron emission

Table 1 Studies on Neural and Cortical Analysis of Swallowing

Category, Reference, Modality	Subjects and Cue, Data	Study Contents	Key Findings
Hamdy et al. (1996), TMS, Cortical network for swallowing	20 Healthy subj. (12/8: male/female, mean: 34); 2 stroke pat. (51 and 68, unilateral hemispheric stroke; 1 with/1 without dysphagia	To study cortical topography of human oral, pharyngeal, and esophageal musculature in healthy subj.; and topography of pharyngeal musculature in stroke pat. Apply single magnetoelectric stimuli to cortex to excite EMG responses. 3 stimuli for each scalp site	○ Swallowing musculature was represented by motor and premotor cortex, showed interhemispheric asymmetry, independent of handedness ○ Topography of the mylohyoid muscles was most lateral and that of pharynx and esophagus appeared to be more rostromedial ○ Dysphagia was associated with smaller pharyngeal representation on intact hemisphere and increased with the recovery of swallowing
Hamdy et al. (1999a), fMRI, Cortical network for swallowing	10 Healthy volunteers (7/3: male/female, mean age: 32 years); water bolus	To study cortical activations and lateralization Injecting water bolus into the oral cavity every 30 s	○ Areas with increased signal changes: caudal sensorimotor cortex, anterior insula, premotor cortex, frontal operculum, anterior cingulate and prefrontal cortex, anterolateral and posterior parietal cortex ○ Activations were bilateral, and lateralization was observed at premotor, insular, and frontal opercular cortices ○ Multidimensional cortical activity implied recruiting brain areas for processing motor, sensory, and attention/affective aspects of task
Martin et al. (2004), fMRI, Brain activations for swallowing and tongue	14 Healthy subj. (12/2: female/male, 28±6.5 years), performed voluntary saliva swallowing, tongue mov., finger opposition Visual cues	Single-event-related fMRI, laryngeal, and tongue movements were recorded 12-min imaging runs, 3 tasks in each run: voluntary swallowing of saliva, voluntary tongue elevation, and finger opposition, 6 times for each task	○ Both swallowing and tongue elevation activated left lateral pericentral and anterior parietal cortex; anterior cingulate cortex and adjacent SMA. Tongue activation was larger than swallowing at ACC, SMA, right precentral and postcentral gyri, premotor cortex, right putamen, and thalamus ○ 60% of the subjects showed lateralization of the postcentral gyrus toward left hemisphere for swallowing. 40% showed lateralization toward left for tongue elevation

Continued

Table 1 Studies on Neural and Cortical Analysis of Swallowing—cont'd

Category, Reference, Modality	Subjects and Cue, Data	Study Contents	Key Findings
Furlong et al. (2004), MEG, Brain activations for swallowing and tongue	8 Healthy subj. (6/2: male/female, aged 28–45), 151-channel whole cortex MEG data were collected	To study temporal characteristics of cortical activity of swallowing using MEG. Oral water infusion, volitional wet swallowing (5 mL bolus), tongue thrust, or rest. Each condition lasted for 5 s and was repeated 20 times. SAM analysis was performed	○ Water infusion preferentially activated caudolateral sensorimotor cortex. Volitional swallowing and tongue movement activated superior sensorimotor cortex ○ Time–frequency wavelet analysis showed that sensory input from tongue simultaneously activated caudolateral sensorimotor and primary gustatory cortex (prime areas for volitional phase of swallowing)
Satow et al. (2004), scalp EEG and epicortical EEG Brain activations for swallowing and tongue	8 Healthy subj. (7/1: male/female, 24–38), scalp EEG. 6 epilepsy pat. (2/4: male/female, 15–34), implanted Subdural elec., self-paced, each sess. 10 min, 8–10 sess.	To investigate face/tongue SMI and SMA in volitional swallowing by MRCPs. To determine hemispheric dominance from preparatory phase of swallowing (scalp EEG). Swallow: keep 2–3 mL water in mouth and swallow with jaw kept relaxed and slightly open. Tongue: jaw was kept relaxed, to make brisk forward protrusion of tongue	○ Scalp EEG for normal subjects revealed that premovement BP was largest at vertex and lateralized ○ Epicortical EEG in patients confirmed that face/tongue SMI and SMA were involved in swallowing and tongue protrusion. SMA played a supplementary role to face/tongue SMI in swallowing and tongue ○ No difference in BP amplitude between swallowing and tongue, whereas PMP was significantly larger in tongue than swallowing at face/tongue SMI, suggesting cerebral cortex does not play a significant role in postmovement processing of swallowing
Teismann et al. (2011) Cortical activity of swallowing for patients	7 Controls (3/4: female/male, mean: 57.6), 14 ALS (9/5: male/female, mean: 58.9), mildly (MDG, 7) and severely dysphagic (SDG, 7) patients	Investigated cortical activation during deglutition in MDG and SDG ALS using MEG. Performed time–frequency analysis and SAM. 15 min of MEG recording, swallowed in self-paced manner, no external cue. Data were collected by 275-channel SQUID array	○ Reduction in cortical swallowing-related activation in ALS, the response was stronger for SDG group ○ Healthy subjects showed bilateral cortical activation, whereas the right sensorimotor cortex was dominant for ALS patients ○ The cortical plasticity demonstrated by the right hemisphere lateralization (RHL) of volitional swallowing can be used as compensational mechanisms, where the RHL is known to predominantly coordinate the pharyngeal phase of deglutition

Notes: subj., subjects; pat., patients; mov., movements; sess., session; elec., electrodes; ALS, amyotrophic lateral sclerosis; ACC, anterior cingulate cortex; SMA, supplementary motor area; BP, Bereischaftspotentials; PMP, postmovement potential; MDG, mildly dysphagic patients; SDG, severely dysphagic patients; SMI, face/tongue area of primary sensorimotor.

tomography (PET) (Hamdy et al., 1999a,b). A review of the swallowing problems and how the organization of the cortical projections to swallowing muscles can account for many clinical observations on swallowing after stroke has been reported (Hamdy et al., 2000, 2001). The central nervous system of the brain controls the regulation of swallowing (Hamdy et al., 2000). Specifically, the reflective component of swallowing depends on the swallowing center in the brain stem, whereas the initiation of swallowing is voluntary involving the integrity of motor areas of cerebral cortex (Hamdy et al., 2000). Furthermore studies showed that one of the hemispheres was dominant on the control of swallowing for humans (Hamdy et al., 2000). Asymmetry was found in the size of responses evoked by a constant stimulus to each hemisphere (Hamdy et al., 1997a, 1998, 2000, 2001), ie, the responses from one hemisphere tended to be larger than that of another. Analysis of the electromyogram (EMG) response from stimulation of a single shocks given several seconds apart showed that the EMG had a latency comparable to the pathway from the cortex via brain stem to the muscles (Hamdy et al., 2000), demonstrating the somatotopically arranged swallowing muscles such as the oral muscles, and the pharynx and esophagus were arranged laterally and medially, respectively. The PET results on swallowing showed strong activations in the sensorimotor cortices, insula, and cerebellum (Hamdy et al., 2000). Other cerebral regions that were recruited in an asymmetric manner are right orbitofrontal cortex, left medial premotor cortex and cingulate, right and left caudolateral sensorimotor cortex, right anterior insular, left temporopolar cortex merging with left amygdala, right temporopolar cortex, and left medial cerebellum.

The physiological characteristics of the corticofugal pathways to oral, pharyngeal, and esophageal muscles help identify their topographic relations and explore the evidence for interhemispheric asymmetries described (Hamdy et al., 1996). TMS was given by single magnetoelectric stimuli to the cortex of fully conscious subjects, which evoked the EMG responses in each of the individual muscle groups active in the swallowing. The evoked EMG responses show that the individual muscle groups respond bilaterally and are asymmetrically represented in the motor and premotor cortex (Hamdy et al., 1996). This finding inferred an important role of the motor cortex in the control of the complex swallowing process. It is anticipated that the specific areas of the motor cortex may be related to each phase of swallowing, which may act differently from the brain stem swallowing center and can be modulated individually to control and monitor the swallowing process.

To understand how the cerebral cortex operates in controlling the complex swallowing function, the cortical activity associated with human volitional swallowing using single-event-related functional magnetic resonance imaging (fMRI) was identified (Hamdy et al., 1999a). The water boluses of 5 mL were injected into the oral cavity every 30 s via a plastic infusion catheter, and the subject was instructed to initiate swallowing. Each subject performed 20 wet swallows. The analysis results showed that the peak activation occurred at least 12 s after onset of swallow. Most subjects showed a significant decrease in signal change immediately after swallow. Consistent activations are observed in ACC, caudolateral sensorimotor cortex, anterior insula, frontal opercular cortex, superior premotor cortex, anteromedial temporal cortex, anterolateral somatosensory cortex, and precuneus (Hamdy et al., 1999a). Activations were bilateral for most subjects; however, they were lateralized at insular, opercular, and premotor cortices, which was consistent with the results reported in Hamdy et al. (1996, 1999b), showing that the motor projections of pharyngeal and esophageal from areas anterior to the primary motor strip are asymmetrically represented (Hamdy et al., 1999a,b). These results furthermore imply that the cortical control mechanisms are more important for pharyngeal and esophageal motility than oral stage functions.

Compensatory reorganization of the undamaged hemisphere has been suggested for the recovery of swallowing function in the throat (Hamdy et al., 2000). One possible therapy to speed up the recovery is to manipulate the sensory input to the cortex. Another way is to induce changes in the excitation of motor cortex with prolonged electrical stimulation of the pharynx for up to 15 min (Hamdy et al., 1998, 2000). These findings can be exploited for the treatment of the dysphagia patients by noting the asymmetry on the connections of each hemisphere, increasing the involvement of the projections from the undamaged hemisphere, and involving the stimulation of sensory and afferent inputs from the pharynx (Hamdy et al., 2000, 2001). The pharyngeal responses to swallowing show a remarkable increase in amplitude and area for unaffected hemisphere, compared with the little changes showed in the affected hemisphere (Hamdy et al., 2000).

The key points of these findings are summarized in the reviews (Hamdy et al., 2000, 2001). Cerebral cortex plays an important role in regulation of swallowing and the reflexive component of swallowing depends on swallowing centers in brain stem. Initiation of swallowing involves the integrity of motor areas of cerebral cortex. The locus of cortical control of swallowing lies anterior caudal to the face area of primary motor cortex. The most effective site for stimulation is slightly anterior to the best points for obtaining responses in muscles of hand or arm. Repetitive electrical stimulation of cortex in animals or humans can help induce swallowing (Hamdy et al., 2001). One of the hemispheres is dominant, whereas stimulation of undamaged hemisphere of dysphagia patients produces smaller responses in pharynx and esophagus than that of the undamaged hemisphere in nondysphagic patients. This finding can be used to determine the presence or absence of dysphagia. Good recovery of swallowing function depends on compensatory reorganization of the undamaged hemisphere. Future therapies could target at interventions for reorganization on the intact side to enhance swallowing.

2.2 BRAIN ACTIVATIONS OF SWALLOWING AND TONGUE

Swallowing and tongue are relevant but distinct actions, whereas tongue movement is an integral part of swallowing process. Hence, investigations have been carried out to study the brain activations during swallowing and tongue movements based on fMRI (Martin et al., 2004), magnetoencephalography (MEG) (Furlong et al., 2004) and movement-related cortical potentials (MRCPs) (Satow et al., 2004). Trials of single swallowing and tongue elevation were verified based on profiles of laryn-geal movements (Martin et al., 2001, 2004). The brain activations for swallowing and tongue elevation were contrasted and identified (Martin et al., 2004). The inclusion of tongue elevation lies in that it is an integral part of swallowing and can be pro-duced volitionally. The inclusion of finger opposition task is to verify that the brain regions activated by swallow or tongue elevation is specific to an oral sensorimotor task, and not to the limb movements. The common activated regions of swallowing and tongue elevation were interpreted as the motor planning and motor execution shared by them. The brain regions activated by swallowing but not tongue elevation were interpreted as the functional role performed specific to swallowing regulation (Martin et al., 2002, 2004). The results showed that the most consistent shared com-mon activation regions were the lateral pericentral cortex, frontoparietal operculum, and ACC. The pericentral activation common to both tasks may show the mechanical sensory stimulation of the oral cavity by moving the bolus during swallow, as well as by the tongue contacting with other oral tissues (Martin et al., 2004). The distinct activation regions of swallowing and tongue movements from that of finger tapping were consistent with previous findings that the orofacial representation within sen-sorimotor cortex was lateral to that of the hand (Mosier et al., 1999). The common activated frontoparietal operculum suggests that the presence of the mediation of the similar processing during simple voluntary oral movements such as tongue elevation (Martin et al., 2001). Furthermore, the common activated region of somatosensory association areas may also suggest that the mechanical sensory processing (rather than gustatory processing) is involved in tongue elevation since tongue movement does not involve the manipulation of the bolus (Martin et al., 2004). The regions activated by swallowing alone were left lateral pericentral cortex immediately lateral to the area activated by tongue movement, left postcentral gyrus, ACC, precuneus/cuneus, and right insula/operculum (Martin et al., 2004).

A synthetic aperture magnetometry (SAM)-based technique for MEG data was employed to dissociate the cortical contributions of each separable component of swallowing in the sensorimotor sequence and identify the spatiotemporal character-istics of cortical activity during swallowing (Furlong et al., 2004). The MEG data were analyzed in the frequency bands of 5–15 Hz, 15–25 Hz, and 25–40 Hz. The ac-tive epochs windowed at 5 s following the cues to receive water, swallow, or tongue thrust were referenced to the passive epochs of 5 s before cue to rest. The event-related paradigm makes it possible to separate the components of swallowing. Time–frequency plots based on wavelet analysis were employed to examine the tem-poral sequencing of activation within regions of interest (ROIs). SAM was then used to dissociate both the spatial and temporal characteristics of cortical activity within an interconnected cortical swallowing network (Furlong et al., 2004).

Comparison of time–frequency wavelet plots for all subjects from left caudolat-eral precentral gyrus (dot in the image) before nonparametric statistical analysis is shown in Fig. 3. In the figure, the MRI-SAM group mean images for all eight subjects were shown in the right, where each active phase vs rest phase for the 15–25 Hz bands is shown. Significant activation within the left and right superior precentral

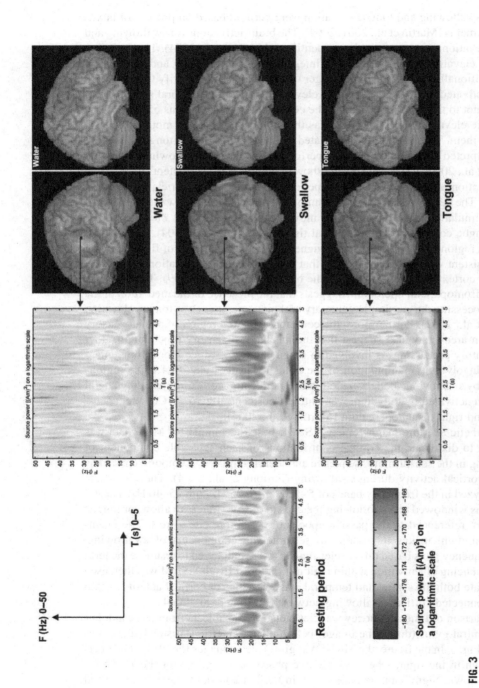

FIG. 3

Comparison of time–frequency plots for all subjects from left caudolateral precentral gyrus. Colors represented the level of frequency power difference between active and passive phases, with *blues* (*dark gray* in the print version)/*purples* (*gray* in the print version), and *reds* (*gray* in the print version)/*yellows* (*light gray* in the print version) indicating a decrease (ERD) and an increase (ERS) in power, respectively. Time 0 on the x-axis corresponds to the onset of the visual cue for each condition.

Reprinted from Furlong, P.L., Hobson, A.R., Aziz, Q., Barnes, G.R., Singh, K.D., Hillebrand, A., Thompson, D.G., and Hamdy, S., 2004. Dissociating the spatiotemporal characteristics of cortical neuronal activity associated with human volitional swallowing in the healthy adult. Neuroimage 22, 1447–1455, with permission from Elsevier.

gyrus (BA 4) together with the right postcentral gyrus in the 5–15 Hz frequency band and a larger area of activation in the inferior precentral cortex which appeared bilaterally was observed. The time–frequency wavelet plot for multiple cortical sites for one representative individual is shown in Fig. 4. Significant changes in power ($p < 0.05$) with respect to the mean level in the passive phase are indicated. The pattern of activation over time at an inferior precentral gyrus site was revealed. The selection of this site was due to the involvement of the precentral in all three active phases across all subjects. A dominant resting frequency in 15–25 Hz band was observed. The group SAM images showed the event-related desynchronization (ERD) throughout the water infusion and tongue thrust phases and the ERD during swallowing phase but with an event-related synchronization (ERS) rebound upon completion of swallowing.

The results showed that activation of superior sensorimotor cortex occurred during volitional swallowing and tongue movement, and caudolateral sensorimotor cortex was activated during water infusion. The ERD/ERS associated with swallowing was similar to those described by other functional imaging techniques. The findings with oral infusion of water confirmed that the sensation played a major role in central regulatory feedback of swallowing, acting at both brain stem and cortical levels (Furlong et al., 2004). The results revealed that the superior regions of precentral cortex were an important contributor to swallowing. The pericentral cortical loci activated during tongue movements was the same as that activated by swallowing, demonstrating that the significant contribution of tongue during swallowing was sensory. The temporal analysis of ROIs showed significant ERD following water infusion at the caudolateral pericentral cortex.

MRCPs preceding voluntary movements are known to reflect a central control process with superior temporal resolution (Satow et al., 2004). To clearly distinguish the motor components and sensory feedback, MRCPs at face/tongue area of primary sensorimotor (SMI) cortex and supplementary motor area (SMA) were employed to clarify the sequential cerebral processing of swallowing (Satow et al., 2004), where scalp EEG was recorded for normal subjects and epicortical EEG was recorded for patients. The changes of cortical activity in different phases of swallowing were also studied by MRCPs (Satow et al., 2004). As indicated, the pre- and postmovement activities of MRCPs reflected motor components without and with sensory feedback. Electrooculograms, EMG, and glossokinetic potential were recorded to monitor the eye movements and other swallow-related movements. Artifactual and incomplete trials were excluded, and the EEG signal was baseline corrected. The Bereitschaft-spotentials (BP) onset time was determined visually at the time when slow potential shift started to arise from baseline (Satow et al., 2004). Two electrodes at the left (C3) and right (C4) central were used to determine the dominant side. The results revealed that the BP was maximal at the midline vertex for both swallow and tongue, and asymmetrically distributed, but the dominant side was not consistent across subjects, with the distribution of tongue to a lesser degree. The face/tongue SMI or its adjacent area was involved in BP generation for tongue but not for swallow. The amplitude of postmovement potential (PMP) on lateral for tongue was

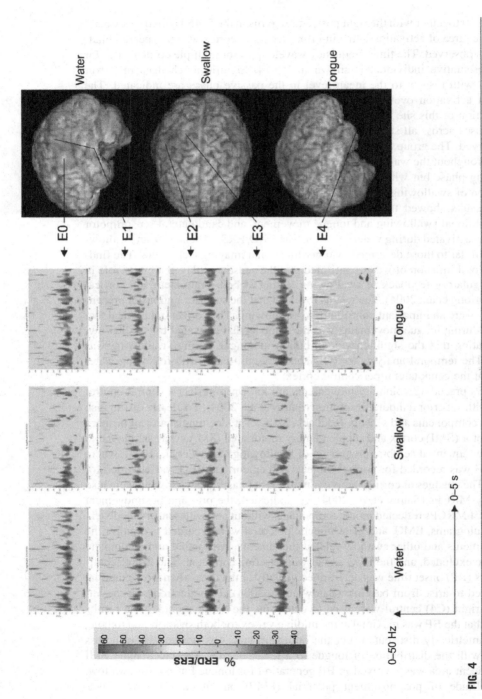

FIG. 4

Time–frequency wavelet plots for multiple cortical sites in one representative individual. Spectrograms calculated for a single subject. Voxels in positions E0, E1, E2, E3 represented the precentral gyrus, inferior parietal lobule, postcentral gyrus (Brodmann area 2), and postcentral gyrus (Brodmann area 5), respectively. MRI-SAM images (right) for the active water (25–40 Hz), swallow, and tongue thrust (15–25 Hz) phases vs rest. Time 0 on the x-axis indicates the end of the 5 s of the passive period and 0 s for the commencement of the 5 s of the active phase.

Reprinted from Furlong, P.L., Hobson, A.R., Aziz, Q., Barnes, G.R., Singh, K.D., Hillebrand, A., Thompson, D.G., and Hamdy, S., 2004. Dissociating the spatiotemporal characteristics of cortical neuronal activity associated with human volitional swallowing in the healthy adult. Neuroimage 22, 1447–1455, with permission from Elsevier.

significantly larger than that for swallow, despite the fact that swallowing is comprised of a sequence of motor and sensory processing. This suggests that the brain stem reflex mechanism is the main driving force for swallowing after initial volitional swallowing (Satow et al., 2004). Caudal SMA and rostral SMA were active in both swallow and tongue. No consistent difference on the distribution of BP and PMP between swallow and tongue on lateral or medial was found. The active areas for swallow and tongue overlapped to certain degrees, which may suggest that the face/tongue SMI played an equally important role in both the preparation for voluntary swallowing and tongue protrusion at least for the initial stage (Satow et al., 2004). The onset time of BP for swallow is earlier than that for tongue. The results furthermore demonstrated the engagement of face/tongue SMI in the preparation for volitional swallowing as well as tongue movement. Medial frontal cortex (caudal/rostral SMA) was commonly involved in volitional swallowing and tongue movements (Satow et al., 2004).

2.3 CORTICAL ACTIVITY OF SWALLOWING FOR PATIENTS

MEG has been employed to monitor the cortical activity with a high temporal and spatial resolution. The SAM-based whole-head MEG has been demonstrated as a reliable method to examine complex function of swallowing in humans (Furlong et al., 2004; Teismann et al., 2011). Along the same line, a whole-head MEG and SAM were employed to study the cortical activity during self-paced volitional swallowing for the amyotrophic lateral sclerosis (ALS) patients, aiming at discovering the effects of neuron degeneration of ALS to the cortical processing of human swallowing (Teismann et al., 2011). MEG data recorded from three groups of subjects, ie, control, mildly dysphagic patients (MDG), and severely dysphagic patients (SDG) were analyzed. The individual SAM results showed that ERD of beta and low gamma frequency band was bilateral in the sensorimotor cortices during swallowing execution phase for the controls. Left hemispheric lateralization was also observed for beta activation in the controls. Beta ERD was found in MDG and SDG patients, and most of them showed right hemispheric lateralization. No symmetric activation was found in all three groups. Group comparisons revealed significantly stronger activation of bilateral primary sensorimotor cortex in the control group compared with the patient groups. The significant reduction in cortical sensorimotor activation in ALS compared with controls increased with the progression of the disease. Furthermore, clear right hemispheric lateralization was observed in both patient groups (Teismann et al., 2011). The lack of involvement of the mesial areas or the secondary sensorimotor cortex but only the central area of the primary motor cortex might reflect the disturbance of the swallowing network (Teismann et al., 2011). Reasons for the reduction of the bilateral cortical ERD during swallowing may be due to the degeneration of the upper motor function or the compensation for the disordered pharyngeal swallowing by an increase in the number of active neurons at the right hemisphere (Teismann et al., 2011).

3 DETECTION OF MI-SW

In this section, we review different approaches on the detection and analysis of MI-SW and MI-TM based on EEG and near-infrared spectroscopy (NIRS). The details of these methods are summarized in Table 2.

3.1 OVERVIEW OF DETECTION OF MI-SW

Detection of MI-SW in comparison with the detection of MI-TM for the purpose of stroke dysphagia rehabilitation was investigated (Yang et al., 2012, 2013a,b, 2014, 2015a). BCI-based motor imagery of upper limb (eg, grasping, stretching, finger-typing, finger opposition, supination, pronation, etc.) and motor imagery of lower limb (eg, walking and foot dorsiflexion.) have been employed for stroke rehabilitation (Ang and Guan, 2015; Ang et al., 2014a,b; de Vries and Mulder, 2007; Dickstein et al., 2004; Do et al., 2011, 2013; Dunsky et al., 2008; Prasad et al., 2010; Sharma et al., 2006; Silvoni et al., 2011; Yang et al., 2015b). The principle is based on the shared common brain activation areas for motor imagery and motor execution of the same actions, eg, hand grasping and walking. The clinical trials based on 21 chronic hemiplegic stroke patients in BCI-haptic knob intervention, and the one based on 26 stroke patients in BCI-Manus therapy achieved significant higher motor gain compared with standard arm therapy, supporting its potential use in stroke rehabilitation coupled with physical rehabilitation therapy (Ang et al., 2014a,b). The engagement of the patients was measured during an MI practice by the neurofeedback, which was performed as part of the poststroke rehabilitation protocol, in conjunction with the physical practice (Prasad et al., 2010). Hemispheric asymmetry in both mu and beta bands contributed to BCI classification accuracies as demonstrated by the high correlation between classification accuracies and ERD/ERS ratios. Employing MI of upper limb or lower limb for the training of stroke patients has been investigated extensively in the past decades. However, there are only a few approaches that detected MI-SW for the rehabilitation of stroke dysphagia patients (Yang et al., 2012, 2013a,b, 2014). Possible reasons are as follows. First, swallowing is a complex process which involves the three phases of oral, pharyngeal, and esophageal and requires the integration from central nervous system, motor planning and control, attention, etc. It is difficult to imagine such a complex process especially for the dysphagia patients (Ertekin and Aydogdu, 2003; Yang et al., 2012, 2014). Second, detection of MI-SW is also difficult compared with that of motor imagery of upper limb and lower limb, where a single or only a few motor actions are involved.

The use of MI-SW for dysphagia rehabilitation was first investigated (Yang et al., 2012, 2013a,b, 2014, 2015a,b). In these studies, they investigated the following: (1) to test the hypotheses that MI-SW and MI-TM could be detected from the background idle state for their possible use in stroke dysphagia rehabilitation, (2) to build a model based on a simple yet relevant modality of MI-TM EEG signals to detect MI-SW, (3) to test the hypotheses by determining the classification accuracies across

Table 2 Studies on the Detection and Analysis of Motor Imagery of Swallow

Study	# of Subjects, Trials, Classes, and Cue	Modalities/ Electrodes	Features, Classifiers	Accuracies/Statistical Analysis Results and Key Findings
Yang et al. (2012)	6 Healthy subj, Cue: images; 60 trials/sess., 2 classes. MI-SW vs idle: 2 sess.; ME-TM vs idle: 1 sess.	EEG (MI-SW, ME-TM, Idle), 30 channels	Features: DTCWT; classifier: SVM	CV acc.: 69.96% Selecting the time segments based on the initiation from EEG signal of tongue movements is effective
Yang et al. (2013a)	6 Healthy subj, whose CV acc. > 60%. Cue: Videos; 160 trials/sess. 2 sess., 2 classes: MI-SW vs idle	EEG (MI-SW, idle), 30 channels	Features: DTCWT; Laplacian power; classifier: SVM	○ S2S acc. using MI-SW model: 74.29% (power fea.) 72.64% (wavelet fea.) ○ Feature consistency and cluster impurity-based model adaptation (MA-FCCI) was effective for session-to-session classification based on MI-SW model
Yang et al. (2013b)	6 Healthy subj., CV acc. > 60%. Cue: videos; 160 trials/sess., 2 classes. MI-SW vs idle: 2 sess.; MI-TM vs idle: 1 sess.	EEG, (MI-SW vs idle; MI-TM vs idle), 30 channels	Features: DTCWT; classifier: SVM	○ S2S acc.: 72.12% (using MI-SW model.) and 71.81% (using MI-TM model) ○ Using MI-TM model to classify MI-SW and model adaption using MA-FCCI was effective for session-to-session classification
Yang et al. (2014)	10 Healthy subj., 1 stroke patient. Cue: videos; 160 trials/sess., 2 classes. MI-SW vs idle: 2 sess.; MI-TM vs idle: 1 sess.	EEG (MI-SW vs idle; MI-TM vs idle), 30 channels	Features: DTCWT; classifier: SVM	○ CV acc.: 70.89% (MI-SW; 73.79% (MI-TM; S2S acc.: 66.40% (using MI-SW model); 70.24% (using MI-TM model) ○ MI-SW and MI-TM were detectable for healthy and dysphagia patient, using MI-TM and MI-SW model. Model adaptation by maximizing the ratio of the between-classes distance and within-class distances (MA-RBWD) was effective

Continued

Table 2 Studies on the Detection and Analysis of Motor Imagery of Swallow—cont'd

Study	# of Subjects, Trials, Classes, and Cue	Modalities/ Electrodes	Features, Classifiers	Accuracies/Statistical Analysis Results and Key Findings
Yang et al. (2015a,b)	10 Healthy subj., 1 stroke patient; cue: videos; 80 trials/class, 3 classes: MI-SW, ME-SW, MI-TM	EEG (MI-SW, MI-TM, ME-SW), selected channels (C3, C4)	Bin-based spectral power, baseline removed, smoothed, spike trials corrected	o Group analysis results demonstrated that MI-SW and MI-TM, and MI-SW and ME-SW were strongly correlated (p-value < 0.001, examined at "C3") for both mu and low beta frequency bands o Correlation was weaker but still significant for MI-SW and ME-SW (p-value < 0.05), and MI-SW and MI-TM (p-value < 0.01) for the dysphagia patient
Kober and Wood (2014)	14 Healthy subj; Cue: text; 20 trials/MI-SW and 20 trials/ME-SW (swallow water)	NIRS (oxy-Hb, deoxy-Hb), 48 channels	PASW statistics 18 was used for statistical analysis	o MI and ME showed strongest changes in inferior frontal gyrus. Changes in deoxy-Hb were comparable between kinesthetic MI and ME o ME: oxy-Hb significantly increased, peak at 15 s after task onset. MI: oxy-Hb decreased during MI compared to a rest period
Kober et al. (2015)	Patients: 2 with cerebral lesions, 2 with lesions in brain stem; 2 healthy subj.; Cue: text; 10 trials/MI-SW, 10 trials/ME-SW, 2 classes, swallow saliva	NIRS (oxy-Hb, deoxy-Hb), 20 channels	Artifacts correction, high-pass and low-pass filtering, baseline correction, averaging task period	o Patients with lesions in brain stem showed bilateral hemodynamic changes in inferior frontal gyrus during ME-SW o Patients with cerebral lesion showed more unilateral activation patterns during ME-SW and showed a prolonged time course during MI-SW and ME-SW compared to controls o Patients with brain stem lesions, activation patterns were largely comparable, especially for changes in deoxy-Hb (ME-SW and MI-SW)

Notes: S2S, *session-to-session*; CV, *crossvalidation*; DTCWT, *dual-tree complex wavelet transform*; SVM, *support vector machine*; oxy-Hb, *oxyhemoglobin*; deoxy-Hb, *deoxygenated hemoglobin*; PASW, *predictive analytics software*.

sessions and modalities, and (4) to determine the classification accuracies in a sample of 10 healthy volunteers and 1 subject with chronic stroke. Dual-tree complex wavelet transform (DTCWT) was employed for feature extraction (FE), in particular, the energy and phases of the wavelet coefficients at different levels and directions, and coarse representation of the EEG signal were used as the features. These signals are expected to contain the EEG rhythms at different frequency ranges, ie, the ERS and ERD. The dynamic initiation location identified using the EMG signal of tongue movements was employed to extract the effective time segment for the detection of MI-SW. This is possible since swallowing and tongue movements shared some common brain activation areas (Martin et al., 2004; Yang et al., 2014), whereby the tongue movements are an integral part of the whole swallowing process (Yang et al., 2012, 2014). Furthermore, the initiations to the motor imagery of two relevant tasks are expected to be similar for a person. Based on the selected six healthy subjects, an average classification accuracy (ie, by classifying MI-SW vs idle) of 69.96% was achieved by using the time segment centered at the dynamically identified initiation location of tongue movements. This was significantly higher than that obtained by using a fixed time segment with different time intervals, as well as the three existing methods, namely, common spatial pattern (CSP), filter bank CSP (FBCSP), and sliding window discriminative CSP (SWDCSP)-based methods. It should be noted that the timing for performing MI-SW was only 6 s in this experimental protocol, which is relatively short for a subject to complete the whole complex MI-SW process. The results also showed that choosing different sizes of moving window to detect the dynamic initiation time did not affect the detection rate significantly.

Furthermore investigations on how to improve the detection accuracies of classifying MI-SW vs idle based on MI-SW model (ie, the training model generated by classifying MI-SW vs idle) as well as MI-TM model (ie, the training model generated by classifying MI-TM vs idle) from earlier sessions were investigated (Yang et al., 2013a,b, 2014). The nonstationarity of EEG signal leads to the degradation of the classification performance, especially when the model was built using the data collected in a session which was far from the testing session. Two novel methods for model adaptation for the detection of MI-SW was proposed (Yang et al., 2013a,b, 2014), namely, model adaption based on the feature consistency and cluster impurity (MA-FCCI) (Yang et al., 2013a,b) and model adaptation by maximizing the ratio of between-classes distance and within-class distance (MA-RBWD) (Yang et al., 2014). A small amount of calibration-testing data collected on the same day as the testing data were employed to select the best training models to classify the testing data. The model adaptation methods were tested for classifying MI-SW vs idle using both MI-SW model and MI-TM model. These two methods will be discussed in more details in Section 3.2.2.

Moving the research from laboratory to clinical trials, in another attempt, detection of MI-SW and MI-TM was investigated based on 10 healthy subjects and 1 dysphagia patient (Yang et al., 2014). The session-to-session classification accuracy was boosted by adaptively selecting the trained models. In this investigation,

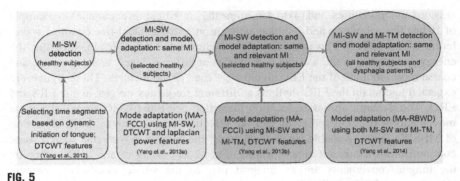

FIG. 5

Schematic illustration of the progression of DTCWT-based detection of MI-SW and MI-TM.

10 healthy subjects with the mean age of 35.9 ± 7.7 years old (mean $\pm$ standard deviation), and one stroke dysphagia patient of 56-year-old Chinese male participated in the experiments (Yang et al., 2014). The experimental protocol consisted of 17 s including 2 s of preparation and 15 s of performing MI-SW or MI-TM (tongue protrusion). This long time interval allowed the subject to finish the imagination of the complex swallowing process. Two sessions of MI-SW and one session of MI-TM EEG data were collected. These data were used to test the session-to-session classification accuracy using the proposed adaptive model selection method and to test the possibility of using MI-TM model to classify MI-SW. In these experiments, Neuroscan NuAmps cap and EEG acquisition software were employed. EMG activity was also monitored by recording the activities at the submental and infrahyoid muscles. A schematic illustration of the progression of the detection of MI-SW and MI-TM for dysphagia rehabilitation based on EEG signals is shown in Fig. 5.

3.2 FEATURE EXTRACTION AND MODEL ADAPTATION

3.2.1 Feature extraction

CSP has been widely employed in extracting features for EEG signals (Blankertz et al., 2008; Ramoser et al., 2000). CSP transforms the data into the two classes such that they have the same principle components, and their eigen values added up to a unit matrix (Ge et al., 2014). The basic idea in CSP is to optimize the spatial filters such that the variance of the projected signal is maximum for one class and minimum for another class (Blankertz et al., 2008; Ge et al., 2014; Ramoser et al., 2000). CSP is originally proposed for binary classification, which has been extended to multi-classes by pairing any two classes (Dornhege et al., 2006; Ge et al., 2014) or considering any one-vs-the-rest classes (Blankertz et al., 2003; Ge et al., 2014). This is a supervised method and mostly suitable for the two-class classification problem. Despite its most popular use in the EEG classification, CSP-based features have shown some vulnerability in the presence of noise, artifacts, and nonstationarity, which are normally present in the EEG recordings. Hence, a lot of algorithms were subsequently proposed to address this problem by employing a regularization strategy to reduce the variability of the features between training and testing sessions (Quionero-Candela et al., 2009; Sugiyama et al., 2007) and to transfer the changes between subjects performing the same experiments (Kang et al., 2009; Lotte and Guan, 2010, 2011; Samek et al., 2013b). To address the robustness issue, a recent approach formulated the problem as extracting the spatial filter computation as a divergence maximization problem (Samek et al., 2013a,b,c, 2014). This formulation integrated many state-of-the-art CSP variants and provides an information geometric interpretation.

Different from the CSP-based FE method, in which the label information of the training data is needed to guide the FE process, the complex wavelet transform (DTCWT)-based approach is an unsupervised FE method (Yang et al., 2012, 2013a,b, 2014). The wavelets were designed such that the two wavelets of the first pair were offset from one another, and another pair formed an approximate Hilbert transform pair (Yang et al., 2014). The selection of the DTCWT not only lies in the general advantages of wavelet transform, eg, EEG data at different frequency bands as well as time localization can be obtained, but also lies in the special properties that DTCWT possesses, ie, shift-invariant, approximately analytic for real and imagery parts of the filters and antialiasing effects (Yang et al., 2014). In the experiments, the EEG signal sampled at 250 Hz was decomposed into five levels; in this way, the EEG data at level 5, 4, and 3, and level 2 and 1 would represent the theta, alpha, beta, and gamma rhythms, respectively. The final features for the detection of ERD/ERS were formulated by the powers and phases at different levels and directions, coarse representation of the EEG signals, and higher order statistics such as skewness and kurtosis of the powers and phases.

3.2.2 Model adaptation

How to improve the detection accuracies of MI-SW based on MI-SW model as well as MI-TM model built using data recorded from earlier sessions were investigated (Yang et al., 2013a,b, 2014). The nonstationarity of the EEG signal leads to different distributions of the features for the training and testing data (Krusienski et al., 2011; Lotte and Guan, 2011; Lotte et al., 2009; Quionero-Candela et al., 2009; Samek et al., 2013a,b,c; Shenoy et al., 2006; Sugiyama et al., 2007; Yang et al., 2014). This nonstationarity was caused by the changes in electrode locations, variations in the electrodes impedance over time, and using and not using the feedback for online testing and training sessions. Existing approaches to address the unsupervised adaptation include unsupervised covariate shift minimization by estimating the shift in distribution based on a least-square fitting, adapting the parameters of the FE methods, unsupervised classifier adaptation, and debiasing the classifier output (Krusienski et al., 2011). The nonstationarity of EEG signal leads to the degradation of the classification performance, especially when the model was built using the data collected in a session which was far from the testing session in time. Two model adaptation methods were proposed to address the nonstationarity issue (Yang et al., 2013a,b, 2014).

Different from existing methods, the proposed method built many training models by randomly sampling the training set of the data, which can be obtained during crossvalidation evaluation. Hence, no extra process is required. In the first model adaptation method (Yang et al., 2013a), the model adaptation is done based on the feature consistency and cluster impurity (MA-FCCI). A small amount of calibration-testing data collected on the same day as the testing data were employed. The features of the training data and the calibration-testing data were first clustered. The cluster impurity was then measured. The cluster with the minimum impurity was selected, and the number of features that were consistent with the cluster label was calculated for both training and calibration-testing data. Finally, the cluster with the maximum consistency was selected. The model that was built based on the selected chunk of training data was then used to classify the testing data. This method was tested on the training model obtained by MI-SW model, ie, model obtained by classifying MI-SW vs idle, and MI-TM model, ie, model obtained by classifying MI-TM vs idle (Yang et al., 2013b). Two types of features were employed in using the MI-SW model (Yang et al., 2013a), ie, Laplacian derivatives of power (LAD-P) and DTCWT wavelet (DTCWT-W) features. Based on the selected six healthy subjects, the average accuracies of 74.29% and 72.64% were achieved for the classification of MI-SW vs idle by using LAD-P and DTCWT-W features, respectively. Model adaptation using wavelet features resulted in significant increase compared with those without model adaptation. Surprisingly, classification of MI-SW vs idle with model adaptation using the MI-TM model resulted in comparable classification accuracies for the selected six subjects, ie, 71.81%, compared with that obtained using MI-SW model, ie, 72.12%. These results were better than that obtained without model adaptation, ie, 68.75% (using MI-SW model) and 69.74% (using MI-TM model) (Yang et al., 2013b).

In the second model adaptation method, the within-class and between-class distances were calculated between the training and calibration-testing features. The maximum separation hyperplane was then calculated by the difference of the within-class and between-classes distances, which was normalized by the average covariance of them. Subsequent projecting the within- and between-classes distances to this hyperplane was done. The final ratio of projected between-classes vs within-class distances was used to determine which model to be selected, ie, MA-RBWD (Yang et al., 2014). The detection of MI-SW and MI-TM showed significant higher performance compared with existing methods such as the FBCSP, CSP, and SWDCSP, with the average cross-validation accuracy across subjects as: 70.89% and 73.79% for classifying MI-SW vs idle and classifying MI-TM vs idle, respectively. The session-to-session classification results indicated that the use of model adaptation increased the classification accuracy compared with that of no model adaptation and selecting the model with the best cross-validation accuracy, especially for the MI-TM. These results confirmed the detectability of MI-SW and MI-TM, which also validated the use of MI-TM for stroke dysphagia rehabilitation.

3.3 NEURAL CORTICAL CORRELATES OF MI-SW WITH ME-SW

In the last several years, several groups have conducted experiments to examine the correlates of MI-SW and motor execution of swallow (ME-SW) based on different modalities such as EEG (Yang et al., 2015a,b) and NIRS (Kober and Wood, 2014; Kober et al., 2015). Identifying the neural cortical correlates of MI-SW with that of ME-SW is important so as to employ MI-SW for the treatment of dysphagia patients. Comparable and overlapping activation of brain areas for MI-SW and ME-SW may help promote the use of MI-SW in developing practical rehabilitation tools for the training of stroke dysphagia patients. The first attempt was to use NIRS to study the hemodynamic changes in the brain that respond to MI-SW and ME-SW (Kober and Wood, 2014; Kober et al., 2015). NIRS is a noninvasive optical imaging technique which measures the concentration changes of oxyhemoglobin (oxy-Hb) and deoxygenated hemoglobin (deoxy-Hb) in the cerebral vessels based on the absorption spectra for light in the near-infrared range (Kober et al., 2015). oxy-Hb and deoxy-Hb are important indicators of the changes in the cerebral blood flow, which are also the indicators of cortical brain activation (Kober et al., 2015). Compared with other neuroimaging modalities such as fMRI, NIRS is cheaper, more portable, and offer better temporal resolution, thus allowing it to be used in patient's home.

Fourteen healthy subjects participated in this experiment (Kober and Wood, 2014). The subjects were asked to swallow a cup of water at room temperature or to imagine swallowing the same cup of water without actually drinking it. The action time for each task is 15 s, interspaced with a rest period of 28–32 s between any two tasks. Sixteen photodetectors and 16 light emitters were used to assess the relative concentration changes of oxy-Hb and deoxy-Hb. The false discovery rate (FDR) method was used to control the proportion of false positives among the channels that are detected as significant. Preprocessing of the NIRS signal was performed before the analysis, which includes rejecting the artifactual trials based on amplitude, and filtering the signal with 0.01 Hz high-pass filter and 0.90 Hz low-pass filter. The signal was then baseline corrected (eg, using the signal from -5 to 0 s) and averaged for each task (eg, MI-SW and ME-SW) separately for the time period after the task. Fig. 6 illustrates the topographical distribution of relative concentration changes in oxy- and deoxy-Hb for the different tasks.

Results from Fig. 6 revealed that the relative concentration changes in oxy- and deoxy-Hb were the strongest for channels 4 and 31 during ME and MI ($p >$ FDR 0.05). Channels 1, 27, 8, 34, 5, 30, 11, and 38 showed the second strongest signal change. These results demonstrated that changes in oxy-Hb and deoxy-Hb during MI and ME were the most pronounced in the inferior frontal gyrus including the Broca's area. Specifically, oxy-Hb was higher during ME than during MI, and oxy-Hb was significantly higher during pause than that during ME. The oxy-Hb was significantly increased during and after ME, whereas a decrease in oxy-Hb for MI was observed due to the inhibition mechanisms of motor imagery. Furthermore, the responses of deoxy-Hb of ME and MI were similar, eg, changes in deoxy-Hb showed strong positive correlation during ME-SW and MI-SW. An illustration of the time course of oxy- and deoxy-Hb during MI and ME is shown in Fig. 7.

Another interesting finding from this work was that the same deoxy-Hb level during MI and ME was observed for the group with kinesthetic MI strategy, whereas significant higher deoxy-Hb during MI than during ME was observed for the group with no strategy. It should be noted that the sensorimotor cortex, the supplementary

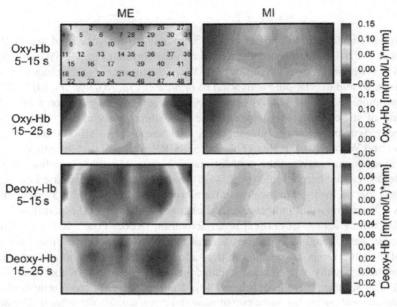

FIG. 6

Topographical distribution of relative concentration changes in oxy- and deoxy-Hb for the different tasks.

Reprinted from Kober, S.E., Wood, G., 2014. Changes in hemodynamic signals accompanying motor imagery and motor execution of swallowing: a near-infrared spectroscopy study. Neuroimage 93 (Pt. 1), 1–10, with permission from Elsevier.

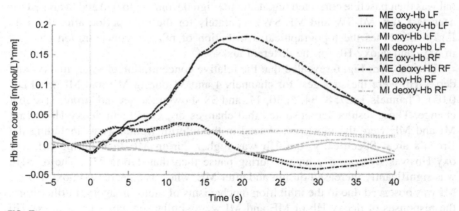

FIG. 7

Mean activation changes in oxy- and deoxy-Hb in response to motor execution (ME, *black lines*) and motor imagery (MI, *gray lines*), for the left inferior frontal (LF) and right inferior frontal (RF) brain regions.

Reprinted from Kober, S.E., Wood, G., 2014. Changes in hemodynamic signals accompanying motor imagery and motor execution of swallowing: a near-infrared spectroscopy study. Neuroimage 93 (Pt. 1), 1–10, with permission from Elsevier.

motor cortex, and anterior cingulate gyrus that were usually activated in previous imaging studies were not found in this work (Furlong et al., 2004, Martin et al., 2004). Possible reasons maybe the use of water swallowing instead of saliva swallowing that were used in earlier work, where different sensorimotor processing was employed. Distilled water may invoke gustatory sensations, reflexive swallowing such as saliva swallowing was mainly represented at the sensorimotor cortex, whereas voluntarily initiated swallowing was represented in multiple cortical regions.

Furthermore to the correlations analyzed using NIRS, the correlations between MI-SW and MI-TM, and the correlations between MI-SW and ME-SW based on 10 healthy subjects and 1 dysphagia patient were analyzed using EEG signals (Yang et al., 2015a,b). The spectral power for each trial was calculated for the EEG signal epoched at the selected time segment and electrode, and filtered at the specified frequency band. Note that the power of the baseline of 2 s was removed in calculating the spectral power. The spectral powers were averaged across trials and divided into bins for different time points, and then the accumulated spectral power at each bin, namely, the bin-based accumulated spectral powers (BASPs) was calculated. The Pearson correlation coefficients were calculated between the BASPs of MI-SW and BASPs of MI-TM, and between the BASPs of MI-SW and BASPs of ME-SW for the selected pair of channels. In the analysis, "C3" and "C4" were selected due to the reason that these regions are close to the activation regions of swallowing and tongue movements (Furlong et al., 2004, Martin et al., 2004). Significant ERD was observed at the primary motor cortex and primary somatosensory motor cortex (eg, broadmann areas 4 and 2) for water infusion and tongue thrust (Furlong et al., 2004). Furthermore, the overlapping activation for swallow and tongue movements was observed in the SMA (Martin et al., 2004). The group analysis results of using bin-based spectral powers demonstrated that MI-SW and MI-TM, and MI-SW and ME-SW were strongly correlated (p-value < 0.001, examined at "C3") for both mu and low beta frequency bands. The correlation was decreased for the dysphagia patient; nevertheless, it was still significant for MI-SW and ME-SW (p-value < 0.05) and MI-SW and MI-TM (p-value < 0.01). These results furthermore validate the use of MI-SW and MI-TM for dysphagia rehabilitation.

3.4 IMPLICATIONS FOR CLINICAL USE

To move the research from the laboratory to clinical trials, and home care of the dysphagia patients, one stroke dysphagia patient of 56-year-old male participated in the investigation (Yang et al., 2014). The patient has severe brain stem hemorrhagic stroke involving the right hemipons and midbrain. He has tetraparesis and severe poststroke dysphagia with complete dependence on nasogastric tube feeding. FEES showed the presence of moderate oropharyngeal dysphagia with reduced orolingual control, delayed swallows, mild reduced hyolaryngeal excursion, and pharyngeal stripping (Yang et al., 2014). Two sessions of EEG data were collected for both

MI-SW data and MI-TM data. In particular, each session consisted of 40 trials of MI-SW and 40 trials of idle, and 40 trials of MI-TM and 40 trials of idle for MI-SW data and MI-TM data, respectively. Not surprisingly, the accuracies of this patient on the classification of MI-SW vs idle for the two sessions were 54.95% and 77.86%, and the accuracies of classifying MI-TM vs idle for the two sessions were 78.28% and 62.19%. This observation furthermore validated the detectability of the MI-SW and MI-TM from baseline idling state for stroke dysphagia patient.

Another study on the hemodynamic signal changes during MI-SW and ME-SW for four stroke dysphagia patients and two healthy subjects using NIRS was conducted (Kober et al., 2015). The objective of this study was to observe the differences in cerebral activation patterns during swallowing for different lesion locations. The assumption was that lesions at the cerebral regions would impair voluntary swallowing and lesions at the brain stem would impair more voluntary phases of swallowing. In this work, two stroke patients with cerebral lesions in the right hemisphere, two stroke patients with lesions in the brain stem, and two healthy subjects with comparable age and gender to that of patients participated in the experiments. The protocol was similar to their earlier work (Kober and Wood, 2014), 20 trials which consisted of half MI and half ME were performed, each trial took 15 s, and there were 28–32 s of rest between any two trials. Eight photodetectors and eight light emitters were employed, resulting in 20 channels in total. The dysphagia patients with lesions in the brain stem showed bilateral hemodynamic signal changes in the inferior frontal gyrus during ME-SW compared with healthy subjects, whereas dysphagia patients with cerebral lesions in the right hemisphere showed stronger increase in oxy-Hb and deoxy-Hb during swallowing (Kober et al., 2015). This was in line with previous findings that the healthy hemisphere showed a lower activation as compared with the affected hemisphere. In addition, prolonged response time was required for patients with cerebral lesions compared to the other two groups. In summary, the topographical distribution patterns and the time course of the hemodynamic response depend on the lesion location. The increased activation during swallowing in the inferior frontal gyrus including the Broca's area, which may be due to the activation in the insula lying in the proximal area deeper inside the brain structures. Insula has been reported to be involved in the swallowing process in many earlier studies (Hamdy et al., 1999a,b, Martin et al., 2001). Overall, MI-SW and ME-SW led to comparable brain activation patterns in stroke patients, especially for the deoxy-Hb, which was consistent with the findings for young healthy subjects (Kober and Wood, 2014). The relative concentration change of oxy-Hb is stronger for ME compared with that of MI.

The limitation of the research to date is the small sample sizes for stroke dysphagia patients. In order to bring the technology from laboratory to home care, a large population of patients with various loci of lesion should be recruited in the future clinical trials. This not only to validate the hypothesis of detectability of MI-SW and MI-TM from baseline idling state but also to validate the difference in topographical distribution patterns and the time course of the hemodynamic response for stroke patients with different lesion locations.

4 DETECTION OF MI-TM

It is noticeable that there is little research work that is dedicated for detection of MI-TM for rehabilitation. Most research employed the competition data, eg, BCI competition IV dataset 2a (Ang et al., 2012; Coyle et al., 2010; Naeem et al., 2006; Tangermann et al., 2012). Dataset 2a comprised 22 channels of 9 subjects performing 4 classes of motor imagery of left hand (MI-LH), motor imagery of right hand (MI-RH), motor imagery of feet movement (MI-FM) and MI-TM (Ang et al., 2012; Coyle et al., 2010; Ge et al., 2014; Morash et al., 2008; Naeem et al., 2006). The use of independent components analysis (ICA) for the classification of multiclass of motor imagery of EEG signals was investigated (Naeem et al., 2006); however, the performance was not good compared with that of CSP. The investigation on the use of time segment before movements or imagery execution to predict the task could be useful to shorten the waiting time especially for an online training scenario (Morash et al., 2008). The combination of neural time-series prediction preprocessing (NTSPP), along with spectral filtering (SF) and CSP can significantly improve the classification performance (Coyle et al., 2010). Furthermore, none of these approaches have compared the detectability of MI-SW and MI-TM, not to mention their use for the rehabilitation of dysphagia patients. A summary of the methods for the detection of multiclass motor imagery of EEG signals including MI-TM is presented in Table 3 and discussed in detail later. It is worth noting that the focus of this section is to review existing methods that performed classification or detection of motor imagery of tongue signals in a two-class or multiclass settings; hence, it may not cover all relevant methods for a particular technique.

4.1 ICA AND FBCSP-BASED DETECTION

Different ICA methods were studied on the classification of four-classes motor imagery of EEG signals for BCI competition IV dataset 2a (Naeem et al., 2006). Three ICA methods were investigated: Infomax, FastICA, and second-order blind identification (SOBI). Infomax tries to minimize the mutual information among the extracted components, FastICA separately maximizes the negentropy of each mixture, and SOBI relies on the stationary second-order statistics that are obtained by joint diagonalization of covariance matrices (Naeem et al., 2006). CSP computes the spatial filters such that the variances of the band-pass filtered time series are maximized and optimally discriminable with respect to the different motor imagery classes. To apply CSP for the classification of multiple classes, multiple one-vs-rest filters are to be computed. Selection of the important components in ICA was done by visual inspection based on the priori knowledge of the physiological processes underlying the motor imagery (Naeem et al., 2006). Such priori knowledge can be the contralateral regions over motor cortex containing mu or beta rhythms for hand motor imagery, the midcentral or parietal components containing localized and prominent activity for foot or tongue imagery. Once the important components were selected, the logarithmic band power features for the frequency bands of alpha

Table 3 Detection of Motor Imagery of Tongue (in Multiclass Settings)

Study, Type	# of Subjects, Trials, Classes, Cue, Modality	Features, Classifiers	Accuracy/Statistical Analysis Result	Key Findings
Naeem et al. (2006) ICA	8 Healthy subj.; ; cue: arrow, EEG, BCI Comp. IV2a, 288 trials, 2 sess., 4 classes	All and selected components, band power features ICA (Infomax, FastICA, and SOBI)	CV (s1/s2): 59.8%/63.3% (Info) 70%/73.7% (fast), 56.1%/ 67.6% (SOBI), 69.2%/67.0% (CSP), S2S (s1/s2): 59.7%/66.7% (Info), 61.5%/65.6% (fast), 55.6%/51.7% (SOBI), 60.0%/ 63.6% (CSP)	○ Infomax performed better than FastICA and SOBI, but still lower than CSP ○ SOBI has fewer parameters to tune
Ang et al. (2012) FBCSP	9 Healthy subj.; ; cue: arrow, EEG, BCI Comp. IV2a (288 trials, 2 sess., 4 classes) & 2b (train: 240 trials/no feedback; 160 trials/feedback, eval.: 320 trials, 2 sess.)	FBCSP features, feature selection, multiclass FBCSP	Avg. Kappa: CV DS2a: 0.613 (DC), 0.658 (PW), and 0.663 (OVR); CV DS2b: 0.493 (MIBIF), 0.502 (MIRSR); S2S DS2a: 0.52 (DC), 0.57 (PW), and 0.57 (OVR); S2S DS2b: 0.59 (MIBIF), 0.60 (MIRSR)	○ Automatic feature selection of subject-specific frequency bands based on MIBIF and MIRSR yielded better results ○ Extending to multiclass classification of FBCSP still yielded good results
Morash et al. (2008) Pred.-BCI	8 Healthy subj. (5/3: male/female); cue: arrow & diamond; EEG for MI/ME of LH-SZ, RH-SZ, Ton-P, RF-TC, 29 electrodes at central and parietal areas; 300 trials (ME), 300 trials (MI), 4 classes	CNV visu.: low-pass filt., avg. volt. ERS/ ERD visu.: power spectra Classification: ICA & DWT filt., norm., FS: Bayesian CV and Bhat. dist. NBC classifier	4-class ME/MI, Avg. Acc.: ME: 40.88% MI: 37.63% 2-class ME/MI, Avg. Acc.: ME: 63.33%, best pair-RL: 66% MI: 60.5%, best pair-RF: 63%	○ Independence between CNV and ERD/ERS. Best pairs for classification were not consistent ○ Preparation ERD/ERS correlated better with MI prediction accuracy than ME ○ For best subject, right foot and left hand signals were the easiest to differentiate, difficult to differentiate tongue movements and other preparations

Study	Subjects/Dataset	Features	Results	Findings
Coyle et al. (2010) PSSP-MBCI	9 Healthy subj. for BCI IV 2a (288 trials, 2 sess., 4 class), 22 electrodes; 5 healthy subj; for BCI IIIa (360 trials-first subj;; 240 trials-next 4 subj;, 4 classes), 22 electrodes were chosen	NTSPP-SF, SF-CSP, NTSPP-SF-CSP LDA classifier	5×5 CV: NTSPP-SF (3 electrodes): 57.12% ± 11.66; SF-CSP (22 electrodes); 65.31% ± 14.23; NTSPP-SF-CSP (22 electrodes): 67.55% ± 11.79; Train-Test: NTSPP-SF (3): 54.85% ± 11.17; SF-CSP (22): 63.80% ± 14.15; NTSPP-SF-CSP (22): 67.01% ± 13.79	o Extend the work that combines prediction based on NTSPP along with SF and CSP for 4-class MI-BCI o NTSPP and CSP can be combined as complementary approaches o NTSPP can minimize the number of channels required o Computation time should be minimized when NTSPP is deployed
Ge et al. (2014) STFT	3 Healthy subj. Cue: arrow, EEG, single channel, total used 6 channels; BCI Comp. IIIa, 360 trials for first subj;, 240 trials second & third subj;, 4 classes	Short-time fourier transform-based CSP features	STFT+CSP: 73.4%, 78.3%, and 75.2% (FP2, for subj. K3, K6, L1); 71.3%, 88.1%, and 71.2% (C4, for subj. K3, K6, L1)	o No significant differences in accuracies using C3, Cz, and C4, compared with Fp1, Fpz, and Fp2 o Using STFT to transform time domain signal of a single channel to multiple frequency-domain signals is effective

Sess., session; subj., subject; eval., evaluation; visu., visualization; avg., average; volt., voltage; DS, dataset; Bhat., Bhattacharyya; filt., filtered/filtering; norm., normalization; FS, feature selection; NBC, naive Bayesian classifier; hemi., hemisphere; comp., competition; pred., prediction; DC, divide-and-conquer; PW, pair-wise; OVR, one-vs-rest; MIBIF, mutual information-based best individual feature selection; MIRSR, mutual information-based rough set reduction.

(eg, 10–12 Hz) and beta (eg, 16–24 Hz) rhythms were computed, forming 12 band power features for 6 components (Naeem et al., 2006). Comparison of the performance for different ICA algorithms showed that Infomax performed best by using all 22 components and the 6 selected components, but the performance was still not better than that of CSP. This better performance of CSP may be due to its supervisory nature. SOBI's overall performance was poor, which was even worse than that of Laplacian or bipolar derivations, indicating that the time delay model may not be suitable to represent ERD/RES-related brain dynamics. Robustness was also an issue for Infomax and FastICA which might be due to the optimization process, eg, the global minimum was sensitive to the choice of the initial values. On the other hand, SOBI was fast with the least number of tunable parameters that need to be adjusted. Laplacian derivations performed comparably to that of Infomax and better than that of FastICA and SOBI. Future research using automatic component selection based on a carefully designed objective measure may improve ICA-based methods. The low performance of this method may hinder its deployment for practical rehabilitation systems.

The FBCSP was proposed to optimize the subject-specific frequency band for CSP based on dataset 2a and 2b of BCI competition IV (Ang et al., 2012). Noted that dataset 2b consisted of 3 bipolar EEG channels for 9 subjects performing MI-LH and MI-RH. Extending FBCSP for the classification of multiclasses EEG signals was made by divide-and-conquer (DC), pair-wise (PW), and one-vs-rest (OVR) approaches. Two methods were proposed to select the subject-specific frequency bands by mutual information-based best individual feature (MIBIF) selection, and the mutual information-based rough set reduction (MIRSR). The experimental evaluation showed that FBCSP yielded the best performance among all the submitted algorithms for both cross-validation and session-to-session transfer.

4.2 PREDICTIVE-SPECTRAL-SPATIAL PREPROCESSING FOR A MULTICLASS BCI, PREDICTION BCI, AND SHORT-TIME FOURIER TRANSFORM-BASED DETECTION

Combination NTSPP, along with SF and CSP for multiclass BCI, namely, predictive-spectral-spatial preprocessing for a multiclass BCI (PSSP-MBCI), was investigated (Coyle et al., 2010). NTSPP exploited the differences in prediction outputs produced by different prediction networks to help improve the separability of the EEG data. The self-organizing fuzzy network was employed for prediction. The EEG signal was preprocessed with NTSPP and spectrally filtered in the subject-specific frequency bands, eg, the frequency which covers mu and beta bands were employed to detect the ERD and ERS during MI. Finally, CSP was applied to reduce the dimensionality of the data as well as to extract the effective features. The results showed that NTSPP combined with SF and CSP yielded significantly better performance than that obtained by NTSPP for the montages with 2 and 3 channels. Furthermore, NTSPP-SF without CSP also yielded better results than SF-CSP, which implied that NTSPP could be an alternative to CSP for preprocessing.

The viability of a movement/imagery prediction BCI to discover the best EEG signals for controlling a device was investigated (Morash et al., 2008). A prediction BCI was proposed that used the brain signals preceding movements execution and imagery to predict which of the four movements, ie, left hand squeeze (LH-SZ), right hand squeeze (RH-SZ), tongue press (Ton-P), and right foot toe curl (RF-TC) would occur. This prediction could potentially reduce the waiting time between a patient's action and BCI's response. Two stimulus were employed (S1 and S2), where the instruction was given at S1 to instruct the subject which action to perform. The contingent negative variation (CNV) and the ERD/ERS were unique to movement and imagery preparation. Their assumption was that the ERD/ERS would work better than that of CNV due to its straightforward relationship with motor cortex activities (Morash et al., 2008). CNV visualizations were created by low-pass filtering and averaging voltages. ERD/ERS visualizations were created by computing power spectra for each trial with hanning window and averaged at 3.9 Hz, 256 ms bins of power spectra. The data were filtered using ICA and DWT and then normalized to zero mean and unit variance. Bayesian crossvalidation and Bhattacharyya distances were employed to identify the best features for classification of movements/imagery preparations during 1.5 s before action appearance. A naive Bayesian classifier was employed as the classifier. Results showed that the CNVs and ERD/ERS were independent from each other. Each subject had particular pairs of movement/imagery that produced better results, which were not consistent among the subjects. Furthermore, less M1 activity was involved in motor imagery preparation compared with that of motor movements. The preparatory ERD/ERS correlated better with the accuracy of MI than that of ME. It was expected that the BCI would perform best when using ERD/ERS ME/MI from M1. Furthermore, they expected that classification of RH-SZ and RF-TC pair should perform better since their representations were in left and right hemispheres, respectively. However, the results showed that the best pair was the classification of LH-SZ and RF-TC pair.

How to extract the effective features of motor imagery from a system comprising only a few channels is an interesting problem. The short-time Fourier transform (STFT) was employed for the detection of motor imagery of EEG signals from few channels or a single channel (Ge et al., 2014). CSP would fail if the EEG signal only has one single channel even if it can be applied to the signal with small number of channels. The authors proposed to treat the multiple frequency bands (8–30 Hz) as a variable, thus obtained the multifrequency time varying inputs, for which the CSP can be applied. BCI competition dataset IIIa which consisted of three subjects performing MI-LH, MI-RH, MI-FM, and MI-TM was employed for evaluation. In this study, channels of C3, Cz, C4, FP1, FPz, and FP2 were selected. Experimental evaluation showed that there were no significant difference in the accuracies obtained by using channels located at the motor cortex (eg, C3, Cz, and C4) compared with those obtained using channels located far from the motor cortex (eg, FP1, FPz, and FP2). This finding coincides with the findings that high correlations in the event-related potential and spectral perturbation were found at the forehead area and sensorimotor area EEGs during a motor imagery task (Li et al., 2009). Furthermore, employing STFT to transform the time domain signal of a single channel into multiple frequency-domain signals is effective for the detection of motor imagery EEG signals.

Other approaches that employed STFT to extract features for EEG signals of MI-LH and MI-RH were investigated (Coyle et al., 2005). Features were extracted by interpolating the spectrum obtained by calculating the norm of power in the subject-specific frequency bands. Two windows, ie, the FE window and STFT window, were employed. The temporal resolution was achieved within each FE window by sliding the STFT window along the data sequence with certain overlapping. Parameters that had a significant effect on the performance were to be tuned, which were width of the frequency bands, window length of the FE window and STFT window, overlapping between STFT windows and interpolation interval. Comparable performance was achieved by tuning the parameters compared with other existing approaches. How to develop a fully automated procedure to select the subject-specific frequency bands as well as to optimize the subject-specific parameters is an interesting research direction.

5 IMPLICATIONS AND FUTURE DIRECTIONS
5.1 FUTURE DIRECTIONS FOR NEURAL ANALYSIS OF SWALLOWING

Future studies can look at the functional interactions between the cortical swallowing regions and their relation with the brain stem central pattern generator (Hamdy et al., 1996). The poor temporal resolution and good spatial resolution of fMRI, and the poor spatial resolution and good temporal resolution of EEG, may suggest the use of a multimodal approach for the detection and analysis of the swallowing and MI-SW for stroke rehabilitation. The strong sensory input from the tongue engaged in the whole cortical swallowing network may be the primary driver of the temporal concordance between each of the cortical loci for sensory preswallow and sensory motor swallow phases (Furlong et al., 2004). The importance of the sensory input may imply that future treatments of swallowing problems after stroke might be more effective if sensory stimulation techniques are used (Furlong et al., 2004). For example, some forms of oral/tongue stimulation may help accelerate the swallowing recovery. The difference in the activation for mild and severe dysphagic patients and controls can also be due to their behavioral differences (Teismann et al., 2011). As a result, a parametric scanning design can be designed with different levels of swallowing tasks. No significant difference in BP and PMP amplitude between volitional swallowing and tongue protrusion was found (Satow et al., 2004), which may imply that the SMA may not play any specific role in volitional swallowing. Hence, future work on functional significance of SMA in swallowing on larger number of patients is needed. Current work has investigated the neural correlates MI-SW and ME-SW based on NIRS; future work can concentrate on investigating the neural correlates between MI-SW and MI-TM, and between MI-SW and ME-SW, which will form the neural basis in the use of BCI-based rehabilitation for dysphagia patients.

Combining sensory stimulation with BCI-based training techniques may also benefit the recovery of the dysphagia patients.

5.2 FUTURE DIRECTIONS ON THE REHABILITATION OF STROKE DYSPHAGIA PATIENTS

The main challenges in employing the motor imagery for the rehabilitation of stroke dysphagia patients lie in the followings. First, it is relatively difficult to imagine the complex swallowing process compared with that of motor imagery of upper limb and low limb. This is especially true for the dysphagia patients who might have difficulty initiating the swallow process. Hence, we suggest the rehabilitation should be targeting at those patients with mild dysphagia considering the safety and efficacy of the technique. An example of the suggested rehabilitation for dysphagia patient by incorporating the motor imagery technique is shown in Fig. 8.

Two strategies for rehabilitation are suggested in this review. In the first strategy, the engagement of the patients during motor imagery process is measured by coupling the MI-SW or MI-TM with the traditional swallowing therapies, eg, using the detected MI-SW or MI-TM signal to trigger an actual swallow and provide feedback to the patient (Ang et al., 2014a,b; Prasad et al., 2010; Silvoni et al., 2011). In this way, a speech and language therapist is required to assist the patient with the actual swallowing. It is reasonable to employ MI-TM instead of MI-SW if the patient is unable to perform MI-SW or in a severe situation. A practical deployment is to perform MI-TM in the training sessions, and perform MI-SW in online rehabilitation sessions. In the second strategy, the detected MI-SW or MI-TM signal can be used as a switch or trigger for subsequent neuromuscular or oral sensory stimulation (Kiger et al., 2006; Langdon and Blacker, 2010; Silvoni et al., 2011). The stimulation

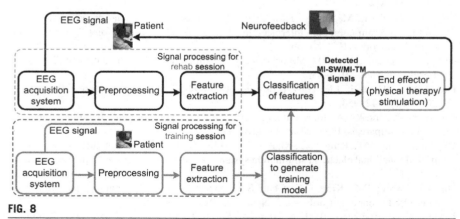

FIG. 8

Block diagram illustrating a motor imagery-based rehabilitation system for dysphagia patients.

location should be carefully selected, eg, the hyoid bone for neuromuscular stimulation. Furthermore, the strength of the stimulation should be varied according to the severeness of the patient. The patient to use the stimulation therapy should be able to establish the basic swallow pattern for the sake of safety. Consultation with the speech and language therapist and doctors is required regarding the safety on the use of stimulation technique for the patients (Langdon and Blacker, 2010).

REFERENCES

Ang, K.K., Guan, C., 2015. Brain–computer interface for neuro-rehabilitation of upper limb after stroke. Proc. IEEE 103 (6), 944–953. 06/2015.

Ang, K.K., Chin, Z.Y., Wang, C., Guan, C., Zhang, H., 2012. Filter bank common spatial pattern algorithm on BCI competition IV datasets 2a and 2b. Front. Neurosci. 6, 39.

Ang, K.K., Chua, K.S.G., Phua, K.S., Wang, C., Chin, Z.Y., Kuah, C.W.K., Low, W., Guan, C., 2014a. A randomized controlled trial of EEG-based motor imagery brain-computer interface robotic rehabilitation for stroke. Clin. EEG Neurosci. 45, 1–11.

Ang, K.K., Guan, C., Phua, K.S., Wang, C., Zhou, L., Tang, K.Y., Joseph, G.J.E., Kuah, C.W.K., Chua, K.S.G., 2014b. Brain computer interface-based robotic end effector system for wrist and hand rehabilitation: results of a three-armed randomized controlled trial for chronic stroke. Front. Neuroeng. 7, 30.

Blankertz, B., Dornhege, G., Schafer, C., Krepki, R., Kohlmorgen, J., et al., 2003. Boosting bit rates and error detection for the classification of fast-paced motor commands based on single-trial EEG analysis. IEEE Trans. Neural Syst. Rehabil. Eng. 11, 127–131.

Blankertz, B., Tomioka, R., Lemm, S., Kawanabe, M., Muller, K.-R., January 2008. Optimizing spatial filters for robust EEG single-trial analysis. IEEE Signal Process. Mag. 41, 41–56.

Coyle, D., Prasad, G., McGinnity, T.M., 2005. A time-frequency approach to feature extraction for a brain-computer interface with a comparative analysis of performance measures. EURASIP J. Adv. Signal Process. 2005 (19), 3141–3151. http://dx.doi.org/10.1155/ASP.2005.3141.

Coyle, D., Satti, A., Mcginnity, T.M., 2010. Predictive-spectral-spatial preprocessing for a multiclass brain-computer interface. In: The 2010 International Joint Conference on Neural Networks (IJCNN), pp. 1–8.

de Vries, S., Mulder, T., 2007. Motor imagery and stroke rehabilitation: a critical discussion. J. Rehabil. Med. 39, 5–13.

Dickstein, R., Deutsch, J.E., 2007. Motor imagery in physical therapist practice. Phys. Ther. 2007 (87), 942–953.

Dickstein, R., Dunsky, A., Marcovitz, E., 2004. Motor imagery for gait rehabilitation in poststroke hemiparesis. Phys. Ther. 84, 1167–1177.

Do, A.H., Wang, P.T., King, C.E., Abiri, A., Nenadic, Z., 2011. Brain–computer interface controlled functional electrical stimulation system for ankle movement. J. Neuroeng. Rehabil. 8, 1–14.

Do, A.H., Wang, P.T., King, C.E., Chun, S.N., Nenadic, Z., 2013. Brain–computer interface controlled robotic gait orthosis. J. Neuroeng. Rehabil. 10, 111.

Dornhege, G., Blankertz, B., Krauledat, M., Losch, F., Curio, G., et al., 2006. Combined optimization of spatial and temporal filters for improving brain computer interfacing. IEEE Trans. Biomed. Eng. 53, 2274–2281.

Dunsky, A., Dickstein, R., Marcovitz, E., Levy, S., 2008. Home-based motor imagery training for gait rehabilitation of people with chronic post-stroke hemiparesis. Arch. Phys. Med. Rehabil. 89, 1580–1588.

Ertekin, C., Aydogdu, I., 2003. Neurophysiology of swallowing. Clin. Neurophysiol. 114 (12), 2226–2244.

Furlong, P.L., Hobson, A.R., Aziz, Q., Barnes, G.R., Singh, K.D., Hillebrand, A., Thompson, D.G., Hamdy, S., 2004. Dissociating the spatio-temporal characteristics of cortical neuronal activity associated with human volitional swallowing in the healthy adult brain. Neuroimage 22, 1447–1455.

Ge, S., Wang, R., Yu, D., 2014. Classification of four-class motor imagery employing single-channel electroencephalography. PLoS One 9, e98019.

Hamdy, S., Aziz, Q., Rothwell, J.C., Singh, K.D., Barlow, J., Hughes, D.G., Tallis, R.C., Thompson, D.G., 1996. The cortical topography of human swallowing musculature in health and disease. Nat. Med. 2 (11), 1217–1224.

Hamdy, S., Aziz, Q., Rothwell, J.C., Crone, R., Hughes, D., Tallis, R.C., Thompson, D.G., 1997a. Explaining oropharyngeal dysphagia after unilateral hemispheric stroke. Lancet 350, 686–692.

Hamdy, S., Aziz, Q., Rothwell, J.C., Power, M., Singh, K.D., Nicholson, D.A., et al., 1998. Recovery of swallowing after dysphagic stroke relates to functional reorganization in the intact motor cortex. Gastroenterology 115, 1104–1112.

Hamdy, S., Mikulis, D.J., Crawley, A., Xue, S., Lau, H., Henry, S., Diamant, N.E., 1999a. Cortical activation during human volitional swallowing: an event-related fMRI study. Am. J. Physiol. 277 (1 Pt. 1), G219–G225.

Hamdy, S., Rothwell, J.C., Brooks, D.J., Bailey, D., Aziz, Q., Thompson, D.G., 1999b. Identification of the cerebral loci processing human swallowing with H2(15)O PET activation. J. Neurophysiol. 81 (4), 1917–1926.

Hamdy, S., Rothwell, J.C., Aziz, Q., Thompson, D.G., 2000. Organization and reorganization of human swallowing motor cortex: implications for recovery after stroke. Clin. Sci. (Lond.) 99 (2), 151–157.

Hamdy, S., Aziz, Q., Thompson, D.G., Rothwell, J.C., 2001. Physiology and pathophysiology of the swallowing area of human motor cortex. Neural Plast. 8 (1–2), 91–97.

Jestrovic, I., Coyle, J.L., Sejdic, E., 2015. Decoding human swallowing via electroencephalography: a state-of-the-art review. J. Neural Eng. 12, 051001. 15 pp.

Kang, H., Nam, Y., Choi, S., 2009. Composite common spatial pattern for subject-to-subject transfer. IEEE Signal Process. Lett. 16 (8), 683–686.

Kiger, M., Brown, C.S., Watkins, L., 2006. Dysphagia management: an analysis of patient outcomes Using VitalStim™ therapy compared to traditional swallow therapy. Dysphagia 21, 243–253.

Kober, S.E., Wood, G., 2014. Changes in hemodynamic signals accompanying motor imagery and motor execution of swallowing: a near-infrared spectroscopy study. Neuroimage 93 (Pt. 1), 1–10.

Kober, S.E., Bauernfeind, G., Woller, C., Sampl, M., Grieshofer, P., Neuper, C., Wood, G., 2015. Hemodynamic signal changes accompanying execution and imagery of swallowing in patients with dysphagia: a multiple single-case near-Infrared spectroscopy study. Front. Neurol. 6, 151.

Krusienski, D.J., Grosse-Wentrup, M., Galán, F., Coyle, D., Miller, K.J., Forney, E., Anderson, C.W., 2011. Critical issues in state-of-the-art brain-computer interface signal processing. J. Neural Eng. 8 (2), 025002. http://dx.doi.org/10.1088/1741-2560/8/2/025002.

Langdon, C., Blacker, D., 2010. Dysphagia in stroke: a new solution. Stroke Res. Treat. 2010. http://dx.doi.org/10.4061/2010/570403. 570403, 6 pages. Published online 2010 Jun 30, PMCID, PMC2915662.

Li, K.D., Sun, G.F., Zhang, B.F., Wu, S.C., Wu, G.F., 2009. Correlation between forehead EEG and sensorimotor area EEG in motor imagery task. In: Eighth IEEE International Conference on Dependable, Autonomic and Secure Computing, IEE DASC'09, pp. 430–435.

Lotte, F., Guan, C., 2010. Learning from other subjects helps reducing brain-computer interface calibration time. In: IEEE International Conference on Acoustics, Speech, and Signal Processing (ICASSP), pp. 614–617.

Lotte, F., Guan, C., 2011. Regularizing common spatial patterns to improve BCI designs: unified theory and new algorithms. IEEE Trans. Biomed. Eng. 58 (2), 355–362.

Lotte, F., Guan, C., Ang, K.K., 2009. Comparison of designs towards a subject-independent brain-computer interface based on motor imagery. IEEE EMBC 2009, 4543–4546.

Martin, R.E., Goodyear, B.G., Gati, J.S., Menon, R.S., 2001. Cerebral cortical representation of automatic and volitional swallowing in humans. J. Neurophysiol. 85 (2), 938–950.

Martin, R.E., MacIntosh, B.J., Thomas, C., Gati, J.S., Menon, R.S., 2002. Comparison of brain activation during swallowing and tongue movement: event-related fMRI. Soc. Neurosci. Abstr. 163 (12), 2002.

Martin, R.E., MacIntosh, B.J., Smith, R.C., Barr, A.M., Stevens, T.K., Gati, J.S., Menon, R.S., 2004. Cerebral areas processing swallowing and tongue movement are overlapping but distinct: a functional magnetic resonance imaging study. J. Neurophysiol. 92, 2428–2443.

Matsuo, K., Palmer, J.B., 2008. Anatomy and physiology of feeding and swallowing: normal and abnormal. Phys. Med. Rehabil. Clin. N. Am. 19 (4), 691–707.

McKeown, M.J., Torpey, D.C., Gehm, W.C., 2002. Non-invasive monitoring of functionally distinct muscle activations during swallowing. Clin. Neurophysiol. 113, 354–366.

Morash, V., Bai, O., Furlani, S., Lin, P., Hallett, M., 2008. Classifying EEG signals preceding right hand, left hand, tongue, and right foot movements and motor imageries. Clin. Neurophysiol. 119, 2570–2578.

Mosier, K., Patel, R., Liu, W., Kalnin, A., Maldjian, J., Baredes, S., 1999. Cortical representation of swallowing in normal adults: functional implications. Laryngoscope 109, 1417–1423.

Naeem, M., Brunner, C., Leeb, R., Graimann, B., Pfurtscheller, G., 2006. Seperability of four-class motor imagery data using independent components analysis. J. Neural Eng. 3, 208.

Prasad, G., Herman, P., Coyle, D., McDonough, S., Crosbie, J., 2010. Applying a brain-computer interface to support motor imagery practice in people with stroke for upper limb recovery: a feasibility study. J. Neuroeng. Rehabil. 7 (1), 60. http://dx.doi.org/10.1186/1743-0003-7-60.

Quionero-Candela, J., Sugiyama, M., Schwaighofer, A., Lawrence, N.D. (Eds.), 2009. Dataset Shift in Machine Learning. MIT Press, Cambridge, MA.

Ramoser, H., Muller-Gerking, J., Pfurtscheller, G., 2000. Optimal spatial filtering of single trial EEG during imagined hand movement. IEEE Trans. Rehabil. Eng. 8 (4), 441–446.

Samek, W., Blythe, D., Müller, K.-R., Kawanabe, M., 2013a. Robust spatial filtering with beta divergence. In: Advances in Neural Information Processing Systems 26 (NIPS), pp. 1007–1015.

Samek, W., Binder, A., Muller, K.-R., 2013b. Multiple kernel learning for brain-computer interfacing. In: International Conference of the IEEE Engineering in Medicine and Biology Society (EMBC), pp. 7048–7051.

Samek, W., Meinecke, F., Muller, K.-R., 2013c. Transferring subspaces between subjects in brain-computer interfacing. IEEE Trans. Biomed. Eng. 60 (8), 2289–2298.

Samek, W., Kawanabe, M., Muller, K.-R., 2014. Divergence-based framework for common spatial patterns algorithms. IEEE Rev. Biomed. Eng. 7, 50–72.

Satow, T., Ikeda, A., Yamamoto, J., Begum, T., Thuy, D.H., Matsuhashi, M., Mima, T., Nagamine, T., Baba, K., Mihara, T., Inoue, Y., Miyamoto, S., Hashimoto, N., Shibasaki, H., 2004. Role of primary sensorimotor cortex and supplementary motor area in volitional swallowing: a movement-related cortical potential study. Am. J. Physiol. Gastrointest. Liver Physiol. 287 (2), G459–G470.

Sharma, N., Pomeroy, V.M., Baron, J.-C., 2006. Motor imagery: a backdoor to the motor system after stroke? Stroke 37 (7), 1941–1952.

Shenoy, P., Krauledat, M., Blankertz, B., Rao, R.P., Muler, K.R., 2006. Towards adaptive classification for BCI. J. Neural Eng. 3 (1), R13–R23.

Silvoni, S., Ramos-Murguialday, A., Cavinato, M., Volpato, C., Cisotto, G., Turolla, A., Piccione, F., Birbaumer, N., 2011. Brain-computer interface in stroke: a review of progress. Clin. EEG Neurosci. 42 (4), 245–252. http://dx.doi.org/10.1177/155005941104200410.

Sugiyama, M., Krauledat, M., Muller, K.-R., 2007. Covariate shift adaptation by importance weighted cross validation. J. Mach. Learn. Res. 8, 985–1005.

Tangermann, M., Muller, K.R., Aertsen, A., Birbaumer, N., Braun, C., Brunner, C., Leeb, R., Mehring, C., Miller, K.J., Muller-Putz, G.R., Nolte, G., Pfurtscheller, G., Preissl, H., Schalk, G., Schlogl, A., Vidaurre, C., Waldert, S., Blankertz, B., 2012. Review of the BCI competition IV. Front. Neurosci. 6, 55.

Teismann, I.K., Warnecke, T., Suntrup, S., Steinstrater, O., Kronenberg, L., Ringelstein, E.B., Dengler, R., Petri, S., Pantev, C., Dziewas, R., 2011. Cortical processing of swallowing in ALS patients with progressive dysphagia—a magnetoencephalographic study. PLoS One 6 (5), e19987.

Wolpaw, J.R., Birbaumer, N., McFarland, D.J., Pfurtscheller, G., Vaughan, T.M., 2002. Brain-computer interfaces for communication and control. Clin. Neurophysiol. 113 (6), 767–791.

Yang, H., Guan, C., Ang, K.K., Wang, C., Phua, K.S., Yu, J., 2012. Dynamic initiation and dual-tree complex wavelet feature-based classification of motor imagery of swallow EEG signals. In: The 2012 International Joint Conference on Neural Networks (IJCNN), pp. 1–6.

Yang, H., Guan, C., Ang, K.K., Wang, C., Phua, K.S., Tang, C.K.Y., Zhou, L., 2013a. Feature consistency-based model adaptation in session-to-session classification: a study using motor imagery of swallow EEG signals. In: The 35th Annual International Conference of the IEEE Engineering in Medicine and Biology Society (EMBC), pp. 429–432.

Yang, H., Guan, C., Ang, K.K., Wang, C., 2013b. Detection of motor imagery of swallow with model adaptation: swallow or tongue. In: Abstract in Fifth International Brain Computer Interface Meeting 56.

Yang, H., Guan, C., Chua, K.S.G., Wang, C., Phua, K.S., Tang, C.K.Y., Ang, K.K., 2014. Detection of motor imagery of swallow EEG signals based on the dual-tree complex wavelet transform and adaptive model selection. J. Neural Eng. 11 (3), 035016.

Yang, H., Guan, C., Wang, C., Ang, K.K., Phua, K.S., Chok, S.S., Tang, C.K.Y., Chua, K.S.G., 2015a. On the correlations of motor imagery of swallow with motor imagery of tongue movements and actual swallow. In: Proceedings of the fifth International Conference on Cognitive Neurodynamics. Advances in Cognitive Neurodynamics, vol. V, pp. 397–404. Chapter 55, June 3–7, China, 2015.

Yang, H., Guan, C., Wang, C., Ang, K.K., 2015b. Detection of motor imagery of brisk walking from electroencephalogram. J. Neurosci. Methods 244, 33–44.

[illegible faded reference text]

A cognitive brain–computer interface for patients with amyotrophic lateral sclerosis

M.R. Hohmann*,†,1, T. Fomina*,†, V. Jayaram*,†, N. Widmann†, C. Förster†, J. Just‡,§, M. Synofzik‡, B. Schölkopf†, L. Schöls‡,§, M. Grosse-Wentrup†

*International Max Planck Research School for Cognitive and Systems Neuroscience, Tübingen, Germany
†Max Planck Institute for Intelligent Systems, Tübingen, Germany
‡Hertie Institute for Clinical Brain Research, Tübingen, Germany
§German Center for Neurodegenerative Diseases (DZNE), Tübingen, Germany
1Corresponding author: Tel.: +49-7071-601-558; Fax: +49-7071-601-616, e-mail address: matthias.hohmann@tuebingen.mpg.de

Abstract

Brain–computer interfaces (BCIs) are often based on the control of sensorimotor processes, yet sensorimotor processes are impaired in patients suffering from amyotrophic lateral sclerosis (ALS). We devised a new paradigm that targets higher-level cognitive processes to transmit information from the user to the BCI. We instructed five ALS patients and twelve healthy subjects to either activate self-referential memories or to focus on a process without mnemonic content while recording a high-density electroencephalogram (EEG). Both tasks are designed to modulate activity in the default mode network (DMN) without involving sensorimotor pathways. We find that the two tasks can be distinguished after only one experimental session from the average of the combined bandpower modulations in the theta-(4–7 Hz) and alpha-range (8–13 Hz), with an average accuracy of 62.5% and 60.8% for healthy subjects and ALS patients, respectively. The spatial weights of the decoding algorithm show a preference for the parietal area, consistent with modulation of neural activity in primary nodes of the DMN.

Keywords

EEG, Brain–computer interface, Brain–machine interface, ALS, locked-in.

Progress in Brain Research, Volume 228, ISSN 0079-6123, http://dx.doi.org/10.1016/bs.pbr.2016.04.022
© 2016 Elsevier B.V. All rights reserved.

1 INTRODUCTION

1.1 AMYOTROPHIC LATERAL SCLEROSIS

Amyotrophic Lateral Sclerosis (ALS) describes a variety of conditions that have the progressive degeneration of upper and lower motor neurons in common (Wijesekera and Leigh, 2009). There is no known cure for ALS. The progressive paralysis leads to death due to respiratory failure within an average of 3–5 years (Aggarwal and Cudkowicz, 2008). While modern life-support technology like artificial respiration and nutrition allows for a prolonged life, it in turn also prolongs the psychological and social burden of being in a paralyzed and eventually totally locked-in state. In this state, all voluntary muscle control is lost, including oculomotor functions (Wijesekera and Leigh, 2009; Wolpaw et al., 2002).

The crucial ability lost in 80–95% of ALS patients over the course of the disease is communication (Leigh, 2003). The inability to communicate emotions, thoughts, and needs is the most daunting problem that both ALS patients and the social environment inevitably have to face during the progress of the disease (Kübler et al., 2001). Establishing and maintaining communication may not prolong survival, but it greatly increases the quality of life for ALS patients (Bach, 1993).

1.2 BRAIN–COMPUTER INTERFACES

One way to enable communication via nonmuscular modalities is a brain–computer interface (BCI). The term refers to a direct interface with the nervous system through a range of techniques, currently limited by technical and surgical constraints (Wander and Rao, 2014). A BCI communication system delivers the messages or commands of an individual to the external world without peripheral nerves and muscles through the understanding of brain activity (Wolpaw et al., 2002), the most commonly used of which is noninvasive electroencephalography (EEG). The acquired signals are processed and classified as digital commands to control an application (Kübler et al., 2009).

BCIs have already been used successfully in clinical settings, eg, for stroke rehabilitation, the treatment of mental illness, and early-stage ALS patients (Mak and Wolpaw, 2009). This has raised hopes that BCIs could also provide autonomy for and enable communication with late-stage ALS patients. However, this mission has proven to be very challenging, as BCIs are often based on motor and sensory processes, such as the voluntary modulation of sensorimotor rhythms (Pfurtscheller and Neuper, 2001). Patients suffering from ALS show degeneration of neurons in the primary motor cortex (Nihei et al., 1993) and are impaired in their ability to modulate these rhythms in later stages of the disease (Birbaumer et al., 2012). Visual speller systems, like the P300 speller or the SSVEP system, require subjects to fixate on target stimuli through gaze. They can be used during the progress of the disease, but fail in the latest stages due to the loss of oculomotor control (Jacobs et al., 1981). BCIs that rely on covert attention can be operated without gazing movements (Aloise et al., 2012; Aricò et al., 2014; Treder et al., 2011), but the retinal jitter that is necessary to perceive a visual stimulus could be affected by the disease as well. Circumventing the visual modality by porting the P300 speller to an auditory (Kübler et al., 2009) or tactile setting (Brouwer and van Erp, 2010), or using acoustic odd-ball BCIs for yes/no communication (Nijboer et al., 2008) have mostly been tested on healthy subjects and patients in earlier stages of the disease. One study reported a promising results when testing a word-based acoustic odd-ball paradigm in two later-stage ALS patients; however, they were not completely locked-in (Hill et al., 2014). The usefulness of slow cortical potentials (Kübler et al., 1999) for establishing a reliable communication with completely locked-in patients remains unclear as well. A recent meta-study (Marchetti and Priftis, 2015) addressed these issues and concludes that, to this day, no reliable EEG-based communication method has been established for completely locked-in patients.

Some of the cortical processes impaired in ALS can be avoided by training subjects via neurofeedback to self-regulate neural activity in cortical areas that subserve higher functions (Grosse-Wentrup and Schölkopf, 2014; Vansteensel et al., 2010). One major issue with this approach is the amount of training that is needed for patients to successfully modulate activity. The need for extensive training decreases the feasibility of the system, especially for patients in later stages of the disease. Another issue is the use of visual stimuli, which only works if the patient is not yet completely locked-in. Additionally, if the training starts too late in the progress of the disease the patient may be unable to achieve a classification accuracy that is necessary for communication.

Finally, the state of consciousness in completely locked-in patients remains unclear. It has been argued that the long-term paralysis in the final stages of the disease extinguishes goal-directed thinking (Kübler and Birbaumer, 2008), and patients may reside in a state-of-mind similar to REM sleep (Birbaumer et al., 2012).

1.3 THE CURRENT WORK

We propose to employ a cognitive strategy for realizing a BCI that targets higher cognitive functions without relying on neurofeedback-driven learning mechanisms. This cognitive strategy should fulfill three important criteria: First, it should target processes that are at the very basis of human nature and therefore be immediately accessible for everyone. Second, these processes should be generally unrelated to motor processes, circumventing the issues with previous BCIs in ALS patients. And third, they should remain accessible to ALS patients for as long as they possess the cognitive capacity for communication.

While most brain areas are eventually affected by ALS, with the possible exception of the occipital lobe, parietal and prefrontal areas appear to be affected later in the course of disease progression than sensorimotor regions (Braak et al., 2013). Based on these findings, we chose to target the Default Mode Network (DMN), a large-scale cortical network that has first been discovered in PET (Shulman et al., 1997) and later in fMRI recordings (Raichle et al., 2001). It consists of three major subdivisions: the medial prefrontal cortex (MPC); the temporoparietal junction (TPJ); and its most important hub, the posterior cingulate cortex, combined with the precuneus. The DMN has been connected to social behavior, mood control, motivational drive, self-referential judgments, and recollection of prior experiences (Fransson and Marrelec, 2008; Raichle, 2015; Simpson et al., 2001). Therefore, it plays an important role in the human ability to generate "spontaneous cognition," like daydreaming or mind wandering, which is a basic and nonmotor related human ability.

Recently, the DMN has also been connected to consciousness in brain-damaged patients: Connectivity patterns within the DMN during resting state have been found to be negatively correlated with the degree of clinical consciousness impairment. Participants in the study ranged from fully conscious healthy controls over locked-in patients with spinal cord injuries or stroke to minimally conscious and comatose patients (Vanhaudenhuyse et al., 2010). While comatose and vegetative patients showed the least connectivity within the DMN, patients with spinal cord injuries and stroke damage showed almost no difference to healthy controls. Therefore, the successful modulation of brain activity in this network could serve as an indicator for the state of consciousness of a patient. Under the assumption that completely locked-in ALS patients are not in a comatose, unconscious state, and goal-directed thinking is still possible, we hypothesize that the DMN will still exhibit activity patterns as described in Vanhaudenhuyse et al. (2010). If this is not the case, attempts to communicate would probably be meaningless.

To target processes in the DMN, we devised a novel, stimulus-independent cognitive strategy that modulates the activation and deactivation of the DMN by taking its self-referential properties into account. Based on previous, stimulus-driven studies in fMRI, we instructed subjects to alternate between self-referential thoughts, which activate the DMN (Andreasen et al., 1995; Greicius et al., 2003; Weissman et al., 2006), and focusing on their breathing, which we expect to deactivate the DMN because it is devoid of self-referential mnemonics (Raichle et al., 2001). The current work investigates the hypothesis that this strategy elicits bandpower changes in the EEG over areas consistent with the DMN regions found in fMRI. These changes should be sufficiently strong to enable above chance-level decoding accuracies in healthy subjects and patients with ALS, without the need of any subject training. A preliminary version of this work has been published recently in conference proceedings (Hohmann et al., 2015).

2 METHODS
2.1 EXPERIMENTAL PARADIGM

Healthy subjects were placed in a chair approximately 1.25 m away from a 17" LCD screen with a resolution of 1280 × 1024 pixels and a 60 Hz refresh rate. The background of the screen was black, with a white fixation cross appearing in the center.

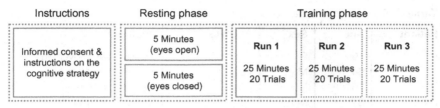

FIG. 1

The experimental procedure. During all trials and the eyes open resting phase, a fixation cross appeared in the center of the screen. ALS patients were only asked to perform the two resting states and the first training run (depicted as boxes with *solid borders*).

Prior to the experimental session, two 5-min resting state EEGs were recorded. Subjects were asked to let their mind wander and to keep their eyes open in the first resting state and closed in the second one.

After the resting state sessions, subjects performed three experimental blocks with brief intermissions. Each experimental block consisted of ten trials in which the participants were asked to "remember a positive experience" and ten trials in which the participants were asked to "focus on their breathing," in pseudorandomized order. We chose a trial time of 60 s to give participants enough time to concentrate on the high-level tasks that they were asked to do in each trial. Each trial began with 5.5 ± 0.50 s rest, followed by a 60 s trial, in the beginning of which acoustic and visual instructions were given to indicate which of the two cognitive tasks should be performed. To ensure comprehension, both cognitive tasks were explained to participants in a briefing before the experiment. For ALS patients, the experimental paradigm remained the same. However, they were asked to only perform one experimental block. Fig. 1 illustrates the paradigm.

2.2 EXPERIMENTAL DATA

The study was conducted at the Max Planck Institute for Intelligent Systems in Tübingen, Germany. Recordings with ALS patients were conducted in their homes. Twelve healthy subjects (eight male and three female, mean age 29.3 ± 8.3 years) and five ALS patients (cf Table 1) were recruited from the local community and in cooperation with the University Clinics Tübingen. Participants received 12 Euro per hour for their participation. One healthy subject was excluded due to noisy recordings. This left eleven healthy subjects for the final analysis. All participants were naive to the setup. They were informed by the experimenter about the procedure with standardized instructions and signed a consent form to confirm their voluntary participation in advance. For subject P1, informed consent was given by her legal guardian. The study was approved by the ethics committee of the Max Planck Society.

A 124-channel EEG was recorded at a sampling frequency of 500 Hz using acti-CAP active electrodes and a QuickAmp amplifier (BrainProducts GmbH, Gilching, Germany). Electrodes were placed according to the extended 10–20 system with the

Table 1 ALS Patient Data

Patient	Age	Sex	ALSFRS-R[a]	Impairment
P1	59	F	0	Residual eye-movements
P2	54	M	48	Mild limb impairments
P3	75	M	42	Mild limb impairments
P4	81	M	23	No limb functionality
P5	51	F	12	Locked-in, eye-movements

[a]*Revised amyotrophic lateral sclerosis functional rating scale (Cedarbaum et al., 1999). The rating scale was filled out after the recording session by the experimenter.*

left mastoid electrode as the initial reference. All recordings were converted to common average reference. The application was realized with the BCI2000 and BCPy2000 toolboxes (Schalk et al., 2004).

2.3 EEG ANALYSIS

We performed an offline analysis of the acquired data to attenuate confounding electromyographic activity, to investigate differentiability of the activity patterns associated with self-referential thoughts and focus on breathing, and to analyze the spatial distribution as well as the dynamics of the induced bandpower changes.

2.3.1 Attenuation of EMG Artifacts

EEG recordings are likely to be contaminated by scalp-muscle artifacts (Shackman et al., 2009). Subjects may have been able to involuntarily influence the EEG signal by altering the tonus of their scalp muscles. In order to identify such EMG confounds, we employed independent component analysis (ICA) (McMenamin et al., 2011). The continuous data of one session was first reduced to 64 components by principal component analysis, and then separated into independent components (ICs) using the SOBI algorithm (Belouchrani et al., 1997). We then sorted the ICs according to their neurophysiological plausibility (Grosse-Wentrup et al., 2013), manually inspected the topography, spectrum, and time series of each component, and rejected those for which at least one of the following criteria applied: (1) Components displayed a monotonic increase in spectral power starting around 20 Hz. This is characteristic of muscle activity. (2) Eye-blinks were detectable in the time series. (3) The topography did not show a dipolar pattern. (4) The time series seemed to be contaminated by other sources of noise, like large spikes and 50 Hz line noise (adapted from Onton et al., 2006). The remaining ICs were reprojected onto the scalp. As discussed in McMenamin et al. (2011), it is unreasonable to expect a complete removal of artifacts using ICA, but careful application "is a useful means of rejecting the most dubious results on the scalp."

2.3.2 Preprocessing

We restricted our analysis to the time window of 4.5–60 s per trial, as instructions were played back for the first 2 s and were shown on the screen for the first 4 s of each trial. To reduce the feature space for later classification and to capture the effect of self-referential processing, we restricted our analysis to the θ- and α-frequency bands of the EEG signal. Mu and Han (2010) found that self-referential processing correlates with θ and α spectral power in a stimulus-driven task. θ-band activity is generally modulated by memory load and retrieval of episodic information from long-term memory (Klimesch, 1999). α-bandpower is linked to inner-directed attention demand in self-referential processing (Mu and Han, 2010). In particular, parietal α-power has been associated with the DMN in EEG studies (Knyazev, 2013). As our classification algorithm will be trained on all subjects simultaneously, we used standard boundaries for θ- and α-bandpower. Based on Klimesch (1999), θ-bandpower ranges from 4 to 7 Hz, and α-bandpower was set to 7–13 Hz. For each trial, we windowed every channel's time series with a Hann window. We then computed the trial-wise log-bandpower of the averaged, combined θ- and α-range at every channel location using the Fourier transform. This served as the 124-dimensional feature space.

2.3.3 Pattern Classification

Due to the long trial duration, the number of trials was limited to 60 and 20 for healthy subjects and ALS patients, respectively. With a 124-dimensional feature space, standard machine learning techniques are unlikely to learn a good decoder when trained on each subject's data individually. We resolved this problem by using a transfer learning technique, which is capable of simultaneously learning decoders for all subjects while accounting for inter-individual differences (Jayaram et al., 2015). In this framework, a linear regression model is learned for each subject individually, while penalizing deviations of the regression weights from a Gaussian prior that is learned on the data of all other subjects. This leads to the following loss function,

$$\min_{W,\boldsymbol{\mu},\Sigma} LP(W,\boldsymbol{\mu},\Sigma;X,Y,\lambda) = \min_{W,\boldsymbol{\mu},\Sigma} \frac{1}{\lambda}\sum_s \| X_s w_s - y_s \|^2$$
$$+ \sum_s \frac{1}{2}\Big[(w_s - \boldsymbol{\mu})^{\mathrm{T}}\Sigma^{-1}(w_s - \boldsymbol{\mu})\Big]. \tag{1}$$

Here, y_s denotes a vector containing all trials' stimuli for one subject, which we represent by $\{-1,1\}$ for the two cognitive tasks "focus on your breathing" and "remember a positive memory," respectively. X_s denotes the feature matrix for subject s with dimensionality [number of trials] × [number of features], in our case 60 trials (20 for patients) and one bandpower estimate at each of the 124 channels. w_s denotes the regression weights for each subject, and $\boldsymbol{\mu}$ and Σ refer to the mean and the covariance matrix of the unknown Gaussian prior over w. Finally, λ refers to the importance of the subjects' individual information relative to the prior. It is determined by a maximum likelihood estimation on the whole dataset.

The prior is updated iteratively though an expectation-maximization procedure in two steps. First, we keep μ and Σ constant and solve with respect to w_s for a given subject,

$$w_s = \left(\frac{1}{\lambda}\Sigma X_s^T X_s + I\right)^{-1}\left(\frac{1}{\lambda}\Sigma X_s^T y_s + \mu\right). \tag{2}$$

In the second step, we update our information about the prior by updating its parameters μ and Σ,

$$\mu^* = \frac{1}{S}\sum_s w_s, \tag{3}$$

$$\Sigma^* = \frac{\sum_s (w_s - \mu)(w_s - \mu)^T}{\mathrm{Tr}\left(\sum_s (w_s - \mu)(w_s - \mu)^T\right)} + \varepsilon I. \tag{4}$$

We add εI to (4), with ε set to $\frac{1}{10}$ of the smallest nonzero eigenvalue, to ensure a full rank matrix.

For each subject, we computed the parameters of the prior across all other subjects. We then used a fivefold cross-validation procedure within the test subject with a random separation of the data into folds while balancing the number of trials for each class in every fold, to obtain an estimate of the classification accuracy given the computed parameters. To account for the high variance of cross-validation with such few trials, we repeated this procedure 1000× and averaged the classification accuracy across these repetitions.

2.3.4 Statistical Test on Decoding Accuracy

As discussed in Coyle et al. (2015), it cannot be assumed that the chance-level decoding accuracy matches the theoretical chance-level of 50% when performing cross-validation on a small number of trials. To test whether our strategy achieved above chance-level decoding accuracies, we compared the decoding accuracy during trial time with the accuracy obtained on the pretrial baseline. Specifically, we tested the null-hypothesis H0: trial-time classification accuracy = baseline classification accuracy by a two-tailed pair-wise t-test, given the mean classification-accuracy value of each subject during baseline and during trial time.

2.3.5 Spatial Distribution

To investigate the spatial distribution of induced bandpower modulations, we averaged all 16 priors that were obtained by the transfer learning algorithm and multiplied it with the covariance matrix of the averaged 16 feature sets, as described by Haufe et al. (2014). This results in a topography that depicts the components within the feature space that are modulated by the cognitive strategy.

2.3.6 Dynamics of Induced Bandpower Changes and Timecourse of Classification Accuracy

In a further post-hoc analysis, we investigated the effect of our strategy on event-related (de-)synchronization (ERD/ERS) during the course of a trial. We computed log-bandpower changes over time, relative to the last 3 s of the rest phase before each trial. We used a sliding window of 1 s with a step size of 100 ms to compute bandpower in frequencies from 1 to 40 Hz. We restricted this analysis to channel Pz due to its central parietal position over the posterior cingulate cortex.

Lastly, we investigated cumulative classification accuracy over the course of the trial. First, we employed the previously described pattern classification algorithm to train on the averaged, combined θ- and α-bandpower during the baseline and instruction phase of each trial, respectively. Second, we used an expanding window starting at 4.5 s, with an increment of 1 s, until it span the whole trial. We repeated the classification procedure at each increment $100\times$, with random splits of the data into training- and test set, and averaged the resulting accuracy across these repetitions.

3 RESULTS

We rejected an average of 57 ICs ($\pm$ 1.7) per subject during artifact attenuation. Fig. 2 shows the accuracy of the classification on the combined, averaged α and θ-bandpower for the ALS patients and healthy subjects in red and blue, respectively. ALS patients and healthy subjects achieved a decoding accuracy of 60.8% and 62.5%, respectively, with an across-group average of 62.0%. A two-tailed pair-wise t-test between trial-time and pretrial baseline classification accuracies rejected the null-hypothesis with $t = -3.87$, $p = 0.0015$ for the combined subject groups.

Fig. 3 shows the spatial distribution of bandpower modulation. We observe that the cognitive strategy leads to bandpower modulations that are concentrated over parietal areas.

The first row of Fig. 4 shows the ERS/ERD patterns, averaged across all trials of the healthy subjects, at channel Pz for the self- and nonself-referential condition, respectively. In the self-referential condition, we observe a distinct ERS in the α-range and, to a lesser extent, in the β-range ($\sim$20 Hz), while the nonself-referential conditions shows an ERD first, followed by an ERS. All other frequencies display an ERD. In the self-referential condition, the α-ERS starts with stimulus presentation and remains roughly constant throughout the whole trial. In the nonself-referential condition, the α-bandpower first shows an ERD, until the effect turns into an ERS around 30 s. These different dynamics are also visible in the ERS/ERD differences between conditions (Fig. 4, second row), in which an initial α-ERS diminishes at around 20 s. Subject-specific differences in ERD/ERS patterns are shown in Fig. 5. It is apparent that some subjects show a stronger α-ERS in the self-referential condition (S6, S9, and S11), while other subjects exhibit a stronger α-ERS in the nonself-referential condition (S4 and S5). The transfer learning approach, that we used for decoding, is flexible enough to accommodate these subject-specific

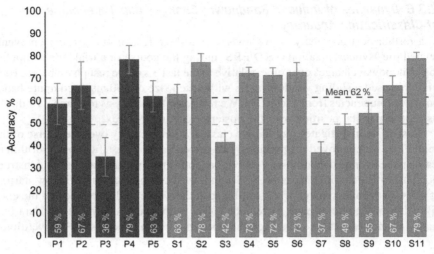

FIG. 2

Classification accuracies for both patients and healthy subjects. The dashed *grey line* represents chance-level classification accuracy at 50%, the *black reference line* represents the mean classification accuracy of 62.0%. P1–P5 are patients and S1–S11 are healthy subjects.

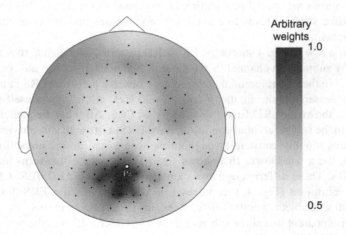

FIG. 3

Classifier topography (see Section 2.3.5). A higher weight indicates a stronger modulation of combined θ- and α-power across conditions.

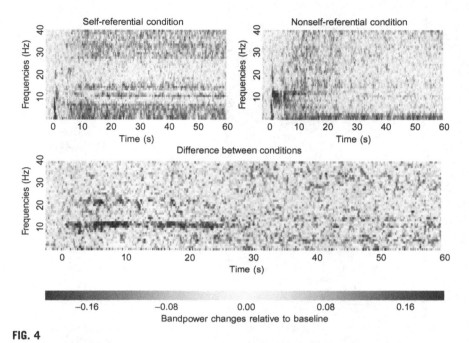

FIG. 4

Average ERD/ERS in healthy subjects over the course of the trial. Time $t = 0$ denotes the presentation of the stimulus.

differences, resulting in high classification accuracies in subjects S4 and S6 in spite of a reversed α-ERD/ERD.

The ALS patients exhibit a slightly different pattern (Fig. 6). Both, the non- and the self-referential conditions, show a distinct ERS in the θ- and in the α-range. In contrast to the healthy subjects, the α-ERD is on average stronger in the nonself-referential condition throughout the whole time course of a trial. As indicated by the patient-specific ERD/ERS shown in Fig. 7, however, these observations are primarily driven by patient P1 (it is noteworthy that patient P1 is the only patient in this study with an ALS-FRS score of zero).

Fig. 8 displays the classification performance over the course of the trial, based on the combined, averaged α- and θ-bandpower for the ALS patients and healthy subjects in red and blue, respectively. ALS patients achieved a peak decoding accuracy of 61.8% after 59 s trial time. Healthy subjects achieved a peak accuracy of 62.4% after 55 s trial time. Several differences in the course of classification performance can be seen between the two groups. Healthy subjects show a steep increase in performance shortly after the instruction phase, while the performance of ALS patients increases more gradually after about 35 s into the trial. Also, the standard error of measurement is noticeably smaller in healthy subjects compared to ALS patients.

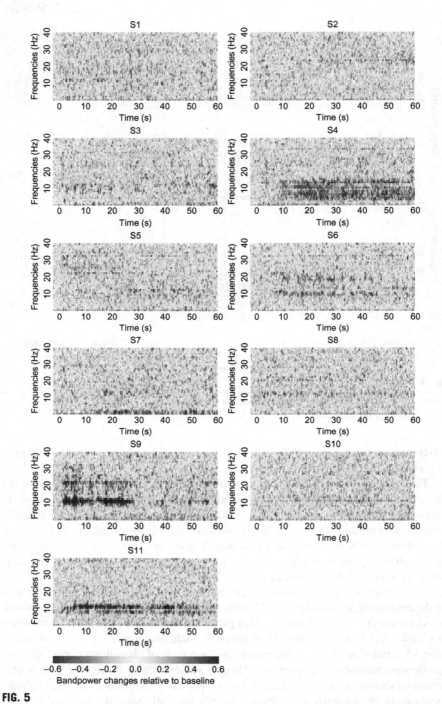

FIG. 5

Bandpower differences between conditions for each healthy subject over the course of the trial. Time $t = 0$ denotes the presentation of the stimulus.

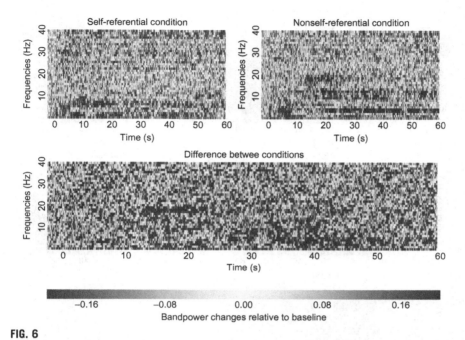

FIG. 6

Average ERD/ERS in ALS patients over the course of a trial. Time $t = 0$ denotes the presentation of the stimulus.

4 DISCUSSION

The current study tested whether healthy subjects and ALS patients in various stages of the disease are able to use a cognitive paradigm for BCI control. Using a linear classifier in a transfer learning approach, we were able to successfully distinguish a self-referential from a nonself-referential condition with an average decoding of 62.5% and 60.8% for the healthy subjects and ALS patients, respectively. We found that the cognitive strategy primarily induced θ- and α-ERD/ERS over parietal areas. Most importantly, we found that even ALS patients in the latest stages of disease progression (P1 and P5) were capable of self-modulating activity in the targeted areas without any training.

It has been argued that completely locked-in ALS patients reside in a state-of-mind similar to unconsciousness or REM sleep (Kübler and Birbaumer, 2008). Therefore, they would be incapable of goal-directed thinking and hence unable to operate any BCI. In our current work, we targeted high-level cognitive processes that are associated with the DMN. This network has been related to the level of consciousness in clinical populations. We therefore hypothesized that a conscious state-of-mind is necessary to voluntarily modulate activity in this network.

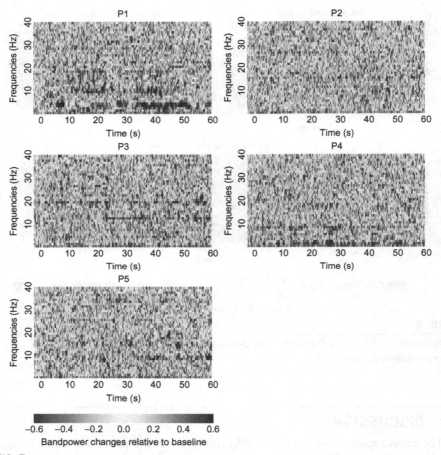

FIG. 7

Bandpower differences between conditions for each ALS patient over the course of the trial. Time $t = 0$ denotes the presentation of the stimulus.

In agreement with our hypothesis, we found that neural activity between the two employed conditions significantly differed in both patients and healthy controls. This indicates that both groups were able to voluntarily modulate neural activity according to the experimental conditions. Importantly, we found a strong ERD/ERS in patient P1 with a ALS-FRS score of zero; this patient only retained minimal residual ocular control for communication. Based on this positive result, we argue that the unreliability of previous attempts to establish BCI control in late-stage ALS may have been caused by the employed paradigms that mostly relied on the subjects' responses to external stimuli or the modulation of SMRs. We point out, however, that previous fMRI studies found weakened activity in several regions of the DMN in

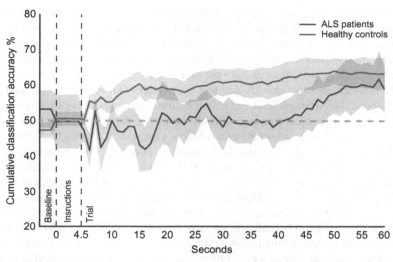

FIG. 8

Mean classification performance over the course of the trial. Accuracy during baseline and instruction phase was computed with a single window. Accuracy during trial time was computed with an expanding window, starting at 4.5 s, in steps of 1 s. The *grey line* represents chance-level. The *shaded area* around the mean represents the standard error of measurement.

ALS patients (Mohammadi et al., 2009). Specifically, areas that are involved in stimulus perception and recognition as well as in working memory were shown to be affected. This included the precuneus that may be responsible for the α-ERD/ERS elicited in this study. It thus remains an open question for how long late-stage ALS patients can maintain BCI control based on the cognitive paradigm introduced here.

We note that, due to the long trial time of 60 s and the decoding accuracies of 62.5% and 60.8% for the healthy subjects and ALS patients, respectively, the resulting information transfer rate (ITR) is low. Fig. 8 indicates that this long trial time is needed by patients to execute the cognitive strategy. While the maximum ITR of our novel paradigm is thus well below those achieved by other paradigms in healthy subjects, we note that the ITR is of secondary importance when working with severely paralyzed patients in late stages of ALS. Instead, the primary challenge remains to establish any form of communication with completely locked-in ALS patients. Our work establishes a novel cognitive paradigm for achieving this goal.

The successful implementation of this novel cognitive strategy has a number of implications for further development of BCI systems for ALS patients. First, recordings were conducted with a 124-channel wet-electrode EEG system. Such conventional EEG systems are often only accessible in clinical environments. They are not very cost efficient or portable. Also, nursing staff or family members of the ALS patient may not have the necessary expertise to setup such a conventional EEG system for online communication. To create a communication method that is available to everyone, it would be beneficial to transfer the paradigm to a commercially available, less expensive, and portable EEG system. As our novel paradigm primarily induces bandpower changes over parietal areas (cf Fig. 3), we expect that it can also be realized on a low-density and low-cost system that focuses on parietal areas only. Second, our strategy achieved classification accuracies above baseline without the need for prior subject training. Still, the results of the post-hoc analysis indicate that the induced effect varies between subjects. One reason for this finding could be the choice of the nonself-referential condition. Focusing on breathing has been shown to decrease overall activity in the DMN, but it also increases synchronization within the DMN (Brewer et al., 2011). These two effects may be difficult to separate when investigating EEG bandpower values, as an increase in synchronization can lead to an increase in spectral power, indistinguishable from the self-referential activation. Focusing on breathing could also be prone to distractions and mind wandering, which in turn also increases DMN activity. A potential direction to address this problem in future studies could be the choice of a different nonself-referential strategy. One candidate could be a verbal spelling task, as verbal execution has been found to lower DMN activity (Koshino et al., 2014). It may also be sufficiently demanding to avoid involuntary mind wandering.

REFERENCES

Aggarwal, S., Cudkowicz, M., 2008. ALS drug development: reflections from the past and a way forward. Neurotherapeutics 1933-7213. 5 (4), 516–527. http://dx.doi.org/10.1016/j.nurt.2008.08.002.

Aloise, F., Aricò, P., Schettini, F., Riccio, A., Salinari, S., Mattia, D., Babiloni, F., Cincotti, F., 2012. A covert attention P300-based brain-computer interface: geospell. Ergonomics 1366-5847. 55 (5), 538–551. http://dx.doi.org/10.1080/00140139.2012.661084.

Andreasen, N.C., O'Leary, D.S., Cizadlo, T., Arndt, S., Rezai, K., Watkins, G.L., Ponto, L.L.B., Hichwa, R.D., 1995. Remembering the past: two facets of episodic memory explored with positron emission tomography. Am. J. Psych. 0002953X. 152 (11), 1576–1585.

Aricò, P., Aloise, F., Schettini, F., Salinari, S., Mattia, D., Cincotti, F., 2014. Influence of P300 latency jitter on event related potential-based brain-computer interface performance. J. Neural Eng. 1741-2552. 11 (3), 035008. http://dx.doi.org/10.1088/1741-2560/11/3/035008.

Bach, J.R., 1993. Amyotrophic lateral sclerosis. Communication status and survival with ventilatory support. Am. J. Phys. Med. Rehab. 0894-9115. 72 (6), 343–349.

Belouchrani, A., Abed-Meraim, K., Cardoso, J.F., Moulines, E., 1997. A blind source separation technique using second-order statistics. IEEE Trans. Sign. Proc. 1053-587X. 45 (2), 434–444. http://dx.doi.org/10.1109/78.554307.

Birbaumer, N., Piccione, F., Silvoni, S., Wildgruber, M., 2012. Ideomotor silence: the case of complete paralysis and brain-computer interfaces (BCI). Psychol. Res. 76 (2), 183–191. http://dx.doi.org/10.1007/s00426-012-0412-5.

Braak, H., Brettschneider, J., Ludolph, A.C., Lee, V.M., Trojanowski, J.Q., Del Tredici, K., 2013. Amyotrophic lateral sclerosis-a model of corticofugal axonal spread. Nat. Rev. Neurol. 1759-4766. 9 (12), 708–714. http://dx.doi.org/10.1038/nrneurol.2013.221.

Brewer, J.A., Worhunsky, P.D., Gray, J.R., Tang, Y.Y., Weber, J., Kober, H., 2011. Meditation experience is associated with differences in default mode network activity and connectivity. Proc. Nat. Acad. Sci. 0027-8424. 108 (50), 20254–20259. http://dx.doi.org/10.1073/pnas.1112029108.

Brouwer, A.M., van Erp, J.B.F., 2010. A tactile P300 brain-computer interface. Front. Neurosci. 16624548. 4 (MAY), 19. http://dx.doi.org/10.3389/fnins.2010.00019.

Cedarbaum, J.M., Stambler, N., Malta, E., Fuller, C., Hilt, D., Thurmond, B., Nakanishi, A., 1999. The ALSFRS-R: a revised ALS functional rating scale that incorporates assessments of respiratory function. J. Neurol. Sci. 0022510X. 169 (1-2), 13–21. http://dx.doi.org/10.1016/S0022-510X(99)00210-5.

Coyle, D., Stow, J., McCreadie, K., McElligott, J., Carroll, Á., 2015. Sensorimotor modulation assessment and brain-computer interface training in disorders of consciousness. Arch. Phys. Med. Rehabil. 1532-821X. 96 (3 Suppl), S62–S70. http://dx.doi.org/10.1016/j.apmr.2014.08.024.

Fransson, P., Marrelec, G., 2008. The precuneus/posterior cingulate cortex plays a pivotal role in the default mode network: Evidence from a partial correlation network analysis. NeuroImage 10538119. 42 (3), 1178–1184. http://dx.doi.org/10.1016/j. neuroimage.2008.05.059.

Greicius, M.D., Krasnow, B., Reiss, A.L., Menon, V., 2003. Functional connectivity in the resting brain: a network analysis of the default mode hypothesis. Proc. Nat. Acad. Sci. USA 0027-8424. 100 (1), 253–258. http://dx.doi.org/10.1073/pnas.0135058100.

Grosse-Wentrup, M., Schölkopf, B., 2014. A brain-computer interface based on self-regulation of gamma-oscillations in the superior parietal cortex. J. Neural Eng. 1741-2552. 11 (5), 056015. http://dx.doi.org/10.1088/1741-2560/11/5/ 056015.

Grosse-Wentrup, M., Harmeling, S., Zander, T., Hill, J., Schölkopf, B., 2013. How to test the quality of reconstructed sources in independent component analysis (ICA) of EEG/MEG data. In: Proceedings–2013 3rd International Workshop on Pattern Recognition in Neuroimaging, PRNI 2013, pp. 102–105.

Haufe, S., Meinecke, F., Görgen, K., Dähne, S., Haynes, J.D., Blankertz, B., Bießmann, F., 2014. On the interpretation of weight vectors of linear models in multivariate neuroimaging. NeuroImage 1095-9572. 87, 96–110. http://dx.doi.org/10.1016/j.neuroimage.2013.10.067.

Hill, N.J., Ricci, E., Haider, S., McCane, L.M., Heckman, S., Wolpaw, J.R., Vaughan, T.M., 2014. A practical, intuitive brain-computer interface for communicating 'yes' or 'no' by listening. J. Neural Eng. 1741-2552. 11 (3), 035003. http://dx.doi.org/10.1088/1741-2560/11/3/035003.

Hohmann, M.R., Fomina, T., Jayaram, V., Widmann, N., Förster, C., Müller vom Hagen, J., Synofzik, M., Schölkopf, B., Schölz, L., Grosse-Wentrup, M., 2015. A cognitive brain-computer interface for patients with amyotrophic lateral sclerosis. In: Proceedings of the 2015 IEEE International Conference on Systems, Man, and Cybernetics (SMC2015), Hong Kong.

Jacobs, L., Bozian, D., Heffner, R.R., Barron, S.A., 1981. An eye movement disorder in amyotrophic lateral sclerosis. Neurology 0028-3878. 31 (10), 1282–1287. http://dx.doi.org/10.1212/WNL.31.10. 1282.

Jayaram, V., Alamgir, M., Altun, Y., Schölkopf, B., Grosse-Wentrup, M., 2015. Transfer learning in brain-computer interfaces. IEEE Computat. Intell. Mag.

Klimesch, W., 1999. EEG alpha and theta oscillations reflect cognitive and memory performance: a review and analysis. Brain Res. Rev. 01650173. 29 (2-3), 169–195. http://dx.doi.org/10.1016/S0165-0173(98) 00056-3.

Knyazev, G.G., 2013. EEG correlates of self-referential processing. Front. Human Neurosci. 7, 264. http://dx.doi.org/10.3389/fnhum.2013.00264.

Koshino, H., Minamoto, T., Yaoi, K., Osaka, M., Osaka, N., 2014. Coactivation of the default mode network regions and working memory network regions during task preparation. Scient. Rep. 2045-2322. 4, 5954. http://dx.doi.org/10.1038/srep05954.

Kübler, A., Birbaumer, N., 2008. Brain-computer interfaces and communication in paralysis: extinction of goal directed thinking in completely paralysed patients? Clin. Neurophys. 1388-2457. 119 (11), 2658–2666. http://dx.doi.org/10.1016/j. clinph.2008.06.019.

Kübler, A., Kotchoubey, B., Hinterberger, T., Ghanayim, N., Perelmouter, J., Schauer, M., Fritsch, C., Taub, E., Birbaumer, N., 1999. The thought translation device: a neurophysiological approach to communication in total motor paralysis. Exper. Brain Res. 0014-4819. 124 (2), 223–232.

Kübler, A., Kotchoubey, B., Kaiser, J., Wolpaw, J.R., Birbaumer, N., 2001. Brain-computer communication: unlocking the locked in. Psychol. Bull. 0033-2909. 127 (3), 358–375. http://dx.doi.org/10.1037/0033-2909.127.3. 358.

Kübler, A., Furdea, A., Halder, S., Hammer, E.M., Nijboer, F., Kotchoubey, B., 2009. A brain-computer interface controlled auditory event-related potential (p300) spelling system for locked-in patients. Ann. N. Y. Acad. Sci. 1157, 90–100. http://dx.doi.org/10.1111/j.1749-6632.2008.04122.x.

Leigh, P.N., 2003. The management of motor neurone disease. J. Neurol. Neuros. Psych. 0022-3050. 74 (90004), 32–47. http://dx.doi.org/10.1136/jnnp.74.suppl_4.iv32.

Mak, J.N., Wolpaw, J.R., 2009. Clinical applications of brain-computer interfaces: current state and future prospects. IEEE Rev. Biomed. Eng. 1941-1189. 2, 187–199. http://dx. doi.org/10.1109/RBME.2009.2035356.

Marchetti, M., Priftis, K., 2015. Brain-computer interfaces in amyotrophic lateral sclerosis: a metanalysis. Clin. Neurophysiol. 1872-8952. 126 (6), 1255–1263. http://dx.doi.org/10.1016/j.clinph.2014.09.017.

McMenamin, B.W., Shackman, A.J., Greischar, L.L., Davidson, R.J., 2011. Electromyogenic artifacts and electroencephalographic inferences revisited. NeuroImage 10538119. 54 (1), 4–9. http://dx.doi.org/10.1016/j.neuroimage.2010.07. 057.

Mohammadi, B., Kollewe, K., Samii, A., Krampfl, K., Dengler, R., Münte, T.F., 2009. Changes of resting state brain networks in amyotrophic lateral sclerosis. Exp. Neurol. 1090-2430. 217 (1), 147–153. http://dx.doi.org/10.1016/j.expneurol.2009.01.025.

Mu, Y., Han, S., 2010. Neural oscillations involved in self-referential processing. NeuroImage 10538119. 53 (2), 757–768. http://dx.doi.org/10.1016/j.neuroimage. 2010.07.008.

Nihei, K., McKee, A.C., Kowall, N.W., 1993. Patterns of neuronal degeneration in the motor cortex of amyotrophic lateral sclerosis patients. Acta Neuropathol. 0001-6322. 86 (1), 55–64. http://dx.doi.org/10.1007/BF00454899.

Nijboer, F., Furdea, A., Gunst, I., Mellinger, J., McFarland, D.J., Birbaumer, N., Kübler, A., 2008. An auditory brain-computer interface (BCI). J. Neurosci. Meth. 01650270. 167 (1), 43–50. http://dx.doi.org/10.1016/j.jneumeth.2007.02.009.

Onton, J., Westerfield, M., Townsend, J., Makeig, S., 2006. Imaging human EEG dynamics using independent component analysis. Neurosci. Biobehav. Rev. 0149-7634. 30 (6), 808–822. http://dx.doi.org/10.1016/j.neubiorev.2006. 06.007.

Pfurtscheller, G., Neuper, C., 2001. Motor imagery and direct brain-computer communication. Proc. IEEE 0018-9219. 89 (7), 1123–1134. http://dx.doi.org/10.1109/5. 939829.

Raichle, M.E., 2015. The brain's default mode network. Ann. Rev. Neurosci. 0147-006X. 38 (1), 433–447. http://dx.doi.org/10.1146/annurev-neuro-071013-014030.

Raichle, M.E., MacLeod, A.M., Snyder, A.Z., Powers, W.J., Gusnard, D.A., Shulman, G.L., 2001. A default mode of brain function. Proc. Nat. Acad. Sci. USA 0027-8424. 98 (2), 676–682. http://dx.doi.org/10.1073/pnas. 98.2.676.

Schalk, G., McFarland, D.J., Hinterberger, T., Birbaumer, N., Wolpaw, J.R., 2004. BCI2000: A general-purpose brain-computer interface (BCI) system. IEEE Trans. Biomed. Eng. 00189294. 51 (6), 1034–1043. http://dx.doi.org/10.1109/TBME.2004.827072.

Shackman, A.J., McMenamin, B.W., Slagter, H.A., Maxwell, J.S., Greischar, L.L., Davidson, R.J., 2009. Electromyogenic artifacts and electroencephalographic inferences. Brain Topogr. 0896-0267. 22 (1), 7–12. http://dx.doi.org/10.1007/s10548-009-0079-4.

Shulman, G.L., Fiez, J.A., Corbetta, M., Buckner, R.L., Miezin, F.M., Raichle, M.E., Petersen, S.E., 1997. Common blood flow changes across visual tasks: II. Decreases in cerebral cortex. J. Cogn. Neurosci. 0898-929X. 9 (5), 648–663. http://dx.doi.org/10.1162/jocn.1997.9.5.648.

Simpson, J.R., Snyder, A.Z., Gusnard, D.A., Raichle, M.E., 2001. Emotion-induced changes in human medial prefrontal cortex: I. During cognitive task performance. Proc. Natl. Acad. Sci. USA 0027-8424. 98 (2), 683–687. http://dx.doi.org/10.1073/pnas.98.2. 683.

Treder, M., Schmidt, N., Blankertz, B., 2011. Gaze-independent brain-computer interfaces based on covert attention and feature attention. J. Neur. Eng. 1741-2560. 8 (6), 066003. http://dx.doi.org/10.1088/1741-2560/8/6/066003.

Vanhaudenhuyse, A., Noirhomme, Q., Tshibanda, L.J.F., Bruno, M.A., Boveroux, P., Schnakers, C., Soddu, A., Perlbarg, V., Ledoux, D., Brichant, J.F., Moonen, G., Maquet, P., Greicius, M.D., Laureys, S., Boly, M., 2010. Default network connectivity reflects the level of consciousness in non-communicative brain-damaged patients. Brain 00068950. 133 (1), 161–171. http://dx.doi.org/10.1093/brain/awp313.

Vansteensel, M.J., Hermes, D., Aarnoutse, E.J., Bleichner, M.G., Schalk, G., van Rijen, P.C., Leijten, F.S.S., Ramsey, N.F., 2010. Brain-computer interfacing based on cognitive control. Ann. Neurol. 1531-8249. 67 (6), 809–816. http://dx.doi.org/10.1002/ana. 21985.

Wander, J.D., Rao, R.P.N., 2014. Brain-computer interfaces: a powerful tool for scientific inquiry. Curr. Opin. Neurobiol. 1873-6882. 25, 70–75. http://dx.doi.org/10.1016/j.conb. 2013.11.013.

Weissman, D.H., Roberts, K.C., Visscher, K.M., Woldorff, M.G., 2006. The neural bases of momentary lapses in attention. Nat. Neurosci. 1097-6256. 9 (7), 971–978. http://dx.doi.org/10.1038/nn1727.

Wijesekera, L.C., Leigh, P.N., 2009. Amyotrophic lateral sclerosis. Orphanet J. Rare Dis. 1750-1172. 4 (1), 3. http://dx.doi.org/10.1186/1750-1172-4-3.

Wolpaw, J.R., Birbaumer, N., McFarland, D.J., Pfurtscheller, G., Vaughan, T.M., 2002. Brain-computer interfaces for communication and control. Clin. Neurophysiol. 13882457. 113 (6), 767–791. http://dx.doi.org/10.1016/S1388-2457(02)00057-3.

Brain–computer interfaces for patients with disorders of consciousness

R.M. Gibson[*,†,1], **A.M. Owen**[*,†], **D. Cruse**[‡]

*The Brain and Mind Institute, University of Western Ontario, London, ON, Canada
†University of Western Ontario, London, ON, Canada
‡School of Psychology, University of Birmingham, Birmingham, United Kingdom
[1]Corresponding author: Tel.: +1-519-661-2111; Fax: +1-519-661-3613,
e-mail address: rgibso5@uwo.ca

Abstract

The disorders of consciousness refer to clinical conditions that follow a severe head injury. Patients diagnosed as in a vegetative state lack awareness, while patients diagnosed as in a minimally conscious state retain fluctuating awareness. However, it is a challenge to accurately diagnose these disorders with clinical assessments of behavior. To improve diagnostic accuracy, neuroimaging-based approaches have been developed to detect the presence or absence of awareness in patients who lack overt responsiveness. For the small subset of patients who retain awareness, brain–computer interfaces could serve as tools for communication and environmental control. Here we review the existing literature concerning the sensory and cognitive abilities of patients with disorders of consciousness with respect to existing brain–computer interface designs. We highlight the challenges of device development for this special population and address some of the most promising approaches for future investigations.

Keywords

Disorders of consciousness, Vegetative state, Minimally conscious state, Awareness detection, Covert cognition

1 THE DISORDERS OF CONSCIOUSNESS

Severe head injury can result in clinical conditions characterized by absent or reduced awareness—known as the vegetative state (VS, or unresponsive wakefulness syndrome, UWS) and the minimally conscious state (MCS), respectively (Bernat, 2006; Laureys et al., 2010). These conditions, along with coma, are known as the disorders of consciousness (DoC; refer to Table 1 for a summary). The comatose state is an acute condition (4 weeks or less) in which a patient lacks both

Progress in Brain Research, Volume 228, ISSN 0079-6123, http://dx.doi.org/10.1016/bs.pbr.2016.04.003
© 2016 Elsevier B.V. All rights reserved.

Table 1 Overview of the Disorders of Consciousness

Diagnosis	Characteristics	Defining Behavior	Behavioral Command Following and Communication
Coma (Bernat, 2006)	The absence of wakefulness and responsiveness to stimulation for a period of no more than about 4 weeks	Closed eyes with no responsiveness to stimulation	None
Vegetative state/unresponsive wakefulness syndrome [VS/UWS] (Bernat, 2006; Laureys et al., 2010; Multi-Society Task Force on PVS, 1994a,b; Royal College of Physicians Working Group, 2003)	Wakefulness with reflexive behavior	Spontaneous eye-opening behavior with no reproducible responsiveness to stimulation, excluding the following reflexive behavior: startle responses (auditory or visual); abnormal posturing; withdrawal (motor); reflexive oral movements; and/or localization to sound	None
Minimally conscious state *minus* [MCS−] (Bruno et al., 2011, 2012; Giacino et al., 2002)	Wakefulness with nonreflexive behavior	Reproducible, nonreflexive behavior including at least one of: visual fixation or pursuit; object localization, recognition, or manipulation; orientation to noxious stimulation; or automatic motor responses	None
Minimally conscious state *plus* [MCS+] (Bruno et al., 2011, 2012; Giacino et al., 2002)	Wakefulness with nonreflexive behavior and command following	Behavioral command following generally accompanied by behavior indicative of an MCS−	At least one of: reproducible or consistent movement to command; intelligible verbalization; or nonfunctional, intentional communication
Emergence from a minimally conscious state (EMCS) (Giacino et al., 2002)	Wakefulness with sophisticated nonreflexive behavior including functional object use and/or accurate functional communication	Accurate functional communication and/or functional object use generally accompanied by behavior indicative of an MCS+	At least one of: accurate functional communication; or functional object use

Notes. *All behavioral criteria (third and fourth columns) are taken from the revised version of the Coma Recovery Scale (Kalmar and Giacino, 2005).*

awareness and wakefulness (Bernat, 2006). Following emergence from coma, patients diagnosed as in either a VS/UWS or an MCS demonstrate eye opening that reflects the preservation of the ascending reticular activating system (Fernández-Espejo and Owen, 2013; Giacino et al., 2014; Royal College of Physicians Working Group, 2003). Critically, however, a patient must produce evidence of purposeful behavior in a formal clinical assessment to be considered aware. Patients in a VS/UWS do not generate purposeful behavior and are thus considered to lack awareness (Multi-Society Task Force on PVS, 1994a,b). Conversely, patients in an MCS generate variable, but reproducible, behavior and are considered to possess awareness (Giacino et al., 2002).

A critical diagnostic marker in DoC is whether or not a patient can follow commands. While purposeful behavior is considered sufficient to denote awareness of one's external environment, command following indicates beyond reasonable doubt that the patient is conscious (Fernández-Espejo and Owen, 2013; Gosseries et al., 2014; Owen, 2013). For patients diagnosed as in an MCS, the ability to follow commands can be indicated by a diagnostic qualifier of "+" (ie, MCS+, Bruno et al., 2011, 2012). Similarly, patients in an MCS who do not demonstrate evidence of command following can be categorized as in an MCS − (Bruno et al., 2011, 2012). Emergence from an MCS (EMCS) occurs when a patient demonstrates functional object use and/or accurate communication (Giacino et al., 2002).

Given that patients diagnosed as in a VS/UWS do not produce any evidence of overt, purposeful behavior, such a patient could not follow commands in a behavioral assessment. However, factors such as fluctuating arousal, fatigue, lack of interest, and concurrent cognitive and sensory limitations from brain injury may reduce responsiveness in any patient (Giacino et al., 2014; Whyte et al., 2013). In fact, using only medical observation, misdiagnosis of a patient's conscious state is estimated at rates as high as 43% (Andrews et al., 1996; Schnakers et al., 2009b). Furthermore, there is a risk that a patient who retains awareness, but lacks the ability to respond in a behavioral assessment due to motor impairments, could be inaccurately diagnosed as in a vegetative, ie, unconscious, state. This possibility, with its implied legal, ethical, and moral challenges (Jennett, 2002; Peterson et al., 2013; Racine and Illes, 2007), has been the subject of increasing attention in scientific and clinical research for the past 20 years (Fernández-Espejo and Owen, 2013; Giacino et al., 2014; Gosseries et al., 2014).

2 THE CHALLENGES OF COMMUNICATING WITH A DAMAGED BRAIN

To address the diagnostic challenges of the DoC, researchers have used measures of brain function to determine if an outwardly nonresponsive patient can volitionally modulate their brain activity and provide evidence of their ability to follow commands. One well-established paradigm to assess so-called covert command following in the DoC involves asking a patient to engage in mental imagery during a functional magnetic resonance imaging (fMRI) scan (Bardin et al., 2011;

Boly et al., 2007; Fernández-Espejo and Owen, 2013; Gibson et al., 2014b; Monti et al., 2010; Owen et al., 2006; Stender et al., 2014). The patient's engagement in the mental task is quantified by the patient's ability to generate specific, reliable modulations of their brain activity identified from validation studies (Adapa et al., 2014; Boly et al., 2007; Davis et al., 2007; Fernández-Espejo et al., 2014; Naci et al., 2013; Owen and Coleman, 2007). Similar approaches using electroencephalographic (EEG) responses to imagined movement have also been used successfully in this patient population (Cruse et al., 2011a, 2012; Gibson et al., 2014b; Goldfine et al., 2011).

Given this large body of evidence that a subset of patients with DoC possess covert awareness, these patients are candidates for intervention with brain–computer interfaces (BCIs). However, an important difference between the DoC and other BCI target populations is that the DoC arise from severe and often diffuse acquired brain injury (Bernat, 2006). Most patients with DoC lack oculomotor control, which reduces the feasibility of visual information in BCI applications (Kalmar and Giacino, 2005). Significantly, the sensory and cognitive abilities of any patient with a DoC are potentially compromised by their acquired brain injuries and concurrent medical complications (Giacino et al., 2014; Whyte et al., 2013). For instance, patients in an MCS in particular are susceptible to aphasia (Majerus et al., 2009), and patients with severe brain injury, even with sophisticated abilities consistent with EMCS, can have difficultly answering yes/no questions (Nakase-Richardson et al., 2008). Patients with DoC also suffer from fatigue and fluctuating arousal (Fernández-Espejo and Owen, 2013; Giacino et al., 2014; Laureys et al., 2004). Together, these factors restrict many aspects of BCI development and anticipated BCI literacy in this population.

Despite these challenges, BCI development for patients with DoC can fulfill important clinical diagnostic functions, such as cognitive assessment and awareness detection (Boly et al., 2007; Kirschner et al., 2015; Naci and Owen, 2013; Owen et al., 2006; Rodriguez Moreno et al., 2010). In a rehabilitation context, when a purposeful external behavior is identified, efforts are focused on training the patient to employ this purposeful behavior for communication. Consequently, if a purposeful ability to covertly follow commands can be identified with BCI methods—reflecting the preservation of at least minimal consciousness—we are compelled to conduct additional investigations into feasible communication options for these patients. However, Gabriel and colleagues (2015) recently evaluated the sensitivity of fMRI- and EEG-based assessments of command following and communication using the mental imagery approaches originally reported by Owen (Boly et al., 2007; Monti et al., 2010; Owen et al., 2006) and Cruse (Cruse et al., 2011a). In the EEG assessments, positive evidence of command following and successful communication was only achieved by 6 of the 20 healthy volunteers. From the fMRI assessment, positive evidence of command following was obtained for 17 of 20 participants, but only 12 of 20 participants were able to communicate (Gabriel et al., 2015). These findings emphasize the difficulties of translating methods for the detection of command following into methods for functional communication, despite the potential diagnostic benefits.

3 BCIs FOR PATIENTS WITH DoC

In this chapter, we review the existing literature concerning the assessment of cognitive and sensory abilities for patients with DoC. We focus our review on neural signals that have also been used in BCI applications outside of DoC, including both healthy and patient populations. Indeed, relatively few investigations have directly evaluated BCI use in patients with DoC. Accordingly, here we highlight the available literature and discuss the feasibility of eventual BCI use in patients with DoC. We have structured our review according to the technology used to obtain the BCI control signal of interest (see Fig. 1); given the extensive study of EEG data in BCI applications to date, the majority of our review focuses on control signals acquired using this approach. In each section, we begin with a brief discussion of the neural basis of the control signal of interest, and we then discuss each subtype of paradigm according to its relevance for patients with DoC. We conclude with specific recommendations for future BCI development in patients with DoC.

3.1 ELECTROENCEPHALOGRAPHY

Even for healthy users, BCIs based on EEG are widely regarded as the most practical for regular use (Chatelle et al., 2012, 2015; Naci et al., 2012; Nicolas-Alonso and Gomez-Gil, 2012). EEG signals have a very high temporal resolution alongside a minimally invasive acquisition protocol. Importantly, these signals can be acquired from most individuals with minimal health risks. One of the only physical or medical attributes of a person that would render EEG measurements uninformative is a skull breach; EEG data acquired over a breached area of a skull are usually contaminated by sharp, high-frequency bursts known as breach rhythm (Lee et al., 2010). Breach rhythm occurs in some patients with DoC (eg, due to traumatic brain injury).

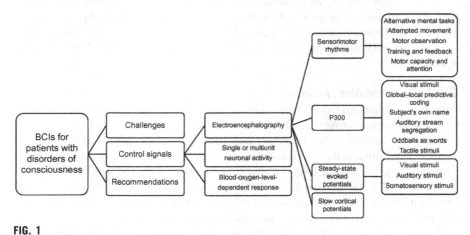

FIG. 1

Graphical overview of the contents of this chapter.

EEG signals are used routinely in clinical practice. Some clinical applications of EEG include the detection of epileptiform activity and monitoring during various stages of recovery from coma (Brown et al., 2010). From this clinical literature as reviewed in Bagnato et al. (2014), a reduction in EEG amplitude is associated with poor outcomes in comatose patients following cardiac arrest (Cloostermans et al., 2012; Hofmeijer et al., 2014; Synek, 1988). With respect to patients with chronic DoC (ie, those diagnosed as in a VS/UWS or MCS), several investigations have concluded that there are no general patterns of EEG responses that are specific to only one of these disorders (Bagnato et al., 2010; Boccagni et al., 2011; Kulkarni et al., 2007). Nevertheless, other researchers and clinicians have noted that patients recover more power in the alpha (8–12 Hz) and beta (13–30 Hz) bands of the EEG signal as they emerge from coma toward a VS/UWS, MCS, and recovery (Brown et al., 2010).

The EEG signal arises from summated postsynaptic potentials that occur in cortical layers known as dipole sheets (Nunez and Srinivasan, 2006). As these measures are acquired at the scalp, EEG signals are susceptible to nonneuronal electrical signals (Srinivasan, 2012). One such signal is high-frequency line noise from the alternating current of powerline electricity, although line noise is typically eliminated during acquisition (or offline) with a notch filter. Other physical sources of nonneuronal electrical signals in EEG recordings include mechanical sources, such as low-frequency signal due to the physical movement of cables or other recording devices, and transient high-frequency activity from the electrodes themselves (Srinivasan, 2012). Finally, another nonneuronal signal source that is particularly important for BCI applications with patients who lack voluntary motor control are other biological electrical signals. Biological artifacts in the EEG arise from the heart and other muscles and may also present as low-frequency drifts due to sweating. Contamination of the EEG by motion or sweating artifacts is especially problematic in studies of patients with DoC.

In BCI applications, EEG signals are frequently evaluated after being time-locked to a stimulus or response of interest and averaged over repeated presentations. This averaged, time-locked EEG signal is known as an event-related potential (ERP; Luck, 2014). ERP studies of patients with DoC were recently reviewed by Lehembre et al. (2012).

3.1.1 Sensorimotor rhythms

Sensorimotor rhythms (SMRs) are oscillations in magnetic or electric fields recorded over sensorimotor cortex in the mu (8–12 Hz), beta (18–30 Hz), and gamma (30–200 Hz) frequency bands (Jasper and Pendfield, 1949; Lopes da Silva, 1991; Neuper and Pfurtscheller, 2001). An event-related desynchronization (ERD) is a reduction in oscillatory activity related to a sensorimotor event (Pfurtscheller and Aranibar, 1977). An increase in oscillatory activity known as an event-related synchronization (ERS) can also occur, and this increase in activity may be a correlate of a disinhibited/deactivated cortical network (Pfurtscheller, 1992).

Low-frequency mu ERDs (8–10 Hz) occur with almost any motor behavior and are widespread over sensorimotor cortex (Pfurtscheller et al., 2000b). These oscillations are thought to reflect general motor preparation, low-level bottom-up stimulus processing, and basic attentional processing (Klimesch, 1999). In contrast, higher frequency mu ERDs (10–13 Hz) are topographically restricted and related to specific aspects of task performance (Pfurtscheller et al., 2000b). Beta rhythms have been extensively studied in cognitive neuroscience; for a review, see Kilavik et al. (2013). Beta ERDs with a rebound ERS occur following movement (Brovelli et al., 2004). Beta ERDs are similar for active/passive movements (Cassim et al., 2001), electrical nerve stimulation (Neuper and Pfurtscheller, 2001), and motor imagery (Pfurtscheller et al., 2005). These responses also coincide with decreased excitability of motor cortical neurons, as measured using transcranial magnetic stimulation (TMS; Chen et al., 1998).

3.1.1.1 Neural basis of SMRs

Using depth electrodes, it has been shown that SMRs occur in both cortical and subcortical structures. For example, mu and beta activity occurs in the thalamus, subthalamic nucleus, and pedunculopontine area (Androulidakis et al., 2008; Klostermann et al., 2007; Williams et al., 2002). The relationships among these brain regions and neural rhythms when movement occurs are complicated: for instance, a mu ERD occurs in motor cortex, a mu ERS occurs in subthalamic nuclei, and a beta ERS occurs in motor cortex, the thalamus, and subthalamic nuclei (Klostermann et al., 2007). Using simultaneous EEG-fMRI, SMRs have been localized to the primary sensorimotor cortex during actual and imagined movement (Yuan et al., 2010a). ERD magnitude is also proportional to positive blood-oxygen-level-dependent (BOLD) responses (Yuan et al., 2010b, 2011), and temporal variations in SMRs are highly correlated with the BOLD signal in the contralateral sensorimotor cortex (Logothetis et al., 2001; Yuan et al., 2011). Gamma activity is also strongly correlated with the firing rate of single neurons, and this finding has been confirmed using several electrical and magnetic neuroimaging methodologies (Ball et al., 2008; Brookes et al., 2005; Lachaux et al., 2007; Logothetis et al., 2001).

3.1.1.2 SMR-based BCIs

SMR-based BCIs have been extensively studied. In fact, BCIs based on responses to motor imagery were the most widely studied type of BCI between 2007 and 2011 according to a recent meta-analysis (Hwang et al., 2013). There have been many studies of SMRs for BCI applications, including cursor control (Bai et al., 2008), communication (Blankertz et al., 2006; Rohani et al., 2013), games (Marshall et al., 2013), and the restoration of motor function (Pfurtscheller et al., 2000a, 2003). Notably, better performance has been reported in the general population with the P300-based BCIs to be discussed in a subsequent section (Guger et al., 2009) than with SMR-based BCIs (Guger et al., 2003). Some investigators have recommended P300-based BCIs over SMR-based BCIs for patient applications (Nijboer et al., 2010). Nonetheless, and despite possible changes in the cortical motor system due to prolonged immobility, there is evidence that people with severe and long-term motor impairments retain SMRs and can even operate SMR-based BCIs in some cases. For example, although amyotrophic lateral sclerosis (ALS) impacts cortical motor neurons (Kiernan et al., 2011), Kübler and colleagues showed that four patients with ALS could operate a SMR-based BCI (Kübler et al., 2005). Likewise, successful SMR-based BCI use has been reported for people with muscular dystrophy (Cincotti et al., 2008), cerebral palsy (Neuper et al., 2003), spinal cord injuries (Wolpaw and McFarland, 2004), and tetraplegia (Pfurtscheller et al., 2000a). It is therefore not surprising that some patients with DoC have been found to generate reliable SMRs.

One cohort study of SMR modulations in patients with DoC was conducted by Cruse et al. (2011a). Sixteen patients and 12 healthy volunteers were instructed to imagine moving their right hand in a squeezing motion and wiggling their toes on separate trials. On other trials, participants were instructed to relax. Each experimental block consisted of fifteen 600-Hz tones every few seconds after the instruction to cue the participants to engage in motor imagery or relaxation, as instructed. Data were analyzed from 25 electrodes over motor cortex. Classification analyses employed a linear support vector machine with block-wise cross-validation. The features were log power values of the EEG data taken from 0.5 to 3.5 s after the cue, and spectral power was analyzed in four frequency bands (7–13, 13–19, 19–25, and 25–30 Hz). Accuracy was calculated with a binomial test. Above-chance classification accuracy was obtained for three patients diagnosed as in a VS/UWS (range: 61–78%, mean of 70%). These findings were taken as evidence of the abilities of these patients to follow commands (Cruse et al., 2011a).

More recently, Coyle and colleagues reported a BCI based on SMRs using visual and stereo auditory feedback with a sample of four patients diagnosed as in an MCS (Coyle et al., 2015). SMRs were obtained by asking the patients to imagine movements of the right hand or the toes with simultaneous visual and auditory cues (an arrow presented on a computer screen and a tone presented binaurally). The patients were trained in multiple sessions and provided with both visual and auditory feedback. Visual feedback consisted of visually presented games; in one version, participants had to direct a ball to a basket using hand or toe imagery to move the ball left or right, respectively. Auditory feedback consisted of a short clip of music or pink noise moved between the left or right earphones using the same imagined movements. The patients produced significant, appropriate, and consistent responses across multiple assessments. Auditory feedback seemed to enhance arousal more than visual feedback, and the music feedback resulted in better performance than pink noise. Overall, this study provides strong evidence that a true BCI is feasible for use by patients with DoC (Coyle et al., 2015).

An important consideration with respect to machine learning methods to identify subject-specific responses in the absence of overt behavior (or other means to confirm the subject-specific effects) is that these techniques are susceptible to task-irrelevant changes in the EEG. In response to the previously discussed work of Cruse et al. (2011a), Goldfine and colleagues highlighted the potential problems of blocked mental imagery tasks (Goldfine et al., 2013). Using blocks circumvents the potential for so-called automatic responses due to task instructions (Owen et al., 2007), but also introduces potential violations of certain statistical assumptions that may lead to high rates of false positives (Cruse et al., 2011b; Goldfine et al., 2013). Notably, the rate of false positives can be reduced by increasing the amount of features available from the EEG data for these machine learning approaches (Noirhomme et al., 2014). However, as has been discussed elsewhere (Cruse et al., 2014a; Peterson et al., 2015), applications intended to inform the diagnosis of the DoC especially require a case-by-case trade-off between an acceptable rate of false alarms (ie, evidence of command following when the patient lacks awareness) and misses (ie, no evidence of command following when the patient is aware).

3.1.1.2.1 Alternative mental tasks. Despite the interest and reasonable success of SMR-based BCIs, there have been some concerns over the practicality of their use. As noted in two recent reviews, SMR-based BCI performance is quite variable in healthy samples (Grosse-Wentrup and Schölkopf, 2013; Yuan and He, 2014). Some investigators have employed motor imagery questionnaires to determine if these measures predict BCI performance success (Hammer et al., 2012; Vuckovic and Osuagwu, 2013). Unfortunately, these approaches are not appropriate for patients with DoC. It has also been proposed that using different mental tasks, including more complex or familiar actions, could improve performance (Chatelle et al., 2012; Curran and Stokes, 2003; Curran et al., 2004). In fact, Gibson and colleagues found that more complex bimanual movements and certain types of familiar movements led to more robust SMR modulations in a sample of healthy individuals (Gibson et al., 2014a). Similarly, one recent study of patients who had suffered strokes found an advantage for user-selected mental tasks over experimenter-selected tasks (Scherer et al., 2015). These alternative mental task approaches have also been evaluated in patients with DoC.

One of the first reports of alternative motor imagery tasks to evaluate SMR modulations in patients with DoC was that of Goldfine et al. (2011). Two patients with DoC (one diagnosed as in an MCS and the other diagnosed as EMCS) and one patient with locked-in syndrome (LIS; León-Carrión et al., 2002; Smith and Delargy, 2005) were asked to imagine swimming and to imagine moving around their homes. In this approach, alternating instructions to start and stop imagination were presented approximately every 15 s. EEG data were analyzed from 29 or 37 electrodes, and these electrodes were converted to a Laplacian montage to improve source localization (Hjorth, 1975). Power spectral density was calculated from 4 to 24 Hz. In the univariate approach to the statistical analysis of the spectral data, z-statistics were calculated using the two-group test (Bokil et al., 2007). In the multivariate approach, the investigators employed Fisher's linear discriminant analysis (LDA). A randomization test with a false discovery rate-corrected probability threshold was used to assess the statistical significance of these analyses (Goldfine et al., 2011).

The healthy volunteers generated statistically reliable, but variable (across participants), SMR modulations to imagined swimming and spatial navigation (Goldfine et al., 2011). The most common finding from the healthy volunteers for imagined swimming was an ERD from 6 to 9 Hz and 13 to 15 Hz in central channels. For spatial navigation, however, no two healthy volunteers generated the same type of SMR modulation. From the patient sample, the patient with LIS and one patient diagnosed as in an MCS also generated reliable SMR modulations for imagined swimming (Goldfine et al., 2011). One patient produced a reliable ERS from

11 to 20 Hz that was maximal at parietal sites, while the other patient produced a reliable ERS from 8 to 12 Hz alongside a reliable ERD from 15 to 17 Hz. The investigators noted that these two patients, as well as the third patient, produced indeterminate results on some runs (Goldfine et al., 2011).

The investigators speculated about the reason for the indeterminate results from some of the patients in their sample (Goldfine et al., 2011). Possible sources of variability include differences in task performance between runs, diminished EEG signals, and, in the case of the third patient (with no determinant results on any run), subclinical seizure activity. The presence of a statistically reliable modulation of the SMR from the two patients in this report was taken as evidence of their ability to follow commands (Goldfine et al., 2011). In a subsequent fMRI study, one patient diagnosed as in an MCS, one patient diagnosed as in an EMCS, and one patient with LIS generated responses in the supplementary motor area (SMA) and premotor cortex (like healthy volunteers) when instructed to perform motor imagery involving actions from tennis, swimming, or another subject-specific activity (Bardin et al., 2011). Taken together, these studies confirm the utility of different types of motor imagery to detect SMRs from patients with DoC.

Using a similar approach, a small sample of patients with DoC completed motor imagery tasks in separate evaluations with fMRI and EEG (Gibson et al., 2014b). In the EEG assessment, the patients were asked to imagine squeezing their right hand or to imagine performing a hand action from a sport or other action that was familiar to them based on consultation with a family member. In the fMRI task, the patients were asked to imagine playing tennis and moving around their home, as has been previously reported (Boly et al., 2007; Monti et al., 2010; Owen et al., 2006). EEG data were analyzed in a bipolar montage over sensorimotor cortex from sites C3' (FC3-CP3) and C4' (FC4-CP4) between 7 and 30 Hz. A spectral analysis procedure consisting of a nonparametric t-test with a Monte Carlo approach for estimating p values was used to assess the presence or absence of SMRs (Maris, 2004; Maris and Oostenveld, 2007).

One patient diagnosed as in an MCS+ (ie, with behavioral command following) and one patient diagnosed as in a VS/UWS generated robust SMR modulations for imagined movements of their right hand (Gibson et al., 2014b). Both patients produced ERDs that were statistically significant over the contralateral hemisphere in the mu (7–13 Hz) range. Only the patient diagnosed as in a VS produced evidence of reliable and appropriate responses to the two imagery tasks during the functional scans; these findings were taken as corroborative evidence for the patient's ability to follow commands. The patient diagnosed as in an MCS+ did not produce reliable and appropriate brain responses during the fMRI assessment, and this finding was interpreted as reflective of the patient's fluctuating ability to sustain attention and arousal. An overview of these findings is presented in Fig. 2 (Gibson et al., 2014b).

3.1.1.2.2 Attempted movement. Another approach to SMR modulation assessment for patients with DoC is to ask the patients to attempt to complete a motor action. Cruse and colleagues evaluated this paradigm in a case report of a patient diagnosed as in a VS/UWS (Cruse et al., 2012). The patient was instructed to try to move his left or right hand with alternating periods of rest. Classification of SMR modulation was performed using a Naïve Bayes classifier with 10-fold cross-validation. The features for classification were logarithmic power values from 7 to 30 Hz. Only EEG data from sites C3′ (FC3-CP3) and C4′ (FC4-CP4) were analyzed, and statistical significance of the classification procedure was determined using a familywise permutation test (Maris, 2004).

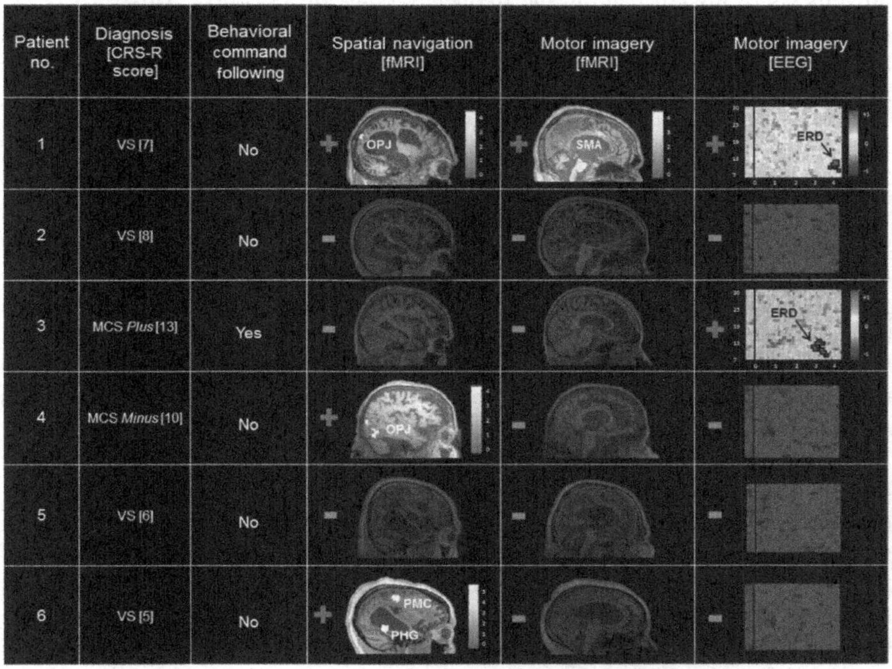

FIG. 2

Summary of the results of six patients with DoC on behavioral, fMRI, and EEG-based assessments of command following. Significant BOLD responses for the fMRI mental imagery tasks are indicated by region on each patient's T1 image. Significant SMR modulations from the EEG motor imagery task are enclosed with a black outline on each spectrogram. Note that both patients with statistically significant SMR modulations generated ERDs over contralateral motor cortex from 7 to 13 Hz. CRS-R, Coma Recovery Scale—Revised; VS, vegetative state; MCS, minimally conscious state; OPJ, occipito-parietal junction; SMA, supplementary motor area; PMC, premotor cortex; PHG, parahippocampal gyrus; ERD, event-related desynchronization.

Reproduced with permission from R. Gibson from the original open-source publication (Gibson R.M., Chennu S., Owen A.M. and Cruse D., Complexity and familiarity enhance single-trial detectability of imagined movements with electroencephalography, Clin. Neurophysiol. 125, 2014a, 1556–1567; Gibson R.M., Fernández-Espejo D., Gonzalez-Lara L.E., Kwan B.Y., Lee D.H., Owen A.M. and Cruse D., Multiple tasks and neuroimaging modalities increase the likelihood of detecting covert awareness in patients with disorders of consciousness, Front. Hum. Neurosci. 8, 2014b, 1–9).

As in the previously discussed investigations, the SMR modulations from the healthy volunteers were variable (Cruse et al., 2012). For example, two volunteers produced statistically significant ERDs in the 7–13 Hz band, while three other volunteers produced only statistically significant ERSs in different frequency bands (Fig. 3; Cruse et al., 2012). Importantly, however, significant SMR modulations only occurred for attempted movement and never for the rest periods. The patient generated a statistically significant ERS over the ipsilateral hemisphere for attempted movements of his left hand in the frequency range of 25–30 Hz. This ERS began about 0.5 s after the instruction and dissipated about 1 s later (Fig. 4; Cruse et al., 2012). This finding was taken as evidence for the patient's abilities to follow commands (Cruse et al., 2012).

Attempted movement paradigms for patients with DoC have also been evaluated using fMRI (Bekinschtein et al., 2011). In this study, all patients first underwent a separate assessment with fMRI to determine whether or not they had the ability to process basic speech stimuli. Five patients diagnosed as in a VS/UWS with preserved auditory processing were identified using this approach. These five patients then underwent an fMRI scan while receiving verbal instructions to move their left or right hand with alternating periods of rest. Interestingly, two of the five patients diagnosed as in a VS/UWS generated premotor activity in response to the commands to attempt movement, like healthy volunteers. These findings were again taken as evidence of the abilities of the two patients with positive results to follow commands (Bekinschtein et al., 2011).

Another report of alternative mental tasks intended to elicit reliable SMR modulations from patients with DoC, including attempted movement, is that of Horki et al. (2014). A sample of six patients diagnosed as in an MCS were asked to perform mental imagery for certain sports, spatial navigation, and attempted movement of their feet. Four patients participated in an offline paradigm, while four patients (two from the offline paradigm) participated in an online paradigm with feedback. Classification analyses were performed using an LDA classifier. Features were computed from logarithmic band power in five frequency bands from 4 to 30 Hz, and data were converted to a Laplacian montage. Nested block-wise cross-validation was applied in both the online and offline analyses; the offline procedure involved a 10×10 inner fold and a leave-one-out-block outer fold, and the online procedure involved a 10×10 inner fold, leave-one-out-block outer fold, and microaveraging of confusion matrices. Online analyses were only applied to the motor imagery conditions (imagined movement of the feet and sport imagery). For feedback, correctly classified trials were followed by "Sport/feet correctly recognized," while other trials (incorrect or indeterminate due to artifacts) were followed by "Pause" (Horki et al., 2014).

All three mental tasks rendered classification accuracy above 50% in all four patients (Horki et al., 2014). Significant results were obtained for sport imagery in 10/18 sessions; attempted feet movement in 7/14 sessions; and spatial navigation in 4/12 sessions. In the online procedure, three of the four patients also produced classification accuracy above chance in either the attempted movement or sport imagery tasks. Of note, all classification analyses actually conducted online in the

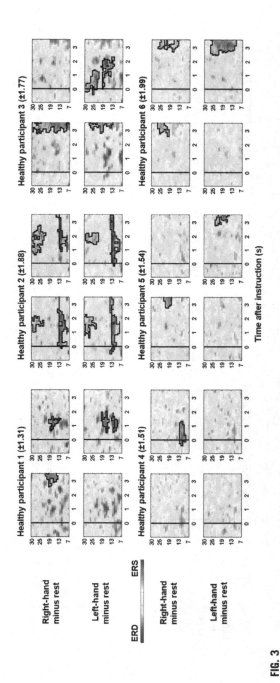

FIG. 3

Single-subject modulations of SMRs in a sample of six healthy young adults. The participants engaged in imagined movements of their left and right hands, with significant modulations enclosed in black on each spectrogram. The range of power values (log ratio vs rest) that are plotted is indicated in parentheses. Plots on the left and right for each participant reflect left- and right-hemisphere EEG channels (C3' and C4' respectively). Time is measured relative to the offset of the verbal instructions. Frequency (Hz) is indicated on the vertical axis.

*Reproduced with permission from D. Cruse from the original open-source publication (Cruse D., Chennu S., Fernández-Espejo D., Payne W.L., Young G.B. and Owen A.M., Detecting awareness in the vegetative state: electroencephalographic evidence for attempted movements to command, PLoS One **7**, 2012, e49933).*

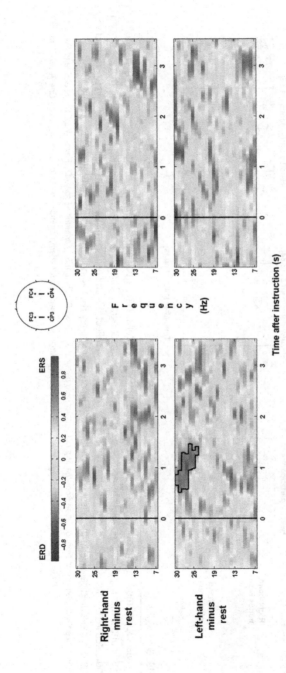

FIG. 4

Modulation of SMRs in one patient diagnosed as in a VS/UWS. The patient produced a reliable ERS for attempted movements of his left hand from 25 to 30 Hz from about 0.5 to 1.5 s after the cue, as indicated with a black outline on the appropriate spectrogram. Plots on the left and right reflect left- and right-hemisphere EEG channels (C3′ and C4′ respectively). Time is measured relative to the offset of the verbal instructions. Color scale denotes the log ratio of power versus rest.

*Reproduced with permission from D. Cruse from the original open-source publication (Cruse D., Chennu S., Fernández-Espejo D., Payne W.L., Young G.B. and Owen A.M., Detecting awareness in the vegetative state: electroencephalographic evidence for attempted movements to command, PLoS One **7**, 2012, e49933).*

online portion of the task were below chance, and the reported above-chance classification analyses of this session were calculated offline. The authors speculate that a shorter detection period after the instruction to engage in mental imagery was needed to detect the SMR changes online. Additionally, as in previous reports (Cruse et al., 2011a; Goldfine et al., 2011), the SMR modulations generated by the patients were variable in terms of both topography and frequency (Horki et al., 2014).

3.1.1.2.3 Motor observation.
Another approach to examine SMR modulations in patients with DoC has combined motor observation with motor imagination. In a sample of nine patients diagnosed as in a VS/UWS and seven patients diagnosed as in an MCS, Lechinger and colleagues presented participants with a short film of a person reaching for, and then drinking from, a mug (Lechinger et al., 2013). As participants watched the video, they were instructed to imagine completing the same movement. Once the video ended, the participants were asked to engage in motor imagery of the same action again. Following this, an image of two resting arms was presented. EEG data were analyzed over three topographies: frontal, F3 and F4; central, C3 and C4; and parieto-occipital, PO7 and PO8. SMRs were evaluated from complex Morlet waves calculated between 1 and 30 Hz, and statistical significance was determined using an ANOVA with factors of diagnostic group, scalp location, and time (baseline, motor observation, and motor imagery; Lechinger et al. 2013).

None of the patients diagnosed as in a VS/UWS showed a reliable response to motor observation, while all patients diagnosed as in an MCS showed reliable ERDs for this condition (Lechinger et al., 2013). The SMR modulations generated by the patients were different from healthy volunteers in that the patients produced reliable patterns as an ERD from 8 to 10 Hz alongside an ERS from 12 to 15 Hz, while the volunteers produced an ERD from 8 to 15 Hz only. Nevertheless, the significant SMR modulations from the patients were taken as evidence of the ability of those patients to follow commands (Lechinger et al., 2013).

3.1.1.2.4 The importance of training and feedback.
Another body of work that explores performance variations in SMR-based BCIs involves the role and type of user training and feedback. One study reported that a 2-min pretraining was required to achieve a state of mind for optimal SMR-based BCI use in a healthy sample (Blankertz et al., 2010). Another investigation employed three types of feedback during SMR-based BCI training, including an animated visual bar and anatomically congruent feedback of animated hand movements (Ono et al., 2013). All types of feedback improved performance relative to users who received no feedback (Ono et al., 2013).

Coyle and colleagues have explicitly investigated the role of feedback for SMR-based BCI use in two case reports about a patient diagnosed as in an MCS (Coyle et al., 2012, 2013) and a recent cohort study of patients diagnosed as in an MCS (Coyle et al., 2015). The BCI paradigm involved imagined squeezes of the right hand and wiggling of the toes with the same stimulus presentation parameters as used in the cohort study by Cruse et al. (2011a). In Coyle's version, instructions were also given visually, with text for imagery instructions and arrows to reinforce the auditory cues to begin imagery (Coyle et al., 2012, 2013, 2015). For classification, frequency bands were selected automatically from 1 to 30 Hz using neural time-series prediction preprocessing (Coyle, 2009; Coyle et al., 2005) with neural networks and common spatial patterns with LDA (Coyle et al., 2005, 2011). A 20-fold inner–outer cross-validation was performed for parameter optimization. The final time point of the peak mean classification accuracy was used for the real-time feedback.

In the first case report, feedback consisted of visual animations (Coyle et al., 2012). The patient tried to direct a ball into a basket (first run) and to move a spaceship to dodge asteroids (second run) using toe or hand imagery to move the ball/spaceship left and right, respectively. The significance of the classification analyses was determined with a parametric *t*-test and a Wilcoxon signed-rank test. The patient generated robust SMR modulation during this task. For example, in channel C4, the patient produced an ERS during hand imagery and an ERD during toe imagery, while an upper band ERD was evident in channel C3 during hand imagery. Notably, the patient also produced significant classification accuracy during the task, with accuracy surpassing chance 3-s after the feedback (Coyle et al., 2012).

In a follow-up study, Coyle and colleagues extended their feedback and paradigm to the auditory modality (Coyle et al., 2013). In addition to the visual feedback procedure reported in Coyle et al. (2012), a secondary auditory feedback procedure was evaluated using broadband (pink) noise and music. In this case, the sounds were varied from the left to the right earphones as the patient engaged in motor imagery to move the sound left or right, as directed by spoken commands of "LEFT" and "RIGHT." The same protocol for sound movement applied as in the visual task, ie, toe imagery to move left and hand imagery to move right. Classification accuracy was similar for both types of feedback, but the difference between peak and baseline accuracy increased for auditory feedback and decreased for visual feedback. The investigators speculated that this difference may have occurred because the patient was unable to fixate on the visual information. They also noted that the patient seemed to become more alert as he received the auditory feedback (Coyle et al., 2013).

In a subsequent cohort study by Coyle and colleagues, the findings of the two case reports were confirmed and extended to three additional patients (Coyle et al., 2015). Importantly, this body of work provides evidence that feedback protocols are feasible for use by patients with DoC and that feedback can lead to performance gains for these patients (Coyle et al., 2012, 2013, 2015). Moreover, this work also confirms that musical feedback is also feasible for use by, and perhaps even leads to increased arousal from, patients with DoC (Coyle et al., 2012, 2015). Auditory feedback in particular is critical for patients with DoC due to their visual impairments. Importantly, recent investigations involving healthy volunteers have provided evidence that auditory feedback renders similar performance benefits as visual feedback (McCreadie et al., 2014; Nijboer et al., 2008). Altogether, these findings support the use of auditory information as feedback for improved BCI performance and a potentially more engaging user experience for patients with DoC.

3.1.1.2.5 The roles of motor capacity and attention in SMR-based BCI use. An important application of SMR-based BCIs is movement rehabilitation for patients with impaired motor function. One investigation applied TMS to the motor cortex prior to and following SMR-based BCI training over a 4-week period in a sample of healthy people (Pichiorri et al., 2011). SMR training enhanced cortical motor excitability and resulted in functional connectivity changes in the higher-beta frequency range (Pichiorri et al., 2011). In another investigation of healthy volunteers, motor imagery-induced ERDs were associated with enhanced M1 excitability (Takemi et al., 2013). These findings imply that motor imagery, like overt movement, can lead to changes in corticospinal excitability (Takemi et al., 2013). For patients with DoC, poor integrity of white matter tracts between motor cortex and the thalamus prevents patients who can imagine movements from being able to execute these actions (Fernández-Espejo et al., 2015; Osborne et al., 2015). Furthermore, it is unlikely that most patients with DoC have sufficient cognitive and attentional resources to participate in extended training sessions. Nevertheless, motor imagery training interventions are potentially useful for patients with DoC, although there are no reports of such attempts to date.

Another factor in SMR-based BCI use relevant to patients with DoC is performance fluctuations due to variations in attention (Grosse-Wentrup and Schölkopf, 2013). Trial-to-trial variations in SMR modulation correlate with gamma amplitude in healthy volunteers (Grosse-Wentrup and Schölkopf, 2013). This finding implies a causal role of gamma in SMR variability (Grosse-Wentrup et al., 2011). In another study of healthy volunteers, baseline gamma predicted SMR-based BCI performance success (Grosse-Wentrup and Schölkopf, 2012), and the same relationship between SMR-based BCI use and gamma held in a case study of one patient with ALS (Grosse-Wentrup, 2011). Given the prevalence of low-frequency EEG activity in patients with DoC, however, it seems unlikely that a relationship between SMR modulation stability and gamma power will be useful, although this is an empirical issue that requires additional investigation.

3.1.1.3 The feasibility of SMR-based BCIs for long-term use

There are a few issues that need consideration to evaluate the feasibility of long-term use of SMR-based BCIs by patients with DoC. In one report, BCI performance and SMR patterns stayed relatively stable over 10 weeks in a sample of healthy volunteers (Friedrich et al., 2013). The volunteers also reported greater comfort in performance over time (Friedrich et al., 2013). Even with design and alternative classification approaches, however, the variable success of SMR-based BCIs in healthy people has led some researchers to recommend against motor imagery approaches for BCIs in general (Henriques et al., 2014; Nijboer et al., 2010). For functional binary communication, the lower limit of classification accuracy is argued to be 70% (Kübler et al., 2001). In a recent investigation, 38% of healthy users could not achieve performance at or above 70% with an SMR-based BCI (Hammer et al., 2012). In fact, about 20% of healthy users cannot regulate their SMRs well enough to accurately control the intended BCI application (Blankertz et al., 2010). While some reports are optimistic (Kübler et al. 2005), two recent studies of patients with ALS have reported significantly reduced SMR modulation (Kasahara et al., 2012) and abnormal motor imagery abilities (Fiori et al., 2013) in these patients. On this basis, these researchers have cautioned that SMR-based BCI use may not be appropriate for patients with ALS (Fiori et al., 2013; Kasahara et al., 2012). Despite these concerns, SMR-based BCIs are particularly promising when feedback is provided to the user, as evident from some studies of SMR-based BCI use in patients with DoC (Coyle et al., 2011, 2012, 2015). SMR-based BCIs accordingly warrant additional investigation for patients with DoC given that these devices may provide reward, stimulation, and skill development for these patients.

3.1.2 P300 event-related potentials

The P300 is a positive-going ERP that peaks about 300 ms after a rare stimulus (Comerchero and Polich, 1999; Picton, 1992; Polich, 2007). The so-called novelty P300 is elicited by an infrequent, oddball stimulus within a series of events from two classes. P300 amplitude decreases as the frequency of the rare event increases (Comerchero and Polich, 1999; Squires et al., 1977) and positively correlates with the time interval (up to about 8 s) between stimuli (Polich, 1990; Polich and Bondurant, 1997). Importantly, the P300 (or P3a) reflects bottom-up, preconscious processing (Comerchero and Polich, 1999; Squires et al., 1977). There is some evidence that the P300 can even be elicited during sleep (Cote, 2002) and sedation (Koelsch et al., 2006). Finally, the P300 tends to be lower amplitude in BCI applications than standard scientific investigations due to the rapid rate of stimulus presentation (Martens et al., 2009; Woldorff, 1993). This tendency is exacerbated in patients with DoC, who often produce ERPs with reduced amplitude due to cortical atrophy (Goldfine et al., 2011).

In some variations of the typical oddball paradigm with a response or attentional contingency, both P3a and P3b ERPs can be elicited (see Fig. 5). In this context, attended, task-relevant target stimuli elicit the P3b potential (Comerchero and Polich, 1999; Squires et al., 1977). The P3b differs from the P3a in that it is usually largest over parietal sites and tends to occur at a longer interval from the eliciting stimulus than the P3a (Comerchero and Polich, 1999; Polich, 2007). Importantly, the P3b reflects top-down, conscious information processing (Comerchero and Polich, 1999; Squires et al., 1977), although one very recent investigation challenges this view (Silverstein et al., 2015). With the novel and controversial work of Silverstein and colleagues aside (Silverstein et al., 2015), P3b paradigms are often employed for awareness detection applications.

3.1.2.1 Neural basis of the P300

From combined EEG-fMRI investigations of the typical P300 auditory oddball task, this ERP is associated with increased activity in the SMA, anterior cingulate cortex (ACC), temporoparietal junction (TPJ), insula, and inferior frontal gyrus (Bledowski et al., 2004; Li et al., 2009; Mulert et al., 2004). From a few seminal lesion studies reviewed in Soltani and Knight (2000), it was observed that lesions in the TPJ abolished the auditory P300, whereas lesions in the lateral parietal cortex did not impact

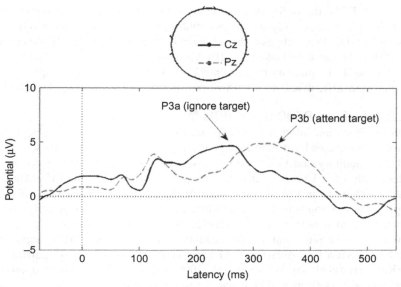

FIG. 5

Sample P3a and P3b grand-averaged event-related potentials as measured at scalp locations Cz and Pz, respectively. These responses were calculated from unpublished data acquired from 16 healthy volunteers by Gibson and Cruse. The locations of Cz and Pz on the scalp are depicted in the topographic map at the top of the figure. Time is measured relative to the onset of the target stimulus. Targets were presented as 10% of all stimuli, and participants were instructed to either attend to or ignore these targets in separate blocks. Unattended targets elicited P3a responses, while attended targets elicited P3b responses, as indicated.

P300 amplitude (Knight et al., 1989). Similarly, lesions in the prefrontal and lateral parietal cortex did not impair auditory, visual, or somatosensory P300s, whereas lesions of the TPJ abolished both auditory and somatosensory P300s and reduced the visual P300 (Knight and Scabini, 1998). Overall, this work suggests the P300 has a distributed set of generators in the brain and reflects complex information processing.

3.1.2.2 Visual P300-based BCIs

The first report of the P300 for a communication BCI application was the [visual] P300 speller described by Farwell and Donchin (1988). This speller used a 6 × 6 grid of incrementally flashed letters, and while spelling rates were relatively low by modern BCI standards (2.3 characters per minute), this early approach was effective. Since its original report, several subsequent studies have reported modifications and variations of this original design. For example, an innovative variation of the original speller paradigm used a checkerboard pattern (rather than a grid) to eliminate issues of simultaneously flashing targets, and this led to fewer errors due to users selecting an unintended item within the same row or column as the intended target letter (Townsend et al., 2010). Despite the promise and relative success of the visual

P300-based BCIs, the utility of these approaches for patients who lack voluntary motor control, and especially oculomotor control, is limited. For example, a few studies have found that variable gaze direction tends to reduce P300 amplitude (Brunner et al., 2010b; Treder and Blankertz, 2010). Most patients with DoC are unable to fixate their eyes and lack voluntary motor control; on this basis, one would expect very diminished (and difficult to detect) P300 responses to visual stimuli from these patients.

3.1.2.3 Auditory P300-based BCIs for patients with DoC

Given the limitations of visual P300 speller BCIs for patients who lack oculomotor control, investigators have attempted to develop auditory versions of these BCIs. By combining auditory and visual stimuli, researchers have presented modified P300 spellers with a 5×5 visual matrix that maps onto auditory stimuli (Furdea et al., 2009). Another research group presented a P300 BCI with a 6×6 visual matrix that mapped onto environmental sounds (Klobassa et al., 2009). One entirely auditory approach provided users with a five-choice set of response options by giving each stimulus a unique pitch and spatial location (Schreuder et al., 2010). Importantly, there have been a few assessments of auditory P300-based BCIs for patients with LIS (Kaufmann et al., 2013; Kübler et al., 2009) and several tests of these approaches in patients with DoC, as will be discussed in detail next.

3.1.2.3.1 Global–local predictive coding. One approach to assess P300s from patients with DoC employs hierarchical predictive coding (Friston, 2008). The first study of the ERP global–local predictive coding framework including patients with DoC was conducted by Bekinschtein et al. (2009). Bekinschtein's paradigm employed auditory stimuli to evaluate brain responses to violations of temporal regularity. In this approach, local violations arise following the unexpected occurrence of a deviant sound in a train of standard sounds, while global violations follow the detection of a deviation in the higher-order pattern of the stimuli. For patients with DoC, this approach can dissociate between automatic, stimulus-driven information processing and higher-order, top-down expectations about incoming sensory information (Bekinschtein et al., 2009).

From healthy volunteers, it was determined that the ERP response to local deviations was an early response in auditory cortex known as the mismatch negativity (MMN; Bekinschtein et al., 2009). Conversely, global deviations led to a P3b. In a second sample of healthy volunteers, the same local response occurred even when participants were instructed to mind-wander and ignore the sounds. Furthermore, the local response also occurred when participants were engaged in a concurrent rapid serial visual response task. In contrast, the global response was abolished in both the inattentive and visual distraction conditions, confirming that the detection of global violations only occurs when subjects are attentive and aware of the violations (Bekinschtein et al., 2009). Most importantly for our purposes, Bekinschtein and colleagues evaluated responses to the global–local framework in a sample of four patients with DoC (Bekinschtein et al., 2009; see Table 2). Interestingly, the global responses were detected only in three of the four patients diagnosed as in an MCS. These three patients showed subsequent clinical improvement such that all

Table 2 Overview of the Patient Outcomes from the Global–Local Predictive Coding Investigations Discussed in This Subsection

Investigation	Local Response	Global Response
Bekinschtein et al. (2009)	3/4 VS/UWS	0/4 VS/UWS
	4/4 MCS	3/4 MCS
Faugeras et al. (2011)	22/22 VS/UWS	2/22 VS/UWS
Faugeras et al. (2012)	6/24 VS/UWS	2/24 VS/UWS
	9/28 MCS	4/28 MCS
	8/13 Conscious patients	7/13 Conscious patients

three patients had progressed to a fully conscious state several weeks after their assessment with the global–local paradigm. Overall, the absence of the global effect in the patients diagnosed as in a VS/UWS suggests that this effect is a measure of subjective conscious content and awareness (Bekinschtein et al., 2009).

Since the original report of this global–local paradigm (Bekinschtein et al., 2009), there has been a high correspondence between global prediction errors and consciousness (Faugeras et al., 2011, 2012; King et al., 2013). Faugeras and colleagues used the same analysis of the ERP effects as in the original publication (Bekinschtein et al., 2009) alongside permutation testing (Faugeras et al., 2011). Local effects were detected in all of the patients, but global effects were only detected in two patients. Both patients with global effects had progressed to a diagnosis of MCS within 4 days of their assessments with the global–local paradigm (Faugeras et al., 2011).

In Faugeras et al. (2012), a large sample of patients with DoC were evaluated with the global–local paradigm. As reported in previous work, patients diagnosed as in a VS/UWS with global effects progressed to an MCS within a few days of their assessment with the global–local paradigm (Faugeras et al., 2012). Additionally, Faugeras and colleagues reported on an early effect of sound processing by examining the averaged ERPs from electrode Cz across an entire trial (Faugeras et al., 2012). A significant negative deflection corresponding to a contingent negative variation (CNV) was detected in all healthy volunteers, most of the patients in the conscious group, many of the patients in the MCS group, and some of the patients in the VS/UWS group (see Table 2). Importantly, all patients with a significant CNV had global effects, and all patients without significant CNV effects did not have global effects. There was no apparent correspondence between the presence or absence of the CNV and the local effect. This finding suggests that the CNV reflected the participant's expectations of the stimulus regularity (Faugeras et al., 2012). Use of the CNV in BCI applications will be discussed in more detail in the subsection concerning BCIs based on slow cortical potentials (SCPs).

3.1.2.3.2 *Subject's own name.*
There have been several studies concerning P300 responses from patients with DoC that utilize the patient's responses to their own first name (vs other sounds, or other/unfamiliar names). These studies are often referred to as subject's own name, or SON, approaches. Prior to their utilization in assessments of patients with DoC, it was documented that healthy volunteers

produce enhanced P300 responses to SON vs other unfamiliar names (Berlad and Pratt, 1995; Wood and Cowan, 1995). During sleep stage II and paradoxical sleep, healthy volunteers also produced enhanced, but delayed, P300s to SON stimuli vs unfamiliar names (Perrin et al., 1999).

One of the earliest reports of responses to SONs in a sample of patients with DoC and LIS was that of Perrin et al. (2006). In this approach, eight prerecorded, spoken first names were presented to patients and healthy volunteers. Names included SON and seven unfamiliar, high-frequency names. In the healthy control group, SON evoked early perceptual ERP components and P300 responses (Perrin et al., 2006). For the patient sample, all patients other than two patients diagnosed as in a VS/UWS generated the same set of ERP responses including a P300. In both the healthy and patient samples, P300 responses were larger for SON than for unfamiliar names. In terms of latency, the P300 was significantly delayed in the VS/UWS group relative to the healthy group and LIS group; likewise, the P300 was significantly delayed in the MCS group relative to the control group (Perrin et al., 2006).

In a follow-up study, researchers added an attentional manipulation to the SON task for patients with DoC (Schnakers et al., 2008b). In all blocks, eight first names were presented to the patient, including SON and seven unfamiliar, high-frequency names. In the passive listening blocks, patients were simply presented with all names without any task instructions. In one set of active blocks, patients were asked to count one of the unfamiliar target names. In another set of active blocks, patients were asked to count SON (Perrin et al., 2006; see also Risetti et al., 2013).

There were no differences in any of the early perceptual ERP components for any of the diagnostic groups (Schnakers et al., 2008b). P300 waveforms differed between the healthy and MCS groups only. In the follow-up analyses, healthy individuals produced larger P300 responses for passive SON vs unfamiliar names and for counted vs uncounted targets in the active conditions. All of these group effects were also consistent at the single-subject level. For the patient sample, 9 of 14 patients diagnosed as in an MCS made a larger P300 to counted targets in one of the two active conditions; this enhanced P300 effect was used to infer command following from those patients. The P300 was significantly delayed in patients diagnosed as in an MCS relative to the healthy volunteers. The authors suggest that this latency difference from the MCS patients reflected an information processing delay (Schnakers et al., 2008b).

Using a similar paradigm, some patients with DoC generated distinct ERPs (MMN) to SON presented among tones and other names (Qin et al., 2008). Early perceptual responses and MMN to SON were detected in the EEG data from all healthy participants. For the patient sample, SON-MMN was present in two patients diagnosed as in a comatose state, three patients diagnosed as in a VS/UWS, and two patients diagnosed as in an MCS. Interestingly, at a 3-month follow-up assessment, six of the patients with SON-MMN responses had behavioral responses consistent with an MCS, while one patient (diagnosed as comatose at the initial assessment) had behavioral abilities consistent with a VS/UWS (Qin et al., 2008).

As in a previous case report (Schnakers et al., 2009a), some patients in an acutely comatose state also produced reliable P300 responses in a combined SON and tone task (Fischer et al., 2008; Schnakers et al., 2009a). Furthermore, the presence of the P300 had a high predictive value such that most patients with a preserved P300 response awakened (Fischer et al., 2008). Similar results were obtained in the cohort study of patients with chronic DoC (Fischer et al., 2010). P300 responses to SON were detected in most patients diagnosed as in a VS/UWS and half of the patients diagnosed as in an MCS. Interestingly, these components did not significantly differ in amplitude or latency between MCS and VS/UWS. Finally, fewer patients with anoxic brain injuries than with traumatic brain injuries generated P300 responses (Fischer et al., 2010).

A recent variation on the SON P300 paradigm using the subject's own face rather than name employed steady-state visual-evoked potentials, SSVEPs (Pan et al., 2014). (Note that evoked potentials for BCI applications with the DoC are discussed in a subsequent subsection.) Patients were presented with their own and unfamiliar photographs and asked to count photos on one side of the screen (left or right) as the pairs of photographs changed in a random order. The flashing frames were intended to elicit SSVEP responses, while the flashing target (left or right) was used to elicit P300 responses. After 10 s, a feedback photo was selected based on the classification procedure. Correct feedback photos were presented with a 4-s sound clip of applause (Pan et al., 2014).

Data were collected and analyzed across three experimental runs. In the first run, the patients were asked to focus on their own photo. Five patients achieved accuracy greater than 64% in this run (two VS/UWS, two MCS, and one LIS). In the second run, patients were instructed to attend to the unfamiliar photos. Three of the five patients with above-chance accuracy in the first run also achieved accuracy greater than 64% in this run (one VS/UWS, one MCS, and one LIS). In the third run, patients were asked to attend to their own or the unfamiliar photo in a random order, and the same three patients again generated classification accuracy greater than 64%. The investigators concluded that these three patients were able to follow commands and thus possessed awareness (Pan et al., 2014).

To infer the brain areas involved in brain responses to SON, a few previous studies have measured brain responses from patients with DoC while participating in similar versions of the EEG paradigms described previously and undergoing an fMRI scan. Some patients with DoC generated responses in the ACC (Qin et al., 2010), auditory association cortex (Di et al., 2007), and medial prefrontal cortex (Staffen et al., 2006) when attending to their own vs unfamiliar names and/or sounds. Additionally, two patients diagnosed as in a VS/UWS who produced activation in association temporal cortex to SON, ie, areas involved in the higher-order processing of sounds, showed clinical improvement at a 3-month follow-up visit (Di et al., 2007). Altogether, these studies support the utility of SON approaches for detection of command following in patients with DoC.

3.1.2.3.3 Auditory stream segregation. A number of other P300-based BCI-like frameworks have also been evaluated for use by patients with DoC. In a study by Halder and colleagues, an oddball task based on auditory stimuli was used for binary communication with healthy volunteers (Halder et al., 2010). The binary response options were given with two low-frequency deviant tones such that participants directed their attention to the deviant tone type that corresponded with their desired response (Halder et al., 2010). In another study of only healthy volunteers, Kanoh and colleagues developed a P300-based BCI using responses to auditory stream segregation (Kanoh et al., 2008). Concurrent streams of two different tones (ie, high or low pitched) were presented to the right ear with occasional deviants in each stream. Participants were able to direct their attention to one of the two streams such that they produced P300s to the deviant tones in the attended stream (Kanoh et al., 2008).

Pokorny and colleagues sought to develop a P300-based BCI with auditory stimuli that allowed for binary decisions (as in Halder et al., 2010) and did not rely on binaural hearing (as in Kanoh et al., 2008; Pokorny et al., 2013). This paradigm was assessed in a sample of healthy volunteers and 12 patients diagnosed as in an MCS. A stream of high and low tones with occasional deviants in each stream was presented to both ears. EEG data were acquired from 15 sites in the healthy volunteers, but only from 9 sites in the patients due to time constraints and the challenges of positioning electrodes on participants who were lying in bed. Healthy participants were always presented with the two concurrent streams of tones, while the patients were always initially assessed using only one of the two streams in order to assess a P300 response in the traditional manner (Pokorny et al., 2013).

Pokorny and colleagues used a machine learning approach to identify P300 responses (Pokorny et al., 2013). P300 classification was conducted for deviant vs standard tones only in the single stream condition (baseline); deviant tones were compared to standard tones in each stream separately; and deviant tones from the attended stream were compared to deviant tones from the unattended stream. Classification accuracy for the healthy volunteers ranged from 59% to 64.5% in all comparisons. For patients, however, classification accuracy was always below chance. On this basis, none of the 12 patients diagnosed as in an MCS generated reliable P300 responses, and thus did not demonstrate command following, with this approach (Pokorny et al., 2013). We speculate that the cognitive demands of stream segregation are too high for patients with DoC.

3.1.2.3.4 Oddballs as words.
As is necessary for most BCI paradigms, some patients with DoC retain normal (or nearly normal) language comprehension (Coleman et al., 2007, 2009; Davis et al., 2007; Fernández-Espejo et al., 2008). Partly capitalizing on this finding, one approach to P300-based BCIs for patients with DoC employed word stimuli (Chennu et al., 2013). The stimuli consisted of emotionally neutral, monosyllabic, spoken words. In a block, about two-thirds of the words were assigned as irrelevant distractors, while "YES" and "NO" were presented repeatedly among these distractors. "YES" was always presented to the left ear, while "NO" was always presented to the right ear to allow participants to allocate spatial attention differently between the two targets. This differential allocation of spatial attention was intended to facilitate a participant's ability to selectively attend to one word or the other. Across blocks, either "YES" or "NO" was assigned as

the target word such that the other word became an implicit target due to its high frequency and distinct spatial orientation (Chennu et al., 2013).

Chennu and colleagues evaluated each patient's data for the presence or absence of P3a responses to implicit targets and P3b responses to explicit targets (Chennu et al., 2013). ERPs were identified using a nonparametric *t*-test (Maris and Oostenveld, 2007) comparing global field power, GFP (Lehmann and Skrandies, 1980; Skrandies, 1990), from both conditions with a Monte Carlo approach for estimating *p* values (Maris, 2004). The comparison of the GFP difference at each time point to the maximal GFP difference obtained in each iteration controls for familywise error and multiple comparisons. These controls are important in studies that employ high-density electrode arrays (in this case, 129 channels). The GFP data were compared between the −300 to 0 ms prestimulus window and the 100–400 ms poststimulus for the P3a and with 400–700 ms poststimulus for the P3b (Chennu et al., 2013).

Explicit target words were associated with P3b responses (Chennu et al., 2013). Specifically, implicit targets elicited only P3a responses, while explicit targets elicited only P3b responses in the group analyses of the EEG data from the healthy volunteers. These results were consistent at the single-subject level for all healthy volunteers, with the exception that P3a responses were also elicited by explicit targets for five of eight volunteers. At the group level, both explicit and implicit targets elicited P3a responses from the patients, while neither type of target elicited a P3b from the patients. At the single-subject level, 17 of the 21 patients did not show significantly different ERP effects for standard vs deviant stimuli. However, both a P3b response to explicit targets and an (abnormally) early P3a response to implicit targets were identified in one patient diagnosed as in a VS/UWS. This patient also generated evidence of covert command following in an fMRI motor imagery paradigm (Boly et al., 2007; Monti et al., 2010; Owen et al., 2006). The remaining three patients, all diagnosed as in an MCS, only generated evidence of P3a responses, but none of these patients generated quantifiably different responses to explicit and implicit targets (Chennu et al., 2013).

Another variation on the oddball word paradigm intended for patients with DoC involves a more limited set of auditory stimuli (Lulé et al., 2013). This approach was developed for healthy volunteers and patients with ALS (Furdea et al., 2009; Sellers and Donchin, 2006). Four words ("YES," "NO," "STOP," and "GO") were presented with two speakers positioned in front of the participants (Lulé et al., 2013). In a block, each word was presented 15 times in a pseudo-random order, and participants were asked to count the occurrences of either "YES" or "NO" to detect their ability to follow commands. Subsequently, participants were asked to answer yes/no questions by attending to the desired response. P300 responses were detected using a permutation test and the robust average method (Litvak et al., 2011). Classification analyses were performed using stepwise LDA (Lulé et al., 2013).

P300 responses were detected in 12 of 16 healthy volunteers (Lulé et al., 2013). Communication accuracy from the healthy volunteers was 73% online on average. P300 responses were also detected in one patient diagnosed as in an MCS and one patient with LIS, although the P300 response from the patient diagnosed as in an

MCS was only significant at one electrode (T8). For communication, one patient with LIS achieved classification accuracy of 60%, while the other patient with LIS achieved classification accuracy of only 20%. None of the patients with DoC, including four patients diagnosed as in an MCS+, achieved above-chance classification accuracy during the communication task and thus could not use the BCI (Lulé et al., 2013).

Similar paradigms involving word stimuli have been evaluated for patients with DoC using fMRI. In one approach involving similar word stimuli as in Chennu et al. (2013), each patient was asked to select and maintain an arbitrary target word in mind throughout an experimental block (Monti et al., 2009). One patient diagnosed as in an MCS generated activation in the frontoparietal network during this task, which implied that the patient had both working memory and target detection abilities (Monti et al., 2009). Similar evidence that some patients with DoC can sustain their attention was reported by Naci and colleagues in two other fMRI studies (Naci and Owen, 2013; Naci et al., 2013). As in Chennu et al. (2013), patients were asked to count "YES" or "NO" presented among other words. Two patients diagnosed as in an MCS and one patient diagnosed as in a VS/UWS produced similar frontoparietal responses as healthy individuals during this task (Naci and Owen, 2013; Naci et al., 2013). Furthermore, one patient diagnosed as in a VS/UWS and one patient diagnosed as in an MCS could answer two yes/no questions with this approach (Naci and Owen, 2013). Overall, these studies confirm that a small number of patients with DoC are capable of sustaining attention to word stimuli and can even follow commands, despite their inability to respond with their overt behavior.

3.1.2.4 Tactile P300-based BCIs for patients with DoC

Another promising alternative to auditory P300-based BCIs are a family of BCIs that use tactile stimulation. These approaches have value in that they do not engage the auditory or visual systems, which leave these sensory systems available for other activities. Frontal lobe lesions have been associated with diminished oddball P300s, but preserved P3bs, to tactile stimulation (Yamaguchi and Knight, 1991). This implies that tactile stimulation may tax the attentional mechanisms that generate the P300 more so than other types of stimulation. In one early report, tactile stimulation was applied at the waist with two, four, or six tactors, and all three versions of this paradigm led to significant classification accuracy in a sample of healthy volunteers (Brouwer and van Erp, 2010).

Another study compared a tactile P300 speller BCI, in which healthy users counted vibrations on their fingers to select letters of the alphabet, to a conventional visual P300-based BCI speller (van der Waal et al., 2012). In another recent report, classification accuracy for P300 responses to tactile stimulation was substantially higher in a sample of healthy volunteers when stimulation was applied to different limbs rather than to adjacent fingers (Ortner et al., 2013). Finally, in one case study of a patient with LIS, the patient reported low practical use in daily life for the tactile BCI, and online classification accuracy was lower for this paradigm than for the auditory or visual alternatives (Kaufmann et al., 2013). However, offline accuracy was higher with tactile vs visual or auditory stimulation in this case report (Kaufmann et al., 2013).

In one recent report, some patients with LIS were able to communicate using a tactile P300-based BCI (Lugo et al., 2014). As a baseline test for the P300, tactile stimulation was applied at two places on the body; 90% of stimuli were applied at one site as the standard stimuli, while 10% of stimuli were applied at the other site to elicit the P300 response. For communication, stimulation was applied at three locations on the body such that two sites received infrequent stimulation (5% per site) to allow the patient with a binary response option. EEG data were analyzed from Fz, FC1, FC2, C3, Cz, C4, CP1, and CP2 using an LDA classifier. The first five trials served as the training data, and every subsequent five stimuli served as the test set for online classification. Feedback was given as the class with the highest sum of weight parameters from the test set (Lugo et al., 2014).

To test for the P300, the investigators conducted an ANOVA comparing voltages across all eight electrodes using a moving window of 50 ms (Lugo et al., 2014). A P300 was considered present for a significant difference between target/nontarget stimuli at a minimum of two electrodes between 200 and 600 ms poststimulus. P300 responses were detected in five of six patients with LIS in the single deviant condition and in all six patients in the two-deviant condition. However, these results varied between the testing (postfeedback) and training (prefeedback) phases. For communication, accuracy was 55.3% on average and required three to seven stimuli (Lugo et al., 2014). The feasibility of this approach for patients with DoC has yet to be assessed.

3.1.2.5 P300-based BCI optimization and feasibility of long-term use

Given the popularity and efficacy of the P300-based BCIs, there is a tremendous amount of literature about the optimization of these approaches. For example, one report explicitly compared classification accuracy across different recording montages (Krusienski et al., 2008). It was found that a montage consisting of Fz, Pz, Cz, PO7, PO8, and Oz generated the best performance accuracy (Krusienski et al., 2008). Subsequently, another research group proposed an algorithm to optimize classification accuracy for P300 BCI data (Cecotti et al., 2011). In terms of classification algorithms, stepwise LDA and Fisher's linear discriminant classifiers consistently produce the best performance for this type of BCI (Krusienski et al., 2006). It has also been acknowledged that these algorithms perform optimally when the parameter settings are customized to the individual user (Sellers and Donchin, 2006). These attributes have been incorporated into some studies of patients with DoC, as discussed previously (Lugo et al. 2014; Lulé et al. 2013; Pokorny et al. 2013).

A number of sophisticated applications have been developed for P300-based BCIs. Examples include creative applications like painting (Münßinger et al., 2010) and Internet browser control (Bensch et al., 2007; Mugler et al., 2008). Given the limited cognitive abilities of most patients with DoC, these more sophisticated BCIs have not been tested in this population to date. Nonetheless, these outlets could potentially benefit a suitable patient. Additionally, Kirschner and colleagues recently proposed a battery of auditory P300-based assessments for patients with DoC that probes increasingly complex cognitive processing, including verbal reasoning and working memory (Kirschner et al., 2015). Unfortunately, this approach has yet to be evaluated in a sample of patients with DoC (Kirschner et al., 2015).

Given the popularity of the P300-based BCIs, it is not surprising that some investigators have developed tools to assess the practicality of these approaches for people with severe disabilities, such as patients with ALS (Mccane et al., 2014). In studies of long-term use, P300 amplitude changes for healthy volunteers vary within a session (Pan et al., 2000; Ravden and Polich, 1999) and over several months (Kinoshita et al., 1996). Conversely, other studies have found no change in P300 amplitude from healthy volunteers tested over 2 weeks (Polich, 1986; Williams et al., 2005). Patients with ALS had stable P300s when assessed repeatedly over 10 weeks (Sellers and Donchin, 2006), and in a single patient, over daily use for 3 years (Sellers et al., 2010). Longitudinal studies of P300-based BCIs in patients with DoC are encouraged.

3.1.3 Steady-state evoked potentials

A steady-state evoked potential (SSEP) is a repetitive series of voltage deflections phase-locked to a sensory event (Picton et al., 2003; Vialatte et al., 2010). A SSEP consists of a fundamental frequency corresponding to the frequency of the stimulus and its harmonics (Herrmann, 2001). SSEPs can be detected in single trials (Quian Quiroga et al., 2001) and enhanced with averaging (Dawson, 1954). More recent study has found improvements in the SSEP as a BCI control signal by classifying three harmonic peaks, including higher harmonics and subharmonics of the stimulation frequency, rather than only one or two peaks (Brunner et al., 2010a; Müller-Putz et al., 2005).

SSEPs derive from sensory cortex. Using high-density EEG, dipole modeling, and simultaneous fMRI, it was found that visually evoked SSEPs (SSVEPs) arise from the primary visual cortex, motion-sensitive association cortex (MT/V5), and, to a lesser extent, both mid- and ventral occipital areas (Di Russo et al., 2007). Using MEG and high-density EEG source localization protocols, the auditory SSEP (SSAEP) arises from primary auditory cortex (Makela and Hari, 1987; Pantev et al., 1996); these findings are supported by fMRI-based evidence that the medial primary auditory cortex in humans is always activated by sound (Petkov et al., 2004). Similarly, SSEPs to somatosensory stimulation (SSSEPs) derive from primary somatosensory cortex as assessed using surface and depth electrodes in humans (Allison et al., 1989a,b) and in animal models (Arezzo et al., 1981; McCarthy et al., 1991).

3.1.3.1 Visual SSEP-based BCIs

For BCI applications, SSEPs were initially evaluated using visual stimulation. In one of the earliest investigations, users were able to move a cursor in one of four directions to navigate through a maze (Vidal, 1977). Later attempts employed a large grid, which gave the user 64 response options (Sutter, 1992). A recent study of a small group of healthy volunteers and one patient with ALS reported modest success (bit rate of 10.83 bits/min and single-subject accuracy of 80% in the patient) with a modified SSVEP paradigm in which the user could have their eyes closed while flashes were presented in a pair of glasses (Lim et al., 2013). Importantly, this eyes-closed approach could provide a binary communication option for a patient with a DoC without the need for visual fixation, but replication and validation studies are needed. Moreover, this type of BCI may be less promising for noncommunicative patients given that the flashing lights in the eyes could be irritating, especially if the patient did not wish to participate.

3.1.3.2 Auditory SSEP-based BCIs

SSAEPs occur in humans for stimulation rates between 1 and 200 Hz (Picton et al., 2003). Even during sleep, SSAEPs remain relatively consistent for stimulation frequencies up to 70 Hz (Cohen et al., 1991). SSAEP-based BCIs are relatively rare. Two recent investigations (Baek et al., 2013; Kim et al., 2011) presented binary communication BCIs based on SSAEPs, but the information transfer rates of these approaches were lower than the visual equivalents. Another recent attempt combined SSAEPs with a standard oddball paradigm to elicit P300s, but found superior performance for P300 (vs SSAEP) classification (Hill and Schölkopf, 2012).

3.1.3.3 Somatosensory SSEP-based BCIs

As with other sensory modalities, SSSEPs can be reliably detected following only a few seconds of stimulation (Noss et al., 1996). When elicited using vibrations (rather than nerve stimulation), cortical SSSEP amplitude is maximal with stimulation from approximately 20 to 26 Hz (Snyder, 1992; Tobimatsu et al., 1999). In clinical work, the absence of cortical SSSEPs to median nerve stimulation is predictive of poor recovery from coma (Cruse et al., 2014b; Zandbergen et al., 1998).

BCI applications of SSSEPs have only been recently addressed. Müller-Putz and colleagues present evidence that two of four users could selectively direct their attention to two different modulation frequencies of fingertip vibrations with success rates greater than 70% (Müller-Putz et al., 2006). Another proposed BCI framework combined SSSEPs with SSVEPs; performance in this framework was better than in single-modality designs (Maye et al., 2011; Zhang et al., 2007). Recently, one SSSEP-based BCI helped a healthy user control a wheelchair, although follow-up studies in a larger sample and a patient cohort are needed (Kim and Lee, 2014). As another alternative, users report that tactile feedback in other BCI paradigms feels more natural, and future applications of tactile feedback may be useful in BCI development (Chatterjee et al., 2007; Cincotti et al., 2007).

To date, exclusively SSEP-based BCIs have not been evaluated for use by patients with DoC.

3.1.4 Slow cortical potentials

SCPs are time-locked and phase-locked ERPs elicited by sensorimotor events (Birbaumer et al., 1990). Most SCPs are negative deflections that arise in a latency range from 0.5 s or more preceding an actual or imagined movement (Birbaumer et al., 1990; Shibasaki and Hallett, 2006). There are several subtypes of SCPs, including: (1) the movement-related potential, a biphasic wave that follows an actual movement (Colebatch, 2007); (2) the readiness potential, a waveform that precedes a voluntary movement by about 0.5 s (Shibasaki and Hallett, 2006); and (3) the CNV, a deflection elicited by an imperative, ie, warning, stimulus that precedes a response-contingent stimulus (Rohrbaugh et al., 1976; Walter et al., 1964).

There is strong evidence from both cortical surface and depth electrodes that SCPs derive from the excitatory postsynaptic potentials of apical dendrites (Birbaumer et al., 1990; Mitzdorf, 1985). Moreover, troughs in SCPs correlate with high-frequency field potentials (Vanhatalo et al., 2004) and multiunit neural activity (Birbaumer et al., 1990). Most SCPs are movement related, and SCPs correlate with fluctuations in the fMRI-derived BOLD signal from sensorimotor cortex (He et al., 2008) and widespread activation in central, prefrontal, and parietal cortex (Hinterberger et al., 2003). The CNV, however, can mark both upcoming motor and cognitive actions; it is therefore not surprising that this response arises from the SMA and certain parts of the frontoparietal network (Gómez et al., 2007; Hultin et al., 1996; Nagai et al., 2004).

Early attempts to employ SCPs in BCI-like applications were similar to attempted applications of P300s and SMRs. For example, one approach involved using SCPs to control a cursor-like object in a neurofeedback framework (Elbert et al., 1980; Lutzenberger et al., 1979). Unfortunately, the rate of the system response to the user was slow such that a user could make one selection only every 10 s or so (Elbert et al., 1980; Lutzenberger et al., 1979). Subsequent attempts to employ SCPs for BCI applications focused on improving the rate of response. Two attempts included a case study of a SCP-based speller in a patient with ALS (Birbaumer et al., 1999) and a similar paradigm for healthy controls (Hinterberger et al., 2004). Unfortunately, it was noted in subsequent studies involving patients with ALS that many months of training were required for the patients to learn to regulate their SCPs sufficiently for cursor control (Neumann and Kübler, 2003; Neumann et al., 2004).

While the SCP-based BCIs require low cognitive demands, these approaches have several critical limitations for use by patients with DoC. First, the SCP signal is slow (Birbaumer et al., 1990; Chatelle et al., 2012; Shibasaki and Hallett, 2006). Second, SCP-based BCIs generally require extensive training for successful use. In studies of patients with ALS, training periods for successful BCI use range from a few weeks (Kübler et al., 2001) to several months (Neumann and Kübler, 2003; Neumann et al., 2004). Finally, SCPs occur in the same EEG frequency range as nonneuronal electrical signals from slow drift, sweating, and movement (He and Raichle, 2009). For this reason, these responses are often excluded from EEG data with filtering. As suggested in previous work, the most useful application of SCPs for future BCIs is likely the incorporation of this signal into another BCI framework to mark anticipatory responses (Boehm et al., 2014; Faugeras et al., 2012; Haagh and Brunia, 1985). Otherwise, given the slow rate of this signal, the high training demands of these BCIs, and the co-occurrence of this signal with nonneuronal electrical signals, SCP-based BCIs are impractical for use by patients with DoC.

3.2 SINGLE- OR MULTIUNIT NEURONAL ACTIVITY

Some investigators have developed BCIs based on signals acquired from electrodes on the surface of the brain or within brain tissue itself. The aim of BCI control signals from within the cranium is to achieve better control than is possible with the external signals (Andersen et al., 2004; Donoghue, 2008, 2012). For example, spikes recorded from a single neuron in the primary motor cortex can encode information about movement parameters such as force and velocity (Georgopoulos, 1988), while spikes from a single neuron in parietal and frontal areas can encode information such as plans for upcoming movements and limb kinematics (Achtman et al., 2007). Overall, such a control signal should allow for lower attentional and learning demands during BCI operation.

As reviewed in Yuan and He (2014), early reports of BCIs based on implanted sensors were tested with nonhuman primates (Ethier et al., 2012; Serruya et al., 2002; Taylor et al., 2002; Wessberg et al., 2000). However, implant-based BCIs have also been tested in several individuals with severe motor impairments. For example, one BCI allowed a user to execute multidimensional control of a computer cursor (Hochberg et al., 2006; Kim et al., 2008). Another promising BCI even allowed a user to control a robotic arm (Collinger et al., 2013, 2015; Hochberg et al., 2012).

Unfortunately, there are several issues that restrict the feasibility of these internal signals for regular BCI use. For example, single unit electrodes must be very small and require very high sampling rates (Buzsaki, 2004). In most applications, one must tether the electrode to the skull, which results in movement of the electrode due to cardiac or respiratory pulsations (Buzsaki, 2004). There can be difficulties with biocompatibility due to the immune response of the brain tissue to the implant (Shain et al., 2003) and biostability due to the degradation of the implant while it is exposed to the warm, salty environment of the human brain (Hsu et al., 2009). Furthermore, regular implant-based BCI use generally requires a technician for device calibration, and device failures could require repeated surgeries for repairs (Donoghue, 2012). Overall, these issues limit the clinical applications of implant-based BCIs for patients with DoC and other motor impairments (Simeral et al., 2011).

3.3 BOLD RESPONSE

The BOLD responses refer to changes in hemoglobin (Hb) that occur with brain activity (Ogawa et al., 1990). The two techniques to measure the BOLD response most relevant to BCI applications are fMRI and functional near-infrared spectroscopy (fNIRS). fMRI measures the BOLD response by tracking the relative amounts of oxygenated and deoxygenated Hb in the brain based on the magnetic properties of this molecule (Ogawa et al., 1990). fNIRS measures the BOLD response by passing near-infrared light through the skull and measuring the amount of light absorbed in the unique frequencies that correspond with the two types of Hb (Villringer et al., 1993). While both approaches are informative for BCI research and development, BCIs based on the BOLD response are somewhat impractical because blood flow changes are slow (Toronov et al., 2007).

fMRI approaches to BCIs are useful to provide anatomically specific feedback to users. In fact, fMRI is often used to explore and develop better BCI systems, for example, by localizing the brain signature of a particular mental task to determine the optimal placement of electrodes for EEG-based BCIs (Formaggio et al., 2010). fMRI has been used in several investigations of patients with DoC to assess a patient's ability to follow commands using mental imagery (Bardin et al., 2011; Boly et al., 2007; Fernández-Espejo and Owen, 2013; Gibson et al., 2014b; Monti et al., 2010; Owen et al., 2006; Stender et al., 2014). Unfortunately, fMRI technology is expensive to obtain, operate, and maintain, and these approaches are impractical for use in daily life (Birbaumer et al., 2008).

fNIRS has several appealing attributes for BCI applications. This technique is safe, noninvasive, portable, and not as sensitive to stray electrical signals as EEG (Naseer and Hong, 2015). In studies of healthy individuals, fNIRS-based BCIs have been employed successfully with motor imagery paradigms (Coyle et al., 2007) and more cognitively demanding tasks (Hwang et al., 2014). fNIRS-based BCIs have also been proposed for spelling (Sitaram et al., 2007) and binary communication (Naseer et al., 2014). One investigation of an fNIRS-based BCI intended to allow patients with ALS to communicate had moderate success, although results were better for patients who were not completely locked-in (Naito et al., 2007). Unfortunately, BCIs based on fNIRS have not been extensively tested in patients with DoC.

4 SUMMARY AND RECOMMENDATIONS

It is evident that a subset of patients with DoC retains a range of cognitive abilities that could be exploited for BCI-based communication, such as attention orienting and motor imagery. Indeed, BCIs based on P300 and SMRs are by far the most extensively tested types of EEG-based BCIs, even for patients with DoC. Importantly, BCIs based on P300 responses are feasible for this population, with a number of existing paradigms based on auditory stimuli already evaluated in patient samples (Bekinschtein et al., 2009; Chennu et al., 2013; Morlet and Fischer, 2014). Future work with tactile stimulation for P300-based BCIs is promising. Conversely, BCIs based on SMRs have rendered mixed results in both healthy users and patient samples. Although SMRs have proved useful for awareness detection applications in patients with DoC (Cruse et al., 2011a; Gibson et al., 2014a; Goldfine et al.,

2011), additional investigation concerning appropriate feedback protocols for these patients will likely render more consistent BCI outcomes, as evident in several recent investigations (Coyle et al., 2011, 2012, 2015).

While BCIs based on SSEPs have had reasonable success in healthy samples, the feasibility of these approaches for patients with DoC is not yet known. A potential concern about SSEPs for patients with DoC is that the repetitive stimulation required in these designs could be irritating and uncomfortable for patients (Chatelle et al., 2012). The nature of this fast stimulation also limits the practicality of use in daily life. SSEP responses to tactile stimulation may be more feasible, particularly as feedback, because this type of stimulation frees the auditory and visual systems for other purposes. Indeed, some users report that tactile feedback feels more natural than other types of feedback in BCI settings (Chatterjee et al., 2007; Cincotti et al., 2007). Lastly, one work involving a P300-based BCI achieved reasonable success in a patient sample by incorporating an SSVEP into their framework (Pan et al., 2014). Future hybrid BCIs approaches warrant additional consideration.

BCIs based on SCPs are not extensively studied because this signal is slow (Birbaumer et al., 1990; Chatelle et al., 2012; Shibasaki and Hallett, 2006). Additionally, users require extensive training to learn to regulate their SCPs (Kübler et al., 2001; Neumann and Kübler, 2003; Neumann et al., 2004). The occurrence of this signal in the same frequency band as several types of nonneuronal electrical signals limits it practicality for use in BCI applications in general (He and Raichle, 2009). However, SCPs could be incorporated into BCIs based on another EEG control signal to mark anticipatory responses (Boehm et al., 2014; Haagh and Brunia, 1985). There is even evidence that this sort of response may occur in some patients with DoC in certain types of oddball paradigms intended to elicit the P300 (Faugeras et al., 2012).

Although BCIs based on signals aside from EEG have received less attention in the literature to date, these approaches have some utility for patients with DoC. For example, fMRI has been used successfully to assess command following in patients with DoC (Bardin et al., 2011; Boly et al., 2007; Fernández-Espejo and Owen, 2013; Gibson et al., 2014b; Monti et al., 2010; Owen et al., 2006; Stender et al., 2014). Although fMRI-based BCIs are impractical for daily life use, fNIRS provides a promising and practical alternative to fMRI. fNIRS-based BCIs are garnering more attention from BCI developers (for a recent review, see Naseer and Hong, 2015). Unfortunately, aside from one report in a sample of patients with ALS (Naito et al., 2007), these approaches have not yet been evaluated in many patient samples. We are optimistic about BCIs based on fNIRS control signals in future work involving patients with DoC.

BCIs based on implanted electrodes have achieved impressive performance in a few case reports (Collinger et al., 2013, 2015; Hochberg et al., 2006, 2012; Kim et al., 2008). Indeed, internal control signals seem to provide superior control over those acquired from outside of the cranium (Andersen et al., 2004; Donoghue, 2008). However, the risks associated with these invasive approaches necessitate a careful cost–benefit analysis, particularly for patients unable to provide consent for themselves. An implant-based BCI may be suitable for a patient who demonstrates consistent evidence of command following and communication by other means, but the potential risks of these BCIs are likely to outweigh the potential benefit of such devices for most patients with DoC.

Across all types of BCIs, long-term evaluations in patients with DoC are needed. It is not yet known if the cortical control signals from these patients will remain consistent over time. Moreover, inconsistency seems probable given that these patients are likely to undergo functional reorganization due to their acquired brain injuries. The role and type of feedback that is most feasible for this population is especially in need of study. Indeed, feedback has received little attention in BCIs tested in patients with DoC, although most existing studies confirm that auditory feedback is feasible and may even improve the user experience (ie, lead to increased arousal) in some patients compared to visual feedback (Coyle et al., 2012, 2013, 2015). Additionally, the inability to regulate eye movements is a diagnostic criterion for the DoC (Kalmar and Giacino, 2005). For this reason, approaches based on visual information are inappropriate for most patients with DoC. Perhaps more importantly, the cognitive, sensory, and arousal/attentional impairments of patients with severe brain injuries varies on a case-by-case basis with the particular brain regions compromised. While user customization is important for most BCI designs, these issues require special consideration in BCIs developed for patients with DoC.

Finally, an important pragmatic consideration relates to how often we should expect a patient with a DoC to communicate with a BCI. Indeed, patients who are able to follow commands are placed in a different diagnostic category (ie, MCS+) from those patients who can functionally communicate (ie, EMCS). Furthermore, the neural mechanisms that underlie these abilities are distinct (Fernández-Espejo et al., 2015; Osborne et al., 2015). Therefore, it should not surprise us that the same is also apparently true for signs of covert command following—ie, there will be patients who exhibit command following with BCI, but who are unable to use a BCI for functional communication. As a result, those patients with DoC who will be able to operate a BCI for functional communication are necessarily a subset of those patients with DoC who can follow commands. It is clear, therefore, that the primary benefit of BCI methods in DoC is the identification of covert cognition and awareness. Nevertheless, when an ability to follow commands has been identified, it behooves the clinical and BCI worlds to develop methods to allow those patients to try to exploit their residual abilities for communication.

REFERENCES

Achtman, N., Afshar, A., Santhanam, G., Yu, B.M., Ryu, S.I., Shenoy, K.V., 2007. Free-paced high-performance brain–computer interfaces. J. Neural Eng. 4, 336.

Adapa, R.M., Davis, M.H., Stamatakis, E.A., Absalom, A.R., Menon, D.K., 2014. Neural correlates of successful semantic processing during propofol sedation. Hum. Brain Mapp. 35, 2935–2949.

Allison, T., McCarthy, G., Wood, C.C., Darcey, T.M., Spencer, D.D., Williamson, P.D., 1989a. Human cortical potentials evoked by stimulation of the median nerve. I. Cytoarchitectonic areas generating short-latency activity. J. Neurophysiol. 62, 694–710.

Allison, T., McCarthy, G., Wood, C.C., Williamson, P.D., Spencer, D.D., 1989b. Human cortical potentials evoked by stimulation of the median nerve. II. Cytoarchitectonic areas generating long-latency activity. J. Neurophysiol. 62, 711–722.

Andersen, R.A., Musallam, S., Pesaran, B., 2004. Selecting the signals for a brain-machine interface. Curr. Opin. Neurobiol. 14, 720–726.

Andrews, K., Murphy, L., Munday, R., Littlewood, C., 1996. Misdiagnosis of the vegetative state: retrospective study in a rehabilitation unit. BMJ 313, 13–16.

Androulidakis, A.G., Mazzone, P., Litvak, V., Penny, W., Dileone, M., Gaynor, L.M., Tisch, S., Di Lazzaro, V., Brown, P., 2008. Oscillatory activity in the pedunculopontine area of patients with Parkinson's disease. Exp. Neurol. 211, 59–66.

Arezzo, J.C., Vaughan Jr., H.G., Legatt, A.D., 1981. Topography and intracranial sources of somatosensory evoked potentials in the monkey. II. Cortical components. Electroencephalogr. Clin. Neurophysiol. 51, 1–18.

Baek, H.J., Kim, H.S., Heo, J., Lim, Y.G., Park, K.S., 2013. Brain-computer interfaces using capacitive measurement of visual or auditory steady-state responses. J. Neural Eng. 10, 024001.

Bagnato, S., Boccagni, C., Prestandrea, C., Sant'Angelo, A., Castiglione, A., Galardi, G., 2010. Prognostic value of standard EEG in traumatic and non-traumatic disorders of consciousness following coma. Clin. Neurophysiol. 121, 274–280.

Bagnato, S., Boccagni, C., Sant'Angelo, A., Prestandrea, C., Mazzilli, R., Galardi, G., 2014. EEG predictors of outcome in patients with disorders of consciousness admitted for intensive rehabilitation. Clin. Neurophysiol. 126, 959–966.

Bai, O., Lin, P., Vorbach, S., Floeter, M.K., Hattori, N., Hallett, M., 2008. A high performance sensorimotor beta rhythm-based brain-computer interface associated with human natural motor behavior. J. Neural Eng. 5, 24–35.

Ball, T., Demandt, E., Mutschler, I., Neitzel, E., Mehring, C., Vogt, K., Aertsen, A., Schulze-Bonhage, A., 2008. Movement related activity in the high gamma range of the human EEG. Neuroimage 41, 302–310.

Bardin, J.C., Fins, J.J., Katz, D.I., Hersh, J., Heier, L.A., Tabelow, K., Dyke, J.P., Ballon, D.J., Schiff, N.D., Voss, H.U., 2011. Dissociations between behavioural and functional magnetic resonance imaging-based evaluations of cognitive function after brain injury. Brain 134, 769–782.

Bekinschtein, T.A., Dehaene, S., Rohaut, B., Tadel, F., Cohen, L., Naccache, L., 2009. Neural signature of the conscious processing of auditory regularities. Proc. Natl. Acad. Sci. U.S.A. 106, 1672–1677.

Bekinschtein, T.A., Manes, F.F., Villarreal, M., Owen, A.M., Della-Maggiore, V., 2011. Functional imaging reveals movement preparatory activity in the vegetative state. Front. Hum. Neurosci. 5, 1–5.

Bensch, M., Karim, A.A., Mellinger, J., Hinterberger, T., Tangermann, M., Bogdan, M., Rosenstiel, W., Birbaumer, N., 2007. Nessi: an EEG-controlled web browser for severely paralyzed patients. Comput. Intell. Neurosci. 2007, 71863.

Berlad, I., Pratt, H., 1995. P300 in response to the subject's own name. Electroencephalogr. Clin. Neurophysiol. 96, 472–474.

Bernat, J.L., 2006. Chronic disorders of consciousness. Lancet 367, 1181–1192.

Birbaumer, N., Elbert, T., Canavan, A.G., Rockstroh, B., 1990. Slow potentials of the cerebral cortex and behavior. Physiol. Rev. 70, 1–41.

Birbaumer, N., Ghanayim, N., Hinterberger, T., Iversen, I., Kotchoubey, B., Kubler, A., Perelmouter, J., Taub, E., Flor, H., 1999. A spelling device for the paralysed. Nature 398, 297–298.

Birbaumer, N., Murguialday, A.R., Cohen, L., 2008. Brain–computer interface in paralysis. Curr. Opin. Neurol. 21, 634–638.

Blankertz, B., Dornhege, G., Krauledat, M., Schröder, M., Williamson, J., Murray-Smith, R., Muller, K.R., 2006. The Berlin brain-computer interface presents the novel mental typewriter hex-o-spell. In: Proceedings of the 3rd International Brain-Computer Interface Workshop and Training Course.

Blankertz, B., Sannelli, C., Halder, S., Hammer, E.M., Kübler, A., Müller, K.-R., Curio, G., Dickhaus, T., 2010. Neurophysiological predictor of SMR-based BCI performance. Neuroimage 51, 1303–1309.

Bledowski, C., Prvulovic, D., Hoechstetter, K., Scherg, M., Wibral, M., Goebel, R., Linden, D.E., 2004. Localizing P300 generators in visual target and distractor processing: a combined event-related potential and functional magnetic resonance imaging study. J. Neurosci. 24, 9353–9360.

Boccagni, C., Bagnato, S., Sant'Angelo, A., Prestandrea, C., Galardi, G., 2011. Usefulness of standard EEG in predicting the outcome of patients with disorders of consciousness after anoxic coma. J. Clin. Neurophysiol. 28, 489–492.

Boehm, U., van Maanen, L., Forstmann, B., van Rijn, H., 2014. Trial-by-trial fluctuations in CNV amplitude reflect anticipatory adjustment of response caution. Neuroimage 96, 95–105.

Bokil, H., Purpura, K., Schoffelen, J.-M., Thomson, D., Mitra, P., 2007. Comparing spectra and coherences for groups of unequal size. J. Neurosci. Methods 159, 337–345.

Boly, M., Coleman, M.R., Davis, M.H., Hampshire, A., Bor, D., Moonen, G., Maquet, P.A., Pickard, J.D., Laureys, S., Owen, A.M., 2007. When thoughts become action: an fMRI paradigm to study volitional brain activity in non-communicative brain injured patients. Neuroimage 36, 979–992.

Brookes, M.J., Gibson, A.M., Hall, S.D., Furlong, P.L., Barnes, G.R., Hillebrand, A., Singh, K.D., Holliday, I.E., Francis, S.T., Morris, P.G., 2005. GLM-beamformer method demonstrates stationary field, alpha ERD and gamma ERS co-localisation with fMRI BOLD response in visual cortex. Neuroimage 26, 302–308.

Brouwer, A.-M.M., van Erp, J.B.F., 2010. A tactile P300 brain-computer interface. Front. Neurosci. 4, 19.

Brovelli, A., Ding, M., Ledberg, A., Chen, Y., Nakamura, R., Bressler, S.L., 2004. Beta oscillations in a large-scale sensorimotor cortical network: directional influences revealed by Granger causality. Proc. Natl. Acad. Sci. U.S.A. 101, 9849–9854.

Brown, E.N., Lydic, R., Schiff, N.D., 2010. General anesthesia, sleep, and coma. N. Engl. J. Med. 363, 2638–2650.

Brunner, C., Allison, B.Z., Krusienski, D.J., 2010a. Improved signal processing approaches in an offline simulation of a hybrid brain–computer interface. J. Neurosci. Methods 188, 165–173.

Brunner, P., Joshi, S., Briskin, S., Wolpaw, J.R., Bischof, H., Schalk, G., 2010b. Does the "P300" speller depend on eye gaze? J. Neural Eng. 7, 056013.

Bruno, M.-A., Vanhaudenhuyse, A., Thibaut, A., Moonen, G., Laureys, S., 2011. From unresponsive wakefulness to minimally conscious PLUS and functional locked-in syndromes:

recent advances in our understanding of disorders of consciousness. J. Neurol. 258, 1373–1384.

Bruno, M.-A., Majerus, S., Boly, M., Vanhaudenhuyse, A., Schnakers, C., Gosseries, O., Boveroux, P., Kirsch, M., Demertzi, A., Bernard, C., Hustinx, R., Moonen, G., Laureys, S., 2012. Functional neuroanatomy underlying the clinical subcategorization of minimally conscious state patients. J. Neurol. 259, 1087–1098.

Buzsaki, G., 2004. Large-scale recording of neuronal ensembles. Nat. Neurosci. 7, 446–451.

Cassim, F., Monaca, C., Szurhaj, W., Bourriez, J.L., Defebvre, L., Derambure, P., Guieu, J.D., 2001. Does post-movement beta synchronization reflect an idling motor cortex? Neuroreport 12, 3859–3863.

Cecotti, H., Rivet, B., Congedo, M., Jutten, C., Bertrand, O., Maby, E., Mattout, J., 2011. A robust sensor-selection method for P300 brain-computer interfaces. J. Neural Eng. 8, 016001.

Chatelle, C., Chennu, S., Noirhomme, Q., Cruse, D., Owen, A.M., Laureys, S., 2012. Brain-computer interfacing in disorders of consciousness. Brain Inj. 26, 1510–1522.

Chatelle, C., Lesenfants, D., Guller, Y., Laureys, S., Noirhomme, Q., 2015. In: Brain-Computer Interface for Assessing Consciousness in Severely Brain-Injured Patients. Clinical Neurophysiology in Disorders of Consciousness: Brain Function Monitoring in the ICU and Beyond; Springer, Vienna.

Chatterjee, A., Aggarwal, V., Ramos, A., Acharya, S., Thakor, N.V., 2007. A brain-computer interface with vibrotactile biofeedback for haptic information. J. Neuroeng. Rehabil. 4, 40.

Chen, R., Yaseen, Z., Cohen, L.G., Hallett, M., 1998. Time course of corticospinal excitability in reaction time and self-paced movements. Ann. Neurol. 44, 317–325.

Chennu, S., Finoia, P., Kamau, E., Monti, M.M., Allanson, J., Pickard, J.D., Owen, A.M., Bekinschtein, T.A., 2013. Dissociable endogenous and exogenous attention in disorders of consciousness. Neuroimage Clin. 3, 450–461.

Cincotti, F., Kauhanen, L., Aloise, F., Palomaki, T., Caporusso, N., Jylanki, P., Mattia, D., Babiloni, F., Vanacker, G., Nuttin, M., Marciani, M.G., Del, R., Millan, J., 2007. Vibrotactile feedback for brain-computer interface operation. Comput. Intell. Neurosci. 2007, 12. Article ID 48937, http://dx.doi.org/10.1155/2007/48937; http://www.hindawi.com/journals/cin/2007/048937/cta/.

Cincotti, F., Mattia, D., Aloise, F., Bufalari, S., Schalk, G., Oriolo, G., Cherubini, A., Marciani, M.G., Babiloni, F., 2008. Non-invasive brain–computer interface system: towards its application as assistive technology. Brain Res. Bull. 75, 796–803.

Cloostermans, M.C., van Meulen, F.B., Eertman, C.J., Hom, H.W., van Putten, M.J., 2012. Continuous electroencephalography monitoring for early prediction of neurological outcome in postanoxic patients after cardiac arrest: a prospective cohort study. Crit. Care Med. 40, 2867–2875.

Cohen, L.T., Rickards, F.W., Clark, G.M., 1991. A comparison of steady-state evoked potentials to modulated tones in awake and sleeping humans. J. Acoust. Soc. Am. 90, 2467–2479.

Colebatch, J.G., 2007. Bereitschaftspotential and movement-related potentials: origin, significance, and application in disorders of human movement. Mov. Disord. 22, 601–610.

Coleman, M.R., Rodd, J.M., Davis, M.H., Johnsrude, I.S., Menon, D.K., Pickard, J.D., Owen, A.M., 2007. Do vegetative patients retain aspects of language comprehension? Evidence from fMRI. Brain 130, 2494–2507.

Coleman, M.R., Davis, M.H., Rodd, J.M., Robson, T., Ali, A., Owen, A.M., Pickard, J.D., 2009. Towards the routine use of brain imaging to aid the clinical diagnosis of disorders of consciousness. Brain 132, 2541–2552.

Collinger, J.L., Wodlinger, B., Downey, J.E., Wang, W., Tyler-Kabara, E.C., Weber, D.J., McMorland, A.J.C., Velliste, M., Boninger, M.L., Schwartz, A.B., 2013. 7 degree-of-freedom neuroprosthetic control by an individual with tetraplegia. Lancet 381, 557–564.

Collinger, J.L., Wodlinger, B., Downey, J.E., Wang, W., Tyler-Kabara, E.C., Weber, D.J., McMorland, A.J.C., Velliste, M., Boninger, M.L., Schwartz, A.B., 2015. High-performance neuroprosthetic control by an individual with tetraplegia. Lancet 381, 557–564.

Comerchero, M.D., Polich, J., 1999. P3a and P3b from typical auditory and visual stimuli. Clin. Neurophysiol. 110, 24–30.

Cote, K.A., 2002. Probing awareness during sleep with the auditory odd-ball paradigm. Int. J. Psychophysiol. 46, 227–241.

Coyle, D., 2009. Neural network based auto association and time-series prediction for bio-signal processing in brain-computer interfaces. IEEE Comput. Intell. Mag. 4, 47–59.

Coyle, D., Prasad, G., McGinnity, T.M., 2005. A time-series prediction approach for feature extraction in a brain-computer interface. IEEE Trans. Neural Syst. Rehabil. Eng. 13, 461–467.

Coyle, S.M., Ward, T.E., Markham, C.M., 2007. Brain-computer interface using a simplified functional near-infrared spectroscopy system. J. Neural Eng. 4, 219–226.

Coyle, D., Garcia, J., Satti, A.R., McGinnity, T.M., 2011. EEG-based continuous control of a game using a 3 channel motor imagery BCI: BCI game. In: 2011 IEEE Symposium on Computational Intelligence, Cognitive Algorithms, Mind, Brain (CCMB).

Coyle, D., Carroll, A., Stow, J., McCann, A., 2012. Enabling control in the minimally conscious state in a single session with a three channel BCI. In: The 1st International DECODER Workshop, pp. 1–4.

Coyle, D., Carroll, Á., Stow, J., Mccreadie, K., Mcelligott, J., 2013. Visual and stereo audio sensorimotor rhythm feedback in the minimally conscious state. In: Proceedings of the 5th International Brain-Computer Interface Meeting, pp. 2–3.

Coyle, D., Stow, J., McCreadie, K., McElligott, J., Carroll, Á, 2015. Sensorimotor modulation assessment and brain-computer interface training in disorders of consciousness. Arch. Phys. Med. Rehabil. 96, S62–S70.

Cruse, D., Chennu, S., Chatelle, C., Bekinschtein, T.A., Fernández-Espejo, D., Pickard, J.D., Laureys, S., Owen, A.M., 2011a. Bedside detection of awareness in the vegetative state: a cohort study. Lancet 378, 2088–2094.

Cruse, D., Chennu, S., Chatelle, C., Bekinschtein, T.A., Fernández-Espejo, D., Pickard, J.D., Laureys, S., Owen, A.M., 2011b. Reanalysis of "bedside detection of awareness in the vegetative state: a cohort study"—authors' reply. Lancet 381, 291–292.

Cruse, D., Chennu, S., Fernández-Espejo, D., Payne, W.L., Young, G.B., Owen, A.M., 2012. Detecting awareness in the vegetative state: electroencephalographic evidence for attempted movements to command. PLoS One 7, e49933.

Cruse, D., Gantner, I.S., Soddu, A., Owen, A.M., 2014a. Lies, damned lies, and diagnoses: estimating the clinical utility of assessments of covert awareness in the vegetative state. Brain Inj. 28, 1197–1201.

Cruse, D., Norton, L., Gofton, T., Young, G.B., Owen, A.M., 2014b. Positive prognostication from median-nerve somatosensory evoked cortical potentials. Neurocrit. Care 21, 238–244.

Curran, E., Stokes, M.J., 2003. Learning to control brain activity: a review of the production and control of EEG components for driving brain–computer interface (BCI) systems. Brain Cogn. 51, 326–336.

Curran, E., Sykacek, P., Stokes, M.J., Roberts, S.J., Penny, W., Johnsrude, I., Owen, A.M., 2004. Cognitive tasks for driving a brain-computer interfacing system: a pilot study. IEEE Trans. Neural Syst. Rehabil. Eng. 12, 48–54.

Davis, M.H., Coleman, M.R., Absalom, A.R., Rodd, J.M., Johnsrude, I.S., Matta, B.F., Owen, A.M., Menon, D.K., 2007. Dissociating speech perception and comprehension at reduced levels of awareness. Proc. Natl. Acad. Sci. U.S.A. 104, 16032–16037.

Dawson, G., 1954. A summation technique for the detection of small evoked potentials. Electroencephalogr. Clin. Neurophysiol. 6, 65–84.

Di, H.B., Yu, S.M., Weng, X.C., Laureys, S., Yu, D., Li, J.Q., Qin, P.M., Zhu, Y.H., Zhang, S.Z., Chen, Y.Z., 2007. Cerebral response to patient's own name in the vegetative and minimally conscious states. Neurology 68, 895–899.

Di Russo, F., Pitzalis, S., Aprile, T., Spitoni, G., Patria, F., Stella, A., Spinelli, D., Hillyard, S.A., 2007. Spatiotemporal analysis of the cortical sources of the steady-state visual evoked potential. Hum. Brain Mapp. 28, 323–334.

Donoghue, J.P., 2008. Bridging the brain to the world: a perspective on neural interface systems. Neuron 60, 511–521.

Donoghue, J.P., 2012. BCIs that use signals recorded in motor cortex. In: Wolpaw, J.R., Wolpaw, E.W. (Eds.), Brain-Computer Interfaces: Principles and Practice. Oxford University Press, New York, pp. 265–288.

Elbert, T., Rockstroh, B., Lutzenberger, W., Birbaumer, N., 1980. Biofeedback of slow cortical potentials. I. Electroencephalogr. Clin. Neurophysiol. 48, 293–301.

Ethier, C., Oby, E., Bauman, M., Miller, L., 2012. Restoration of grasp following paralysis through brain-controlled stimulation of muscles. Nature 485, 368–371.

Farwell, L.A., Donchin, E., 1988. Talking off the top of your head: toward a mental prosthesis utilizing event-related brain potentials. Electroencephalogr. Clin. Neurophysiol. 70, 510–523.

Faugeras, F., Rohaut, B., Weiss, N., Bekinschtein, T.A., Galanaud, D., Puybasset, L., Bolgert, F., Sergent, C., Cohen, L., Dehaene, S., Naccache, L., 2011. Probing consciousness with event-related potentials in the vegetative state. Neurology 77, 264–268.

Faugeras, F., Rohaut, B., Weiss, N., Bekinschtein, T.A., Galanaud, D., Puybasset, L., Bolgert, F., Sergent, C., Cohen, L., Dehaene, S., Naccache, L., 2012. Event related potentials elicited by violations of auditory regularities in patients with impaired consciousness. Neuropsychologia 50, 403–418.

Fernández-Espejo, D., Owen, A.M., 2013. Detecting awareness after severe brain injury. Nat. Rev. Neurosci. 14, 801–809.

Fernández-Espejo, D., Junqué, C., Vendrell, P., Bernabeu, M., Roig, T., Bargalló, N., Mercader, J.M., 2008. Cerebral response to speech in vegetative and minimally conscious states after traumatic brain injury. Brain Inj. 22, 882–890.

Fernández-Espejo, D., Norton, L., Owen, A.M., 2014. The clinical utility of fMRI for identifying covert awareness in the vegetative state: a comparison of sensitivity between 3 T and 1.5 T. PLoS One 9, e95082.

Fernández-Espejo, D., Rossit, S., Owen, A.M., 2015. A thalamocortical mechanism for the absence of overt motor behavior in covertly aware patients. JAMA Neurol. 72, 1442–1450.

Fiori, F., Sedda, A., Ferre, E.R., Toraldo, A., Querzola, M., Pasotti, F., Ovadia, D., Piroddi, C., Dell'aquila, R., Lunetta, C., Corbo, M., Bottini, G., 2013. Exploring motor and visual imagery in amyotrophic lateral sclerosis. Exp. Brain Res. 226, 537–547.

Fischer, C., Dailler, F., Morlet, D., 2008. Novelty P3 elicited by the subject's own name in comatose patients. Clin. Neurophysiol. 119, 2224–2230.

Fischer, C., Luaute, J., Morlet, D., 2010. Event-related potentials (MMN and novelty P3) in permanent vegetative or minimally conscious states. Clin. Neurophysiol. 121, 1032–1042.

Formaggio, E., Storti, S.F., Cerini, R., Fiaschi, A., Manganotti, P., 2010. Brain oscillatory activity during motor imagery in EEG-fMRI coregistration. Magn. Reson. Imaging 28, 1403–1412.

Friedrich, E.V.C., Scherer, R., Neuper, C., 2013. Long-term evaluation of a 4-class imagery-based brain–computer interface. Clin. Neurophysiol. 124, 916–927.

Friston, K., 2008. Hierarchical models in the brain. PLoS Comput. Biol. 4, e1000211.

Furdea, A., Halder, S., Krusienski, D.J., Bross, D., Nijboer, F., Birbaumer, N., Kübler, A., 2009. An auditory oddball (P300) spelling system for brain-computer interfaces. Psychophysiology 46, 617–625.

Gabriel, D., Henriques, J., Comte, A., Grigoryeva, L., Ortega, J.-P., Cretin, E., Brunotte, G., Haffen, E., Moulin, T., Aubry, R., Pazart, L., 2015. Substitute or complement? Defining the relative place of EEG and fMRI in the detection of voluntary brain reactions. Neuroscience 290C, 435–444.

Georgopoulos, A.P., 1988. Neural integration of movement: role of motor cortex in reaching. FASEB J. 2, 2849–2857.

Giacino, J.T., Ashwal, S., Childs, N.L., Cranford, R., Jennett, B., Katz, D.I., Kelly, J.E., Rosenberg, J., Whyte, J., Zafonte, R.D., Zasler, N.D., 2002. The minimally conscious state: definition and diagnostic criteria. Neurology 58, 349–353.

Giacino, J.T., Fins, J.J., Laureys, S., Schiff, N.D., 2014. Disorders of consciousness after acquired brain injury: the state of the science. Nat. Rev. Neurol. 10, 99–114.

Gibson, R.M., Chennu, S., Owen, A.M., Cruse, D., 2014a. Complexity and familiarity enhance single-trial detectability of imagined movements with electroencephalography. Clin. Neurophysiol. 125, 1556–1567.

Gibson, R.M., Fernández-Espejo, D., Gonzalez-Lara, L.E., Kwan, B.Y., Lee, D.H., Owen, A.M., Cruse, D., 2014b. Multiple tasks and neuroimaging modalities increase the likelihood of detecting covert awareness in patients with disorders of consciousness. Front. Hum. Neurosci. 8, 1–9.

Goldfine, A.M., Victor, J.D., Conte, M.M., Bardin, J.C., Schiff, N.D., 2011. Determination of awareness in patients with severe brain injury using EEG power spectral analysis. Clin. Neurophysiol. 122, 2157–2168.

Goldfine, A.M., Bardin, J.C., Noirhomme, Q., Fins, J.J., Schiff, N.D., Victor, J.D., 2013. Reanalysis of "Bedside detection of awareness in the vegetative state: a cohort study". Lancet 381, 289–291.

Gómez, C.M., Flores, A., Ledesma, A., 2007. Fronto-parietal networks activation during the contingent negative variation period. Brain Res. Bull. 73, 40–47.

Gosseries, O., Di, H., Laureys, S., Boly, M., 2014. Measuring consciousness in severely damaged brains. Annu. Rev. Neurosci. 37, 457–478.

Grosse-Wentrup, M., 2011. The neural correlates of BCI performance variations in ALS: a pilot study. Conference Abstract: BC11: Computational Neuroscience & Neurotechnology Bernstein Conference & Neurex Annual Meeting 2011. Front. Comput. Neurosci. http://dx.doi.org/10.3389/conf.fncom.2011.53.00117.

Grosse-Wentrup, M., Scholkopf, B., 2012. High gamma-power predicts performance in sensorimotor-rhythm brain-computer interfaces. J. Neural Eng. 9, 46001.

Grosse-Wentrup, M., Schölkopf, B., 2013. A review of performance variations in SMR-based brain-computer interfaces (BCIs). In: Guger, C., Allison, B.Z., Edlinger, G. (Eds.), Brain-

Computer Interface Research. SpringerBriefs in Electrical and Computer Engineering, Springer, Berlin, Heidelberg, pp. 39–51.

Grosse-Wentrup, M., Scholkopf, B., Hill, J., 2011. Causal influence of gamma oscillations on the sensorimotor rhythm. Neuroimage 56, 837–842.

Guger, C., Edlinger, G., Harkam, W., Niedermayer, I., Pfurtscheller, G., 2003. How many people are able to operate an EEG-based brain-computer interface (BCI)? IEEE Trans. Neural Syst. Rehabil. Eng. 11, 145–147.

Guger, C., Daban, S., Sellers, E.W., Holzner, C., Krausz, G., Carabalona, R., Gramatica, F., Edlinger, G., 2009. How many people are able to control a P300-based brain-computer interface (BCI)? Neurosci. Lett. 462, 94–98.

Haagh, S.A., Brunia, C.H., 1985. Anticipatory response-relevant muscle activity, CNV amplitude and simple reaction time. Electroencephalogr. Clin. Neurophysiol. 61, 30–39.

Halder, S., Rea, M., Andreoni, R., Nijboer, F., Hammer, E.M., Kleih, S.C., Birbaumer, N., Kübler, A., 2010. An auditory oddball brain–computer interface for binary choices. Clin. Neurophysiol. 121, 516–523.

Hammer, E.M., Halder, S., Blankertz, B., Sannelli, C., Dickhaus, T., Kleih, S.C., Müller, K.-R., Kübler, A., 2012. Psychological predictors of SMR-BCI performance. Biol. Psychol. 89, 80–86.

He, B.J., Raichle, M.E., 2009. The fMRI signal, slow cortical potential and consciousness. Trends Cogn. Sci. 13, 302–309.

He, B.J., Snyder, A.Z., Zempel, J.M., Smyth, M.D., Raichle, M.E., 2008. Electrophysiological correlates of the brain's intrinsic large-scale functional architecture. Proc. Natl. Acad. Sci. U.S.A. 105, 16039–16044.

Henriques, J., Gabriel, D., Grigoryeva, L., Haffen, E., Moulin, T., Aubry, R., Pazart, L., Ortega, J.-P., 2014. Protocol design challenges in the detection of awareness in aware subjects using EEG signals. Clin. EEG Neurosci., 1–10.

Herrmann, C.S., 2001. Human EEG responses to 1–100 Hz flicker: resonance phenomena in visual cortex and their potential correlation to cognitive phenomena. Exp. Brain Res. 137, 346–353.

Hill, N., Schölkopf, B., 2012. An online brain–computer interface based on shifting attention to concurrent streams of auditory stimuli. J. Neural Eng. 9, 1–23.

Hinterberger, T., Veit, R., Strehl, U., Trevorrow, T., Erb, M., Kotchoubey, B., Flor, H., Birbaumer, N., 2003. Brain areas activated in fMRI during self-regulation of slow cortical potentials (SCPs). Exp. Brain Res. 152, 113–122.

Hinterberger, T., Weiskopf, N., Veit, R., Wilhelm, B., Betta, E., Birbaumer, N., 2004. An EEG-driven brain-computer interface combined with functional magnetic resonance imaging (fMRI). IEEE Trans. Biomed. Eng. 51, 971–974.

Hjorth, B., 1975. An on-line transformation of EEG scalp potentials into orthogonal source derivations. Electroencephalogr. Clin. Neurophysiol. 39, 526–530.

Hochberg, L.R., Serruya, M.D., Friehs, G.M., Mukand, J.A., Saleh, M., Caplan, A.H., Branner, A., Chen, D., Penn, R.D., Donoghue, J.P., 2006. Neuronal ensemble control of prosthetic devices by a human with tetraplegia. Nature 442, 164–171.

Hochberg, L.R., Bacher, D., Jarosiewicz, B., Masse, N.Y., Simeral, J.D., Vogel, J., Haddadin, S., Liu, J., Cash, S.S., van der Smagt, P., Donoghue, J.P., 2012. Reach and grasp by people with tetraplegia using a neurally controlled robotic arm. Nature 485, 372–375.

Hofmeijer, J., Tjepkema-Cloostermans, M.C., van Putten, M.J.A.M., 2014. Burst-suppression with identical bursts: a distinct EEG pattern with poor outcome in postanoxic coma. Clin. Neurophysiol. 125, 947–954.

Horki, P., Bauernfeind, G., Klobassa, D.S., Pokorny, C., Pichler, G., Schippinger, W., Müller-Putz, G.R., 2014. Detection of mental imagery and attempted movements in patients with disorders of consciousness using EEG. Front. Hum. Neurosci. 8, 1009.

Hsu, J.-M., Rieth, L., Normann, R.A., Tathireddy, P., Solzbacher, F., 2009. Encapsulation of an integrated neural interface device with Parylene C. IEEE Trans. Biomed. Eng. 56, 23–29.

Hultin, L., Rossini, P., Romani, G.L., Hogstedt, P., Tecchio, F., Pizzella, V., 1996. Neuromagnetic localization of the late component of the contingent negative variation. Electroencephalogr. Clin. Neurophysiol. 98, 435–448.

Hwang, H.-J., Kim, S., Choi, S., Im, C.-H., 2013. EEG-based brain-computer interfaces: a thorough literature survey. Int. J. Hum. Comput. Interact. 29, 814–826.

Hwang, H.-J., Lim, J.-H., Kim, D.-W., Im, C.-H., 2014. Evaluation of various mental task combinations for near-infrared spectroscopy-based brain-computer interfaces. J. Biomed. Opt. 19, 77005.

Jasper, H., Pendfield, W., 1949. Electrocorticograms in man: effect of voluntary movement upon the electrical activity of the precentral gyrus. Arch. Psychiatr. Z. Neurol. 183, 163–174.

Jennett, B., 2002. The Vegetative State. Medical Facts, Ethical and Legal Dilemmas. Cambridge University Press, Cambridge.

Kalmar, K., Giacino, J.T., 2005. The JFK coma recovery scale—revised. Neuropsychol. Rehabil. 15, 454–460.

Kanoh, S., Miyamoto, K., Yoshinobu, T., 2008. A brain-computer interface (BCI) system based on auditory stream segregation. In: 30th Annual International Conference of the IEEE Engineering in Medicine and Biology Society. IEEE, Vancouver, BC, pp. 642–645.

Kasahara, T., Terasaki, K., Ogawa, Y., Ushiba, J., Aramaki, H., Masakado, Y., 2012. The correlation between motor impairments and event-related desynchronization during motor imagery in ALS patients. BMC Neurosci. 13, 66.

Kaufmann, T., Holz, E.M., Kübler, A., 2013. Comparison of tactile, auditory, and visual modality for brain-computer interface use: a case study with a patient in the locked-in state. Front. Neurosci. 7, 1–12.

Kiernan, M.C., Vucic, S., Cheah, B.C., Turner, M.R., Eisen, A., Hardiman, O., Burrell, J.R., Zoing, M.C., 2011. Amyotrophic lateral sclerosis. Lancet 377, 942–955.

Kilavik, B.E., Zaepffel, M., Brovelli, A., MacKay, W.A., Riehle, A., 2013. The ups and downs of β oscillations in sensorimotor cortex. Exp. Neurol. 245, 15–26.

Kim, K.-T., Lee, S.-W., 2014. Steady-state somatosensory evoked potentials for brain-controlled wheelchair. In: 2014 International Winter Workshop on Brain-Computer Interface (BCI).

Kim, S.-P., Simeral, J.D., Hochberg, L.R., Donoghue, J.P., Black, M.J., 2008. Neural control of computer cursor velocity by decoding motor cortical spiking activity in humans with tetraplegia. J. Neural Eng. 5, 455–476.

Kim, D.-W., Cho, J.-H., Hwang, H.-J., Lim, J.-H., Im, C.-H., 2011. A vision-free brain-computer interface (BCI) paradigm based on auditory selective attention. In: Annual International Conference of the IEEE Engineering in Medicine and Biology Society, pp. 3684–3687.

King, J.R., Faugeras, F., Gramfort, A., Schurger, A., El Karoui, I., Sitt, J.D., Rohaut, B., Wacongne, C., Labyt, E., Bekinschtein, T., Cohen, L., Naccache, L., Dehaene, S., 2013. Single-trial decoding of auditory novelty responses facilitates the detection of residual consciousness. Neuroimage 83, 726–738.

Kinoshita, S., Inoue, M., Maeda, H., Nakamura, J., Morita, K., 1996. Long-term patterns of change in ERPs across repeated measurements. Physiol. Behav. 60, 1087–1092.

Kirschner, A., Cruse, D., Chennu, S., Owen, A.M., Hampshire, A., 2015. A P300-based cognitive assessment battery. Brain Behav. 5, e00336.

Klimesch, W., 1999. EEG alpha and theta oscillations reflect cognitive and memory performance: a review and analysis. Brain Res. Rev. 29, 169–195.

Klobassa, D.S., Vaughan, T.M., Brunner, P., Schwartz, N.E., Wolpaw, J.R., Neuper, C., Sellers, E.W., 2009. Toward a high-throughput auditory P300-based brain–computer interface. Clin. Neurophysiol. 120, 1252–1261.

Klostermann, F., Nikulin, V.V., Kuhn, A.A., Marzinzik, F., Wahl, M., Pogosyan, A., Kupsch, A., Schneider, G.-H., Brown, P., Curio, G., 2007. Task-related differential dynamics of EEG alpha- and beta-band synchronization in cortico-basal motor structures. Eur. J. Neurosci. 25, 1604–1615.

Knight, R.T., Scabini, D., 1998. Anatomic bases of event-related potentials and their relationship to novelty detection in humans. J. Clin. Neurophysiol. 15, 3–13.

Knight, R.T., Scabini, D., Woods, D.L., Clayworth, C.C., 1989. Contributions of temporal-parietal junction to the human auditory P3. Brain Res. 502, 109–116.

Koelsch, S., Heinke, W., Sammler, D., Olthoff, D., 2006. Auditory processing during deep propofol sedation and recovery from unconsciousness. Clin. Neurophysiol. 117, 1746–1759.

Krusienski, D.J., Sellers, E.W., Cabestaing, F., Bayoudh, S., McFarland, D.J., Vaughan, T.M., Wolpaw, J.R., 2006. A comparison of classification techniques for the P300 Speller. J. Neural Eng. 3, 299–305.

Krusienski, D.J., Sellers, E.W., McFarland, D.J., Vaughan, T.M., Wolpaw, J.R., 2008. Toward enhanced P300 speller performance. J. Neurosci. Methods 167, 15–21.

Kübler, A., Neumann, N., Kaiser, J., Kotchoubey, B., Hinterberger, T., Birbaumer, N.P., 2001. Brain-computer communication: self-regulation of slow cortical potentials for verbal communication. Arch. Phys. Med. Rehabil. 82, 1533–1539.

Kübler, A., Nijboer, F., Mellinger, J., Vaughan, T.M., Pawelzik, H., Schalk, G., McFarland, D.J., Birbaumer, N., Wolpaw, J.R., 2005. Patients with ALS can use sensorimotor rhythms to operate a brain-computer interface. Neurology 64, 1775–1777.

Kübler, A., Furdea, A., Halder, S., Hammer, E.M., Nijboer, F., Kotchoubey, B., 2009. A brain-computer interface controlled auditory event-related potential (p300) spelling system for locked-in patients. Ann. N.Y. Acad. Sci. 1157, 90–100.

Kulkarni, V.P., Lin, K., Benbadis, S.R., 2007. EEG findings in the persistent vegetative state. J. Clin. Neurophysiol. 24, 433–437.

Lachaux, J.-P., Fonlupt, P., Kahane, P., Minotti, L., Hoffmann, D., Bertrand, O., Baciu, M., 2007. Relationship between task-related gamma oscillations and BOLD signal: new insights from combined fMRI and intracranial EEG. Hum. Brain Mapp. 28, 1368–1375.

Laureys, S., Owen, A.M., Schiff, N.D., 2004. Brain function in coma, vegetative state, and related disorders. Lancet 3, 537–546.

Laureys, S., Celesia, G.G., Cohadon, F., Lavrijsen, J., Leon-Carrion, J., Sannita, W.G., Sazbon, L., Schmutzhard, E., von Wild, K.R., Zeman, A., Dolce, G., 2010. Unresponsive wakefulness syndrome: a new name for the vegetative state or apallic syndrome. BMC Med. 8, 68.

Lechinger, J., Chwala-Schlegel, N., Fellinger, R., Donis, J., Michitsch, G., Pichler, G., Schabus, M., 2013. Mirroring of a simple motor behavior in disorders of consciousness. Clin. Neurophysiol. 124, 27–34.

Lee, J.W., Tanaka, N., Shiraishi, H., Milligan, T.A., Dworetzky, B.A., Khoshbin, S., Stufflebeam, S.M., Bromfield, E.B., 2010. Evaluation of postoperative sharp waveforms through EEG and magnetoencephalography. J. Clin. Neurophysiol. 27, 7–11.

Lehembre, R., Gosseries, O., Lugo, Z., Jedidi, Z., Chatelle, C., Sadzot, B., Laureys, S., Noirhomme, Q., 2012. Electrophysiological investigations of brain function in coma, vegetative and minimally conscious patients. Arch. Ital. Biol. 150, 122–139.

Lehmann, D., Skrandies, W., 1980. Reference-free identification of components of checkerboard-evoked multichannel potential fields. Electroencephalogr. Clin. Neurophysiol. 48, 609–621.

León-Carrión, J., van Eeckhout, P., Domínguez-Morales, M.D.R., 2002. The locked-in syndrome: a syndrome looking for a therapy. Brain Inj. 16, 555–569.

Li, Y., Wang, L.-Q., Hu, Y., 2009. Localizing P300 generators in high-density event-related potential with fMRI. Med. Sci. Monit. 15, 47–53.

Lim, J.-H., Hwang, H.-J., Han, C.-H., Jung, K.-Y., Im, C.-H., 2013. Classification of binary intentions for individuals with impaired oculomotor function: "eyes-closed" SSVEP-based brain-computer interface (BCI). J. Neural Eng. 10, 026021.

Litvak, V., Mattout, J., Kiebel, S., Phillips, C., Henson, R., Kilner, J., Barnes, G., Oostenveld, R., Daunizeau, J., Flandin, G., Penny, W., Friston, K., 2011. EEG and MEG data analysis in SPM8. Comput. Intell. Neurosci. 2011, 1–32.

Logothetis, N.K., Pauls, J., Augath, M., Trinath, T., Oeltermann, A., 2001. Neurophysiological investigation of the basis of the fMRI signal. Nature 412, 150–157.

Lopes da Silva, F.H., 1991. Neural mechanisms underlying brain waves: from neural membranes to networks. Electroencephalogr. Clin. Neurophysiol. 79, 81–93.

Luck, S.J., 2014. An Introduction to the Event-Related Potential Technique, second ed. MIT Press, Cambridge, MA.

Lugo, Z.R., Rodriguez, J., Lechner, A., Ortner, R., Gantner, I.S., Laureys, S., Noirhomme, Q., Guger, C., 2014. A vibrotactile P300-based brain-computer interface for consciousness detection and communication. Clin. EEG Neurosci. 45, 14–21.

Lulé, D., Noirhomme, Q., Kleih, S.C., Chatelle, C., Halder, S., Demertzi, A., Bruno, M.-A., Gosseries, O., Vanhaudenhuyse, A., Schnakers, C., Thonnard, M., Soddu, A., Kübler, A., Laureys, S., 2013. Probing command following in patients with disorders of consciousness using a brain-computer interface. Clin. Neurophysiol. 124, 101–106.

Lutzenberger, W., Elbert, T., Rockstroh, B., Birbaumer, N., 1979. The effects of self-regulation of slow cortical potentials on performance in a signal detection task. Int. J. Neurosci. 9, 175–183.

Majerus, S., Bruno, M.A., Schnakers, C., Giacino, J.T., Laureys, S., 2009. The problem of aphasia in the assessment of consciousness in brain-damaged patients. Prog. Brain Res. 177, 49–61.

Makela, J.P., Hari, R., 1987. Evidence for cortical origin of the 40 Hz auditory evoked response in man. Electroencephalogr. Clin. Neurophysiol. 66, 539–546.

Maris, E., 2004. Randomization tests for ERP topographies and whole spatiotemporal data matrices. Psychophysiology 41, 142–151.

Maris, E., Oostenveld, R., 2007. Nonparametric statistical testing of EEG- and MEG-data. J. Neurosci. Methods 164, 177–190.

Marshall, D., Coyle, D., Wilson, S., Callaghan, M., 2013. Games, gameplay, and BCI: the state of the art. IEEE Trans. Comput. Intell. AI Games 5, 82–99.

Martens, S.M.M., Hill, N.J., Farquhar, J., Schölkopf, B., 2009. Overlap and refractory effects in a brain–computer interface speller based on the visual P300 event-related potential. J. Neural Eng. 6, 026003.

Maye, A., Zhang, D., Wang, Y., Gao, S., Engel, A.K., 2011. Multimodal brain-computer interfaces. Tsinghua Sci. Technol. 16, 133–139.

Mccane, L.M., Sellers, E.W., Mcfarland, D.J., Mak, J.N., Steve, C., Zeitlin, D., Wolpaw, J.R., Vaughan, T.M., Hayes, H., Hospital, R., Haverstraw, W., City, J., Kong, H., 2014. Brain-computer interface (BCI) evaluation in people with amyotrophic lateral sclerosis. Amyotroph. Lateral Scler. Frontotemporal Degener. 15, 207–215.

McCarthy, G., Wood, C.C., Allison, T., 1991. Cortical somatosensory evoked potentials. I. Recordings in the monkey *Macaca fascicularis*. J. Neurophysiol. 66, 53–63.

McCreadie, K.A., Coyle, D.H., Prasad, G., 2014. Is sensorimotor BCI performance influenced differently by mono, stereo, or 3-D auditory feedback? IEEE Trans. Neural Syst. Rehabil. Eng. 22, 431–440.

Mitzdorf, U., 1985. Current source-density method and application in cat cerebral cortex: investigation of evoked potentials and EEG phenomena. Physiol. Rev. 65, 37–100.

Monti, M.M., Coleman, M.R., Owen, A.M., 2009. Executive functions in the absence of behavior: functional imaging of the minimally conscious state. In: Coma Science: Clinical and Ethical Implications. Progress in Brain Research, vol. 177, Elsevier, Oxford, pp. 1–425.

Monti, M.M., Vanhaudenhuyse, A., Coleman, M.R., Boly, M., Pickard, J.D., Tshibanda, L., Owen, A.M., Laureys, S., 2010. Willful modulation of brain activity in disorders of consciousness. N. Engl. J. Med. 362, 579–589.

Morlet, D., Fischer, C., 2014. MMN and novelty P3 in coma and other altered states of consciousness: a review. Brain Topogr. 27, 467–479.

Mugler, E., Bensch, M., Halder, S., Rosenstiel, W., Birbaumer, N., Kübler, A., 2008. Control of an internet browser using the P300 event-related potential. Int. J. Bioelectromagn. 10, 56–63.

Mulert, C., Jäger, L., Schmitt, R., Bussfeld, P., Pogarell, O., Möller, H.-J., Juckel, G., Hegerl, U., 2004. Integration of fMRI and simultaneous EEG: towards a comprehensive understanding of localization and time-course of brain activity in target detection. Neuroimage 22, 83–94.

Müller-Putz, G.R., Scherer, R., Brauneis, C., Pfurtscheller, G., 2005. Steady-state visual evoked potential (SSVEP)-based communication: impact of harmonic frequency components. J. Neural Eng. 2, 123–130.

Müller-Putz, G.R., Scherer, R., Neuper, C., Pfurtscheller, G., 2006. Steady-state somatosensory evoked potentials: suitable brain signals for brain-computer interfaces? IEEE Trans. Neural Syst. Rehabil. Eng. 14, 30–37.

Multi-Society Task Force on PVS, 1994a. Medical aspects of the persistent vegetative state (first part). N. Engl. J. Med. 330, 1499–1508.

Multi-Society Task Force on PVS, 1994b. Medical aspects of the persistent vegetative state (second part). N. Engl. J. Med. 330, 1572–1579.

Münßinger, J.I., Halder, S., Kleih, S.C., Furdea, A., Raco, V., Hösle, A., Kübler, A., 2010. Brain painting: first evaluation of a new brain-computer interface application with ALS-patients and healthy volunteers. Front. Neurosci. 4, 1–11.

Naci, L., Owen, A.M., 2013. Making every word count for nonresponsive patients. JAMA Neurol. 70, 1–7.

Naci, L., Monti, M.M., Cruse, D., Kübler, A., Sorger, B., Goebel, R., Kotchoubey, B., Owen, A.M., 2012. Brain computer interfaces for communication with non-responsive patients. Ann. Neurol. 72, 312–323.

Naci, L., Cusack, R., Jia, V.Z., Owen, A.M., 2013. The brain's silent messenger: using selective attention to decode human thought for brain-based communication. J. Neurosci. 33, 9385–9393.

Nagai, Y., Critchley, H.D., Featherstone, E., Fenwick, P.B.C., Trimble, M.R., Dolan, R.J., 2004. Brain activity relating to the contingent negative variation: an fMRI investigation. Neuroimage 21, 1232–1241.

Naito, M., Michioka, Y., Ozawa, K., Ito, Y., Kiguchi, M., Kanazawa, T., 2007. A communication means for totally locked-in ALS patients based on changes in cerebral blood volume measured with near-infrared light. IEICE Trans. Inf. Syst. E90-D, 1028–1037.

Nakase-Richardson, R., Yablon, S.A., Sherer, M., Evans, C.C., Nick, T.G., 2008. Serial yes/no reliability after traumatic brain injury: implications regarding the operational criteria for emergence from the minimally conscious state. J. Neurol. Neurosurg. Psychiatry 79, 216–218.

Naseer, N., Hong, K.-S., 2015. fNIRS-based brain-computer interfaces: a review. Front. Hum. Neurosci. 9, 3.

Naseer, N., Hong, M., Hong, K.-S., 2014. Online binary decision decoding using functional near-infrared spectroscopy for the development of brain–computer interface. Exp. Brain Res. 232, 555–564.

Neumann, N., Kübler, A., 2003. Training locked-in patients: a challenge for the use of brain-computer interfaces. IEEE Trans. Neural Syst. Rehabil. Eng. 11, 169–172.

Neumann, N., Hinterberger, T., Kaiser, J., Leins, U., Birbaumer, N., Kubler, A., 2004. Automatic processing of self-regulation of slow cortical potentials: evidence from brain-computer communication in paralysed patients. Clin. Neurophysiol. 115, 628–635.

Neuper, C., Pfurtscheller, G., 2001. Event-related dynamics of cortical rhythms: frequency-specific features and functional correlates. Int. J. Psychophysiol. 43, 41–58.

Neuper, C., Müller, G.R., Kübler, A., Birbaumer, N., Pfurtscheller, G., 2003. Clinical application of an EEG-based brain–computer interface: a case study in a patient with severe motor impairment. Clin. Neurophysiol. 114, 399–409.

Nicolas-Alonso, L.F., Gomez-Gil, J., 2012. Brain computer interfaces, a review. Sensors 12, 1211–1279.

Nijboer, F., Furdea, A., Gunst, I., Mellinger, J., McFarland, D.J., Birbaumer, N., Kübler, A., 2008. An auditory brain-computer interface (BCI). J. Neurosci. Methods 167, 43–50.

Nijboer, F., Birbaumer, N., Kubler, A., 2010. The influence of psychological state and motivation on brain-computer interface performance in patients with amyotrophic lateral sclerosis—a longitudinal study. Front. Neurosci. 4, 55.

Noirhomme, Q., Lesenfants, D., Gomez, F., Soddu, A., Schrouff, J., Garraux, G., Luxen, A., Phillips, C., Laureys, S., 2014. Biased binomial assessment of cross-validated estimation of classification accuracies illustrated in diagnosis predictions. Neuroimage Clin. 4, 687–694.

Noss, R.S., Boles, C.D., Yingling, C.D., 1996. Steady-state analysis of somatosensory evoked potentials. Electroencephalogr. Clin. Neurophysiol. 100, 453–461.

Nunez, P.L., Srinivasan, R., 2006. Electric Fields of the Brain: The Neurophysics of EEG, second ed. Oxford University Press, New York.

Ogawa, S., Lee, T.M., Kay, A.R., Tank, D.W., 1990. Brain magnetic resonance imaging with contrast dependent on blood oxygenation. Proc. Natl. Acad. Sci. U.S.A. 87, 9868–9872.

Ono, T., Kimura, A., Ushiba, J., 2013. Daily training with realistic visual feedback improves reproducibility of event-related desynchronisation following hand motor imagery. Clin. Neurophysiol. 124, 1779–1786.

Ortner, R., Prückl, R., Guger, C., 2013. A tactile P300-based BCI for communication and detection of awareness. Biomed. Tech. 58, 1–2.

Osborne, N.R., Owen, A.M., Fernández-Espejo, D., 2015. The dissociation between command following and communication in disorders of consciousness: an fMRI study in healthy subjects. Front. Hum. Neurosci. 9, 1–9.

Owen, A.M., 2013. Detecting consciousness: a unique role for neuroimaging. Annu. Rev. Psychol. 64, 109–133.

Owen, A.M., Coleman, M.R., 2007. Functional MRI in disorders of consciousness: advantages and limitations. Curr. Opin. Neurol. 20, 632–637.

Owen, A.M., Coleman, M.R., Boly, M., Davis, M.H., Laureys, S., Pickard, J.D., 2006. Detecting awareness in the vegetative state. Science 313, 1402.

Owen, A.M., Coleman, M.R., Boly, M., Davis, M.H., Laureys, S., Jolles, D., Pickard, J.D., 2007. Response to comments on "Detecting awareness in the vegetative state". Science 315, 1221.

Pan, J., Takeshita, T., Morimoto, K., 2000. P300 habituation from auditory single-stimulus and oddball paradigms. Int. J. Psychophysiol. 37, 149–153.

Pan, J., Xie, Q., He, Y., Wang, F., Di, H., Laureys, S., Yu, R., Li, Y., 2014. Detecting awareness in patients with disorders of consciousness using a hybrid brain-computer interface. J. Neural Eng. 11, 056007.

Pantev, C., Roberts, L.E., Elbert, T., Ross, B., Wienbruch, C., 1996. Tonotopic organization of the sources of human auditory steady-state responses. Hear. Res. 101, 62–74.

Perrin, F., García-Larrea, L., Mauguière, F., Bastuji, H., 1999. A differential brain response to the subject's own name persists during sleep. Clin. Neurophysiol. 110, 2153–2164.

Perrin, F., Schnakers, C., Schabus, M., Degueldre, C., Goldman, S., Brédart, S., Faymonville, M.-E., Lamy, M., Moonen, G., Luxen, A., Maquet, P.A., Laureys, S., 2006. Brain response to one's own name in vegetative state, minimally conscious state, and locked-in syndrome. Arch. Neurol. 63, 562–569.

Peterson, A., Naci, L., Weijer, C., Cruse, D., Fernández-Espejo, D., Graham, M., Owen, A.M., 2013. Assessing decision-making capacity in the behaviorally nonresponsive patient with residual covert awareness. AJOB Neurosci. 4, 3–14.

Peterson, A., Cruse, D., Naci, L., Weijer, C., Owen, A.M., 2015. Risk, diagnostic error, and the clinical science of consciousness. Neuroimage Clin. 7, 588–597.

Petkov, C.I., Kang, X., Alho, K., Bertrand, O., Yund, E.W., Woods, D.L., 2004. Attentional modulation of human auditory cortex. Nat. Neurosci. 7, 658–663.

Pfurtscheller, G., 1992. Event-related synchronization (ERS): an electrophysiological correlate of cortical areas at rest. Electroencephalogr. Clin. Neurophysiol. 83, 62–69.

Pfurtscheller, G., Aranibar, A., 1977. Event-related cortical desynchronization detected by power measurements of scalp EEG. Electroencephalogr. Clin. Neurophysiol. 42, 817–826.

Pfurtscheller, G., Guger, C., Müller, G.R., Krausz, G., Neuper, C., 2000a. Brain oscillations control hand orthosis in a tetraplegic. Neurosci. Lett. 292, 211–214.

Pfurtscheller, G., Neuper, C., Krausz, G., 2000b. Functional dissociation of lower and upper frequency mu rhythms in relation to voluntary limb movement. Clin. Neurophysiol. 111, 1873–1879.

Pfurtscheller, G., Müller, G.R., Pfurtscheller, J., Gerner, H.J., Rupp, R., 2003. "Thought"—control of functional electrical stimulation to restore hand grasp in a patient with tetraplegia. Neurosci. Lett. 351, 33–36.

Pfurtscheller, G., Neuper, C., Brunner, C., da Silva, F.L., 2005. Beta rebound after different types of motor imagery in man. Neurosci. Lett. 378, 156–159.

Pichiorri, F., De Vico Fallani, F., Cincotti, F., Babiloni, F., Molinari, M., Kleih, S.C., Neuper, C., Kubler, A., Mattia, D., 2011. Sensorimotor rhythm-based brain-computer interface training: the impact on motor cortical responsiveness. J. Neural Eng. 8, 25020.

Picton, T.W., 1992. The P300 wave of the human event-related potential. J. Clin. Neurophysiol. 9, 456–479.

Picton, T.W., John, M.S., Dimitrijevic, A., Purcell, D., 2003. Human auditory steady-state responses. Int. J. Audiol. 42, 177–219.

Pokorny, C., Klobassa, D.S., Pichler, G., Erlbeck, H., Real, R.G.L., Kübler, A., Lesenfants, D., Habbal, D., Noirhomme, Q., Risetti, M., Mattia, D., Müller-Putz, G.R., 2013. The auditory P300-based single-switch brain-computer interface: paradigm transition from healthy subjects to minimally conscious patients. Artif. Intell. Med. 59, 81–90.

Polich, J., 1986. Normal variation of P300 from auditory stimuli. Electroencephalogr. Clin. Neurophysiol. 65, 236–240.

Polich, J., 1990. P300, probability, and interstimulus interval. Psychophysiology 27, 396–403.

Polich, J., 2007. Updating P300: an integrative theory of P3a and P3b. Clin. Neurophysiol. 118, 2128–2148.

Polich, J., Bondurant, T., 1997. P300 sequence effects, probability, and interstimulus interval. Physiol. Behav. 61, 843–849.

Qin, P., Di, H., Yan, X., Yu, S., Yu, D., Laureys, S., Weng, X., 2008. Mismatch negativity to the patient's own name in chronic disorders of consciousness. Neurosci. Lett. 448, 24–28.

Qin, P., Di, H., Liu, Y., Yu, S., Gong, Q., Duncan, N., Weng, X., Laureys, S., Northoff, G., 2010. Anterior cingulate activity and the self in disorders of consciousness. Hum. Brain Mapp. 31, 1993–2002.

Quian Quiroga, R., Sakowitz, O.W., Basar, E., Schurmann, M., 2001. Wavelet transform in the analysis of the frequency composition of evoked potentials. Brain Res. Brain Res. Protoc. 8, 16–24.

Racine, E., Illes, J., 2007. Emerging ethical challenges in advanced neuroimaging research: review, recommendations and research agenda. J. Empir. Res. Hum. Res. Ethics 2, 1–10.

Ravden, D., Polich, J., 1999. On P300 measurement stability: habituation, intra-trial block variation, and ultradian rhythms. Biol. Psychol. 51, 59–76.

Risetti, M., Formisano, R., Toppi, J., Quitadamo, L.R., Bianchi, L., Astolfi, L., Cincotti, F., Mattia, D., 2013. On ERPs detection in disorders of consciousness rehabilitation. Front. Hum. Neurosci. 7, 775.

Rodriguez Moreno, D., Schiff, N.D., Giacino, J., Kalmar, K., Hirsch, J., 2010. A network approach to assessing cognition in disorders of consciousness. Neurology 75, 1871–1878.

Rohani, D.A., Henning, W.S., Thomsen, C.E., Kjaer, T.W., Puthusserypady, S., Sorensen, H.B.D., 2013. BCI using imaginary movements: the simulator. Comput. Methods Programs Biomed. 111, 300–307.

Rohrbaugh, J.W., Syndulko, K., Lindsley, D.B., 1976. Brain wave components of the contingent negative variation in humans. Science 191, 1055–1057.

Royal College of Physicians Working Group, 2003. The vegetative state: guidance on diagnosis and management. Clin. Med. (Northfield) 3, 249–254.

Scherer, R., Faller, J., Friedrich, E.V.C., Opisso, E., Costa, U., Kübler, A., Müller-Putz, G.R., 2015. Individually adapted imagery improves brain-computer interface performance in end-users with disability. PLoS One 10, e0123727.

Schnakers, C., Perrin, F., Schabus, M., Majerus, S., Ledoux, D., Damas, P., Boly, M., Vanhaudenhuyse, A., Bruno, M., Moonen, G., Laureys, S., 2008b. Voluntary brain processing in disorders of consciousness. Neurology 71, 1614–1620.

Schnakers, C., Perrin, F., Schabus, M., Hustinx, R., Majerus, S., Moonen, G., Boly, M., Vanhaudenhuyse, A., Bruno, M.-A., Laureys, S., 2009a. Detecting consciousness in a total locked-in syndrome: an active event-related paradigm. Neurocase 15, 271–277.

Schnakers, C., Vanhaudenhuyse, A., Giacino, J., Ventura, M., Boly, M., Majerus, S., Moonen, G., Laureys, S., 2009b. Diagnostic accuracy of the vegetative and minimally conscious state: clinical consensus versus standardized neurobehavioral assessment. BMC Neurol. 9, 35.

Schreuder, M., Blankertz, B., Tangermann, M., 2010. A new auditory multi-class brain-computer interface paradigm: spatial hearing as an informative cue. PLoS One 5, e9813.

Sellers, E.W., Donchin, E., 2006. A P300-based brain-computer interface: initial tests by ALS patients. Clin. Neurophysiol. 117, 538–548.

Sellers, E.W., Vaughan, T.M., Wolpaw, J.R., 2010. A brain-computer interface for long-term independent home use. Amyotroph. Lateral Scler. 11, 449–455.

Serruya, M.D., Hatsopoulos, N.G., Paninski, L., Fellows, M.R., Donoghue, J.P., 2002. Instant neural control of a movement signal. Nature 416, 141–142.

Shain, W., Spataro, L., Dilgen, J., Haverstick, K., Retterer, S., Isaacson, M., Saltzman, M., Turner, J.N., 2003. Controlling cellular reactive responses around neural prosthetic devices using peripheral and local intervention strategies. IEEE Trans. Neural Syst. Rehabil. Eng. 11, 186–188.

Shibasaki, H., Hallett, M., 2006. What is the Bereitschaftspotential? Clin. Neurophysiol. 117, 2341–2356.

Silverstein, B.H., Snodgrass, M., Shevrin, H., Kushwaha, R., 2015. P3b, consciousness, and complex unconscious processing. Cortex 73, 216–227.

Simeral, J.D., Kim, S.-P., Black, M.J., Donoghue, J.P., Hochberg, L.R., 2011. Neural control of cursor trajectory and click by a human with tetraplegia 1000 days after implant of an intracortical microelectrode array. J. Neural Eng. 8, 25027.

Sitaram, R., Zhang, H., Guan, C., Thulasidas, M., Hoshi, Y., Ishikawa, A., Shimizu, K., Birbaumer, N., 2007. Temporal classification of multichannel near-infrared spectroscopy signals of motor imagery for developing a brain–computer interface. Neuroimage 34, 1416–1427.

Skrandies, W., 1990. Global field power and topographic similarity. Brain Topogr. 3, 137–141.

Smith, E., Delargy, M., 2005. Locked-in syndrome. Br. Med. J. 330, 3–6.

Snyder, A.Z., 1992. Steady-state vibration evoked potentials: description of technique and characterization of responses. Electroencephalogr. Clin. Neurophysiol. 84, 257–268.

Soltani, M., Knight, R.T., 2000. Neural origins of the P300. Crit. Rev. Neurobiol. 14, 199.

Squires, K.C., Donchin, E., Herning, R.I., McCarthy, G., 1977. On the influence of task relevance and stimulus probability on event-related-potential components. Electroencephalogr. Clin. Neurophysiol. 42, 1–14.

Srinivasan, R., 2012. Acquiring signals from outside the brain. In: Wolpaw, J.R., Wolpaw, E.W. (Eds.), Brain-Computer Interfaces: Principles and Practice. Oxford University Press, New York, pp. 105–122.

Staffen, W., Kronbichler, M., Aichhorn, M., Mair, A., Ladurner, G., 2006. Selective brain activity in response to one's own name in the persistent vegetative state. J. Neurol. Neurosurg. Psychiatry 77, 1383–1384.

Stender, J., Gosseries, O., Bruno, M.-A., Charland-Verville, V., Vanhaudenhuyse, A., Demertzi, A., Chatelle, C., Thonnard, M., Thibaut, A., Heine, L., Soddu, A., Boly, M., Schnakers, C., Gjedde, A., Laureys, S., 2014. Diagnostic precision of PET imaging and functional MRI in disorders of consciousness: a clinical validation study. Lancet 384, 514–522.

Sutter, E.E., 1992. The brain response interface: communication through visually-induced electrical brain responses. J. Microcomput. Appl. 15, 31–45.

Synek, V.M., 1988. Prognostically important EEG coma patterns in diffuse anoxic and traumatic encephalopathies in adults. J. Clin. Neurophysiol. 5, 161–174.

Takemi, M., Masakado, Y., Liu, M., Ushiba, J., 2013. Event-related desynchronization reflects downregulation of intracortical inhibition in human primary motor cortex. J. Neurophysiol. 110, 1158–1166.

Taylor, D.M., Tillery, S.I.H., Schwartz, A.B., 2002. Direct cortical control of 3D neuroprosthetic devices. Science 296, 1829–1832.

Tobimatsu, S., Zhang, Y.M., Kato, M., 1999. Steady-state vibration somatosensory evoked potentials: physiological characteristics and tuning function. Clin. Neurophysiol. 110, 1953–1958.

Toronov, V.Y., Zhang, X., Webb, A.G., 2007. NIH A spatial and temporal comparison of hemodynamic signals measured using optical and functional magnetic resonance imaging during activation in the human primary visual cortex. Neuroimage 34, 1136–1148.

Townsend, G., LaPallo, B.K., Boulay, C.B., Krusienski, D.J., Frye, G.E., Hauser, C.K., Schwartz, N.E., Vaughan, T.M., Wolpaw, J.R., Sellers, E.W., 2010. A novel P300-based brain–computer interface stimulus presentation paradigm: moving beyond rows and columns. Clin. Neurophysiol. 121, 1109–1120.

Treder, M.S., Blankertz, B., 2010. (C)overt attention and visual speller design in an ERP-based brain-computer interface. Behav. Brain Funct. 6, 28.

van der Waal, M., Severens, M., Geuze, J., Desain, P., 2012. Introducing the tactile speller: an ERP-based brain-computer interface for communication. J. Neural Eng. 9, 045002.

Vanhatalo, S., Palva, J.M., Holmes, M.D., Miller, J.W., Voipio, J., Kaila, K., 2004. Infraslow oscillations modulate excitability and interictal epileptic activity in the human cortex during sleep. Proc. Natl. Acad. Sci. U.S.A. 101, 5053–5057.

Vialatte, F.-B., Maurice, M., Dauwels, J., Cichocki, A., 2010. Steady-state visually evoked potentials: focus on essential paradigms and future perspectives. Prog. Neurobiol. 90, 418–438.

Vidal, J.J., 1977. Real-time detection of brain events in EEG. In: Proceedings of the IEEE.

Villringer, A., Planck, J., Hock, C., Schleinkofer, L., Dirnagl, U., 1993. Near infrared spectroscopy (NIRS): a new tool to study hemodynamic changes during activation of brain function in human adults. Neurosci. Lett. 154, 101–104.

Vuckovic, A., Osuagwu, B.A., 2013. Using a motor imagery questionnaire to estimate the performance of a brain-computer interface based on object oriented motor imagery. Clin. Neurophysiol. 124, 1586–1595.

Walter, W.G., Cooper, R., Aldridge, V.J., McCallum, W.C., Winter, A.L., 1964. Contingent negative variation: an electric sign of sensori-motor association and expectancy in the human brain. Nature 203, 380–384.

Wessberg, J., Stambaugh, C.R., Kralik, J.D., Beck, P.D., Laubach, M., Chapin, J.K., Kim, J., Biggs, S.J., Srinivasan, M.A., Nicolelis, M.A., 2000. Real-time prediction of hand trajectory by ensembles of cortical neurons in primates. Nature 408, 361–365.

Whyte, J., Nordenbo, A.M., Kalmar, K., Merges, B., Bagiella, E., Chang, H., Yablon, S., Cho, S., Hammond, F., Khademi, A., Giacino, J., 2013. Medical complications during inpatient rehabilitation among patients with traumatic disorders of consciousness. Arch. Phys. Med. Rehabil. 94, 1877–1883.

Williams, D., Tijssen, M., Van Bruggen, G., Bosch, A., Insola, A., Di Lazzaro, V., Mazzone, P., Oliviero, A., Quartarone, A., Speelman, H., Brown, P., 2002. Dopamine-dependent changes in the functional connectivity between basal ganglia and cerebral cortex in humans. Brain 125, 1558–1569.

Williams, L.M., Simms, E., Clark, C.R., Paul, R.H., Rowe, D., Gordon, E., 2005. The test-retest reliability of a standardized neurocognitive and neurophysiological test battery: "Neuromarker" Int. J. Neurosci. 115, 1605–1630.

Woldorff, M.G., 1993. Distortion of ERP averages due to overlap from temporally adjacent ERPs: analysis and correction. Psychophysiology 30, 98–119.

Wolpaw, J.R., McFarland, D.J., 2004. Control of a two-dimensional movement signal by a noninvasive brain-computer interface in humans. Proc. Natl. Acad. Sci. U.S.A. 101, 17849–17854.

Wood, N., Cowan, N., 1995. The cocktail party phenomenon revisited: how frequent are attention shifts to one's name in an irrelevant auditory channel? J. Exp. Psychol. Learn. Mem. Cogn. 21, 255–260.

Yamaguchi, S., Knight, R.T., 1991. Anterior and posterior association cortex contributions to the somatosensory P300. J. Neurosci. 11, 2039–2054.

Yuan, H., He, B., 2014. Brain-computer interfaces using sensorimotor rhythms: current state and future perspectives. IEEE Trans. Biomed. Eng. 61, 1425–1435.

Yuan, H., Liu, T., Szarkowski, R., Rios, C., Ashe, J., He, B., 2010a. Negative covariation between task-related responses in alpha/beta-band activity and BOLD in human sensorimotor cortex: an EEG and fMRI study of motor imagery and movements. Neuroimage 49, 2596–2606.

Yuan, H., Perdoni, C., He, B., 2010b. Relationship between speed and EEG activity during imagined and executed hand movements. J. Neural Eng. 7, 26001.

Yuan, H., Perdoni, C., Yang, L., He, B., 2011. Differential electrophysiological coupling for positive and negative BOLD responses during unilateral hand movements. J. Neurosci. 31, 9585–9593.

Zandbergen, E.G., de Haan, R.J., Stoutenbeek, C.P., Koelman, J.H., Hijdra, A., 1998. Systematic review of early prediction of poor outcome in anoxic-ischaemic coma. Lancet 352, 1808–1812.

Zhang, Q., Damian, M.F., Yang, Y., 2007. Electrophysiological estimates of the time course of tonal and orthographic encoding in Chinese speech production. Brain Res. 1184, 234–244.

Non-Medical Applications

IV

A passive brain–computer interface application for the mental workload assessment on professional air traffic controllers during realistic air traffic control tasks

10

P. Aricò[*,†,‡,2], **G. Borghini**[*,†,‡,2], **G. Di Flumeri**[*,†,‡,2], **A. Colosimo**[*],
S. Pozzi[§], **F. Babiloni**[*,†,1]

University of Rome "Sapienza", Rome, Italy
†*BrainSigns srl, Rome, Italy*
‡*Neuroelectrical Imaging and BCI Lab, IRCCS Fondazione Santa Lucia, Rome, Italy*
§*DeepBlue srl, Rome, Italy*
1*Corresponding author: Tel.: +39-3287697914, e-mail address: fabio.babiloni@uniroma1.it*

Abstract

In the last decades, it has been a fast-growing concept in the neuroscience field. The *passive brain–computer interface* (p-BCI) systems allow to improve the *human–machine interaction* (HMI) in operational environments, by using the covert brain activity (eg, mental workload) of the operator. However, p-BCI technology could suffer from some practical issues when used outside the laboratories. In particular, one of the most important limitations is the necessity to recalibrate the p-BCI system each time before its use, to avoid a significant reduction of its reliability in the detection of the considered mental states. The objective of the proposed study was to provide an example of p-BCIs used to evaluate the users' mental workload in a real operational environment. For this purpose, through the facilities provided by the *École Nationale de l'Aviation Civile* of Toulouse (France), the cerebral activity of 12 professional *air traffic control officers* (ATCOs) has been recorded while performing high realistic air traffic management scenarios. By the analysis of the ATCOs' brain activity (*electroencephalographic signal—EEG*) and the subjective workload perception (*instantaneous self-assessment*) provided by both the examined ATCOs and external air traffic control experts,

---

[2]These authors contributed equally to this work.

it has been possible to estimate and evaluate the variation of the mental workload under which the controllers were operating. The results showed (i) a high significant correlation between the neurophysiological and the subjective workload assessment, and (ii) a high reliability over time (up to a month) of the proposed algorithm that was also able to maintain high discrimination accuracies by using a low number of EEG electrodes (~3 EEG channels). In conclusion, the proposed methodology demonstrated the suitability of p-BCI systems in operational environments and the advantages of the neurophysiological measures with respect to the subjective ones.

Keywords

Passive brain–computer interface, Augmented cognition, Air traffic management, Electroencephalogram, Mental workload, Automatic-stop stepwise linear discriminant analysis, Stepwise linear discriminant analysis, Instantaneous self-assessment, Human factor, Neuroergonomic

1 INTRODUCTION

In some operational environments, the safety of the people relies on the attentional and cognitive efforts of the operator(s). In such challenging contexts, human errors could have serious and dramatic consequences. For example, in the transportations domain the safety of the passengers depends on the performance of the pilot(s), of the (eg, air, train, vessel) traffic controller(s), or of the driver(s) of private vehicles.

In general, human error has consistently been identified as one of the main factors in workplaces accidents. In particular, it has been estimated that up to 90% of accidents list human errors as the principal cause (Feyer and Williamson, 1998).

Human error is an extremely common phenomenon: people, regardless of abilities, skills, and expertise, make errors daily. It can be defined as the execution of an incorrect or inappropriate action, or a failure to perform a particular action. The main causes of human errors have to be sought within the internal or psychological factors of the operator (Reason, 2000). In fact, errors could arise from aberrant mental processes, such as inattention, poor motivation, loss of vigilance, mental overload, and fatigue, that negatively affect the user's performance. For example, cognitive psychology literature demonstrated that the mental workload has an "inverted U-shape" relationship with performance. In other words, some levels of mental workload may help the user to reach high-performance level (Calabrese, 2008), since it stimulates positively the user and it keeps him/her awake with high attention level. On the contrary, a period of mental inactivity and "understimulation" can cause a monotonous and boring state (underload), a low level of vigilance and attention, with low cognitive resources demand. Additionally, an operative condition characterized by demanding multitasks can lead the user to an overload condition and to a likely occurrence of errors (Kirsh, 2000). It is interesting to note that all the mentioned causes produced a reduction of the operator's performance and the concomitant change of the spectral properties of his/her cerebral signals.

In this regard, the *augmented cognition* research field aims at developing systems to avoid performance degradation by adapting the user's interface and reducing the task demand/complexity, or by intervening directly on the system (Fuchs et al., 2007). Over the past two decades, researchers in the field of augmented cognition developed novel technologies to both monitor and enhance human cognition and performance. Most of those works were based on research findings coming from cognitive science and cognitive neuroscience (Decades, 2008). On the basis of such findings and technological improvements in measuring human biosignals, it has been possible to evaluate operators' mental states unobtrusively and in realistic contexts. The neurophysiological indexes have then been used as inputs for the interface the operator was interacting with. Such application is usually named *passive brain–computer interface* (p-BCI).

1.1 PASSIVE BRAIN–COMPUTER INTERFACE

In its classical assumption, a BCI is "a communication system in which messages or commands do not pass through the brain normal output pathways of peripheral nerves and muscles" (Wolpaw et al., 2002). More recently, Wolpaw and Wolpaw (2012) defined a BCI as "a system that measures central nervous system (CNS) activity and converts it into artificial output that replaces, restores, enhances, supplements, or improves natural CNS output and thereby changes the ongoing interactions between the CNS and its external or internal environment."

In the BCI community, the possibility of using the BCI systems in different contexts for communication and system control (Allison and Pineda, 2003; Aloise et al., 2010, 2013; Blankertz et al., 2010; Riccio et al., 2015; Schettini et al., 2015), developing applications in realistic and operational environments, is not just a theory but something very close to real applications (Blankertz et al., 2010; Müller et al., 2008; Zander et al., 2009). In fact, in the classic BCI applications the user modulates voluntarily its brain activity to interact with the system. In the p-BCI implementation, the system itself recognizes the spontaneous brain activity of the user related to the considered mental state (eg, emotional state, workload, attention levels) and uses such information to improve and modulate the interaction between the operator and the system.

Systems based on passive BCI technology can provide objective information about covert aspects of the user's cognitive state, since conventional methods, such as behavioral measures, could only detect such mental states with weak reliability (Zander and Jatzev, 2012). The information extracted by the p-BCIs is then employed to improve man–machine interactions and to achieve potentially novel types of skills. Anyhow, the quantification of mental states by using this technology is far from trivial. In fact, it requires a combination of knowledge in different fields (Brouwer et al., 2015), such as neurophysiology (to acquire and manage biosignals), experimental psychology (to find out the right way to assess mental states), machine learning (to develop innovative classification techniques), and human factor (to develop real applications).

Neuroimaging methods and cognitive neuroscience have steadily improved their technical sophistication and breadth of application over the past decade, and there has been growing interest in their use to examine the neural circuits supporting complex tasks representative of perception, cognition, and action as they occur in operational settings. At the same time, many fields in the biological sciences, including neuroscience, are being challenged to demonstrate their relevance to practical real-world problems (Parasuraman, 2003).

In this context, the most studied mental state has been the mental workload due to its strong relationship with the increasing or degrading of user's performance. In fact, mental workload is a complex construct that is assumed to be reflective of an individual's level of attentional engagement and mental effort (Wickens, 1984). Measurement of mental workload essentially represents the quantification of mental activity resulting from performance of a task or set of tasks. As mentioned previously, several empirical investigations have suggested that performance declines at either extreme of the workload demand profile (ie, when event rates are excessively high or extremely low). Consequently, it is important to preserve a proper level of the user's mental workload, avoiding under- or overload state, with the aim to maintain optimal levels of performance and reducing the risk of errors (Borghini et al., 2014a,b, 2015a). For these reasons, the mental workload is an important and central construct in ergonomics and human factor researches.

1.2 MENTAL WORKLOAD: THE MEAN AND ITS NEUROPHYSIOLOGICAL MEASUREMENTS

Various mental workload definitions have been given during the last decades:

- "Mental workload refers to the portion of operator information processing capacity or resources that is actually required to meet system demands" (Eggemeier et al., 1991).
- "Workload is not an inherent property, but rather it emerges from the interaction between the requirements of a task, the circumstances under which it is performed, and the skills, behaviors, and perceptions of the operator" (Hart and Staveland, 1988).
- "Mental workload is a hypothetical construct that describes the extent to which the cognitive resources required to perform a task have been actively engaged by the operator" (Gopher and Donchin, 1986).
- The reason to specify and evaluate the mental workload is to quantify the mental cost involved during task performance "in order to predict operator and system performance" (Cain, 2007).

These definitions show that mental workload may not be a unitary concept because it is the result of different interacting aspects. In fact, several mental processes, such as alertness, vigilance, mental effort, attention, mental fatigue, drowsiness, and so on, can be involved in the meanwhile of a task execution, and they could be affected in each moment by specific task demands.

In general, mental workload theory assumes that: (a) people have a limited cognitive and attentional capacity, (b) different tasks will require different amounts of processing resources, and (c) two individuals might be able to perform a given task equally well, but differently in terms of brain activation (Baldwin, 2003).

Mental workload assessment techniques must be sensitive to cognitive fluctuations in task demands without intruding on primary task performance (O'Donnell and Eggemeier, 1986). In this regard, measuring the mental workload by using subjective measures during the execution of the main task could negatively affect the user's performances. Additionally, it has been widely demonstrated that neurophysiological measurements transcend both behavioral and subjective measures in discriminating cognitive demand fluctuations (Di Flumeri et al., 2015; Mühl et al., 2014; Wierwille and Eggemeier, 1993).

Thus, the online neurophysiological measurements of the mental workload could become very important not only as monitoring techniques but mainly as support tools to the user during operative activities. In fact, as the changes in cognitive activity can be measured in real time, it should also be possible to manipulate the task demand in order to help the user in maintaining optimal levels of mental workload during the work. In other words, the neurophysiological workload assessment could be used to realize p-BCI applications in real operational environments.

Many neurophysiological measures have been used for the mental workload assessment, including *electroencephalography* (EEG), *functional near-infrared* (fNIR) imaging, *functional magnetic resonance imaging* (fMRI), and *magnetoencephalography* (MEG), and other types of biosignals such as *electrocardiography* (ECG), *electrooculography* (EOG), and *galvanic skin response* (GSR) (Borghini et al., 2014b; Ramnani and Owen, 2004; Toppi et al., 2016; Wood and Grafman, 2003). The size, weight, and power constraints outlined above limit the types of neurofeedback that can be used to realize p-BCI applications. For example, fMRI (Cabeza and Nyberg, 2000) and MEG techniques require room-size equipment; thus they would not be portable. EOG, ECG, and GSR activities highlighted correlations with some mental states (stress, mental fatigue, drowsiness), but they were demonstrated to be useful only in combination with other neuroimaging techniques directly linked to the CNS, ie, the brain (Borghini et al., 2014b, 2015b; Ryu and Myung, 2005). Consequently, the EEG and fNIR are the most likely candidates that can be straightforwardly employed to realize passive BCI applications usable in operational environments.

Regarding the EEG measurements, most part of the studies showed that the brain electrical activities mainly considered for the mental workload analysis are the theta and alpha brain rhythms typically gathered from the *prefrontal cortex* (PFC) and the *posterior parietal cortex* (PPC) regions. Previous studies demonstrated as the EEG theta rhythm over the PFC present a positive correlation with the mental workload (Gevins and Smith, 2003; Smit et al., 2005). Moreover, published literature stressed the inverse correlation between the EEG power in the alpha frequency band over the

PPC and the mental workload (Brookings et al., 1996; Gevins et al., 1997; Jaušovec and Jaušovec, 2012; Klimesch et al., 1997; Venables and Fairclough, 2009). Only few studies have reported significant results about the modulation of the EEG power in other frequency bands, ie, the delta, beta, and gamma (Borghini et al., 2014b; Gevins et al., 1997; Smith and Gevins, 2005). More specifically, most of the studies are focalized on the EEG power modulation occurring in theta (4–8 Hz) and alpha (8–12 Hz) frequency bands, usually associated with cognitive processes such as working memory and attention, typically involved in mental workload. Onton et al. (2005) reported that the frontal midline theta rhythm increases with memory load, confirming previous results about the correlation between the frontal theta EEG activity and mental effort (Gevins et al., 1997; Smit et al., 2005). Mental workload is also known to suppress EEG alpha rhythm and to increase theta rhythm during activity of information encoding and retrieval (Klimesch, 1999; Klimesch et al., 1997; Vecchiato et al., 2014).

According to the idea that the higher the mental workload level is, the greater the brain blood oxygenation will be, the functional near-infrared spectroscopy (fNIRs) has been demonstrated to be another reliable mental workload measurement technique (Cui et al., 2011; Derosière et al, 2013). fNIRs is safe, highly portable, user-friendly, and relatively inexpensive, with rapid application times and near-zero run-time costs, so it could be a potential portable system for measuring mental workload in realistic settings. The most common fNIR system uses infrared light introduced in the scalp to measure changes in blood oxygenation. Oxyhemoglobin (HbO_2) converts into deoxyhemoglobin (HbR) during neural activity, that is, the cerebral hemodynamic response. This phenomenon is called *blood-oxygen-level-dependent* (BOLD) signal. fNIRs has been shown to compare favorably with other functional imaging methods (Huppert et al., 2006) and demonstrates solid test–retest reliability for task-specific brain activation (Herff et al., 2013; Plichta et al., 2006). Thus, the primary hypothesis was that blood oxygenation in the PFC, as assessed by fNIR, would rise with increasing task load and would demonstrate a positive correlation with the mental workload. In fact, Izzetoglu et al. (2004) indicated clearly that the rate of changes in blood oxygenation was significantly sensitive to task load variations.

1.3 AN EXAMPLE OF MENTAL WORKLOAD MEASURE IN REALISTIC SETTINGS: THE AIR TRAFFIC MANAGEMENT CASE

In the last 20 years, it has been widely documented that 70% of civil aviation accidents were linked with human errors (Bellenkes, 2007). Recently, the Aviation Safety Network reported 37 accidents with 564 casualties. Moreover, air traffic is growing exponentially, and it has been predicted to double in 2020 (Flight Safety Foundation). It is easy to understand how this factor would increase the work difficulty of *air traffic control officers* (ATCOs). In fact, they have to perform a variety of tasks, including monitoring air traffic, anticipating loss of separation between aircraft, and intervening to resolve conflicts and minimize disruption to air traffic flow (for an extensive compilation of the tasks and goals of en route control, see Rodgers and Drechsler, 1993). In this domain, the ATCO's behavior could already be measured through several human factor tools, such as the explicit measurement of errors committed during the execution of the task, or by using questionnaires related to the subjective workload perception such as the *instantaneous self-assessment* (ISA, Kirwan et al., 2001), *NASA—task load index* (Hart and Staveland, 1988), or the *subjective workload assessment technique* (Reid and Nygren, 1988). Because of their inherently subjective nature, none of such questionnaires allows to have an objective and reliable measure of the actual cognitive demand for the operator in a real environment. All the described questionnaires have pros and cons, but there is not a generally accepted standard (Rubio et al., 2004). Therefore, the need of an objective measure became fundamental for reliable workload evaluations.

Several researches in the air traffic management (ATM) domain treated the neurophysiological measurements of ATCOs' mental workload in realistic settings with the aim of developing *human–machine interaction* (HMI) systems, by using both EEG and fNIRs techniques. In the following examples, it has been discussed how each technique was able to provide reliable estimations of mental workload. The propensity in using EEG or fNIRs techniques in such kind of HMI applications has not been clarified yet. In fact, there are several factors to take into account in real operational scenarios. For example, both EEG and *fast optical signal* (FOS)-based fNIR have similar bandwidth and sample rate requirements, as the FOS appears to directly reflect aggregated neural spike activity in real time and can be used as a high-bandwidth signal akin to EEG (Medvedev et al., 2008). However, EEG and fNIRs systems have different physical interfaces, sizes, weights, and power budgets, thus different wearability and usability in real operational contexts. Specifically, the physical interface merits scrutiny as it is nontrivial to maintain a good contact between the sensors (ie, electrodes or optodes) and the brain scalp in freely moving tasks. It is worth noticing that fNIRs is not affected by motion artifacts and does not require both scalp abrasion and conductive gel. In addition, there is not the necessity to wear a cap but only a headband. Furthermore, unlike EEG, fNIRs recordings are not affected by electroculographic and environmental electrical noise, and less sensitive to facial muscular activity, which are undoubtedly ubiquitous in human–computer interactions. Thus, fNIR technology could appear more suitable in realistic environments (Durantin et al., 2014; Goldberg et al., 2011; Izzetoglu et al., 2004; Owen et al., 2005).

However, in a recent study, Harrison et al. (2014) reported how the BOLD signal showed a lower resolution than the subjective measures (ISA; Kirwan et al., 2001) to evaluate the mental workload of ATCOs involved in the experiment. In particular, while the task was becoming more difficult, the subjective measure was still increasing, and the BOLD signal (neurophysiological index) reached its maximum, lingering on this value. Furthermore, the BOLD signal, used as workload index, was shown to be not reliable over time since the workload measurements performed in different days were significantly different and in discordance with the subjective measures.

In addition, since the presence of hair may impact on both photon absorption (Murkin and Arango, 2009) and the coupling of the probes with the underlying scalp, the fNIRs technique is very reliable only on those unhairy brain areas, like the PFC.

As quoted earlier, the parietal brain sites also play a key role in the mental workload evaluation, and Derosière et al. (2013) pointed out how some fNIRs-measured hemodynamic variables were relatively insensitive to certain changes in mental workload and attentional states.

Due to its higher temporal resolution and usability, in comparison with the fNIRs technique, the EEG technique overcomes such kind of issues. In addition, there are several studies in ATM domain that highlighted the high reliability of EEG-based mental workload indexes (W_{EEG}; Brookings et al., 1996). The results showed that the effects of the task demand were evident on the EEG rhythms variations. EEG power spectra increased in the theta band, while significantly decreased in the alpha band as the task difficulty increased, over central, parietal, frontal, and temporal brain sites. In a recent study, Shou et al. (2012) evaluated the mental workload during an air traffic control (ATC) experiment using a new *time–frequency-independent component analysis* (tfICA) method for the analysis of the EEG signal. They found that "the frontal theta EEG activity was a sensitive and reliable metric to assess workload and time-on-task effect during an ATC task at the resolution of minute(s)." In other recent studies involving professional and trainees ATCOs (Aricò et al., 2014b, 2015c; Di Flumeri et al., 2015), it was demonstrated how it was possible to compute an EEG-based workload index able to significantly discriminate the workload demands of the ATM task by using machine-learning techniques and frontal–parietal brain features. In those studies, the ATM tasks were developed with a continuously varying difficulty levels in order to ensure realistic ATC conditions, ie, starting form an easy level, then increasing up to a hard one and finishing with an easy one again. The EEG-based mental workload indices showed to be directly and significantly correlated with the actual mental demand experienced by the ATCOs during the entire task.

The same EEG-based workload index was also used to evaluate and compare the impact of different avionic technologies on the mental workload of professional helicopter pilots (Borghini et al., 2015b). Furthermore, the machine-learning techniques have been successfully used in other real environments for the evaluation of mental states (Müller et al., 2008) and mental workload (Berka et al., 2004, 2007). Another interesting application of the neurophysiological workload evaluation was proposed by Borghini et al. (2014a), where a neuroelectrical metric was defined and used for the training assessment of subjects while learning to execute correctly a new task.

Even if the main limitation of the EEG is its wearability, technology improvements (Liao et al., 2012) have being developed and tested in terms of dry electrodes (no gel and impedances adaptation issues), comfort, ergonomic, and wireless communications (no cables between EEG sensors and the recording system).

In conclusion, the EEG technique seems to be the appropriate solution to evaluate the mental workload in realistic and operational settings, and to be integrated in passive BCI systems. Such systems will support the operator during his/her working activity in order to improve the works wellness and, most of all, the safety standards of the whole environment.

1.4 PRESENT STUDY

EEG-based p-BCI system potentially appears as the best solution for the user's mental workload estimation in real operational environments. However, this technology could suffer from some practical issues, such as the necessity to be recalibrated each time before its use, reduction of reliability over time (Christensen et al., 2012; Pollock et al., 1991), and intrusiveness due to the high number of EEG electrodes.

The objective of the proposed study was to provide an example of passive BCI-based methodology to evaluate the users' mental workload in operational environment, and to overcome the issues described previously. For such purposes, the brain activity was recorded on 12 professional ATCOs while performing high realistic ATM scenarios. From the EEG signals, a W_{EEG} was computed by means of the *automatic-stop stepwise linear discriminant analysis* (asSWLDA) (Aricò et al., 2015a), a modified version of the standard SWLDA.

To summarize, the proposed study has been organized in order to investigate two important key issues to use neurophysiological measurements in operational environments: the overtime reliability of the measure and the accuracy of the methodology in comparison with the standard (ie, subjective) workload measures.

2 MATERIALS AND METHODS
2.1 EXPERIMENTAL PROTOCOL
2.1.1 Subjects

Twelve professional (40.41 ± 5.54 years old) ATCOs from the *École Nationale de l'Aviation Civile* (ENAC) of Toulouse (France) have been involved in this study. They were selected in order to have a homogeneous experimental group in terms of age and expertise. The ENAC represents one of the most important training schools for pilots and ATCOs in the world. The experimental procedures involving human subjects described in this chapter were approved by the Institutional Review Board.

2.1.2 Experimental task

ATCOs have been asked to perform a series of ATM scenarios in realistic settings. Such particular settings, developed and hosted at ENAC (Fig. 1A), consisted in a functional simulated ATM environment with a 30″ screen (RADAR screen) to display radar image and a 21″ screen (ATM interface) to interact with the radar image (zoom, move, clearances, and information). The experiments have also been attended by two pseudopilots (Fig. 1B) who have interacted with the ATCOs with the aim to simulate real-flight communications.

The complexity of the task could be modulated according to how many aircraft the ATCO had to control the number and type of clearances required over the time and the number/trajectory of other interfering flights. The experiments have taken place in two different sessions, a month on, named hereafter as *Day 1* and *Day 30*.

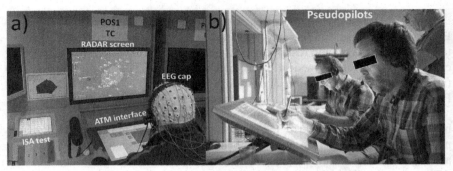

FIG. 1

(A) The ENAC simulator platform, composed of two screens, a 30″ (RADAR) screen to display radar image and a 21″ screen to interact with the radar image (ATM interface). On the little screen on the *left bottom*, the ISA test was proposed every 3 min. (B) Pseudopilots have interacted with the ATCOs with the aim to simulate real-flight communications.

For each session, ATCOs have been asked to perform a different 45-min ATM scenario enclosing three different levels of complexity (15 min for each complexity condition) associated to three different mental workload demands (EASY, MEDIUM, and HARD). For each scenario, the presentation of the difficulty conditions has been randomized. In addition, although the two ATM scenarios were different, in order to avoid any habituation or expectation effect, they have been designed identically in terms of complexity within the same difficulty levels (ie, for instance EASY Day 1 vs EASY Day 30), to make them comparable between sessions, and to avoid any bias in the results. Such scenarios have been validated and tested by a *subject-matter expert* (SME) from ENAC before the experiments.

It has to be stressed that air traffic shape was not constant, and the transitions between the different difficulty levels were smoothly organized, in order to have ATM scenarios as much realistic as possible. Fig. 2 shows a representative scenario's complexity shape.

2.1.3 Collected data related to the mental workload of ATCOs
2.1.3.1 Neurophysiological data
For each ATCO, scalp EEG signals have been recorded by the digital monitoring *BEmicro* system (EBNeuro system) with a sampling frequency of 256 (Hz) by 8 Ag/AgCl passive wet electrodes (Fz, F3, F4, AF3, AF4, Pz, P3, and P4) referenced to both the earlobes and grounded to the Cz electrode, according to the 10–20 standard (Jurcak et al., 2007). In addition, the vertical EOG signal has been recorded concurrently with the EEG, and with the same sampling frequency (256 Hz), by a bipolar channel over the left eye, in order to collect the eyes blink of the subjects during the execution of the task.

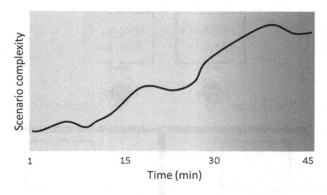

FIG. 2

Representative scenario's complexity shape.

2.1.3.2 Subjective workload assessment (self-assessment)

Simultaneously to the execution of the ATM task, ATCOs have been asked to fill the ISA. In particular, the ISA (Kirwan et al., 2001) is a technique that has been developed to provide immediate subjective ratings of workload demands, from 1 (very easy) to 5 (very difficult), during the execution of a task. The ISA technique has provided a profile of the operator's workload perception throughout the ATM scenarios. The ISA test scale has been presented to the ATCOs every 3 min in the form of a color-coded keypad on a screen placed on the left of the main monitor (Fig. 1A). The keypad flashed and sounded when the workload rating was required, and the participants simply pushed the button related to their workload perception.

2.1.3.3 Subjective Workload Assessment (SME Assessment)

ATC experts (SMEs) seated behind the ATCO, and they have been asked to provide independent rate, from 1 to 5 according to the ISA scale, of the ATCO's mental workload (by filling the paper version of the ISA), in order to have an extra mental workload evaluation experienced by the ATCOs. In particular, SMEs have been asked to express their continuous judgment depending on the ongoing overall performance of the examined ATCO. Such judgment took into account the quality and time of the indications/information provided to the pilots, separation planning strategy, response responsiveness, and general management of the air traffic condition.

ISA scores provided by experimental subjects and by the SMEs are named hereafter, respectively, *SELF-ISA* and *SME-ISA*.

2.1.4 People involved and study organization

The experimental setting consisted in two ATC positions (Fig. 3), two external ATC experts (SMEs), two biosignal measurements experts, and two pseudopilots.

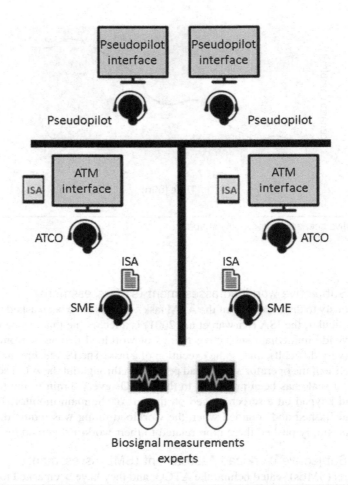

FIG. 3

Experimental settings, involving two experimental subjects (ATCOs), two external ATC Experts (SMEs), two biosignal measurement experts, and two pseudopilots at the same time.

The experimental study has been organized in two main phases:

– *Reliability over time of the neurophysiological workload measure.* The first phase of the study had the aim to test the reliability over time (1 month) of the neurophysiological workload measure, by using two different models (see Section 2.2.2). Five of the 12 mentioned ATCOs gave their availability to take part in both the experimental sessions (Day 1 and Day 30), while the remaining controllers attended only the last experimental session (Day 30).

– *Comparison between neurophysiological and subjective workload assessment.* The second phase of the study had the aim to test the effectiveness of the neurophysiological workload measure in comparison with the subjective assessment (ISA and SME workload scores). To investigate this point, only the last experimental session (Day 30) has been used, where all the ATOCs participated to the experiment (12 professional ATCOs in total).

2.2 NEUROPHYSIOLOGICAL DATA ANALYSIS

2.2.1 *EEG signal processing*

For each session (Day 1 and Day 30) and for each difficulty level (EASY, MEDIUM, and HARD), the biosignal data set (EEG and EOG signals) has been segmented in five consecutive parts (named hereafter as "runs") of 3 min each, in order to have five EASY runs (E1, E2, E3, E4, and E5), five MEDIUM runs (M1, M2, M3, M4, and M5), and five HARD runs (H1, H2, H3, H4, and H5), and to have the same time resolution of the ISA scores provided by both the ATCOs and the SMEs (SELF-ISA and SME-ISA), and therefore allowing a more direct comparison between all the collected measures.

The recorded EEG signal has been firstly band-pass filtered with a fourth-order Butterworth filter (low-pass filter cutoff frequency: 30 (Hz), high-pass filter cutoff frequency: 1 (Hz)). The EOG signal, band-pass filtered too with a fourth-order Butterworth filter (low-pass filter cutoff frequency: 7 (Hz), high-pass filter cutoff frequency: 1 (Hz)), has then been used to remove eyes-blink contributions from each epoch of the EEG signal, by using the Gratton et al. (1983) algorithm available on the EEGLab toolbox (Delorme and Makeig, 2004). This last step has been performed because the eyes-blink contribution could affect the frequency bands correlated to the mental workload, in particular the theta EEG band. For other sources of artifacts (ie, ATC-operators normally communicate verbally and perform several movements during their operational activity), specific procedures of the EEGLAB toolbox have been used (Delorme and Makeig, 2004). First, the EEG signal has been segmented into epochs of 2 s (*Epoch length*), shifted of 0.125 s (*Shift*). This windowing have been chosen with the compromise to have both a high number of observations (see Eq. 1), in comparison with the number of variables (see Eq. 2) and to respect the condition of stationarity of the EEG signal (Elul, 1969). In fact, this is a necessary hypothesis in order to proceed with the spectral analysis of the signal. The EEG epochs where the signal amplitude exceeds ± 100 μV (*threshold criteria*) have been marked as "artifact." Then, each EEG epoch has been interpolated in order to check the slope of the trend within the considered epoch (*trend estimation*). If such slope was higher than 3, the considered epoch was marked as "artifact." The last artifact check has been based on the EEG *sample-to-sample* difference. If such difference, in terms of amplitude, was higher than 25 μV, it meant that an abrupt variation (no-physiological) happened, and the EEG epoch has been marked as "artifact." All the previous values have been chosen following the guidelines reported in Delorme and Makeig (2004). At the end, the EEG epochs marked as "artifact" have been removed from the EEG data set with the aim to have a clean EEG signal from which estimate the brain parameters for the different analyses.

The percentage (with respect to the total number of epochs averaged on all the subjects) of EEG epochs containing artifacts and removed from the EEG data set was 20% (±13%).

From the clean EEG data set, the *power spectral density* (PSD) was calculated for each EEG epoch using a Hanning window of the same length of the considered epoch (2 s length (that means 0.5 Hz of frequency resolution)). The application of a Hanning window helped to smooth the contribution of the signal close to the end of the segment (Epoch), improving the accuracy of the PSD estimation (Harris, 1978).

Then, the EEG frequency bands of interest have been defined for each ATCO by the estimation of the *individual alpha frequency* (IAF) value (Babiloni et al., 2000, 2001; De Vico Fallani et al., 2010; Klimesch, 1999). In order to have a precise estimation of the alpha peak, hence of the IAF, the subjects have been asked to keep the eyes closed for a minute before starting with the experiments. Finally, a spectral features matrix (EEG channels × frequency bins) has been obtained in the frequency bands directly correlated to the mental workload. In particular, only the theta rhythm (IAF $-$ 6:IAF $-$ 2), over the EEG frontal channels (Fz, F3, F4, AF3, and AF4), and the alpha rhythm (IAF $-$ 2:IAF+2), over the EEG parietal channels (Pz, P3, and P4), have been considered as variables for the mental workload evaluation.

In the considered case, the number of observations (#Observations) and number of variables (Variables) are as follows:

$$\#Observations = \frac{RunDuration - EpochLength}{Shift} = 1424 \tag{1}$$

where $RunDuration = 180$ s (E_k, M_k, H_k), $k = [1,2, ..., 5]$, $EpochLength = 2$ s, and $Shift = 0.125$ s.

$$\#Variables = (\#FrontalSites * \#ThetaFrequencyBins) + (\#ParietalSites * \#AlphaFrequencyBins) = 72 \tag{2}$$

where #FrontalSites $= 5$ (namely Fz, F3, F4, AF3, and AF4), #ParietalSites $= 3$ (namely Pz, P3, and P4), #ThetaFrequencyBins $= (IAF - 6:IAF - 2) \cdot 0.5 = 9$, and #AlphaFrequencyBins $= (IAF - 2:IAF + 2) \cdot 0.5 = 9$.

2.2.2 EEG-based mental workload index

Fig. 4 shows the algorithm steps used in this study for the estimation of the user's W_{EEG}.

The effectiveness of two linear classifiers, in particular the standard *stepwise linear discriminant analysis*, SWLDA (Aloise et al., 2012; Draper, 1998), and the asSWLDA (Aricò et al., 2015a), was investigated in terms of reliability over a month. In particular, with respect to the standard SWLDA approach, the asSWLDA algorithm embeds an automatic procedure to select the best number of relevant features to keep into the discrimination model. This property was demonstrated so far to increase the robustness to the under and the overfitting phenomenon, over a week.

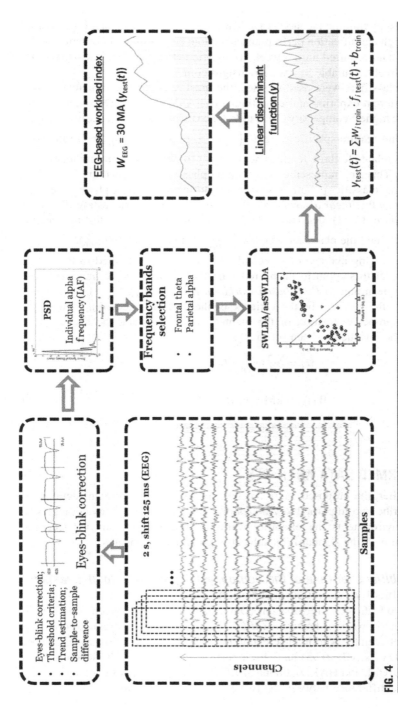

FIG. 4

EEG-based mental workload index (W_{EEG}). The figure explains the algorithm for the EEG-based workload index estimation. The band-pass filtered (1–30 Hz) EEG signal has been segmented into epochs of 2 s, shifted of 0.125 s, and the band-pass filtered (1–7 Hz) EOG signal has been used to remove the eyes-artifact contribution from the EEG signal. Other sources of artifacts have been deleted by using specific algorithms. Then, the *power spectral density* (PSD) has been evaluated for each epoch ($Epoch_{PSD}$), taking into account only the EEG frequency bands and channels correlated with the mental workload variations (frontal theta and parietal alpha bands). Two linear classifiers (SWLDA and asSWLDA) have then been used to select the most relevant brain spectral features for the discrimination of the mental workload levels. The linear discriminant function has been calculated on the EEG testing data sets, and the W_{EEG} has been defined as the moving average of 30 s (30 MA) applied to the linear discriminant function.

In other words, by training the asSWLDA with data acquired on a day, it is possible to maintain high classification performances without any further recalibration of the algorithm on data acquired until a week after (Aricò et al., 2015a). The asSWLDA algorithm is freely available in www.brainsigns.com.

Both the classifiers were used to select the most relevant discriminant features within the different experimental conditions (ie, EASY and HARD), related to the lowest and the highest complexity of the task. Once identified, each classifier assigns to each relevant feature-specific weights $\left(w_{i_{\text{train}}}\right)$, plus a bias ($b_{\text{train}}$). On the contrary, weights related to those features not relevant for the classification model have been set to 0. This step represented the training phase of the algorithm.

Later on, the classifier parameters estimated during the training phase have been used to calculate the *linear discriminant function* ($y_{\text{test}}(t)$) over the testing EEG data set (testing phase, Eq. 3), defined as the linear combination of the testing spectral features $\left(f_{i_{\text{test}}}\right)$ and the classifier weights $\left(w_{i_{\text{train}}}\right)$, plus the bias ($b_{\text{train}}$).

Finally, a moving average of k seconds (kMA) has been applied to the $y_{\text{test}}(t)$ function in order to smooth it out by reducing the variance of the measures, and the result has been named *EEG-based workload index* (W_{EEG}, Eq. 4). The higher is the k value, the less will be the variance of the measure. Accordingly with the SMEs, for a proper evaluation of the mental workload during the execution of ATM tasks, the k value has been set to 30 s:

$$y_{\text{test}}(t) = \sum_i w_{i_{\text{train}}} {}^* f_{i_{\text{test}}}(t) + b_{\text{train}} \tag{3}$$

$$W_{\text{EEG}} = \text{kMA}(y_{\text{test}}(t)) \quad k = 30\,\text{s} \tag{4}$$

2.3 PERFORMED DATA ANALYSES

As stated earlier, the proposed study has been organized in two main sections, in order to describe two important key issues of using passive BCI methodologies in operational environments: the reliability over time of the measure, and the accuracy in comparison with the standard (ie, subjective) workload measures.

2.3.1 Reliability over time of the neurophysiological workload measure
2.3.1.1 Subjective workload assessment
Firstly, the two EEG recording sessions (Day 1 and Day 30) have been compared in terms of subjective workload measure (*SELF-ISA* and *SME-ISA* scores), to check any differences between the workload perception of the ATCOs and of the SMEs. Three two-way ANOVAs (CI = 0.95) have been performed, one for each difficulty level (EASY, MEDIUM, and HARD), on the *SELF-ISA* and the *SME-ISA* scores in order to find out the difference between the two experimental sessions.

2.3.1.2 EEG-based workload assessment

After demonstrating that the two sessions (Day 1 and Day 30) did not differ in terms of perceived workload (see Section 2.3.1.1) for each considered difficulty level (EASY, MEDIUM, and HARD), the stability of the neurophysiological workload measures (W_{EEG}) has been investigated over a month, by using the two classifiers, the SWLDA and the asSWLDA. In particular, two different kinds of cross-validations have been defined: (i) the *Intra*-cross-validation type, where the training and testing data belonged to the same day, and (ii) the *Inter*-cross-validation type, where the training data belonged to Day 1 and the testing data to Day 30.

The third couple of runs (E3 and H3) of the first session (Day 1) has been chosen to calibrate the classifiers. In fact, since the ATM scenarios' profile has been designed without any constant traffic samples or sudden transitions, the easy (E3) and hard (H3) conditions in the middle of each difficulty level have been considered the best choice for training the classifier. Such choice is the best compromise in terms of stable difficulty level to represent the lowest and the highest air traffic complexity condition (and related workload demand), respectively.

To evaluate the reliability of each classifier in discriminating EASY and HARD difficulty levels along the different cross-validation types, *area under curve* (AUC) values of the *receiver operating characteristic* (ROC; Bamber, 1975) have been calculated by considering couple of W_{EEG} distributions (E vs H). An ROC curve is a graphical plot that illustrates the performance of a binary classifier to discriminate two classes. The area under an ROC curve (AUC, which can assumes values comprised between 0.5 and 1) quantifies the overall ability of a binary classifier to discriminate between two conditions (ie, EASY and HARD). If the two conditions are not discriminable, the AUC assumes value of 0.5. On the contrary, if the two conditions are perfectly discriminable, the AUC assumes value of 1.

A two-way repeated measures ANOVA (CI $= 0.95$) analysis has been performed on the AUC values, by considering as *within* factors the "classifiers" (asSWLDA and SWLDA) and the "cross-validation types" (Intra and Inter). Furthermore, Duncan post hoc tests (a multiple comparison procedure, Duncan, 1955) have been performed to assess significant differences between all pairs of levels of the considered factors.

2.3.1.2.1 EEG features selection analysis. As stated earlier, both the SWLDA and the asSWLDA algorithms set to 0 all the weights related to the brain features not significant for the classification model. In addition, the asSWLDA algorithm has the ability to automatically select the lowest number of features from the EEG training data set to optimize the regression model. This property has been demonstrated to make the model able to overcome both the under and the overfitting phenomena (Aricò et al., 2015a). On the contrary, the standard SWLDA has not this property and the algorithm selects, from the EEG training data set, the maximum number of brain features that optimize the regression model until the features selection criteria are satisfied (Draper, 1998).

The hypothesis of the study was that the asSWLDA might be able to achieve high discrimination accuracy, by using a lower number of features (and of EEG channels) than the standard SWLDA algorithm. In this regard, it is easy to realize that for a practical use of p-BCI systems in operational environments, the less is the number of EEG channels, the smaller and less intrusive will be the EEG system.

Two-tailed paired t-tests ($\alpha = 0.05$) have been performed: (i) the first to compare the number of total features among the considered algorithms, and (ii) the second one to compare the related number of EEG channels selected by the two models (standard SWLDA and asSWLDA). For the analyses, both the number of features and the EEG channels used in the two sessions have been averaged for each model (SWLDA and asSWLDA).

2.3.2 Comparison between neurophysiological and subjective workload evaluation

As reported earlier, the analyses have been performed by considering only the last session (Day 30), where all the 12 ATCOs participated to the experiment.

2.3.2.1 Self-workload assessment

First, the three difficulty conditions (EASY, MEDIUM, and HARD) have been compared in terms of perceived workload, by using both *SELF-ISA* and *SME-ISA* scores, to assess if the three difficulty conditions had been perceived differently by the ATCOs. In addition, the two subjective scores have been compared for each difficulty condition. In particular, a two-way ANOVA (CI = 0.95) has been conducted on the *SELF-ISA* and *SME-ISA* score, by considering as *within* factors the "difficulty conditions" (EASY, MEDIUM, and HARD) and the "subjective workload scores" (SELF-ISA and SME-ISA), and by averaging the scores across each difficulty level. Furthermore, Duncan post hoc tests have been performed to assess differences between all pairs of levels of the considered factors.

2.3.2.2 EEG-based workload assessment

The E3 and H3 runs of the second session (*Day 30*) have been selected to calibrate the asSWLDA classifier and the W_{EEG} has then been estimated for each ATCO (as ascribed earlier) over the remaining runs (E1, E2, E4, E5, M1, M2, M3, M4, M5, H1, H2, H4, and H5).

A one-way ANOVA (CI = 0.95) has been performed on the W_{EEG} index, by considering as *within* factor the "difficulty conditions" (EASY, MEDIUM, and HARD), by averaging for each ATCO all the W_{EEG} indexes for each difficulty level. Finally, Duncan post hoc tests have been performed to assess differences between all pairs of levels of the considered factor.

2.3.2.3 Accuracy of neurophysiological measurement in comparison with standard workload assessment

In order to assess the accuracy of the proposed methodology for the mental workload assessment, in comparison with standard subjective workload measures (eg, ISA), a *Pearson's correlation* analysis has been done between the W_{EEG} index and both the subjective scores (*SELF-ISA* and *SME-ISA*). Thus, the *Fisher's R-to-Z* transformation (Fisher, 1921) has been performed in order to assess possible differences between the correlation coefficients (W_{EEG} vs *SELF-ISA and* W_{EEG} vs *SME-ISA*).

Before every statistical analysis, the *z*-score transformation (Zhang et al., 1999) has been used to normalize the data.

3 RESULTS
3.1 OVERTIME STABILITY OF THE EEG-BASED WORKLOAD MEASURE
3.1.1 Self-workload assessment
The three two-way ANOVAs (CI $=0.95$) did not highlight any significant difference between the two sessions (Day 1 and Day 30) in terms of both *SELF-ISA and SME-ISA* (EASY: $F(1,16) = 0.015, p = 0.90$; MEDIUM: $F(1,16) = 2.48, p = 0.13$; HARD: $F(1,16) = 1.77, p = 0.20$) scores (Fig. 5). The results replicate perfectly the correctness of the ATM scenarios designed by the ATC Experts from ENAC. In fact, the requirements were to define different realistic ATM scenarios with comparable difficulty conditions (EASY, MEDIUM, and HARD), with the aim to avoid habituation and expectation effects.

3.1.2 EEG-based workload assessment
The two-way repeated measures ANOVA (CI $=0.95$) highlighted a significant interaction effect between the two (classifiers and cross-validations) factors ($F(1,4) = 10.6, p = 0.03$). The post hoc test highlighted a significant decrement ($p = 0.005$)

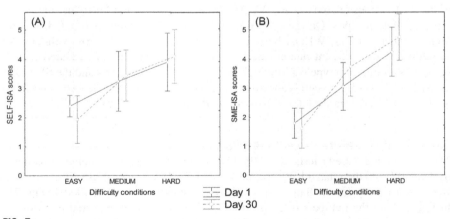

FIG. 5

Error bars related to the *SELF-ISA* and the *SME-ISA* scores for each session (Day 1 and Day 30) and difficulty condition (EASY, MEDIUM, and HARD). The two-way ANOVAs did not show any significant differences between the two experimental sessions for each difficulty level (EASY, MEDIUM, and HARD).

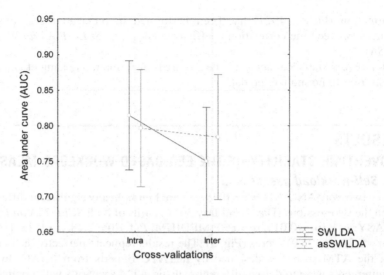

FIG. 6

Error bars (CI = 0.95) related to the AUC values of the SWLDA and asSWLDA classifiers calculated on the EASY and HARD conditions over the two cross-validation types (*Intra* and *Inter*). In particular, regarding the SWLDA, there is a significant AUC decrement ($p = 0.005$) between the *Intra*- and *Inter*-cross-validation types. On the contrary, there is no significant difference ($p = 0.33$) between the two cross-validation types, concerning the asSWLDA. Focusing on the *inter*-cross-validation type, the SWLDA performance (ie, AUC) is significantly ($p = 0.04$) poorer that the asSWLDA one.

of the AUC values related to the SWLDA classifier between the *Intra*- and the *inter*-cross-validation types. On the contrary, no significant differences ($p = 0.33$) were highlighted for the asSWLDA between the *Intra*- and the *Inter*-cross-validations. In addition, a significant decrement ($p = 0.04$) of the AUC values related to the *Inter*-cross-validation type was highlighted between the asSWLDA and the SWLDA classifiers. Instead, no significant differences ($p = 0.2$) between the two classifiers were highlighted regarding the *Intra*-cross-validation type (Fig. 6).

3.1.2.1 EEG features selection analysis

The 2 two-tailed paired t-tests ($\alpha = 0.05$) highlighted that both the number of features ($p = 0.0007$) and the related EEG channels ($p = 0.0003$) used by the asSWLDA model were significantly lower than those used by the standard SWLDA model (Fig. 7). In Fig. 7, both the numbers of features and EEG channels are reported in terms of percentage in respect to the total number of features (72) and EEG channels (8). In particular, the asSWLDA selected the 5.2% of the available features by using the data from the 37% of EEG channels. This means that asSWLDA algorithm selected for each ATCO about four features on three EEG channels. On the contrary, the standard SWLDA used the 44% of the available features by using the 100% of EEG channels.

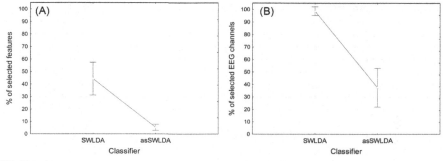

FIG. 7

Error bars related to the number of features (A) and related number of EEG channels (B) selected by the two classification models (SWLDA and asSWLDA). As expected, both the number of features and related number of EEG channels used by the asSWLDA were significantly lower than those used by the standard SWLDA algorithm ($p=0.0007$ and $p=0.0003$, respectively).

This means that the standard SWLDA used for each ATCO 32 features on all the 8 EEG channels. It could be concluded that the asSWLDA algorithm used roughly the 10% of the information employed by the SWLDA, achieving higher performance than the standard SWLDA. This result is important in the perspective of practical usage of such neurophysiological workload assessment in working environment.

3.1.3 Comparison between EEG-based and subjective workload assessment

3.1.3.1 Subjective assessment

The two-way repeated measures ANOVA (CI$=0.95$) highlighted a significant interaction effect ($F(2,22)=10.88$, $p=0.005$) between the two factors, difficulty conditions (EASY, MEDIUM, and HARD) and subjective workload scores (*SELF-ISA* and *SME-ISA*). The post hoc test highlighted significant differences (all $p<0.001$) between the difficulty conditions (ie, EASY lower than MEDIUM, MEDIUM lower than HARD, EASY lower than HARD) for both the *SELF-ISA* and the *SME-ISA* scores. In addition, the *SME-ISA* scores over the MEDIUM ($p=0.0007$) and HARD ($p=0.00007$) conditions were significantly higher than those related to the *SELF-ISA* scores (Fig. 8).

3.1.3.2 EEG-based workload assessment

As for the subjective workload assessment, the one-way ANOVA (Fig. 9) on the neurophysiological workload measures (W_{EEG} data) highlighted a significant effect ($F(2,22)=27.4$, $p=0.000001$) between the three levels (EASY, MEDIUM, and HARD). In particular, the post hoc test highlighted significant differences (all $p<0.001$) between the W_{EEG} score related to the difficulty conditions (ie, EASY lower than MEDIUM, MEDIUM lower than HARD, EASY lower than HARD).

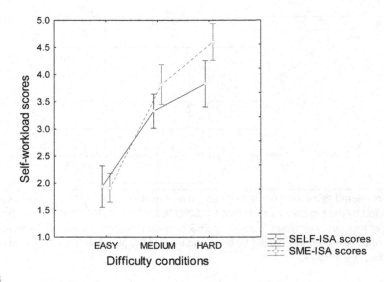

FIG. 8

Error bars (CI=0.95) related to the *SELF-ISA* and the *SME-ISA* scores along the three difficulty conditions (EASY, MEDIUM, and HARD). Results showed significant differences ($p < 0.003$) between all the difficulty conditions for both the *SELF-ISA* and *SME-ISA* scores. In addition, the *SME-ISA* scores related to the MEDIUM and HARD conditions were significantly higher than those related to the *SELF-ISA* ones ($p = 0.0007$ and $p = 0.00007$, respectively).

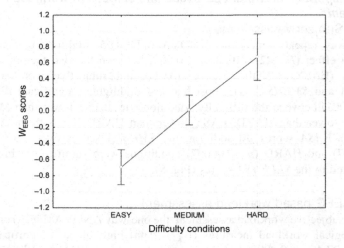

FIG. 9

Error bars (CI=0.95) related to the W_{EEG} scores along the three difficulty conditions (EASY, MEDIUM, and HARD). Results showed significant differences between all the difficulty conditions ($p < 0.001$).

Table 1 Pearson's Correlation Coefficient (R) and Significance (p) Level Between the Neurophysiological (W_{EEG}) Workload Index and Both the Subjective Measures (ISA and SME Scores)

Statistical Analysis of the Correlation		Pearson's Correlation Index	
		R	p
12 subjects	W_{EEG} vs SELF-ISA	0.856	0.0002
	W_{EEG} vs SME-ISA	0.797	0.0011
Statistical Analysis of the Correlation		Fisher's Transformation	
		Z	p
12 subjects	$R_1 = 0.856$, $R_2 = 0.797$ $n = 13$, 2 tails	0.418	0.676

The Fisher's R-to-Z transformation showed no significant difference between the two correlation values.

3.1.3.3 Accuracy of neurophysiological measurement in comparison with standard workload assessment

The correlation analysis (Table 1), by means of the Pearson's correlation coefficient, highlighted a high and positive correlation between the EEG-based workload index (W_{EEG}) and both the ISA (SELF and SME) indexes. In particular the correlation analyses reported $R = 0.856$ and $p = 0.0002$ for the *SELF-ISA data*, and $R = 0.797$ and $p = 0.0011$ for the *SME-ISA* data. In other words, the shape of the three indexes was very similar; that is, the W_{EEG} was able to follow the variation of the mental workload demanded by the ATM scenarios and experienced by the ATCOs during the execution of the task (Fig. 10).

Finally, the Fisher's R-to-Z analysis (Table 1) on the two correlation indexes showed no differences between them ($p = 0.676$).

The scatter plot in Fig. 11 highlighted a high and positive correlation between the neurophysiological and the subjective workload indexes.

4 DISCUSSION

Passive BCI systems can provide reliable information about covert aspects of the user's mental state and overcome the low resolution and limitations of the conventional methods, such as behavioral or subjective measures (Zander and Jatzev, 2012). The information obtained by BCI techniques could then be employed to exploit novel information to improve HMIs. As a consequence, the human performance could be enhanced, and novel operative skills could be potentially achieved. There are many examples in which p-BCIs could be really useful. For example, p-BCI technology can reveal valuable information about the user's mental state in safety-critical applications, such as driving (Borghini et al., 2012; Welke et al., 2009), industrial environments (Venthur et al., 2010), or security surveillance (Marcel and Millan, 2007). With

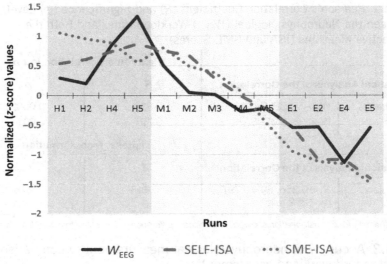

FIG. 10

Shape of the three workload indexes, the neurophysiologic (W_{EEG}), and the subjective (SELF- and SME-ISA) ones, across the experimental task. The three measures were able to follow the mental workload variation along the ATM scenarios.

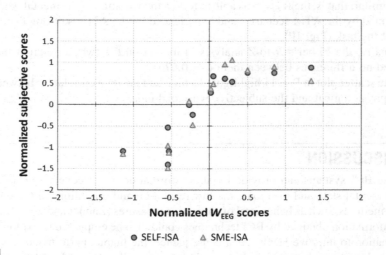

FIG. 11

Scatter plot of the subjective workload measures (*SELF-ISA* and *SME-ISA*) with respect to the neurophysiological workload measure. On *the x-axis* the normalized W_{EEG} index, on the *y-axis* the normalized *SELF-* and S*ME-ISA* indexes. The results of the correlation analyses showed a high and significant correlation among all the workload measures (Table 1).

respect to driving assistance applications, recent studies demonstrated the utility of p-BCI systems during driving simulation for assessing driving performance and inattentiveness (Schubert and Tangermann, 2008), as well as for robustly detecting emergency brakes before braking onset (Welke et al., 2009). In addition, p-BCI systems can potentially be used for real-time cognitive monitoring of the operator's mental workload (Aricò et al., 2014a,b; Kohlmorgen et al., 2007).

Anyhow, the application of the p-BCI technology outside research laboratories (eg, operational environments) has to face several practical issues, such as the reliability over time of the measure (unless a frequent recalibration of the system), or the intrusiveness of the equipment (eg, EEG sensors and recording system).

The purpose of the proposed study was to investigate the effectiveness of a methodology for the user's mental workload assessment in ATM environment, by using neurophysiological measures. The brain activity (EEG) and subjective measures (*SELF-ISA* and *SME-ISA* scores) of 12 professional ATCOs from ENAC (Toulouse, France) have been gathered while managing high-realistic ATM scenarios and analyzed by a machine-learning approach.

The asSWLDA, a modified version of the standard SWLDA (Aricò et al., 2015a), has been used to compute a mental workload index based on the EEG activity of the user (W_{EEG}). The SWLDA model has been chosen because it has been demonstrated to be one of the best outperforming linear classifiers (Aloise et al., 2012; Craven et al., 2006; Krusienski et al., 2006). In fact, in comparison with other linear methods, it has the advantage of having automatic features extraction, so that insignificant terms will be statistically removed from the model.

As stated earlier, the proposed study has been organized in order to investigate two important key issues to use neurophysiological measurements in operational environments: (1) the reliability over time of the measure, and (2) the accuracy in comparison with the standard (ie, subjective) workload measures.

Regarding the first issue, despite the low sample size (only five ATCOs took part to the whole experimental protocol), results demonstrated that the proposed algorithm has been able to maintain a high reliability across a month. It has been already demonstrated the reliability of the model over a week in a previous study (Aricò et al., 2015a). In other words, unlike the standard SWLDA algorithm, it is possible to calibrate the asSWLDA model and then use it every day without accuracy reductions in the mental workload evaluation up to a month after the calibration.

In addition, the asSWLDA model has been able to select a lower number of brain features and EEG channels (37%, that means three EEG channels in the specific study), to be used for the workload assessment, in comparison with the standard SWLDA (100%, that means eight EEG channels). In this regard, in the standard SWLDA algorithm it could be possible to force the model to select less features (that means less EEG channels; Aricò et al., 2015b). However, with the standard SWLDA, it became tricky to empirically (and manually) find out, so that it might change from subject to subject. On the contrary, the asSWLDA is able to automatically select the right number of brain features and to optimize the final model (Aricò et al., 2015a). More important, the results suggested that the selected features for the asSWLDA could be almost an order of magnitude less than those selected by using the standard SWLDA. As a direct consequence, a lower number of EEG channels will be necessary with the asSWLDA than with the standard SWLDA. Since one of the big limitations in using p-BCI systems in operational environments is represented by wearing the EEG cap, it is simple to conclude that the less is the number of EEG channels included in the classification model, the less intrusive will be the system for the final user. In this regard, just moving to a plausible operational showcase, the proposed algorithm will be calibrated once with many electrodes to select the specific subjective features and then used online by assume a lighter EEG configuration (eg, two or three electrodes).

Concerning the second issue, the EEG-based workload measure has been compared with two subjective workload measures, one provided by the ATCOs (*SELF-ISA* scores) and the second provided by two ATC Experts (SMEs), who have been asked to fill the ISA questionnaire at the same time of the ATCOs (*SME-ISA* scores). Results highlighted high and significant correlations between the neurophysiological and both the subjective workload measurements. Such result is very important, since it showed how the W_{EEG} and both the subjective indexes (*SELF-ISA* and *SME-ISA*) were able to follow the actual fluctuations of the mental workload experienced by the ATCOs during the experimental task. In addition, the *SELF-ISA* scores showed a higher workload perception during the MEDIUM and the HARD conditions in comparison with the *SME-ISA* ones. This result highlighted the main limitation of the subjective measures: they are highly operator dependent, and they cannot be used to quantify objectively the operators' mental states (ie, mental workload). On the contrary, the neurophysiological measures can provide, with high resolution, an objective evaluation of the operator's mental workload.

Finally, it has to be underlined that the proposed algorithms do not require a priori information about consecutive data; that is, the calibration of the classifier can be performed on a different day than the testing. As a consequence, the proposed methodologies can also be used for online applications, for example, to improve the HMIs by using information derived by the operator's mental workload states.

To summarize, it has been possible to calibrate the proposed algorithm by using EEG training data and then to evaluate the ATCO's mental workload during workshift across different days (up to a month).

The results reported in the present study do not exclude the possibility to achieve similar or even better results by using other machine-learning techniques, but they have demonstrated the possibility to use p-BCI systems in operational environments to measure the operators' mental workload during the execution of a realistic ATM task.

5 CONCLUSION

In this study, a passive BCI technique for the assessment of ATCOs mental workload has been proposed and tested in a high-realistic operational environment. In particular, the ATM environment imposes multiple concurrent demands on the ATCO, including air traffic monitoring, anticipating loss of separation between aircraft, and intervening to resolve conflicts. The objective assessment of the mental workload associated with operative activities in such a complex environment has long been recognized as an important issue (Gopher and Donchin, 1986).

Results showed that (i) the proposed algorithm maintained a high reliability over time (up to a month), (ii) high and significant correlations between the EEG-based and the subjective (*SELF-ISA* and *SME-ISA* scores) workload measures, and (iii) in comparison with other machine-learning techniques, the proposed algorithm (asSWLDA) was able to reduce the number of brain features and EEG channels, in other words, to reduce the intrusiveness of the p-BCI system.

One of the practical issues of machine learning approaches for their application outside of laboratory setting (ie, operational environments) is the necessity to calibrate the system every time before using it. In addition, it might not be always possible to find the right conditions (eg, EASY and HARD) to calibrate the system in operational environments. Different studies tried to address such issue in laboratory setting and only one in operational environment (Harrison et al., 2014) by using fNIRs technique. However, authors reported conflicting results related to the correlation between neurophysiological and self-assessed mental workload measures. We addressed partially this issue in the present study, since the asSWLDA algorithm can be calibrated once and then used over time (until a month) without requiring any calibration.

Taking into account these limitations, there is the need to perform further experiments to test the possibility to select brain features during the execution of short standard and controlled tasks (that enhance the considered mental state) and then to use such brain features to calibrate the classification algorithm that will be used later in the operative situation.

ACKNOWLEDGMENTS

This work is in part supported by a grant of the European Union through the Horizon2020—HCO funding scheme with the project "SmokeFreeBrain" GA no. 681120. The grant provided by the Italian Minister of University and Education under the PRIN 2012, Grant no. 2012WAANZJ scheme to F.B. is also gratefully acknowledged. The facilities provided by the ENAC, Toulouse, France under the WPE-SESAR research project "NINA", the precious support of Drs. R. Benhacene, G. Granger, and J.P. Imbert from ENAC and S. Bonelli from DeepBlue srl, Rome are also gratefully acknowledged.

REFERENCES

Allison, B.Z., Pineda, J.A., 2003. ERPs evoked by different matrix sizes: implications for a brain computer interface (BCI) system. IEEE Trans. Neural Syst. Rehabil. Eng. 11, 110–113. http://dx.doi.org/10.1109/TNSRE.2003.814448.

Aloise, F., Schettini, F., Aricò, P., Bianchi, L., Riccio, A., Mecella, M., Babiloni, F., Mattia, D., Cincotti, F., 2010. Advanced brain computer interface for communication and control. In: Proceedings of the International Conference on Advanced Visual Interfaces, pp. 399–400.

Aloise, F., Schettini, F., Aricò, P., Salinari, S., Babiloni, F., Cincotti, F., 2012. A comparison of classification techniques for a gaze-independent P300-based brain-computer interface. J. Neural Eng. 9, 045012. http://dx.doi.org/10.1088/1741-2560/9/4/045012.

Aloise, F., Aricò, P., Schettini, F., Salinari, S., Mattia, D., Cincotti, F., 2013. Asynchronous gaze-independent event-related potential-based brain–computer interface. Artif. Intell. Med. 59, 61–69. http://dx.doi.org/10.1016/j.artmed.2013.07.006 (Special Issue: Brain-computer interfacing).

Aricò, P., Aloise, F., Schettini, F., Salinari, S., Mattia, D., Cincotti, F., 2014a. Influence of P300 latency jitter on event related potential-based brain-computer interface performance. J. Neural Eng. 11, 035008. http://dx.doi.org/10.1088/1741-2560/11/3/035008.

Aricò, P., Borghini, G., Graziani, I., Taya, F., Sun, Y., Bezerianos, A., Thakor, N.V., Cincotti, F., Babiloni, F., 2014b. Towards a multimodal bioelectrical framework for the online mental workload evaluation. Conf. Proc. IEEE Eng. Med. Biol. Soc. 2014, 3001–3004. http://dx.doi.org/10.1109/EMBC.2014.6944254.

Aricò, P., Borghini, G., Di Flumeri, G., Babiloni, F., 2015a. Metodo per stimare uno stato mentale, in particolare un carico di lavoro, e relativo apparato (A method for the estimation of mental state, in particular of the mental workload and its device). P1108IT00.

Aricò, P., Borghini, G., Di Flumeri, G., Colosimo, A., Graziani, I., Imbert, J.P., Granger, G., Benhacene, R., Terenzi, M., Pozzi, S., Babiloni, F., 2015b. Reliability over time of EEG-based mental workload evaluation during air traffic management (ATM) tasks. Conf. Proc. IEEE Eng. Med. Biol. Soc. 2015, 7242–7245. http://dx.doi.org/10.1109/EMBC.2015.7320063.

Aricò, P., Borghini, G., Graziani, I., Imbert, J.P., Granger, G., Benhacene, R., Pozzi, S., Napolitano, L., Di Flumeri, G., Colosimo, A., Babiloni, F., 2015c. ATCO: neurophysiological analysis of the training and of the workload. Ital. J. Aerosp. Med. 12, 18–34.

Babiloni, F., Carducci, F., Cincotti, F., Del Gratta, C., Roberti, G.M., Romani, G.L., Rossini, P.M., Babiloni, C., 2000. Integration of high resolution EEG and functional magnetic resonance in the study of human movement-related potentials. Methods Inf. Med. 39, 179–182.

Babiloni, C., Babiloni, F., Carducci, F., Cincotti, F., Rosciarelli, F., Rossini, P., Arendt-Nielsen, L., Chen, A., 2001. Mapping of early and late human somatosensory evoked brain potentials to phasic galvanic painful stimulation. Hum. Brain Mapp. 12, 168–179.

Baldwin, C.L., 2003. Commentary. Theor. Issues Ergon. Sci. 4, 132–141. http://dx.doi.org/10.1080/14639220210159807.

Bamber, D., 1975. The area above the ordinal dominance graph and the area below the receiver operating characteristic graph. J. Math. Psychol. 12, 387–415. http://dx.doi.org/10.1016/0022-2496(75)90001-2.

Bellenkes, C.A.H., 2007. Contemporary issues in human factors and aviation safety. Ergonomics 50, 963–965. http://dx.doi.org/10.1080/00140130600971093.

Berka, C., Levendowski, D.J., Cvetinovic, M.M., Petrovic, M.M., Davis, G., Lumicao, M.N., Zivkovic, V.T., Popovic, M.V., Olmstead, R., 2004. Real-time analysis of EEG indexes of alertness, cognition, and memory acquired with a wireless EEG headset. Int. J. Hum. Comput. Interact. 17, 151–170. http://dx.doi.org/10.1207/s15327590ijhc1702_3.

Berka, C., Levendowski, D.J., Lumicao, M.N., Yau, A., Davis, G., Zivkovic, V.T., Olmstead, R.E., Tremoulet, P.D., Craven, P.L., 2007. EEG correlates of task engagement and mental workload in vigilance, learning, and memory tasks. Aviat. Space Environ. Med. 78, B231–B244.

Blankertz, B., Tangermann, M., Vidaurre, C., Fazli, S., Sannelli, C., Haufe, S., Maeder, C., Ramsey, L., Sturm, I., Curio, G., Müller, K.-R., 2010. The Berlin brain–computer interface: non-medical uses of BCI technology. Front. Neurosci. 4, 198. http://dx.doi.org/10.3389/fnins.2010.00198.

Borghini, G., Vecchiato, G., Toppi, J., Astolfi, L., Maglione, A., Isabella, R., Caltagirone, C., Kong, W., Wei, D., Zhou, Z., Polidori, L., Vitiello, S., Babiloni, F., 2012. Assessment of mental fatigue during car driving by using high resolution EEG activity and neurophysiologic indices. Conf. Proc. IEEE Eng. Med. Biol. Soc. 2012, 6442–6445. http://dx.doi.org/10.1109/EMBC.2012.6347469.

Borghini, G., Aricò, P., Ferri, F., Graziani, I., Pozzi, S., Napoletano, L., Imbert, J.P., Granger, G., Benhacene, R., Babiloni, F., 2014a. A neurophysiological training evaluation metric for air traffic management. Conf. Proc. IEEE Eng. Med. Biol. Soc. 2014, 3005–3008. http://dx.doi.org/10.1109/EMBC.2014.6944255.

Borghini, G., Astolfi, L., Vecchiato, G., Mattia, D., Babiloni, F., 2014b. Measuring neurophysiological signals in aircraft pilots and car drivers for the assessment of mental workload, fatigue and drowsiness. Neurosci. Biobehav. Rev. 44, 58–75. http://dx.doi.org/10.1016/j.neubiorev.2012.10.003.

Borghini, G., Aricò, P., Di Flumeri, G., Salinari, S., Colosimo, A., Bonelli, S., Napoletano, L., Ferreira, A., Babiloni, F., 2015a. Avionic technology testing by using a cognitive neurometric index: a study with professional helicopter pilots. Conf. Proc. IEEE Eng. Med. Biol. Soc. 2015, 6182–6185. http://dx.doi.org/10.1109/EMBC.2015.7319804.

Borghini, G., Aricò, P., Graziani, I., Salinari, S., Sun, Y., Taya, F., Bezerianos, A., Thakor, N.V., Babiloni, F., 2015b. Quantitative assessment of the training improvement in a motor-cognitive task by using EEG, ECG and EOG signals. Brain Topogr. 29, 149–161. http://dx.doi.org/10.1007/s10548-015-0425-7.

Brookings, J.B., Wilson, G.F., Swain, C.R., 1996. Psychophysiological responses to changes in workload during simulated air traffic control. Biol. Psychol. 42, 361–377.

Brouwer, A.-M., Zander, T.O., van Erp, J.B.F., Korteling, J.E., Bronkhorst, A.W., 2015. Using neurophysiological signals that reflect cognitive or affective state: six recommendations to avoid common pitfalls. Front. Neurosci. 9, 136. http://dx.doi.org/10.3389/fnins.2015.00136.

Cabeza, R., Nyberg, L., 2000. Imaging cognition II: an empirical review of 275 PET and fMRI studies. J. Cogn. Neurosci. 12, 1–47.

Cain, B., 2007. A Review of the Mental Workload Literature. Defence Research and Development Canada Toronto Human System Integration Section, Toronto, Canada. Report No.: RTO-TR-HFM-121-Part-II.

Calabrese, E.J., 2008. Neuroscience and hormesis: overview and general findings. Crit. Rev. Toxicol. 38, 249–252. http://dx.doi.org/10.1080/10408440801981957.

Christensen, J.C., Estepp, J.R., Wilson, G.F., Russell, C.A., 2012. The effects of day-to-day variability of physiological data on operator functional state classification. NeuroImage 59, 57–63. http://dx.doi.org/10.1016/j.neuroimage.2011.07.091.

Craven, P.L., Belov, N., Tremoulet, P., et al., 2006. Cognitive workload gauge development: comparison of real-time classification methods. In: Schmorrow, D., Stanney, K., Reeves, L. (Eds.), Augmented Cognition: Past, Present and Future, Foundations of Augmented Cognition. Strategic Analysis, Inc., Arlington, pp. 66–74.

Cui, X., Bray, S., Bryant, D.M., Glover, G.H., Reiss, A.L., 2011. A quantitative comparison of NIRS and fMRI across multiple cognitive tasks. Neuroimage 54, 2808–2821. http://dx.doi.org/10.1016/j.neuroimage.2010.10.069.

Delorme, A., Makeig, S., 2004. EEGLAB: an open source toolbox for analysis of single-trial EEG dynamics including independent component analysis. J. Neurosci. Methods 134, 9–21. http://dx.doi.org/10.1016/j.jneumeth.2003.10.009.

Derosière, G., Mandrick, K., Dray, G., Ward, T.E., Perrey, S., 2013. NIRS-measured prefrontal cortex activity in neuroergonomics: strengths and weaknesses. Front. Hum. Neurosci. 7. http://dx.doi.org/10.3389/fnhum.2013.00583.

De Vico Fallani, F., Nicosia, V., Sinatra, R., Astolfi, L., Cincotti, F., Mattia, D., Wilke, C., Doud, A., Latora, V., He, B., Babiloni, F., 2010. Defecting or not defecting: how to "read" human behavior during cooperative games by EEG measurements. PLoS One 5, e14187. http://dx.doi.org/10.1371/journal.pone.0014187.

Di Flumeri, G., Borghini, G., Aricò, P., Colosimo, A., Pozzi, S., Bonelli, S., Golfetti, A., Kong, W., Babiloni, F., 2015. On the use of cognitive neurometric indexes in aeronautic and air traffic management environments. In: Blankertz, B., Jacucci, G., Gamberini, L., Spagnolli, A., Freeman, J. (Eds.), Symbiotic Interaction. Springer International Publishing, Cham, pp. 45–56.

Draper, N.R., 1998. Applied regression analysis. Commun. Stat. Theory Methods 27, 2581–2623. http://dx.doi.org/10.1080/03610929808832244.

Duncan, D.B., 1955. Multiple range and multiple F tests. Biometrics 11, 1–42.

Durantin, G., Gagnon, J.-F., Tremblay, S., Dehais, F., 2014. Using near infrared spectroscopy and heart rate variability to detect mental overload. Behav. Brain Res. 259, 16–23. http://dx.doi.org/10.1016/j.bbr.2013.10.042.

Eggemeier, F.T., Wilson, G.F., Kramer, A.F., Damos, D.L., 1991. Workload assessment in multi-task environments. In: Multiple-Task Performance. Taylor & Francis, London, pp. 207–216.

Elul, R., 1969. Gaussian behavior of the electroencephalogram: changes during performance of mental task. Science 164, 328–331.

Feyer, A., Williamson, A.M., 1998. Human factors in accident modelling. In: Stellman, J.M. (Ed.), Encyclopedia of Occupational Health and Safety, fourth ed., International Labor Organization, Geneva.

Fisher, R.A., 1921. On the "probable error" of a coefficient of correlation deduced from a small sample. Metron 1, 3–32.

Fuchs, S., Hale, K.S., Stanney, K.M., Juhnke, J., Schmorrow, D.D., 2007. Enhancing mitigation in augmented cognition. J. Cogn. Eng. Decis. Mak. 1, 309–326. http://dx.doi.org/10.1518/155534307X255645.

Gevins, A., Smith, M.E., 2003. Neurophysiological measures of cognitive workload during human-computer interaction. Theor. Issues Ergon. Sci. 4, 113–131. http://dx.doi.org/10.1080/14639220210159717.

Gevins, A., Smith, M.E., McEvoy, L., Yu, D., 1997. High-resolution EEG mapping of cortical activation related to working memory: effects of task difficulty, type of processing, and practice. Cereb. Cortex 1991 (7), 374–385.

Goldberg, D.H., Vogelstein, R.J., Socolinsky, D.A., Wolff, L.B., 2011. Toward a wearable, neurally-enhanced augmented reality system. In: Schmorrow, D.D., Fidopiastis, C.M. (Eds.), Foundations of Augmented Cognition. Directing the Future of Adaptive Systems. Springer, Berlin, Heidelberg, pp. 493–499.

Gopher, D., Donchin, E., 1986. Workload: an examination of the concept. In: Handbook of Perception and Human Performance. Cognitive Processes and Performance, vol. 2. John Wiley & Sons, Oxford, England, pp. 1–49.

Gratton, G., Coles, M.G., Donchin, E., 1983. A new method for off-line removal of ocular artifact. Electroencephalogr. Clin. Neurophysiol. 55, 468–484.

Harris, F.J., 1978. On the use of windows for harmonic analysis with the discrete Fourier transform. Proc. IEEE 66, 51–83. http://dx.doi.org/10.1109/PROC.1978.10837.

Harrison, J., Izzetoglu, K., Ayaz, H., Willems, B., Hah, S., Ahlstrom, U., Woo, H., Shewokis, P.A., Bunce, S.C., Onaral, B., 2014. Cognitive workload and learning assessment during the implementation of a next-generation air traffic control technology using functional near-infrared spectroscopy. IEEE Trans. Hum.-Mach. Syst. 44, 429–440. http://dx.doi.org/10.1109/THMS.2014.2319822.

Hart, S.G., Staveland, L.E., 1988. Development of NASA-TLX (Task Load Index): Results of empirical and theoretical research. In: Hancock, P.A., Meshkati, N. (Eds.), Human Mental Workload. Amsterdam, North-Holland Press.

Herff, C., Heger, D., Fortmann, O., Hennrich, J., Putze, F., Schultz, T., 2013. Mental workload during n-back task-quantified in the prefrontal cortex using fNIRS. Front. Hum. Neurosci. 7, 935. http://dx.doi.org/10.3389/fnhum.2013.00935.

Huppert, T.J., Hoge, R.D., Diamond, S.G., Franceschini, M.A., Boas, D.A., 2006. A temporal comparison of BOLD, ASL, and NIRS hemodynamic responses to motor stimuli in adult humans. NeuroImage 29, 368–382. http://dx.doi.org/10.1016/j.neuroimage.2005.08.065.

Izzetoglu, K., Bunce, S., Onaral, B., Pourrezaei, K., Chance, B., 2004. Functional optical brain imaging using near-infrared during cognitive tasks. Int. J. Hum. Comput. Interact. 17, 211–227. http://dx.doi.org/10.1207/s15327590ijhc1702_6.

Jaušovec, N., Jaušovec, K., 2012. Working memory training: improving intelligence—changing brain activity. Brain Cogn. 79, 96–106. http://dx.doi.org/10.1016/j.bandc.2012.02.007.

Jurcak, V., Tsuzuki, D., Dan, I., 2007. 10/20, 10/10, and 10/5 systems revisited: their validity as relative head-surface-based positioning systems. NeuroImage 34, 1600–1611. http://dx.doi.org/10.1016/j.neuroimage.2006.09.024.

Kirsh, D., 2000. A few thoughts on cognitive overload. Intellectica 30, 19–52.

Kirwan, B., Scaife, R., Kennedy, R., 2001. Investigating complexity factors in UK air traffic management. Hum. Factors Aerosp. Saf. 1, 125–144.

Klimesch, W., 1999. EEG alpha and theta oscillations reflect cognitive and memory performance: a review and analysis. Brain Res. Brain Res. Rev. 29, 169–195.

Klimesch, W., Doppelmayr, M., Pachinger, T., Ripper, B., 1997. Brain oscillations and human memory: EEG correlates in the upper alpha and theta band. Neurosci. Lett. 238, 9–12.

Kohlmorgen, J., Dornhege, G., Braun, M., Blankertz, B., Müller, K.R., Curio, G., Hagemann, K., Bruns, A., Schrauf, M., Kincses, W., 2007. Improving human performance in a real operating environment through real-time mental workload detection. Toward brain-computer interfacing, MIT Press.

Krusienski, D.J., Sellers, E.W., Cabestaing, F., Bayoudh, S., McFarland, D.J., Vaughan, T.M., Wolpaw, J.R., 2006. A comparison of classification techniques for the P300 Speller. J. Neural Eng. 3, 299–305. http://dx.doi.org/10.1088/1741-2560/3/4/007.

Liao, L.-D., Lin, C.-T., McDowell, K., Wickenden, A.E., Gramann, K., Jung, T.-P., Ko, L.-W., Chang, J.-Y., 2012. Biosensor technologies for augmented brain–computer interfaces in the next decades. Proc. IEEE 100, 1553–1566. http://dx.doi.org/10.1109/JPROC.2012.2184829.

Marcel, S., Millan, J.D.R., 2007. Person authentication using brainwaves (EEG) and maximum a posteriori model adaptation. IEEE Trans. Pattern Anal. Mach. Intell. 29, 743–752. http://dx.doi.org/10.1109/TPAMI.2007.1012.

Medvedev, A.V., Kainerstorfer, J., Borisov, S.V., Barbour, R.L., VanMeter, J., 2008. Event-related fast optical signal in a rapid object recognition task: improving detection by the independent component analysis. Brain Res. 1236, 145–158. http://dx.doi.org/10.1016/j.brainres.2008.07.122.

Mühl, C., Jeunet, C., Lotte, F., 2014. EEG-based workload estimation across affective contexts. Front. Neurosci. 8, 114. http://dx.doi.org/10.3389/fnins.2014.00114.

Müller, K.-R., Tangermann, M., Dornhege, G., Krauledat, M., Curio, G., Blankertz, B., 2008. Machine learning for real-time single-trial EEG-analysis: from brain-computer interfacing to mental state monitoring. J. Neurosci. Methods 167, 82–90. http://dx.doi.org/10.1016/j.jneumeth.2007.09.022.

Murkin, J.M., Arango, M., 2009. Near-infrared spectroscopy as an index of brain and tissue oxygenation. Br. J. Anaesth. 103 (Suppl. 1), i3–i13. http://dx.doi.org/10.1093/bja/aep299.

National Research Council (US) Committee on Military and Intelligence Methodology for Emergent Neruophysiological and Cognitive/Neural Research in the Next Two Decades, 2008. Emerging Areas of Cognitive Neuroscience and Neurotechnologies. National Academies Press, Washington, DC.

O'Donnell, R.D., Eggemeier, F.T., 1986. Workload Assessment Methodology. Handbook of Perception and Human Performance. John Wiley and Sons, Inc., New York, NY.

Onton, J., Delorme, A., Makeig, S., 2005. Frontal midline EEG dynamics during working memory. NeuroImage 27, 341–356. http://dx.doi.org/10.1016/j.neuroimage.2005.04.014.

Owen, A.M., McMillan, K.M., Laird, A.R., Bullmore, E., 2005. N-back working memory paradigm: a meta-analysis of normative functional neuroimaging studies. Hum. Brain Mapp. 25, 46–59. http://dx.doi.org/10.1002/hbm.20131.

Parasuraman, R., 2003. Neuroergonomics: research and practice. Theor. Issues Ergon. Sci. 4, 5–20. http://dx.doi.org/10.1080/14639220210199753.

Plichta, M.M., Herrmann, M.J., Baehne, C.G., Ehlis, A.-C., Richter, M.M., Pauli, P., Fallgatter, A.J., 2006. Event-related functional near-infrared spectroscopy (fNIRS): are the measurements reliable? NeuroImage 31, 116–124. http://dx.doi.org/10.1016/j.neuroimage.2005.12.008.

Pollock, V.E., Schneider, L.S., Lyness, S.A., 1991. Reliability of topographic quantitative EEG amplitude in healthy late-middle-aged and elderly subjects. Electroencephalogr. Clin. Neurophysiol. 79, 20–26.

Ramnani, N., Owen, A.M., 2004. Anterior prefrontal cortex: insights into function from anatomy and neuroimaging. Nat. Rev. Neurosci. 5, 184–194. http://dx.doi.org/10.1038/nrn1343.

Reason, J., 2000. Human error. West. J. Med. 172, 393–396.

Reid, G.B., Nygren, T.E., 1988. The subjective workload assessment technique: a scaling procedure for measuring mental workload. In: Hancock, P.A., Meshkati, N. (Eds.), Human Mental Workload. Advances in Psychology, Amsterdam, North-Holland, pp. 185–218.

Riccio, A., Holz, E.M., Aricò, P., Leotta, F., Aloise, F., Desideri, L., Rimondini, M., Kübler, A., Mattia, D., Cincotti, F., 2015. Hybrid P300-based brain-computer interface to improve usability for people with severe motor disability: electromyographic signals for error correction during a spelling task. Arch. Phys. Med. Rehabil. 96, S54–S61. http://dx.doi.org/10.1016/j.apmr.2014.05.029.

Rodgers, M.D., Drechsler, G.K., 1993. Conversion of the CTA, Inc., En Route Operations Concepts Database into a Formal Sentence Outline Job Task Taxonomy.

Rubio, S., Díaz, E., Martín, J., Puente, J.M., 2004. Evaluation of subjective mental workload: a comparison of SWAT, NASA-TLX, and workload profile methods. Appl. Psychol. 53, 61–86. http://dx.doi.org/10.1111/j.1464-0597.2004.00161.x.

Ryu, K., Myung, R., 2005. Evaluation of mental workload with a combined measure based on physiological indices during a dual task of tracking and mental arithmetic. Int. J. Ind. Ergon. 35, 991–1009. http://dx.doi.org/10.1016/j.ergon.2005.04.005.

Schettini, F., Riccio, A., Simione, L., Liberati, G., Caruso, M., Frasca, V., Calabrese, B., Mecella, M., Pizzimenti, A., Inghilleri, M., Mattia, D., Cincotti, F., 2015. Assistive device with conventional, alternative, and brain-computer interface inputs to enhance interaction with the environment for people with amyotrophic lateral sclerosis: a feasibility and usability study. Arch. Phys. Med. Rehabil. 96, S46–S53. http://dx.doi.org/10.1016/j.apmr.2014.05.027.

Schubert, R., Tangermann, M., 2008. Parieto-occipital alpha power indexes distraction during simulated car driving. Abstracts of the 14th World Congress of Psychophysiology. Int. J. Psychophysiol. 69. http://dx.doi.org/10.1016/j.ijpsycho.2008.05.033.

Shou, G., Ding, L., Dasari, D., 2012. Probing neural activations from continuous EEG in a real-world task: time-frequency independent component analysis. J. Neurosci. Methods 209, 22–34. http://dx.doi.org/10.1016/j.jneumeth.2012.05.022.

Smit, A.S., Eling, P.A., Hopman, M.T., Coenen, A.M., 2005. Mental and physical effort affect vigilance differently. Int. J. Psychophysiol. 57, 211–217.

Smith, M.E., Gevins, A., 2005. Neurophysiologic monitoring of mental workload and fatigue during operation of a flight simulator. Proc. SPIE 5797, 116–126. http://dx.doi.org/10.1117/12.602181.

Toppi, J., Borghini, G., Petti, M., He, E.J., Giusti, V.D., He, B., Astolfi, L., Babiloni, F., 2016. Investigating cooperative behavior in ecological settings: an EEG hyperscanning study. PLoS One 11, e0154236. http://dx.doi.org/10.1371/journal.pone.0154236.

Vecchiato, G., Di Flumeri, G., Maglione, A.G., Cherubino, P., Kong, W., Trettel, A., Babiloni, F., 2014. An electroencephalographic peak density function to detect memorization during the observation of TV commercials. Conf. Proc. IEEE Eng. Med. Biol. Soc. 2014, 6969–6972. http://dx.doi.org/10.1109/EMBC.2014.6945231.

Venables, L., Fairclough, S.H., 2009. The influence of performance feedback on goal-setting and mental effort regulation. Motiv. Emot. 33, 63–74. http://dx.doi.org/10.1007/s11031-008-9116-y.

Venthur, B., Blankertz, B., Gugler, M.F., Curio, G., 2010. Novel applications of BCI technology: Psychophysiological optimization of working conditions in industry. 2010 IEEE International Conference on Systems Man and Cybernetics (SMC). Presented at the 2010 IEEE International Conference on Systems Man and Cybernetics (SMC), 417–421. http://dx.doi.org/10.1109/ICSMC.2010.5641772.

Welke, S., Jurgensohn, T., Roetting, M., 2009. Single-trial detection of cognitive processes for increasing traffic safety. In: Proceedings of the 21st (Esv) International Technical Conference on the Enhanced Safety of Vehicles. Held June 2009 Stuttgart, Germany.

Wickens, C.D., 1984. Processing resources in attention. In: Parasuraman, R., Davies, R. (Eds.), Varieties of attention. Academic Press, Orlando, FL, pp. 62–102.

Wierwille, W.W., Eggemeier, F.T., 1993. Recommendations for mental workload measurement in a test and evaluation environment. Hum. Factors J. Hum. Factors Ergon. Soc. 35, 263–281. http://dx.doi.org/10.1177/001872089303500205.

Wolpaw, J., Wolpaw, E.W., 2012. Brain-Computer Interfaces: Principles and Practice. Oxford University Press.

Wolpaw, J.R., Birbaumer, N., McFarland, D.J., Pfurtscheller, G., Vaughan, T.M., 2002. Brain-computer interfaces for communication and control. Clin. Neurophysiol. 113, 767–791.

Wood, J.N., Grafman, J., 2003. Human prefrontal cortex: processing and representational perspectives. Nat. Rev. Neurosci. 4, 139–147. http://dx.doi.org/10.1038/nrn1033.

Zander, T.O., Jatzev, S., 2012. Context-aware brain-computer interfaces: exploring the information space of user, technical system and environment. J. Neural Eng. 9, 016003. http://dx.doi.org/10.1088/1741-2560/9/1/016003.

Zander, T.O., Kothe, C., Welke, S., Roetting, M., 2009. Utilizing secondary input from passive brain-computer interfaces for enhancing human-machine interaction. In: Schmorrow, D.D., Estabrooke, I.V., Grootjen, M. (Eds.), Foundations of Augmented Cognition. Neuroergonomics and Operational Neuroscience. Springer, Berlin, Heidelberg, pp. 759–771.

Zhang, J.H., Chung, T.D., Oldenburg, K., 1999. A simple statistical parameter for use in evaluation and validation of high throughput screening assays. J. Biomol. Screen. 4, 67–73.

3D graphics, virtual reality, and motion-onset visual evoked potentials in neurogaming

11

R. Beveridge[1], S. Wilson, D. Coyle

Intelligent Systems Research Centre, Ulster University, Derry,
Northern Ireland, United Kingdom
[1]*Corresponding author: Tel.: +44-28-71671195; Fax: +44-28-71675570,*
e-mail address: beveridge-r@email.ulster.ac.uk

Abstract

A brain–computer interface (BCI) offers movement-free control of a computer application and is achieved by reading and translating the cortical activity of the brain into semantic control signals. Motion-onset visual evoked potentials (mVEP) are neural potentials employed in BCIs and occur when motion-related stimuli are attended visually. mVEP dynamics are correlated with the position and timing of the moving stimuli. To investigate the feasibility of utilizing the mVEP paradigm with video games of various graphical complexities including those of commercial quality, we conducted three studies over four separate sessions comparing the performance of classifying five mVEP responses with variations in graphical complexity and style, in-game distractions, and display parameters surrounding mVEP stimuli. To investigate the feasibility of utilizing contemporary presentation modalities in neurogaming, one of the studies compared mVEP classification performance when stimuli were presented using the oculus rift virtual reality headset. Results from 31 independent subjects were analyzed offline. The results show classification performances ranging up to 90% with variations in conditions in graphical complexity having limited effect on mVEP performance; thus, demonstrating the feasibility of using the mVEP paradigm within BCI-based neurogaming.

Keywords

Brain–computer interface, Motion-onset visually evoked potentials, Electroencephalography, Video gaming, 3-Dimensional, Graphics, Liquid crystal display, Oculus rift, Virtual reality

© 2016 Elsevier B.V. All rights reserved.

1 INTRODUCTION

Brain–computer interfaces (BCIs) offer an alternative method of human–computer interaction and may replace input devices that require muscle control such as mice, keyboards, and gaming joysticks. A BCI-controlled computer system translates electrophysiological activity of the brain, measured either invasively or noninvasively that is modulated by a user as they sense stimuli presented visually (Farwell and Donchin, 1988), auditorily (Sellers and Donchin, 2006), tactilely (Müller-Putz et al., 2006), or if they intentionally modulate brain activity using mental imagery (Wolpaw et al., 2002). Due to its high temporal resolution, low inter- and intrasubject variability, ease of use, low cost, and user safety (Chancellor, 2009), electroencephalography (EEG) is the most widely used method to measure cortical activity. EEG is recorded for analysis by placing electrodes on the scalp of the user. BCIs have been researched for a number of decades (Wolpaw et al., 2000) with a major focus on clinical and assistive technology applications; however, recent advances in computing technology have broadened both its application domain and user base. BCI training paradigms have traditionally used gameplay elements in video games to challenge and motivate users. Brain–computer game interaction (BCGI) represents an obvious target application domain for BCI and research in the area has grown significantly in recent years (Coyle et al., 2015; Marshall et al., 2013).

Video gamers are traditionally early adopters of new and novel interaction modalities such as the Nintendo Wii (Nintendo, 2006), Microsoft Kinect (Microsoft, 2010), and PlayStation Move (Sony, 2010). The oculus rift (OCR) (Oculus, 2014b) is a technological breakthrough and represents the state of the art in virtual reality (VR) technology, spurring the development of similar VR platforms such as the HTC VIVE (HTC, 2016) and Samsung Gear VR (Samsung, 2015). The OCR is a virtual reality head-mounted display and by using the concept of stereopsis (Hubel, 1995) can provide the user with the sense of depth in a virtual scene. By combining information from the right and left eyes concerning the right and left fields of view, the human visual processing system provides us with stereoscopic depth perception. The OCR operates on the same principle to reproduce a stereoscopic view of a virtual world using two separate images rendered onto two different LCD screens—one for each eye (Oculus, 2014a). Aside from its technological underpinnings, the financial and commercial strengths of the video gaming industry may help to propel BCI technology to commercial success (Nijholt, 2008).

Most BCI studies involving the use of video games have been used as a means of training the user on how to use a BCI system (Marshall et al., 2013), to keep them motivated and challenged while they learn BCI control and served mainly as an interesting or novel training environment in order to cloak the mundane nature of training to use a BCI paradigm. Inevitably, a trade-off exists between user-centered and data-centered BCI design which refers to the fact that BCI designers sometimes sacrifice gameplay and esthetics to focus on data gathering. As a consequence, most BCI games employ rudimentary graphics and can therefore lack immersion. In the interests of promoting BCI technology to the wider gaming population, it is necessary to improve their esthetics, functional, and technological appeal.

There are a number of brain signatures that can be used for BCI and BCGI often referred to as "BCI paradigms." The motor imagery paradigm involves intentional modulation of sensorimotor oscillations or rhythms (SMRs) by imagining various limb movements (Allison et al., 2010; Pfurtscheller, 2001; Pfurtscheller and Lopes da Silva, 1999). In Coyle et al. (2015), SMRs are used to control three different BCI action games. In Asensio-Cubero et al. (2015), SMRs are employed to control left and right movements of a game character in a BCI action game. The authors in Rao et al. (2014) developed and tested a cooperative two-player BCI action game based on SMR control. Although SMRs offer an interesting control strategy that can be learned and improved over time, lengthy training periods are common before reliable control can be acquired. Also, there appears to be a nonnegligible portion of the population that cannot gain reliable control in this paradigm (Nijholt et al., 2009; Sannelli et al., 2008; Vidaurre and Blankertz, 2010). Other techniques for BCI control which subvert the requirement for user training and BCI learning problem involve evoking a response through visual, auditory, or tactile stimulation.

For example, steady-state visual evoked potentials (SSVEPs) utilize flashing visual stimuli presented on a screen or light array via a light source such as light-emitting diodes or filament bulbs which are presented to the user to invoke a response in the cortical activity and readable when EEG sensors are focused around the visual cortex (Bin et al., 2009; Cheng et al., 2002; Gao et al., 2003). Each of the stimuli flashes at a different but fixed frequency and each can be related to a command for the BCI system to process. The fundamental blinking frequency of the users' target stimulus is observed in the EEG signal. Recent BCI-gaming research which has exploited the SSVEP paradigm includes giving user control over a virtual cart in order to collect monetary rewards (Wong et al., 2015) where four SSVEP stimuli offer control representing Up, Down, Left, and Right motion of the cart. In Koo et al. (2015) the authors utilize SSVEPs to control a maze game. SSVEP control of a game character in a popular video game was shown in Kapeller et al. (2012). In Lalor et al. (2005) users were able to control the left- and right-balanced motion of a computer character in an immersive action game. To investigate the feasibility of utilizing the OCR within an SSVEP-based BCI, Koo and Choi (2015) demonstrated that lower frequencies (those <10 Hz) were able to provide better SSVEP control than the use of higher frequencies (>10 Hz). SSVEP use within an action game was investigated in Martinez et al. (2007) where the user navigates a racing car around a racing track using four chequer-board patterns representing Up, Down, Left, and Right commands. Although SSVEP BCIs are capable of providing high information transfer rates and a large number of stimuli can be presented within the field of view of the user, the use of flashing stimuli can cause visual fatigue for users, especially after long-term use (Punsawad and Wongsawat, 2013).

The P300 BCI paradigm also utilizes flashing stimuli to evoke a response in the EEG. A positive peak is produced in the EEG around 300 ms after the flash of a stimulus the BCI user attends to (the oddball stimulus) among frequent stimuli which the user ignores (Bos et al., 2009; Finke et al., 2009; Kathner et al., 2015; Pires et al., 2011). The user gazes at their required target among multiple on-screen stimuli, each relating to a specific command for the BCI system to execute. In Korczowski et al. (2015) a P300 version of the popular arcade game "Space Invaders" was controlled by flashing random groups of six on-screen targets and the role of the player was to select the single target item out of the 36 items available. A P300-based puzzle control paradigm employed in a game targeting treatment of children with attention deficit hyperactive disorder was investigated in Rohani et al. (2014) where users also have to contend with other visual distractions in a complete 3D scene of a school classroom. A P300-based game was presented in Finke et al. (2009) where users attempted to control an avatar between flashing trees in the shortest possible route. P300 use has been successful in BCI-gaming studies, and the presentation of multiple stimuli is possible within the field of view of the user but, as with the SSVEP paradigm, P300 depends on continuously flashing stimuli to evoke responses in the EEG which can be visually fatiguing for the user and perhaps may have limited appeal and performance in games that are graphically complex with fast-paced graphical changes. An alternative to these paradigms is the motion-onset visual evoked potential (mVEP) paradigm.

An mVEP response is evoked by motion-related stimuli (Guo et al., 2008a,b; Marshall et al., 2015a,b). The saliency of a sudden movement of an object or stimuli produces responses in the dorsal pathway of the brain. The dorsal pathway extends from the primary visual cortex to the parietal cortex and is known as the "where" pathway; it processes actions such as motion, spatial location, shape, and orientation (Hebart and Hesselmann, 2012). The mVEP response comprises three main peaks. The "P100" peak, a positive deflection in the EEG at between 70 and 110 ms poststimulus followed by the motion-specific "N200" peak, a negative deflection between 160 and 200 ms, and finally the "P200" peak, a positive deflection which occurs between 240 and 500 ms after the evoking stimulus whose amplitude can be increased with more complex stimuli (Guo et al., 2008a,b). Fig. 1 depicts the typical mVEP response (target vs nontarget).

Clear and robust features such as N200 and P200 constitute the neural response exploited in the mVEP-based BCI paradigm. mVEP stimuli may consist of a black

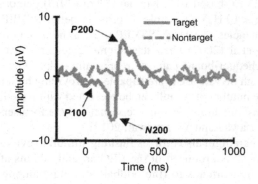

FIG. 1

Signal features of the mVEP response.

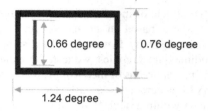

FIG. 2

Visual angles used for mVEP stimuli.

rectangle containing a white center and a moving red vertical line placed within the center subtending a visual field of 0.76 degree height × 1.24 degree width (Guo et al., 2008a,b; Marshall et al., 2015a,b). The moving red line is 0.66 degree in height as shown in Fig. 2. The red vertical line begins motion (motion-onset) starting on the right-hand side of the vacant rectangle and continues to the left-hand side in one continuous motion lasting 140 ms (motion-offset). A number of stimuli can be delineated by positioning at different locations on the screen.

The use of motion rather than flashing stimuli renders mVEP a more elegant visual paradigm than SSVEP or P300, and as a consequence, mVEP does not induce visual fatigue making it apposite for use in visually rich BCI video games. Also, due to the natural ability of the brain to capture the onset of motion (Abrams and Christ, 2003), mVEP can be used without the need for long training sessions. It is also possible to present more compact visual stimuli onto the game environment allowing more of the screen space to be used for the game.

As the mVEP is a relatively new BCI paradigm, it has been relatively understudied, especially in BCI-controlled games. mVEP, however, may offer beneficial characteristics which are suitable for use within visually rich video games. In a previous study by Marshall et al. (2015a,b), the mVEP paradigm was evaluated with three games belonging to the sports, puzzle, and action genres, each with five control options, ie, five stimuli to select from. Their findings demonstrated when users trained within a dedicated (plain) training level, average offline, and online accuracies of 74% and 66%, respectively, were possible across all three game levels. In a further study by Marshall et al. (2015a,b), they investigated the use of online mVEP control within the same three game genres with stimuli presented on a heads-up-display as opposed to overlaid onto the game graphics when users were trained within the same level as they were tested in. The study concluded that the average online accuracy had improved to 85% compared to the findings of the previous study (74%).

Here, we present three studies which investigate the influence on the mVEP paradigm using various components of video games namely graphical variations, visual parameters, and presentation modalities.

Study 1: The aim of study 1 is to investigate the effects on mVEP system accuracies on video game presentations when using graphics and in-game distractions of various complexities. mVEP stimuli were placed overlying the game scene to test the effects of in-game distractions surrounding the stimuli. Rudimentary game graphics based on the action genre were utilized.

Study 2: As an extension to study 1, we utilized the same mVEP system setup, but instead of the rudimentary graphics, we tested popular commercially available video game presentations of increasingly advanced graphical fidelities. In order to test if mVEP accuracies were affected by in-game distractions, the stimuli were placed within a dedicated controller area consisting of a plain white background.

Study 3: Using the findings gained from studies 1 and 2, we developed two game level presentations, one with basic and one with complex graphics both based on the action genre. We also compared the use of two different presentation environments for the mVEP stimuli—one where the stimuli were presented within a plain white background (dedicated stimuli area) and one where the stimuli were located within the game scene. Moreover, to investigate the effects of utilizing VR technology with mVEP-based BCI games and prove the concept of mVEP stimuli in VR for the first time, we compared the use of two display modalities namely the OCR and LCD computer screen.

2 METHODOLOGY

2.1 DATA ACQUISITION

All data were recorded in an electrostatically shielded, acoustic noise insulated room, and participants were seated in a comfortable chair 50 cm in front of a 56-cm (width 47.7 cm and height 29.8 cm) LCD screen (except in study 3 when using OCR as the display modality). During the course of each game level, each of five mVEP stimuli was active 60 times yielding data from 300 trials, ie, 60 target trials for each stimulus per game level. In order to avoid habituation, during each trial the stimuli were activated in random order. A stimulus onset asynchrony of 200 ms was employed. We refer to each of the five stimuli as buttons to be selected. The motion of the mVEP button activation was from the right-hand side of the vacant rectangle, continuing to the left-hand side in one continuous motion lasting 140 ms; therefore, the time between individual button activations and the next random stimulus activation was 60 ms as shown in Fig. 3.

Using a g.BSamp signal amplifier (g.Tec, 2016a) and g.Gammasys (g.Tec, 2016b) active electrode system connected to an Easycap (Easycap, 2016) electrode cap, a 12-channel montage was used for recording the EEG signals. Electrodes were placed surrounding the occipital areas (Cz, TP7, CPz, TP8, P7, P3, Pz, P4, P8, O1, Oz, and O2). These positions cover the primary visual cortex area (V1) (Tootell et al., 1998) involved in lower level visual processing and the dorsal pathway (middle temporal (MT) area) which is said to be involved in the detection of motion (Hebart and Hesselmann, 2012). FPz served as the reference voltage and left mastoid as ground as shown in Fig. 4.

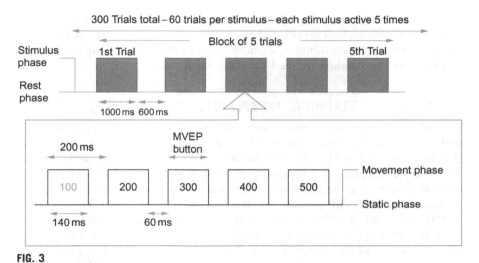

FIG. 3

Trial timing details utilized in our mVEP studies.

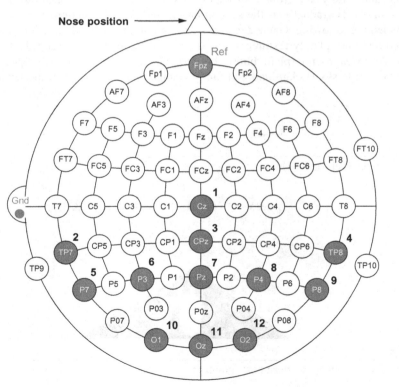

FIG. 4

Twelve channel EEG montage covering occipital areas.

The data were stored using Matlab Simulink (Mathworks, 2016), and Unity 3D (Unity, 2016) was utilized to present the visual stimuli and gaming environment. As Unity 3D activated each stimulus, a unique stimulus identifier and timing information were sent to Simulink via the User Datagram Protocol.

2.2 STUDY 1—GRAPHICAL COMPLEXITY (BASIC GAMES)

Ten subjects (two females, eight males—age range 25–37 years) participated in study 1–two subjects had previous BCI experience, and eight were BCI naïve. We compared the use of five different action game level presentations using increasingly complex graphics over the course of the session. The stimuli in study 1 were overlaid directly onto the game scene such that any in-game distractors around the stimuli may affect mVEP response and thus classification accuracies. The first game level (Game 1) was used for training and presented no graphical distractions. It consisted of a plain white colored background with the mVEP stimuli in a central position at the top of the screen (Fig. 5). Each of the remaining four game levels comprised a 3D game environment containing the following visual distractions: (1) yellow-colored capsule-shaped main character, (2) road surface, (3) roadside verge, and (4) sky background. Visual distractions were added to each of the remaining four levels gradually as the session progressed. The distractions for each level included the following: Game 2, character motion in the forward direction at a slow speed and only plainly textured surfaces used for the roadside verge (plain white) and sky background (plain blue) (Fig. 6); Game 3, the characters speed was increased, the sky background constantly changed color throughout the level, and

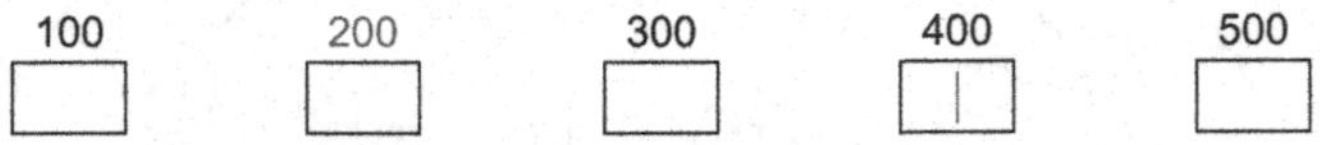

| 100 | 200 | 300 | 400 | 500 |

FIG. 5

The training level (Game 1).

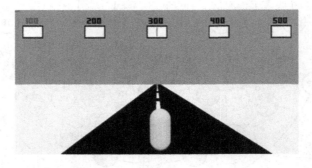

FIG. 6

Game 2 representing the most basic graphics.

the roadside verge was colored in plain green (Fig. 7); Game 4, in addition to level 2 characteristics the sky texture returned to a constant plain blue color and there were barrel-shaped objects placed directly at the side of the road (Fig. 8). The barrel objects each contained a number directly above to add text as a visual distractor; Game 5 was as level 3 but instead of having the barrel objects placed at the side of the road, cube-shaped items were added directly onto the road surface and the game character moved left and right automatically to avoid them. In addition, the sky background for Game 5 used a realistic texture (Fig. 9). The graphics used in study 1 across all levels were rudimentary in contrast to currently available commercial games on the market but still allowed for a comparison to a number of visual distractions typically associated with commercially available games such as 3D graphics, character motion, flashing imagery, textured objects, text, and vivid colors. Participants had no input control over the game levels. All levels were automatically controlled by the Unity 3D game engine. The task of the participants was to focus on the target stimulus indicated by its red-colored text.

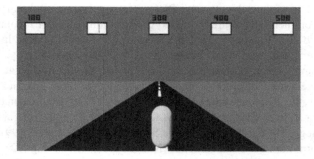

FIG. 7

Game 3.

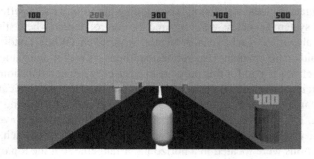

FIG. 8

Game 4.

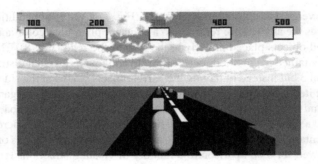

FIG. 9

Game 5 representing the most complex graphics.

2.3 STUDY 2—GRAPHICAL COMPLEXITY (COMMERCIAL GAMES)

Study 2 took place on another day involving 10 male participants (age range 21–38 years), three of which were retained from study 1 and the remaining seven were new to this study. Six of the subjects were BCI naïve. We compared the graphical complexities of commercially available video games within an mVEP control environment. To keep visual distractions to a minimum, the stimuli resided in a dedicated "controller area"—a plain white background above the game display. We selected five video games, each representing a different genre and graphical complexity. The game levels used in order of the most basic to the most graphically complex were: Game 1, the 2D arcade game Pacman (Namco, 1984) (Fig. 10) on the Nintendo Entertainment System (Nintendo, 1983); Game 2, the 2D platform game Sonic the Hedgehog (Sega, 1991b) (Fig. 11) on the Sega Mega Drive (Sega, 1991a); Game 3, the 3D platform game Crash Bandicoot (NaughtyDog, 1996) (Fig. 12) for the Sony PlayStation (Sony, 1995); Game 4, the 3D car racing simulation Gran Turismo 3 (PolyphonyDigital, 2001) (Fig. 13) for the Sony PlayStation 2; and Game 5, the first-person shooter Call of Duty: Advanced Warfare (Activision, 2014) (Fig. 14) on the Microsoft Xbox 360 (Microsoft, 2005).

To investigate if visual distractions surrounding the stimuli had an effect on mVEP detection and system accuracy, we compared the controller area where stimuli buttons were placed above the game in a dedicated white area (White condition—W) vs stimuli overlaid on the graphics (No White condition—NW) for one game genre (only one game level was tested for this purpose to ensure the session duration was not too long for participants). Crash Bandicoot was tested with both the dedicated stimulus presentation area and the dedicated white background surrounding the stimuli removed (Fig. 15). Crash Bandicoot was selected as it represented the average graphical complexity among the five game levels under evaluation. In each game level, the mVEP buttons were located in a horizontal arrangement at the top of the screen. To avoid confounding results due to the participants becoming fatigued during the session, the sequence of game levels was randomized for each participant. As in study 2, the participants were directed to stimuli to focus on, while the game graphics were played and had no direct input control over the game levels.

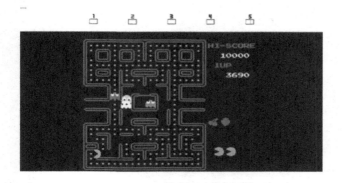

FIG. 10

Pacman representing the most basic graphics (NES).

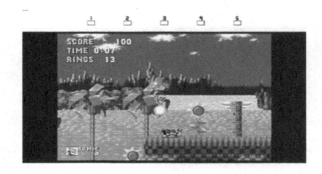

FIG. 11

Sonic the Hedgehog (Mega Drive).

FIG. 12

Crash Bandicoot (PlayStation).

FIG. 13

Gran Turismo 3 (PlayStation 2).

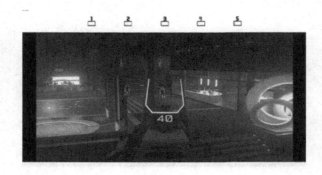

FIG. 14

COD representing the most complex graphics.

FIG. 15

Crash Bandicoot level without dedicated controller area.

2.4 STUDY 3—OCR VS LCD SCREEN

Two female and 12 male participants (age range 19–38 years) took part in study 3 which took place on another day. Eleven subjects were BCI naïve and three had previous BCI experience from study 1 or study 2. We compared the use of two modalities as visual display methods for mVEP games. We utilized the contemporary OCR (Oculus, 2014b) (Development Kit 2 (DK2)) headset to present four mVEP game levels to the participants based on the action genre (Levels OCR1, OCR2, OCR3, and OCR4). We then used the more widely utilized LCD screen to present the same four levels to the participants (Levels LCD1, LCD2, LCD3, and LCD4). As in study 2, in order to offer a fair comparison between the two display modalities, we compared the use of two different mVEP stimuli background types—one which offers a dedicated white "controller area" (W) in which to present the mVEP stimuli (Levels OCR1, OCR3, LCD1, and LCD3) (Figs. 16 and 17), and the other which presented the mVEP stimuli overlaid onto the game environment (NW) (Levels OCR2, OCR4, LCD2, and LCD4) (Figs. 18 and 19). The basic game level

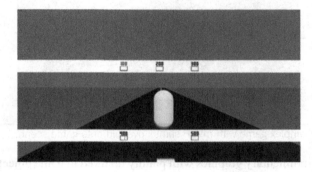

FIG. 16

Level 1—Basic game with dedicated mVEP stimuli area.

FIG. 17

Level 3—Complex game with dedicated mVEP stimuli area.

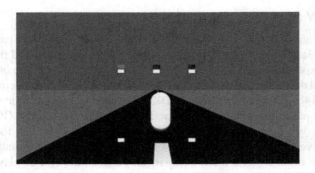

FIG. 18

Level 2 NW—Basic game level with stimuli overlaid onto game scene.

FIG. 19

Level 4 NW—Complex game with mVEP stimuli overlaid onto game scene.

offered only rudimentary graphics with plainly textured in game objects representing the game character, road, sky, and roadside. The capsule-shaped game character moved in a constant forward direction at a slow pace. More realistic graphics were used for the complex game level and included a realistic 3D car model, fully textured road and roadside surfaces, 3D models of buildings, and realistic sky. The car moved in a constant forward direction and automatically avoided traffic cone objects placed on the road by turning left and right. The OCR and EEG setup is shown in Fig. 20.

3 DATA ANALYSIS
3.1 DATA PREPROCESSING

Data from all studies were analyzed offline. The data for each stimulus were epoched at 1200 ms, triggered 200 ms prior to motion-onset. Using the 200 ms preceding motion-onset of the five stimuli, the mean voltage was baseline corrected. Using a low-pass Butterworth filter (order 5, cutoff at 10 Hz) the data were digitally

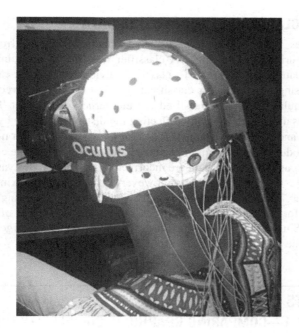

FIG. 20

Participant wearing the EEG/OCR setup as used in study 3.

filtered and then subsequently resampled at 20 Hz. The most reactive mVEP components, ie, P100, N200, and P200, appear in the EEG between 70 and 500 ms; therefore, features were extracted using this epoch yielding 9 features for each of the 12 channels. Data were averaged over 5 trials yielding 12 feature vectors per stimulus for each level. The time epochs associated with each trial were initially used to split the data into target and nontarget items. As an mVEP response in the EEG is time and phase locked to the onset of the motion stimuli, the induced mVEP response is detectable using the above-mentioned processing procedure (Guo et al., 2008a,b).

3.2 mVEP CLASSIFICATION—TRAINING DATA

Initially, a binary linear discriminant analysis (LDA) classifier is trained to distinguish between target and nontarget (2-class) feature vectors from single channels. A leave-one-out (LOO) cross-validation was performed on 50% of the data (training data) and the final 50% of data were held out for use as testing data. LOO classification was performed on each of the 12 channels, and the channels were subsequently ranked based on the mean LOO classification accuracy. The three highest-ranked channels were selected for further tests. These average cross-validation results are reported as "LOO-CV (training)." Also reported is the 5-class discrimination accuracy on the training data based on the classifier trained on the target vs nontarget training data "Validation 5-class (Training)."

3.3 mVEP CLASSIFICATION—TESTING DATA

Using features from the three best-ranked channels selected from the cross-validation described earlier, an LDA classifier was trained on training data (first 50% of user data for each level). To classify individual mVEP for each of the five symbols in a single trial (5-class classification), first each feature vector associated with each stimulus in a trial is classified as either target or nontarget. The LDA classifier produces a distance value, D, reflecting the distance from the hyperplane separating target and nontarget features ($D > 0$ for target and $D < 0$ for nontarget). The vector that produces the maximum distance value is selected as the classified stimulus. In some cases nontarget data are incorrectly classified if we evaluate, D, ie, in some cases $D > 0$ for nontarget data; however, D is normally maximal among the target stimulus, ie, the stimulus on which the user is focused. Single-trial results are reported for 5-class classification using the remaining 50% of the data and reported as "Single-trial 5-class (Testing)." We also report the target vs nontarget accuracy on the test data, ie, "Single-trial 2-class (Testing)."

4 RESULTS

4.1 STUDY 1—COMPARING GRAPHICAL COMPLEXITY (BASIC GAMES)

Results for study 1 are presented in Fig. 21. Here, we compare the basic game level 1 (white background—no graphics) with each of the other levels. Across all the tests there is a drop in accuracy between the basic level game graphic (Game 1) to the

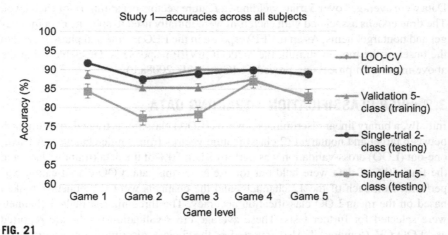

FIG. 21

Study 1 results. 2-Class and 5-class (training and testing) mVEP accuracies across all game levels.

Game 2 level graphics; however, these drops are only significant for the 2-class results ($p < 0.05$). For all tests, there is no difference between the Game 1 and Game 3 or 4, however, comparing the results of the most basic vs most complex Game levels (Game 1 vs Game 5), the results were found to be significant for both the 2-class assessments ($p < 0.05$). For both of the 5-class assessments, the differences between the most basic vs the most complex graphical levels were found to be insignificant ($p > 0.05$). The 5-class training and testing accuracies are lower than the 2-class assessment accuracies as expected (for two classes, random data would produce a chance accuracy of 50%, whereas for five classes, the chance accuracy is 20%).

4.2 STUDY 2—COMPARING GRAPHICAL COMPLEXITY (COMMERCIAL GAMES)

The results for study 2 are presented in Fig. 22. As with study 1, results for study 2 show the homogeneity of accuracies for the 2-class and 5-class training and testing assessments. The maximum accuracies were obtained with Gran Turismo 3 on three of the assessments. Gran Turismo 3 constitutes the second most graphically complex game level. All differences in performance were found to be insignificant; however, Crash Bandicoot level with no white surrounding the controller area consistently produced the lowest accuracy, indicating that having the controller overlaid on the graphics may have an impact on performance, particularly in a fast-paced game with fast moving characters, objects, and scrolling screen.

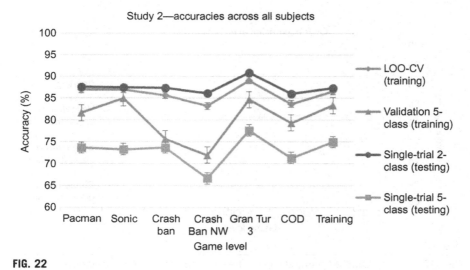

FIG. 22

Study 2 results. 2-Class and 5-class (training and testing) mVEP accuracies across all game levels.

4.3 STUDY 3—OCR VS LCD SCREEN

Offline results for the LCD and OCR tests are presented in Figs. 23 and 24, respectively. Fig. 23 shows the superior performance of the 2-class tests, continuing the trend of 2-class accuracy dominance across all three studies, which is expected given probability of misclassifying in a 2-class problem (50% chance) is much

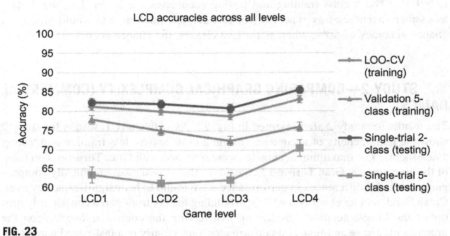

FIG. 23

Study 3 results for LCD screen. 2-Class and 5-class (training and testing) mVEP accuracies across all game levels.

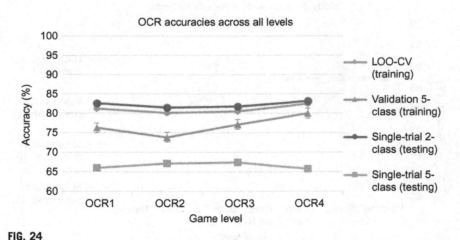

FIG. 24

Study 3 results for OCR. 2-Class and 5-class (training and testing) mVEP accuracies across all game levels.

lower compared to 5-class problem (20% chance). As with studies 1 and 2, the 5-class accuracies are lowest. Trends between all tests were similar across all game levels with game level 4 producing the maximum accuracies; however, difference in accuracies given by level 4 is not significant ($p > 0.05$). This result is somewhat encouraging as the more complex graphics using the dedicated controller area surrounding the stimuli is not detrimental to performance.

Fig. 24 shows the results for the OCR. Trends are analogous with the LCD test with level OCR4 showing the highest accuracy achieved for each assessment. Again, the 5-class accuracies are significantly lower than the 2-class results, but there are no significant differences in game levels. When compared with the LCD screen presentation modality, the differences for all assessments are insignificant ($p > 0.05$).

For both the LCD screen and OCR presentation modalities, the use of dedicated controller area surrounding the stimuli vs no controller area showed no significant difference ($p > 0.05$). The differences between the best and worst performing game levels for each of the analysis methods for both the LCD screen and OCR were compared and no significant differences were found ($p > 0.05$).

4.4 STUDIES 1–3—BEST CHANNELS

A cross-validation test performed on the EEG electrode channels yielded the three highest-ranked electrode averages across all three studies to be channels *P7*, *O1*, and *P3* (in descending order). This is depicted in the topographic plot in Fig. 25.

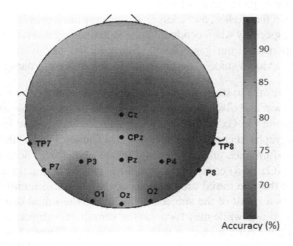

FIG. 25

Topographic representation of the three highest-ranked channels averaged across all three studies.

5 DISCUSSION

We have studied the effects on classification accuracies using various graphical properties in games based on the mVEP and compared the use of two different approaches for presenting the mVEP stimuli namely the dedicated "controller area" (W) vs the stimuli overlaid onto the game scene (NW). Results suggest that graphics containing various complexities including high-end graphics as seen in popular commercial video games can be used in an mVEP-based BCI environment while still maintaining acceptable BCI accuracy. Consistent with the study in Marshall et al. (2015a,b), the two approaches tested here to investigate the optimum display method for presenting mVEP stimuli have shown that the use of a dedicated "controller area" does indeed improve classification accuracies in certain cases. For example, in study 2, the Crash Bandicoot level performance was reduced when the graphics were overlaid on the games environment, while in study 3, there were no differences found when comparing dedicated controller area vs overlaid graphics for both basic and complex game graphics.

We have also studied BCI video game integration within a VR environment utilizing the OCR and compared its use with the more commonly utilized LCD screen. Results between these two modalities suggest the feasibility of utilizing novel display technologies within mVEP BCI games with different graphic complexities and controller types.

The studies presented here using the mVEP paradigm do, however, have a number of limitations. Across all three studies, the addition of feedback may have engaged the participants to perform better and thus may have contributed to higher accuracies. A limited number of participants ($n = 10$, 10, and 14 for studies 1, 2, and 3, respectively) took part in the studies, and a larger cohort may have provided a more diverse range of results especially when conducting the Wilcoxon signed-rank test to compare the various properties in our game levels. Some further discussion and limitations relating to the individual studies are presented in the following paragraphs.

Study 1: The results in study 1 comparing graphical complexities suggest that the mVEP detection and discrimination are affected when moving from plain white background in Game 1 to a low complexity background in Game 2; however, as graphical complexity increases (in Games 3 and 4) there is less of an impact on performance until a threshold where complexity does affect performance (Game 5) compared to baseline with no distractions. It is hypothesized that the initial drop in accuracy when transitioning from a plain background is a result of the subjects adjusting to the initial distraction of the moving background while they focus on the stimuli, ie, subjects are distracted by basic complexity initially, but as they move through Games 3 and 4, they have more experience with the main graphical interface and the changes in graphical complexity do not have any further impact on their ability to focus on the stimuli. However, with the increase in graphical complexity in Game 5, there is an impact on performance which again is significant.

However, this summarization of findings is only relevant for the 2-class (target vs nontarget) results. For the 5-class results, graphical complexity is shown to have an insignificant impact on performance. The variations in accuracies for the 5-class results are as indicated by the standard error bars (which are correlated with standard deviation), and therefore, the statistical methods may be impacted by this variation and the limited number of trials and subjects in the analysis. The game levels were presented to the participants from lowest complexity to highest complexity; therefore, we cannot rule out the possibility of user fatigue or the drying of EEG electrode gel during the course of the session correlating with changes in results associated with complexity. To avoid confounding results, it would have been prudent to have the sequence of game levels randomized for each participant (this limitation was addressed in study 2). Additionally, although 1500 trials were recorded for each participant (300 trials per game level—60 trials for each target stimulus and five game levels), each level was analyzed independently and five trials were averaged for each classified stimulus; therefore, there were only 12 trials per stimulus per game level. This was split between training and testing. We trained on target vs nontarget, so had 6 training exemplars × 5 target classes resulting in 30 training examples per game level for training. This is a relatively low number of trials for training.

Study 2: This provides an indication that there are types of graphics that may be best for mVEP (Grand Turismo type car games), while the fast-paced games such as Crash Bandicoot may be less apposite; however, the results are inconclusive. The results indicate that overlaying the stimuli onto the game graphics can result in poorer performance but again the performance drop is not shown to be significant. Only one of the game levels was used to compare the two mVEP stimuli background types. Further tests comparing each of the five game levels using both background types would produce a clearer picture of the optimum mVEP stimuli background type to use within the commercially available video games assessed in this study.

Study 3: LCD presentation and OCR presentation of mVEP stimuli do not differ. This finding is positive indicating for the first time the mVEP paradigm can not only be used for playing video games, but the paradigm can also be deployed in a virtual reality environment. However, the DK2 OCR headset, as used in this study, is a cumbersome headset and, when coupled with the EEG electrode cap as in this study, did make a number of the participants feel uncomfortable. This caveat was especially important over the course of the session where some participants commented on the bulky nature of the EEG/OCR setup toward the end of the session. Also, the OCR offers an immersive gaming experience by allowing players to look around and explore the 3D environment. During the session, noise artifacts in the EEG may have been caused by participants moving their head to look around the virtual world. In future studies, careful consideration to signal processing may help to recognize and remove such motion-related activity from the EEG so the user can make full use of the VR technology.

Our findings corroborate earlier research (Guo et al., 2008a,b) demonstrating that the left hemisphere of visual cortex showed dominance in neural activity when using leftward motion of the stimuli. This finding also replicates those in Heinze et al. (1994) where the authors report cortical activations in the contralateral hemisphere when subjecting 10 participants to flashing stimuli in the left and right visual fields. We have found further evidence that a small subset of electrodes placed over the left hemisphere of the visual cortex may provide enough information to classify mVEPs. This reduced setup would be convenient to apply mVEP for neurogaming and testing with a large participant pool. Future work will explore this reduced montage of three electrodes with a large study population.

6 CONCLUSION

Considering the vast range of video games currently available which span many genres, platforms, demographic groups, and complexity, it is clear that video games do not wholly depend on rich 3D, realistic or state-of-the-art graphics to be attractive. Other properties of video games are just as important such as but not limited to gameplay mechanics, rewarding gameplay social interaction, and novel interaction technology. However, for BCI technology to be shown in the best possible light and appeal to a wide range of users, we find it necessary to study not only the effects of different graphical complexities but also contemporary presentation modalities and interaction techniques such as the OCR. An important finding of the mVEP studies presented here can be seen from study 2, where the video games with the more complex, realistic, and state-of-the-art graphics such as in the Gran Turismo 3 game level did not adversely affect mVEP classification accuracies compared to games with less complex graphics. This is a positive finding as we can proceed to develop and test a more diverse range of BCI games which offer esthetically pleasing, immersive, and engaging graphics. We chose the mVEP paradigm as it offers a low visual fatigue, esthetically pleasing, and feature-rich paradigm that avoids the need for long user training periods and demonstrated that mVEP may be apposite for use within not only graphically rudimentary, slow paced video games, but also visually rich, immersive, and fast-paced BCI video games on a par with those commercially available. However, these findings come in the early stages of BCI game research, and if the BCI game developer is to succeed in commercializing BCI technology as control modality, more work still needs to be done to explore effects on BCI classification accuracies while using video games with various genres, graphics, and other properties such as speed, pace, colors, and contemporary presentation modalities.

REFERENCES

Abrams, R.A., Christ, S.E., 2003. Motion onset captures attention. Psychol. Sci. 14 (5), 427–432.

Activision, 2014. Call of Duty: Advanced Warfare. Available at: https://www.callofduty.com/uk/en/advancedwarfare (Accessed May 31, 2016).

Allison, B.Z., et al., 2010. Toward a hybrid brain-computer interface based on imagined movement and visual attention. J. Neural Eng. 7 (2), 26007.

Asensio-Cubero, J., Gan, J.Q., Palaniappan, R., 2015. Multiresolution analysis over graphs for a motor imagery based online BCI game. Comput. Biol. Med. 68, 21–26.

Bin, G., et al., 2009. An online multi-channel SSVEP-based brain-computer interface using a canonical correlation analysis method. J. Neural Eng. 6 (4), 1–6.

Bos, D.P., et al., 2009. Bacteria hunt: a multimodal, multiparadigm BCI game. In: Workshop Report for the Enterface Workshop in Genova, Italy, pp. 1–22.

Chancellor, A., 2009. Electroencephalography: maturing gracefully. Pract. Neurol. 9 (3), 130–132.

Cheng, M., et al., 2002. Design and implementation of a brain-computer interface with high transfer rates. IEEE Trans. Biomed. Eng. 49 (10), 1181–1186.

Coyle, D., et al., 2015. Action games, motor imagery, and control strategies: toward a multibutton controller. In: Nakatsu, R., Rauterberg, M., Ciancarini, P. (Eds.), Handbook of Digital Games and Entertainment Technologies. Springer, Singapore, pp. 1–34.

Easycap, 2016. Easycap EEG Cap. Available at: http://easycap.brainproducts.com/ (Accessed May 31, 2016).

Farwell, L.A., Donchin, E., 1988. Talking off the top of your head: toward a mental prosthesis utilizing event-related brain potentials. Electroencephalogr. Clin. Neurophysiol. 70 (6), 510–523.

Finke, A., Lenhardt, A., Ritter, H., 2009. The MindGame: a P300-based brain-computer interface game. Neural Netw. 22 (9), 1329–1333.

g.Tec, 2016a. g.tec—g.BSamp Biosignal Amplifier. Available at: http://www.gtec.at/Products/Hardware-and-Accessories/g.BSamp-Specs-Features (Accessed May 31, 2016).

g.Tec, 2016b. g.Tec—g.GAMMAsys. Available at: http://www.gtec.at/Products/Electrodes-and-Sensors/g.GAMMAsys-Specs-Features (Accessed May 31, 2016).

Gao, X., et al., 2003. A BCI-based environmental controller for the motion-disabled. IEEE Trans. Neural Syst. Rehabil. Eng. 11 (2), 137–140.

Guo, F., et al., 2008a. A brain computer interface based on motion-onset VEPs. In: 30th Annual International IEEE EMBS Conference, pp. 4478–4481.

Guo, F., et al., 2008b. A brain–computer interface using motion-onset visual evoked potential. J. Neural Eng. 5 (4), 477–485.

Hebart, M.N., Hesselmann, G., 2012. What visual information is processed in the human dorsal stream? J. Neurosci. 32 (24), 8107–8109.

Heinze, H.J., et al., 1994. Combined spatial and temporal imaging of brain activity during visual selective attention in humans. Nature 372, 543–546.

HTC, 2016. HTC VIVE. Available at: https://www.htcvive.com/uk/ (Accessed May 31, 2016).

Hubel, D.H., 1995. Eye, Brain and Vision, second ed. Henry Holt and Company, New York, USA.

Kapeller, C., Hintermüller, C., Guger, C., 2012. Augmented control of an avatar using an SSVEP based BCI. In: Proceedings of the 3rd Augmented Human International Conference on–AH'12, pp. 1–2.

Kathner, I., Kubler, A., Halder, S., 2015. Rapid P300 brain-computer interface communication with a head-mounted display. Front. Neurosci. 9 (June), 1–13.

Koo, B., Choi, S., 2015. SSVEP response on oculus rift. In: The 3rd International Winter Conference on Brain-Computer Interface, pp. 1–4.

Koo, B., et al., 2015. Immersive BCI with SSVEP in VR head-mounted display. In: 2015 37th Annual International Conference of the IEEE Engineering in Medicine and Biology Society (EMBC), pp. 1103–1106.

Korczowski, L., et al., 2015. Single-trial classification of multi-user P300-based brain-computer interface using Riemannian geometry. 37TH Annual International Conference of the IEEE Engineering in Medicine and Biology Society (EMBC) 2015, 1769–1772.

Lalor, E.C., et al., 2005. Steady-state VEP-based brain–computer interface control in an immersive 3D gaming environment. EURASIP J. Adv. Signal Process. 2005 (19), 3156–3164.

Marshall, D., et al., 2013. Games, gameplay, and BCI: the state of the art. IEEE Trans. Comput. Intell. AI Games 5 (2), 82–99.

Marshall, D., Beveridge, R., et al., 2015a. Interacting with multiple game genres using motion onset visual evoked potentials. In: The 20th International Conference on Computer Games, pp. 18–27.

Marshall, D., Wilson, S., Coyle, D., 2015b. Motion-onset visual evoked potentials for gaming. In: 8th International Conference on Computer Games, Multimedia and Allied Technology, pp. 155–164.

Martinez, P., Bakardjian, H., Cichocki, A., 2007. Fully online multicommand brain-computer interface with visual neurofeedback using SSVEP paradigm. Comput. Intell. Neurosci. 2007 (i), 1–9.

Mathworks, 2016. MATLAB Simulink. Available at: http://uk.mathworks.com/products/matlab/?requestedDomain=uk.mathworks.com (Accessed May 31, 2016).

Microsoft, 2005. Xbox 360. Available at: http://www.xbox.com/en-gb/ (Accessed May 31, 2016).

Microsoft, 2010. Xbox 360 Kinect (Microsoft). Available at: http://www.xbox.com/en-gb/kinect (Accessed May 31, 2016).

Müller-Putz, G.R., et al., 2006. Steady-state somatosensory evoked potentials: suitable brain signals for brain-computer interfaces? IEEE Trans. Neural Sys. Rehabil. Eng. 14 (1), 30–37.

Namco, 1984. PACMAN. Available at: http://pacman.com/en/pac-man-history/ (Accessed May 31, 2016).

NaughtyDog, 1996. Crash Bandicoot. Available at: https://www.playstation.com/en-gb/games/crash-bandicoot-ps3/ (Accessed May 31, 2016).

Nijholt, A., 2008. BCI for games: a "state of the art" survey. In: Entertainment Computing—ICEC 2008, pp. 225–228.

Nijholt, A., Bos, D.P.-O., Reuderink, B., 2009. Turning shortcomings into challenges: brain–computer interfaces for games. Entertain. Comput. 1 (2), 85–94.

Nintendo, 1983. NES. Available at: https://www.nintendo.co.uk/index.html (Accessed May 31, 2016).

Nintendo, 2006. Nintendo Wii. Available at: https://www.nintendo.co.uk/Wii/Wii-94559.html (Accessed May 31, 2016).

Oculus, 2014a. Binocular vision, stereoscopic imaging and depth cues. Available at: https://developer.oculus.com/documentation/intro-vr/latest/concepts/bp_app_imaging/ (Accessed May 31, 2016).

Oculus, 2014b. Oculus Rift. Available at: http://www.oculus.com/ (Accessed May 31, 2016).

Pfurtscheller, G., 2001. Functional brain imaging based on ERD/ERS. Vis. Res. 41 (10–11), 1257–1260.

Pfurtscheller, G., Lopes da Silva, F.H., 1999. Event-related EEG/MEG synchronization and desynchronization: basic principles. Clin. Neurophysiol. 110 (11), 1842–1857.

Pires, G., et al., 2011. Playing Tetris with non-invasive BCI. In: 2011 IEEE 1st International Conference on Serious Games and Applications for Health (SeGAH), pp. 1–6.

PolyphonyDigital, 2001. Gran Turismo 3. Available at: http://www.gran-turismo.com/gb/ (Accessed May 31, 2016).

Punsawad, Y., Wongsawat, Y., 2013. Hybrid SSVEP-motion visual stimulus based BCI system for intelligent wheelchair. In: Conference Proceedings: Annual International Conference of the IEEE Engineering in Medicine and Biology Society. IEEE Engineering in Medicine and Biology Society. Conference, pp. 7416–7419.

Rao, R.P.N., et al., 2014. A direct brain-to-brain interface in humans. PLoS One 9 (11), 1–12.

Rohani, D.A.D., Sorensen, H.B.D., Puthusserypady, S., 2014. Brain-computer interface using P300 and virtual reality: a gaming approach for treating ADHD. In: Conference Proceedings: Annual International Conference of the IEEE Engineering in Medicine and Biology Society. IEEE Engineering in Medicine and Biology Society. Annual Conference, pp. 3606–3609.

Samsung, 2015. Samsung gear VR. Available at: http://www.samsung.com/global/galaxy/wearables/gear-vr/ (Accessed May 31, 2016).

Sannelli, C., et al., 2008. Estimating noise and dimensionality in BCI data sets: towards BCI illiteracy comprehension. In: International Brain-Computer Interface Workshop and Training Course. vol. 1, pp. 26–31.

Sega, 1991a. Sega UK. Available at: http://www.sega.co.uk/ (Accessed May 31, 2016).

Sega, 1991b. Sonic the Hedgehog. Available at: http://www.sonicthehedgehog.com/en/ (Accessed May 31, 2016).

Sellers, E.W., Donchin, E., 2006. A P300-based brain–computer interface: initial tests by ALS patients. Clin. Neurophysiol. 117 (3), 538–548.

Sony, 1995. Playstation. Available at: http://uk.playstation.com/ (Accessed May 31, 2016).

Sony, 2010. PlayStation Move. Available at: https://www.playstation.com/en-us/explore/accessories/playstation-move/ (Accessed May 31, 2016).

Tootell, R.B., et al., 1998. Functional analysis of primary visual cortex (V1) in humans. Proc. Natl. Acad. Sci. U.S.A. 95 (3), 811–817.

Unity, 2016. Unity 3D. Available at: http://unity3d.com/ (Accessed May 31, 2016).

Vidaurre, C., Blankertz, B., 2010. Towards a cure for BCI illiteracy. Brain Topogr. 23 (2), 194–198.

Wolpaw, J.R., et al., 2000. Brain–computer interface technology: a review of the first international meeting. IEEE Trans. Rehabil. Eng. 8 (2), 164–173.

Wolpaw, J.R., et al., 2002. Brain-computer interfaces for communication and control. Clin. Neurophysiol. 113 (6), 767–791.

Wong, C.M., et al., 2015. A multi-channel SSVEP-based BCI for computer games with analogue control. In: 2015 IEEE International Conference on Computational Intelligence and Virtual Environments for Measurement Systems and Applications, CIVEMSA, pp. 1–6.

BCI in Practice and Usability Considerations

Interfacing brain with computer to improve communication and rehabilitation after brain damage

12

A. Riccio*,², F. Pichiorri*,†,², F. Schettini*, J. Toppi*,†, M. Risetti*,
R. Formisano‡, M. Molinari§, L. Astolfi*,†, F. Cincotti*,†, D. Mattia*,¹

*Neuroelectrical Imaging and Brain-Computer Interface Laboratory,
Fondazione Santa Lucia IRCCS, Rome, Italy*
†*Sapienza University of Rome, Rome, Italy*
‡*Post-Coma Unit, Fondazione Santa Lucia IRCCS, Rome, Italy*
§*Spinal Cord Unit, IRCCS Santa Lucia Foundation, Rome, Italy*
¹*Corresponding author: Tel.: +39-06-51501167, e-mail address: d.mattia@hsantalucia.it*

Abstract

Communication and control of the external environment can be provided via brain–computer interfaces (BCIs) to replace a lost function in persons with severe diseases and little or no chance of recovery of motor abilities (ie, amyotrophic lateral sclerosis, brainstem stroke). BCIs allow to intentionally modulate brain activity, to train specific brain functions, and to control prosthetic devices, and thus, this technology can also improve the outcome of rehabilitation programs in persons who have suffered from a central nervous system injury (ie, stroke leading to motor or cognitive impairment). Overall, the BCI researcher is challenged to interact with people with severe disabilities and professionals in the field of neurorehabilitation. This implies a deep understanding of the disabled condition on the one hand, and it requires extensive knowledge on the physiology and function of the human brain on the other. For these reasons, a multidisciplinary approach and the continuous involvement of BCI users in the design, development, and testing of new systems are desirable. In this chapter, we will focus on noninvasive EEG-based systems and their clinical applications, highlighting crucial issues to foster BCI translation outside laboratories to eventually become a technology usable in real-life realm.

---

²These two authors equally contributed to this chapter.

Progress in Brain Research, Volume 228, ISSN 0079-6123, http://dx.doi.org/10.1016/bs.pbr.2016.04.018
© 2016 Elsevier B.V. All rights reserved.

Keywords

Brain–computer interface, Communication, Rehabilitation, User-centered design, EEG

1 INTRODUCTION

Despite the increasing number of applications for healthy individuals in recent years, most brain–computer interface (BCI)-related research remains focused on clinical applications.

Communication and control of the external environment can be provided to severely disabled people through direct brain–computer communication, bypassing the conventional channels that are mediated by neuromuscular integrity. In these applications, BCIs are designed to replace a lost function (eg, speaking, writing, and moving around the house on a brain-controlled wheelchair) in persons with severe diseases and little or no chance of recovery.

BCIs have the potential to increase our understanding of brain function. By offering the possibility to intentionally modulate brain activity, train specific brain functions through online feedback, and control prosthetic devices, BCIs have made inroads into neurorehabilitation (ie, motor and cognitive). In this context, the aim of BCI applications is to *enhance* brain function-related signals to eventually improve functional outcomes in persons who have suffered from a central nervous system (CNS) injury, such as stroke.

In replacing communication and control and improving motor and cognitive function (Wolpaw and Wolpaw, 2012), the BCI researcher is challenged to interact with people with severe disabilities, in some cases with little or no chance of recovery [eg, spinal cord injury (SCI) patients] and very often with life-threatening conditions [eg, amyotrophic lateral sclerosis (ALS)]. This interaction has important implications—it demands a thorough understanding of the disabled condition and its effects on a personal and social level (Schicktanz et al., 2015) and requires extensive knowledge on the physiology and function of the human brain to design specific BCI-based interventions for neurorehabilitation following CNS injury.

For these reasons, clinical applications of BCIs need a multidisciplinary approach and the continuous involvement of BCI users in the design, development, and testing of new systems.

To stress the importance of a multidisciplinary and user-centered approach (ISO 9241-210:2010) in BCI applications that target disability and neurorehabilitation, we begin this chapter with an overview of currently available reports on user needs, highlighting successful examples of user-centered approaches in BCI research and suggesting strategies to optimize synergies with nearby fields and thus favoring its translation to the clinical environment (Section 2). In Section 3, we will summarize current BCI applications in replacing communication and control, highlighting their potential, limitations, and challenges. In Section 4, we review BCI applications for motor and cognitive rehabilitation—the clinical relevance of current systems will be discussed, as will the potential contribution of BCI research in this field toward increasing our understanding of the pathophysiology of CNS damage.

Whereas invasive BCIs have been proposed and tested for communication and rehabilitation (Leuthardt et al., 2004; Ramsey et al., 2014), in this chapter, we will focus on noninvasive EEG-based systems. The results that have been obtained in the past several years have demonstrated the possibility of performing complex tasks by relying on noninvasive EEG systems, highlighting the potential of BCI as an assistive technology (AT) option (Kleih et al., 2011; McFarland et al., 2008; Riccio et al., 2015; Schettini et al., 2015). Similarly, encouraging results have been generated with noninvasive BCI systems in stroke rehabilitation (Pichiorri et al., 2015; Ramos-Murguialday et al., 2013).

2 MULTIDISCIPLINARY APPROACH TO BCI DESIGN
2.1 BCI USERS IN CLINICAL CONTEXTS

Establishing a clear and comprehensive definition of users in a BCI context is the first step toward an integrated approach. "User-centered design" (UCD) is a broad term that describes design processes in which end-users influence how a product design takes shape (ISO 9241-210:2010). In the UCD approach, three types of users can be identified: (i) end-users (or primary users), persons who actually use the product; (ii) secondary users, persons who will occasionally use the product or those who use it through an intermediary; and (iii) tertiary users (professional users or other stakeholders), persons who will be affected by the use of the product or make decisions about its purchase. Applied to BCIs in clinical applications, this definition implies the involvement of several professional and nonprofessional figures (eg, caregivers, medical doctors, therapists, health care providers, companies, and insurance companies), in addition to the end-users, identified as persons with disabilities or patients who are undergoing rehabilitation.

The UCD approach is an iterative process in which the understanding and specification of user needs, in a given context of use, precedes the evaluation of the proposed system against the defined requirements. Once the context of use has been identified, the iterative process comprises three main stages that are repeated until a user-adapted product can be released: (i) specify the user requirements, (ii) produce design solutions to meet these requirements, and (iii) evaluate the designs against the requirements. Several instruments can be used to collect user requirements, such as surveys, questionnaires, interviews, and focus groups. The analysis of the requirements should involve all system stakeholders (ie, those who can affect or are affected by a given product) and thus include various user classes (end-users, professional users, companies, and policy makers). Moreover, it is important that the appropriate method by which user requirements are gathered is used—eg, survey and questionnaires produce results that are replicable and generalizable to a broader population (scientific methods); structured interviews are less replicable and generalizable (systematic methods); and focus groups (impressionistic methods) range from simple brainstorming sessions to group discussions, the results of which are not generalizable (Roadmap BNCI Horizon 2020, 2015).

Altogether, these considerations imply a comprehensive understanding, by the BCI researcher, of the wide range of users who participate in the development of a BCI system and knowledge of the correct instruments (some of which are derived by UCD approaches and theories) that can be adopted to address such a complex environment. In a clinical context, these requirements necessitate interaction with health professionals, medical companies, caregivers, and patients with specific deficits and impairments that are related to their medical condition. Thus, a multidisciplinary approach is essential. Experts from nearby fields, such as AT, human–computer interaction, robotics, psychology, rehabilitation, and clinical neurophysiology, should be continuously consulted and involved in BCI research.

In the following section, we will summarize the existing reports on user requirements and the evaluation of usability of BCIs for clinical applications and discuss the importance of an integrated multidisciplinary approach and synergies with nearby fields with regard to successful application of BCIs in clinical contexts.

2.2 USER NEEDS AND USABILITY EVALUATION

2.2.1 Communication and control applications

In recent years, an increasing number of studies have adopted the UCD approach to evaluate the usability of BCI systems (Kübler et al., 2014) and investigate BCI end-users' needs. Most of these studies involved persons with ALS, their caregivers, and other stakeholders in the field. Several instruments have been used, ranging from surveys (Geronimo et al., 2015; Huggins et al., 2011) to focus groups (Blain-Moraes et al., 2012), for which the following technical issues emerged: simplicity and reliability of particular hardware and software characteristics and accuracy of command identification (at least 90% was required). Moreover, personal and relational factors were identified as barriers to successful BCI use: personal factors included psychological (cognitive fatigue, anxiety, participant attitude, and managing distraction), physiological (fatigue and endurance), and physical (pain and discomfort) issues, whereas among relational factors (corporeal, technological, and social relations), the importance of maintaining a sense of agency during the progression of the illness was highlighted. Thus, participants insisted on the importance of the accuracy of a BCI system. Further, behavioral deficits influenced the level of acceptance of the BCI as an AT in end-users with ALS (Geronimo et al., 2015).

Recently, Nijboer (2015) interviewed 28 stakeholders, who stressed the issue of the possible presence of cognitive and physical constraints in target users that could limit BCI control, implying the need to develop AT solutions that are designed by taking into account cognitive and sensory disabilities. Liberati et al. (2015) performed a focus group involving persons with ALS, their caregivers, and health care assistants and reported the following factors as being essential for BCI development: the need for information on BCI systems, on their capabilities and limitations, and on the differences between those with ALS and healthy persons in BCI control. Another factor was the modularity of BCIs: participants stressed the importance of a modular and customizable system to support a wide range of users. Other factors included the importance of taking into account the emotions of persons with ALS and their need to retain a sense of agency when using a BCI.

In Section 3, we will report more on BCI studies for communication and control applications with the participation of end-users in the testing.

2.2.2 Rehabilitation applications

Collecting user needs with regard to BCIs for rehabilitation implies continuous interaction with rehabilitation experts (eg, medical doctors and therapists). The founding principles of neurorehabilitation must be embodied in the BCI applications, which should be specifically designed and tailored to the pathology and clinical setting (hospital, rehabilitation clinic, home-based rehabilitation of the chronic patient). Complementing this perspective, BCI technology should be integrated into a comprehensive rehabilitation program, subserving the specific objectives of each patient and his/her rehabilitator during recovery.

As in communication and control applications, the system characteristics and the psychophysiological factors of end-users must be taken into account. An important issue of rehabilitation applications is the acceptability of the technologically advanced tool by elderly patients; Lee et al. (2013) tested this aspect with a BCI for cognitive rehabilitation. Acceptability by rehabilitators is also critical, especially for systems that are designed for inpatient rehabilitation. The feasibility and acceptability of an inpatient rehabilitation system for upper limb motor recovery (Cincotti et al., 2012) have been tested with admitted patients and their therapists (Morone et al., 2015)—in this study, the acceptability of the proposed system by therapists was related to the subjective technical confidence and attitude toward the use of technologies. This result implies that improvements in hardware and software components that increase ease of use are needed, even in this field.

Positive feedback on the use of BCIs for motor rehabilitation in general were recently collected in a focus group setting, involving primary users (stroke patients), professionals (medical doctors and therapists), and other stakeholders (health care providers, company representatives; Roadmap BNCI Horizon 2020, 2015). The discussion brought up interesting near-future scenarios for home-based rehabilitation that is supported by BCIs (chronic phase) and for inpatient rehabilitation with BCI as an adjunct to standard therapy (subacute phase); although the application was undoubtedly judged to be promising, it clearly emerged that large clinical trials are needed to define the parameters of the intervention (eg, duration, quantity, and indications). More details on the state of the art of current applications for BCIs in rehabilitation will be presented in Section 4.

3 REPLACING COMMUNICATION AND CONTROL

Communication with others is the first step toward building a relationship in society. Communication is related to social activity, social networks, and social support; accordingly, it has a considerable impact on quality of life (QoL).

Persons with acquired neurological conditions eventually lose the ability to communicate. To compensate for this loss and restore basic communication abilities, they rely on ATs. ATs increase their independence and reduce social isolation, significantly improving their QoL. Despite the progress in the development of ATs, there are many who lack functionally valid residual muscular activity, preventing them from fully benefiting from ATs. BCIs exploit brain activity as an input channel to control external devices: they have the potential to enable severely disabled individuals to communicate with other people and control their environment, without relying on muscular outputs. This potential was confirmed in many studies on noninvasive BCIs for communication in those with severe motor disabilities, as reported in the following section.

In recent years, the development of communication systems that are based on BCI technology has relied on the UCD principles (Kübler et al., 2014; Millán et al., 2010; Pasqualotto et al., 2012; Powers et al., 2015), in which end-users were the focus of the development of BCIs and the UCD iterative process was adopted (Section 2).

Primary users (end-users) of BCIs for communication and interaction with the environment are persons with functional deficits affecting their capacity to communicate and interact with the environment. Several classes of end-users have been defined by researchers (Mak and Wolpaw, 2009) and rehabilitation professionals (Nijboer, 2015); individuals who suffer from ALS, multiple sclerosis, cerebral palsy (CP), brain stem stroke, SCI, muscular dystrophy, Duchenne muscular dystrophy (DMD), Rett syndrome, peripheral neuropathy, and locked-in syndrome (LIS) might benefit from BCIs. The extent of end-users' residual neuromuscular control, in addition to the etiology of their pathology, has been considered to be the main factor in categorizing them for BCI applications. However, in the past several years, the importance of end-users' cognitive abilities in their interaction with BCI paradigms has been noted (Nijboer, 2015; Riccio et al., 2012, 2013; Schreuder et al., 2013).

Secondary users are nonprofessional users who would be influenced indirectly by BCI use, such as family members, caregivers, and people who interact with end-users.

Tertiary users are professional users, such as manufacturers, AT professionals, researchers, and other stakeholders—eg, insurance firms and public health systems.

The following section will survey current applications of BCIs that aim to replace the ability to communicate and interact with the environment in end-users. Studies will be considered with regard to their adherence to the UCD approach; thus, reports that primarily involve potential end-users as testers of BCI technology and include evaluations on usability will be considered. For the latter, we refer to the approach that is applied in BCI studies that include assessments of effectiveness, efficiency, and user satisfaction. Effectiveness is expressed as the accuracy and completeness with which the intended goals are achieved; efficiency refers to the amount of human, economic, and temporal resources that are expended in obtaining the required level of product effectiveness; and satisfaction is a measure of the immediate and long-term comfort and acceptability of the overall system (ISO 9241-210:2010).

Altogether, these parameters aim to establish the acceptability of BCI prototypes in bridging the gap in translating BCI technologies from the laboratory to real-life use (Kübler et al., 2014, 2015b).

3.1 BCIs FOR COMMUNICATION IN END-USERS

The first studies on end-users in the evaluation of the feasibility of BCIs for communication involved people with advanced ALS, who were trained to control a virtual speller with slow cortical potentials (SCPs) (Birbaumer et al., 1999, 2000; Hinterberger et al., 2003; Kübler et al., 1999, 2001; Neumann et al., 2003). SCPs are slow polarization shifts that are recorded over the sensorimotor cortex in association with various cognitive tasks. By learning to perform mental tasks to effect changes in SCPs and thereby control the movement of an object on a computer screen, end-users were able to select letters that were presented dichotomously. The alphabet was gradually split into two subsets of letters, successively presented in five levels, until the single intended letter was presented for selection (Kübler et al., 2001).

Similarly, BCIs that are based on sensorimotor rhythms (SMRs) are operated by voluntary modulation of rhythms that are recorded over sensorimotor areas but exclusively related to limb movement execution and imagination (Pfurtscheller and Neuper, 1992). In brief, motor imagery induces a desynchronization (ie, a reduction in spectral power) that occurs within specific EEG frequency ranges (alpha 8–12 Hz and beta 18–26 Hz), above sensorimotor cortical regions contralateral to the imagined part of the body (Pfurtscheller and Lopes da Silva, 1999). The consequent modulation of SMRs of two brain states that were associated with two types of motor imagery (eg, right vs left hand and right hand vs both feet) or with one type of motor imagery and relaxation was exploited to control a cursor (presented in visual modality) in patients with spinal cord lesions (SCI; McFarland et al., 2008; Pfurtscheller et al., 2003; Wolpaw and McFarland, 2004) and ALS (Kübler et al., 2005). Subsequently, SMR-based BCIs were used to control spelling (Neuper et al., 2003, 2006), environmental control (Babiloni et al., 2009; Cincotti et al., 2008), and assistive mobility applications (Leeb et al., 2013) in people with motor disabilities due to diseases such as CP, DMD, ALS, SCI, and SMA. Although, these studies on end-users focused on one of the three domains of usability, namely the device effectiveness they clearly demonstrated the feasibility of SCP- and SMR-based BCIs to replace communication and control in various populations of end-users.

Alternative feedback modalities for SMR-based BCIs were also evaluated with healthy participants (Chatterjee et al., 2007; McCreadie et al., 2014; Nijboer et al., 2008a).

Most studies on communication that have involved potential end-users evaluated P3-based BCIs (P3-BCIs). The P3 wave is a positive deflection that arises in the EEG approximately 300 ms after the presentation of a task relevant visual, auditory, or somatosensory stimulus (Sutton et al., 1965). The first P3 paradigm comprised a virtual keyboard that was organized in a 6×6 matrix (Farwell and Donchin, 1988), the rows and columns of which were randomly intensified. The user had to focus on the desired item, which was the "rare event" of an oddball paradigm (Fabiani et al., 2007) and elicited the P3 event-related potential (ERP) that was exploited by the BCI to identify the item. After its introduction people with ALS could communicate through the P3-BCI (Birbaumer, 2006; McCane et al., 2015), maintaining stable performance over time (Nijboer et al., 2008b; Silvoni et al., 2013), but approximately 30% of the population did not demonstrate adequate control (McCane et al., 2014).

In addition to the assessment of the system effectiveness, the types of stimulation exploited to elicit the P3 (Kaufmann et al., 2013; Townsend et al., 2010), the user's motivation (Nijboer et al., 2010), and selective attention (Riccio et al., 2013) were shown to influence the BCI performance of people with neurodegenerative diseases.

Moreover, simplifications of the P3 speller, resulting in 4-choice (Piccione et al., 2006; Sellers and Donchin, 2006) and 6-choice paradigms (Hoffmann et al., 2008), were evaluated in terms of their effectiveness with users who suffered from various pathologies.

The performance of the P3 speller was recently demonstrated to depend on eye gaze on the intended letter (Brunner et al., 2010; Treder and Blankertz, 2010). Accordingly, impairments to oculomotor control and visual function can affect the performance of BCIs that rely on visual abilities. This finding prompted research that emphasized the needs of eye gaze-independent BCIs, exploiting visual, auditory, and tactile channels. Although many of these alternatives have been presented (Acqualagna and Blankertz, 2011; Aloise et al., 2013; Hohne et al., 2010; Schreuder et al., 2011), few have been tested on potential end-users (for a review, see Riccio et al., 2012). In Marchetti et al. (2013), 10 users with ALS were involved to evaluate 2 visual 4-choice ERP-based interfaces based on covert attention, and showed that they were able to control a cursor with both interfaces.

In parallel, visual eye gaze-independent BCIs which exploited steady-state visual evoked potentials (SSVEP) were proposed (Zhang et al., 2010). SSVEPs are stable oscillations in voltage elicited by rapid repetitive visual stimulation. When the user directs his/her attention to one of the presented stimuli, SSVEP responses are elicited at the corresponding frequency. An independent covert two-class SSVEP paradigm was evaluated with six end-users with severe disorders of behavioral communication (LIS due to traumatic brainstem lesion and stroke). Two of them obtained accuracies above chance level (evaluated at 63%) in the training session and one was able to functionally communicate online (Lesenfants et al., 2014). An SSVEP-based BCI to be controlled with eyes closed was tested with one end-user with ALS (Han et al., 2013) who controlled the system with an 80% of accuracy.

Although no direct reference to UCD was reported in these SSVEP studies, they represent a notable effort in developing eye-gaze-independent visual paradigms, which would improve performance and satisfaction in end-users with impaired oculomotor control. A special focus on hardware characteristics was further reported in Lesenfants et al. (2014) where the stimulation pattern was described as small, portable, easy to use and adapted for bedside use.

Auditory BCIs have been controlled by participants with motor disabilities in certain cases (Kleih et al., 2015; Sellers and Donchin, 2006) but not others (Kübler et al., 2009; Schreuder et al., 2013; Simon et al., 2015). The unsuccessful clinical trials were attributed to the excessive cognitive workload that was required to control these BCIs, which presented multiclass paradigms, underscoring the need to develop BCIs that are adaptable to various end-users and cope with user needs in accordance with the UCD approach. In particular, in Schreuder et al. (2013), the participant, who had suffered from an ischemic brain stem stroke, was presented with an auditory and a visual ERP paradigm, only the latter of which she successfully controlled, possibly due to the user's neuropsychological deficit.

The relevance of adapting BCIs individually in accordance with the UCD principle was also highlighted in a case study by Kaufmann et al. (2013). With the LIS participant, tactually evoked ERP modality was clearly more reliable than visual and auditory modality. Again, this discrepancy showed the need to identify the best stimulus modality for each end-user.

In an effort to bring the BCIs outside the laboratory, initial steps were made toward the integration of BCI-based systems with existing technologies following a UCD approach (see Fig. 1).

Thompson et al. (2014) showed that an unmodified commercial AT, operated through a plug-and-play BCI keyboard, can be controlled by end-users with ALS. In this study, the system was evaluated only in terms of its effectiveness. Conversely, a comprehensive approach to measuring usability (effectiveness, efficiency, and satisfaction) was adopted to evaluate a P3-based BCI that was integrated—as an

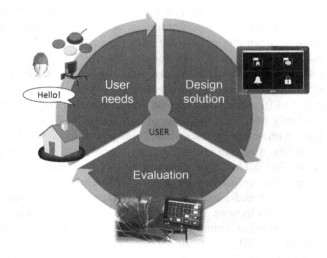

FIG. 1

The user-centered design (UCD) cycle foresees three main stages: collection of needs and requirements, design and development of solutions accordingly, and evaluation against the designed requirements.

additional control option—into a commercial AT software program over the course of the UCD iterative cycle. The system was initially tested with healthy (Riccio et al., 2011) and potential end-users (Zickler et al., 2011). In the first part of the evaluation, end-user feedback was collected and addressed in a second version of the system, which was endowed with a *hybrid* control. The hybrid control contained an additional channel, exploiting the electromyographic (EMG) signals that were generated by the end-user's residual muscular activity to delete incorrect selections. To close the UCD cycle, the system usability was reevaluated, involving end-users with severe motor disabilities (Riccio et al., 2015).

Another attempt to follow the complete UCD cycle (from collecting needs and requirements to testing and evaluating a specifically designed BCI systems) is represented by an AT prototype (Caruso et al., 2013) that could be accessed and operated through several conventional and alternative aids in combination with a P3-based BCI channel. The functions of the AT prototype in terms of communication and domotic control were selected based on the results of a preliminary survey (Schettini et al., 2015) and focus group (Liberati et al., 2015) with end-users. The prototype was sufficiently adaptable to manage progressive impairments to muscular function (as in the case of a neurodegenerative disease, such as ALS). The feasibility and usability of the proposed prototype were evaluated by people with ALS (Schettini et al., 2015).

Full usability was also assessed to evaluate a P3-based brain-painting BCI (Zickler et al., 2013), operated with high effectiveness and efficiency by four end-users with severe disabilities.

The usability of an EMG-based command to delete incorrect selections was also demonstrated for a SMR-based speller in eight end-users maintaining some usable muscle reliability (Leeb et al., 2013; Perdikis et al., 2014). The EMG-based command was proved to be reliable and flexible to end-users functional profile, confirming the adaptability of UCD to BCI devices development.

Although the results of these studies are encouraging, they often involved end-users who had not lost their motor abilities completely and could thus take advantage of conventional ATs (ie, they could rely on communication channels other than a BCI). A recent study addressed the issue of considering a P3-BCI-based internet browser for users with severe physical disabilities who could still use conventional ATs. An eye tracker was faster, more accurate, and more usable than the BCI (Pasqualotto et al., 2015). One of the principal targets of research on BCIs for communication has been the replacement of communication in people with no other such means; yet, few cases of end-users with complete LIS (CLIS) have been described. However, promising results were reported in two studies that demonstrated that BCI can be used to reestablish communication in people with CLIS due to ALS (Gallegos-Ayala et al., 2014) and brainstem stroke (Sellers et al., 2014). Using near-infrared spectroscopy (NIRS), Gallegos and colleagues obtained significantly above chance level binary (yes vs no) answers in a woman who was diagnosed with ALS and had lost the ability to communicate with eye movements, other muscles, and assistive communication devices.

Conversely, Sellers and colleagues reported on a case of CLIS due to brainstem stroke who was able to control an adapted P3 speller BCI to produce messages for his family: the patient was unable to control the eye tracker but could still communicate through a low-tech solution, requiring an assistant. Over 13 months, the operators visited the participant for 62 recording sessions. In 40 sessions, he was able to spell words accurately and to initiate dialogs with his family. Several paradigms were tested to allow him to communicate, and the number of flashes and stimulus onset asynchrony were varied between visits and sessions to optimize performance. BCI technology represented an additional means of volitional communication providing the participant with his only method of unassisted communication, possibly helping him to regain a sense of autonomy from an otherwise dependent situation.

The final aim of BCI research is to bring usable BCIs for communication from the laboratory to severely disabled users' homes. The potential of long-term independent home use for severely disabled people with ALS was demonstrated in a case report (Sellers et al., 2010); daily BCI use contributed significantly to the end-user's QoL and productivity, as informally reported by the end-user and his caregivers. A comprehensive approach to the evaluation of the usability and the impact of the BCI on the QoL of persons with LIS was adopted in Holz et al. (2015a,b). The long-term independent use of the brain-painting application controlled by a P3-based BCI (Kübler et al., 2013; Zickler et al., 2013) was evaluated at two end-users' home. Usability of such a BCI used in daily life was evaluated in terms of effectiveness, efficiency, and user's satisfaction as expected from UCD. Special emphasis was placed on the impact of the BCI on the lives of the two end-users. Results showed that the proposed BCI could be reliably used as an assistive device over a long period of time with a positive impact on the QoL.

The studies reported in this section showed the potential of BCIs for communication and control for end-users with several diseases leading to severe disabilities. Although the evaluation studies with the participation of end-users are not definitive, the introduction of the UCD in the BCI field represents an effort of the BCI community to bring the end-users into the focus of BCI development. UCD provides a framework to promote BCI development together with the end-users (Kübler et al., 2015b) and allowed a first delineation of user needs, preparing the ground to finally bring BCIs outside the laboratories.

The BCI community is continuously working on the simplicity and the reliability of hardware and software characteristics (Aricò et al., 2014; Brunner et al., 2011; Kaufmann et al., 2012; Nijboer et al., 2015; Renard et al., 2010; Schettini et al., 2014), promptly meeting the requirements for modular and customizable systems (Riccio et al., 2015; Schettini et al., 2015) which take into account cognitive (Riccio et al., 2013; Schreuder et al., 2013) and physical constrains (Lesenfants et al., 2014; Marchetti et al., 2013) of end-users.

Despite the overall efforts made by the researchers in the developmental phase, the acceptance of the technology by the end-user is unpredictable; a full multidisciplinary approach reduces the risk of future equipment abandonment. Also a greater involvement of secondary and especially tertiary users in BCI development would probably increase the acceptance rate of BCI systems in a domestic environment and their translation to market.

4 IMPROVING MOTOR AND COGNITIVE FUNCTION

BCI offers the possibility to detect, monitor, and reinforce specific brain activities. Brain activity that is recorded via, eg, EEG can be related to specific functions, one example above all is the mu rhythm for sensorimotor activation (Pfurtscheller and Lopes da Silva, 1999). In medical conditions that affect the CNS, brain activity can be altered, paralleling the impairment of the specific related function. The potential to guide altered brain activity back to a physiological condition through the BCI and the assumption that this recovery of brain activity leads to restoration of behavior—ie, function (McFarland et al., 2015)—constitute one of the rationale behind the use of BCI systems in rehabilitation.

To propose and successfully evaluate BCI-based interventions for rehabilitation that are rational, feasible, and effective, multidisciplinary expertise is required. Extensive knowledge in neurophysiology is needed to decode the relationship between brain activity and function, and how this relationship is altered in CNS conditions and the proper neurophysiological indicators that should be used to evaluate the effects of the BCI. The clinical and rehabilitative aspects of each specific condition must be taken into account to set reasonable rehabilitative objectives and establish the metrics that are apt to evaluate the achievement of these goals. Also, the technical aspects of BCIs are paramount in applying the best possible setting, using the fittest brain signal, and deploying the most appropriate algorithm to subserve the specific objectives of rehabilitation.

Provided that all of these aspects are considered, BCI technology can be used as a rehabilitative intervention, besides other neuromodulation (eg, noninvasive brain stimulation) and neurofeedback paradigms.

Most current work on BCIs in neurorehabilitation is targeted toward improving motor deficits due to stroke. Stroke is an acute injury of the CNS that is affected by sudden ischemia or hemorrhage in the brain. Causing a wide range of deficits (motor, cognitive), depending on lesion location and extension, stroke is a leading cause of long-term disability (Go et al., 2013). Although research suggests that most poststroke recovery mechanisms occur within the first several months after the injury (Zeiler and Krakauer, 2013), clinical experience supports the importance of maintaining the benefits of rehabilitation in the chronic phase (Teasell et al., 2014), and many studies on noninvasive brain stimulation suggest that such techniques are effective, even in the chronically damaged brain (Di Pino et al., 2014). Thus, the epidemiological profile of stroke implies that the target population of BCI-based interventions in this area is wide (compared with BCIs for communication and control applications).

In this chapter, we will survey the current applications of BCIs as rehabilitative interventions in motor and cognitive disabilities (primarily due to stroke) and discuss the potential and limitations of this approach. Like other neurophysiological techniques, BCIs can increase our understanding of the pathophysiology of CNS lesions and subsequent recovery, providing insight into brain function and plasticity (Dimyan and Cohen, 2011; Grosse-Wentrup et al., 2011). This topic will be outlined in a dedicated section, in which we will describe how BCI systems can influence brain reorganization after stroke (Section 4.3).

4.1 MOTOR REHABILITATION

Existing applications for motor rehabilitation have been based on a twofold mechanism (Daly and Wolpaw, 2008): on the one side, the goal is to modify brain activity to improve motor behavior (Pichiorri et al., 2015; Prasad et al., 2010); on the other, brain activity can be used to control devices that assist movement (eg, robotic orthosis, peripheral stimulation devices), and thus, by improving the quality of movement and reestablishing the connection between the brain and periphery (ie, limb) in a motor context, motor function is ultimately benefited (Buch et al., 2008). The two approaches are not mutually exclusive—their combination fosters the full exploitation of the potential of BCI (Kim et al., 2016; Ramos-Murguialday et al., 2013).

Notably, the possibility of integrating neuromodulation techniques to boost neuroplasticity by optimizing the substratum on which they operate at the CNS level has also been explored—one example is the use of transcranial direct current stimulation (tDCS) to increase sensorimotor reactivity in a BCI setting (Ang et al., 2015; Kasashima et al., 2012). This approach has been developed further to use the information on brain activity derived from the BCI to trigger the neuromodulation paradigm with the optimal timing and condition (Plow et al., 2009; Soekadar et al., 2014; Walter et al., 2012). This "brain-to-brain" approach, which has demonstrated outstanding potential when studied invasively in animals (Jackson et al., 2006), could be listed as a third strategy besides the previously mentioned "brain-to-function" and "brain-to-limb" approaches (see Fig. 2). Even more, the three strategies should not be considered as separate, because their mutual interaction is not only inevitable but desirable; the "perfect blend" of these components should be adjusted to address each specific medical condition, or even each specific patient at the specific time when the BCI intervention is applied to target optimal motor recovery.

The initial reports on the use of BCIs systems in motor rehabilitation after stroke were case reports (Daly et al., 2009) or small group studies (Buch et al., 2008); these studies delineated the fundamental approaches and highlighted several important aspects, such as the modulation of brain activity in response to training (Buch et al., 2008); the possibility of obtaining functionally relevant achievements even in a chronic, severely impaired patient (Daly et al., 2009); and the advantages of combining BCIs with physical therapy to obtain further benefits (Broetz et al., 2010). More recent studies have tested specific BCI approaches in randomized controlled trials to

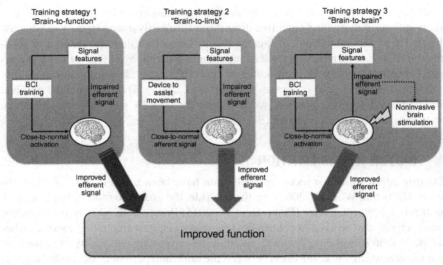

FIG. 2

The diagram is deliberately modified from Daly and Wolpaw (2008) and illustrates three possible training strategies currently employed in brain–computer interfaces (BCI) for neurorehabilitation after stroke: in the "brain-to-function" strategy the goal is to train a close-to-normal brain activation to improve motor behavior; in the "brain-to-limb" approach the BCI is used to control devices that assist movement and reestablish the connection between the brain and periphery (close-to-normal afferent signal) ultimately improving motor function; and in the "brain-to-brain" strategy the information on brain activity derived from the BCI triggers the neuromodulation paradigm (noninvasive brain stimulation) to finally improve brain activation and motor function. The three approaches are not mutually exclusive, and their interaction is desirable to address each specific medical condition, patient, and timing of rehabilitation.

demonstrate the benefits of the BCI intervention per se more soundly. Positive results have been shown for upper limb motor recovery in the chronic (Ramos-Murguialday et al., 2013) and subacute phase (Pichiorri et al., 2015) and for approaches that target lower limb recovery (Mrachacz-Kersting et al., 2016). In all of these studies, the control conditions were designed to highlight the significance of the contingency between the mental task and the feedback that is provided by the BCI system to induce plasticity and thus improve motor recovery.

Another important aspect is the combination of BCI approaches and standard therapies as to foster a priming effect of the BCI, intended here as a form of neuromodulation strategy—ie, putting the brain in the optimal condition to boost the functional gains that are obtained with physical therapy (Kim et al., 2016; Naros and Gharabaghi, 2015; Ramos-Murguialday et al., 2013). To this aim, it is crucial that only the brain activity that is related to the targeted function is reinforced in the BCI paradigm—that physiologically relevant features are selected for BCI control.

This precondition also implies a change in the BCI classification approach, from a pursuit of maximum accuracy toward a balanced reward of correct brain activity that takes into account physiological learning principles (Naros and Gharabaghi, 2015).

Technology-based approaches, ranging from telemedicine to virtual reality approaches and robotics, are constantly gaining attraction in poststroke rehabilitation (Chang and Kim, 2013; Laver et al., 2013, 2015) in gait rehabilitation (Mehrholz et al., 2013) and upper limb motor recovery (Pollock et al., 2014). Technology-assisted therapy offers the possibility to increase exercise repetition and intensity while reducing the workload of therapists. In this context, the possibility of integrating a BCI system with other technologies is invaluable (Belda-Lois et al., 2011; Ramos-Murguialday et al., 2013). We have mentioned the combination of BCIs with noninvasive brain stimulation techniques, such as tDCS (Ang et al., 2015); peripheral electrical stimulation in the form of functional electrical stimulation can also be controlled safely through the BCI for upper and lower limbs (Cincotti et al., 2012; Daly et al., 2009; McCrimmon et al., 2015). BCIs and other technology-based strategies should be considered instruments in the hands of rehabilitation professionals (ie, therapists and medical doctors) (Morone et al., 2015) and evaluated in light of the multifaceted and complex environment of current rehabilitation options for poststroke patients.

There is no clear evidence to support any specific rehabilitation strategy as being superior to the many that have been proposed (Quinn et al., 2009). However, new rehabilitation interventions—in our case, BCIs—must be evaluated, taking into account the indications for progressively staged pilot trials, leading to successful randomized controlled trials on efficacy—notable examples include constraint-induced motion therapy and body weight-supported treadmill training (Dobkin, 2009). Clinical trials must have a rational design to ensure acceptance of BCI interventions in actual clinical environments and assess essential clinical aspects, such as the dose–response relationship (Young et al., 2015).

4.2 COGNITIVE REHABILITATION

Compared with the advancements in BCI application for motor recovery after stroke, the literature on BCI systems that target cognitive deficits is limited (Burke et al., 2014). To outline reasonable approaches, BCI researchers should refer to current treatment strategies for neuropsychological deficits and to the wide literature on neurofeedback approaches for cognitive enhancement. An extensive review on neurofeedback is beyond the scope of this chapter (see Gruzelier, 2014a,b,c).

Most neuropsychological treatments for cognitive deficits are based on restitution mechanisms. Restitution consists of improvements in behavioral performance that is induced by repetitive training procedures (Milewski-Lopez et al., 2014; Zucchella et al., 2014). The positive effects of this approach were demonstrated in a longitudinal PET and fMRI study, in which a standardized behavioral training program of alertness resulted in changes in functional activity in brain areas related to the specific trained function (Sturm et al., 2004). However, the cognitive enhancement that is effected by such techniques is limited to the specific behavioral exercise, and patients encounter difficulties in generalizing the benefits to daily life situations (Owen et al., 2010).

Recent findings on stroke, along with progress in brain–computer interfacing, have led to the development of a new class of devices for improving cognitive functions, such as executive planning, directed and sustained attention, and several types of memory (Serruya and Kahana, 2008). Several EEG neurofeedback studies have shown that a range of cognitive functions might be enhanced using this approach (for a review, see Gruzelier and Egner, 2005). Applications have included cognitive abilities such as attention (Egner and Gruzelier, 2004), working memory (Hoedlmoser et al., 2008; Kober et al., 2013; Vernon et al., 2003), and mood enhancement (Raymond et al., 2005). The brain features that are used to provide the neurofeedback include SCP or specific EEG rhythms (Lutzenberger et al., 1993).

Training persons to increase negative SCP shifts improves basic attentional performance and enables individuals to focus on tasks, inhibiting the processing of internal or external distractors. Instead, providing feedback of specific EEG frequency bands, such as upper alpha, theta, and beta, enhances the performance of specific cognitive functions, such as encoding and retrieving new material from memory, sustaining attention, and inhibiting prepotent actions (for a review, see Gruzelier, 2014a,b,c).

BCI neurofeedback systems for cognitive rehabilitation are rare. Notable exceptions include attention deficit/hyperactivity disorder (Gevensleben et al., 2014; Leins et al., 2007; Zuberer et al., 2015) and concentration deficits after stroke (Cho et al., 2015).

4.3 HARNESSING BRAIN REORGANIZATION VIA BCI

Stroke is defined as a focal, acute lesion in the brain that is caused by ischemia or hemorrhage. Nevertheless, the natural clinical evolution of stroke and the process of recovery teach us how focal damage affects activity in remote areas, and in turn, reorganization of brain activity that involves "unaffected" regions contributes to the recovery of function (Dimyan and Cohen, 2011). Brain connectivity from advanced neuroimaging and neurophysiological techniques is particularly suited to examine the phenomena that occur early after focal brain damage and the compensatory mechanisms of the recovery phase (Grefkes and Fink, 2014). These mechanisms might involve the peri-infarct region (ipsilesional hemisphere)—for example, with activation of nonprimary motor areas to compensate for neuronal loss in M1— and even the contralesional hemisphere, especially in cases in which damage to the affected hemisphere is vast (Buetefisch, 2015). Specific rehabilitative interventions have been shown to promote specific reorganization patterns—eg, distal limb training facilitates ipsilesional reorganization, whereas bilateral limb training restores interhemispheric balance (Plow et al., 2009).

Based on their ability to capture and modulate specific brain activities, BCIs for rehabilitation should be evaluated in the framework of brain connectivity to target specific reorganization patterns that lead to better motor and cognitive outcomes. Several BCI studies have already addressed this aspect, primarily referring to connectivity from magnetic resonance imaging (MRI). Buch et al. (2012) examined whether specific network characteristics are necessary to voluntarily modulate specific brain activities related to hand grasping, and thus be capable of controlling a BCI system for hand grasping restoration. Connectivity was estimated from magnetoencephalography data in a group of chronic stroke patients who were participating in a BCI training program for upper limb rehabilitation, and lesions were characterized by MRI. The characteristics of the network (described by a graph theoretical approach) and BCI control skills were then correlated. The authors concluded that successful operation of a BCI requires integrity of the ipsilesional and contralesional parietofrontal pathways that mediate visuomotor control, which implied that specific brain (and lesion) characteristics determine the likelihood of a patient to benefit from a specific BCI intervention.

Another possibility that is offered by connectivity studies is the ability to determine the changes in brain network organization that are induced by the BCI training and evaluate whether they are related to functional improvements. This approach highlights the identification of neurophysiological parameters (represented by connectivity indices) to assess and quantify the effects of the BCI intervention on the brain. The characteristics of the brain network at rest (MRI-derived)—more precisely, increased connectivity in primary and nonprimary motor areas—correlate with improvements in upper extremity function in chronic patients after a specific robotic-assisted BCI training (Várkuti et al., 2013).

In our laboratory we have applied advanced methods for estimating effective connectivity (Astolfi et al., 2008), combined with a state-of-the-art approach to extract synthetic indexes that describe brain networks that are derived from EEG signals (Sporns et al., 2004) in evaluating BCI interventions for motor and cognitive rehabilitation.

We have demonstrated that BCI training for upper limb motor recovery specifically modulates interhemispheric and intrahemispheric connectivity at rest and that this modulation is specific for the trained EEG frequency bands (specific for sensorimotor activation). By correlating the increase in the connectivity of the affected hemisphere (at sensorimotor-relevant EEG frequency intervals) with the observed motor recovery, we demonstrated that certain changes in brain organization are due to reinforcement of specific EEG rhythms (induced by the BCI training) and that this modulation of activity and connectivity is the substratum of functional recovery (Pichiorri et al., 2015).

The diagnosis of cognitive impairments after stroke and their treatment efficacy rely on a neuropsychological assessment battery (Strauss et al., 2007). However, neuroimaging studies indicate that the adaptive neuroplasticity that occurs after stroke is better understood by examining changes in brain networks (Cramer et al., 2011). In a recent study, we provided neurophysiological descriptors that were sensitive to various training intervention outcomes and supported the neuropsychological assessment in evaluating the efficacy of a BCI-controlled neurofeedback training for memory function deficits after stroke (Toppi et al., 2014). The study was developed under the aegis of the EU-funded CONTRAST project (http://www.con trast-project.eu), which deployed a brain–neural computer interface-based technology to provide cognitive training modules to improve cognitive rehabilitation outcomes in institutionalized patients and support the patient's training at home by remote controlled supervision.

These studies on motor and cognitive rehabilitation represent proof of concept of the use of connectivity in evaluating BCI-supported interventions. The success of our connectivity approach was ensured by the use of a powerful method for statistically validating the connectivity patterns (Toppi et al., 2012b), which, by discarding spurious links, secured the accuracy and reliability of the estimated networks and related graph indices. Moreover, the development of an accurate time-varying connectivity approach that follows connectivity changes over time with fast dynamics (Toppi et al., 2012a) allowed us to track the rapid brain processes that are elicited in cognitive tasks and thus evaluate a BCI-based intervention for memory rehabilitation.

Albeit promising, connectivity approaches require further refinement to provide accurate, stable, and reliable connectivity networks, taking into account intersubject variability (location and extension of the lesion and motor or cognitive impairment) that is typical in stroke individuals. To further promote the use of connectivity indices as neurophysiological markers of the modulation of BCI-induced brain activity, we are proposing methodological advancements to allow the evaluation of connectivity changes at the level of the single subject (Petti et al., 2014)—this approach should account for intersubject variability and will be validated by correlation with functional improvements during the recovery period.

5 CONCLUSION AND FUTURE PERSPECTIVES

In this chapter, we have provided an overview of the current status of clinical application of noninvasive, EEG-based BCI systems. The recent literature on communication and control applications indicates that early involvement of end-users in their design, testing, and evaluation is crucial. The modalities of inclusion of BCI end-users in long-term BCI translational and longitudinal studies have been defined in the form of a decision algorithm taking into account the interest and need of BCI, the possibility to give formal consent and finally the cognitive abilities and the characteristics of the environment (Kübler et al., 2015a). In addition, we recommend an early involvement of end-users and stakeholders in the design process, to avoid worthless efforts in the development phase and prevent disappointment of end-users expectations. This implies that BCI technology should be designed and/or integrated in the context of current AT principles to compensate for the shortcomings and limitations of current solutions, to eventually provide an alternative augmentative communication channel in a wide range of potential end-users. The improvement in the customizability and adaptability of BCIs to user capabilities (ie, cognitive resources) is also crucial for a full exploitation of this technology on a variety of potential users who could benefit from this technology.

The main lesson from the recent literature on BCIs for stroke rehabilitation is that the interventions should be designed taking into account relevant rehabilitation and neurophysiological principles. Thus, the technical aspects of BCIs (such as features extraction and classification algorithms) should be adapted to fulfill the specifications of the clinical and functional objectives. Clinical trials must be designed according to current standards to provide solid evidence of efficacy and thus foster the integration of BCI-based intervention in the rehabilitation program of patients. The aging population determines an increased need of effective rehabilitation strategies targeting motor and cognitive impairment, which goes together with an inevitable increase in the costs. Technology-supported interventions (including BCI based) have the potential to reduce such costs by increasing the intensity and efficacy of training with no added charge on human resources (ie, therapists). The possibility of bringing BCI-based training into the home of patients is even more attractive in this perspective.

The roadmap that was recently presented by the consortium involved in the European project "BNCI Horizon 2020" is structured upon a series of use case scenarios based on a future perspectives for several BCI applications including those discussed in this chapter. For each application the primary, secondary, and tertiary users, the size of the target group and relative market, the current treatments/options and their cost, and advantages and disadvantages, were reported together with the expected advantages/disadvantages of the proposed BCI solutions and the related ethical issues. Here, we have highlighted near-future research pathways in the clinical application of BCIs with regard to technical improvements and interactions with nearby disciplines (clinical and scientific). Provided that lessons are learned from the UCD approach and that integration with the clinical counterpart is pursued (Roadmap BNCI Horizon 2020, 2015), we believe that noninvasive EEG-based BCI systems will have a brilliant future as clinical devices for communication and rehabilitation purposes.

ACKNOWLEDGMENTS

Partially supported by the Italian Ministry of Healthcare (Grant: RF-2010-2319611), the European ICT Program (Project FP7-224631), and the Italian Agency for Research on ALS–ARiSLA (project "Brindisys"). This paper only reflects the authors' views and funding agencies are not liable for any use that may be made of the information contained herein.

REFERENCES

Acqualagna, L., Blankertz, B., 2011. A gaze independent spelling based on rapid serial visual presentation. Conf. Proc. IEEE Eng. Med. Biol. Soc. 2011, 4560–4563. http://dx.doi.org/10.1109/IEMBS.2011.6091129.

Aloise, F., Aricò, P., Schettini, F., Salinari, S., Mattia, D., Cincotti, F., 2013. Asynchronous gaze-independent event-related potential-based brain-computer interface. Artif. Intell. Med. 59, 61–69. http://dx.doi.org/10.1016/j.artmed.2013.07.006.

Ang, K.K., Guan, C., Phua, K.S., Wang, C., Zhao, L., Teo, W.P., Chen, C., Ng, Y.S., Chew, E., 2015. Facilitating effects of transcranial direct current stimulation on motor imagery brain-computer interface with robotic feedback for stroke rehabilitation. Arch. Phys. Med. Rehabil. 96, S79–S87. http://dx.doi.org/10.1016/j.apmr.2014.08.008.

Aricò, P., Aloise, F., Schettini, F., Salinari, S., Mattia, D., Cincotti, F., 2014. Influence of P300 latency jitter on event related potential-based brain-computer interface performance. J. Neural Eng. 11, 035008. http://dx.doi.org/10.1088/1741-2560/11/3/035008.

Astolfi, L., Cincotti, F., Mattia, D., De Vico Fallani, F., Tocci, A., Colosimo, A., Salinari, S., Marciani, M.G., Hesse, W., Witte, H., Ursino, M., Zavaglia, M., Babiloni, F., 2008. Tracking the time-varying cortical connectivity patterns by adaptive multivariate estimators. IEEE Trans. Biomed. Eng. 55, 902–913. http://dx.doi.org/10.1109/TBME.2007.905419.

Babiloni, F., Cincotti, F., Marciani, M., Salinari, S., Astolfi, L., Aloise, F., De Vico Fallani, F., Mattia, D., 2009. On the use of brain–computer interfaces outside scientific laboratories: toward an application in domotic environments. International Review of Neurobiology, vol. 86. Academic Press, pp. 133–146. Chapter 10. ISSN 0074-7742, ISBN 9780123748218, http://dx.doi.org/10.1016/S0074-7742(09)86010-8.

Belda-Lois, J.-M., Mena-del Horno, S., Bermejo-Bosch, I., Moreno, J.C., Pons, J.L., Farina, D., Iosa, M., Molinari, M., Tamburella, F., Ramos, A., Caria, A., Solis-Escalante, T., Brunner, C., Rea, M., 2011. Rehabilitation of gait after stroke: a review towards a top-down approach. J. Neuroeng. Rehabil. 8, 66. http://dx.doi.org/10.1186/1743-0003-8-66.

Birbaumer, N., 2006. Breaking the silence: brain-computer interfaces (BCI) for communication and motor control. Psychophysiology 43, 517–532. http://dx.doi.org/10.1111/j.1469-8986.2006.00456.x.

Birbaumer, N., Ghanayim, N., Hinterberger, T., Iversen, I., Kotchoubey, B., Kübler, A., Perelmouter, J., Taub, E., Flor, H., 1999. A spelling device for the paralysed. Nature 398, 297–298. http://dx.doi.org/10.1038/18581.

Birbaumer, N., Kübler, A., Ghanayim, N., Hinterberger, T., Perelmouter, J., Kaiser, J., Iversen, I., Kotchoubey, B., Neumann, N., Flor, H., 2000. The thought translation device (TTD) for completely paralyzed patients. IEEE Trans. Neural Syst. Rehabil. Eng. 8, 190–193.

Blain-Moraes, S., Schaff, R., Gruis, K.L., Huggins, J.E., Wren, P.A., 2012. Barriers to and mediators of brain–computer interface user acceptance: focus group findings. Ergonomics 55, 516–525. http://dx.doi.org/10.1080/00140139.2012.661082.

Broetz, D., Braun, C., Weber, C., Soekadar, S.R., Caria, A., Birbaumer, N., 2010. Combination of brain-computer interface training and goal-directed physical therapy in chronic stroke: a case report. Neurorehabil. Neural Repair 24, 674–679. http://dx.doi.org/10.1177/1545968310368683.

Brunner, P., Joshi, S., Briskin, S., Wolpaw, J.R., Bischof, H., Schalk, G., 2010. Does the "P300" speller depend on eye gaze? J. Neural Eng. 7, 056013. http://dx.doi.org/10.1088/1741-2560/7/5/056013.

Brunner, P., Bianchi, L., Guger, C., Cincotti, F., Schalk, G., 2011. Current trends in hardware and software for brain-computer interfaces (BCIs). J. Neural Eng. 8, 025001. http://dx.doi.org/10.1088/1741-2560/8/2/025001.

Buch, E., Weber, C., Cohen, L.G., Braun, C., Dimyan, M.A., Ard, T., Mellinger, J., Caria, A., Soekadar, S., Fourkas, A., Birbaumer, N., 2008. Think to move: a neuromagnetic brain-computer interface (BCI) system for chronic stroke. Stroke 39, 910–917. http://dx.doi.org/10.1161/STROKEAHA.107.505313.

Buch, E.R., Modir Shanechi, A., Fourkas, A.D., Weber, C., Birbaumer, N., Cohen, L.G., 2012. Parietofrontal integrity determines neural modulation associated with grasping imagery after stroke. Brain J. Neurol. 135, 596–614. http://dx.doi.org/10.1093/brain/awr331.

Buetefisch, C.M., 2015. Role of the contralesional hemisphere in post-stroke recovery of upper extremity motor function. Front. Neurol. 6, 214. http://dx.doi.org/10.3389/fneur.2015.00214.

Burke, J.F., Merkow, M.B., Jacobs, J., Kahana, M.J., Zaghloul, K.A., 2014. Brain computer interface to enhance episodic memory in human participants. Front. Hum. Neurosci. 8, 1055. http://dx.doi.org/10.3389/fnhum.2014.01055.

Caruso, M., Cincotti, F., Leotta, F., Mecella, M., Riccio, A., Schettini, F., Simione, L., Catarci, T., 2013. My-world-in-my-tablet: an architecture for people with physical impairment. In: Kurosu, M. (Ed.), Human-Computer Interaction. Interaction Modalities and Techniques. Springer, Berlin, Heidelberg, pp. 637–647.

Chang, W.H., Kim, Y.-H., 2013. Robot-assisted therapy in stroke rehabilitation. J. Stroke 15, 174–181. http://dx.doi.org/10.5853/jos.2013.15.3.174.

Chatterjee, A., Aggarwal, V., Ramos, A., Acharya, S., Thakor, N.V., 2007. A brain-computer interface with vibrotactile biofeedback for haptic information. J. Neuroeng. Rehabil. 4, 40.

Cho, H.-Y., Kim, K., Lee, B., Jung, J., 2015. The effect of neurofeedback on a brain wave and visual perception in stroke: a randomized control trial. J. Phys. Ther. Sci. 27, 673–676. http://dx.doi.org/10.1589/jpts.27.673.

Cincotti, F., Mattia, D., Aloise, F., Bufalari, S., Schalk, G., Oriolo, G., Cherubini, A., Marciani, M.G., Babiloni, F., 2008. Non-invasive brain-computer interface system: towards its application as assistive technology. Brain Res. Bull. 75, 796–803. http://dx.doi.org/10.1016/j.brainresbull.2008.01.007.

Cincotti, F., Pichiorri, F., Aricò, P., Aloise, F., Leotta, F., de Vico Fallani, F., Millán, J.D.R., Molinari, M., Mattia, D., 2012. EEG-based brain-computer interface to support post-stroke motor rehabilitation of the upper limb. Conf. Proc. IEEE Eng. Med. Biol. Soc. 2012, 4112–4115. http://dx.doi.org/10.1109/EMBC.2012.6346871.

Cramer, S.C., Sur, M., Dobkin, B.H., O'Brien, C., Sanger, T.D., Trojanowski, J.Q., Rumsey, J.M., Hicks, R., Cameron, J., Chen, D., Chen, W.G., Cohen, L.G., deCharms, C., Duffy, C.J., Eden, G.F., Fetz, E.E., Filart, R., Freund, M., Grant, S.J., Haber, S., Kalivas, P.W., Kolb, B., Kramer, A.F., Lynch, M., Mayberg, H.S., McQuillen, P.S., Nitkin, R., Pascual-Leone, A., Reuter-Lorenz, P., Schiff, N., Sharma, A., Shekim, L., Stryker, M., Sullivan, E.V., Vinogradov, S., 2011. Harnessing neuroplasticity for clinical applications. Brain J. Neurol. 134, 1591–1609. http://dx.doi.org/10.1093/brain/awr039.

Daly, J.J., Wolpaw, J.R., 2008. Brain-computer interfaces in neurological rehabilitation. Lancet Neurol. 7, 1032–1043. http://dx.doi.org/10.1016/S1474-4422(08)70223-0.

Daly, J.J., Cheng, R., Rogers, J., Litinas, K., Hrovat, K., Dohring, M., 2009. Feasibility of a new application of noninvasive brain computer interface (BCI): a case study of training for recovery of volitional motor control after stroke. J. Neurol. Phys. Ther. 33, 203–211. http://dx.doi.org/10.1097/NPT.0b013e3181c1fc0b.

Di Pino, G., Pellegrino, G., Assenza, G., Capone, F., Ferreri, F., Formica, D., Ranieri, F., Tombini, M., Ziemann, U., Rothwell, J.C., Di Lazzaro, V., 2014. Modulation of brain plasticity in stroke: a novel model for neurorehabilitation. Nat. Rev. Neurol. 10, 597–608. http://dx.doi.org/10.1038/nrneurol.2014.162.

Dimyan, M.A., Cohen, L.G., 2011. Neuroplasticity in the context of motor rehabilitation after stroke. Nat. Rev. Neurol. 7, 76–85. http://dx.doi.org/10.1038/nrneurol.2010.200.

Dobkin, B.H., 2009. Progressive staging of pilot studies to improve phase III trials for motor interventions. Neurorehabil. Neural Repair 23, 197–206. http://dx.doi.org/10.1177/1545968309331863.

Egner, T., Gruzelier, J.H., 2004. EEG biofeedback of low beta band components: frequency-specific effects on variables of attention and event-related brain potentials. Clin. Neurophysiol. 115, 131–139.

Fabiani, M., Gratton, G., Federmeier, K.D., 2007. Event-related brain potentials: methods, theory, and applications. Handbook of Psychophysiology. Cambridge University Press, Cambridge, UK.

Farwell, L.A., Donchin, E., 1988. Talking off the top of your head: toward a mental prosthesis utilizing event-related brain potentials. Electroencephalogr. Clin. Neurophysiol. 70, 510–523.

Gallegos-Ayala, G., Furdea, A., Takano, K., Ruf, C.A., Flor, H., Birbaumer, N., 2014. Brain communication in a completely locked-in patient using bedside near-infrared spectroscopy. Neurology 82, 1930–1932. http://dx.doi.org/10.1212/WNL.0000000000000449.

Geronimo, A., Stephens, H.E., Schiff, S.J., Simmons, Z., 2015. Acceptance of brain-computer interfaces in amyotrophic lateral sclerosis. Amyotroph. Lateral Scler. Frontotemporal Degener. 16, 258–264. http://dx.doi.org/10.3109/21678421.2014.969275.

Gevensleben, H., Kleemeyer, M., Rothenberger, L.G., Studer, P., Flaig-Röhr, A., Moll, G.H., Rothenberger, A., Heinrich, H., 2014. Neurofeedback in ADHD: further pieces of the puzzle. Brain Topogr. 27, 20–32. http://dx.doi.org/10.1007/s10548-013-0285-y.

Go, A.S., Mozaffarian, D., Roger, V.L., Benjamin, E.J., Berry, J.D., Borden, W.B., Bravata, D.M., Dai, S., Ford, E.S., Fox, C.S., Franco, S., Fullerton, H.J., Gillespie, C., Hailpern, S.M., Heit, J.A., Howard, V.J., Huffman, M.D., Kissela, B.M., Kittner, S.J., Lackland, D.T., Lichtman, J.H., Lisabeth, L.D., Magid, D., Marcus, G.M., Marelli, A., Matchar, D.B., McGuire, D.K., Mohler, E.R., Moy, C.S., Mussolino, M.E., Nichol, G., Paynter, N.P., Schreiner, P.J., Sorlie, P.D., Stein, J., Turan, T.N., Virani, S.S., Wong, N.D., Woo, D., Turner, M.B., American Heart Association Statistics Committee and Stroke Statistics Subcommittee, 2013. Executive summary: heart disease and stroke statistics—2013 update: a report from the American Heart Association. Circulation 127, 143–152. http://dx.doi.org/10.1161/CIR.0b013e318282ab8f.

Grefkes, C., Fink, G.R., 2014. Connectivity-based approaches in stroke and recovery of function. Lancet Neurol. 13, 206–216.

Grosse-Wentrup, M., Mattia, D., Oweiss, K., 2011. Using brain-computer interfaces to induce neural plasticity and restore function. J. Neural Eng. 8, 025004. http://dx.doi.org/10.1088/1741-2560/8/2/025004.

Gruzelier, J.H., 2014a. EEG-neurofeedback for optimising performance. I: a review of cognitive and affective outcome in healthy participants. Neurosci. Biobehav. Rev. 44, 124–141. http://dx.doi.org/10.1016/j.neubiorev.2013.09.015. special issue.

Gruzelier, J.H., 2014b. EEG-neurofeedback for optimising performance. II: creativity, the performing arts and ecological validity. Neurosci. Biobehav. Rev. 44, 142–158. http://dx.doi.org/10.1016/j.neubiorev.2013.11.004.

Gruzelier, J.H., 2014c. EEG-neurofeedback for optimising performance. III: a review of methodological and theoretical considerations. Neurosci. Biobehav. Rev. 44, 159–182. http://dx.doi.org/10.1016/j.neubiorev.2014.03.015.

Gruzelier, J., Egner, T., 2005. Critical validation studies of neurofeedback. Child Adolesc. Psychiatr. Clin. N. Am. 14, 83–104. http://dx.doi.org/10.1016/j.chc.2004.07.002. vi.

Han, C.-H., Hwang, H.-J., Lim, J.-H., Im, C.-H., 2013. Development of an "eyes-closed" brain-computer interface system for communication of patients with oculomotor impairment. Conf. Proc. IEEE Eng. Med. Biol. Soc. 2013, 2236–2239. http://dx.doi.org/10.1109/EMBC.2013.6609981.

Hinterberger, T., Kübler, A., Kaiser, J., Neumann, N., Birbaumer, N., 2003. A brain-computer interface (BCI) for the locked-in: comparison of different EEG classifications for the thought translation device. Clin. Neurophysiol. 114, 416–425.

Hoedlmoser, K., Pecherstorfer, T., Gruber, G., Anderer, P., Doppelmayr, M., Klimesch, W., Schabus, M., 2008. Instrumental conditioning of human sensorimotor rhythm (12–15 Hz) and its impact on sleep as well as declarative learning. Sleep 31, 1401–1408.

Hoffmann, U., Vesin, J.-M., Ebrahimi, T., Diserens, K., 2008. An efficient P300-based brain-computer interface for disabled subjects. J. Neurosci. Methods 167, 115–125. http://dx.doi.org/10.1016/j.jneumeth.2007.03.005.

Hohne, J., Schreuder, M., Blankertz, B., Tangermann, M., 2010. Two-dimensional auditory p300 speller with predictive text system. Conf. Proc. IEEE Eng. Med. Biol. Soc. 2010, 4185–4188. http://dx.doi.org/10.1109/IEMBS.2010.5627379.

Holz, E.M., Botrel, L., Kaufmann, T., Kübler, A., 2015a. Long-term independent brain-computer interface home use improves quality of life of a patient in the locked-in state: a case study. Arch. Phys. Med. Rehabil. 96, S16–S26. http://dx.doi.org/10.1016/j.apmr.2014.03.035.

Holz, E.M., Botrel, L., Kübler, A., 2015b. Independent home use of brain painting improves quality of life of two artists in the locked-in state diagnosed with amyotrophic lateral sclerosis. Brain-Comput. Interfaces 2, 117–134. http://dx.doi.org/10.1080/2326263X.2015.1100048.

Huggins, J.E., Wren, P.A., Gruis, K.L., 2011. What would brain-computer interface users want? Opinions and priorities of potential users with amyotrophic lateral sclerosis. Amyotroph. Lateral Scler. 12, 318–324. http://dx.doi.org/10.3109/17482968.2011.572978.

ISO 9241-210:2010, n.d. Ergonomics of human-system interaction—Part 210: Human-centred design for interactive systems [WWW document]. http://www.iso.org/iso/home/store/catalogue_tc/catalogue_detail.htm?csnumber=52075 (accessed 01.11.16).

Jackson, A., Mavoori, J., Fetz, E.E., 2006. Long-term motor cortex plasticity induced by an electronic neural implant. Nature 444, 56–60. http://dx.doi.org/10.1038/nature05226.

Kasashima, Y., Fujiwara, T., Matsushika, Y., Tsuji, T., Hase, K., Ushiyama, J., Ushiba, J., Liu, M., 2012. Modulation of event-related desynchronization during motor imagery with transcranial direct current stimulation (tDCS) in patients with chronic hemiparetic stroke. Exp. Brain Res. 221, 263–268. http://dx.doi.org/10.1007/s00221-012-3166-9.

Kaufmann, T., Völker, S., Gunesch, L., Kübler, A., 2012. Spelling is just a click away—a user-centered brain-computer interface including auto-calibration and predictive text entry. Front. Neurosci. 6, 72. http://dx.doi.org/10.3389/fnins.2012.00072.

Kaufmann, T., Holz, E.M., Kübler, A., 2013. Comparison of tactile, auditory, and visual modality for brain-computer interface use: a case study with a patient in the locked-in state. Front. Neurosci. 7, 129. http://dx.doi.org/10.3389/fnins.2013.00129.

Kim, T., Kim, S., Lee, B., 2016. Effects of action observational training plus brain–computer interface-based functional electrical stimulation on paretic arm motor recovery in patient with stroke: a randomized controlled trial. Occup. Ther. Int. 23, 39–47. http://dx.doi.org/10.1002/oti.1403.

Kleih, S.C., Kaufmann, T., Zickler, C., Halder, S., Leotta, F., Cincotti, F., Aloise, F., Riccio, A., Herbert, C., Mattia, D., Kübler, A., 2011. Out of the frying pan into the fire—the P300-based BCI faces real-world challenges. Prog. Brain Res. 194, 27–46. http://dx.doi.org/10.1016/B978-0-444-53815-4.00019-4.

Kleih, S.C., Herweg, A., Kaufmann, T., Staiger-Sälzer, P., Gerstner, N., Kübler, A., 2015. The WIN-speller: a new intuitive auditory brain-computer interface spelling application. Front. Neurosci. 9. http://dx.doi.org/10.3389/fnins.2015.00346.

Kober, S.E., Witte, M., Ninaus, M., Neuper, C., Wood, G., 2013. Learning to modulate one's own brain activity: the effect of spontaneous mental strategies. Front. Hum. Neurosci. 7, 695. http://dx.doi.org/10.3389/fnhum.2013.00695.

Kübler, A., Kotchoubey, B., Hinterberger, T., Ghanayim, N., Perelmouter, J., Schauer, M., Fritsch, C., Taub, E., Birbaumer, N., 1999. The thought translation device: a neurophysiological approach to communication in total motor paralysis. Exp. Brain Res. 124, 223–232.

Kübler, A., Neumann, N., Kaiser, J., Kotchoubey, B., Hinterberger, T., Birbaumer, N.P., 2001. Brain-computer communication: self-regulation of slow cortical potentials for verbal communication. Arch. Phys. Med. Rehabil. 82, 1533–1539.

Kübler, A., Nijboer, F., Mellinger, J., Vaughan, T.M., Pawelzik, H., Schalk, G., McFarland, D.J., Birbaumer, N., Wolpaw, J.R., 2005. Patients with ALS can use sensorimotor rhythms to operate a brain-computer interface. Neurology 64, 1775–1777. http://dx.doi.org/10.1212/01.WNL.0000158616.43002.6D.

Kübler, A., Furdea, A., Halder, S., Hammer, E.M., Nijboer, F., Kotchoubey, B., 2009. A brain-computer interface controlled auditory event-related potential (p300) spelling system for locked-in patients. Ann. N. Y. Acad. Sci. 1157, 90–100.

Kübler, A., Holz, E., Botrel, L., 2013. Addendum. Brain 136, 2005–2006. http://dx.doi.org/10.1093/brain/awt156.

Kübler, A., Holz, E.M., Riccio, A., Zickler, C., Kaufmann, T., Kleih, S.C., Staiger-Sälzer, P., Desideri, L., Hoogerwerf, E.-J., Mattia, D., 2014. The user-centered design as novel perspective for evaluating the usability of BCI-controlled applications. PLoS One 9, e112392. http://dx.doi.org/10.1371/journal.pone.0112392.

Kübler, A., Holz, E.M., Sellers, E.W., Vaughan, T.M., 2015a. Toward independent home use of brain-computer interfaces: a decision algorithm for selection of potential end-users. Arch. Phys. Med. Rehabil. 96, S27–S32. http://dx.doi.org/10.1016/j.apmr.2014.03.036.

Kübler, A., Müller-Putz, G., Mattia, D., 2015b. User-centred design in brain–computer interface research and development. Ann. Phys. Rehabil. Med. 58, 312–314. http://dx.doi.org/10.1016/j.rehab.2015.06.003.

Laver, K.E., Schoene, D., Crotty, M., George, S., Lannin, N.A., Sherrington, C., 2013. Telerehabilitation services for stroke. Cochrane Database Syst. Rev. 12, CD010255. http://dx.doi.org/10.1002/14651858.CD010255.pub2.

Laver, K.E., George, S., Thomas, S., Deutsch, J.E., Crotty, M., 2015. Virtual reality for stroke rehabilitation. Cochrane Database Syst. Rev. 2, CD008349. http://dx.doi.org/10.1002/14651858.CD008349.pub3.

Lee, T.-S., Goh, S.J.A., Quek, S.Y., Phillips, R., Guan, C., Cheung, Y.B., Feng, L., Teng, S.S. W., Wang, C.C., Chin, Z.Y., Zhang, H., Ng, T.P., Lee, J., Keefe, R., Krishnan, K.R.R., 2013. A brain-computer interface based cognitive training system for healthy elderly: a randomized control pilot study for usability and preliminary efficacy. PLoS One 8, e79419. http://dx.doi.org/10.1371/journal.pone.0079419.

Leeb, R., Perdikis, S., Tonin, L., Biasiucci, A., Tavella, M., Creatura, M., Molina, A., Al-Khodairy, A., Carlson, T., Millán, J.D.R., 2013. Transferring brain-computer interfaces beyond the laboratory: successful application control for motor-disabled users. Artif. Intell. Med. 59, 121–132. http://dx.doi.org/10.1016/j.artmed.2013.08.004.

Leins, U., Goth, G., Hinterberger, T., Klinger, C., Rumpf, N., Strehl, U., 2007. Neurofeedback for children with ADHD: a comparison of SCP and Theta/Beta protocols. Appl. Psychophysiol. Biofeedback 32, 73–88. http://dx.doi.org/10.1007/s10484-007-9031-0.

Lesenfants, D., Habbal, D., Lugo, Z., Lebeau, M., Horki, P., Amico, E., Pokorny, C., Gómez, F., Soddu, A., Müller-Putz, G., Laureys, S., Noirhomme, Q., 2014. An independent SSVEP-based brain-computer interface in locked-in syndrome. J. Neural Eng. 11, 035002. http://dx.doi.org/10.1088/1741-2560/11/3/035002.

Leuthardt, E.C., Schalk, G., Wolpaw, J.R., Ojemann, J.G., Moran, D.W., 2004. A brain-computer interface using electrocorticographic signals in humans. J. Neural Eng. 1, 63–71. http://dx.doi.org/10.1088/1741-2560/1/2/001.

Liberati, G., Pizzimenti, A., Simione, L., Riccio, A., Schettini, F., Inghilleri, M., Mattia, D., Cincotti, F., 2015. Developing brain-computer interfaces from a user-centered perspective: assessing the needs of persons with amyotrophic lateral sclerosis, caregivers, and professionals. Appl. Ergon. 50, 139–146. http://dx.doi.org/10.1016/j.apergo.2015.03.012.

Lutzenberger, W., Roberts, L.E., Birbaumer, N., 1993. Memory performance and area-specific self-regulation of slow cortical potentials: dual-task interference. Int. J. Psychophysiol. 15, 217–226.

Mak, J.N., Wolpaw, J.R., 2009. Clinical applications of brain-computer interfaces: current state and future prospects. IEEE Rev. Biomed. Eng. 2, 187–199. http://dx.doi.org/10.1109/RBME.2009.2035356.

Marchetti, M., Piccione, F., Silvoni, S., Gamberini, L., Priftis, K., 2013. Covert visuospatial attention orienting in a brain-computer interface for amyotrophic lateral sclerosis patients. Neurorehabil. Neural Repair 27, 430–438. http://dx.doi.org/10.1177/1545968312471903.

McCane, L.M., Sellers, E.W., McFarland, D.J., Mak, J.N., Carmack, C.S., Zeitlin, D., Wolpaw, J.R., Vaughan, T.M., 2014. Brain-computer interface (BCI) evaluation in people with amyotrophic lateral sclerosis. Amyotroph. Lateral Scler. Frontotemporal Degener. 15, 207–215. http://dx.doi.org/10.3109/21678421.2013.865750.

McCane, L.M., Heckman, S.M., McFarland, D.J., Townsend, G., Mak, J.N., Sellers, E.W., Zeitlin, D., Tenteromano, L.M., Wolpaw, J.R., Vaughan, T.M., 2015. P300-based brain-computer interface (BCI) event-related potentials (ERPs): people with amyotrophic lateral sclerosis (ALS) vs. age-matched controls. Clin. Neurophysiol. 126, 2124–2131. http://dx.doi.org/10.1016/j.clinph.2015.01.013.

McCreadie, K.A., Coyle, D.H., Prasad, G., 2014. Is sensorimotor BCI performance influenced differently by mono, stereo, or 3-D auditory feedback? IEEE Trans. Neural Syst. Rehabil. Eng. 22, 431–440. http://dx.doi.org/10.1109/TNSRE.2014.2312270.

McCrimmon, C.M., King, C.E., Wang, P.T., Cramer, S.C., Nenadic, Z., Do, A.H., 2015. Brain-controlled functional electrical stimulation therapy for gait rehabilitation after stroke: a safety study. J. Neuroeng. Rehabil. 12, 57. http://dx.doi.org/10.1186/s12984-015-0050-4.

McFarland, D.J., Krusienski, D.J., Sarnacki, W.A., Wolpaw, J.R., 2008. Emulation of computer mouse control with a noninvasive brain-computer interface. J. Neural Eng. 5, 101–110. http://dx.doi.org/10.1088/1741-2560/5/2/001.

McFarland, D.J., Sarnacki, W.A., Wolpaw, J.R., 2015. Effects of training pre-movement sensorimotor rhythms on behavioral performance. J. Neural Eng. 12, 066021. http://dx.doi.org/10.1088/1741-2560/12/6/066021.

Mehrholz, J., Elsner, B., Werner, C., Kugler, J., Pohl, M., 2013. Electromechanical-assisted training for walking after stroke. Cochrane Database Syst. Rev. 7, CD006185. http://dx.doi.org/10.1002/14651858.CD006185.pub3.

Milewski-Lopez, A., Greco, E., van den Berg, F., McAvinue, L.P., McGuire, S., Robertson, I.H., 2014. An evaluation of alertness training for older adults. Front. Aging Neurosci. 6, 67. http://dx.doi.org/10.3389/fnagi.2014.00067.

Millán, J.D.R., Rupp, R., Müller-Putz, G.R., Murray-Smith, R., Giugliemma, C., Tangermann, M., Vidaurre, C., Cincotti, F., Kübler, A., Leeb, R., Neuper, C., Müller, K.-R., Mattia, D., 2010. Combining brain–computer interfaces and assistive technologies: state-of-the-art and challenges. Front. Neurosci. 4, 161. http://dx.doi.org/10.3389/fnins.2010.00161.

Morone, G., Pisotta, I., Pichiorri, F., Kleih, S., Paolucci, S., Molinari, M., Cincotti, F., Kübler, A., Mattia, D., 2015. Proof of principle of a brain-computer interface approach to support poststroke arm rehabilitation in hospitalized patients: design, acceptability, and usability. Arch. Phys. Med. Rehabil. 96, S71–S78. http://dx.doi.org/10.1016/j.apmr.2014.05.026.

Mrachacz-Kersting, N., Jiang, N., Stevenson, A.J.T., Niazi, I.K., Kostic, V., Pavlovic, A., Radovanovic, S., Djuric-Jovicic, M., Agosta, F., Dremstrup, K., Farina, D., 2016. Efficient neuroplasticity induction in chronic stroke patients by an associative brain-computer interface. J. Neurophysiol. 115, 1410–1421. http://dx.doi.org/10.1152/jn.00918.2015.

Naros, G., Gharabaghi, A., 2015. Reinforcement learning of self-regulated β-oscillations for motor restoration in chronic stroke. Front. Hum. Neurosci. 9, 391. http://dx.doi.org/10.3389/fnhum.2015.00391.

Neumann, N., Kübler, A., Kaiser, J., Hinterberger, T., Birbaumer, N., 2003. Conscious perception of brain states: mental strategies for brain-computer communication. Neuropsychologia 41, 1028–1036.

Neuper, C., Müller, G.R., Kübler, A., Birbaumer, N., Pfurtscheller, G., 2003. Clinical application of an EEG-based brain–computer interface: a case study in a patient with severe motor impairment. Clin. Neurophysiol. 114, 399–409. http://dx.doi.org/10.1016/S1388-2457(02)00387-5.

Neuper, C., Müller-Putz, G.R., Scherer, R., Pfurtscheller, G., 2006. Motor imagery and EEG-based control of spelling devices and neuroprostheses. In: Neuper, C., Klimesch, W. (Eds.), Progress in Brain Research, Event-Related Dynamics of Brain Oscillations. Elsevier, Amsterdam, pp. 393–409.

Nijboer, F., 2015. Technology transfer of brain-computer interfaces as assistive technology: barriers and opportunities. Ann. Phys. Rehabil. Med. 58, 35–38. http://dx.doi.org/10.1016/j.rehab.2014.11.001.

Nijboer, F., Furdea, A., Gunst, I., Mellinger, J., McFarland, D.J., Birbaumer, N., Kübler, A., 2008a. An auditory brain-computer interface (BCI). J. Neurosci. Methods 167, 43–50. http://dx.doi.org/10.1016/j.jneumeth.2007.02.009.

Nijboer, F., Sellers, E.W., Mellinger, J., Jordan, M.A., Matuz, T., Furdea, A., Halder, S., Mochty, U., Krusienski, D.J., Vaughan, T.M., Wolpaw, J.R., Birbaumer, N., Kübler, A., 2008b. A P300-based brain-computer interface for people with amyotrophic lateral sclerosis. Clin. Neurophysiol. 119, 1909–1916. http://dx.doi.org/10.1016/j.clinph.2008.03.034.

Nijboer, F., Birbaumer, N., Kübler, A., 2010. The influence of psychological state and motivation on brain-computer interface performance in patients with amyotrophic lateral sclerosis—a longitudinal study. Front. Neurosci. 4. http://dx.doi.org/10.3389/fnins.2010.00055.

Nijboer, F., van de Laar, B., Gerritsen, S., Nijholt, A., Poel, M., 2015. Usability of three electroencephalogram headsets for brain–computer interfaces: a within subject comparison. Interact. Comput. 27, 500–511. http://dx.doi.org/10.1093/iwc/iwv023.

Owen, A.M., Hampshire, A., Grahn, J.A., Stenton, R., Dajani, S., Burns, A.S., Howard, R.J., Ballard, C.G., 2010. Putting brain training to the test. Nature 465, 775–778. http://dx.doi.org/10.1038/nature09042.

Pasqualotto, E., Federici, S., Belardinelli, M.O., 2012. Toward functioning and usable brain–computer interfaces (BCIs): a literature review. Disabil. Rehabil. Assist. Technol. 7, 89–103. http://dx.doi.org/10.3109/17483107.2011.589486.

Pasqualotto, E., Matuz, T., Federici, S., Ruf, C.A., Bartl, M., Belardinelli, M.O., Birbaumer, N., Halder, S., 2015. Usability and workload of access technology for people with severe motor impairment a comparison of brain-computer interfacing and eye tracking. Neurorehabil. Neural Repair 29, 950–957. http://dx.doi.org/10.1177/1545968315575611.

Perdikis, S., Leeb, R., Williamson, J., Ramsay, A., Tavella, M., Desideri, L., Hoogerwerf, E.-J., Al-Khodairy, A., Murray-Smith, R., Millán, J.d.R., 2014. Clinical evaluation of BrainTree, a motor imagery hybrid BCI speller. J. Neural Eng. 11, 036003. http://dx.doi.org/10.1088/1741-2560/11/3/036003.

Petti, M., Pichiorri, F., Toppi, J., Cincotti, F., Salinari, S., Babiloni, F., Mattia, D., Astolfi, L., 2014. Individual cortical connectivity changes after stroke: a resampling approach to enable statistical assessment at single-subject level, 2014 36th Annual International Conference of the IEEE Engineering in Medicine and Biology Society, 2785–2788.

Pfurtscheller, G., Lopes da Silva, F.H., 1999. Event-related EEG/MEG synchronization and desynchronization: basic principles. Clin. Neurophysiol. 110, 1842–1857.

Pfurtscheller, G., Neuper, C., 1992. Simultaneous EEG 10 Hz desynchronization and 40 Hz synchronization during finger movements. Neuroreport 3, 1057–1060.

Pfurtscheller, G., Neuper, C., Müller, G.R., Obermaier, B., Krausz, G., Schlögl, A., Scherer, R., Graimann, B., Keinrath, C., Skliris, D., Wörtz, M., Supp, G., Schrank, C., 2003. Graz-BCI: state of the art and clinical applications. IEEE Trans. Neural Syst. Rehabil. Eng. 11, 177–180. http://dx.doi.org/10.1109/TNSRE.2003.814454.

Piccione, F., Giorgi, F., Tonin, P., Priftis, K., Giove, S., Silvoni, S., Palmas, G., Beverina, F., 2006. P300-based brain computer interface: reliability and performance in healthy and paralysed participants. Clin. Neurophysiol. 117, 531–537. http://dx.doi.org/10.1016/j.clinph.2005.07.024.

Pichiorri, F., Morone, G., Petti, M., Toppi, J., Pisotta, I., Molinari, M., Paolucci, S., Inghilleri, M., Astolfi, L., Cincotti, F., Mattia, D., 2015. Brain-computer interface boosts motor imagery practice during stroke recovery. Ann. Neurol. 77, 851–865. http://dx.doi.org/10.1002/ana.24390.

Plow, E.B., Carey, J.R., Nudo, R.J., Pascual-Leone, A., 2009. Invasive cortical stimulation to promote recovery of function after stroke a critical appraisal. Stroke 40, 1926–1931. http://dx.doi.org/10.1161/STROKEAHA.108.540823.

Pollock, A., Farmer, S.E., Brady, M.C., Langhorne, P., Mead, G.E., Mehrholz, J., van Wijck, F., 2014. Interventions for improving upper limb function after stroke. Cochrane Database Syst. Rev. 11, CD010820. http://dx.doi.org/10.1002/14651858.CD010820.pub2.

Powers, J.C., Bieliaieva, K., Wu, S., Nam, C.S., 2015. The human factors and ergonomics of P300-based brain-computer interfaces. Brain Sci. 5, 318–356. http://dx.doi.org/10.3390/brainsci5030318.

Prasad, G., Herman, P., Coyle, D., McDonough, S., Crosbie, J., 2010. Applying a brain-computer interface to support motor imagery practice in people with stroke for upper limb recovery: a feasibility study. J. Neuroeng. Rehabil. 7, 60. http://dx.doi.org/10.1186/1743-0003-7-60.

Quinn, T.J., Paolucci, S., Sunnerhagen, K.S., Sivenius, J., Walker, M.F., Toni, D., Lees, K.R., European Stroke Organisation (ESO) Executive Committee, ESO Writing Committee,

2009. Evidence-based stroke rehabilitation: an expanded guidance document from the European Stroke Organisation (ESO) guidelines for management of ischaemic stroke and transient ischaemic attack 2008. J. Rehabil. Med. 41, 99–111. http://dx.doi.org/10.2340/16501977-0301.

Ramos-Murguialday, A., Broetz, D., Rea, M., Läer, L., Yilmaz, O., Brasil, F.L., Liberati, G., Curado, M.R., Garcia-Cossio, E., Vyziotis, A., Cho, W., Agostini, M., Soares, E., Soekadar, S., Caria, A., Cohen, L.G., Birbaumer, N., 2013. Brain-machine interface in chronic stroke rehabilitation: a controlled study. Ann. Neurol. 74, 100–108. http://dx.doi.org/10.1002/ana.23879.

Ramsey, N.F., Aarnoutse, E.J., Vansteensel, M.J., 2014. Brain implants for substituting lost motor function: state of the art and potential impact on the lives of motor-impaired seniors. Gerontology 60, 366–372. http://dx.doi.org/10.1159/000357565.

Raymond, J., Varney, C., Parkinson, L.A., Gruzelier, J.H., 2005. The effects of alpha/theta neurofeedback on personality and mood. Brain Res. Cogn. Brain Res. 23, 287–292. http://dx.doi.org/10.1016/j.cogbrainres.2004.10.023.

Renard, Y., Lotte, F., Gibert, G., Congedo, M., Maby, E., Delannoy, V., Bertrand, O., Lécuyer, A., 2010. OpenViBE: an open-source software platform to design, test, and use brain–computer interfaces in real and virtual environments. Presence Teleoperators Virtual Environ. 19, 35–53. http://dx.doi.org/10.1162/pres.19.1.35.

Riccio, A., Leotta, F., Bianchi, L., Aloise, F., Zickler, C., Hoogerwerf, E.-J., Kübler, A., Mattia, D., Cincotti, F., 2011. Workload measurement in a communication application operated through a P300-based brain–computer interface. J. Neural Eng. 8, 025028. http://dx.doi.org/10.1088/1741-2560/8/2/025028.

Riccio, A., Mattia, D., Simione, L., Olivetti, M., Cincotti, F., 2012. Eye-gaze independent EEG-based brain-computer interfaces for communication. J. Neural Eng. 9, 045001. http://dx.doi.org/10.1088/1741-2560/9/4/045001.

Riccio, A., Simione, L., Schettini, F., Pizzimenti, A., Inghilleri, M., Belardinelli, M.O., Mattia, D., Cincotti, F., 2013. Attention and P300-based BCI performance in people with amyotrophic lateral sclerosis. Front. Hum. Neurosci. 7. http://dx.doi.org/10.3389/fnhum.2013.00732.

Riccio, A., Holz, E.M., Aricò, P., Leotta, F., Aloise, F., Desideri, L., Rimondini, M., Kübler, A., Mattia, D., Cincotti, F., 2015. Hybrid P300-based brain-computer interface to improve usability for people with severe motor disability: electromyographic signals for error correction during a spelling task. In: The Fifth International Brain-Computer Interface Meeting Presents Clinical and Translational Developments in Brain-Computer Interface Research. Arch. Phys. Med. Rehabil., 96, pp. S54–S61. http://dx.doi.org/10.1016/j.apmr.2014.05.029.

Roadmap BNCI Horizon 2020, 2015. The Future in Brain/Neural-Computer Interaction. http://dx.doi.org/10.3217/978-3-85125-379-5.

Schettini, F., Aloise, F., Aricò, P., Salinari, S., Mattia, D., Cincotti, F., 2014. Self-calibration algorithm in an asynchronous P300-based brain–computer interface. J. Neural Eng. 11, 035004. http://dx.doi.org/10.1088/1741-2560/11/3/035004.

Schettini, F., Riccio, A., Simione, L., Liberati, G., Caruso, M., Frasca, V., Calabrese, B., Mecella, M., Pizzimenti, A., Inghilleri, M., Mattia, D., Cincotti, F., 2015. Assistive device with conventional, alternative, and brain-computer interface inputs to enhance interaction with the environment for people with amyotrophic lateral sclerosis: a feasibility and usability study. In: The Fifth International Brain-Computer Interface Meeting Presents Clinical and Translational Developments in Brain-Computer Interface Research. Arch. Phys. Med. Rehabil., 96, pp. S46–S53. http://dx.doi.org/10.1016/j.apmr.2014.05.027.

Schicktanz, S., Amelung, T., Rieger, J.W., 2015. Qualitative assessment of patients' attitudes and expectations toward BCIs and implications for future technology development. Front. Syst. Neurosci. 9, 64. http://dx.doi.org/10.3389/fnsys.2015.00064.

Schreuder, M., Rost, T., Tangermann, M., 2011. Listen, you are writing! Speeding up online spelling with a dynamic auditory BCI. Front. Neurosci. 5, 112. http://dx.doi.org/10.3389/fnins.2011.00112.

Schreuder, M., Riccio, A., Risetti, M., Dähne, S., Ramsay, A., Williamson, J., Mattia, D., Tangermann, M., 2013. User-centered design in brain-computer interfaces-a case study. Artif. Intell. Med. 59, 71–80. http://dx.doi.org/10.1016/j.artmed.2013.07.005.

Sellers, E.W., Donchin, E., 2006. A P300-based brain-computer interface: initial tests by ALS patients. Clin. Neurophysiol. 117, 538–548. http://dx.doi.org/10.1016/j.clinph.2005.06.027.

Sellers, E.W., Vaughan, T.M., Wolpaw, J.R., 2010. A brain-computer interface for long-term independent home use. Amyotroph. Lateral Scler. 11, 449–455. http://dx.doi.org/10.3109/17482961003777470.

Sellers, E.W., Ryan, D.B., Hauser, C.K., 2014. Noninvasive brain-computer interface enables communication after brainstem stroke. Sci. Transl. Med. 6, 257re7–257re7. http://dx.doi.org/10.1126/scitranslmed.3007801.

Serruya, M.D., Kahana, M.J., 2008. Techniques and devices to restore cognition. Behav. Brain Res. 192, 149–165. http://dx.doi.org/10.1016/j.bbr.2008.04.007.

Silvoni, S., Cavinato, M., Volpato, C., Ruf, C.A., Birbaumer, N., Piccione, F., 2013. Amyotrophic lateral sclerosis progression and stability of brain-computer interface communication. Amyotroph. Lateral Scler. Front. Degener. 14, 390–396. http://dx.doi.org/10.3109/21678421.2013.770029.

Simon, N., Käthner, I., Ruf, C.A., Pasqualotto, E., Kübler, A., Halder, S., 2015. An auditory multiclass brain-computer interface with natural stimuli: usability evaluation with healthy participants and a motor impaired end user. Front. Hum. Neurosci. 8, http://dx.doi.org/10.3389/fnhum.2014.01039.

Soekadar, S.R., Birbaumer, N., Slutzky, M.W., Cohen, L.G., 2014. Brain–machine interfaces in neurorehabilitation of stroke. Neurobiol. Dis. 83, 172–179. http://dx.doi.org/10.1016/j.nbd.2014.11.025.

Sporns, O., Chialvo, D.R., Kaiser, M., Hilgetag, C.C., 2004. Organization, development and function of complex brain networks. Trends Cogn. Sci. 8, 418–425. http://dx.doi.org/10.1016/j.tics.2004.07.008.

Strauss, E., Sherman, E.M.S., Spreen, O., 2007. A compendium of neuropsychological tests: administration, norms, and commentary. Appl. Neuropsychol. 14, 62–63.

Sturm, W., Longoni, F., Weis, S., Specht, K., Herzog, H., Vohn, R., Thimm, M., Willmes, K., 2004. Functional reorganisation in patients with right hemisphere stroke after training of alertness: a longitudinal PET and fMRI study in eight cases. Neuropsychologia 42, 434–450.

Sutton, S., Braren, M., Zubin, J., John, E.R., 1965. Evoked-potential correlates of stimulus uncertainty. Science 150, 1187–1188. http://dx.doi.org/10.1126/science.150.3700.1187.

Teasell, R.W., Murie Fernandez, M., McIntyre, A., Mehta, S., 2014. Rethinking the continuum of stroke rehabilitation. Arch. Phys. Med. Rehabil. 95, 595–596. http://dx.doi.org/10.1016/j.apmr.2013.11.014.

Thompson, D.E., Gruis, K.L., Huggins, J.E., 2014. A plug-and-play brain-computer interface to operate commercial assistive technology. Disabil. Rehabil. Assist. Technol. 9, 144–150. http://dx.doi.org/10.3109/17483107.2013.785036.

Toppi, J., Babiloni, F., Vecchiato, G., De Vico Fallani, F., Mattia, D., Salinari, S., Milde, T., Leistritz, L., Witte, H., Astolfi, L., 2012a. Towards the time varying estimation of complex brain connectivity networks by means of a General Linear Kalman Filter approach. Conf. Proc. IEEE Eng. Med. Biol. Soc. 2012, 6192–6195. http://dx.doi.org/10.1109/EMBC.2012.6347408.

Toppi, J., De Vico Fallani, F., Vecchiato, G., Maglione, A.G., Cincotti, F., Mattia, D., Salinari, S., Babiloni, F., Astolfi, L., 2012b. How the statistical validation of functional connectivity patterns can prevent erroneous definition of small-world properties of a brain connectivity network. Comput. Math. Methods Med. 2012, 130985. http://dx.doi.org/10.1155/2012/130985.

Toppi, J., Mattia, D., Anzolin, A., Risetti, M., Petti, M., Cincotti, F., Babiloni, F., Astolfi, L., 2014. Time varying effective connectivity for describing brain network changes induced by a memory rehabilitation treatment. Conf. Proc. IEEE Eng. Med. Biol. Soc. 2014, 6786–6789. http://dx.doi.org/10.1109/EMBC.2014.6945186.

Townsend, G., LaPallo, B.K., Boulay, C.B., Krusienski, D.J., Frye, G.E., Hauser, C.K., Schwartz, N.E., Vaughan, T.M., Wolpaw, J.R., Sellers, E.W., 2010. A novel P300-based brain-computer interface stimulus presentation paradigm: moving beyond rows and columns. Clin. Neurophysiol. 121, 1109–1120. http://dx.doi.org/10.1016/j.clinph.2010.01.030.

Treder, M.S., Blankertz, B., 2010. (C)overt attention and visual speller design in an ERP-based brain-computer interface. Behav. Brain Funct. 6, 28. http://dx.doi.org/10.1186/1744-9081-6-28.

Várkuti, B., Guan, C., Pan, Y., Phua, K.S., Ang, K.K., Kuah, C.W.K., Chua, K., Ang, B.T., Birbaumer, N., Sitaram, R., 2013. Resting state changes in functional connectivity correlate with movement recovery for BCI and robot-assisted upper-extremity training after stroke. Neurorehabil. Neural Repair 27, 53–62. http://dx.doi.org/10.1177/1545968312445910.

Vernon, D., Egner, T., Cooper, N., Compton, T., Neilands, C., Sheri, A., Gruzelier, J., 2003. The effect of training distinct neurofeedback protocols on aspects of cognitive performance. Int. J. Psychophysiol. 47, 75–85.

Walter, A., Ramos Murguialday, A., Spüler, M., Naros, G., Leão, M.T., Gharabaghi, A., Rosenstiel, W., Birbaumer, N., Bogdan, M., 2012. Coupling BCI and cortical stimulation for brain-state-dependent stimulation: methods for spectral estimation in the presence of stimulation after-effects. Front. Neural Circuits 6, 87. http://dx.doi.org/10.3389/fncir.2012.00087.

Wolpaw, J.R., McFarland, D.J., 2004. Control of a two-dimensional movement signal by a noninvasive brain-computer interface in humans. Proc. Natl. Acad. Sci. U.S.A. 101, 17849–17854. http://dx.doi.org/10.1073/pnas.0403504101.

Wolpaw, J., Wolpaw, E.W., 2012. Brain-Computer Interfaces: Principles and Practice. Oxford University Press, New York.

Young, B.M., Nigogosyan, Z., Walton, L.M., Remsik, A., Song, J., Nair, V.A., Tyler, M.E., Edwards, D.F., Caldera, K., Sattin, J.A., Williams, J.C., Prabhakaran, V., 2015. Dose–response relationships using brain-computer interface technology impact stroke rehabilitation. Front. Hum. Neurosci. 9, 361. http://dx.doi.org/10.3389/fnhum.2015.00361.

Zeiler, S.R., Krakauer, J.W., 2013. The interaction between training and plasticity in the poststroke brain. Curr. Opin. Neurol. 26, 609–616. http://dx.doi.org/10.1097/WCO.0000000000000025.

Zhang, D., Maye, A., Gao, X., Hong, B., Engel, A.K., Gao, S., 2010. An independent brain-computer interface using covert non-spatial visual selective attention. J. Neural Eng. 7, 16010. http://dx.doi.org/10.1088/1741-2560/7/1/016010.

Zickler, C., Riccio, A., Leotta, F., Hillian-Tress, S., Halder, S., Holz, E., Staiger-Sälzer, P., Hoogerwerf, E.-J., Desideri, L., Mattia, D., Kübler, A., 2011. A brain-computer interface as input channel for a standard assistive technology software. Clin. EEG Neurosci. 42, 236–244. http://dx.doi.org/10.1177/155005941104200409.

Zickler, C., Halder, S., Kleih, S.C., Herbert, C., Kübler, A., 2013. Brain painting: usability testing according to the user-centered design in end users with severe motor paralysis. Artif. Intell. Med. 59, 99–110. http://dx.doi.org/10.1016/j.artmed.2013.08.003.

Zuberer, A., Brandeis, D., Drechsler, R., 2015. Are treatment effects of neurofeedback training in children with ADHD related to the successful regulation of brain activity? A review on the learning of regulation of brain activity and a contribution to the discussion on specificity. Front. Hum. Neurosci. 9, 135. http://dx.doi.org/10.3389/fnhum.2015.00135.

Zucchella, C., Capone, A., Codella, V., Vecchione, C., Buccino, G., Sandrini, G., Pierelli, F., Bartolo, M., 2014. Assessing and restoring cognitive functions early after stroke. Funct. Neurol. 29, 255–262.

BCI in practice

13

D.J. McFarland[1], T.M. Vaughan

National Center for Adaptive Neurotechnologies, Wadsworth Center, Albany, NY, United States
[1]Corresponding author: Tel.: +1-518-473-4680, e-mail address: dennis.mcfarland@health.ny.gov

Abstract

Brain–computer interfaces are systems that use signals recorded from the brain to enable communication and control applications for individuals who have impaired function. This technology has developed to the point that it is now being used by individuals who can actually benefit from it. However, there are several outstanding issues that prevent widespread use. These include the ease of obtaining high-quality recordings by home users, the speed, and accuracy of current devices and adapting applications to the needs of the user. In this chapter, we discuss some of these unsolved issues.

Keywords

Brain–computer interface, Home use, Neurotechnologies

People with severe motor disabilities require alternative methods for communication and control. A brain–computer interface (BCI) is a system that does not depend on the brain's normal output pathways of peripheral nerves and muscles. It measures brain activity and converts it into an artificial output that replaces, restores, enhances, supplements, or improves natural CNS output (Wolpaw and Wolpaw, 2012).

Given the complexity of recording and interpreting brain signals, it is not surprising that most BCI studies take place in a laboratory with healthy subjects or with target populations with expert supervision. To be useful, a BCI must be available, reliable, and serviceable outside the laboratory. Further, the application must be useful to the target population. That is, a BCI must provide a safe and effective solution to an important problem most of the time for most of the people who need it. This chapter seeks to provide information and insight into the practical matters that must be addressed for BCIs to be useful in the everyday lives of people who need them.

Progress in Brain Research, Volume 228, ISSN 0079-6123, http://dx.doi.org/10.1016/bs.pbr.2016.06.005
© 2016 Elsevier B.V. All rights reserved.

1 OVERVIEW OF COMMON BCI SYSTEMS

In this section, we present a brief overview of several BCI systems that could be used for practical applications. Our intent is not an exhaustive review, but rather to highlight some of the features of these systems. A variety of signals can be measured and have the potential for use in a BCI. They include electrical, magnetic, metabolic, chemical, thermal, and mechanical responses to brain activity and signals recorded from the spinal cord. Questions about which kind of brain signal are best for which application is an empirical question. The overall goal is to use the brain signal that provides sufficient information content for controlling the BCI device with required reliability, safety, longevity, and cost effectiveness (Wolpaw and Wolpaw, 2012; Wolpaw et al., 2002). To date, most BCI studies have focused on replacing or augmenting communication and control using electrophysiological signals recorded from the scalp (electroencephalography, EEG), from the surface of the cortex (electrocorticography, ECoG), or from the activity recorded from single cortical neurons. The ultimate usefulness of each of these methods hinges on the range of communication and control applications it can support and on the extent to which its disadvantages can be overcome.

Here, we wish only to provide a brief summary of the more common alternatives and focus on issues that arise when one tries to apply these to end users. It is worth noting that improvements in these methods are continually being proposed.

BCI methods that rely on epidural or subdural recordings (Schalk et al., 2008) as well as those involving electrodes penetrating the brain (Hochberg et al., 2006; reviewed in Homer et al., 2013) offer superior spatial resolution over surface recordings. Whether or not increased spatial resolution is of sufficient benefit for communication and control and outweighs the cost and the increased health risk to the subject remains uncertain (McFarland et al., 2010). In addition, current invasive methodologies have not yet solved problems rising from long-term stable recordings (Groothuis et al., 2014; Kozai et al., 2015). To date, all clinical studies involving these methods have required expert supervision. Advances in materials and methods may reduce the risks, and further study may demonstrate increased utility (reviewed in Huggins et al., 2014).

Sensorimotor rhythm or SMR-based BCI has been the focus of research and development for over two decades (Pfurtscheller and McFarland, 2012). These BCIs rely on the fact that the execution, or imagined execution, of limb movement induces changes in rhythmic activity recorded over sensorimotor cortex (Pfurtscheller and Aranibar, 1979). Changes in SMRs can be detected on the scalp by EEG (eg, McFarland et al., 2000) and magnetoencephalography (MEG) (eg, Jurkiewicz et al., 2006) or on the surface of the brain by ECoG (eg, Graimann et al., 2002; Leuthardt et al., 2004; reviewed in Pfurtscheller and McFarland, 2012). Most often, BCIs that rely on SMRs use linear regression algorithms to translate SMR amplitudes into cursor movements on a computer display (eg, Wolpaw et al., 1991). More recent developments of this approach have produced the most complex multidimensional SMR-based BCI control realized to date (McFarland et al., 2010; Wolpaw and

McFarland, 2004). Using an approach based on classification, Guger et al. (2003) report that 56 of 60 nondisabled subjects achieved classification accuracies of 60% or better on a two-choice task after two sessions of training. In one example, an SMR-based BCI spelling application realized spelling by dividing the alphabet into four parts. Users reached a single letter through a series of three successive selections (Wolpaw et al., 2003). Importantly, these users required many days of training to master this task.

Some researchers have suggested the use of various cognitive strategies as alternatives to the use of motor imagery (eg, Curran et al., 2003; Vansteensel et al., 2010). However, it is important that a communication and control devices not co-opt cognitive resources that would normally be involved in how the user decides to use the device. In this regard, use of motor systems normally used in functions such as typing or speaking become automatic with practice. This also appears to be the case with SMR control (McFarland et al., 2010).

Like SMRs, movement or movement imagery is associated with relatively slow changes in the voltages recorded over the sensorimotor cortex, called slow cortical potentials (SCPs). SCPs typically consist of negative potential shifts that precede actual or imagined movement or cognitive tasks (eg, mental arithmetic Birbaumer et al., 1990). An SCP is typically followed by a biphasic wave referred to as the movement-related potential (Colebatch, 2007). SCP BCI users learn to produce SCP changes that can be detected by a BCI and used for control. This training requires repeated sessions over weeks or months (Birbaumer et al., 1999). In a typical SCP-based BCI, the user communicates through a series of binary selections until the alphabet is parsed (Perelmouter et al., 1999). While Krepki et al. (2007) described improvements, Allison et al. (2012) emphasize that compared with other methods, SCP-based BCIs remain slow.

Steady state visual evoked potential (SSVEP)-based BCIs depend on changes in SSVEPs (eg, Gao et al., 2003; Middendorf et al., 2000). In this approach, the subject views one or more stimuli that each oscillate at a unique constant frequency. When the subject focuses attention on one stimulus, the corresponding frequency can be detected in the EEG activity recorded over occipital areas of the brain. Hence, an SSVEP-based BCI can infer a user's intent by measuring the EEG activity at a specific frequency or frequencies recorded over occipital areas of the brain and achieve high information transfer rates (Chen et al., 2013; Nakanishi et al., 2014). BCIs using SSVEPs have been described as dependent; ie, they use EEG features that depend on the ocular-motor muscles that control eye movements and thus not appropriate for individuals who lack muscle control (Wolpaw et al., 2002). Allison et al. (2008) reported that two spatially overlapping stimuli produced differences in SSVEPs, and Zhang et al. (2010) reported that subjects using a similar approach averaged online classification accuracy of $72.6 \pm 16.1\%$ after 3 days of use. In addition, several groups have reported that people can use a binary SSVEP-based device with eyes closed (Hwang et al., 2015; Lim et al., 2013). Thus, SSVEP-based BCIs might support BCI control in people who are currently considered locked in. Guger et al. (2012a) report that 96% of

53 able-bodied subjects attained an accuracy of 80% or above with a four-choice SSVEP BCI that required virtually no training.

The P300-based matrix speller, originally described by Farwell and Donchin (1988), holds promise for providing BCI-based communication to users with severe motor disabilities (Vaughan et al., 2006). A P300 is the response that occurs when a subject recognizes a rare target stimulus (Sutton et al., 1965). Since the P300 signals the subject's recognition of the target event without the requirement for an overt response, it represents a useful signal for BCI. In the original P300-based BCI speller paradigm, a 6×6 matrix of 36 items (ie, characters and numbers) is presented on a screen and the user attends to the desired item (ie, the target), while different groups of items flash rapidly. About 300 ms after the target item flashes, a positive deflection occurs in the EEG, the P300 event-related potential (ERP). The P300-based BCI can usually identify the target item with a high rate of accuracy. Guger et al. (2009) reported that 89% of 81 able-bodied subjects were able to spell with an accuracy greater than 80% after just 5 min of data collection for system calibration. The P300 speller paradigm has been well studied. According to an Ovid search in early 2016, over 80 studies have examined aspects of P300-based BCI control and applied it to problems like communication, environmental, wheelchair, and robotic control.

P300 spelling devices generally average EEG over multiple stimulus sequences in order to improve accuracy. This creates a speed-accuracy trade-off since longer sequence runs produce more accuracy at the expense of speed. Schreuder et al. (2013) evaluated rules for the early termination of stimulus sequences based on dynamic determination of the discriminability of the data collected from the current trial. Most methods worked well. Mainsah et al. (2015) showed that dynamic stopping could increase communication rates in patients with amyotrophic lateral sclerosis (ALS). Furthermore, the patients preferred this method.

The design of the P300 speller matrix also has a considerable impact on performance. For example, Townsend et al. (2010) reported on use of a paradigm that used virtual matrices that were reordered prior to display on the screen. This procedure prevented a given potential target from flashing twice on successive epochs and minimizes the extent to which adjacent stimuli flash within the same epoch. Townsend et al. (2010) found that the use of the virtual matrix paradigm resulted in better performance and user acceptance in both healthy volunteers and ALS participants. Zhang et al. (2012) showed that the use of facial stimuli produced superior classification over simply highlighting an icon. Allison and Pineda (2003) showed that larger matrices with more elements evoked larger P300 responses. This effect could be due in part to the fact that increases in target-to-target interval enhance P300-based performance (McFarland et al., 2011).

Each of the BCI approaches discussed so far has its strengths and weaknesses. For example, an SMR-based BCI can provide relatively rapid graded multidimensional control. However, available methods require extensive training, and the training requires expert supervision. Furthermore, it is unknown if people with severe disabilities can tolerate such training regimes. SSVEP-based BCIs allow for a relatively high information transfer rate without extensive training, but there are concerns about the requirement of good eye control. Invasive methods pose some medical risk. However, many people with disabilities express a desire to use implanted devices (Blabe et al., 2015).

The P300-based method designed by Farwell and Donchin (1988) has great advantages. The ERPs appear to be stable over time (Sellers et al., 2010), do not require extensive training (Guger et al., 2009), and have information transfer rates that compare to other augmentative and assistive communication devices. Yeom et al. (2014) report about 50 bits per minute, and more recently, Townsend and Platsko (2016) report 100 bpm. A P300-based BCI also has several important disadvantages. The matrix-based speller requires vision (McCane et al., 2014). Furthermore, such methods may rely, in part, on the users' ability to move their eyes (Brunner et al., 2010; Treder and Blankertz, 2010). Thus, this method may be especially problematic for people with ALS who, late in disease, have both impaired vision and weakened oculomotor control. For example, McCane et al. (2014) report that visual impairment was the principal obstacle for about 30% of individuals with ALS who were unable to use a P300-based visual speller. These visual impairments primarily involved some aspect of motor control (eg, diplopia, nystagmus, ptosis) that could potentially interfere with seeing the flashing items well enough to achieve high accuracy.

2 SOME ISSUES IN APPLICATIONS FOR END USERS

Nijboer (2015) suggests that BCI technology should be designed for usability rather than reliability. From this perspective, it is important to consider the needs of a potential patient population in designing a BCI system as user acceptance is the ultimate test of success. Studies using questionnaires indicate that patients are interested in using BCI systems (Huggins et al., 2011, 2015), but that current systems do not meet their requirements for speed, accuracy, and ease of use. While system performance (ie, speed and accuracy) is important to end users, other aspects of usability also need to be considered. For example, Liberati et al. (2015) report that participants in a focus group emphasized the need for ALS patients to retain their sense of agency by being able to control their environment without asking for help (eg, turn the lights on and off, control the television, answer the doorbell, regulate the temperature in a room, and get somebody's attention).

There are several possible ways to evaluate the impact of BCI systems on the needs of users. Perhaps the most straightforward approach is to determine how often the BCI devices are used. The assumption here is that individuals will use devices that meet their needs more often. However, BCI researchers should be aware that all assistive technologies face certain barriers to acceptance and that these should be taken into account (Baxter et al., 2012).

Another approach is to consider how BCI systems impact the quality of life of users. However, this approach is not so simple, and many psychologists have opted for evaluating constructs related to mood and affect. For example, depression is related to quality-of-life ratings. Kübler et al. (2005) report that the incidence of depression in ALS is quite variable, ranging from none to clinically depressed. Yet, quality of life was rated by Kübler as satisfactory. In a review of the literature, McLeod and Clarke (2007) found that quality of life as assessed by questionnaire varied more with social support and hopelessness than with the physical state of the patient. Well-being is often treated as synonymous with quality of life and happiness. However, it is important to consider whether questionnaires can effectively measure these constructs (World Health Organization, 2012). Indeed, it may be very difficult to validate constructs for which there are not established criteria. Questionnaires designed to measure the quality of life of someone with a particular diagnosis, for example, ALS, may reflect the investigators' point of view rather than validated psychological constructs (eg, Simmons et al., 2006). There are complex relationships between measures purported to assess satisfaction with life, subjective happiness, and self-reflection (Lyke, 2009). A further complicating factor is that the value an individual might place on life may change as death appears closer (King et al., 2009).

Perhaps the most common BCI study involves the evaluation of potential prediction algorithms (Lotte et al., 2007; Pasqualotto et al., 2012), often using data from archived BCI competitions that involve healthy subjects (eg, Blankertz et al., 2006; Sajda et al., 2003). For the most part, these data sets do not involve transfer between sessions. Data set 1 described by Blankertz et al. (2006) is an exception in that training and test sets were recorded on different days. Likewise, data set 2b described by Tangermann et al. (2012) was concerned with session-to-session transfer. Both of these competition data sets involved motor imagery without feedback. In general, the competition data sets do not approximate data that would be encountered in the field. Individuals who could actually benefit from use of a BCI would most likely have a neurological disorder, and the data would be collected over many separate sessions, often under less than favorable recording conditions. In addition, feedback would be inevitable. In any case, the results reported in these studies vary widely (eg, fig. 1 from Blankertz et al., 2006), due in large part to the skill of the analysts. Further, when prediction algorithms are compared within the same group, the differences are often not large (eg, Krusienski et al., 2006).

Optimizing recordings is one of the more important issues in adapting BCI systems to individuals who might actually benefit from their use. Potential users have expressed concerns about the mess, inconvenience, and discomfort of wet electrodes (Peters et al., 2015). As these same users also expressed concerns about system accuracy, potential alternative sensors should be developed to produce quality recordings. While it has been stated that current wet gel recordings provide an excellent signal (Chi et al., 2010), they are probably less than optimal for several reasons. If the electrode density is too great, bridging can occur so that two or more sensors are electrically coupled (Alschuler et al., 2014). In addition, current generation surface sensors are susceptible to a variety of noise sources due to variations in impedance. Ferree et al. (2001) have asserted that high electrode impedance has little effect beyond power-line noise that can be easily filtered out. However, Kappenman and Luck (2010) showed that high impedance increased the noise level of the EEG primarily at lower frequencies and reduced the signal-to-noise ratio of the P3 response.

In addition to overall impedance levels, fluctuations due to unstable electrode contact can produce large artifacts in the EEG. While it might seem that completely paralyzed subjects are unlikely to produce movement artifacts, use of a respirator can produce rather large movement-related artifacts and involuntary reflexes may be present.

There are a number of alternative sensor designs that might be used in a BCI system. The emotive EPOC system uses moistened felt pads and a semirigid support that is less accurate but quicker than conventional electrode positioning (Mayaud et al., 2013). The locations of the pads are also largely restricted to sites on the perimeter of traditional recording montages which are more prone to EMG contamination (Goncharova et al., 2003). Guger et al. (2012b) describe the g.SAHARA dry electrode that consists of a series of eight gold-plated pins that are mounted in a conventional cap that does not limit electrode locations. Both of these rely on low impedance resistive contact with the scalp. In contrast, Sellers et al. (2009) describe a sensor by QUASAR that uses hybrid combination of high impedance resistive and capacitive contact with the scalp.

Guger et al. (2012b) report that dry and gel-based electrodes (g.SAHARA vs g.BUTTERFLY wet electrodes) produced similar results with a P300-spelling device used by healthy individuals. Nijboer et al. (2015) report that a 32-channel BioSemi headset produced higher accuracy than 8-channel g.SAHARA and 14-channel Emotive systems. There was no significant difference between the BioSemi system and the g.SAHARA system when performance based on the same eight electrodes was compared. Hairston et al. (2014) compared the EPOC and QUASAR systems as well as the B-Alert X-10, with the BioSemi system, which they considered a "gold standard." They report on usability and comfort, but did not consider quality of the signal or how it might impact performance. Hairston et al. (2014) state that only the BioSemi system accommodates variations in both head size and shape. They rated the B-Alert system next in terms of accommodation. The EPOC and QUASAR systems could produce uncomfortable pressure points and movement artifacts when they do not fit properly. As noted by Chi et al. (2010), dry electrodes require that new mechanical solutions be devised since they are much more difficult to secure to the patient's scalp. This may create a potential trade-off between comfort and recording quality.

Design of the BCI user interface can also have a considerable impact on usability. Mason and Birch (2000) noted that many user applications require infrequent, asynchronous input. In contrast, existing BCI applications require a user response synchronized with a regularly occurring BCI system stimulus display. Asynchronous input can be a challenge as many EEG signals can generate a high rate of false positives. The solution to this problem depends on the task design as well as the particular EEG signal used. Mason and Birch (2000) based their approach on producing a system with a low false-alarm rate. In contrast, Kaiser et al. (2001) trained two paralyzed patients to learn to regulate SCPs in order to turn the BCI system on.

Communication rates can also be enhanced by the use of information available in the sequential probabilities in language. For example, Da Silva-Sauer et al. (2016)

found increased communication rates using the T9 system and word prediction similar to that employed by many mobile phones. Another alternative is to use language priors in the classifier that determines the users' intent (Delgado Saa et al., 2015).

Even with all of these various enhancements, some severely disabled patients cannot use current BCI systems. As discussed earlier, visual impairments appear to be a major factor in preventing some individuals with ALS from using a P300-based speller (McCane et al., 2014). This has led to considerable effort to develop BCI systems based on alternative sensory modalities (eg, Halder et al., 2010; Nijboer et al., 2008a). So far these systems that use alternative sensory modalities do not appear to provide communication rates comparable to the visual P300 speller. In addition, the logic of using alternative sensory modalities assumes that these will provide a solution to the difficulties that prevent effective BCI operation for some users with ALS. This assumption requires additional study. There is some evidence that ALS may also be associated with auditory processing difficulties (Pekkonen et al., 2004). Furthermore, poor BCI performance might also be associated with ALS-related dementia (Swinnen and Robberecht, 2014) which would not be corrected by substitution of sensory modalities.

3 STUDIES WITH END USERS

Over the past decade, BCI researchers have begun to explore the BCI capacities of people severely disabled by injury or disease. The results to date indicate that many people with severe disabilities might use BCIs for communication and control (eg, Jarosiewiczn et al., 2015; reviewed in Vaughan et al., 2012). By far the largest number of BCI studies to date has included people with ALS (Marchetti and Priftis, 2015). People with ALS have learned to use P300-based BCIs (eg, Nijboer et al., 2008b; Silvoni et al., 2013), SCPs (eg, Birbaumer et al., 1999), and SMR-based BCIs (eg, Neuper et al., 2003; Kübler et al., 2005) to operate spelling devices. Recently, one study reported success with an individual with ALS who was completely locked in (Gallegos-Ayala et al., 2014). Many aspects of the paradigm have been manipulated in on- and off-line studies, eg, rate (McFarland et al., 2011) and stimulus presentation (Townsend and Platsko, 2016; Yeom et al., 2014). These studies suggest strongly that customization may be an important factor for success and indicate that ERPs from the entire time interval used for classification are likely involved in classifier performance (Bianchi et al., 2010; McCane et al., 2015).

However, not all individuals with ALS are able to use these BCI systems. In fact, many of those who have participated in BCI studies retained alternative means to communicate (Kübler and Birbaumer, 2008). As discussed earlier, several factors could account for this lack of success for individuals with advanced ALS, including oculomotor dysfunction (reviewed in Sharma et al., 2011); extinction of goal-oriented behavior (Kübler and Birbaumer, 2008) and dementia (Hochberg and Anderson, 2012). Designs that capitalize on the P300 and related ERPs, but do not require visual acuity, have reduced information transfer rates but have not been tested extensively in populations they are meant to serve (eg, Hill et al., 2014Klobassa et al., 2009; Sellers and Donchin, 2006; Treder et al., 2010).

More recently, P300 spelling devices have been installed in users' homes and maintained by their caregivers (Holz et al., 2015; Sellers et al., 2010; Wolpaw et al., 2016). While these systems still require technical support, most of the day-to-day support for use is handled by the caregivers. These systems face all the problems that face BCI researchers, and in addition, some that are the purview of assistive technology (Huggins and Zeitlin, 2012).

Like any device deployed in the home, components must be safe and simple to use and maintain. However, monitoring success and providing ongoing training and technical support present some issues that are unique to BCI devices (eg, placement and care of the cap). Without capable and motivated caregivers, long-term BCI home use is currently not possible (Wilkins et al., 2009). Current BCIs available for home use also require some ongoing technical support. This is dependent on consistent Internet connections for data transfer and regular contact if support is to be done remotely.

Successful home use of a BCI system requires a home environment that can support its use. The immediate environments of people with severe disabilities are often crowded with much essential equipment, including ventilators, mechanical beds, wheelchairs, and so forth. Thus, significant sources of electrical noise and intermittent artifacts may be present. For example, the ventilators essential to the survival of many prospective BCI users often cause high-frequency electromagnetic and low-frequency mechanical (ie, movement) artifacts (Young and Campbell, 1999).

System reliability for EEG-based BCI depends on good signal quality. Fig. 1 represents impedances recorded over 23 months of BCI home use by two different home users (for details of the method, see Krusienski et al., 2006; McCane et al., 2015). In every session represented here, the caregiver positioned an eight-channel cap and started the system after using diagnostic software (Wolpaw et al., 2016).

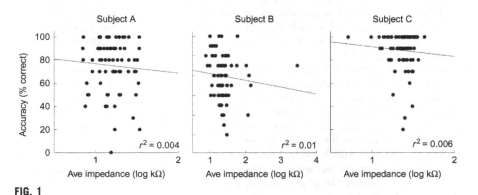

FIG. 1

The log of average impedance over eight channels for a copy-spelling calibration task for three BCI-24/7 home users over A (12 mos), B (11 mos), and C (12 mos).

This diagnostic software allows caregivers to measure impedance and regard EEG traces in order to judge record quality in order to determine BCI readiness. BCI performance on this copy-spelling task was unaffected at averaged impedances well over the laboratory standard. Likely, there are both system and subject qualities not currently captured by home system measures.

BCIs are currently used mainly by researchers in the laboratory. To see BCI realize its full potential BCIs must work well not only in the laboratory but also in real life. To meet these requirements, they must be simple to operate, require minimal expert oversight, be usable by the people who need them (ie, the BCI user, their caregivers, and/or their healthcare providers). Much more translational research is required if BCI is to fulfill its promise to its funders and to the people who need it.

ACKNOWLEDGMENTS

Supported by NIBIB/NINDS, NIH (EB00856, 1P41EB018783); NCMRR, NICHD, NIH (HD30146), James S. McDonnell Foundation; Altran Foundation, ALS Hope Foundation; NEC Foundation; and the Department of Veterans Affairs (VA) and coordinated by the Hines VA Cooperative Studies Program Coordinating Center (CSPCC) in Hines, Illinois.

REFERENCES

Allison, B.Z., Pineda, J.A., 2003. ERPs evoked by different matrix sizes: implications for a brain computer interface (BCI) system. IEEE Trans. Neural Syst. Rehabil. Eng. 11, 110–113.

Allison, B.Z., McFarland, D.J., Schalk, G., Zheng, S.D., Moore, M.M., Wolpaw, J.R., 2008. Towards an independent brain-computer interface using steady state visual evoked potentials. Clin. Neurophysiol. 119, 399–408.

Allison, B.Z., Dunne, S., Leeb, R., Millan, J. del R., Nijholt, A., 2012. Recent and upcoming BCI progress: overview, analysis and recommendations. In: Allison, B.Z., Dunne, S., Leeb, R., Millan, J. del R., Nijholt, A. (Eds.), Towards Practical Brain–Computer Interfaces: Bridging the Gap from Research to Real-World Applications. Springer, Heidelberg, pp. 1–16.

Alschuler, D.M., Tenke, C.E., Bruder, G.E., Kayser, J., 2014. Identifying electrode bridging from electrical distance distributions: a survey of publicly-available EEG data using a new method. Clin. Neurophysiol. 125, 484–490.

Baxter, S., Enderby, P., Judge, S., Evans, P., 2012. Barriers and facilitators to use of high technology augmentative and alternative communication devices: a systematic review and qualitative synthesis. Int. J. Lang. Commun. Disord. 47, 115–129.

Bianchi, L., Sami, S., Hillebrand, A., Fawcett, I.P., Quitadamo, L.R., Seri, S., 2010. Which physiological components are more suitable for visual ERP based brain-computer interface? A preliminary MEG/EEG study. Brain Topogr. 23, 180–185.

Birbaumer, N., Elbert, T., Canavan, A.G., Rockstroh, B., 1990. Slow potentials of the cerebral cortex. Physiol. Rev. 70, 1–41.

Birbaumer, N., Ghanayim, N., Hinterberger, T., Iversen, I., Kotchoubey, B., Kübler, J., Perelmouter, J., Taub, E., Flor, H., 1999. A spelling device for the paralysed. Nature 398, 297–298.

Blabe, C.H., Gilja, V., Chestek, C.A., Shenoy, K.V., Anderson, K.D., Henderson, J.M., 2015. Assessment of brain-machine interfaces from the perspective of people with paralysis. J. Neural Eng. 12, 04302.

Blankertz, B., Muller, K.-R., Krusienski, D.J., Schalk, G., Wolpaw, J.R., Schogl, A., Pfurtscheller, G., Millan, J.R., Schroder, M., Birbaumer, N., 2006. The BCI competition III: validating alternative approaches to actual BCI problems. IEEE Trans. Neural Syst. Rehabil. Eng. 14, 153–159.

Brunner, P., Joshi, S., Briskin, S., Wolpaw, J.R., Bischof, H., Schalk, G., 2010. Does the 'P300' speller depend on eye gaze? J. Neural Eng. 7, 056013.

Chen, X., Chen, Z., Gao, S., Gao, X., 2013. Brain–computer interface based on intermodulation frequency. J. Neural Eng. 10 (6), 066009.

Chi, Y.M., Jung, T.-P., Cauwenberghs, G., 2010. Dry-contact and noncontact biopotential electrodes: methodological review. IEEE Rev. Biomed. Eng. 3, 106–119.

Colebatch, J.G., 2007. Bereitschaftspotential and movement-related potentials: origin, significance, and application in disorders of human movement. Mov. Disord. 22, 601–610.

Curran, E., Sykacek, P., Stokes, M., Roberts, S., Penny, W., Johnsrude, I., Owen, A.M., 2003. Cognitive tasks for driving a brain-computer interfacing system: a pilot study. IEEE Trans. Neural Syst. Rehabil. Eng. 12, 48–54.

Da Silva-Sauer, L., Valero-Aguayo, L., de la Torre-Luque, A., Ron-Angevin, R., Varona-Moya, S., 2016. Concentration on performance with P300-based BCI systems: a matter of interface features. Appl. Ergon. 52, 325–332.

Delgado Saa, J.F., de Pesters, A., McFarland, D., Cetin, M., 2015. World-level language modeling for P300 spellers based on discriminative graphical models. J. Neural Eng. 12, 026007.

Farwell, L.A., Donchin, E., 1988. Talking of the top of your head: toward a mental prosthesis utilizing event-related brain potentials. Electroencephalogr. Clin. Neurophysiol. 70, 510–523.

Ferree, T.C., Luu, P., Russell, G.S., Tucker, D.M., 2001. Scalp electrode impedance, infection risk, and EEG data quality. Clin. Neurophysiol. 112, 536–544.

Gallegos-Ayala, G., Furdea, A., Takano, K., Ruf, C.A., Flor, H., Birbaumer, N., 2014. Brain communication in a completely locked-in patient using bedside near-infrared spectroscopy. Neurology 82, 1930–1932.

Gao, X., Xu, D., Cheng, M., Gao, S., 2003. A BCI-based environmental controller for the motion-disabled. IEEE Trans. Neural Syst. Rehabil. Eng. 11, 137–140.

Goncharova, I.I., McFarland, D.J., Vaughan, T.M., Wolpaw, J.R., 2003. EMG contamination of EEG: spectral and topographical characteristics. Clin. Neurophysiol. 114, 1580–1593.

Graimann, B., Huggins, J.E., Levine, S.P., Pfurtscheller, G., 2002. visualization of significant ERD/ERS patterns in multichannel EEG and ECoG data. Clin. Neurophysiol. 113, 43–47.

Groothuis, J., Ramsey, N.F., Ramakers, G.M.J., van der Plasse, G., 2014. Physiological challenges for intracortical electrodes. Brain Stimul. 7, 1–6.

Guger, C., Edlinger, G., Harkam, W., Niedermayer, I., Pfurtscheller, G., 2003. How many people are able to operate an EEG-based brain-computer interface (BCI)? IEEE Trans. Neural Syst. Rehabil. Eng. 11, 145–147.

Guger, C., Daban, S., Sellers, E., Holzner, C., Krausz, G., Carabalona, R., Gramatica, F., Edlinger, G., 2009. How many people are able to control a P300-based brain-computer interface (BCI)? Neurosci. Lett. 462, 95–98.

Guger, C., Allison, B., Grosswindhager, B., Pruckl, R., Hintermuller, C., Kapeller, C., Bruckner, M., Krausz, G., Edlinger, G., 2012a. How many people could use an SSVEP BCI? Front. Neurosci. 19, 169.

Guger, C., Krausz, G., Allison, B.Z., Edlinger, G., 2012b. Comparison of dry and gel based electrodes for P300 brain–computer interfaces. Front. Neurosci. 6, 60.

Hairston, W.D., Whitaker, K.W., Ries, A.J., Vettel, J.M., Bradford, J.C., Kerick, S.E., McDowell, K., 2014. Usability of four commercially-oriented EEG systems. J. Neural Eng. 11, 046018.

Halder, S., Rea, M., Andreoni, R., Nijboer, F., Hammer, E.M., Kleih, S.C., Birbaumer, N., Kübler, A., 2010. An auditory oddball brain-computer interface for binary choices. Clin. Neurophysiol. 121, 516–523.

Hill, N.J., Ricci, E., Hailder, S., McCane, L.M., Heckman, S., Wolpaw, J.R., Vaughan, T.M., 2014. A practical, intuitive brain–computer interface for communicating 'yes' and 'no' by listening. J. Neural Eng. 11, 035003.

Hochberg, L.R., Anderson, K.D., 2012. BCI users and their needs. In: Wolpaw, J.R., Wolpaw, E.W. (Eds.), Brain–Computer Interfaces: Principles and Practice. Oxford University Press, New York, pp. 317–323.

Hochberg, L.R., Serruya, M.D., Friehs, G.M., Mukand, J.A., Saleh, M., Caplan, A.H., Branner, A., Chen, D., Penn, R.D., Donoghue, J.P., 2006. Neuronal ensemble control of prosthetic devices by a human with tetraplegia. Nature 442, 164–171.

Holz, E.M., Botrel, L., Kaufmann, T., Kübler, A., 2015. Long-term independent brain-computer interface home use improves quality of life of a patient in the locked-in state: a case study. Arch. Phys. Med. Rehabil. 96 (3 Suppl.), S16–S26.

Homer, M.L., Nurmikko, A.V., Donoghue, J.P., Hochberg, L.R., 2013. Sensors and decoding for intracortical brain computer interfaces. Annu. Rev. Biomed. Eng. 15, 383–405.

Huggins, J.E., Zeitlin, D., 2012. BCI applications. In: Wolpaw, J.R., Winter-Wolpaw, E. (Eds.), Brain-Computer Interfaces: Principles and Practice. Oxford University Press, New York, pp. 197–214.

Huggins, J.E., Wren, P., Gruis, K.L., 2011. What would brain-computer interface users want? Opinions and priorities of potential users with amyotrophic lateral sclerosis. Amyotroph. Lateral Scler. 12, 318–324.

Huggins, J.E., Guger, C., Allison, B., Anderson, C.W., Batista, A., Brouwer, A.-M., Brunner, C., Chavarriaga, R., Fried-Oken, M., Gunduz, A., Gupta, D., Kübler, A., Leeb, R., Lotte, F., Miller, L.E., Müller-Putz, G., Rutkowski, T., Tangermann, M., Thompson, D.E., 2014. Workshops of the fifth international brain–computer interface meeting: defining the future. Brain Comput. Interfaces 1, 27–49.

Huggins, J.E., Moinuddin, A.A., Chiodo, A.E., Wren, P.A., 2015. What would brain-computer interface users want: opinions and priorities of potential useras with spinal cord injury. Arch. Phys. Med. Rehabil. 96 (Suppl. 1), S38–S45.

Hwang, H.-J., Ferreria, V.Y., Ulrich, D., Kilic, T., Chatziliadis, X., Blankertz, B., Trederb, M., 2015. A gaze independent brain-computer interface based on visual stimulation through closed eyelids. Sci. Rep. 5, 15890.

Jarosiewiczn, B., Sarma, A.A., Bacher, D., Masse, N.Y., Simeral, J.D., Sorice, B., Oakley, E.M., Blabe, C., Pandarinath, C., Gilja, V., Cash, S.S., Eskandar, E.N.,

Friehs, G., Henderson, J.M., Shenoy, K.V., Donoghue, J.P., Hochberg, L.R., 2015. Virtual typing by people with tetraplegia using a self-calibrating intracortical brain-computer interface. Sci. Transl. Med. 7, 313ra179.

Jurkiewicz, M.T., Gaetz, W.C., Bostan, A.C., Cheyne, D., 2006. Post-movement beta rebound is generated in motor cortex: evidence from neuromagnetic recordings. Neuroimage 32, 1281–1289.

Kaiser, J., Perelmouter, J., Iversen, I.H., Neumann, N., Ghanayim, N., Hinterberger, T., Kübler, A., Kotchoubey, B., Birbaumer, N., 2001. Self-initiation of EEG-based communication in paralyzed patients. Clin. Neurophysiol. 112, 551–554.

Kappenman, E.S., Luck, S., 2010. The effects of electrode impedance on data quality and statistical significance in ERP recordings. Psychophysiology 47, 888–904.

King, L.A., Hicks, J.A., Abdelkhalik, J., 2009. Death, life, scarcity, and value: an alternative perspective on the meaning of death. Psychol. Sci. 20, 1459–1462.

Klobassa, D.S., Vaughan, T.M., Brunner, P., Schwartz, N.E., Wolpaw, J.R., Neuper, C., Sellers, E.W., 2009. Toward a high-throughput auditory P300-based brain-computer interface. Clin. Neurophysiol. 120, 1252–1261.

Kozai, T.D., Jaquins-Gerstl, A.S., Vazquez, A.L., Michael, A.C., Cui, X.T., 2015. Brain tissue response to neural implants impact signal sensitivity and intervention strategies. ACS Chem. Neurosci. 6, 48–67.

Krepki, R., Curio, G., Blankertz, B., Muller, K.-R., 2007. Berlin brain-computer interface—the HCL communication channel for discovery. Int. J. Hum. Comput. Stud. 65, 460–477.

Krusienski, D.J., Sellers, E.W., Cabestaing, F.C., Bayoudh, S., McFarland, D.J., Vaughan, T.M., Wolpaw, J.R., 2006. A comparison of classification techniques for the P300 speller. J. Neural Eng. 3, 299–305.

Kübler, A., Birbaumer, N., 2008. Brain-computer interfaces and communication in paralysis: extinction of goal directed thinking in completely paralysed patients. Clin. Neurophysiol. 119, 2658–2666.

Kübler, A., Winter, S., Ludolph, A.C., Hautzinger, M., Birbaumer, N., 2005. Severity of depressive symptoms and quality of life in patients with amyotrophic lateral sclerosis. Neurorehabil. Neural Repair 19, 182–193.

Leuthardt, E.C., Schalk, G., Wolpaw, J.R., Ojemann, J.G., Moran, D.W., 2004. A brain–computer interface using electrocorticographic signals in humans. J. Neural Eng. 1, 63–71.

Liberati, G., Pizzimenti, A., Simione, L., Riccio, A., Schettini, F., Inghilleri, M., Mattia, D., Cincotti, F., 2015. Developing brain–computer interfaces from a user-centered perspective: assessing the needs of persons with amyotrophic lateral sclerosis, caregivers, and professionals. Appl. Ergon. 50, 139–146.

Lim, J.H., Hwang, H.J., Han, C.H., Jung, K.Y., Im, C.H., 2013. Classification of binary intentions for individuals with impaired oculomotor function: 'eyes-closed' SSVEP-based brain-computer interface (BCI). J. Neural Eng. 10, 026021.

Lotte, F., Congedo, M., Lecuyer, A., Lamarche, F., Arnaldi, B., 2007. A review of classification algorithms for EEG-based brain-computer interfaces. J. Neural Eng. 4, R1–R13.

Lyke, J.A., 2009. Insight, but not self-reflection, is related to subjective well-being. Personal. Individ. Differ. 46, 66–70.

Mainsah, B.O., Collins, L.M., Colwell, K.A., Sellers, E.W., Ryan, D.B., Caves, K., Throckmorton, C.S., 2015. Increasing BCI communication rates with dynamic stopping towards more practical use: an ALS study. J. Neural Eng. 12 (1), 016013.

Marchetti, M., Priftis, K., 2015. Brain-computer interfaces in amyotrophic lateral sclerosis: a metanalysis. Clin. Neurophysiol. 126, 1255–1263.

Mason, S.G., Birch, G.E., 2000. A brain-controlled switch for asynchronous control applications. IEEE Trans. Biomed. Eng. 47, 1297–1307.

Mayaud, L., Congedo, M., Van Laghenhove, A., Orlikowski, D., Figere, M., Azabou, E., Cheliout-Heraut, F., 2013. A comparison of recording modalities of P300 event-related potentials (ERP) for brain-computer interface (BCI) paradigm. Neurophysiol. Clin. 43, 217–227.

McCane, L.M., Sellers, E.W., McFarland, D.J., Mak, J.N., Carmack, C.S., Zeitlin, D., Wolpaw, J.R., Vaughan, T.M., 2014. Brain-computer interface (BCI) evaluation in people with amyotrophic lateral sclerosis. Amyotroph. Lateral Scler. Frontotemporal Degener. 15, 207–215.

McCane, L.M., Heckman, S.M., McFarland, D.J., Townsend, G., Mak, J.N., Sellers, E.W., Zeitlin, D., Tenteromano, L.M., Wolpaw, J.R., Vaughan, T.M., 2015. P300-based brain-computer interface (BCI) event-related potentials (ERPs): people with amyotrophic lateral sclerosis (ALS) vs. age-matched controls. Clin. Neurophysiol. 126, 2124–2131.

McFarland, D.J., Miner, L.A., Vaughan, T.M., Wolpaw, J.R., 2000. Mu and beta rhythm topographies during motor imagery and actual movement. Brain Topogr. 12, 177–186.

McFarland, D.J., Sarnacki, W.A., Wolpaw, J.R., 2010. Electroencephalographic (EEG) control of three-dimensional movement. J. Neural Eng. 7, 036007.

McFarland, D.J., Sarnacki, W.A., Townsend, G., Vaughan, T., Wolpaw, J.R., 2011. The P300-based brain–computer interface (BCI): effects of stimulus rate. Clin. Neurophysiol. 122, 731–737.

McLeod, J.E., Clarke, D.M., 2007. A review of psychosocial aspects of motor neuron disease. J. Neurol. Sci. 258, 4–10.

Middendorf, M., McMillan, G., Calhoun, G., Jones, K.S., 2000. Brain-computer interfaces based on steady-state visual-evoked response. IEEE Trans. Rehabil. Eng. 8, 211–214.

Nakanishi, M., Wang, Y., Wang, Y.-T., Mitsukura, Y., Jung, T.-P., 2014. A high-speed brain speller using steady-state visual evoked potentials. Int. J. Neural Syst. 24, 1450019.

Neuper, C., Muller, G.R., Kubler, A., Birbaumer, N., Pfurtscheller, G., 2003. Clinical application of an EEG-based brain-computer interface: a case study in a patient with severe motor impairment. Clin. Neurophysiol. 114, 399–409.

Nijboer, F., 2015. Technology transfer of brain–computer interfaces as assistive technology: barriers and opportunities. Ann. Phys. Rehabil. Med. 58, 35–38.

Nijboer, F., Furdea, A., Gunst, I., Mellinger, J., McFarland, D.J., Birbaumer, N., Kübler, A., 2008a. An auditory brain-computer interface (BCI). J. Neurosci. Methods 167, 43–50.

Nijboer, F., Sellers, E.W., Mellinger, J., Jordan, M.A., Matuz, T., Furdea, A., Halder, S., Mochty, U., Krusienski, D.J., Vaughan, T.M., Wolpaw, J.R., Birbaumer, N., Kübler, A., 2008b. A P300-based brain-computer interface for people with amyotrophic lateral sclerosis. Clin. Neurophysiol. 119, 1909–1916.

Nijboer, F., Van De Laar, B., Gerritsen, S., Nijholt, A., Poel, M., 2015. Usability of three electroencephalogram headsets for brain–computer interfaces: a within subject comparison. Interact. Comput. 27, 500–511.

Pasqualotto, E., Federici, S., Belardinelli, M., 2012. Towards functioning and usable brain–computer interfaces (BCIs): a literature review. Disabil. Rehabil. Assist. Technol. 7, 89–103.

Pekkonen, E., Osipova, D., Laaksovirta, H., 2004. Magnetoencephalographic evidence for auditory processing in amyotrophic lateral sclerosis with bulbar signs. Clin. Neurophysiol. 115, 309–315.

Perelmouter, J., Kotchoubey, B., Kübler, A., Taub, E., Birbaumer, N., 1999. Language support program for thought-translation-devices. Automedica 18, 67–84.

Peters, B., Bieker, G., Heckman, S.M., Huggins, J.E., Wolf, C., Zeitlin, D., Fried-Oken, M., 2015. Brain-computer interface users speak up: the virtual users' forum at the 2013 international brain-computer interface meeting. Arch. Phys. Med. Rehabil. 96 (Suppl. 1), S33–S37.

Pfurtscheller, G., Aranibar, A., 1979. Evaluation of event-related desynchronization (ERD) preceding and following voluntary self-paced movement. Electroencephalogr. Clin. Neurophysiol. 46, 138–146.

Pfurtscheller, G., McFarland, D.J., 2012. BCI signal processing: feature translation. In: Wolpaw, J.R., Wolpaw, E.W. (Eds.), Brain–Computer Interfaces: Principles and Practice. Oxford University Press, New York, pp. 147–163.

Sajda, P., Gerson, A., Muller, K.-R., Blankertz, B., Parra, L., 2003. A data analysis competition to evaluate machine learning algorithms for use in brain-computer interfaces. IEEE Trans. Neural Syst. Rehabil. Eng. 11, 184–185.

Schalk, G., Miller, K.J., Anderson, N.R., Wilson, J.A., Smyth, M.D., Ojemann, J.G., Moran, D.W., Wolpaw, J.R., Leuthardt, E.C., 2008. Two-dimensional movement control using electrocorticographic signals in humans. J. Neural Eng. 5, 75–84.

Schreuder, M., Hohne, J., Blankertz, B., Haufe, S., Dickhaus, T., Tangermann, M., 2013. Optimizing event-related potential based brain-computer interfaces: a systematic evaluation of dynamic stopping methods. J. Neural Eng. 10 (3), 036025.

Sellers, E.W., Donchin, E., 2006. A P300-based brain-computer interface: initial tests by ALS patients. Clin. Neurophysiol. 117, 538–548.

Sellers, E.W., Turner, P., Sarnacki, W.A., McManus, T., Vaughan, T.M., Matthews, R., 2009. A novel dry electrode for brain-computer interface. Lect. Notes Comput. Sci 5611, 623–631.

Sellers, E.W., Vaughan, T.M., Wolpaw, J.R., 2010. A brain-computer interface for long-term independent home use. Amyotroph. Lateral Scler. 11, 449–455.

Sharma, R., Hicks, S., Berna, C.M., Kennard, C., Talbot, K., Turner, M.R., 2011. Oculomotor dysfunction in amyotrophic lateral sclerosis: a comprehensive review. Arch. Neurol. 68, 857–861.

Silvoni, S., Cavinato, M., Volpato, C., Ruf, C.A., Birbaumer, N., Piccione, F., 2013. Amyotropic lateral sclerosis progression and stability of brain-computer interface communication. Amyotroph. Lateral Scler. Frontotemporal Degener. 14, 390–396.

Simmons, Z., Felgoise, S.H., Bremer, B.A., Walsh, S.M., Hufford, D.J., Bromberg, M.B., David, W., Forshew, D.A., Heiman-Patterson, T.D., Lai, E.C., McCluskey, L., 2006. The ALSSQOL: balancing physical and nonphysical factors in assessing quality of life in ALS. Neurology 67, 1659–1664.

Sutton, S., Braren, M., Zubin, J., John, E.R., 1965. Evoked-potential correlates of stimulus uncertainty. Science 150, 1187–1188.

Swinnen, B., Robberecht, W., 2014. The phenotypic variability of amyotrophic lateral sclerosis. Nat. Rev. Neurol. 10, 661–670.

Tangermann, M., Muller, K.-L., Aertsen, A., Birbaumer, N., Braun, C., Brunner, C., Leeb, R., Mehring, C., Miller, K.J., Muller-Putz, G.R., Nolte, G., Pfurtscheller, G., Preissl, H., Schalk, G., Schlogl, A., Vidaurre, C., Waldert, S., Blankertz, B., 2012. Review of the BCI competition IV. Front. Neurosci. 6, 55.

Townsend, G., Platsko, V., 2016. Pushing the P300-based brain–computer interface beyond 100 bpm: extending performance guided constraints into the temporal domain. J. Neural Eng. 13, 026024.

Townsend, G., LaPollo, B.K., Boulay, C.B., Krunsienski, D.J., Frye, G.E., Hauser, C.K., Schartz, N.E., Vaughan, T.M., Wolpaw, J.R., Sellers, E.W., 2010. A novel P300-based brain-computer interface stimulus presentation paradigm: moving beyond rows and columns. Clin. Neurophysiol. 121, 1109–1120.

Treder, M.S., Blankertz, B., 2010. Covert attention and visual speller design in an ERP-based brain-computer interface. Behav. Brain Funct. 6, 28.

Vansteensel, M.J., Hermes, D., Aarnoutse, E.J., Bleichner, M.G., Schalk, G., van Rijen, P.C., Leijten, F.S., Ramsey, N.F., 2010. Brain-computer interfacing based on cognitive control. Ann. Neurol. 67, 809–816.

Vaughan, T.M., McFarland, D.J., Schalk, G., Sarnacki, W.A., Krusienski, D.J., Sellers, E.W., Wolpaw, J.R., 2006. The Wadsworth BCI research and development program: at home with BCI. IEEE Trans. Neural Syst. Rehabil. Eng. 14, 229–233.

Vaughan, T.M., Sellers, E.W., Wolpaw, J.R., 2012. Clinical evaluation of BCIs. In: Wolpaw, J.R., Winter-Wolpaw, E. (Eds.), Brain–Computer Interfaces: Principles and Practice. Oxford University Press, New York, pp. 325–336.

Wilkins, V.M., Bruce, M.L., Sirey, J.A., 2009. Caregiving tasks and training interest of family caregivers of medically ill homebound older adults. J. Aging Health 21, 528–542.

Wolpaw, J.R., McFarland, D.J., 2004. Control of a two-dimensional movement signal by a non-invasive brain-computer interface. Proc. Natl. Acad. Sci. U.S.A. 51, 17849–17854.

Wolpaw, J.R., Wolpaw, E.W., 2012. Brain-computer interfaces: something new under the sun. In: Wolpaw, J.R., Wolpaw, E.W. (Eds.), Brain-Computer Interfaces: Principles and Practice. Oxford University Press, New York.

Wolpaw, J.R., McFarland, D.J., Neat, G.W., Forneris, C.A., 1991. An EEG-based brain-computer interface for cursor control. Electroencephalogr. Clin. Neurophysiol. 78, 252–259.

Wolpaw, J.R., Birbaumer, N., McFarland, D.J., Pfurtscheller, G., Vaughan, T.M., 2002. Brain-computer interfaces for communication and control. Clin. Neurophysiol. 113, 767–791.

Wolpaw, J.R., McFarland, D.J., Vaughan, T.M., Schalk, G., 2003. The Wadsworth Center brain-computer interface (BCI) research and development program. IEEE Trans. Neural Syst. Rehabil. Eng. 11, 204–207.

Wolpaw, J.R., Bedlack, R.S., Reda, D.J., Ringer, R.J., Banks, P.G., Vaughan, T.M., Heckman, S.M., McCane, L.M., Carmak, C.S., Winden, B.S., McFarland, D.J., Sellers, E.W., Hairong, Shi, Paine, T., Higgins, D.S., Lo, A.C., Patwa, H.S., Hill, K.J., Huang, G.D. & Ruff, R.L. (2016). Home use of a brain–computer interface by veterans with amyotrophic lateral sclerosis (in preparation).

World Health Organization. The European health report 2012: chartering the way to well-being. http://www.euro.who.int/__data/assets/pdf_file/0004/197113/EHR2012-Eng.pdf. Accessed September 1, 2015.

Yeom, S.-K., Fazli, S., Muller, K.-R., Lee, S.-W., 2014. An efficient ERP-based brain-computer interface using random set presentation and face familiarity. PLoS One 9 (11). e111157.

Young, G.B., Campbell, V.C., 1999. EEG monitoring in the intensive care unit: pitfalls and caveats. J. Clin. Neurophysiol. 16, 40–45.

Zhang, D., Maye, A., Gao, X., Hong, B., Engel, A.K., Gao, S., 2010. An independent brain–computer interface using covert non-spatial visual selective attention. J. Neural Eng. 7 (1), 16010.

Zhang, Y., Zhao, Q., Jin, J., Wang, X., Cichocki, A., 2012. A novel BCI based on ERP components sensitive to configural processing of human faces. J. Neural Eng. 9, 026018.

Index

Note: Page numbers followed by "*f*" indicate figures, and "*t*" indicate tables.

Volume 167: Stress Hormones and Post Traumatic Stress Disorder: Basic Studies and Clinical
Perspectives, by E.R. de Kloet, M.S. Oitzl and E. Vermetten (Eds.) – 2008,
ISBN 978-0-444-53140-7.

Volume 168: Models of Brain and Mind: Physical, Computational and Psychological Approaches,
by R. Banerjee and B.K. Chakrabarti (Eds.) – 2008, ISBN 978-0-444-53050-9.

Volume 169: Essence of Memory, by W.S. Sossin, J.-C. Lacaille, V.F. Castellucci and S. Belleville
(Eds.) – 2008, ISBN 978-0-444-53164-3.

Volume 170: Advances in Vasopressin and Oxytocin – From Genes to Behaviour to Disease,
by I.D. Neumann and R. Landgraf (Eds.) – 2008, ISBN 978-0-444-53201-5.

Volume 171: Using Eye Movements as an Experimental Probe of Brain Function—A Symposium in
Honor of Jean Büttner-Ennever, by Christopher Kennard and R. John Leigh (Eds.) – 2008,
ISBN 978-0-444-53163-6.

Volume 172: Serotonin–Dopamine Interaction: Experimental Evidence and Therapeutic Relevance, by
Giuseppe Di Giovanni, Vincenzo Di Matteo and Ennio Esposito (Eds.) – 2008,
ISBN 978-0-444-53235-0.

Volume 173: Glaucoma: An Open Window to Neurodegeneration and Neuroprotection, by Carlo Nucci,
Neville N. Osborne, Giacinto Bagetta and Luciano Cerulli (Eds.) – 2008,
ISBN 978-0-444-53256-5.

Volume 174: Mind and Motion: The Bidirectional Link Between Thought and Action, by Markus Raab,
Joseph G. Johnson and Hauke R. Heekeren (Eds.) – 2009, 978-0-444-53356-2.

Volume 175: Neurotherapy: Progress in Restorative Neuroscience and Neurology — Proceedings of the
25th International Summer School of Brain Research, held at the Royal Netherlands
Academy of Arts and Sciences, Amsterdam, The Netherlands, August 25–28, 2008, by
J. Verhaagen, E.M. Hol, I. Huitinga, J. Wijnholds, A.A. Bergen, G.J. Boer and D.F. Swaab
(Eds.) –2009, ISBN 978-0-12-374511-8.

Volume 176: Attention, by Narayanan Srinivasan (Ed.) – 2009, ISBN 978-0-444-53426-2.

Volume 177: Coma Science: Clinical and Ethical Implications, by Steven Laureys, Nicholas D. Schiff
and Adrian M. Owen (Eds.) – 2009, 978-0-444-53432-3.

Volume 178: Cultural Neuroscience: Cultural Influences On Brain Function, by Joan Y. Chiao (Ed.) –
2009, 978-0-444-53361-6.

Volume 179: Genetic models of schizophrenia, by Akira Sawa (Ed.) – 2009, 978-0-444-53430-9.

Volume 180: Nanoneuroscience and Nanoneuropharmacology, by Hari Shanker Sharma (Ed.) – 2009,
978-0-444-53431-6.

Volume 181: Neuroendocrinology: The Normal Neuroendocrine System, by Luciano Martini, George
P. Chrousos, Fernand Labrie, Karel Pacak and Donald W. Pfaff (Eds.) – 2010,
978-0-444-53617-4.

Volume 182: Neuroendocrinology: Pathological Situations and Diseases, by Luciano Martini, George
P. Chrousos, Fernand Labrie, Karel Pacak and Donald W. Pfaff (Eds.) – 2010,
978-0-444-53616-7.

Volume 183: Recent Advances in Parkinson's Disease: Basic Research, by Anders Björklund and
M. Angela Cenci (Eds.) – 2010, 978-0-444-53614-3.

Volume 184: Recent Advances in Parkinson's Disease: Translational and Clinical Research, by Anders
Björklund and M. Angela Cenci (Eds.) – 2010, 978-0-444-53750-8.

Volume 185: Human Sleep and Cognition Part I: Basic Research, by Gerard A. Kerkhof and Hans
P.A. Van Dongen (Eds.) – 2010, 978-0-444-53702-7.

Volume 186: Sex Differences in the Human Brain, their Underpinnings and Implications, by Ivanka
Savic (Ed.) – 2010, 978-0-444-53630-3.

Volume 187: Breathe, Walk and Chew: The Neural Challenge: Part I, by Jean-Pierre Gossard, Réjean
Dubuc and Arlette Kolta (Eds.) – 2010, 978-0-444-53613-6.

Volume 188: Breathe, Walk and Chew; The Neural Challenge: Part II, by Jean-Pierre Gossard, Réjean
Dubuc and Arlette Kolta (Eds.) – 2011, 978-0-444-53825-3.

Volume 189: Gene Expression to Neurobiology and Behaviour: Human Brain Development and
Developmental Disorders, by Oliver Braddick, Janette Atkinson and Giorgio M. Innocenti
(Eds.) – 2011, 978-0-444-53884-0.

Printed in the United States
By Bookmasters